When Men Revolt—and Why

A Reader in Political Violence and Revolution

When men revolt and why

A reader in political violence and revolution

EDITED BY

James Chowning Davies

[Fp] THE FREE PRESS, NEW YORK
COLLIER-MACMILLAN LIMITED,
LONDON

The Free Press
A Division of the Macmillan Company
866 Third Avenue, New York, New York 10022

Collier-Macmillan Canada, Limited,
Toronto, Ontario

Library of Congress
Catalog Card Number: 74–142361

1 2 3 4 5 6 7 8 9

To the Memory of
Crane Brinton

He never fathered a revolution
but he articulated its anatomy in our disjointed time

Contents

Foreword

The title of this collection of readings looks a little absent-minded. However, the "why" part of it is not afterthought. It reflects the state of our knowledge of revolution. We are still not very well able to predict the occasion of revolution, but we are far better able to predict when than to explain why. The disjointed title may serve to remind the reader that the study of revolution has a long way to go before it becomes an exact science. It will become so when we can show rather precisely how the dozens of environmental influences interact with the dozens of influences within human beings to produce political violence. The purpose of this reader is to indicate what some of the major forces are that work on people, from inside and outside, to make them revolt.

There is a continuity between each of the readings. Together they form some kind of logical whole. The introductions to the readings are intended to make this continuity clear. Nevertheless, each of the readings is interesting in its own right, and if one chooses to read only several and not all of them, he will still get at some of the major relevant material on revolution.

In getting these readings together, deciding which to include and which to omit, I was at every stage helped by Hendrik van Dalen, a tactful and sensible critic and a discriminating, responsible adjutant. While I bear final responsibility for the readings that finally were chosen, he and I bear joint responsibility for the extended bibliography at the end of the volume. We suggest that if you have found this reader a good beginning, you may very well like just as much the books and articles cited in the bibliography. They amount to a large second course in the peripatetic feast which the study of revolution amounts to.

JAMES CHOWNING DAVIES

Eugene, Oregon
4 July 1970

Libris Personae

Aristotle (384 B.C.–322 B.C.). Greek philosopher and scientist who was a student of Plato at the Academy in Athens. His works cover an area from the collection of empirical data on Greek constitutions and the study of causation ("metaphysics") to biological and sociological inquiry.

Leonard Berkowitz (b. 1926) is professor of psychology at the University of Wisconsin. He was educated at New York University and the University of Michigan. Dr. Berkowitz has published a number of articles and several books relating to frustration and aggression.

Julius H. Boeke (b. 1884). Dutch economist studying underdeveloped nations. While at the University of Leiden he published a number of works on the economics of developing nations, especially Indonesia.

Clarence Crane Brinton (1898–1969). Crane Brinton was professor of history at Harvard University, where he began teaching in 1923. He has written sensitive and perceptive works on men and ideas as well as history.

Douglas Bwy (b. 1939) was educated at San Diego State College and Northwestern University. He is currently assistant professor of political science at the University of Hawaii. He has served as a consultant to several research firms and has published articles on the behavioral sciences and on revolution.

James C. Davies (b. 1918) was educated at Oberlin College and the University of California, Berkeley. Author of *Human Nature in Politics* and various articles on political theory based on empirical research. He has taught at the California Institute of Technology and is currently at the University of Oregon.

Stanley M. Elkins (b. 1925) is professor of history at Smith College. His published works include a book on the founding fathers.

Friedrich Engels (1820–1895) was a close associate of Karl Marx, with whom he coauthored a number of works. He edited the second and third volumes of Marx's *Das Kapital*. Sensitive to and aware of the plight of workers in Germany and England, he organized the First Socialist International with Marx in 1864.

Ivo K. Feierabend (b. 1927) was educated at the University of California, Berkeley and Yale University. His published works include a study of Czechoslovakia and a monograph, the *Cross-National Data Bank of Political Instability*. He is currently professor of political science at San Diego State College.

Rosalind L. Feierabend is associate professor of psychology at San Diego State College. She has coauthored a book on the order of presentation in persuasion and has published articles on aggression and the frustration–aggression theory.

Lloyd Free is president of the Institute for International Social Research. He collaborated with Hadley Cantril in numerous published analyses of public opinion in developed and developing nations.

Edward W. Gude (b. 1937) was educated at Dartmouth, the London School of Economics and the Massachusetts Institute of Technology. He has taught political science at Northwestern University and Dartmouth.

Ted Robert Gurr (b. 1936) has taught at Princeton University and is now at Northwestern University. Ted Gurr has published articles on the genesis of civil violence, measures for comparing nations and information retrieval in the social sciences. He was coeditor of the first volume of the President's Commission on Violence and author of *Why Men Rebel*.

Dominique Otare Mannoni is a French psychiatrist who worked in what was then the French colony of Madagascar. His observations are derived from that experience.

Karl Marx (1818–1883) was educated at the universities of Bonn and Berlin. He edited newspapers in Germany and France and was expelled from both countries for espousing radical views. Pursued by the authorities, he settled in London where he resumed his support of socialist organizations and wrote *Das Kapital*.

Thomas Garrigue Masaryk (1850–1937), the son of a serf, became a professor in philosophy at the University of Prague. He was elected to the Austrian Reichsrat in 1891 and the Austrian–Hungarian Parliament in 1907. He was the first president of the new Republic of Czechoslovakia established in 1918.

Mancur L. Olson, Jr. (b. 1932) was educated at North Dakota State University, Oxford University, and Harvard. He taught economics at Princeton before he was put in charge of developing social indicators for the Department of Health, Education, and Welfare in Washington. He is now at the University of Maryland. He has written several works that are influential in economics and other social sciences.

Margaret Mann Phillips (b. 1906) is now a reader in French at the University of London, after serving as director of studies in modern languages at Cambridge University and lecturer in French at King's College of the University of London. She has written extensively on Erasmus.

Bruce M. Russett (b. 1935) is professor of political science at Yale University and director of the Yale Political Data Program. He has written several books and articles on world politics, the United Nations, being noted as the principal author of the *World Handbook of Political and Social Indicators*.

David C. Schwartz (b. 1939), assistant professor of political science at the University of Pennsylvania, was educated at Brooklyn College and the Massachusetts Institute of Technology. His published works include articles on the popularization of social science, political recruitment, political gaming, and self-determination.

Georg Simmel (1858–1918) was a German philosopher and sociologist who introduced the teaching of what is now considered sociology at the University of Berlin. Relatively unrecognized in Germany, Simmel's works gained their prominence primarily through English translations and an American readership.

Edgar P. Snow (b. 1905), a journalist, began as a reporter for the Kansas City Star, a free-lance writer and then a sailor. He went to China in 1928 where he edited a weekly in Shanghai. He is noted for his reporting of events and conditions in China both before and after the Chinese Communist revolution.

Alexis de Tocqueville (1805–1859) was a French statesman and writer. He is noted for his perceptive study, *Democracy in America* (1832), a work in some ways still unsurpassed in its depth and quality of analysis of the nature, the strengths, and the weaknesses of democracy in the United States.

George Wada (b. 1927) lived during the Second World War in Manzanar, a relocation center for Japanese, where the riot occurred that is reported in this volume. He was educated at the California Institute of Technology and Stanford University, where he got his doctorate in electrical engineering. He now works as an engineer in Northern California.

Yale School (John Dollard *et al.*). Perhaps the best joint biography of the five principal authors is their classic statement, *Frustration and Aggression*, from which we have included a selection in this volume.

When Men Revolt—and Why

A Reader in Political Violence and Revolution

1

Introduction

Introduction

Violence among men goes back to the beginnings of human history, when Cain slew his brother Abel and later asked the question: "Am I my brother's keeper?" Violence among citizens, of which revolution is the most extreme sort, probably goes as far back in the history of government. Indeed it may be argued that violence of citizen against citizen, government against citizen, and citizen against government has always come before orderly political processes. If so, political development may be called a movement not from violence to nonviolence but rather from the sharing by all people of the means of violence to a monopoly of violence by those who govern, with the consent of those who are governed. That is, it is a trend from lawless, individual violence toward the kind of violence used only by government acting in accordance with publicly accepted law.

This takes us back to Cain's question: Am I my brother's keeper? When government, Cain-like, has used violence to serve the interests of itself and the governing class, citizens have often responded by taking weapons and the law into their own hands. When government has served the interests of all citizens, most citizens have been willing to surrender the use of violence and its instruments to their government.

In this book we are concerned with finding out when and why people withdraw the surrender to government of their power to kill and coerce. In a developed polity the *right* of government and citizens to do various things is asserted and acknowledged. In every polity the *power* to do things requires assertion but not recognition. Men have always had the power to use violence against government; governments have always had the power to use violence against citizens. The question is not as to the power but as to the reasons people decide to exercise it. When revolution occurs, it is not people who must conform to the demands of governments but governments that must conform to the demands of people. As we learn basic reasons for revolution, we get a better idea of what are the basic human forces to which governments, laws, and constitutions must conform.

Until the beginning of the 20th century, it appeared that the modern era had at last firmly established orderly political ways of doing things, which were voluntarily accepted by citizens almost everywhere. This illusion was broken. In 1900 China experienced the Boxer Rebellion and five years later Russia exploded. The Boxer

3

Rebellion was turned outward, against the world powers that were colonizing China. The 1905 Russian Revolution was turned inward, against the exploitation of Russians by Russians. Both were prototypes of the violent political action that has typified our century. Since 1900—since two world wars and dozens of decolonizings and revolutions—the governments and social systems of perhaps half the world's population have been changed by violent means. Disorderly, nonconstitutional political processes have been the dominant mode of our era.

Except for those who glory in human gore, whether spilled actually in conflicts between or within nations or spilled symbolically on television, this has been a discouraging turn of events. It has led some students of politics to talk grievous nonsense about the inevitability of unlawful force and about the very few years in all recorded history that man has not been killing or maiming man, on battlefields or barricades. This supposedly timeless, long range view is really as ephemeral and myopic as the notion at the end of the Victorian era that nonviolence was here to stay.

The 20th century is surely one of the most violent in history, possibly the second most violent. Top distinction in violence probably goes to the 16th and early 17th centuries. The century of the Protestant Reformation, which preceded by four hundred years the weapons of nuclear fission and computerized overkill, is believed to have reduced the population of Germany by at least a fourth. No actual 20th century war or sum of wars or revolutions has even come close to this proportion—except that the Jewish population of Germany was virtually wiped out in the 1930s and 1940s.

Before we dissolve into a melancholy impotence about how evil and wretched the human condition is, we should take a careful look at when and why all this violence comes about—in the 16th, 20th, or any century. If we find some valid explanations, we may then gain some assurance that diminishing the causes of civil violence will at least reduce its occurrence. And we can hopefully then avoid the naiveté of some governments and citizens who say that certain kinds of people are the cause of revolt and if we eliminate them we will eliminate revolution.

Civil violence, in our ignorance of its causes, often appears to be random, erratic, irrational. This appearance only betokens our ignorance of causes rather than any real randomness of revolutionary behavior. It is the product of natural laws more fundamental than any that men have adopted in writing or by custom—more fundamental than any written or unwritten constitution, any statute or city ordinance against unlawful assembly or disorderly conduct.

Explanations of fundamental, preconstitutional, preinstitutional causes of human behavior have been related to political consequences since Plato's *Republic* and Hobbes's *Leviathan*. In recent decades these fundamental principles have become far more clearly evident than they were even to Hobbes, that most magnificent integrator of speculative psychology and political theory.

As Aristotle observed in the 4th century before Christ and Hobbes twenty centuries later, we are now again becoming aware that civil disorders and revolutions begin in the minds of men. At least that is where revolutions acquire focus and direction. This assertion is so banal as to seem to need no saying, but the most current single assertion about revolution has been that it begins in group (economic, ethic, or religious) conflict. There has been too little awareness of the human mind as a nodal, elemental factor.

Karl Marx was the most tenacious and prescient student of revolution in the 19th century and the most influential in the 20th. For him the unit of analysis was not the human being or his central nervous system but those vast nonindividual units called social classes. Marx did imply the mind, when he spoke of the class-consciousness of the proletariat. But "class-consciousness" and "the collective unconscious" are inexact shorthand terms, appropriate for easy and often monistic generalizations. Consciousness is more exactly a characteristic of individuals than of groups. Nevertheless, newspaper accounts and even academic studies of the civil disturbances among black people in the United States and university students throughout the world remain largely preoccupied with collectivities, rather than individuals, as the units of analysis. Sometimes such studies say that it all started with the demand in black slums for housing and jobs, or in universities for more and better professors and more student participation in making educational policy. They avoid saying that *any* individual, deprived of the steady means of physical survival or frustrated by careers that have been blocked without any visible purpose by tradition or by war, will become restless. They avoid looking into the minds of people.

Just why these demands are made by blacks or students is thus seldom considered on any general level. To many, it seems idle to consider that there may be common explanations applicable to the demands of black people and students and of those who made the Protestant Reformation and the great revolutions of the 20th century. To many, it is awesome and fascinating to read or witness disaster, whether it be the Black Death of early modern times in Europe or a lightning-caused fire in the green forest or a rioter-set fire in a black slum. The awe and the fascination produce little but fear and wonder. Seeing people die of the plague or witnessing a fire does not cure the plague or prevent the fire.

If we can get some understanding of when and why men revolt, we may then be better able to produce social and political conditions that reduce tension below the head-cracking point and emancipate men at a cost less bloodily high than revolution. A search for some basic laws of human behavior can tell us what man-made laws men will obey in accordance with their natural demands and what laws they will not obey. We will then be able to develop better customs, better constitutions, better statutes. This seems a more economic, efficient process than attempting fundamentally to restructure either men or Man, trying to cleanse his supposedly dark soul in some kind of massive brain laundry. Chapter 8 in this book indicates that at least some demands have not changed in the past two and a half millennia. The problem is to identify those of the demands that are basic.

There is not yet consensus about the basic characteristics of men's mental processes, about the nature of man. Indeed until recent years a common assumption has been that man had no nature. By some strange means, man with his highly developed brain was supposed to act like other forms of life whose brains and behavior patterns are less complex and much less amenable to self-analysis and self-control. Man seemed to become Pavlov's dog, nothing but a bundle of conditioned responses to stimuli that together seemed to make him—as Marx put it—the ensemble of his social relations. Even among some people willing to consider the notion that man may have species-wide behavioral tendencies, there have been voices saying that supposed nature is of no concern to social scientists. The idea that the organism contains determinants only messes up their diagrams of political behavior. Just feed into the black box (man's no longer canine but now computerized mind) a class status, a religion, a few other artifacts of culture; then press the computer start button. Out will come the behavior that pops spontaneously from the black box into which you feed the artifacts.

If some social scientists are so programmed by their own preconceptions as to become computers rigorously receiving and rejecting raw data at one end and emitting truth at the other, men at least are not so constructed. Inside the black box, the central nervous system of each individual human being is an enormously complicated but highly integrated and discriminating set of processes that take place systematically in the great network of nerve cells. It has been estimated there are about twenty billion neurons in man. These neurons respond to stimuli not only from the external environment that Marx talked about, but also from the internal environment consisting of the other parts of the anatomy (endocrines, viscera, muscles, bones) other than the brain. The discriminatory and integrative responses, including the decision-making process as it relates to all action including the political, takes place in the brain, which causes the body to act. The inputs into the mind may include a stomach that is empty, a love that is frustrated, adrenalin or noradrenalin which in some summating way demands action. The action may take the form of revolt.

Marx said that man, or at least the proletariat in capitalist society, would revolt when he became so degraded that his share of the product of industry allowed him merely to survive. That is, Marx said man would revolt when his survival was threatened. This would all be very well if chronically hungry men were usually rebels. But hungry men are usually just plain hungry—too hungry to be concerned with anything other than food. They are usually too hungry, when in the condition that Marx described, to form that measure of social solidarity necessary for them to work together to overthrow their government. So hungry men usually live out their truncated lives and die, their annals being short, simple, and, until Marx called the attention of well-fed people to the poor, unnoticed. Revolutions always get recruits from briefly hungry people who break into bakeries and granaries, but they seldom get recruits from those too malnourished to outrun the cops when someone yells "Stop, thief."

Something other than hunger appeared to be behind not only the profound revolution that the Protestant Reformation amounted to but also the more recent great American, French, Russian, and Chinese revolutions. The awesome manifest acts of particular revolutions take our attention away from underlying causes. A stamp tax is not a corvée—is not the tsar's troops firing on workers on 22 January 1905—is not the bloody killing of Communists in Shanghai in 1927, or the cruelty of Japanese or Kuomintang troops as they laid waste a resistant Chinese village.

But the British stamp tax was taxation without representation. The French corvée was an unreasonable, unequal, discriminatory exaction of labor from peasants who got little benefit from the heavy public construction work they performed. When troops fired on peaceful petitioners in Petrograd, human beings were being treated like wild beasts—and so they were when Chinese villagers were killed en masse because they refused to do the bidding of Chinese or Japanese troops. What these various acts of "constituted" governments have in common is the affront to the equal dignity of human beings, who variously happened to receive the affront in America, France, Russia, and China.

When Jefferson premised the argument in 1776 for independence from British rule with the statement that "all men are created equal," he was making an assertion about man's nature. Men who have been denied equality have been highly responsive to the demand by their leaders for equality and have made revolutions to get it. Whether the language was Lutheran, Wesleyan, Calvinist, Jeffersonian, Rousseauean, or Marxian, the frustrated expectation of equality has been a major factor in all major revolutionary upheavals since Luther posted his Ninety-five Theses on the Wittenberg church door. Indeed, since long before that.

"Even as you do it unto these, the least of my brethren, you do it unto me," said Christ nearly two thousand years ago. "Friendship [or love or affection] is among equals," wrote Aristotle some four hundred years before Christ—and as we shall see, he saw a link between equality and revolution. And some seven hundred years before Christ, it was written in a great Jewish law book (Leviticus 19:18): "Thou shalt love thy neighbor as thyself."

It may be that the desire for equality is acquired in the process of putting on the garment of culture. It may be that the idea became imprinted in the mind of Christ by some learned scholar who forgot to footnote the Aristotelian or Hebraic source. It may be that Marx's anger at the brutalizing effects of unbridled capitalism was another Pavlovian product of unconscious conditioning. It may be that Marx could have been conditioned with the notion that all men are or should be unequal. The 19th century culture offered much support for a devout belief in inequality. But such an explanation via cultural determinism is far less plausible than the idea that men naturally desire equality.

Environmental determinism and simple stimulus response psychology leave the black box closed. They neglect what goes on between the time when the stimulus goes in and when the organism acts in response. Pavlov conditioned the response of drooling when his hungry dogs became accustomed to associate the symbolic bell with the reward of real food. The response became established: the hungry dog drooled when the bell rang. And the response became extinguished after a time, when the ringing of the bell was not followed by food. The dogs began to discriminate in their response when the symbolic world lost its link to the real world.

People do indeed respond to symbols far more complexly than dogs. But they do so with relation to things that they want independently of the symbols. If people associate words that express the idea of equality with the practice of equality, they do so because they want real equality. When symbols diverge from practice, the voicing of symbols by priests, prelates, parliamentarians, courtiers, kings, and politicians loses its ability to produce the approving conditioned response. Luther denounces priests and the Church, when their discriminatory acts belie their non-discriminatory universalist and egalitarian ethic. Lenin calls religion (but not equality itself) the opiate of the people. In Chapter 7 we shall see the progression of Mao Tse-tung's growing hatred for his father and his native government.

We can as yet only hypothesize that the desire for equality is innate in all men. But we do know that people who have been degraded and discriminated against (at least since the slave revolts in ancient Rome) are rather likely to join a revolution against the government that is degrading them and discriminating against them.

The need for equality is not the only basic need that relates to revolution. The contemporary American psychologist, Abraham Maslow, has specified a set of basic needs: the physical, security, social or affectional, self-esteem, and self-actualization needs. He orders these basic categories of needs into a hierarchy, saying that the physical needs, when unsatisfied, predominate over all others, even when the others are unsatisfied. The common sense of the idea is evident when you realize what you would concentrate on if you were drowning. It would not likely be love of your fellow man, a demand for a fair trial, an urge to write a poem, or anything other than your desire to breathe.

The editor of this reader believes the Maslow need hierarchy—with the exception of his postulated need for security—to be a very useful starting point in the search for causes of revolution. People who are momentarily hungry will join food riots, as in France in 1789. People who feel socially isolated will join revolutionary movements, as did Hitler when he became a Nazi and drew social rejects (and many others) to the movement that became his own. People whose equal dignity has been denied will become rebellious once they have become fairly well fed and somewhat socially integrated, like relatively well-off blacks in America in the 1960s or Indians in British India in the 1920s. People who are *insecure* in the satisfaction of their physical, social-affectional, or dignity needs form the dry tinder of revolutions. And people whose supply of food, social acceptance, and equal dignity are all quite secure will join revolutions when their career expectations are frustrated—as did many landowners in France in 1789 and Russia in 1905 when the bourgeoisie began to displace them from their accustomed power and prestige—and as did Lenin, the lawyer whose career prospects were destroyed within a few years after his brother was executed as a plotter against the tsar. And as do American college students in the 1960s, when faced not with a challenging career, but with military duty in a conflict in Southeast Asia whose goals have long since been lost from sight.

Without the postulate that people who revolt are doing so in response to very strong, very basic drives, it is impossible to explain their commitment to action so fraught with danger. Without the postulate that such needs are hierarchically arranged, it is at least difficult to explain the collaboration in revolution of people whose immediate hunger is for food with those who have plenty to eat, of people who are beloved by parents and family with those who are not, or who have high self-esteem but cannot pursue the career which they have come to expect they have a right to pursue.

The writings in this collection do not fit a simple theory supporting the idea that men revolt in the name of equality or of any other single basic human need. But they are consistent with the idea that basic needs are always involved. Some of the writings do not even touch on such issues, but in various ways they all relate to what goes on inside the black box, inside the minds of men. Most of the writings relate to inputs into the central nervous system—environmental influences—and use language that has been conventional among philosophers, historians, and social scientists. The writings may not seem to relate particularly to the nature of man or to his fundamental expectations and demands. But they do relate to man's basic characteristics and to an understanding of when and why he invokes fundamental principles in the act of revolt. In earlier eras these principles have been called natural law, and seemingly in all eras they have a natural appeal to men. The hard fact of revolution demonstrates that these principles are more fundamental than the man-made constitutions and laws which revolutionists, once they commence to act, proceed to disregard.

When men revolt, they do so with qualms, trepidation, and guilt. But with all their inner turmoil, they also think themselves to be right and just, both in their actions and in their belief that the established rules and rulers violate equal justice.

The behavior of men in revolutions is in accordance with normal psychological principles that now can be discovered and tested by laboratory and other rigorous scientific analyses. Men who revolt are acting predictably. The writings that follow are a step in the direction of ascertaining the theoretical principles in accordance with which revolutionary action can in time be predicted.

2

How individuals and societies meet the challenge of change

A young man who feared the future

To understand anything in any depth, a person has to experience it and identify with it. When he was about to discover the atomic structure of complicated organic molecules, the Nobel Laureate chemist Linus Pauling said to himself: if I were such a molecule, how would I arrange myself? He then got the insight which became a brilliant basic discovery of a microcosmic process. When he was discovering pre-revolutionary Russia, a Czech sociologist met a young Russian monk who guided him through a monastery and its hermitage named Gethsemane. In this visit the sociologist entered an ancient Russia that still lived and still dominated the modern Russia of factories, railroads, revolutionaries (and a small, weak, diffident middle class).

The Czech sociologist, Thomas Masaryk, was born in Bohemia, the son of a Bohemian mother and a Slovakian father, a serf and coachman on a crown estate of the Austrian emperor. He became one of the earliest social scientists to gather and use quantitative data. He then became the first President of the Czechoslovak Republic. With the young monk, Masaryk reestablished contact with a part of his own past that he had abandoned. The monk huddled in the past, and he peered fearfully, timidly into the fascinating future.

A few years after Masaryk met the monk, Russia exploded, in one of the earth-shaking events of all modern history. Masaryk's young monk must have unwittingly, unwillingly experienced that revolution. If we can understand and identify with what Masaryk reports was going on in the monk's mind, we may then begin to understand the minds of people who are about to witness revolution anxiously from behind curtained windows—or who are about to go into the streets to rebel or fight rebels.

The Russian monk

THOMAS MASARYK

A GENERAL survey of Russian development since the days of Peter the Great shows the country divided into two halves, consisting respectively of an Old Russia with a prepetrine civilization, and a New, European Russia.

An alert observer traveling through Russia will gain a vivid perception of the nature and evolution of this cultural divergence. One entering Russia from Europe (it must be remembered that the Russian crossing the western frontier speaks always of "going to Europe") has first to traverse a non-Russian province or territory. He must pass through Poland, the Baltic provinces, or Finland, through lands annexed from Europe, whose inhabitants are Catholic or Protestant, and who have a European civilization of old date. The connection of these regions with Orthodox Russia is still comparatively superficial. But the further eastward we go, the further do we find ourselves from Europe, until at length Europe is represented only by the railway, the refreshment rooms at the stations, and isolated hotels furnished and managed in European style. The same contrast strikes us between Petrograd and Moscow. In Moscow, and also in Petrograd, it strikes us between the modern portions of the city and the old town which is purely Russian. Odessa, on the other hand, is a new town, quite European.

When compared with the two capitals, and especially when compared with Petrograd, the rural districts, the villages, are Russian. The great landowners, aristocrats, furnish their country-seats in European style. Similarly, many factories in country districts are European oases. Things technical, things practical, are for the most part European: railways, factories, and banks; commerce to some extent (including internal trade); army and navy; in part, also, the bureaucratic machine of state. . . . European elements are everywhere intermingled with Russian, and after a little practice we learn to distinguish the transitional stages and the manifold combinations. . . .

After a time we shall obviously learn to detect the same contrasts in men as well as in things. European and Russian thought and feeling present themselves in the most diversified combinations. Before long the conviction is forced upon us that the Europeanization of Russia does not consist solely in the adoption of isolated ideas and isolated practical institutions, but that we have to do with a characteristic historical process in virtue of which the Old Russian essence, civilization, and modes of life are being transformed and destroyed by the inroad of the European essence, civilization, and modes of life.

The individual Russian undergoing Europeanization experiences this contrast in his own intimate personality. Since the human being cannot live disintegrated, there is forced upon him the attempt to secure an organic connection between the Russian that he is by inheritance and the European that he is by acquirement, to secure as far as possible a unification of the two. The task is difficult! Try to picture to yourself vividly the contrast between the Russian peasant (and the peasant is still Russia), on the one hand, and the writer, the officer, the landowner, or the skilled technician, on the other—men who have been educated in Paris, Berlin, or Zurich, and who are familiar with the life of these cities. People differing thus widely have not merely to live side by side, but must think and work with one another and for one another!

The spiritual contrast between Russia and Europe is displayed in its fullest significance in the Russian monastery. Here we find the most genuine and the oldest Russian life, the feeling and thought of Old Russia. We see this already in the monasteries of Petrograd, but we see it yet more clearly in remoter monasteries and hermitages.

Russia, Old Russia, is the Russian monk. During my first visit to Russia I had a vivid experience of this. In Moscow I was moving in circles where intellectual development was most advanced, but withdrawing one day from this Europeanized environment, I paid a visit to the Troicko-Sergievskaja monastery. With its institutions, its treasures, and its relics, this monastery takes us back into 14th-century Russia; but in the dependent monastery Bethany, and yet more in the hermitage of Gethsemane, we find ourselves in an even remoter historical epoch. In the center of the forest stands the hermitage, with an ancient wooden church—a veritable Gethsemane! The contrast was all the more striking seeing that the previous day I had been debating religious problems with Tolstoi and his friends. Now I found myself at the hermitage of Gethsemane, with its catacombs, its wonder-working relics, and its icons! One of Tolstoi's friends, a man of position, had given me a letter of introduction to the head of the monastery, so that I was able to see everything.

Never shall I forget the man who showed me round the hermitage. This monk was about twenty-five years old. He had grown up in and for the monastery, and his mind was entirely dominated by its Orthodox ideas. To him the world seemed something altogether foreign, whilst I was an emissary from, a part of, the outer world, from which he was a refugee. Now he was to accompany me through the catacombs and to explain what I saw. The things which to him were objects of the most devout contemplation were to be elucidated to the non-Russian, the European, the heretic, the mere sightseer! I could not fail to note and to be sorry for my guide's distress, but I must admit that his uneasiness was a trifle irritating to the European in me. He genuflected before every relic and every icon, at least before the principal ones; he was continually crossing himself; kneeling down he touched the holy precincts with forehead and lips.

As I watched him closely I perceived that alarm was gaining on him, that he was obviously terrified, momentarily expecting that Heaven would punish me for my wickedness and unbelief. But punishment was withheld, and almost without his knowledge and understanding, into the depths of his soul there crept a shadow of doubt. This was obvious in his earnest request that I would at least bow before the chief relic. It was plain that he was no longer anxious about the safety of the heretic, but that the Almighty's failure to send due punishment was troubling him.

After we had finished with the catacombs I wished to return alone, but my guide would not leave me. Before long I realized that the monk on his side wanted to acquire knowledge. He gave free rein to his curiosity, to his eager desire to learn something of the world, of Europe. His world-hunger sparkled in his eyes, and I could not satisfy his appetite for narrative and explanation. At length he, a Russian, began to ask me, a non-Russian, about Moscow, Petrograd, Russia. Several times we paced the distance between the hermitage and the margin of the forest. My companion never wearied in his interrogations. Hitherto he had known the world in the light of the Bible and the legends of the saints, but now he was listening to the unheard of and unsuspected.

At length I had to make my way back to the principal monastery. Despite my repeated and cordial thanks, the monk accompanied me to the very gate; there he continued to stand, and would not take his homeward path after my last words of farewell had been uttered—what on earth did the man want? Did he expect a gratuity? The thought had been worrying me for some little time. I was ashamed of it; it hurt me to entertain it; but in the end I found it impossible to doubt that this strictly religious contemner of the world was accustomed to receive tips! My head was whirling with thoughts about Russia and Europe, belief and unbelief; and I blushed as I slipped a note into the extended palm of the guardian of Gethsemane. . . .

This experience and many similar ones,

especially those gained during a pilgrimage to another leading monastery, and during my intercourse with the "old believers" and the sectaries—in a word, the observation and study of the religious life of the churches, afford ample insight into Old Russia of the days before Peter the Great. To understand European and Europeanized Russia, it is necessary to know what Moscow, the third Rome, has been and still is for Russia in matters of civilization.

I owe to Tolstoi my introduction to the old believer wonderland. One of the best old believer curio dealers in Moscow gave me his personal guidance through the length and breadth of this Old Russia.

Old Russia, Russia in contrast to Europe! Yet the monk in Gethsemane, the pilgrims, the Orthodox, the peasantry—they all carried me back in memory to childhood, when my primitive faith was undisturbed. Such were my own beliefs and such were my own actions when I went on pilgrimage in boyhood; such are still the beliefs and actions of the children and the wives of our Slovak peasants when they visit the shrine of the miracle-working virgin on Mt. Hostein; such were the beliefs and such was the teaching of my own mother. But this childhood has passed away for ever, simply because childhood must yield place to maturity. . . .

Russia has preserved the childhood of Europe; in the overwhelming mass of its peasant population it represents Christian medievalism and, in particular, Byzantine medievalism. It was but a question of time when this middle age would awaken to modernity, and the awakening was in large part due to Peter and his successors.

Two men who (mostly)
welcomed the future

Masaryk's monk lived in passive obscurity through one of the greatest historical epochs, a twig floating downstream and over gigantic falls. Two other monks, living four centuries before their Russian counterpart, entered history's main stream, not only making it resound but also giving it some direction. Both monks were Augustinians, schooled in the Schoolmen and raised on monastic, strict adherence to dogma and ritual. Both broke out of the old channels.

Erasmus, the illegitimate son of a priest and the more radical of the two monks, in his writings ridiculed the stuffiness, the pedantry, the hygroscopic dessication of Europe's intellectual leaders. He rediscovered the classic writings of Rome and Greece. In so doing he rediscovered man and his identity with nature, and he found himself. He became enormously popular among the literate, a kind of more influential Charles Dickens in a more radically changing world. He left the monastery, but he would not leave his Church.

Luther was the legitimate son of a man who lived energetically by the Protestant ethic, before there were in Germany either Protestants or Max Weber. Martin was pushed by his father to improve his social position. His father himself advanced from being a peasant, then a miner, and at last a middle-class proprietor who planned that Martin should become a professional man, a lawyer. The father gave the son beatings, and he gave him affection. And so, lacking the insecurity of Erasmus's bastardy, Luther nevertheless had a soul probably more deeply troubled. Evidently throughout his life he retained mixed feelings of love, awe, and hatred of his authoritarian father. He sought security in the monastic life, made a pilgrimage to Rome. And then he left the cloister forever as an orthodox fundamentalist who was shocked at the Church's urbane worldliness. In October 1517—four hundred years to the month before the Bolsheviks seized the Russian revolution—he posted his indictment of the heterodox actions of a Church that had strayed from Luther's God. Somewhat unintentionally Luther became enormously popular among German noblemen and bourgeoisie. Quite unintentionally, his doctrines became popular among two segments quite lacking in urbanity: peasants and poor people living in cities.

Erasmus and Luther were the most prominent in a movement of religious reform

17

that became a social and then a political revolution that fractured medieval hierarchy. They thus epitomize the profoundest change in Western society in twelve hundred years—since the Christian religion took firm hold in the Roman empire in the year 313.

These gigantic men and their predecessors like John Wycliffe in England and Jan Huss in Bohemia were not simply reforming the Church but restoring the primitive Christian principle of natural equality. Erasmus proposed that people themselves have a new and fresh and natural look at the nonbiblical writings of the great Romans and Greeks, without scholarly pedantry and in the very languages of the ancients. Luther translated the Bible into lay German so that every layman could read it himself. And he insisted that every man must be his own priest.

Erasmus and Luther were thus reasserting the ability of men to look at themselves, to be their own earthly authority, and to bear some responsibility for their own destiny—on earth and beyond. Neither man followed out the logical conclusions of his teaching. Neither advocated modern democracy or universal literacy. Indeed, Erasmus turned against the Reformation and Luther against the peasants who, invoking his belief in equality, revolted against German noblemen and bourgeoisie.

Quite apart from their differing theological principles, both men broke down the churchly and scholarly barriers that for centuries had separated men from their God and from each other. These barriers had blocked people's sensitivity to each other, their creativity, and their ability to act on their own. The work of Erasmus and Luther thus became soon and inevitably political and governmental, because it has been to secure such ends that governments are instituted among men and that they derive their just powers from the consent of the governed.

The Lutheran tragedy

MARGARET M. PHILLIPS

THE similarities between Erasmus and Luther were at first so close as to blind anyone, even themselves, to their fundamental differences. Luther, some 15 years younger than Erasmus, was also an Augustinian monk, though his entry into the monastery had been caused by some violent revulsion of spirit, after a brilliant beginning in the study of law. He was a perfect monk, laboring to fulfil all the duties of an arduous life, and like Erasmus, his support and consolation came from books, though in his case it was particularly the study of the Bible. He had not Erasmus's burning enthusiasm for antiquity, and his Greek never seems to have been carried very far. But he was quick to profit by the critical work of his contemporaries on the text of the Bible, such as that of Lefèvre d'Etaples and Erasmus himself. . . . He was entirely at one with his humanist contemporaries in seeing the key to future development in the right understanding of the texts themselves, and for this purpose the study of the classical languages was essential, though to Luther it was always strictly a means to an end, without the fascination its artistic side had for Erasmus. It was in his own tongue that Luther was to be supremely eloquent, and his identification of himself with the German people provides an easy contrast to Erasmus's Latin cosmopolitanism. But in his beginnings, and to the outward eye, Luther was serving the same cause as the humanists.

His revulsion against medieval philosophy was as strong as Erasmus's. Both of them had been forced to delve into the heritage of the Schoolmen, in order to qualify for their University degrees, and in both the experience produced a lasting horror of the medieval outlook. But Luther was much more theologically minded than Erasmus, and his reaction was a more fundamental one. To Erasmus, sitting through the lectures in Paris and making fun of "Gryllard lecturing from his lofty chair," the stuff he was being asked to follow was merely contemptible; the later medieval philosophers such as Duns Scotus seemed to him equally laughable in form and content, their subjects of argument were so vapid, their methods so hair-splitting, and above all, their Latin so bad! That was the cardinal point: they disgraced the language of Virgil and Cicero.

Erasmus certainly learnt enough medieval philosophy to "satisfy the examiners," but his mind was very little touched by it; his real studies were going on all the time behind the screen of scholastic theology, and as he read the great writers of antiquity he was preparing his own services to a Theology of a different order. In Luther's case this duality was hardly present. Luther read the Schoolmen hoping to discover truth; he must have plunged deeper into the study of the scholastics than Erasmus, for he began by taking them seriously as his masters, and his revulsion from them when he discovered his own point of view was correspondingly acute. He had lectured on them, much to his distaste, and as we have noticed already, their methods had sunk into his mind and he was inclined to use them, even in upholding a point of view diametrically opposed to theirs.

Luther had proclaimed his disagreement with scholastic theology before he stepped into the limelight with his condemnation of indulgences. The theses against the Schoolmen, and against the supremacy of Aristotle, proposed by Luther through his pupils as a subject of disputation in 1516 and 1517, were really more deeply significant of his personal point of view, than those Ninety-five Theses against Indulgences which he posted up on the door of the castle church of Wittenberg on October 31st, 1517. But the practical issue was the one which caught public attention, as indeed Luther intended that it should. Here again, he seemed to be echoing Erasmus. He was not the first person to be shocked by the light-hearted profiteering from religious practices which was being indulged in that time by the Church of Rome, or to condemn what one might call the mechanistic attitude to religion. Had not Erasmus, in his *Enchiridion Militis Christiani*, right at the beginning of the century, written a sincere entreaty to all Christians not to put their faith in mechanical recitation of prayers and masses, kissing of relics, going on pilgrimage, but to try to substitute true charity for the Pharisaism of the time?

And when Luther paid his visit to Rome, probably in 1510, Erasmus had only recently left the Eternal City, as much shocked by some aspects of it as Luther could well be. Differences there certainly were in the impact of Rome on those two powerful individualists. Erasmus, already well known, was received with open arms, and more important, with open libraries, by the learned Cardinals, and his memory of Rome was a mixed one, combining that luxurious welcome, that "fair and fragrant air," and the too-evident abuses and corruption of the Papal Court. He never forgot the sight of Julius II entering Bologna as a conqueror, and it was the un-Apostolic behavior of the Popes rather than their extortions which horrified him. His weapon was satire, and the result of the Italian journey was *The Praise of Folly*. Compare with this picture the memory Luther had of himself, entering Rome as an obscure monk sent by his Order, with a naïve desire to turn this experience to the profit of his soul, and dropping on his knees at sight of the Holy City. He intended to make a complete confession of all the sins of his whole life, and to earn all the benefits promised to those who accomplished pious actions. So he found himself climbing up the steps to the Lateran, saying a paternoster at each step to earn for his grandfather's soul the indulgence promised at the top, and suddenly "coming to" with a great shock as he realized that he had doubts about the spiritual value of such a performance. Already at that time he was beginning to have a glimpse of the revelation which was to underlie all his subsequent work, but his views needed several years of maturing before they were to be proclaimed to the world in the years following 1517.

The practice of indulgences was no new thing. It had gradually developed as part of the penitential system of the Church. Side by side with confession and contrition, penance had been recognized from early days, and in the Middle Ages it became the practice to make satisfaction for sins in some tangible form. The Crusaders were promised remission of sins or at least relaxation of penance; indulgences from penance were offered to people who contributed to the building of a church or founded a charity. The system was extended during the 14th century and in the 15th it included military and financial support in the war against the Turks and in rebuilding St. Peter's. "By the beginning of the 16th century the indulgence system had become one of the most productive devices of papal finance."[1] It was in the 15th century that the efficacy of this method of obtaining money was increased by the extending of the benefit of indulgences to souls in purgatory.

Such a system could not fail to have its critics, and Luther was not alone in his condemnation of it. The Indulgence of 1515–17, which provoked his open attack, was one of the most scandalous of these devices to obtain cash for the Papal treasury. It was an Indulgence proclaimed throughout the lands of the Archbishop of Mainz, and the proceeds were, by a secret arrangement, to be halved between the Archbishop and the Pope, for the express purpose of helping the Archbishop to pay for a dispensation which he needed to allow him to hold three high offices in the Church at once, while under the canonical age. This shady piece of work was camouflaged as a Jubilee indulgence for the building of St. Peter's, and contributors were promised a wide range of benefits, remission of all their sins however heinous, and remission for the dead as well as the living. No methods seem to have been too blatant for the indulgence preachers, especially the Dominican John Tetzel, who was the most successful of them all. It seems clear that these preachers did actually affirm that a mere money payment, apart from prayer or contrition, was enough to free a soul from purgatory, that they painted in lurid colors the agonies of their hearers' deceased relatives from which a small donation would set them free; and that a brisk trade in pardons was going on when Luther posted up his protest on the door of the Church at Wittenberg.

The consequences of this act have made it appear more dramatic than it was, an appeal to popular opinion or a manifesto. It was actually a perfectly normal proceeding, the announcement in the usual manner of a forthcoming academic disputation on the subject of punishment and repentance. Luther was led to it by his reading of the New Testament, and it was evidently by the help of Erasmus that he had come to realize that the words *poenitantiam agere* might have a different meaning than that given them by the Church. Instead of commanding the Christian to make satisfaction for his sins by the fulfilment of certain works of penance, the precept meant "Repent ye"—rend your hearts and not your garments, undergo an inner change brought about by the grace of God. So far, in attacking the materialistic nature of the system of penance, Luther could be sure of the approbation of a spectator like Erasmus; he was speaking exactly in the vein of the *Enchiridion*. There were certainly differences of approach; Luther's was the direct and violent attack, Erasmus's the subtler rapier-thrust of ridicule. But there is no doubt that they would unhesitatingly have condemned the same vices and struggled equally to eliminate them.

Apparently, then, in 1517, Erasmus and Luther represented the same spirit of reform. Fundamentally the contrast was immense. It is well to see this clearly before beginning to study the actual tenor of their relations with each other, since the superficial likeness and the deep antagonism hold between them the key to the understanding of events. No two people could have approached these problems from more different angles or with more dissimilar experience.

The cardinal fact in Luther's life had been the hour of illumination in the tower-room of the monastery at Wittenberg, in 1512 or 1513, when there flashed upon him a new meaning of the words in Romans i, 16–17: "The just shall live by faith." Luther, one of the "twice-born," needed to reverse the direction of his whole life and be reborn into another vision of reality before he could begin his life-work. His years in the monastery had been a time of torment, not of intellectual frustration as in Erasmus's case, but of spiritual agony, because the beliefs which he had accepted from medieval theology were useless to satisfy his soul.

The later Schoolmen, Duns Scotus and Occam, and their followers, who were Luther's first masters in theology, held that man, having free will in himself, can of his own accord, through baptismal grace, turn to God and thus merit the grace which leads to salvation. It is true, they said, that the salvation of man depends on the grace of God and His sovereign will, and the "merit" which man can acquire is only merit in so far as God is pleased to accept it as such. But he has endowed man with free will and has ruled that by exerting it in the right direction, by doing what in him lies to achieve the good life, man can earn or at any rate contribute to his own salvation. This doctrine depended on an optimistic view of human nature and minimized the power of evil and the effects of sin; it virtually did away with the conception of original sin as a fundamental corruption of man's nature, and it put a certain emphasis on the acts of the individual towards his own salvation, rather than on the saving of the world by the Redeemer. It is natural

that such a doctrine should provide a foundation for a mechanistic view of religion, and as philosophy, however recondite, ends in influencing the masses, so there is a direct relation between the intricate theories of the schools and the exaggerated practices which both Erasmus and Luther condemned.

To Erasmus, however, the matter was a question of behavior rather than of doctrine. Dogma was anathema to him. He was no theologian and knew it, and it was in the name of common sense alone that he had made his impassioned plea in the *Enchiridion* for the return to spiritual ideals. Anyone could see by the mere light of reason applied to the teaching of the Gospel, that God did not require ceremonies and observances, but purity of life, peace, brotherly love, an attempt, however feeble, to imitate the character of Jesus. Erasmus does not attempt to go into the doctrinal background of this simplified Christianity. His counsel presupposes certain things: a belief in man's latent power to do right when once enlightened, a close interaction between intelligence and ethical behavior that is almost Cartesian. His introduction of the ancients into the education of a Christian is founded on the idea that their virtues, though unenlightened by Christian revelation, are still valuable and in their way God-given. If tackled on the question, Erasmus would have evaded the issue until it was no longer possible, when he would have retorted that, of course, all virtue and merit must ultimately derive from God. But he usually succeeded in evading all fundamental abstract problems, being eminently practical, especially interested in ethics and really very humble in face of the great mysteries of the spiritual world. He was one of the "once-born"; he began in the way he was to pursue for the rest of his life, and combined elements from different backgrounds to form what was for him a satisfactory working rule for living.

Clearly, if Erasmus hated the Schoolmen, it was not for their fundamental doctrines so much as for their methods and their "barbarism." With Luther it was otherwise. Luther, the inward-looking, was strongly conscious of the gulf which separated him from the righteousness of God; he lived his years in the monastery with the torments of a troubled conscience. His efforts to lead the good life, by fulfilling perfectly all that was required of him, put the philosophy he was taught to the test, and he found it wanting. He was acutely conscious that he *had not* in himself the power to do right, whatever the Schoolmen might say. No efforts of his own could wash away the consciousness of guilt from his soul. In his entourage, no one seemed to understand his restlessness: even the Vicar-General of his Order, John Staupitz, his kindly confessor, was unable to assuage his misery. He came to hate and fear the thought of a righteous God; he went through agonies of rebellion at the thought of the retribution which such a God was bound to visit on the guilty. Christianity as Luther came to conceive it in his period of trial was not a religion of love; it was full of terror and the sky was dark. The effort to discover the road to salvation, to a sense of oneness with the Divine, taxed all his powers and he felt it was completely unavailing.

So he struggled up to the day and hour when, after a long period of intense meditation on the passage of St. Paul in Romans i, 16–17, he had a sudden illumination. Hitherto the idea suggested to him by the phrase "the righteousness of God" had been that of retribution, of a just and terrible God who could not be placated by the puny satisfaction that man could make for his sins. His moment of illumination, as he himself explains it, revealed to him that "the righteousness of God revealed in the Gospel" could only be understood in connection with the following clause, "the just shall live by faith." That righteousness of the Gospel was not the righteousness of the law, the inexorable perfection before which no human soul can stand and which must needs punish the guilty; it was the gift of God to man, the righteousness which God mercifully imputes to the sinner, the garment with which He clothes the naked, the wealth He bestows on the indigent out of His own boundless treasure. Such righteousness has

nothing to do with man's puny efforts towards virtue: they fade into nonexistence in comparison with the great force of God's goodness. The illimitable power of redeeming Providence is substituted for the vain struggles of the soul. From a life of frustration and dissatisfaction with his own useless striving, Luther felt himself to be born again into a life of power; he was like a sinking swimmer, who feels his limbs giving way and his strokes growing weaker, when he is suddenly lifted up and swept to shore by the irresistible swell of the sea.

The idea which lifted Luther out of his personal misery and struck the weight from his shoulders, the doctrine of justification by faith and not by works, was, therefore, at the root of all his subsequent actions. In the light of it he reread Scripture with a sense of freedom and joy. Not all at once, but gradually, he saw how profoundly it struck at the root of the medieval philosophy which had so failed to satisfy him. He now turned against the methods of Aristotle and the ideas of the Schoolmen with a passionate conviction, and in working out his own theology he was as dogmatic and as argumentative as his masters. It was a matter not of philosophy but of experience to him, that man is powerless to help himself until he is illumined by faith; he may wish to do right but he cannot, his will is enslaved, his understanding is dark, his inner conflict holds him bound, his virtue is derisory. It is strange that such a view of human nature should be the result and accompaniment of a psychological release, but so it is; to those like Luther the idea that all good is of God and comes through faith, and all human values are worthless in themselves is a springing source of power and joy.

The process by which this regeneration is brought about by divine grace, transferring to the sinner the effects of the redemption of Christ, was the subject of Luther's commentaries as a lecturer on divinity, and he had already worked out his position by the time he sprang into prominence in 1517. He had discovered by then his mission as a Reformer. It is not possible for us here to go into the details of Luther's theological writings, but two points must be kept in mind for our purpose. One is that Luther's outlook necessarily included the negation of free will, and, therefore, was in direct antagonism not only to the later medieval philosophers but to the humanists. It was a curious fate that led Luther and Erasmus at the same time to attack the Schoolmen and such practices of their own age as the traffic in indulgences, and made them seem to be brothers-in-arms facing the same enemies, when in reality they were doing so from very different motives. When Erasmus condemned mechanical religious practices, he did so because he saw how they were substituted for ethical standards; he wished to see man's desire for salvation translated into a purer form of effort towards the good life. In other words, he thought the effort was valuable, if it was directed into intelligent instead of stupid channels, and that if the simple mind which treasured tangible relics could be led to treasure the precepts of Christ instead, a great advance would be made. But when Luther condemned indulgences, he did so from a deep conviction which counted not only these purely mechanical practices but all works as worthless; trust in indulgences was merely the most glaring instance of a faulty point of view. The higher and purer forms of moral effort, apart from a self-rejecting faith in the mercy of God, would fall for Luther under the same condemnation. And so, necessarily, all the works of antiquity would share the same fate.

The other point arising from Luther's premises which must not be forgotten, is that his view of the corruption of man's nature and man's own helplessness to correct it, led him to develop his belief in predestination. A logical outcome of the negation of free will, the doctrine of predestination is the furthest point of separation between humanist and reformer. It was taken up and developed later by Calvin, and the crystal-clear exposition of the whole doctrine in his *Institution de la Religion Chrétienne* (Latin, 1536, French 1541) marks the completion of the process by which the Revival of Learning and the Reformation branched away from each other. But it was really implicit in Luther's view of Christianity from the beginning. If man's will is vitiated and he cannot raise a finger to help himself, then it is without his volition that the gift of faith descends upon him, transforming his universe of sin into a place of redemption; he will certainly strive towards the good, but only as a result of this free gift of grace, which he cannot in any way attract or deserve. But sin is powerful in the world, and only a certain number of people raise their heads towards the light; it was clear to Luther, following Augustine, that God in His inscrutable wisdom did not bestow the gift of grace on all, but only on the elect. Who they are, he said, and why they are chosen, it is not for man to know; and that any at all should be excepted from the just condemnation for sin, is an extraordinary effect of God's mercy. So the overpowering conviction of sin in Luther's mind led him to this inexorable doctrine, and separated him forever from humanist and Catholic; the one glorying in the inborn love of beauty and virtue in all mankind, the other believing that every baptized Christian has a gift of grace, enough to enable him to turn of his own free will to seek the aid of the Redeemer.

*Some economics, politics, and
warfare in the German
reformation*

The Protestant Reformation has been interpreted by devout Protestants and Catholics as a largely religious controversy, having as a central issue the assertion that every man is his own priest. Luther's assertion is not the only religious issue he raised, nor is it only a religious issue. It is also, as earlier indicated, a human, moral issue having to do with the values which, when men agree on them, provide the basis for rules governing how they act toward each other. The religious doctrine of the priesthood of all believers—a moral issue between laymen and clerics—inevitably has led to an issue in political morality, the principle of equality in the making of decisions on public policy. The value on which this moral issue rests is the equal dignity of men, a principle which Luther accepted but did not consistently practice.

The failure of Luther and his followers to admit to the full logical implications of equality in politics was natural and obvious. Each successive group in any developing society that demands public recognition (and power) does so in the name of the universal principle of equality—whose universality is forgotten when that group gets recognition (and power). The princes, nobles, and propertied townsmen who supported Luther saw the political implications for themselves of his equalitarianism (and nationalism). They could assert and gain, as a matter of right, complete independence from not just the spiritual, but also the temporal power of others—of those acting under the authority of the Roman Church.

But it is easy to fall into the notion that the Protestant Reformation in Germany was only a moral issue, religious and political. To escape this simplism we should look at modern economic developments that were modifying without radically changing the feudal relationships between various segments of German society. By means of trade and simple manufacture, principally of cloth and metal goods, the temporal and visible world was changing. Men's aspirations were rising; they became self-disciplined and future-oriented. Their achievements also rose; they became rich and worldly.

The increase in wealth raised the demand for worldly goods among even the most devout, including nobles whose traditional function was not to create or exchange goods but to protect goods and people from predation. An intraclass war developed

24

between nobles who acknowledged the authority of Rome and its empire and those who acknowledged only their own authority. To support these wars over principalities and goods, the peasants, whom nobles were bound to protect, became the object of rival predatory nobles. Just as German princes gathered under the Lutheran standard in the name of independence from Rome, so German peasants gathered under the same standard in the name of independence from preying German nobles.

Both poverty and warfare threaten the physical survival of people and isolate them from each other in the individual fight to survive. This helps explain why American blacks for a century after the Civil War of 1861–65 were able to establish only a rudimentary group identity. In 1525 there was a vigorous revolt of peasants in Germany. For a time they maintained a remarkable cohesiveness. It was not so strong or enduring as to turn their revolt into a revolution. Luther, the grandson of lifelong peasants and the son of a peasant turned miner, turned savagely against the peasants, saying they lived "pell-mell, like rats in the straw." And he blessed with his righteousness their eradication during the 1525 war.

The bases for German peasant discontent were not identical but similar to those that Tocqueville later described as developing in France before its great revolution and to those which Mao Tse-tung and others emphasized in China before its great revolution. In the 1525 instance, German peasants carried out one of the earliest modern rural revolts and failed. In 1789 French peasants followed the lead of people in the major cities, in effecting not a revolt but a revolution. And in the 1920s and 1930s Chinese peasants took the lead in organizing the basis for the successful 1949 Chinese revolution. The ideologies in these three instances were quite different. The strength and endurance of cohesiveness in the French and Chinese instances appears to have been greater than in the German and to have made a critical difference between failure and success.

The peasant war in Germany

FRIEDRICH ENGELS

LET us first review briefly the situation in Germany at the beginning of the 16th century.

German industry had gone through a considerable process of growth in the 14th and 15th centuries. The local industry of the feudal countryside was superseded by the guild organization of production in the cities, which produced for wider circles and even for remote markets. Weaving of crude woolen stuffs and linens had become a well-established, ramified branch of industry, and even finer woolen and linen fabrics, as well as silks, were already being produced in Augsburg. Outside of the art of weaving, there had arisen those branches of industry, which, approaching the finer arts, were nurtured by the demands for luxuries on the part of the ecclesiastic and lay lords of the late mediæval epoch: gold and silver-smithing, sculpture and woodcarving, etching and wood-engraving, armor-making, medal-engraving, wood-turning, etc., etc. A series of more or less important discoveries culminating in the invention of gunpowder and printing had considerably aided the development of the crafts.

Commerce kept pace with industry. The Hanseatic League, through its century-long monopoly of sea navigation, had brought about the emergence of the entire north of Germany out of mediæval barbarism; and even when, after the end of the 16th century, the Hanseatic League had begun to succumb to the competition of the English and the Dutch, the great highway of commerce from India to the north still lay through Germany, Vasco da Gama's discoveries notwithstanding. Augsburg still remained the great point of concentration for Italian silks, Indian spices, and all Levantine products. The cities of upper Germany, namely, Augsburg and Nürnberg, were the centers of opulence and luxury remarkable for that time. The production of raw materials had equally progressed. The German miners of the 15th century had been the most skillful in the world, and agriculture was also shaken out of its mediæval crudity through the blossoming forth of the cities. Not only had large stretches of land been put under cultivation, but dye plants and other imported cultures had been introduced, which in turn had a favorable influence on agriculture as a whole.

Still, the progress of national production in Germany had not kept pace with the progress of other countries. Agriculture lagged far behind that of England and Holland. Industry lagged far behind the Italian, Flemish and English, and as to sea navigation, the English, and especially the Dutch, were already driving the Germans out of the field. The population was still very sparse. Civilization in Germany existed only in spots, around the centers of industry and commerce; but even the interests of these individual centers diverged widely, with hardly any point of contact. The trade relations and markets of the South differed from those of the North; the East and the West had almost no intercourse. No city had grown to become the industrial and commercial point of gravity for the whole country, such as London was for England. Internal communication was almost exclusively confined to coastwise and river navigation and to a few large commercial highways, like those from Augsburg and Nürnberg through Cologne to the Netherlands, and through Erfurt to the North. Away from the rivers and highways of commerce there was a number of smaller cities which, excluded from the great trade centers, continued a sluggish existence under conditions of late mediæval times, consuming few non-local articles, and yielding few products for export. Of the rural population, only the nobility came into contact with wide circles and new wants; the mass of the peasants never overstepped the boundaries of local relations and local outlook.

While in England, as well as in France, the rise of commerce and industry had brought about a linking of interests over the entire country, the political centralization of Germany had succeeded only in the grouping of interests according to provinces and around purely local centers. This meant political decentralization which later gained momentum through the exclusion of Germany from world commerce. In the degree as the purely feudal empire was falling apart, bonds of unity were becoming weakened, great feudal vassals were turning into almost independent princes, and cities of the empire on the one hand, the knights of the empire on the other, were forming alliances either against each other, or against the princes or the emperor. The imperial power, now uncertain as to its own position, vacillated between the various elements opposing the empire, and was constantly losing authority; the attempt at centralization, in the manner of Louis XI, brought about nothing but the holding together of the Austrian hereditary lands, this in spite of all intrigues and violent actions. The final winners, who could not help winning in this confusion, in this helter-skelter of numerous conflicts, were the representatives of centralization amidst disunion, the representatives of local and provincial centralization, the princes, beside whom the emperor gradually became no more than a prince among princes.

Under these conditions the situation of the classes emerging from mediæval times had considerably changed. New classes had been formed besides the old ones.

Out of the old nobility came the princes. Already they were almost independent of the emperor, and possessed the major part of sovereign rights. They declared war and made peace of their own accord, they maintained standing armies, called local councils, and levied taxes. They had already drawn a large part of the lower nobility and cities under their lordly power; they did everything in their power to incorporate in their lands all the rest of the cities and baronies which still remained under the empire. Towards such cities and baronies they appeared in the role of centralizers, while as far as the imperial power was concerned, they were the decentralizing factor. Internally, their reign was already autocratic, they called the estates only when they could not do without them. They imposed taxes, and collected money whenever they saw fit. The right of the estates to ratify taxes was seldom recognized, and still more seldom practiced. And even when they were called, the princes ordinarily had a majority, thanks to the knights and the prelates which were the two estates freed from taxes, participating, nevertheless, in their consumption. The need of the princes for money grew with the taste for luxuries, with the increase of the courts and the standing armies, with the mounting costs of administration. The taxes were becoming more and more oppressive.

The cities being in most cases protected against them by privileges, the entire weight of the tax burden fell upon the peasants, those under the princes themselves, as well as the serfs and bondsmen of the knights bound by vassalage to the princes; wherever direct taxation was insufficient, indirect taxes were introduced; the most skillful machinations of the art of finance were utilized to fill the gaping holes of the fiscal system. When nothing else availed, when there was nothing to pawn and no free imperial city was willing to grant credit any longer, one resorted to coin manipulations of the basest kind, one coined depreciated money, one set a higher or lower rate of legal tender most convenient for the prince. Trading in city and other privileges, subsequently to be taken away by force, in order that they might again be sold, seizing every attempt at opposition as an excuse for incendiarism and robbery of every kind, etc., etc., were lucrative and quite ordinary sources of income for the princes of those times. The administration of justice was also a constant and not unimportant article of trade for the princes. In brief, the subjects who, besides the princes, had to satisfy the private appetites of their magistrates and bailiffs as well, were enjoying the full taste of the "fatherly" system.

Of the mediæval feudal hierarchy, the knighthood of moderate possessions had almost entirely disappeared; it had either climbed up to the position of independence of small princes, or it had sunk into the ranks of the lower nobility. The lower nobility, the knighthood, was fast moving towards extinction. A large portion of it had already become pauperized, and lived on its services to the princes, either in military or in civil capacity; another portion was bound by vassalage to the sovereignty of the prince; a very small portion was directly under the empire. The development of military science, the rising importance of infantry, the spread of firearms, had dwarfed their military importance as heavy cavalry, at the same time destroying the invincibility of their castles. The knights had become superfluous through the progress of industry, just as the artisans had become obviated by the same progress. The dire need of the knighthood for money added considerably to their ruin. The luxurious life in the castles, the competition in magnificence at tournaments and feasts, the price of armaments and of horses all increased with the progress of civilization, whereas the sources of income of the knights and barons, increased but little, if at all.

Feuds with accompanying plunders and incendiarism, lying in ambush, and similar noble occupations, became in the course of time too dangerous. The cash payments of the knights' subjects brought in hardly more than before. In order to satisfy mounting requirements, the noble masters resorted to the same means as were practiced by the princes; the peasantry was being robbed by the masters with greater dexterity every year. The serfs were being wrung dry. The bondsmen were burdened with ever new payments of various descriptions upon every possible occasion. Serf labor, dues, ground rents, land sale taxes, death taxes, protection moneys and so on, were increased at will in spite of old agreements. Justice was denied or sold for money, and wherever the knight could not obtain the peasant's money otherwise, he threw him into the tower without much ado, and compelled him to pay ransom.

With the other classes, the lower nobility courted no friendly relations either. Vassal knights strove to become vassals of the empire; vassals of the empire strove to become independent. This led to incessant conflicts with the princes. The knighthood looked upon the clergy with their resplendent grandeur as upon a powerful but superfluous class. It envied them their large estates and their riches held secure by celibacy and the church constitution. With the cities, the knighthood was continually on the war path; it owed them money, it fed on plundering their territory, on robbing their merchants, on the ransom paid for prisoners captured in conflicts. The struggle of the knighthood against all these estates became more vehement as the estates themselves began to realize that the money question was a life problem for them.

The clergy, representatives of the ideology of mediæval feudalism, felt the influence of the historic transformation no less acutely. The invention of the art of printing, and the requirements of extended commerce, robbed the clergy not only of its monopoly of reading and writing, but also of that of higher education. Division of labor was being introduced also into the realm of intellectual work. The newly arising class of jurists drove the clergy out of a series of very influential positions. The clergy was also beginning to become largely superfluous, and it acknowledged this fact by growing lazier and more ignorant. The more superfluous it became, the more it grew in numbers, thanks to the enormous riches which it still kept on augmenting by fair means or foul.

The clergy was divided into two distinct groups. The feudal hierarchy of the clergy formed the aristocratic group—bishops and archbishops, abbots, priors and other prelates. These high church dignitaries were either imperial princes themselves, or they reigned as vassals of other princes over large areas with numerous serfs and bondsmen. They not only exploited their subjects as recklessly as the knighthood and the princes, but they practiced this in an even more shameful manner. They used not only brutal force, but all the intrigues of religion as well; not only the horrors of the rack, but also the horror of excommunication, or refusal of absolution; they used all the intricacies of the confessional in order to extract from their subjects the last penny, or to increase the estates of the church. Forging of documents was a widespread and beloved means of extortion in the hands of those worthy men, who, receiving from their subjects feudal payments, taxes and tithes, were still in constant need of money. The manufacture of miracle-producing saints' effigies and relics, the organization of praying-centers endowed with the power of salvation, the trade in indulgences was resorted to in order to squeeze more payments out of the people. All this was practiced long and with not little success.

The prelates and their numerous gendarmerie of monks which grew with the spread of political and religious baiting, were the objects of hatred not only of the people but also of the nobility. Being directly under the empire, the prelates were in the way of the princes. The fast living of the corpulent bishops and abbots with their army of monks, roused the envy of the nobility and the indignation of the people who bore the burden. Hatred was intensified by the fact that the behavior of the clergy was a slap in the face of their own preaching.

The plebeian faction of the clergy consisted of preachers, rural and urban. The preachers were outside the feudal hierarchy of the church and participated in none of its riches. Their activities were less rigorously controlled and, important as they were for the church, they were for the moment far less indispensable than the police services of the barracked monks. Consequently, they were paid much less than the monks, and their prebends were far from lucrative. Being of a middle-class or plebeian origin, they were nearer to the life of the masses, thus being able to retain middle-class and plebeian sympathies, in spite of their status as clergy. While the participation of the monks in the movements of their time was the exception, that of the plebeian clergy was the rule. They gave the movement its theorists and ideologists, and many of them, representatives of the plebeians and peasants, died on the scaffold. The hatred of the masses for the clergy seldom touched this group.

What the emperor was to the princes and nobility, the pope was to the higher and lower clergy. As the emperor received the "common penny," the imperial taxes, so the pope was paid the general church taxes, out of which he defrayed the expenses of the luxurious Roman court. In no country were his taxes collected with such conscientiousness and rigor as in Germany, due to the power and the number of the clergy. The annates were collected with particular severity when a bishopric was to become vacant. With the growth of the court's demands, new means for raising revenues were invented, such as the traffic in relics and indulgences, jubilee collections, etc. Large sums of money were thus yearly transported from Germany to Rome, and the increased pressure fanned not only the hatred towards the clergy, but it also aroused national feelings, particularly among the nobility, the then most national class.

In the cities, the growth of commerce and handicraft produced three distinct groups out of the original citizenry of mediæval times.

The city population was headed by the *patrician families*, the so-called "honorables." Those were the richest families. They alone sat in the council, and held all the city offices. They not only administered all the revenues of the city, but they also consumed them. Strong in their riches and their ancient aristocratic status, recognized by emperor and empire, they exploited in every possible way the city community as well as the peasants belonging to the city. They practiced usury in grain and money; they secured for themselves monopolies of various kinds; they gradually deprived the community of every right to use the city forests and meadows, and used them directly for their own private benefit. They imposed road, bridge and gate payments and other duties; they sold trade and guild privileges, master and citizen rights; and they traded with justice.

The peasants of the city area were treated by them with no more consideration than by the nobility and the clergy. On the contrary, the city magistrates and bailiffs, mostly patricians, brought into the villages, together with aristocratic rigidity and avarice, a certain bureaucratic punctuality in collecting duties. The city revenues thus collected were administered in a most optional fashion; city bookkeeping was as neglectful and confused as possible; defraudation and treasury deficits were the order of the day. How easy it was for a comparatively small caste, surrounded by privileges, and held together by family ties and community of interests, to enrich itself enormously out of the city revenues, will be understood when one considers the numerous frauds and swindles which 1848 witnessed in many city administrations.

The patricians took care to make dormant the rights of the city community everywhere, particularly as regards finance. Later, when the extortions of these gentlemen became too severe, the communities started a movement to bring at least the city administration under their control. In most cities they actually regained their rights, but due, on the one hand, to the eternal squabbles between the guilds and, on the other, to the tenacity of the patricians and their protection by the empire and the governments of the allied cities, the patrician council members soon restored by shrewdness or force their dominance in the councils. At the beginning of the 16th century, the communities of all the cities were again in the opposition.

The city opposition against the patricians was divided into two factions which stood out very clearly in the course of the peasant war.

The *middle-class opposition*, the predecessor of our modern liberals, embraced the richer middle-class, the middle-class of moderate means, and a more or less appreciable section of the poorer elements, according to local conditions. This opposition demanded control over the city administration and participation in the legislative power either through a general assemblage of the community or through representatives (big council, city committee). Further, it demanded modification of the patrician policy of favoring a few families which were gaining an exceptional position inside the patrician group. Aside from this, the middle-class opposition demanded the filling of some council offices by citizens of their own group. This party, joined here and there by dissatisfied elements of impoverished patricians, had a large majority in all the ordinary general assemblies of the community and in the guilds. The adherents of the council and the more radical opposition formed together only a minority among the real citizens.

We shall see how, in the course of the 16th century, this moderate, "law-abiding," well off and intelligent opposition played exactly the same rôle and exactly with the same success as its heir, the constitutional party in the movements of 1848 and 1849. The middle-class opposition had still another object of heated protest: the clergy, whose loose way of living and luxurious habits aroused its bitter scorn. The middle-class opposition demanded measures against the scandalous behavior of those illustrious people. It demanded that the inner jurisdiction of the clergy and its right to levy taxes should be abolished, and that the number of the monks should be limited.

The *plebeian opposition* consisted of ruined members of the middle-class and that mass of the city population which possessed no citizenship rights: the journeymen, the day laborers, and the numerous beginnings of the *lumpenproletariat* which can be found even in the lowest stages of development of city life. This low-grade proletariat is, generally speaking, a phenomenon which, in a more or less developed form, can be found in all the phases of society hitherto observed. The number of people without a definite occupation and a stable domicile was at that time gradually being augmented by the decay of feudalism in a society in which every occupation, every realm of life, was intrenched behind a number of privileges.

In no modern country was the number of vagabonds so great as in Germany, in the first half of the 16th century. One portion of these tramps joined the army in wartime, another begged its way through the country, a third sought to eke out a meager living as day-laborers in those branches of work which were not under guild jurisdiction. All three groups played a rôle in the peasant war; the first in the army of the princes to whom the peasant succumbed, the second in the conspiracies and in the troops of the peasants where its demoralizing influence was manifested every moment; the third, in the struggles of the parties in the cities. It must be borne in mind, however, that a large portion of this class, namely, the one living in the cities, still retained a considerable foundation of peasant nature, and had not developed that degree of venality and degradation which characterize the modern civilized low-grade proletariat.

It is evident that the plebeian opposition of the cities was of a mixed nature. It combined the ruined elements of the old feudal and guild societies with the budding proletarian elements of a coming modern bourgeois society; on the one hand, impoverished guild citizens, who, due to their privileges, still clung to the existing middle-class order, on the other hand, driven out peasants and exofficers who were yet unable to become proletarians. Between these two groups were the journeymen, for the time being outside official society and so close to the standard of living of the proletariat as was possible under the industry of the times and the guild privileges, but, due to the same privileges, almost all prospective middle-class master artisans. The party affiliations of this mixture were, naturally, highly uncertain, and varying from locality to locality.

Before the peasant war, the plebeian opposition appeared in the political struggles, not as a party, but as a shouting, repacious tail-end to the middle-class opposition, a mob that could be bought and sold for a few barrels of wine. It was the revolt of the peasants that transformed them into a party, and even then they were almost everywhere dependent upon the peasants, both in demands and in action—a striking proof of the fact that the cities of that time were greatly dependent upon the country. In so far as the plebeian opposition acted independently, it demanded extension of city trade privileges over the rural districts, and it did like to see the city revenues curtailed by abolition of feudal burdens in the rural area belonging to the city, etc. In brief, in so far as it appeared independently, it was reactionary. It submitted to its own middle-class elements, and thus formed a characteristic prologue to the tragic comedy staged by the modern petty-bourgeoisie in the last three years under the head of democracy.

Only in Thuringia and in a few other localities was the plebeian faction of the city carried away by the general storm to such an extent that its embryo proletarian elements for a brief time gained the upper hand over all the other factors of the movement. This took place under the direct influence of Münzer in Thuringia, and of his disciples in other places. This episode, forming the climax of the entire peasant war, and grouped around the magnificent figure of Thomas Münzer, was of very brief duration. It is easily understood why these elements collapse more quickly than any other, why their movement bears an outspoken, fantastic stamp, and why the expression of their demands must necessarily be extremely indefinite. It was this group that found least firm ground in the then existing conditions.

At the bottom of all the classes, save the last one, was the huge exploited mass of the nation, *the peasants*. It was the peasant who carried the burden of all the other strata of society: princes, officialdom, nobility, clergy, patricians and middle-class. Whether the peasant was the subject of a prince, an imperial baron, a bishop, a monastery or a city, he was everywhere treated as a beast of burden, and worse. If he was a serf, he was entirely at the mercy of his master. If he was a bondsman, the legal deliveries stipulated by agreement were sufficient to crush him; even they were being daily increased. Most of his time, he had to work on his master's estate. Out of that which he earned in his few free hours, he had to pay tithes, dues, ground rents, war taxes, land taxes, imperial taxes, and other payments. He could neither marry nor die without paying the master. Aside from his regular work for the master, he had to gather litter, pick strawberries, pick bilberries, collect snail-shells, drive the game for the hunting, chop wood, and so on. Fishing and hunting belonged to the master. The peasant saw his crop destroyed by wild game. The community meadows and woods of the peasants had almost everywhere been forcibly taken away by the masters.

And in the same manner as the master reigned over the peasant's property, he extended his willfulness over his person, his wife and daughters. He possessed the right of the first night. Whenever he pleased, he threw the peasant into the tower, where the rack waited for him just as surely as the investigating attorney waits for the criminal in our times. Whenever he pleased, he killed him or ordered him beheaded. None of the instructive chapters of the Carolina which speaks of "cutting of ears," "cutting of noses," "blinding," "chopping of fingers," "beheading," "breaking on the wheel," "burning," "pinching with burning tongs," "quartering," etc., was left unpracticed by the gracious lord and master at his pleasure. Who could defend the peasant? The courts were manned by barons, clergymen, patricians, or jurists, who knew very well for what they were being paid. Not in vain did all the official estates of the empire live on the exploitation of the peasants.

Incensed as were the peasants under terrific pressure, it was still difficult to arouse them to revolt. Being spread over large areas, it was highly difficult for them to come to a common understanding; the old habit of submission inherited from generation to generation, the lack of practice in the use of arms in many regions, the unequal degree of exploitation depending on the personality of the master, all combined to keep the peasant quiet. It is for these reasons that, although local insurrections of peasants can be found in mediæval times in large numbers, not one general national peasant revolt, least of all in Germany, can be observed before the peasant war. Moreover, the peasants alone could never make a revolution as long as they were confronted by the organized power of the princes, nobility and the cities. Only by allying themselves with other classes could they have a chance of victory, but how could they have allied themselves with other classes when they were equally exploited by all?

At the beginning of the 16th century the various groups of the empire, princes, nobility, clergy, patricians, middle-class, plebeians and peasants formed a highly complicated mass with the most varied requirements crossing each other in different directions. Every group was in the way of the other, and stood continually in an overt or covert struggle with every other group. A splitting of the entire nation into two major camps, as witnessed in France at the outbreak of the first revolution, and as at present manifest on a higher stage of development in the most progressive countries, was under such conditions a rank impossibility. Something approaching such division took place only when the lowest stratum of the population, the one exploited by all the rest, arose, namely, the plebeians and the peasants. The tangle of interests, views and endeavors of that time will be easily understood when one remembers what a confusion was manifested in the last two years in a society far less complicated and consisting only of feudal nobility, bourgeoisie, petty-bourgeoisie, peasants and proletariat.

Some economics, politics, and warfare in 20th-century Asia

The peasants of Germany in 1525 effected a revolt in one of the first societies to begin the modern process of development. The following selection describes the beginnings of development in a 20th-century Asian context. It bears striking resemblance to what happened four centuries before in Europe—and Boeke is able to probe deeper than Engels in telling what happens to primitive villagers when they are thrust into interaction with the modern world.

The way of life of the 20th-century villagers is indeed similar to that of their 16th-century German precursors. But in the 20th century the confrontation with the new is more sudden and the time available to accept and reject change is much shorter. The attractions and distractions that accompany change now call for making the same frightful leap much more quickly.

In some Asian countries this rapid change from a subsistence to a developing exchange economy has been made relatively peacefully, as in Japan and India. In other countries the change has been made with great and savage violence, most notably in China. Indonesia, in the postcolonial phase of its modernization process, overthrew the Sukarno regime and brutally destroyed native Communists and their followers, most notably in rural villages, starting in October and November 1965. In the following article a Dutch scholar writes mainly from his experience in Indonesia, telling about some basic aspects of development and thereby suggesting why it went through such a violent stage, more than seventeen years after he wrote.

The village community in collision with capitalism

J. H. BOEKE

IT is difficult to picture so small a world as that of the village. In many regions it averages between twenty and fifty households, in others near a hundred. A village with a thousand on more inhabitants is in danger of outgrowing its strength and losing its communal solidarity.

A government keen on a Western policy finds these small and weak units quite unmanageable. Hence the usual policy of forming new units for administrative purposes by consolidating a number of villages. But to make these new units, these municipalities, into living communities is impossible. The original villages live on as quarters or hamlets in the larger units, and within their own modest limits village life goes on as best it can. The two parties, municipality and village, now try as far as possible to work out a compromise, a division of functions. Western institutions— the school, the cooperative society, the municipal bank, the municipal administration, the public works—are taken care of by the Western-type authorities; the genuine village needs are met by the hamlets. Making a rough distinction, one may say that all modern and economic matters are disposed of by the municipal administration, while the traditional and noneconomic matters are left to the old village council. But in reality, the Western institutions remain strange to village life, and the municipal officers remain strangers in the village. For, this is a community of peasants who for generations have lived together, have grown up with their village; while the representatives of Western-type organizations tend to remain birds of passage, outsiders, "foreigners," townspeople.

Sometimes these outsiders huddle together in one village quarter which thereby acquires a new character: something like an advanced urban outpost. In this quarter one will find the municipal hall, the school, the rice mill, the village store, the credit bank, the new building of the agricultural cooperative society. Here live the mayor, the school teachers, the moneylenders, the tailors and other modern artisans. Here the old village customs are not followed, the traditional forms of mutual help are not practiced, the village ceremonials and festivals are not observed. Here people use the Western calendar to determine their weekly rest day and their holidays. Here economy is based on money and exchange. It speaks volumes that in Japan the Shinto service, propagated by the government and turned into national channels, had its sanctuaries, visited only by its priests and by the municipal boards, in the Western quarters of the municipality; while the Buddhist sanctuaries were left in the different hamlets and still remain true village centers where in the day time children play and in the evening young men gather— buildings also used as stopping places by rural visitors from abroad.

The Western-minded ruler cannot leave the concerns of these precapitalistic villages alone. Especially not in countries with direct rule, where Western policy and Western inspired laws have permeated the whole social structure and are applied to the individual villagers. In these countries the government has no understanding or appreciation for the villages; its economic policy interferes with them; its schools only criticize them; its representatives hold them in contempt. Moreover, these civil servants, these Western authorities, feel themselves strangers in the village community, and this often has serious consequences. Whereas in his relations with the village artisans, the menials as he regards them, the peasant holds a strong position, he is utterly helpless in the clutches of the local government representatives. From this springs the universal phenomenon of corruption: "village life," it is said "is moth-eaten with it." Every service of the authorities, be it the apportionment of irrigation water, a police investigation, an inquiry into the cause of crop failure, or anything else, must be bought and paid for. Sometimes this corruption is regularized, as used to be the case in the Netherlands Indies at the time of the East Indian Company. The most a Western-minded government can achieve if it tries to clean up this corruption is to keep it limited to the lower categories of officials who are in immediate contact with the villagers.

However guarded this contact by direct rule may be in practice, its influence always tends in the same direction. The Western government through its institutions isolates the individual, old and young, from the close community with family and village; forces on him all kinds of organizations imported from the Western world—organizations in which he does not feel at home and of which, therefore, he makes use only as an outsider; forbids and combats his social and religious customs; takes a positive interest exclusively in his economic activities; and accentuates his economic wants without being able to procure for him the means, or strengthen such means as he has, to satisfy these wants. As a result, a sense of frustration, of inferiority, and of poverty is awakened in the individual.

Impoverished and individualized, the villagers tend to neglect their social interests and duties. It takes them more time to earn money. Also, there is less occasion for these interests and duties because many of the customary forms of mutual aid and communal cooperation fall into disuse or become superfluous with the introduction of money and exchange.

This crumbling and shrinking of village life is of the utmost importance: all the village festivals and ceremonies gave color and bloom to the peasants' life, took the place of the numerous material comforts of the city dwellers, prevented the villager from feeling poor, kept strong his social ties with his fellow villagers, filled his life, strengthened his sense of social standing, and gave him a fixed place in the world. With the weakening and falling off of all this, the village becomes poorer, emptier. A tie, a support, a content of the individual life has been taken away, and nothing of equal value has been put in its place. Thus it has come about that the economic elements in the farmer's experience have been laid bare and brought into consciousness. And to a large extent these elements are unfavorable. The soil is no longer able to feed the growing population adequately; poverty and malnutrition are universal in the overcrowded rural parts of the oriental countries; the largest part of the heavy taxes rests on the shoulders of the peasant, although he has by far the least opportunity to earn money; the part of the agricultural output that is taken by the urban landlord in the form of rent constantly increases; with the shrinkage of the average landed property and the disappearance of rural industries, it becomes more and more difficult for the peasant to make full use of his own labor power, and seasonal unemployment is on the increase; the burden of debt under which he groans all the time becomes heavier and claims a rapidly increasing part of his agricultural output as interest; excessive use of the soil exhausts its yielding power and makes crop failure more frequent; underfed, the cattle deteriorates or must be abandoned; the family tie is loosened by Western education, factory labor, and military service. In short, for social elements that held together and supported village society, have come to be substituted economic elements that sever and oppress it.

All these symptoms . . . are summed up to support our criticism of an over-Westernized government policy which fails to appreciate and undermines the noneconomic side of village life—which means its most essential side—without being able to raise the members of these rural communities to a level of prosperity that is satisfactory in itself. . . . If village life should prove to be, now and in the future, the only possible way of life for the overwhelming majority of oriental peoples, any policy stands condemned that destroys more of the old than it can replace with new equivalents.

Meanwhile, weakened and confused though it is, village life continues in these oriental countries, and the rural people there remain strongly attached to the environment where they have learned to accept both the sweet and the bitter fruits of life. In this way, the dualism between town and country dominates the scene. Clinging to his village, the oriental peasant feels the urban sphere as a strange and hostile power. Urban life does not attract him as a realization of his dreams; rather, its inconceivable way of life bewilders him. When he is forced to come in contact with it, he longs for the day when he may return to the familiar sphere and the quiet of his village.

This state of mind, so radically different from that in Western countries, this dualism between town and country, has many important economic consequences. These will be seen as we examine ten different aspects of this dualism.

1. Urban industry does not, as far as its labor supply is concerned, depend on an urban proletariat that has left the country for ever and struck roots in the urban centers. To a large extent it remains dependent on rural labor forces (in Japan mostly girls, in India mostly men) that return to village life when, on the expiration of a term of a few years, the necessity of earning a living in the town has passed.

2. Unemployment arising from the fluctuations in demand for the products of industry does not create a problem of urban over-crowding but a problem for the villages, essentially an agrarian problem.

3. In these oriental countries there is no "industrial reserve army" but an "agrarian reserve army," a rural proletariat or semi-proletariat, precapitalistic in nature, traditional and stationary, not yet ripe for modern organization—a reserve army that weighs down the position of the peasant by its land hunger, and that of the wage earner by its low standard of living.

4. At first, there appears a tendency in industry to decentralize: small and medium-sized enterprises seek to increase their opportunities by settling in, and living on, the country, i.e., by choosing their location in the midst of the rural masses which are expected to be satisfied with a bare subsistence wage.

5. The wage level of industrial labor is depressed by the fact that industrial wages often are only accessory revenue, supplementing the family income of the villager.

6. In homogeneous capitalistic countries, the interests of the landed proprietors usually are opposite to those of the industrial employers. In these countries, the flight from the land, the migration of labor to the towns, forces rural wages up and weighs rents down, to the loss of the landlord, but at the same time increases the supply of urban labor for the benefit of the industrial employer. In dualistic countries, on the other hand, the interests of these two groups run parallel: the landed proprietors have the opportunity to screw up rents because their tenants add to their income from the land that of members of their families away from home as mill hands; at the same time, the industrial employer is able to keep his wage scale low because he works with this rural semiproletariat.

7. The rural population's inclination to migrate is very weak. Before that trend can grow, the attachment to village and field has first to be overcome. Therefore, migration is mostly temporary and does not develop into a colonization of foreign lands.

8. As a production factor labor has, generally speaking, little mobility. This is true in even greater measure of rural labor which is bound to the absolutely immobile peasant family and the village. Hence a remarkable disparity of wages that cannot be levelled out. Whereas those industries that settle in rural areas with a high population density can make an unlimited use of the excessive supply of "hands," those industries which are bound to the places where their raw materials are found or to the urban markets for their products are obliged to supply themselves with labor through expensive agencies or by offering high wages, especially when they need qualified labor. This is also the reason while rural

unemployment and an urban shortage of laborers may appear side by side.

9. There is a great distance between Western capitalistic exchange and the pre-capitalistic family household because of the lack of buying power in the home market which makes that exchange dependent on world markets, hence international in character and concentrated in large Western export and import concerns. Because of this distance, a long chain of intermediaries is needed to connect the two extremes. Moreover, lack of capital and, therefore, of stock accumulation, lack also of purchasing and producing power, lead to an extreme scattering of retail trade and of the trade engaged in buying up the farm produce. The small farmer and the small craftsman hardly take part at all in this intermediary trade. The trader has to penetrate to the home of the consumer and petty producer to effect his small transactions. Hence a development of small and intermediary trade wholly out of proportion with the small purchasing power of the bulk of the population and its small need for exchange of any kind; a development characteristic of extreme poverty. Japan especially gives telling proof of this statement. A comparison of the Japanese occupation census reports for 1920 and 1930 shows that the percentage of all the professional classes went down with two exceptions: first that of the free professions and those engaged in government service, which together rose from 5.3 to 6.9 per cent of the total. But the proportion of the second increasing group, those engaged in trade, rose from 11.7 to 15.3 per cent; the last named percentage being only 3.6 per cent below that for all the industrial vocations together. In this country of small buying power, where almost half the population are self-providing peasants, we find one trader for every seventeen persons. That is why the well known economist, Ryoichi Ishii, calls the increase in the number of small traders an economic problem even more serious than that of unemployment.

10. The consequences of both depression and deflation fall on the back of the peasantry. In a society where an urban proletariat furnishes the labor force while a peasantry provides the foodstuffs, depression brings with it reduction of wages and unemployment for the wage earners but at the same time lowers the cost of living; for the peasant the depression means low prices for his produce but also lower wage payments to his laborers. In a dualistic society, on the contrary, where the peasant family furnishes the industrial as well as the rural labor, the disadvantages of wage reduction and unemployment come on top of its suffering from a low price for its crops. Nowhere is the peasant the eternal payer to the extent he is in oriental countries.

In the preceding statements, the oriental village has been considered mainly as a source of labor for the benefit of urban industry. We now have to take account also of its function as a source of agricultural produce. For this purpose we will choose an example from China, which is typical for the other countries of Eastern Asia as well.

A large Chinese village, with three hundred families and some two thousand people, therefore probably a complex of villages, grows peanuts as a secondary crop of small importance. This is cultivated by a few families only which themselves extract the oil and sell it on the local market. Their business activities never extend a radius of one mile. But then it turns out that there is a demand for peanut oil in the neighboring town, and that the export market pays a high price for the product—twenty-three times as much as the local market. The opportunity for easy profit and a substantial money income induces every peasant to try this new market crop. In a few years, the area under peanuts has increased from a third of a hectare (four-fifths of an acre) to more than two hundred hectares (almost five hundred acres). And a new figure has come into the village: the dealer who buys up the crop, a professional trader who represents the city and the market. Moreover, the two well-to-do landlord families in the village begin to take an interest in the business and start collecting peanuts. Now the raw product is no longer pressed by the producers themselves: they sell the nuts to the two major landlords who extract the oil in a primitive plant. Money advances bind the producers to furnish the raw material. This means, they lose a large part of the return from the finished product. Even so, the cultivation of this crop still is a source of income and as such attractive. Money, money from the Western city, forms a new element in the village household. The two landlords make a net profit of a thousand dollars each a year. But this phase does not last long, either. The oil extracted in a rather primitive way in the village does not meet altogether the market's conditions as to standard quality; the amount of raw material supplied by several villages justifies the establishment of a more modern oil mill; the intermediary of the two landlords now is restricted to the function of supplying the raw peanuts to the agent of the factory who similarly collects the product in the neighboring villages. The contact of the village with the oil market is cut: the primary producers now are helplessly subjected to the buying policy of the urban dealer, who pays just enough to keep the cultivation of this crop going and who sees to it that whenever there is a drop in the price of the final product the cultivators of the raw materials will bear the brunt of that drop. And this is none too difficult, because the occasions to earn money are so rare and the need for money has become so great that the small peasants persist to the utmost in cultivating a crop they have found marketable. Yet, now they receive only a small fraction of what they earned at the beginning and of the final price. The position of the producers would have been even weaker if the new cash crop had entirely supplanted the cultivation of food crops and made the cultivators wholly dependent on dealer and market. That state of affairs fortunately is rare.

If this development has taken place in a "colonial" country, yet a fourth phase might have followed: a phase characterized by the intervention of a government that has the interests of the peasants at heart and prevents the dealers from exploiting their economic ascendency to the last degree. In a country like China, however, the chance was that the authorities made common cause with the dealer.

As a result of this relation with an outside market, the village also has come under the influence of the world market fluctuations. A drop in prices is immediately and fully debited to the accounts of those who supply the raw material. In the village here mentioned, it took only two years of depression to run 30 per cent of the villagers into debt. The sham prosperity that spread when first they engaged in cultivation for a market in reality led to their impoverishment: the balance of the village household economy was disturbed, and it is not an easy task to restore it.

Sometimes it happens that a market crop is introduced and propagated by a Western entrepreneur—as, for example, that of Virginia tobacco by a large cigarette manufacturing company. In such a case, the relation with the producers starts with a distribution of seeds or of young plants, and with a promise of fair prices. Soon after, the buyer offers credit. At that point the risks and disadvantages of the new relation begin to make their appearance: growing the new crop involves money expenses; the risks of plant disease or crop failure are the planter's; usually he has to pay interest on the loans without which he cannot operate; when the quality of the produce does not come up to expectation, prices are reduced. In his perpetual need for cash, the poor peasant is like wax in the hands of the large concern and its agents.

When servants sever ties with
masters

Both Engels and Boeke emphasize the consequences of change in the economic system on people who have led a rather isolated existence on the survival level. Engels described developments in Germany that led to the 16th-century peasant war. Boeke analyzed developments in Asia in the early 20th century. Mannoni below goes a step farther. He is a French psychoanalyst who worked as a civil servant in Madagascar, the French possession off the eastern coast of Africa that gained its independence soon after the Second World War. He reports psychologically the result when individuals in a static and primitive society, first involuntarily and then voluntarily, become attached to members of a very advanced culture. And he reports the intensification of anxiety when these asymmetrical attachments are threatened with severance.

The depth of the anguish is suggested by this fact: on the island of Madagascar as it approached independence, there occurred in 1947 one of the most savage of late-colonial rebellions. The island's population was then less than 4.5 million. It is believed that deaths numbered in the hundreds of thousands. Savagery was perpetrated by both colonials and colonized—by categories of people whom colonials respectively deem civilized and savage. One might suppose there was deep anguish on both sides.

Mannoni analyzes the mental situation of both kinds of people as they interact. He concentrates on the tension inside men of ancient and primitive culture who can no more readily return to it after living with people of advanced culture than a teenager can return to childhood. There are similarities to the mental relationship between blacks and whites in America in the 1950s and 1960s. The basic interaction combines love and hate as between fathers and adolescent sons.

39

The threat of abandonment

O. MANNONI

Notes to this section will be found on pages 331–333.

If we were to ask the colonialists for their opinion, they would say: "The Malagasies do not need freedom; they do not know what it is: if you force it on them they become unhappy, and that makes them vicious." This verdict is unacceptable as such because it springs from a biased view. The colonialists' impressions of Malagasy psychology are vitiated by their own psychological defects, which I shall describe later on. They know of the need for dependence, for they exploit it; they live by it. They do not want it to be removed; rather would they maintain it. They do in fact foster it by instinctively adopting a paternalist attitude, with too much affection and too much punishment. The experiment has worked out well for them and therefore, pragmatically speaking, there must be something to be said for it. What that amounts to is this, that living in an untroubled state of dependence would—and does, wherever these conditions occur—give the Malagasies a certain psychological comfort. Even Europeans who are not colonialists, but are susceptible nevertheless to a somewhat old-fashioned style of wisdom, might consider this comfort a good in itself and might hesitate to take it away from people who have up to now undoubtedly enjoyed peace and happiness of a kind, on the pretext that progress was essential—an attitude which might well embarrass us if we were to discuss it at the moral level. There are people of conservative taste, those who favor the *fomba taloha*—the old-time customs—among Europeans as among Malagasies. Among the latter they are usually old people who until recently had the

political support of the French authorities. They are disappearing now and giving place to younger and more active generations. The European conservatives no longer have a voice either: it is too late. Thus there is no need for us to consider this possibility, which we might find it difficult to oppose on philosophical grounds, for it is no longer possible to return to this state of comfort based on dependence of all kinds. We may regret it, but our regrets would be vain.

It seems, then, that there is no alternative to the painful apprenticeship to freedom; that alone will solve all the problems amid which both Malagasies and Europeans are floundering—it is a medicine which will cure them both. If it appears sweet to the one and bitter to the other, it is an illusion in both cases. The way will be much harder for the Malagasies than they imagine, while the Europeans have no idea of the extent to which a genuine and successful liberation of their subject peoples—if it could be brought about without conflict, which unfortunately they make unlikely—would liberate them too, without harming their "interests" to anything like the extent they fear. Needless to say, an essential precondition for the liberation of the individual is the sincere application of a policy of democracy and racial equality. But that is not enough by itself. The colonials who are antidemocratic are not all colonialists. Some, though not many, have adopted a conservative attitude, not out of self-interest or a feeling of racial superiority, but because they are dimly aware of the inadequacy of political reforms to solve psychological problems. They blame the democratic ideal itself for the accidents which are apt to occur when an attempt is made to put it into practice. They believe, not without reason, that a people so thoroughly fixed psychologically in the attitudes I have called dependent, could not pass from this archaic state to a modern one without undergoing some crisis of adolescence. But this conservative attitude—and its adherents are not all Europeans—appears to have had a harmful effect, for it has succeeded in delaying and hindering reforms without preventing them altogether.

The conservatives' opposition, which will avail nothing in the end, has merely aggravated the situation, and the deterioration in relations gives an appearance of proving them right. But as the reader must know in situations of this kind failures can be made to prove anyone right. Obviously if the conservatives had managed to prevent any change at all, there would have been no crisis! But it is equally true that the crisis would have been less serious and more manageable if the reforms proposed had met with less stubborn opposition.

THE DEPENDENT PERSONALITY AND REPRESSION

Although the concept of dependence seems to be the one which will best explain the psychology of the Malagasy who has been "colonized" and is now in course of evolution, it is doubtful whether it would be equally valid with respect to more "primitive" communities, those which have hardly been touched by our civilization, if in fact there are any remaining. . . .

In them we should very probably find some form of dependence, but it is unlikely that it would be dependence on the parental couple alone or that it would be transferred to the same substitutes, the most important of which, for the Malagasy, are the family ancestors. Mythical ancestors, kings living or dead, the group as a whole, the tribe, substituted idols, perhaps, like the *solo*[1] of the ancient Merina—all these would no doubt be found in the rôle of guardians of peace and security and protectors both against external dangers and against feelings of guilt, for the two are always closely linked in the unconscious. A study of these forms of group dependence would be very interesting in itself but would not, I think, help us forward in our investigation of psychological dependence, for in communities of such a kind the individual can hardly be distinguished from the collective, since all the separate conscious minds resemble and reflect each other. Dependence, in such cases, is something solid, universal, and undifferentiated. The bond between mother and child will of course remain and will retain its affective force, but it will necessarily play a less prominent part in a society where all the children of the same age are bound together into a homogeneous group. The village square is as friendly and familiar a place for such children as their own homes, at least during the daytime. The child clings less fiercely to vertical family ties when he feels supported by a whole network of horizontal ties, even if he knows he must wait till he has attained a certain age and pass through a series of initiation ceremonies before they are confirmed. Relations between individuals are consequently very different, and if people of this kind are cut off from their normal environment they will tend to look for a group to which they can belong rather than a person upon whom they can depend. They will also find it easier to make firm friendships with equals.*

We do not know how Malagasy society developed, for we have no means of placing the different types of social organization in chronological order without resorting to hypotheses which are at the best merely plausible. It is a simple matter of fact that among the Merina, who are considered, rightly or wrongly, the more highly developed of the Malagasies, attachments are primarily vertical, and horizontal ties are negligible. We may wonder whether horizontal attachments would spontaneously form—or, it may be, reform—the moment the vertical dependences became dangerously weakened. Observation of Malagasies who have been called up for military service suggests that they would. A farsighted administration ought, in any case, while respecting the vertical relationships, at the same time to try to encourage and strengthen horizontal ties, especially among children, through school friendships, sports societies, scouting, and so on, always guarding, however, as far as possible against their turning into vertical relationships through the appointment of leaders or masters psychologically prepared to accept the projection

* [Cf. Aristotle in Chapter 8, below—ed.]

of parental images.[2] By this means it might be possible to ward off certain difficulties likely to arise in the future, or to moderate their psychological effects by sparing individuals the anxiety resulting from a feeling of abandonment.

It may be objected that the vertical ties are strong and not yet ready to be broken. We cannot be certain about that. Of course there is no question of the parent generations "betraying" their children (in Künkel's sense), but, as we have already seen, a child can experience as betrayal his projection of his own desire for independence, about which he unconsciously feels guilty. For, objectively, anything is enough to make the child feel betrayed, even the lightest and most well earned punishment, if the subjective conditions are ripe.[3] So, then, in the present period of unrest the psychological need for dependence and its unconscious acceptance may be seriously disturbed without there being any change, outwardly at least, in the general sociological structure of the family and the cult of the dead. There is some conflict between the older, conservative generations, and the more progressive-minded youth. The nature of the conflict is, however, rather obscure because the young are both more conservative and more revolutionary than the old.

Meanwhile, dependence continues to give the average Malagasy a greater feeling of security while relieving him of the need to show initiative or assume responsibility. It is easy to see why the Malagasies are lovers of routine. As with some Europeans, it is because it makes them feel safer. To depart from routine is to wander in pathless woods; there you will meet the bull who will send you running helter-skelter home again. No doubt there was a time when routine, adhered to in every detail of life, was a great guarantee of security. But—and we shall see later why—the very existence of the *fady* (taboos) is due to the way in which the feeling of insecurity is assuaged. The Malagasy's routine—which is not the result of conservatism, for he is perfectly ready to adopt a new routine—has something in common with the rituals of the obsessed; it protects

him against his unconscious fear of insecurity. There is more than just this, though, in the Malagasy's kind of routine. A Malagasy will take pleasure in performing some complicated administrative task, observing with pedantic correctness every rule and regulation, and not skipping a single formality, even if it serves no purpose at all. In this he is not very different from some non-Malagasy officials, and the resemblance warrants our saying that in both cases there are probably certain psychological obstacles and that they are of the same kind, whatever form they may have taken at an earlier stage of the individual's development in each case. However, it is not difficult to discover that a respect for red tape in the European civil servant is very often a weapon he uses to defend himself against the public and a means of inflating his own importance—to the extent of being aggressive and malicious at times—in compensation for his feeling of inferiority. The Malagasy, on the other hand, adopts the formalities in order to enter a large family which will afford him a secure place: for him, a scrupulous observance of the rules of the game is his guarantee of the strength of the ties securing that place in the whole structure, and therefore removes the risk of any unforeseen—and consequently dangerous—occurrence.[4] We must guard against oversimplifying the matter and believing that the Malagasy official is scrupulous because he is afraid of "trouble" or of losing his position. There is no deliberate intention; it is his general attitude which compels him to multiply the strong hierarchical bonds of dependence, for he loves to feel anchored by such bonds.

If a situation arises which requires him to show initiative, to settle a question without reference to any rule or precedent, he at once loses his head and appears quite unintelligent. Even at school, pupils may be brilliant at making subtle logical or grammatical analyses but will be unable to deal with questions which are fundamentally quite simple. And in everyday life, opinions on important matters are given only in the form of ready-made formulas, the "proverbs" which enshrine the wisdom of the ancients. Though illogical and extraordinarily elastic, these formulas are always felt to be convincing in arguments or disputes.

The Malagasies may at times appear to be entirely lacking in common sense, but they reveal a remarkable intelligence once it is allowed free exercise within the framework of rules and formulas. Old Malagasy lawyers are formidable practitioners of legal procedure. Every Malagasy can compose poetry by regrouping ready-made phrases in a great variety of ways, and can improvise word-puzzles—like the Hain-Teny—with great subtlety and finesse. Another aspect of this capacity is what the Malagasies call suppleness, a quality which (in their eyes) consists in reaching one's objective without check, without a conflict with anyone, and without violating any of the known rules. To Europeans, of course, this suppleness looks very much like hypocrisy and it shocks those who do not understand its real nature. The Malagasies, for their part, are often shocked and demoralized by the way the Europeans, who brought such detailed and formal regulations into the country, mock and ridicule them and occasionally even violate them.

The words in which D. Westermann, in his *Noirs et Blancs en Afrique*, pp. 45–46, describes the dependence of the African, could very well be applied unchanged to the Malagasy: "The springs of his actions are predominantly social and not individual, and he is profoundly affected by public opinion. His conscience is rooted in the approval of the community; it depends upon the daily security provided by the group and not upon any individual action. Personal responsibility is avoided to the greatest extent possible." It appears, however, that the African group, the tribe, is a more solid unity than Malagasy society, which has a looser general structure, but is rigidly linked to the ancestors.

In spite of his docility, the Malagasy has no real professional conscience, but that is not for the reasons which would account for its absence in Europeans. He lacks it because he personalizes his relationships

where he does not formalize them, and where there is neither formality nor person, there is nothing. Do your best to please the chief and obey the rules; there his ethics ends, and naturally that is not enough to make him conscientious.[5] Even respect for the truth is replaced by consideration for the person to whom he is speaking; he does not say what is true but what he feels it appropriate to say. This is apparent in certain linguistic peculiarities; the word for "yes," for instance, means "I agree with you"; the word for "no" means "I am not in agreement"; to the question, "Has it not rained?" the reply "No" means that it has rained. This mode of conversation reveals a desire to make one's position clear with regard to persons rather than to things.[6]

For the sake of completeness I should perhaps mention in connexion with the dependence complex the fact that semi-evolved Malagasies (and no doubt also, many of those whom we consider "civilized") place absolute faith in divinations. The commonest form of divination practiced at present is that of the *sikidy*. (Seeds are used; the diviner picks up handfuls at random, and according as the handful contains an odd or an even number he lays down one or two, building up groups somewhat like Braille characters. Once the first row is laid down, a second is deduced from it in accordance with certain rather complicated rules. The result is read rather in the way a fortune-teller reads a pack of cards.)[7] The injunctions of the *sikidy* are always strictly obeyed, and this explains the often incomprehensible behavior of Malagasies when they change their plans without apparent reason, give up a profitable enterprise for a less profitable one, and so on. They will never admit that they are following the *sikidy*; to Europeans they invent excuses which are very often absurd and simply irritate him. They also obey the dictates of their dreams.

Sorcerers are very different from the diviners who perform the *sikidy*. They are withdrawn and very difficult to approach. They do as they like and cause horror by disregarding the customs, as for instance by dancing on the tombs at night. By way of reprisal the sorcerer himself is buried, not in a tomb, but at the roadside, where he may be trampled on. He is a sort of voluntary victim, a scapegoat personifying evil, but one who accepts his role. It is easy to see that in order to play this part the sorcerer must have cast off all the bonds of dependence. How does he manage to break free? Does he perhaps transfer his dependence to imaginary beings, in the way we do? His "professional" life is so carefully hidden that it is impossible to find out how a man *becomes* a sorcerer. It would appear, from the energetic way the diviners deny it, that it is possible to pass from "honest" magic to sorcery, and this is probably a temptation the diviners have to guard against. In any case the characteristic feature of the sorcerer is not that he practices magic, but that he is "charged" with evil, in both senses of the word. He is accused of selling poisons more often than of casting spells—although these two branches of activity are not so clearly differentiated by the Malagasies as by ourselves. The most plausible theory that can be put forward to explain the existence of the Malagasy sorcerer is that man spontaneously forms an image of evil and that this image fascinates him; the sorcerer is the man who identifies himself with the image, and there are social paths (ceremonies, initiations, beliefs of various kinds) whereby this identification can be transformed into a "situation" in the community. That is sheer hypothesis, of course, and though it would explain the characteristics of the Malagasy sorcerer, it would not explain those of magicians and witch-doctors.

To return to my main theme—when the Malagasy, with his dependent personality, is confronted with someone whose personality is free and independent, like that of the adult European, he cannot easily adapt himself to it.

The first attempt at adaptation takes place on the mythical level by means of a process of rationalization which I must mention because it is still "true" in the eyes of the Malagasies. They think that the European has no soul. This is a living belief which they do not attempt to reduce to a formula, and it is firmly held because it is linked with the belief in the dead. To them it seems self-evident—a fact which gives us some insight into their concept of the soul. Ironically enough, of course, the very people the Malagasies accuse of having no soul are precisely those who thought to bring them the doctrine of the immortality of the spiritual substance.

The fact is that to the Malagasies the soul is virtually identical with dependence: it is that which requires the observance of the customs and respect for the *fady*; it is that which unites the family and the tribe; it is that which reappears, after death, in the dreams of the living, and so on. Proof of the Europeans' lack of soul is the fact that they have no cult of the dead and no white ghosts. To say that the white man has no conscience, that he does what he likes, that he has no soul, or that he has no ancestors is, for the Malagasy, to say the same thing in four different ways. I have never obtained from a Malagasy an account of a dream in which a white man figured—although this is not conclusive, for a Malagasy would never relate such a dream to a European.

The Malagasy in his way is unhappily aware of the white man's inferiority complex, just as the white man dimly—though to his advantage—comprehends the Malagasy's dependence complex. The Malagasy realizes that there is in the white man some force which drives him to seek constant change, to try out novelties, to make incessant demands, and to accomplish extraordinary things just to "show off." He understands it the more easily since the inferiority complex, though masked in him by his acceptance of dependence, is not entirely absent and in some circumstances becomes clearly apparent. On such occasions his Malagasy comrades say he is "trying to play the *vazaha*," and make fun of him. Playing the *vazaha* and swanking are virtually synonymous, and the Malagasy who begins to act in this way will not get very far or derive any great satisfaction from it unless he has been uprooted from his environment at an early age—for assuredly there is nothing to prevent a Malagasy acquiring a personality of the European type if he has been brought up from infancy in a European environment. But such a Malagasy will be a European and will have the complexes of a European. There may be some traits of character linked with the physical temperament, the manner of expressing emotion, for instance, which persist by way of racial characteristics—but even that is doubtful.

The situation is quite different in those cases, and they are not a few, where a Malagasy has during his youth—and not, be it noted, in infancy—acquired a European personality which is superimposed upon the Malagasy personality he already possessed. If he represses his Malagasy personality he is to all outward appearances a European, but his original personality has not been destroyed and will continue to manifest itself in disguise. If he returns to his own people his repressed personality will be awakened again by the environment. He is then rather in the position of a repressed homosexual among overt homosexuals, a situation which, as is well known, is liable to give rise to hatred, either conscious or otherwise. This explains why "assimilated" natives have so very little influence, why the policy of bringing back to Madagascar Malagasies who have been thoroughly Europeanized in Europe, in the hope of fostering Franco–Malagasy friendship, does not pay off as well as might, *a priori*, be expected. The complexes of the "assimilated" drive them to seek the company of Europeans, but they are never received by them as equals. They are ill at ease in all societies, and the failure they embody heightens rather than diminishes consciousness of racial differences.[8]

If the Europeanized Malagasy is not to repress his Malagasy personality he must integrate his European elements into it—a difficult task for which his own goodwill and skilfulness are not enough; it is necessary in addition that the European and Malagasy environments should not place insurmountable obstacles in his way. If he fails in his task, his European personality will probably be just a slender *persona* and

our "civilized" man will have but a thin European veneer. The unenlightened would see this veneer as the cause of the familiar displays of vanity and manifestations of degradation; their observation of the facts would be correct but their explanation of them wrong: vanity is the price that is paid for failure and is a compensation for inferiority. The Malagasy is better off if he is deliberately hypocritical—and this, too, happens at times. Usually, however, things are less simple, for the original personality does not remain intact under its mask: in place of an almost megalomaniac vanity, resentment and hostility appear. These traits —vanity, hypocrisy, resentment—have sometimes been attributed to the Malagasies as a whole, but this is a mistake, for they are the consequence of unsuccessful Europeanization. Unfortunately, as things are at present —at any rate in Madagascar—Europeanization fails more often than it succeeds. It is more successful in Europe, for European society offers fewer obstacles, and there in any case the Malagasy personality is eventually repressed.

The Malagasy who can be most useful to us in forwarding Franco–Malagasy collaboration is the one who has preserved his Malagasy personality intact, adapting it, but not concealing it. A real understanding of this fact would lead to a total revision of our teaching methods, for all we do at present is to instruct the masses without adapting them to our civilization, and to cultivate the *élite* while suppressing their personalities, neither of which methods really improves the situation.

It is worthy of note that disturbances broke out at the very time when a number of Europeanized Malagasies were returning to Madagascar. Some of them—those who had been truly assimilated—broke with their compatriots, and thereafter had no influence on them. Others, whose assimilation had been incomplete, fomented and led the revolts, for they are the people most likely to develop a real hatred of Europeans. Caliban's dictum:

You taught me language; and my profit on't
Is, I know how to curse . . .,

though oversimplifies the situation, is true in essence. It is not that Caliban has savage and uneducable instincts or that he is such poor so that even good seed would bring forth bad plants, as Prospero believes. The real reason is given by Caliban himself:

... When thou camest first,
Thou strok'dst me, and mad'st much of me ...
... and then I lov'd thee

—and then you abandoned me before I had time to become your equal. ... In other words: you taught me to be dependent, and I was happy; then you betrayed me and plunged me into inferiority. It is indeed in some such situation as this that we must look for the origin of the fierce hatred sometimes shown by "evolved" natives; in them the process of civilization has come to a halt and been left incomplete.

In contrast, the Malagasy whose personality has been neither repressed nor masked, who has preserved his original dependence complex in all its purity, is not generally a prey to hostility towards the European. During the recent rebellion there was a number of cases where Malagasies who came to assassinate isolated Europeans explained that they did so with regret in obedience to their chiefs, to whom they had sworn oaths of allegiance, and not out of any hatred.

From the very beginning of the revolt these assassinations were represented as atrocities; although at the time we had very little information about what was going on we were always given very detailed accounts of any episode that was likely to arouse unconscious sadistic tendencies. ... Such investigations as it has been possible to make since suggest that in almost every case there were distortions and exaggerations which were not even conscious or deliberate. Even where officials of the police department were responsible for circulating these rumors they were impelled rather by their own unconscious sadism than by an official policy. In fact it was not the accounts of Malagasy atrocities only which were exaggerated. Reports of the acts of violence committed by Europeans were exaggerated too, in the same proportions *and by the same people.*

The lawyers defending the Malagasies who were brought to trial took care to mention the ill-treatment inflicted on the prisoners (to make them "confess") only when they could produce positive evidence in the form, say, of medical records or bodily scars. But, surprisingly enough, the Europeans who took a more or less direct part in the ill-treatment boasted about it and, without a thought to the harm they did themselves in the process, represented it as torture of a far more lurid kind than in actual fact it was. (Which is not to say, of course, that it was not adequate to achieve its object, that of making the prisoners sign statements obviously prepared in advance.) A particularly bloody and highly colored description of the Fianarantsoa "chamber of horrors" was so shocking as to provoke an official inquiry: the inquiry revealed nothing more than the abuses—odious, but more prosaic—of police "routine." The description had in fact emanated from certain rather neurotic individuals who had taken part, in a semi-official capacity, in the police interrogations. They had posed as veritable torturers in order to satisfy—relatively cheaply and in imagination only—tendencies to which they had in reality yielded only in a very mild degree. Considerable allowance must therefore be made for a kind of imaginary sadism, and that being so the amount of torture and the number of rapes and cruelties attributed to the rebels will not be so surprising. There was the description, for instance, of the horrible death of a young civil service clerk upon whom a "live autopsy" was said to have been carried out by his own native doctor: he cut him up, it was alleged, exactly according to the rules, tying the arteries as he went along and keeping the man alive right up to the end by injecting him with camphorated oil! (I shall spare the reader the details.) In spite of the absurd improbability of a story of this kind, people were so ready to believe such tales that it was unwise for a European who had retained a modicum of judgment to appear skeptical. In this case, too, an investigation took place some six months later. It revealed that the native doctor had displayed the utmost devotion to his master, who was ill, and had done all in his power to help him escape from the rebels. The Government has since rewarded him for his efforts. There were relatively few cases as extreme as this, but many of a milder kind could be found.

Given this reservation, however, to put us on our guard against all unverified atrocity stories, it must be admitted that the rebellion and its suppression occasioned a great deal of violence in which some streaks of real cruelty can be seen. But the Malagasies' cruelty bears no resemblance to the picture of it which the European spontaneously—and almost inevitably—forms in his imagination. Their ferocity towards their victims was rather that of the "inexperienced" killer, crazed with feelings of guilt, than the skilled refinements of a sadistic torturer. It is obviously difficult, during a period of unrest, to perceive the psychological factor operating in the horrified witnesses, or in those who later peddle these stories for the sake of the unconscious satisfaction they gain from them. Moreover, a murder is in itself cruelty enough, without the addition of torture, to cause a profound disturbance. . . .

We shall be better able to judge exactly what degree of cruelty to attribute to the Malagasies if we consider how they sacrifice their oxen in the course of funeral ceremonies, a practice which, though distasteful to us, is not sadistic. They are fond of the beast they intend to kill. They begin by playing with him; then the game becomes a struggle in earnest, and as the ox defends himself they become indignant and angry, and in the end they kill the "wicked" creature with distressing fury, saying that he "jolly well deserved it." The Spanish toreador's bull is considered noble: whence does it derive its nobility if not from that of the Spanish soul? The Malagasies' sacrificial ox, on the other hand, just before its death, is considered to be intractable, viciously naughty, stupidly disobedient, and all without a hope of success. These characteristics indicate, in projection and by opposites, as it were, the dependence com-

plex. Exactly the same psychological features are to be found in the game children play of sacrificing an ox. A child takes the place of the ox, and he is pretty roughly handled by his comrades. Cailliet notes these facts very accurately in his *Essai sur la psychologie du Hova*, p. 20.

The numerous stories which circulated among the European population, depicting the Malagasies as perpetrators of revolting atrocities (I shall refer later to their sexual ingredients), were not all officially denied or else they were denied too late. Their originators were probably not deliberately seeking to create a lasting misunderstanding between Europeans and Malagasies, but that is what they may well have done. In very truth, however, they *created* nothing; their unconscious feelings of hatred merely *emerged* in the stories and roused in their hearers similar feelings which had up to then been repressed.

The image of the European plays much too big a part in the Malagasy's thoughts for him not to give him a great deal of attention. In normal times the presence of the European is very comforting; he assumes responsibility for so many offences against the customs and looks so strong and easily capable of shouldering the burden of guilt. In him the Malagasy sees at once the absolute master, the protector, and the scapegoat—images which in Europe would never be so completely fused. But in spite of these reassuring factors the European is always a source of ill-defined anxiety for the Malagasy: he can do what he likes and is unpredictable; he has no standards, and his attitudes are extraordinary—he is disappointed if the fruit is not ripe, even if it is the wrong season! He is liable to want the impossible and to demand it. He thereby sets a bad example which may weaken the precepts handed down from the ancestors. Fortunately he is strong; if he were weak, "what on earth would happen to us?" people ask.

Thus everything connected with the European—the way he washes, the way he eats, his habits of life in general—all become the subject of a somewhat legendary learning, as the habits of beavers or ants are to us. This knowledge is to some extent prized among the Malagasies, in the same way as we in Europe prize a knowledge of the habits of the animal societies I have just mentioned. The European, however, who has always something of an inferiority complex, interprets the value set on knowledge of his ways as a valuing of himself; he takes it as a tribute to his immense superiority. But the really typical Malagasy takes an interest in the white man, and even unconsciously identifies himself with him, without actually making any comparison between himself and the other, or feeling inferior, while at the same time adopting a dependent attitude. In these circumstances it is easy to see why "first contacts" are so easy to make; it is easy, too, to see why the observers whom Lévy-Bruhl quotes found the natives first so dependent, then so abusive as if they did not know their "place" —the place, that is, that the observers had assigned to them, as the result of a barely conscious process of valuation to which they alone assented.

If we look at the external facts alone, we cannot help realizing that the dependence relationship is reciprocal in nature: if the master has a servant, the servant likewise has a master, and though he does not compare himself with him, he nevertheless takes pleasure in the value of the thing he possesses. The man Mackenzie cured said distinctly, "You are now *my* white man." The same is probably true in Europe of the psychology of the staff of luxury establishments; they are naïvely devoted to their rich and elegant patrons because they identify themselves with them and no longer suffer from their subservient positions. It is the poor patron who humiliates them. This is an important element in the psychology of dependence. The reader will find many examples of it in Robert Drury's *Journal*, published in 1729. At the time when Robert Drury was living in Madagascar after being shipwrecked, the petty kings of the Malagasies were all very anxious to get possession of a white man.

They attached great value to such a possession, but this value had nothing to do with esteem for the white man himself.

These relationships are difficult to understand properly because we are always too prone to think that they are explained by motives of self-interest. (For instance, people assume that the servant likes the rich patron for his tips, but in fact it is very often the poor man who gives the larger tip out of sheer nervousness, and he is all the more despised for it!) In the case of the petty kings, it has been thought that they considered white men useful possessions because they were knowledgeable about most things. We need only read Drury's *Journal*—which is very interesting in itself—to realize what a mistake that is. Those who offer this explanation overestimate the importance the Malagasies attached to European technique; in fact they saw it as a mere curiosity. No doubt they very much appreciated the manufactured goods the Europeans brought with them, but they had practically no desire to know how to make them. Drury, like a good European, learned much more from the Malagasies than they bothered to learn from him. However, he was perfectly prepared, still like a good European, to teach them all he knew.[9]

The reciprocity in the dependence relationship, whereby the Malagasy, as it were, takes possession of the person upon whom he is dependent, and in that way values him, has certain more obscure psychological foundations. Without trying to elucidate them in their entirety I should like to give some indication of their nature. There is a satisfaction to be gained, as I have said, from knowing about other animal species and their customs, and this, too, might be seen as a kind of appropriation. We are now touching upon the psychological ground in which totemistic beliefs are rooted. Behind the totem lurks the image of the ancestors and, further behind still, the image of the parents as the small child conceives them. Psychoanalysis suggests that this image of the parents, the first of all human images to confront the infant child, is very probably adult man's only means of escaping solipsism—or narcissism—and of apprehending others as real live beings. The strange beliefs collectively known as totemism[10] might then be explained by the need to apprehend even other living species, at least at first, through this human *imago*. In children's dreams or drawings there is a constant recurrence of animal forms representing the mother, so much so as to put the likelihood of assimilation beyond doubt. Totemism thus becomes comprehensible and we find that we are not so far removed from it as we should like to think.

Totemism is the opposite of the mechanistic theory, a theory which was propounded by a philosopher who had been wrestling with the problem of the existence of other people; he was in the habit of seeing them as no more than "hats and coats" and never quite succeeded, in spite of the Princess Elizabeth's questioning, in giving them any more life than that of mechanical toys driven by will and reason, both almost entirely depersonalized—for almost anything can be willed, and reason is identical for all men. The interesting point, however, is that children, instead of treating animals as machines, treat machines as living things, the more highly prized because they are easier to appropriate. Children's appropriation is a virtual identification and they play at being machines (steam-engines, motor cars, airplanes) just as "primitive" peoples play at being the totem. The psychological state in the two cases is probably very similar. The totemic attitude would then be that which occurs when another being is apprehended as living and exjsting, through the naïve projection of the original *imago*. The failure of this projection would lead to narcissism in one of its various forms or to solipsism.

It is against this psychological background, which is barely accessible to the conscious mind, that we must endeavor to sketch in the picture of the white man as the Malagasy may at first see him. We shall then discover —as I shall show later on, and as Emile Cailliet indicated was possible in his *Essai sur la psychologie du Hova*, from which I shall quote[11]—how it may interfere with his image of the ancestors.

At all events it is clear that the dependence relationship contains no element of comparison or self-appraisal, no effort to "situate" oneself otherwise than within that special order of things which is the system of dependence. This is true, of course, only so long as the relationship remains pure, so long, that is, as the feeling of security guaranteed by it remains intact. This is what distinguishes it radically from the attitudes which go to make up the inferiority complex.

When a European child stops "being" an airplane he becomes, in imagination, an airman. He looks at real airmen but does not compare himself with them, and so escapes the feeling of inferiority; on the contrary, he is exalted by his identification of himself with the airman. Moreover, he can later convert his dream into reality and himself become an airman—though this possibility is quite unnecessary to the original game. The Malagasy, however, may suddenly find himself, the instant the bonds of dependence snap, on the brink of an abyss of inferiority, and in danger of falling in. In that case an earlier identification may result in distressingly negative phenomena. In other words, the Malagasy can bear not being a white man; what hurts him cruelly is to have discovered first (by identification) that he is a man and *later* that men are divided into blacks and whites. If the "abandoned" or "betrayed" Malagasy continues his identification he becomes clamorous; he begins to demand *equality* in a way he had never before found necessary. The equality he seeks would have been beneficial before he started asking for it, but afterwards it proves inadequate to remedy his ills—for every increase in equality makes the remaining differences seem the more intolerable, for they suddenly appear agonizingly irremovable. This is the road along which the Malagasy passes from psychological dependence to psychological inferiority.

The idea that the "benefits" of the Malagasy can be increased by our giving him what he lacks, in the way a sum of money can be increased by the addition of other sums, is valid only if it is a matter of material objects such as food and tools. Applied to political, moral, or psychological "advantages" it appears just a trifle silly. . . . If we try to alter only some aspects of a personality which is constructed differently from our own, we ought not to be surprised if the whole personality undergoes a change. Thus, it is just when the Malagasy is beginning to resemble us a little that he turns roughly from us. Our mistake lies in assuming that the personality as a whole can be treated in the way we treat the schoolboy's mind—as an empty vessel waiting to be filled. Those schoolmasters who thought that there was nothing in the mind which had not entered through the doors of the senses—and by that they meant that there was nothing in the memory except what had entered through the ears listening to the teacher or the eyes fastened upon the school-book—were ready to believe that there was nothing good in the personality but what had been put there deliberately, like plants in a garden, and that whatever happened to be growing there could be dug up like weeds. This schoolmaster's philosophy has ruled Europe with a rod of iron and is ultimately responsible for the present character of the European, with all its good and bad qualities. But if it is applied to personalities of a very different type, what is "added" either remains an alien element or else in the long run brings about a modification of the whole personality, some elements being integrated and others repressed.

Thus, an education confined to providing the colonial inhabitant with new tools could be very useful if it left the personality as a whole untouched and had no direct cultural import, but a culturally biased education can disrupt the personality far more than one would expect, unless—and this is probably what most often happens—it is accepted simply at the level of the *persona*, as knowledge for the sake of knowledge, and a source of vanity—purely academic and bookish and not integrated into the whole being. We have yet to find an educational method which is somewhere between these two extremes. For the moment we must be content not to influence the personality or unwittingly undermine it. With all this in mind we can better understand what Christianity could have done for the peoples with dependent personalities—and what it signally failed to do.

DEPENDENCE THREATENED

People say that we do not realize we possess a particular organ until something goes wrong with it. Similarly it may be that the dependence relationship has only now sprung to our notice because it has already been partly undermined. The individuals who have come into contact with representatives of the other civilization—and it applies to both sides—have been more profoundly affected by the encounter than might at first be supposed.[12]

To my mind there is no doubting the fact that colonization has always required the existence of the need for dependence. Not all peoples can be colonized: only those who experience this need. Neither are all peoples equally likely to become colonizers, for, as I shall show later, certain other equally definite predispositions are required for that role. There are other ways of being conquered than that of becoming a subject colony, and other forms of domination than the colonial — assimilation, association, economic exploitation; there is extermination at one end of the scale, and absorption of the victor by the vanquished at the other.

Wherever Europeans have founded colonies of the type we are considering, it can safely be said that their coming was unconsciously expected—even desired—by the future subject peoples. Everywhere there existed legends foretelling the arrival of strangers from the sea, bearing wondrous gifts with them.[13] From the early seventeenth century onwards any shipwrecked sailor was welcomed with open arms, and the chiefs quarreled over possession of them. True, these Europeans were on occasions massacred. But we cannot tell to what extent they may have frightened the natives by their strange behavior and their incomprehensible demands. Certain it is that at the start there was nothing indicative of racial hatred; whatever there was rather favored the white man than otherwise, at least in Madagascar.

When the colonizer first appears, it is not as an enemy but as a stranger, as a guest. In Madagascar he is called *vazaha*, an expression which means as nearly as possible, "honorable stranger."[14] He seizes authority only when at length through his persistent demands—the native finds him insatiable[15]—he has provoked part of the population to display defense reactions. It is in this sense that we can say that the colonies were conquered. But in most cases, in its ordinary meaning, it is a distortion of the facts to make them fit a preconceived pattern, for the armed forces employed would have been inadequate for the task had we not been helped by our unconscious accomplices in the souls of the natives themselves. In 1947, after fifty years of colonial rule, tribes allegedly unwarlike, armed only with pointed sticks—which the communiqués described as assegais—attacked positions defended with Lewis guns and hand grenades. Yet at the time when Madagascar was first conquered the Malagasies had been drawn up in armed formations—and had fled at the first shots fired. It cannot have been force alone, therefore, which vanquished Madagascar; force would not have conquered and kept the island had not the Malagasy people, long before our arrival, been ready for our coming.

Moreover, the Europeans themselves only made a show of believing in military force; they knew instinctively, and barely consciously, where their strength lay—in a certain "weakness" of personality on the part of the Malagasies. They were not to know that their position of dominance was due to the fact that in the network of dependences they occupied roughly the same position as the dead ancestors. . . . But they were aware that the psychological situation favored them, and knew that force alone would be powerless once that situation changed. Proof of this is the alarm and anger with which they greeted any attempt by the natives to gain emancipation. This was not the reasonable reaction of men sure of their own strength preparing to meet a danger with energetic measures. Those few Europeans who, because they were unaffected by the contagion, were able to observe the colonials' reactions dispassionately will confirm that it looked very much like panic and that there was a tendency to take violent, spectacular, rather pointless or downright harmful actions. In the following chapter the reader will find an account of the psychological causes of this attitude.

From the very beginning of the revolt, in March 1947, the Europeans in Madagascar began to behave in a paradoxical and consequently very revealing fashion. Those who were in the area of the revolt displayed great self-possession and courage, and after the initial surprise which caused some loss of life, there were virtually no more casualties. The story is told, for instance, of the colonial who held out single-handed against three hundred assailants, with only a shotgun and twenty rounds, for ten days before being rescued.

In places far from the actual disturbances, however, a mixture of fear, excitement, and anger gained possession of the Europeans. In the capital they took defensive precautions out of all proportion to the real danger, to the extent of depriving other parts of the country which were more closely threatened of the help they badly needed.[16] The emotion generated was evidently unrelated to the degree of real danger. There were many little tell-tale signs: verbal slips, for instance—when the rebellion seemed to be dying down a man, refusing to be reassured, said: "I am not unhopeful of further outbreaks," as if he wanted rather than feared them. The revolt appeared to have some sort of fascination, and the Europeans' actions, which they took to be purely defensive, were, unknown to them, acts of defiance and provocation. They behaved, in fact, rather like an angry schoolmaster whose orders have been disobeyed and who, to gain some psychological satisfaction, resorts to violence, but violence of a peculiar kind, a theatrical sort of violence: he makes a scene, strikes a pose, creates a spectacle for himself and his friends, in accordance with a mode of thinking more superstitious than practical, and derives some inner solace from it. This was the meaning of the noisy sorties of armed men in the evenings; they returned home satisfied and slept soundly for the rest of the night. They justified their behavior by saying that it was necessary to frighten the Malagasies, although what the immense majority of the Malagasies needed far more was to feel that they were not being abandoned. The Europeans knew well enough that their behavior was likely to rouse peaceful Malagasies and drive them into the arms of the rebels. But, irrationally, they derived a certain satisfaction from running this risk.

It could be maintained from the purely psychological point of view, and leaving aside all moral considerations, that the use of force *can* solve problems; we all know that in war the soldier finally makes peace with himself while making peace with the enemy. But he must first have recognized himself in the enemy, have shared his perils, his misfortunes, and his courage: in other words, he must have been a combatant and have seen the combatant in the enemy. This is hardly possible in a colonial war. Anger, threats, defiance, provocation do not bring with them absolution. This was understood somewhat belatedly, and ceremonies of surrender were organized to try to make the pacification of the revolt look like an agreement between opposing forces. Unfortunately nobody believed in it. Even war has its laws which we cannot afford to disobey.

In conclusion, it may be said that the conduct of the Europeans cannot be explained solely in terms of their carefully calculated interests, nor by their fear in the face of danger. On the contrary, it can only be explained by the nature of the complex-determined feelings roused by a colonial situation. In the next part of this book I shall try to indicate the origin of these feelings.

National Independence

O. MANNONI

Notes to this section will be found on page 333.

Further proof of the Malagasies' extreme susceptibility to feelings of guilt, which are always bound up with fear and insecurity, is their belief in the *tody*, according to which the desire to hurt someone else rebounds upon the person guilty of the desire by virtue of a magical *lex talionis*. The root from which the word *tody*[1] derives signifies return to the point of departure. Similar beliefs have doubtless been known in all countries; "evil spirits" can be exorcised, and we talk of an "immanent justice" which will punish "where we have sinned." But the exorcism of evil spirits requires a magical operation, and the idea of immanent justice is a consolation to those who are faced with obvious injustice, while the *tody*, which sees evil intentions as a kind of boomerang, dangerous to hurl because it will spring back unexpectedly, indicates an unconscious feeling of guilt, and is probably the simplest and most primitive expression of remorse.

The only alternative of remorse is resentment, accompanied by hatred and violence. Violence springs from guilt, and guilt from a feeling of abandonment.[2] The most stubborn of the rebels were former soldiers who had come back from Europe; I have already explained what sort of influence Europe may have had on such men. It must be added that for the majority of them the army had been a system of very close-knit and numerous bonds of dependence which replaced the family and social bonds. When these men suddenly found themselves demobilized, in spite of the precautions which had been taken and which for the European would have been enough to cushion the shock, they fell into the emotional state of the abandoned. Their psychological condition was in itself enough, therefore, to lead to feelings of hostility. It remains, however, to discover how these feelings came to be expressed in open hostility, and in particular why they condensed around claims for national independence. The rebels had only the vaguest ideas about the meaning of independence, but they had very clear notions about what kinds of leaders they wanted; they knew them personally and referred to them by name. Political systems and constitutions meant nothing to them. They wanted these particular leaders in order to be able too restore the broken bonds of dependence which they saw no hope of reestablishing with the Europeans. They also wanted them in order to be able to identify themselves with them. And finally they wanted them in order to lay upon their shoulders—but not through hatred—their painful burden of guilt.

Immediately these leaders were arrested, Malagasies who had not taken part in the revolt, but who had nevertheless unconsciously felt rather guilty for having hoped that the nationalists would win, spontaneously demanded the exemplary punishment of the men whom up to then they had looked upon as their models and heroes, without even waiting for a verdict on their actual "guilt." They turned their gods into victims, their heroes into scapegoats, their saints into martyrs, in accordance with an absolutely classical psychological process. Had the French authorities been "primitive" enough themselves, had they offered the Malagasy people their own leaders as expiatory victims (while washing their hands of the whole affair), we should have seen a repetition of those emotional phenomena which occurred in another colony some 20 centuries ago when another people tried to wash away its sins in the blood of its own lamb.

The Malagasy rebels, however, had no such sacrifice in their minds; they wanted only to be delivered of their feelings of guilt by the restoration of clear and firm bonds of dependence on the traditional pattern.

This, I think, is an appropriate point at which to mention the phenomena of identification with the leader. A subject always— and almost always unconsciously—identifies himself with an acclaimed and acknowledged leader. For a leader is never really recognized as such, in any country, unless the man-in-the-street has the feeling—it may be illusory, but that is immaterial—that he understands him, that he can predict what he is going to do, and that he himself would do exactly the same if he were in his place. Whatever qualities a government may have, it will please only that fraction of the population which has the same qualities. It will become popular only when the man-in-the-street has unconsciously identified himself with it and feels that its actions are prompted by feelings akin to his own. If he cannot achieve this identification, though it is easy enough in normal times, then he projects on to it all sorts of low motives and sees it as prompted in all its actions by malice, self-interest, bad faith, and imbecility. If this sort of thing can happen in Europe, where those who govern and those who are governed are of the same nationality and have personalities of similar structure, how much more likely is it to happen in a colonial situation. True, the colonial inhabitants are not very exacting as to the conditions for identification; they were prepared to treat as father and mother governors and administrators not always worthy of that honor; but people dominated by a need for dependence cannot identify themselves with leaders who, they feel— they may be wrong, but no matter—have abandoned them. They saw nothing generous in our proposal to loosen some of their bonds of dependence, at least in the conditions in which the proposal was made, namely, after a war which had made them doubt the power of their overlords, after sharp disputes over domestic policy, and in the midst of a conflict between stern but "tried" colonialists and politicians who, while preaching liberty, did not commit themselves in any way, had nothing either to gain or lose and remained infinitely more "apart" from the Malagasies than the most brutal European foreman.

When the French arrived fifty years ago, the Malagasies did not receive them indifferently in the way people might, say, accept a new employer or a new justice of the peace; their feelings were much warmer, and the French, responding in their fashion,

unwittingly created a situation which, though satisfactory to them, was in fact based on a complete misunderstanding. Many changes have taken place since then. Today the Malagasy wants to project upon us his shortcomings and his ill intentions; he wants to find other leaders with whom to identify himself. We can no longer comfort ourselves with the thought that we are leading our colonial protégés slowly but surely along the path of progress towards a remote but accessible ideal: that of civilization, assimilation, emancipation. . . . For the Malagasies say that they are still following this path, but with other leaders; they do not want us any more. They no longer reproach us for imposing our civilization upon them; they now accuse us of withholding it from them, of barring the path we opened up for them. It is a political reversal—of that there is no doubt—but the political is simply a reflection of the psychological reversal, for at bottom what the Malagasies want is indeed our civilization but not from us.

These aspirations of theirs formed the kernel of the "nationalism" and "patriotism" which backed the program for national independence. The details of that program[3] were borrowed and the ideology was left vague, but neither program nor ideas were required to win adherents. When the leaders the people wanted demanded "independence within the framework of the French Union" the Political Affairs and Police Departments thought themselves positively Machiavellian in allowing another party to be formed and to claim, with impunity, absolute and unconditional independence. In spite of these attractions, however, and in spite of the newspapers placed at its disposal, the party had no success, because its leaders were not the ones the people wanted. The Malagasies took very little interest in programs as such; they did not see themselves as champions of freedom (typical Malagasies, that is, for there are some who approach political problems as we do) but as followers of certain specific leaders. These followers were not rebels; they were "nationalists" and an armed revolt does not appear to have formed part of their plans. The rebels came from more backward tribes, but they adopted the same men as their leaders. Naturally this does not mean that those leaders sanctioned the revolt, but the connexion itself was enough for the Prosecution to maintain that they were responsible, without bothering to go into details.

When the disturbances first began, and although at that time no one knew very much at all about their political causes, the colonialists with one accord and without the slightest hesitation demanded the arrest of the Malagasy chiefs. Subsequently they demanded their execution without trial. There was some sort of minor conspiracy—which failed—to place absolute power in the hands of the military, so that they could be executed under martial law. (This little plot, like all plots, had other motives too, but it was the desire to secure the immediate "punishment" of the leaders which gave it sufficient emotional force to influence public opinion and make it, not a mere conspiracy, but a genuine *movement* among the colonials.) The colonialists were not interested in real responsibility and guilt; they felt, they knew instinctively that their rivals in the hearts of the Malagasies were neither freedom nor independence but the actual persons of the Malagasy leaders, whether or not these men had anything to do with unleashing the revolt.[4]

We shall be returning at a later stage to consider other aspects of these psychological facts. For the moment it is enough to note that nationalism, to the masses, was simply a means of restoring the ancient pattern of dependences. Those woven around the Europeans had not withstood the test of time and change.

Group identity and marginality
as factors in rebellion

The differences in status that Boeke and Mannoni write about are extreme. They are the differences between master and slave, master and servant, colonizer and colonized as these have juxtaposed people in acutely superior–subordinate, benefactor–dependent relationships.

The status differences between the people involved in the following article are those between immigrants and hosts. The interaction between them in its hostile period was neither so intimate nor so intense as that between colonizer and colonized.

Japanese began migrating to the United States around the beginning of the 20th century. By 1941 the original immigrants (Issei) were getting old, had already produced families of native-born Americans (Nisei), and in some cases already had grandchildren (Sansei). On 7 December 1941 their ancestral nation bombed Pearl Harbor, Hawaii. This started a war between Japan and the United States and precipitated in action the prejudice against Japanese immigrants that had existed since their arrival. Within weeks after Pearl Harbor, plans were made to evacuate all Japanese—regardless of country of birth—from the West Coast. Within months they were involuntarily relocated at centers away from the coast, where Japanese attack was believed imminent. Parenthetically, there was no evacuation of Japanese in Hawaii, where roughly a third of the population was Japanese. In the months after the relocation, the internees at first were busy getting physically located and settled. Then they began to form a solidary group, increasingly conscious of their identity vis-à-vis the nearby white guards and the distant white community.

On the first anniversary of Pearl Harbor violent uprisings occurred at several of these Japanese Relocation Centers. One of the coauthors was interned at one of these camps. In an interview-study of former internees, certain differences became clear between those who had taken part in the riots and those who had not. The most striking of these was that the participants were far more likely to be Niseis, caught between loyalty to the country of their ancestry and the country of their birth and upbringing.

The riots at the Japanese Relocation Centers were neither so intense, widespread, nor enduring as the Peasant Revolt in Germany in 1525, the Malagasy uprising in Madagascar in 1947, or the Indonesian violence of 1965–1966. One likely reason is

56

that the degree of subordination to the dominant society was not so great in the Japanese–American case. Another is that very few Japanese were killed by the guards.

But one reason that the rebellion in the camps did take place is that those who were most acutely conscious of their mental proximity to both the old and the new societies were willing to translate their hostility into action. Mental marginality thus emerges as a prominent factor that helps distinguish those who will rebel actively from those who will be (sympathetic) observers. It has been repeatedly noted that the most actively rebellious black people in America in the 1960s have been among those who are socioeconomically the most advanced and who therefore are caught between the lower status of their black brethren and the higher status of the white community.

Riots and rioters

GEORGE WADA
AND
JAMES C. DAVIES

Notes to this section will be found on pages 333–334.

I

A RIOT is one of the rarest types of face-to-face groups, organized to express strongly sensed feelings of protest in violent form. It is a nonlegal, nonroutine, nondeliberative group that is transitory in time and at least semivoluntary in membership. Its members are momentarily conjoined not because they know where they want to go but because they do not like where they have been.

Riots have rarely been subjected to analysis because of the extraordinary difficulty, usually the impossibility, of predicting the time and place of their occurrence, of identifying the people who join this tense crowd which so often gathers under the cover of darkness, and of later locating the participants for inquiry when they have silently merged again into the general populace.

Yet the study of riots is significant because they present in intense form the substance of social unrest which, when widespread, produces rebellion or revolution—which is never an orderly, constitutional process. Finding out what differentiates rioters from nonrioters may offer some clues as to the dynamics of violent, rapid, general political change, which always is initiated by a minority group expressing what it hopes are the discontents of the general public. Research only in the broad causes of unrest does not explain why some people become active participants in a movement of protest while others hang back as more-or-less sympathetic observers of political action.

Before discussing the specific causes and personal composition of the riot we investigated, it may be useful to describe the sense of group identification which pervades a crowd and which makes possible the kinds of action which could not elsewhere be carried out. An individual in a crowd loses perhaps most of the identity and uniqueness that make him an individual. His role as crowd member provides a protective mask behind which he can join in action he would scarcely perform in a gathering of known friends and acquaintances. Losing a measure of identity, a person in a crowd loses a sense of individual responsibility and at the same time gains a sense of power, in the expression of feelings he shares with others present but which he could not express—or express effectively—by himself. This sense of power, which as a release from tension is one aspect of freedom even though it destroys individuality, may in part serve to explain why crowd action may be so satisfying an experience to many individuals. One participant in the riot we studied said with strong emphasis that he "felt *good*" when it was in progress.

Thomas Mann's novella, *Mario and the Magician*, based on the Fascist experience in Italy, gives a more lively sense than scientific articles of the tendency toward the complete preoccupation in group activity that can occur in a crowd. R. C. Myers has presented a vivid report on an anti-Communist riot in 1947, showing how an orderly group became a mob in its simple absorption in a task of violence that its individual members—and leaders—would not have ventured singly.[1]

II

The bombing of Pearl Harbor on 7 December 1941 started the chain of events which made it possible for us to investigate systematically the phenomenon of riots. Very soon thereafter came the decision to remove all persons of Japanese birth or ancestry from the West Coast. During the spring of 1942 their evacuation to hinterland relocation centers was begun. By October 1942, the transfer was completed. The reactions of the Japanese varied from bitterness to resignation. Only one person—an ex-United States Navy man—forcibly resisted to the point of being removed from his home by physical coercion.[2]

At one of the camps, Manzanar, on the eastern slope of the California Sierras, a set of riotous demonstrations took place on the first anniversary of Pearl Harbor. The precipitating cause appears to have been the jailing of several evacuees. These men were believed by the camp administration to have joined in the beating of another evacuee who was reportedly acting as an informer to the administration. At the first protest meeting, blacklists of alleged informers were read, some of the informers being marked for death. Leaders of the meeting went to

the camp administrator, demanding the release of the jailed evacuee. They did not succeed. A second meeting was held, the proposal being to get about ten of the informers. The crowd proceeded to do this, moving excitedly from one point to another in search of intended victims. In trying to move the crowd away from the police station, the soldiers resorted to tear gas. The crowd broke up briefly and then reformed. Without authorization, soldiers then fired into the crowd. Two evacuees later died of wounds and several others were injured. Routine camp work came to a standstill briefly, with at least two-thirds of the evacuees openly mourning the two who had been killed. A month elapsed before the camp got back to normal. Speaking even from thirteen years' retrospect, one of the camp's administrative staff with clearly evident feeling described the atmosphere as being "electric" at the time of the riot.[3]

It was this disturbance that we proposed to study by interviewing people who had been in the camp as evacuees. Most of the people confined at Manzanar had previously lived in metropolitan Los Angeles and returned there after the war. We drew a rather crude area probability sample in 1954 and got successful interviews of 98 Japanese who were in Manzanar at the time of these riots. Of these 98, 26 reported having attended one or more of the demonstrations. We made comparisons between the 26 attendants and the 72 nonattendants. The camp population at Manzanar was about 10,000 at the time of the riots. If our 26 attendants out of 98 respondents corresponded to the total population, it means that about 2500 were present at one or another of the demonstrations. Crowd sizes are notoriously hard to estimate, and we could find no eyewitness conjecture as to the number present. But it is doubtful that more than one internee in four did show up.

Fortunately there are some data that have made it possible to check the reliability of the sample. In our sample and in two earlier ones, the number of families owning their own businesses before the war was determined. In their report of socioeconomic effects of the evacuation, Bloom and Riemer found that 67.2 percent of the 198 families in their sample were engaged in family enterprise as contrasted with 32.8 percent in which the income was wholly derived from wages and salaries.[4] The comparable figure in our sample of 98 is 70 percent reporting family enterprise and 30 percent reporting that no one in the family owned a business.[5] The Bloom–Riemer survey was conducted during March 1947. Ours was conducted from June 1954, to February 1955. Both sets of figures compare with the 68.6 percent of Japanese families who had family enterprises as reported in a 10 percent sample derived by Bloom and Riemer from government forms filled out by Japanese–American families at the time of evacuation. The close consistency of these three sets of figures, from 1942, 1947, and 1954, lends credibility to the responses and to the randomness of our sample.

The problem of accurately recalling a series of events after twelve years naturally raises some question as to the validity of the statements made orally to our three interviewers. We felt, however, that the chances of getting accurate statements were as great as, or greater than, they would have been immediately after the war, when memories and bitterness and fear of white reprisal were stronger than in interracially quite peaceful 1954. Immediately after the riot, investigation would probably have been impossible; there is no published evidence of such having been undertaken.[6]

The rapport between our interviewers and their respondents was in most cases good, with freely given responses. Two of the three interviewers were Nisei—native Americans of Japanese ancestry. One of them was an exchange student in the United States from Japan: he was better able to converse with Issei—native Japanese who migrated to the United States—most of whom think and talk most readily in their native tongue. Unless we assume a systematic error between those who attended the riots and those who stayed home, such as that those who attended have better or worse memories or are more

truthful or less so, we may reasonably suppose that errors in reporting were randomly distributed throughout the entire sample.

The size of the sample is, however, small for statistical reliability and the data are presented with as much diffidence as confidence. They nevertheless are of a reliability so far above that of casual observation or even of documentary search as to merit presentation as reasonably accurate findings in an unusually difficult area of research.

The most obvious cause for the December 1942, demonstrations was a boiling over of resentments against the racial discrimination that had produced the confinement behind barbed wire and armed guards, in a climate that yielded heat, dust, high winds, and severe cold. In having a community-wide effect, this cause is analogous to the chronic dislocation of the agrarian economy that produced the Populist revolt among American farmers in the late nineteenth century. It is analogous to the 1929 depression that put the Republican party out of power in 1933. It is a localized analog of the social and economic conditions that produced the French and Russian Revolutions.

As we have mentioned, the immediate, precipitating cause appears to have been the resentment at the jailing in Manzanar of some people accused of having severely beaten an alleged "dog"—a Japanese collaborator with the white camp administration.

These manifest, self-evident causes or ones similar to them are surely factors without which a series of severe riots would not have occurred. They provided the necessary soil and climate in which the riots briefly flourished. But the obvious fact is that much less than all of the camp population showed up at the riots. What was it about these participants that caused them to assemble, to take action, while the other camp residents, who experienced the same discrimination and enforced confinement, took no such direct action?

No one factor can be singled out as distinguishing the riot participants from those who stayed home. A series of factors which operated jointly appears to distinguish the two categories. The order in which they are presented here indicates no weighting of their comparative importance.

A most striking feature of the rioters appears to be their marginality. They stood betwixt the Japan of the past and the America of the present. Whereas less than a third of the rioters were born in Japan, close to half of the nonrioters were born there![7] But a high proportion of the rioters —two-thirds—had at one time or another returned or gone to Japan for a visit. About half of these visitors had stayed less than two years but the other half had stayed for periods ranging from two to seventeen years and consequently had become deeply immersed in Japanese culture. On the other hand, less than half of the nonrioters ever returned or went to Japan for a visit, and less than a third of those who did return made visits of more than two years.

Yet the rioters had integrated themselves more into American society than the nonrioters. All but one among the rioters who were eligible to vote before the war reported doing so, whereas only three-fourths of the eligible nonrioters reported voting. And somewhat more rioters said they lived in prewar neighborhoods mixed or predominantly white in color than did the nonrioters. Slightly more of the rioters reported having gone to Catholic or Protestant churches (whose congregations were Japanese) before the war than the nonrioters. On the other hand, the nonchurch group memberships held by the rioters were more likely to have been all-Japanese than the group memberships of nonrioters. Less than a third of the rioters as compared with over half of the nonrioters reported joining groups whose membership was mixed or predominantly white.

Thus were the rioters generally more caught between the two cultures of America and Japan: they tended to visit Japan more often, to stay longer, to join all-Japanese clubs in America. Yet they joined Christian churches, voted in American elections, and lived in racially mixed neighborhoods more often than the nonrioters. More often native American than the nonrioters, they were nevertheless more self-consciously Japanese

perhaps than the Japanese in Japan—like the Irish in New York at the turn of the century or the Koreans in Japan after World War II. They were not really at home in either culture.

Another striking characteristic of the rioters was their tendency to be socially active, to join groups and meet people. Almost two-thirds of them were members of some nonchurch organization before the war, compared with less than half of the nonrioters. Four out of five rioters had attended Buddhist or Christian churches, compared with three out of four nonrioters. The larger proportion of rioters eligible to vote who did so has already been mentioned. While at Manzanar, about as many rioters went to church as nonrioters but a third of them were members of some other camp organization as contrasted with only a fifth of the nonrioters. And three-fourths of the rioters reported having contacts with white people outside camp while at Manzanar, compared with less than half of the nonrioters.

Fewer of the rioters had some substantial economic stake in American society. Six out of ten rioters or their families owned a business before the war, ranging from gardening to farms to a hotel, compared with three out of four nonrioters. And the family earnings of the rioters were lower, a third of them making $2000 a year or less before the war compared with a fifth of the nonrioters, and only one of them making over $5000 compared with seven of the nonrioters.

One of the strongest factors weighing in favor of joining the riotous demonstrations was freedom from family responsibility. Almost half of the rioters were unmarried at the time, compared with a third of the nonrioters. Two-thirds of all married rioters had one or more children, compared with over four-fifths of the married nonrioters. Only a third of the married rioters had two or more children, while two-thirds of the nonrioters did, and the rioters' children were older and therefore less dependent on their parents than those of the nonrioters.

Age itself was a somewhat ambiguous

Table 1. *Comparisons of all rioters with all nonrioters.*

	RIOTERS		NONRIOTERS	
Total N, Each Category	26		72	
	N	Percent	N	Percent
Born in Japan	8	31	34	47
Born in U.S. (including Hawaii)	18	69	38	53
Visited Japan after residing in United States	17	65	31	43
Stayed in Japan less than two years	9	53	21	68
Stayed in Japan from two to seventeen years	8	47	10	32
Married at time of riots	14	54	48	67
Had one or more children at time of riots	9	64	41	85
Had two or more children at time of riots	5	36	31	65
Old enough to vote, 1940	11	42	19	26
Voted, if old enough	10	91	14	74
Respondent or his family had prewar business	15	58	53	74
Family prewar earnings under $2000 per year	9	35	15	21
Family prewar earnings $5000 or over per year	1	4	7	10
Lived in prewar white or mixed neighborhood	20	77	49	68
Went to Christian church before war*	12	46	26	36
Went to Buddhist church before war*	11	42	29	40
Member of prewar organized nonchurch group	16	62	30	42
Member of racially mixed group	5	31	16	53
Went to Christian church at Manzanar*	11	42	24	33
Went to Buddhist church at Manzanar*	10	38	27	38
Member of organized nonchurch group at Manzanar	9	35	15	21
Had contacts with outside white people while at Manzanar	19	73	30	42
Expected or hoped Japan would win war, December 1941	16	62	30	42
Expected or hoped Japan would win war, December 1942	14	54	25	35

* Some respondents reported going to both Buddhist and Christian churches. When separate figures above for attendance at each are combined, they do not equal attendance at church of whatever faith as reported in the text of the article.

variable. The mean age of the twenty-six rioters at the time of the riots was 32.6 years and of the seventy-two nonrioters, 34.7. Other comparisons on age were difficult because race prejudice and international diplomacy combined to break the age continuity of Japanese in the United States. In 1907 the Gentleman's Agreement mollified resentment in Japan over segregation of Japanese students in San Francisco public schools when Theodore Roosevelt got the offending city ordinance withdrawn, in return for a promise by the Japanese government virtually to stop emigration of its male nationals to America. A distant ripple of this old tremor, at Manzanar in 1942, produced a population division such that all but two of our forty-two respondents who were born in Japan were also at least 35 years old. It is thus impossible to say that proportionally twice as many respondents in this age category stayed away from the riots because they were older or that they did so because they were Issei, born in Japan. An inconclusive clue is furnished by the fact that the mean age of the eight Issei attending the riots was 48.9 years, compared with 46.5 for the thirty-four nonrioting Issei[8]—a finding that runs contrary to the younger average age for all rioters vis-a-vis all nonrioters. Both age and birthplace among respondents over 34 years old remain ambiguous as factors influencing the decision to attend the riots or not.

It is nevertheless clear that rioters tended to be younger. Fully three-fourths of all rioters were under 35 years and more than half of all rioters were under 30. Correlatively, well over half of the nonrioters were 30 or older, most of this total being 35 or older. And younger respondents as a whole tended to be unmarried, or if married, to have fewer children, and to be members of families with lower incomes. But, as the table below indicates, rioters differed from nonrioters in a wide range of factors in each of the three age groups—under 30, between 30 and 34, and 35 or over. Despite

Table 2. *Rioters and nonrioters compared by age group.*

	RIOTERS UNDER 30		NONRIOTERS UNDER 30		RIOTERS 30–34		NONRIOTERS 30–34		RIOTERS 35 AND OVER		NONRIOTERS 35 AND OVER	
	14		29		6		9		6		34	
Total N, Each Category	N	Percent	N	Percent	N	Percent	N	Percent	N	Percent	N	Percent
Born in Japan	1 of 14	7	0	0	1 of 6	17	1 of 9	11	6 of 6	100	33 of 34	97
Married at time of riots	3/14	21	7/29	24	6/6	100	7/9	78	5/6	83	34/34	100
Had one or more children at time of riots	2/3	67	5/7	71	2/6	33	5/7	71	5/5	100	31/34	91
Had two or more children at time of riots	0/3	0	3/7	43	1/6	17	1/7	14	4/5	80	27/34	79
Number and mean age of all children ( )	2 (1.5)		10 (5.4)		4 (3.5)		6 (3.5)		20 (20.5)		110 (16.4)	
Voted, if old enough	6/6	100	5/10	50	4/5	80	8/8	100	0/0	...	1/1	100
Respondent or his family had prewar business	8/14	57	19/29	66	3/6	50	3/9	33	4/6	67	31/33*	94
Family prewar earnings under $2000 per year	6/13*	46	8/17*	47	1/4*	25	4/9	44	2/5*	40	3/29*	10
Family prewar earnings $5000 or over per year	1/13*	8	1/17*	6	0/4*	0	0/9	0	0/5*	0	6/29*	21
Lived in prewar white or mixed neighborhood	9/14	64	19/29	66	5/6	83	5/9	55	6/6	100	25/34	74
Went to Christian church before war	5/14	36	13/29	45	4/6	67	3/9	33	3/6	50	10/34	29
Member of prewar white or mixed membership group	5/14	36	8/29	28	0/6	0	2/9	22	0/5*	0	6/34	18
Went to Christian church at Manzanar	6/14	43	11/29	38	2/6	33	2/9	22	3/6	50	11/34	32
Member of nonchurch group at Manzanar	6/14	43	9/29	31	1/6	17	1/9	11	2/6	33	5/34	15
Had contacts with outside white people while at Manzanar	14/14	100	14/29	48	4/6	67	4/9	44	1/6	17	12/34	35
Expected or hoped Japan would win war, December 1941	8/14	57	7/29	24	4/6	67	2/9	22	4/6	67	21/34	62
Expected or hoped Japan would win war, December 1942	7/14	50	4/29	14	3/5*	60	1/9	11	4/6	67	20/34	59

* Cases in which information was not ascertained were excluded in the computation of percentages. Since items of nonascertained information were not proportionally distributed between the six categories, percentage computations would not at all have been comparable between the different categories of respondents.

a small number of cases, in most instances rioters in each age group rather consistently tended less often to be married, to have children if married (or have children who were of an age that required much parental supervision), to have been members of families that owned a business before the war and had substantial incomes, and to have lived in racially mixed neighborhoods. In each age group, rioters tended to have voted more often than nonrioters if old enough to vote, to have had contacts with white people outside Manzanar, and to have expected or hoped for Japanese victory in the war. Rioters generally were more gregarious in each age group, but the data on prewar Christian church attendance and prewar nonchurch group membership are not such as to refute or support the notion that age influences the tendency to join groups. As mentioned earlier, a positive relationship of some significance between prewar Christian church and nonchurch groups is evident, when all rioters are compared with all non-rioters—a finding consistent with the more marked tendency of rioters to be joiners.

The rioters differed markedly from the nonrioters in their reactions to their wartime experiences. Subject to the same treatment by the white people and the government both before and during the evacuation and resettlement, they reacted much more strongly—despite the fact that their stake in American society was economically not so large as that of those who stayed away from demonstrations. When asked for what reasons Japanese were evacuated from the coast, nearly a third of the nonrioters listed reasons that could be regarded at least in part as racially unhostile to the Japanese community in California, such as: "to prevent sabotage"; "for the protection of the Japanese"; "to protect Japanese from socalled war terror"; "military reason— more of a precaution; more for Japanese safety, too"; "government says the Americans would be hysterical against the Japanese; they said if we went to camp we'd be loyal." In only two instances did the rioters make such statements. Nevertheless, over half of the nonrioters expressed reasons indicating hostility of whites to Japanese; two-thirds of the rioters expressed such reasons.

There was little difference between the two groups in their appraisal of the attitude of white people generally toward Japanese before the war began, but the rioters were slightly more likely than the nonrioters to indicate that white people became more hostile after Pearl Harbor. First- or second-hand knowledge of "dogs" was greater among the rioters and even from the time-perspective of 1954 rioters were much more sure than nonrioters that "dogs" deserved the beating that some of them got in camp.

A most striking difference in attitude was toward the course of the war with Japan. For every two nonrioters that expected or hoped in December 1941, that Japan would win the war, there were three rioters (the respective absolute percentages: 42 and 62). A year later, at the time of the riots, expectations and hopes had diminished somewhat, but the ratio between the rioters and non-rioters stayed the same, and a majority of the rioters still anticipated Japanese victory.

A rather remarkable instance of the effect of what Le Bon called the suggestibility of a crowd occurred at the camp. Some three weeks before the Manzanar demonstrations, a strike had developed at Poston, another Japanese relocation center in Arizona. Such news surely has impact on the receptive audience that another relocation center would provide, but the ears of the rioters were sharper: over half of them reported having heard before the December demonstrations of the Poston strike, whereas only a third of the nonrioters recalled having heard of it.

III

Rioters appear from this brief analysis to differ from nonrioters primarily in their marginality—their failure to establish strong ties to a meaningful cultural group; the intensity of their search for such ties in group activities; their relative lack of economic stake in the society, their relative youth, and their freedom from responsibilities to that universal group, the child-rearing family. Comparatively speaking they are a restless, dissatisfied category of people, reacting more strongly to the conditions of society which, like rain, fall with an even-handed justice on rich and poor, young and old, skilled and unskilled alike. It is not the conditions but the reaction to conditions which made the difference between a resident of the camp becoming a rioter or staying home. The rioters were the activists, the elite in a discontented society, and in Lippmann's phrase the nonrioters were the interested spectators to action. In some cases accident appeared to be the factor that brought some people to and kept others away from the demonstrations. One person, not included in our category of rioters, was in jail at the time the demonstration took place outside the jail, was briefly freed by the rioters, and then returned to the jail. Some people who were interviewed reported having been deeply involved in a poker game when the riots occurred.

But such factors as marginality, intense social activity, and freedom from family responsibility were not accidental in their operation. If a person has been born into a minority-group family in a not always friendly big society, has spent a half-dozen years or more in school in the land of his ancestors, and then returned to the land of his birth to seek integration and acceptance in the big society, he is rather likely to react strongly to hostility. In quickly weighing whether to accept the invitation, shouted at him from the street, to join a demonstration, he is more likely to respond if he lacks the quieting influences of family, wealth, and substantial income that others have with

similar background and reactions to the background. There was one dramatic border-line case in our sample: a woman headed toward one demonstration but turned back because she was pregnant.

In our account we have described by and large a middle category of people, the minority that in degree of activity lies between the relatively quiescent majority on the one hand and the leaders of the minority on the other. Characteristically, when asked what they did at the demonstrations, our rioters reported having stood in the background just to see what was going on. In a few cases where we thought a prospective respondent might have been a leader in a demonstration, we were refused an interview. But our middle category is significant in that, without it, no demonstrations would have occurred. It takes more than leaders to make a riot or a revolution, or even to effect peaceably at the polls a modification of the power structure of an orderly society.

Our analysis suggests rather clearly that when a society supposedly reaches the boiling point, it is not the society as a whole that does so, but a minority who because of atypical circumstances are free to react with vigor to sensed injustice, since vigorous reaction is less likely to harm these individuals in their home, property, or income. The majority of the society may sympathize with or after the deed support the rebellious minority, but it will not itself man the barricades or shout "Down with the King." It is not alone the existence of intolerable social circumstances which makes people rise in protest. It is perhaps at least as much the existence of individual, private circumstances that make it possible not to tolerate the intolerable.

Revolution in China in
Mao Tse-tung

The modernization of China began with the master–servant and colonial–colonized interactions between people that we have already considered. But China was socially less permeable, with its tight-knit social structure, and so colonialism played a different sort of role and took different forms than elsewhere. Westerners and Japanese colonized Chinese and Chinese colonized Chinese, the latter in a fashion comparable to Africa-born Europeans colonizing Africans in Africa.

The first Westerners who came to China were treated with grand condescension by the rulers. Later arrivals became so established as to secure the immunity of Westerners to Chinese law (extraterritoriality, as it was euphemized). A slowly growing awareness of the *de facto* colonial relationship led to the Boxer Rebellion of 1900, a kind of atavistic attack upon the foreign and the modern intrusions on socioeconomically and culturally static China. The Chinese government could neither contain the rebellion nor expel the foreigners who were the object of the rebels' fury. The imperial court could only sit in its impotent rage and observe the suppression of the rebellion by the Westerners, who then proceeded (with the exception of the United States) to exact reparation from the proud people whom they had humbled.

The deep intimacy of the reaction to modernization is well epitomized in the early life of the man who became the leader of the latest phase of Chinese modernization, Mao Tse-tung. In the selection from Edgar Snow's *Red Star over China* that follows, we can see the same ambivalent respect-and-rage toward his father that Martin Luther felt. We can see the same pride in his native land that Luther felt toward Germany as it haughtily depreciated the urbane culture of the Roman Church. And we see the same enduring anger at wrongs perpetrated by Chinese landlords upon Chinese peasants that animated the 1525 uprisings in Germany. As a small landlord's son, Mao was in marginal contact, positively and negatively, with a wide variety of forces that were colonizing, exploiting, degrading, and modernizing China. He reacted to these processes with a skill showing he had learned well from the mistakes of earlier revolutionaries.

Mao refused to apply dogmatically the Marxist ideology developed to indict a more fully developed industrial economy. He insisted on founding the Chinese revolution among the peasants. He showed an ability to convert enemy troops rather than destroy them. He showed a skill in the use of violence far superior to any earlier leaders in the German Protestant Reformation, the French Revolution, and the Russian Revolution.

Snow's account gives us a close, nearly autobiographical picture of the development of Mao, the successful revolutionary who talked at great length with an American newspaperman in 1936. This was nine years after Chiang Kai-shek firmly established himself in power and destroyed the city-based Chinese Communist party and thirteen years before the establishment of the People's Republic of China. We therefore have an account written in the very midst of a revolution that has fundamentally altered the life style and the value system of the Chinese people. This may be the most profound change that has ever occurred at any one time in history, directly affecting over 500 million Chinese—that is, about one of every five or six people on the entire earth. The indirect effects are even more widespread. And within China itself the revolution is not yet completely established.

Genesis of a Communist: Childhood

EDGAR SNOW

Notes to this section will be found on page 334.

On the five or six sets of questions I had submitted on different matters, Mao had talked for a dozen nights, hardly ever referring to himself or his own role in some of the events described. I was beginning to think it was hopeless to expect him to give me such details: he obviously considered the individual of very little importance. Like other Reds I met he tended to talk only about committees, organizations, armies, resolutions, battles, tactics, "measures," and so on, and seldom of personal experience.

For a while I thought this reluctance to expand on subjective matters, or even the exploits of their comrades as individuals, might derive from modesty, or a fear or suspicion of me, or a consciousness of the price so many of these men had on their heads. Later on I discovered that that was not so much the case as it was that most of them actually did not remember personal details. As I began collecting biographies I found repeatedly that the Communist would be able to tell everything that had happened in his early youth, but once he had become identified with the Red Army he lost himself somewhere, and without repeated questioning one could hear nothing more about *him*, but only stories of the Army, or the Soviets, or the Party—capitalized. These men could talk indefinitely about dates and circumstances of battles, and movements to and from a thousand unheard of places, but those events seemed to have had significance for them only collectively, not because they as individuals had made history there, but because the Red Army had been there, and behind it the whole organic force of an ideology for which they were fighting. It was an interesting discovery, but it made difficult reporting.

One night when all other questions had been satisfied, Mao turned to the list I had headed "Personal History." He smiled at a question, "How many times have you been married?"—and the rumor later spread that I had asked Mao how many wives he had. He was skeptical, anyway, about the necessity for supplying an autobiography. But I argued that in a way that was more important than information on other matters. "People want to know what sort of man you are," I said, "when they read what you say. Then you ought also to correct some of the false rumors circulated."

I reminded him of various reports of his death, how some people believed he spoke fluent French, while others said he was an ignorant peasant, how one report described him as a half-dead tubercular, while others maintained that he was a mad fanatic. He seemed mildly surprised that people should spend their time speculating about him. He agreed that such reports ought to be corrected Then he looked over the items again, as I had written them down.

"Suppose," he said at last "that I just disregard your questions, and instead give you a general sketch of my life? I think it will be more understandable, and in the end all of your questions will be answered just the same."

During the nightly interviews that followed —we were like conspirators indeed, huddled in that cave over the red-covered table, with sputtering candles between us—I wrote until I was ready to fall asleep. Wu Liang-p'ing sat next to me and interpreted Mao's soft southern dialect, in which a chicken, instead of being a good substantial northern *chi*, became a romantic *ghii*, and *Hunan* became *Funan*, and a bowl of *ch'a* turned into *ts'a*, and many much stranger variations occurred. Mao related everything from memory, and I put it down as he talked. It was, as I have said, retranslated and corrected, and this is the result, with no attempt to give it literary excellence, beyond some necessary corrections in the syntax of the patient Mr. Wu:

"I was born in the village of Shao Shan, in Hsiang T'an *hsien*,[1] Hunan province, in 1893. My father's name was Mao Jen-sheng [Mao Shun-sheng], and my mother's maiden name was Wen Ch'i-mei.

"My father was a poor peasant and while still young was obliged to join the army because of heavy debts. He was a soldier for many years. Later on he returned to the village where I was born, and by saving carefully and gathering together a little money through small trading and other enterprise he managed to buy back his land.

"As middle peasants then my family owned fifteen *mou*[2] of land. On this they could raise sixty *tan*[3] of rice a year. The five members of the family consumed a total of thirty-five *tan*—that is, about seven each—which left an annual surplus of twenty-five *tan*. Using this surplus, my father accumulated a little capital and in time purchased seven more *mou*, which gave the family the status of 'rich' peasants. We could then raise eighty-four *tan* of rice a year.

"When I was ten years of age and the family owned only fifteen *mou* of land, the five members of the family consisted of my father, mother, grandfather, younger brother, and myself. After we had acquired the additional seven *mou*, my grandfather died, but there came another younger brother. However, we still had a surplus of forty-nine *tan* of rice each year, and on this my father steadily prospered.

"At the time my father was a middle peasant he began to deal in grain transport and selling, by which he made a little money. After he became a 'rich' peasant, he devoted most of his time to that business. He hired a full-time farm laborer, and put his children to work on the farm, as well as his wife. I began to work at farming tasks when I was six years old. My father had no shop for his business. He simply purchased grain from the poor farmers and then transported it to the city merchants, where he got a higher price. In the winter, when the rice was being ground, he hired an extra laborer to work on the farm, so that at that time there were seven mouths to feed. My family ate frugally, but had enough always.

"I began studying in a local primary school when I was eight and remained there until I was thirteen years old. In the early morning and at night I worked on the farm. During the day I read the Confucian Analects and the Four Classics. My Chinese teacher belonged to the stern-treatment school. He was harsh and severe, frequently beating his students. Because of that I ran away from the school when I was ten. I was afraid to return home for fear of receiving a beating there, and set out in the general direction of the city, which I believed to be in a valley somewhere. I wandered for three days before I was finally found by my family. Then I learned that I had circled round and round in my travels, and in all my walking had got only about eight *li*[4] from my home.

"After my return to the family, however, to my surprise conditions somewhat improved. My father was slightly more considerate and the teacher was more inclined to moderation. The result of my act of protest impressed me very much. It was a successful 'strike.'

"My father wanted me to begin keeping the family books as soon as I had learned a few characters. He wanted me to learn to use the abacus. As my father insisted upon this I began to work at those accounts at night. He was a severe taskmaster. He hated to see me idle, and if there were no books to be kept he put me to work at farm tasks. He was a hot-tempered man and frequently beat both me and my brothers. He gave us no money whatever, and the most meager food. On the fifteenth of every month he made a concession to his laborers and gave them eggs with their rice, but never meat. To me he gave neither eggs nor meat.

"My mother was a kind woman, generous and sympathetic, and ever ready to share what she had. She pitied the poor and often gave them rice when they came to ask for it during famines. But she could not do so when my father was present. He disapproved of charity. We had many quarrels in my home over this question.

"There were two 'parties' in the family. One was my father, the Ruling Power. The Opposition was made up of myself, my mother, my brother, and sometimes even the laborer. In the 'united front' of the Opposition, however, there was a difference of opinion. My mother advocated a policy of indirect attack. She criticized any overt display of emotion and attempts at open rebellion against the Ruling Power. She said it was not the Chinese way.

"But when I was thirteen I discovered a powerful argument of my own for debating with my father on his own ground, by quoting the Classics. My father's favorite accusations against me were of unfilial conduct and laziness. I quoted, in exchange, passages from the Classics saying that the elder must be kind and affectionate. Against his charge that I was lazy I used the rebuttal that older people should do more work than younger, that my father was over three times as old as myself, and therefore should do more work. And I declared that when I was his age I would be much more energetic.

"The old man continued to 'amass wealth,' or what was considered to be a great fortune in that little village. He did not buy more land himself, but he bought many mortgages on other people's land. His capital grew to two or three thousand Chinese dollars.[5]

"My dissatisfaction increased. The dialectical struggle in our family was constantly developing.[6] One incident I especially remember. When I was about thirteen my father invited many guests to his home, and while they were present a dispute arose between the two of us. My father denounced me before the whole group, calling me lazy and useless. This infuriated me. I cursed him and left the house. My mother ran after me and tried to persuade me to return. My father also pursued me, cursing at the same time that he commanded me to come back. I reached the edge of a pond and threatened to jump in if he came any nearer. In this situation demands and counterdemands were presented for cessation of the civil war. My father insisted that I apologize and *k'ou-t'ou*[7] as a sign of submission. I agreed to give a one-knee *k'ou-t'ou* if he would promise not to beat me. Thus the war ended, and from it I learned that when I defended my rights by open rebellion my father relented, but when I remained meek and submissive he only cursed and beat me the more.

"Reflecting on this, I think that in the end the strictness of my father defeated him. I learned to hate him, and we created a real united front against him. At the same time it probably benefited me. It made me most diligent in my work; it made me keep my books carefully, so that he should have no basis for criticizing me.

"My father had had two years of schooling and he could read enough to keep books. My mother was wholly illiterate. Both were from peasant families. I was the family 'scholar.' I knew the Classics, but disliked them. What I enjoyed were the romances of Old China, and especially stories of rebellions. I read the *Yo Fei Chuan* [the *Yo Fei Chronicles*], *Shui Hu Chuan* [*The Water Margin*], *Fan T'ang* [*Revolt Against the T'ang*], *San Kuo* [the *Three Kingdoms*] and *Hsi Yu Chi* [*Travels in the West*, the story of Hsuan Tsang's 7th-century semilegendary pilgrimage to India] while still very young, and despite the vigilance of my old teacher, who hated these outlawed books and called them wicked. I used to read them in school, covering them up with a Classic when the teacher walked past. So also did most of my schoolmates. We learned many of the stories almost by heart, and discussed and rediscussed them many times. We knew more of them than the old men of the village, who also loved them and used to exchange stories with us. I believe that perhaps I was much influenced by such books, read at an impressionable age.

"I finally left the primary school when I was thirteen and began to work long hours on the farm, helping the hired laborer, doing the full labor of a man during the day and at night keeping books for my father. Nevertheless, I succeeded in continuing my reading, devouring everything I could find except the Classics. This annoyed my father, who wanted me to master the Classics, especially after he was defeated in a lawsuit because of an apt Classical quotation used by his adversary in the Chinese court. I used to cover up the window of my room late at night so that my father would not see the light. In this way I read a book called *Sheng-shih Wei-yen* [*Words of Warning*],[8] which I liked very much. The author, one of a number of old reformist scholars, thought that the weakness of China lay in

her lack of Western appliances—railways, telephones, telegraphs, and steamships—and wanted to have them introduced into the country. My father considered such books a waste of time. He wanted me to read something practical like the Classics, which could help him in winning lawsuits.

"I continued to read the old romances and tales of Chinese literature. It occurred to me one day that there was one thing peculiar about such stories, and that was the absence of peasants who tilled the land. All the characters were warriors, officials, or scholars; there was never a peasant hero. I wondered about this for two years, and then I analyzed the content of the stories. I found that they all glorified men of arms, rulers of the people, who did not have to work the land, because they owned and controlled it and evidently made the peasants work it for them.

"My father was in his early days, and in middle age, a skeptic, but my mother devoutly worshiped Buddha. She gave her children religious instruction, and we were all saddened that our father was an unbeliever. When I was nine years old I seriously discussed the problem of my father's lack of piety with my mother. We made many attempts then and later on to convert him, but without success. He only cursed us, and, overwhelmed by his attacks, we withdrew to devise new plans. But he would have nothing to do with the gods.

"My reading gradually began to influence me, however; I myself became more and more skeptical. My mother became concerned about me, and scolded me for my indifference to the requirements of the faith, but my father made no comment. Then one day he went out on the road to collect some money, and on his way he met a tiger. The tiger was surprised at the encounter and fled at once, but my father was even more astonished and afterwards reflected a good deal on his miraculous escape. He began to wonder if he had not offended the gods. From then on he showed more respect to Buddhism and burned incense now and then. Yet when my own backsliding grew worse, the old man did not interfere. He prayed to the gods only when he was in difficulties.

"*Sheng-shih Wei-yen* [*Words of Warning*] stimulated in me a desire to resume my studies. I had also become disgusted with my labor on the farm. My father naturally opposed me. We quarreled about it, and finally I ran away from home. I went to the home of an unemployed law student, and there I studied for half a year. After that I studied more of the Classics under an old Chinese scholar, and also read many contemporary articles and a few books.

"At this time an incident occurred in Hunan which influenced my whole life. Outside the little Chinese school where I was studying, we students noticed many bean merchants coming back from Changsha. We asked them why they were all leaving. They told us about a big uprising in the city.

"There had been a severe famine that year, and in Changsha thousands were without food. The starving sent a delegation to the civil governor to beg for relief, but he replied to them haughtily, 'Why haven't you food? There is plenty in the city. I always have enough.' When the people were told the governor's reply, they became very angry. They held mass meetings and organized a demonstration. They attacked the Manchu yamen, cut down the flagpole, the symbol of office, and drove out the governor. Following this, the Commissioner of Internal Affairs, a man named Chang, came out on his horse and told the people that the government would take measures to help them. Chang was evidently sincere in his promise, but the Emperor disliked him and accused him of having intimate connections with 'the mob.' He was removed. A new governor arrived, and at once ordered the arrest of the leaders of the uprising. Many of them were beheaded and their heads displayed on poles as a warning to future 'rebels.'

"This incident was discussed in my school for many days. It made a deep impression on me. Most of the other students sympathized with the 'insurrectionists,' but only from an observer's point of view. They did not understand that it had any relation to

their own lives. They were merely interested in it as an exciting incident. I never forgot it. I felt that there with the rebels were ordinary people like my own family and I deeply resented the injustice of the treatment given to them.

"Not long afterward, in Shao Shan, there was a conflict between members of the Ke Lao Hui,[9] a secret society, and a local landlord. He sued them in court, and as he was a powerful landlord he easily bought a decision favorable to himself. The Ke Lao Hui members were defeated. But instead of submitting, they rebelled against the landlord and the government and withdrew to a local mountain called Liu Shan, where they built a stronghold. Troops were sent against them and the landlord spread a story that they had sacrificed a child when they raised the banner of revolt. The leader of the rebels was called P'ang the Millstone Maker. They were finally suppressed and P'ang was forced to flee. He was eventually captured and beheaded. In the eyes of the students, however, he was a hero, for all sympathized with the revolt.

"Next year, when the new rice was not yet harvested and the winter rice was exhausted, there was a food shortage in our district. The poor demanded help from the rich farmers and they began a movement called 'Eat Rice Without Charge.'[10] My father was a rice merchant and was exporting much grain to the city from our district, despite the shortage. One of his consignments was seized by the poor villagers and his wrath was boundless. I did not sympathize with him. At the same time I thought the villagers' method was wrong also.

"Another influence on me at this time was the presence in a local primary school of a 'radical' teacher. He was 'radical' because he was opposed to Buddhism and wanted to get rid of the gods. He urged people to convert their temples into schools. He was a widely discussed personality. I admired him and agreed with his views.

"These incidents, occurring close together, made lasting impressions on my young mind, already rebellious. In this period also I began to have a certain amount of political consciousness, especially after I read a pamphlet telling of the dismemberment of China. I remember even now that this pamphlet opened with the sentence: 'Alas, China will be subjugated!' It told of Japan's occupation of Korea and Taiwan, of the loss of suzerainty in Indochina, Burma, and elsewhere. After I read this I felt depressed about the future of my country and began to realize that it was the duty of all the people to help save it.

"My father had decided to apprentice me to a rice shop in Hsiang T'an, with which he had connections. I was not opposed to it at first, thinking it might be interesting. But about this time I heard of an unusual new school and made up my mind to go there, despite my father's opposition. This school was in Hsiang Hsiang *hsien*, where my mother's family lived. A cousin of mine was a student there and he told me of the new school and of the changing conditions in 'modern education.' There was less emphasis on the Classics, and more was taught of the 'new knowledge' of the West. The educational methods, also, were quite 'radical.'

"I went to the school with my cousin and registered. I claimed to be a Hsiang Hsiang man, because I understood that the school was open only to natives of Hsiang Hsiang. Later on I took my true status as a Hsiang T'an native when I discovered that the place was open to all. I paid 1,400 coppers here for five months' board, lodging, and all materials necessary for study. My father finally agreed to let me enter, after friends had argued to him that this 'advanced' education would increase my earning powers. This was the first time I had been as far away from home as 50 *li*. I was 16 years old.

"In the new school I could study natural science and new subjects of Western learning. Another notable thing was that one of the teachers was a returned student from Japan, and he wore a false queue. It was quite easy to tell that his queue was false. Everyone laughed at him and called him the 'False Foreign Devil.'

"I had never before seen so many children together. Most of them were sons of land-lords, wearing expensive clothes; very few peasants could afford to send their children to such a school. I was more poorly dressed than the others. I owned only one decent coat-and-trousers suit. Gowns were not worn by students, but only by the teachers, and none but 'foreign devils' wore foreign clothes. Many of the richer students despised me because usually I was wearing my ragged coat and trousers. However, among them I had friends, and two especially were my good comrades. One of those is now a writer, living in Soviet Russia.[11]

"I was also disliked because I was not a native of Hsiang Hsiang. It was very important to be a native of Hsiang Hsiang and also important to be from a certain district of Hsiang Hsiang. There was an upper, lower, and middle district, and lower and upper were continually fighting, purely on a regional basis. Neither could become reconciled to the existence of the other. I took a neutral position in this war, because I was not a native at all. Consequently all three factions despised me. I felt spiritually very depressed.

"I made good progress at this school. The teachers liked me, especially those who taught the Classics, because I wrote good essays in the Classical manner. But my mind was not on the Classics. I was reading two books sent to me by my cousin, telling of the reform movement of K'ang Yu-wei. One was by Liang Ch'i-ch'ao,[12] editor of the *Hsin-min Ts'ung-pao* [*New People's Miscellany*]. I read and reread those books until I knew them by heart. I worshiped K'ang Yu-wei and Liang Ch'i-ch'ao, and was very grateful to my cousin, whom I then thought very progressive, but who later became a counterrevolutionary, a member of the gentry, and joined the reactionaries in the period of the Great Revolution of 1925–27.

"Many of the students disliked the False Foreign Devil because of his inhuman queue, but I liked hearing him talk about Japan. He taught music and English. One of his songs was Japanese and was called 'The Battle on the Yellow Sea.' I still remember some charming words from it:

The sparrow sings,
The nightingale dances,
And the green fields are lovely in the spring.
The pomegranate flowers crimson,
The willows are green-leaved,
And there is a new picture.

At that time I knew and felt the beauty of Japan, and felt something of her pride and might, in this song of her victory over Russia.[13] I did not think there was also a barbarous Japan—the Japan we know today.

"This is all I learned from the False Foreign Devil.

"I recall also that at about this time I first heard that the Emperor and Tzu Hsi, the Empress Dowager, were both dead, although the new Emperor, Hsuan T'ung [P'u Yi], had already been ruling for two years. I was not yet an antimonarchist; indeed, I considered the Emperor as well as most officials to be honest, good, and clever men. They only needed the help of K'ang Yu-wei's reforms. I was fascinated by accounts of the rulers of ancient China: Yao, Shun, Ch'in Shih Huang Ti, and Han Wu Ti, and read many books about them.[14] I also learned something of foreign history at this time, and of geography. I had first heard of America in an article which told of the American Revolution and contained a sentence like this: 'After eight years of difficult war, Washington won victory and built up his nation.' In a book called *Great Heroes of the World*, I read also of Napoleon, Catherine of Russia, Peter the Great, Wellington, Gladstone, Rousseau, Montesquieu, and Lincoln."

Days in Changsha

EDGAR SNOW

Notes to this section will be found on pages 334–335.

Mao Tse-tung continued:

"I began to long to go to Changsha, the great city, the capital of the province, which was 120 *li* from my home. It was said that this city was very big, contained many, many people, numerous schools, and the yamen of the governor. It was a magnificent place altogether. I wanted very much to go there at this time, and enter the middle school for Hsiang Hsiang people. That winter I asked one of my teachers in the higher primary school to introduce me there. The teacher agreed, and I walked to Changsha, exceedingly excited, half fearing that I would be refused entrance, hardly daring to hope that I could actually become a student in this great school. To my astonishment, I was admitted without difficulty. But political events were moving rapidly and I was to remain there only half a year.

"In Changsha I read my first newspaper, *Min-li-pao* [*People's Strength*], a nationalist revolutionary journal which told of the Canton Uprising against the Manchu Dynasty and the death of the Seventy-two Heroes, under the leadership of a Hunanese named Huang Hsing. I was most impressed with this story and found the *Min-li-pao* full of stimulating material. It was edited by Yu Yu-jen, who later became a famous leader of the Kuomintang. I learned also of Sun Yat-sen at this time, and of the program of the T'ung Meng Hui.[1] The country was on the eve of the First Revolution. I was so agitated that I wrote an article, which I posted on the school wall. It was my first expression of a political opinion, and it was somewhat muddled. I had not yet given up my admiration of K'ang Yu-wei and Liang Ch'i-ch'ao. I did not clearly understand the differences between them. Therefore in my article I advocated that Sun Yat-sen must be called back from Japan to become president of the new government, that K'ang Yu-wei be made premier, and that Liang Ch'i-ch'ao minister of foreign affairs![2]

"The anti-foreign-capital movement began in connection with the building of the Szechuan-Hankow railway, and a popular demand for a parliament became widespread. In reply to it the Emperor decreed merely that an advisory council be created. The students in my school became more and more agitated. They demonstrated their anti-Manchu sentiments by a rebellion against the pigtail.[3] One friend and I clipped off our pigtails, but others, who had promised to do so, afterward failed to keep their word. My friend and I therefore assaulted them in secret and forcibly removed their queues, a total of more than ten falling victim to our shears. Thus in a short space of time I had progressed from ridiculing the False Foreign Devil's imitation queue to demanding the general abolition of queues. How a political idea can change a point of view!

"I got into a dispute with a friend in a law school over the pigtail episode, and we each advanced opposing theories on the subject. The law student held that the body, skin, hair, and nails are heritages from one's parents and must not be destroyed, quoting the Classics to clinch his argument. But I myself and the antipigtailers developed a countertheory, on an anti-Manchu political basis, and thoroughly silenced him.

"After the Wuhan Uprising occurred,[4] led by Li Yuan-hung, martial law was declared in Hunan. The political scene rapidly altered. One day a revolutionary appeared in the middle school and made a stirring speech, with the permission of the principal. Seven or eight students arose in the assembly and supported him with vigorous denunciation of the Manchus, and calls for action to establish the Republic. Everyone listened with complete attention. Not a sound was heard as the orator of the revolution, one of the officials of Li Yuan-hung, spoke before the excited students.

"Four or five days after hearing this speech I determined to join the revolutionary army of Li Yuan-hung. I decided to go to

Hankow with several other friends, and we collected some money from our classmates. Having heard that the streets of Hankow were very wet, and that it was necessary to wear rain shoes, I went to borrow some from a friend in the army, who was quartered outside the city. I was stopped by the garrison guards. The place had become very active, the soldiers had for the first time been furnished with bullets, and they were pouring into the streets.

"Rebels were approaching the city along the Canton-Hankow railway, and fighting had begun. A big battle occurred outside the city walls of Changsha. There was at the same time an insurrection within the city, and the gates were stormed and taken by Chinese laborers. Through one of the gates I reentered the city. Then I stood on a high place and watched the battle, until at last I saw the *Han*[5] flag raised over the yamen. It was a white banner with the character *Han* in it. I returned to my school, to find it under military guard.

"On the following day, a *tutu*[6] government was organized. Two prominent members of the Ke Lao Hui [Elder Brother Society] were made *tutu* and vice-*tutu*. These were Chiao Ta-feng and Chen Tso-hsing, respectively. The new government was established in the former buildings of the provincial advisory council, whose chief had been T'an Yen-k'ai, who was dismissed. The council itself was abolished. Among the Manchu documents found by the revolutionaries were some copies of a petition begging for the opening of parliament. The original had been written in blood by Hsu T'eh-li, who is now commissioner of education in the Soviet Government. Hsu had cut off the end of his finger, as a demonstration of sincerity and determination, and his petition began, 'Begging that parliament be opened, I bid farewell [to the provincial delegates to Peking] by cutting my finger.'

"The new *tutu* and vice-*tutu* did not last long. They were not bad men, and had some revolutionary intentions, but they were poor and represented the interests of the oppressed. The landlords and merchants were dissatisfied with them. Not many days later, when I went to call on a friend, I saw their corpses lying in the street. T'an Yen-k'ai had organized a revolt against them, as representative of the Hunan landlords and militarists.

"Many students were now joining the army. A student army had been organized and among these students was T'ang Sheng-chih.[7] I did not like the student army; I considered the basis of it too confused. I decided to join the regular army instead, and help complete the revolution. The Ch'ing Emperor had not yet abdicated, and there was a period of struggle.

"My salary was seven yuan a month—which is more than I get in the Red Army now, however—and of this I spent two yuan a month on food. I also had to buy water. The soldiers had to carry water in from outside the city, but I, being a student, could not condescend to carrying, and bought it from the water peddlers. The rest of my wages were spent on newspapers, of which I became an avid reader. Among journals then dealing with the revolution was the *Hsiang Chiang Jih-pao* [*Hsiang River Daily News*]. Socialism was discussed in it, and in these columns I first learned the term. I also discussed socialism, really social-reformism, with other students and soldiers. I read some pamphlets written by Kiang K'ang-hu about socialism and its principles. I wrote enthusiastically to several of my classmates on this subject, but only one of them responded in agreement.

"There was a Hunan miner in my squad, and an ironsmith, whom I liked very much. The rest were mediocre, and one was a rascal. I persuaded two more students to join the army, and came to be on friendly terms with the platoon commander and most of the soldiers. I could write, I knew something about books, and they respected my 'great learning.' I could help by writing letters for them or in other such ways.

"The outcome of the revolution was not yet decided. The Ch'ing had not wholly given up power, and there was a struggle within the Kuomintang concerning the leadership. It was said in Hunan that further war was inevitable. Several armies were organized against the Manchus and against Yuan Shih-k'ai.[8] Among these was the Hunan army. But just as the Hunanese were preparing to move into action, Sun Yat-sen and Yuan Shih-k'ai came to an agreement, the scheduled war was called off, North and South were 'unified,' and the Nanking Government was dissolved. Thinking the revolution was over, I resigned from the army and decided to return to my books. I had been a soldier for half a year.

"I began to read advertisements in the papers. Many schools were then being opened and used this medium to attract new students. I had no special standard for judging schools; I did not know exactly what I wanted to do. An advertisement for a police school caught my eye and I registered for entrance to it. Before I was examined, however, I read an advertisement of a soap-making 'school'. No tuition was required, board was furnished and a small salary was promised. It was an attractive and inspiring advertisement. It told of the great social benefits of soap making, how it would enrich the country and enrich the people. I changed my mind about the police school and decided to become a soap maker. I paid my dollar registration fee here also.

"Meanwhile a friend of mine had become a law student and he urged me to enter his school. I also read an alluring advertisement of this law school, which promised many wonderful things. It promised to teach students all about law in three years and guaranteed that at the end of this period they would instantly become mandarins. My friend kept praising the school to me, until finally I wrote to my family, repeated all the promises of the advertisement, and asked them to send me tuition money. I painted a bright picture for them of my future as a jurist and mandarin. Then I paid a dollar to register in the law school and waited to hear from my parents.

"Fate again intervened in the form of an advertisement for a commercial school. Another friend counseled me that the country was in economic war, and that what was most needed were economists who could build up the nation's economy. His argument prevailed and I spent another dollar to register in this commercial middle school. I actually enrolled there and was accepted. Meanwhile, however, I continued to read advertisements, and one day I read one describing the charms of a higher commercial public school. It was operated by the government, it offered a wide curriculum, and I heard that its instructors were very able men. I decided it would be better to become a commercial expert there, paid my dollar and registered, then wrote my father of my decision. He was pleased. My father readily appreciated the advantages of commercial cleverness. I entered this school and remained—for one month.

"The trouble with my new school, I discovered, was that most of the courses were taught in English, and, in common with other students, I knew little English; indeed, scarcely more than the alphabet. An additional handicap was that the school provided no English teacher. Disgusted with this situation, I withdrew from the institution at the end of the month and continued my perusal of the advertisements.

"My next scholastic adventure was in the First Provincial Middle School. I registered for a dollar, took the entrance examination, and passed at the head of the list of candidates. It was a big school, with many students, and its graduates were numerous. A Chinese teacher there helped me very much; he was attracted to me because of my literary tendency. This teacher lent me a book called the *Yu-p'i T'ung-chien* [*Chronicles with Imperial Commentaries*], which contained imperial edicts and critiques by Ch'ien Lung.[9]

"About this time a government magazine exploded in Changsha. There was a huge fire, and we students found it very interesting. Tons of bullets and shells exploded, and gunpowder made an intense blaze. It was better than firecrackers. About a month later T'an Yen-k'ai was driven out by Yuan Shih-k'ai, who now had control of the political machinery of the Republic. T'ang Hsiang-ming replaced T'an Yen-k'ai and he set about making arrangements for Yuan's enthronement [in an attempted restoration of the monarchy, which speedily failed].

"I did not like the First Middle School. Its curriculum was limited and its regulations were objectionable. After reading *Yu-p'i T'ung-chien* I had also come to the conclusion that it would be better for me to read and study alone. After six months I left the school and arranged a schedule of education of my own, which consisted of reading every day in the Hunan Provincial Library. I was very regular and conscientious about it, and the half-year I spent in this way I consider to have been extremely valuable to me. I went to the library in the morning when it opened. At noon I paused only long enough to buy and eat two rice cakes, which were my daily lunch. I stayed in the library every day reading until it closed.

"During this period of self-education I read many books, studied world geography and world history. There for the first time I saw and studied with great interest a map of the world. I read Adam Smith's *The Wealth of Nations*, and Darwin's *Origin of Species*, and a book on ethics by John Stuart Mill. I read the works of Rousseau, Spencer's *Logic*, and a book on law written by Montesquieu. I mixed poetry and romances and, the tales of ancient Greece, with serious study of history and geography of Russia, America, England, France, and other countries.

"I was then living in a guild house for natives of Hsiang Hsiang district. Many soldiers were there also—'retired' or disbanded men from the district, who had no work to do and little money. Students and soldiers were always quarreling in the guild house, and one night this hostility between them broke out in physical violence. The soldiers attacked and tried to kill the students. I escaped by fleeing to the toilet, where I hid until the fight was over.

"I had no money then, my family refusing to support me unless I entered school, and since I could no longer live in the guild house I began looking for a new place to lodge. Meanwhile, I had been thinking seriously of my 'career' and had about

decided that I was best suited for teaching. I had begun reading advertisements again. An attractive announcement of the Hunan Normal School now came to my attention, and I read with interest of its advantages: no tuition required, and cheap board and cheap lodging. Two of my friends were also urging me to enter. They wanted my help in preparing entrance essays. I wrote of my intention to my family and I received their consent. I composed essays for my two friends, and wrote one of my own. All were accepted—in reality, therefore, I was accepted three times. I did not then think my act of substituting for my friends an immoral one; it was merely a matter of friendship.

"I was a student in the normal school for five years, and managed to resist the appeals of all future advertising. Finally I actually got my degree. Incidents in my life here, in the Hunan Provincial First Normal [Teachers' Training] School, were many, and during this period my political ideas began to take shape. Here also I acquired my first experiences in social action.

"There were many regulations in the new school and I agreed with very few of them. For one thing, I was opposed to the required courses in natural science. I wanted to specialize in social sciences. Natural sciences did not especially interest me, and I did not study them, so I got poor marks in most of these courses. Most of all I hated a compulsory course in still-life drawing. I thought it extremely stupid. I used to think of the simplest subjects possible to draw, finish up quickly and leave the class. I remember once, drawing a picture of the 'half-sun, half-rock,'[10] which I represented by a straight line with a semicircle over it. Another time during an examination in drawing I contented myself with making an oval. I called it an egg. I got 40 in drawing, and failed. Fortunately my marks in social sciences were all excellent, and they balanced my poor grades in these other classes.

"A Chinese teacher here, whom the students nicknamed 'Yuan the Big Beard,' ridiculed my writing and called it the work of a journalist. He despised Liang Ch'i-ch'ao, who had been my model, and considered him half-literate. I was obliged to alter my style. I studied the writings of Han Yu, and mastered the old Classical phraseology. Thanks to Yuan the Big Beard, therefore, I can today still turn out a passable Classical essay if required.

"The teacher who made the strongest impression on me was Yang Ch'ang-chi, a returned student from England, with whose life I was later to become intimately related. He taught ethics, he was an idealist and a man of high moral character. He believed in his ethics very strongly and tried to imbue his students with the desire to become just, moral, virtuous men, useful in society. Under his influence I read a book on ethics translated by Ts'ai Yuan-p'ei and was inspired to write an essay which I entitled 'The Energy of the Mind.' I was then an idealist and my essay was highly praised by Professor Yang Ch'ang-chi, from his idealist viewpoint. He gave me a mark of 100 for it.

"A teacher named T'ang used to give me old copies of *Min Pao* [*People's Journal*], and I read them with keen interest. I learned from them about the activities and program of the T'ung Meng Hui. One day I read a copy of the *Min Pao* containing a story about two Chinese students who were traveling across China and had reached Tatsienlu, on the edge of Tibet. This inspired me very much. I wanted to follow their example; but I had no money, and thought I should first try out travelling in Hunan.

"The next summer I set out across the province by foot, and journeyed through five counties. I was accompanied by a student named Hsiao Yu. We walked through these five counties without using a single copper. The peasants fed us and gave us a place to sleep; wherever we went we were kindly treated and welcomed. This fellow, Hsiao Yu, with whom I traveled, later became a Kuomintang official in Nanking, under Yi Pei-ch'i, who was then president of Hunan Normal School. Yi Pei-ch'i became a high official at Nanking and had Hsiao Yu appointed to the office of

custodian of the Peking Palace Museum. Hsiao sold some of the most valuable treasures in the museum and absconded with the funds in 1934.

"Feeling expansive and the need for a few intimate companions, I one day inserted an advertisement in a Changsha paper inviting young men interested in patriotic work to make a contact with me. I specified youths who were hardened and determined, and ready to make sacrifices for their country. To this advertisement I received three and one half replies. One was from Lu Chiang-lung, who later was to join the Communist Party and afterwards to betray it. Two others were from young men who later were to become ultrareactionaries. The 'half' reply came from a noncommittal youth named Li Li-san. Li listened to all I had to say, and then went away without making any definite proposals himself, and our friendship never developed.[11]

"But gradually I did build up a group of students around myself, and the nucleus was formed of what later was to become a society[12] that was to have a widespread influence on the affairs and destiny of China. It was a serious-minded little group of men and they had no time to discuss trivialities. Everything they did or said must have a purpose. They had no time for love or 'romance' and considered the times too critical and the need for knowledge too urgent to discuss women or personal matters. I was not interested in women. My parents had married me when I was fourteen to a girl of twenty, but I had never lived with her—and never subsequently did. I did not consider her my wife and at this time gave little thought to her. Quite aside from the discussions of feminine charm, which usually play an important role in the lives of young men of this age, my companions even rejected talk of ordinary matters of daily life. I remember once being in the house of a youth who began to talk to me about buying some meat, and in my presence called in his servant and discussed the matter with him, then ordered him to buy a piece. I was annoyed and did not see that fellow again. My friends and I preferred to talk only of large matters—the nature of men, of human society, of China, the world, and the universe!

"We also became ardent physical culturists. In the winter holidays we tramped through the fields, up and down mountains, along city walls, and across the streams and rivers. If it rained we took off our shirts and called it a rain bath. When the sun was hot we also doffed shirts and called it a sun bath. In the spring winds we shouted that this was a new sport called 'wind bathing.' We slept in the open when frost was already falling and even in November swam in the cold rivers. All this went on under the title of 'body training.' Perhaps it helped much to build the physique which I was to need so badly later on in my many marches back and forth across South China, and on the Long March from Kiangsi to the Northwest.

"I built up a wide correspondence with many students and friends in other towns and cities. Gradually I began to realize the necessity for a more closely knit organization. In 1917, with some other friends, I helped to found the Hsin-min Hsueh-hui. It had from seventy to eighty members, and of these many were later to become famous names in Chinese communism and in the history of the Chinese Revolution. Among the better-known Communists who were in the Hsin-min Hsueh-hui were Lo Man (Li Wei-han), now secretary of the Party Organization Committee; Hsia Hsi,[13] now in the Second Front Red Army; Ho Shu-heng, who became high judge of the Supreme Court in the Central Soviet regions and was later killed by Chiang Kai-shek (1935); Kuo Liang, a famous labor organizer, killed by General Ho Chien in 1930; Hsiao Chu-chang,[14] a writer now in Soviet Russia; Ts'ai Ho-sen, a member of the Central Committee of the Communist Party, killed by Chang Kai-shek in 1927; Yeh Li-yun, who became a member of the Central Committee, and later 'betrayed' to the

Kuomintang and became a capitalist trade-union organizer; and Hsiao Chen, a prominent Party leader, one of the six signers of the original agreement for the formation of the Party, who died not long ago from illness. The majority of the members of the Hsin-min Hsueh-hui were killed in the counter-revolution of 1927.[15]

"Another society that was formed about that time, and resembled the Hsin-min Hsueh-hui, was the 'Social Welfare Society' of Hupeh. Many of its members also later became Communists. Among them was Yun Tai-ying, who was killed during the counter-revolution by Chiang Kai-shek. Lin Piao, now president of the Red Army University, was a member. So was Chang Hao, now in charge of work among White troops [those taken prisoner by the Reds]. In Peking there was a society called Hu Sheh, some of whose members later became Reds. Elsewhere in China, notably in Shanghai, Hangchow, Hankow, and Tientsin,[16] radical societies were organized by the militant youth then beginning to assert an influence on Chinese politics.

"Most of these societies were organized more or less under the influences of *Hsin Ch'ing-nien* [*New Youth*], the famous magazine of the literary renaissance, edited by Ch'en Tu-hsiu. I began to read this magazine while I was a student in the normal school and admired the articles of Hu Shih and Ch'en Tu-hsiu very much. They became for a while my models, replacing Liang Ch'i-ch'ao and Kang Yu-wei, whom I had already discarded.

"At this time my mind was a curious mixture of ideas of liberalism, democratic reformism, and utopian socialism. I had somewhat vague passions about 'nineteenth-century democracy,' utopianism, and old-fashioned liberalism, and I was definitely antimilitarist and anti-imperialist.

"I had entered the normal school in 1912. I was graduated in 1918."

Prelude to revolution

EDGAR SNOW

Notes to this section will be found on page 335.

DURING Mao's recollections of his past I noticed that an auditor at least as interested as I was Ho Tzu-ch'en, his wife. Many of the facts he told about himself and the Communist movement she had evidently never heard before, and this was true of most of Mao's comrades in Pao An. Later on, when I gathered biographical notes from other Red leaders, their colleagues often crowded around interestedly to listen to the stories for the first time. Although they had all fought together for years, very often they knew nothing of each other's pre-Communist days, which they had tended to regard as a kind of Dark Ages period, one's real life beginning only when one became a Communist.

It was another night, and Mao sat cross-legged, leaning against his dispatch boxes. He lit a cigarette from a candle and took up the thread of the story where he had left off the evening before:

"During my years in normal school in Changsha I had spent, altogether, only $160 —including my numerous registration fees! Of this amount I must have used a third for newspapers, because regular subscriptions cost me about a dollar a month, and I often bought books and journals on the newsstands. My father cursed me for this extravagance. He called it wasted money on wasted paper. But I had acquired the newspaper-reading habit, and from 1911 to 1927, when I climbed up Ching-kangshan, I never stopped reading the daily papers of Peking, Shanghai, and Hunan.

"In my last year in school my mother died, and more than ever I lost interest in returning home. I decided, that summer, to go to Peking. Many students from Hunan were planning trips to France, to study under the 'work and learn' scheme, which France used to recruit young Chinese in her cause during the World War. Before leaving China these students planned to study French in Peking. I helped organize the movement, and in the groups who went abroad were many students from the Hunan Normal School, most of whom were later to become famous radicals. Hsu T'eh-li was influenced by the movement also, and when he was over forty he left his professorship at Hunan Normal School and went to France. He did not become a Communist, however, till 1927.

"I accompanied some of the Hunanese students to Peking. However, although I had helped organize the movement, and it had the support of the Hsin-min Hsueh-hui, I did not want to go to Europe. I felt that I did not know enough about my own country, and that my time could be more profitably spent in China. Those students who had decided to go to France studied French then from Li Shih-tseng, who is now president of the Chung-fa [Sino-French] University, but I did not. I had other plans.

"Peking seemed very expensive to me. I had reached the capital by borrowing money from friends, and when I arrived I had to look for work at once. Yang Ch'ang-chi, my former ethics teacher at the normal school, had become a professor at Peking National University. I appealed to him for help in finding a job, and he introduced me to the university librarian. He was Li Ta-chao, who later became a founder of the Communist Party of China, and was afterwards executed by Chang Tso-lin.[1] Li Ta-chao gave me work as assistant librarian, for which I was paid the generous sum of $8 a month.

"My office was so low that people avoided me. One of my tasks was to register the names of people who came to read newspapers, but to most of them I didn't exist as a human being. Among those who came to read I recognized the names of famous leaders of the renaissance movement, men like Fu Ssu-nien, Lo Chia-lun, and others, in whom I was intensely interested. I tried to begin conversations with them on political and cultural subjects, but they were very busy men. They had no time to listen to an assistant librarian speaking southern dialect.

"But I wasn't discouraged. I joined the Society of Philosophy, and the Journalism Society, in order to be able to attend classes in the university. In the Journalism Society I met fellow students like Ch'en Kung-po, who is now a high official at Nanking; T'an P'ing-shan, who later became a Communist and still later a member of the so-called 'Third Party'; and Shao P'iao-p'ing. Shao, especially, helped me very much. He was a lecturer in the Journalism Society, a liberal, and a man of fervent idealism and fine character. He was killed by Chang Tso-lin in 1926.

"While I was working in the library I also met Chang Kuo-t'ao,[2] now vice-chairman of the Soviet Government; K'ang P'ei-ch'en, who later joined the Ku Klux Klan in California [!!!—E.S.]; and Tuan Hsi-p'eng, now Vice-Minister of Education in Nanking. And here also I met and fell in love with Yang K'ai-hui. She was the daughter of my former ethics teacher, Yang Ch'ang-chi, who had made a great impression on me in my youth, and who afterwards was a genuine friend in Peking.

"My interest in politics continued to increase, and my mind turned more and more radical. I have told you of the background for this. But just now I was still confused, looking for a road, as we say. I read some pamphlets on anarchy, and was much influenced by them. With a student named Chu Hsun-pei, who used to visit me, I often discussed anarchism and its possibilities in China. At that time I favored many of its proposals.

"My own living conditions in Peking were quite miserable, and in contrast the beauty of the old capital was a vivid and living compensation. I stayed in a place called San Yen-ching ["Three-Eyes Well"], in a little room which held seven other people. When we were all packed fast on the *k'ang* there was scarcely room enough for any of us to breathe. I used to have to warn people on each side of me when I wanted to turn over. But in the parks and the old palace grounds I saw the early northern spring, I saw the white plum blossoms flower while the ice still held solid over Pei Hai ["the North Sea"].[3] I saw the willows over Pei Hai with the ice crystals hanging from them and remembered the description of the scene by the T'ang poet Chen Chang, who wrote about Pei Hai's winter-jeweled trees looking 'like ten thousand peach trees blossoming.' The innumerable trees of Peking aroused my wonder and admiration.

"Early in 1919 I went to Shanghai with the students bound for France. I had a ticket only to Tientsin, and I did not know how I was to get any farther. But, as the Chinese proverb says, 'Heaven will not delay a traveler,' and a fortunate loan of ten yuan from a fellow student, who had got some money from the Auguste Comte School in Peking, enabled me to buy a ticket as far as P'u-k'ou. On the way to Nanking I stopped at Ch'u Fu and visited Confucius' grave. I saw the small stream where Confucius' disciples bathed their feet and the little town where the sage lived as a child. He is supposed to have planted a famous tree near the historic temple dedicated to him, and I saw that. I also stopped by the river where Yen Hui, one of Confucius' famous disciples, had once lived, and I saw the birthplace of Mencius. On this trip I climbed T'ai Shan, the sacred mountain of Shantung, where General Feng Yu-hsiang retired and wrote his patriotic scrolls.

"But when I reached P'u-k'ou I was again without a copper, and without a ticket. Nobody had any money to lend me; I did not know how I was to get out of town. But the worst of the tragedy happened when a thief stole my only pair of shoes! *Ai-ya*! What was I to do? But again, 'Heaven will not delay a traveler,' and I had a very good piece of luck. Outside the railway station I met an old friend from Hunan, and he proved to be my 'good angel.' He lent me money for a pair of shoes, and enough to buy a ticket to Shanghai. Thus I safely completed my journey—keeping an eye on my new shoes. At Shanghai I found that a good sum had been raised to help send the students to France, and an allowance had been provided to help me return to Hunan. I saw my friends off on the steamer and then set out for Changsha.

"During my first trip to the North, as I remember it, I made these excursions:

"I walked around the lake of T'ung T'ing, and I circled the wall of Paotingfu. I walked on the ice of the Gulf of Pei Hai. I walked around the wall of Hsuchou, famous in the *San Kuo* [*Three Kingdoms*], and around Nanking's wall, also famous in history. Finally I climbed T'ai Shan and visited Confucius' grave. These seemed to me then achievements worth adding to my adventures and walking tours in Hunan.

"When I returned to Changsha I took a more direct role in politics. After the May Fourth Movement[4] I had devoted most of my time to student political activities, and I was editor of the *Hsiang River Review*, the Hunan students' paper, which had a great influence on the student movement in South China. In Changsha I helped found the Wen-hua Shu-hui [Cultural Book Society], an association for study of modern cultural and political tendencies. This society, and more especially the Hsin-min Hsueh-hui, were violently opposed to Chang Ching-yao, then *tuchun* of Hunan, and a vicious character. We led a general student strike against Chang, demanding his removal, and sent delegations to Peking and the Southwest, where Sun Yat-sen was then active, to agitate against him. In retaliation for the students' opposition, Chang Ching-yao suppressed the *Hsiang River Review*.

"After this I went to Peking, to represent the New People's Study Society and organize an antimilitarist movement there. The society broadened its fight against Chang Ching-yao into a general antimilitarist agitation, and I became head of a news agency to promote this work. In Hunan the movement was rewarded with some success. Chang Ching-yao was overthrown by T'an Yen-k'ai, and a new regime was established in Changsha. About this time the society began to divide into two groups, a right and left wing— the left wing insisting on a program of far-reaching social and economic and political changes.

"I went to Shanghai for the second time in 1919. There once more I saw Ch'en Tu-hsiu.[5] I had first met him in Peking, when I was at Peking National University, and he had influenced me perhaps more than anyone else. I also met Hu Shih at that time, having called on him to try to win his support for the Hunanese students' struggle. In Shanghai I discussed with Ch'en Tu-hsiu our plans for a League for Reconstruction of Hunan. Then I returned to Changsha and began to organize it. I took a place as a teacher there, meanwhile continuing my activity in the New People's Study Society. The society had a program then for the 'independence' of Hunan, meaning, really, autonomy. Disgusted with the Northern Government, and believing that Hunan could modernize more rapidly if freed from connections with Peking, our group agitated for separation. I was then a strong supporter of America's Monroe Doctrine and the Open Door.

"T'an Yen-k'ai was driven out of Hunan by a militarist called Chao Heng-t'i, who utilized the 'Hunan independence' movement for his own ends. He pretended to support it, advocating the idea of a United Autonomous States of China, but as soon as he got power he suppressed the democratic movement with great energy. Our group had demanded equal rights for men and women, and representative government, and in general approval of a platform for a bourgeois democracy. We openly advocated these reforms in our paper, the *New Hunan*. We led an attack on the provincial parliament, the majority of whose members were landlords and gentry appointed by the militarists. This struggle ended in our pulling down the scrolls and banners, which were full of nonsensical and extravagant phrases.

"The attack on the parliament was considered a big incident in Hunan, and frightened the rulers. However, when Chao Heng-t'i seized control he betrayed all the ideas he had supported, and especially he violently suppressed all demands for democracy. Our society therefore turned the struggle against him. I remember an episode in 1920, when the Hsin-min Hsueh-hui organized a demonstration to celebrate the third anniversary of the Russian October Revolution. It was suppressed by the police. Some of the demonstrators had attempted to raise the Red flag at that meeting, but were prohibited from doing so by the police. The demonstrators pointed out that, according to Article 12 of the Constitution, the people had the right to assemble, organize, and speak, but the police were not impressed. They replied that they were not there to be taught the Constitution, but to carry out the orders of the governor, Chao Heng-t'i. From this time on I became more and more convinced that only mass political power, secured through mass action, could guarantee the realization of dynamic reforms.[6]

"In the winter of 1920 I organized workers politically for the first time, and began to be guided in this by the influence of Marxist theory and the history of the Russian Revolution. During my second visit to Peking I had read much about the events in Russia, and had eagerly sought out what little Communist literature was then available in Chinese. Three books especially deeply carved my mind, and built up in me a faith in Marxism, from which, once I had accepted it as the correct interpretation of history, I did not afterwards waver. These books were the *Communist Manifesto*, translated by Ch'en Wang-tao and the first Marxist book ever published in Chinese; *Class Struggle*, by Kautsky; and a *History of Socialism*, by Kirkup. By the summer of 1920 I had become, in theory and to some extent in action, a Marxist, and from this time on I considered myself a Marxist. In the same year I married Yang K'ai-hui."[7]

3

Some general theory

From the brows of ancient
(and modern) Zeuses

Modern social science, unlike old China, is not noted for ancestor worship. Aristotle's work has become neglected scripture and he an ikon. This is understandable; things change in two thousand years. There was only the most rudimentary capitalism and division of labor in ancient Greece. Cities like Athens, Thebes, and Alexandria were the characteristic political units; now they are nation–states, including Greece that has swallowed many of the old city states and has been in rebellious turmoil for at least two decades since the Second World War.

Of the worship of ancestors, this editor wants no part. But the simple ability, in the study of economic and political institutions, to forget continuities in the social behavior of people is awesome. Not only events, but even cause and effect explanations are now viewed as being without precedent. Yet Aristotle too—some 350 years before Christ—noted cause and effect relationships. He observed links between what people want and their tendency to revolt when they failed to get it. His observations at some points read like some statements made by Jefferson, Madison, and Marx. As Aristotle describes the origins of these tendencies in the basic characteristics of men, they read like some of the teachings of Christ and the writings of Freud. In the face of these antecedents of modern phenomena now being researched, modern social science writings appear to have sprung as miraculously from the writer's brow as did Athena, very wise and fully armed, from the brow of her father Zeus.

This is to say neither that Aristotle said everything that has later been identified with Christianity, Marxism, or Freudianism nor to say that Christ, Marx, and Freud are only latter-day Aristotelians. Rather it is to say that these ancients and moderns all were making assertions about the same fundamental phenomenon— man, *Homo sapiens*—and that it would indeed be awesome if their assertions were radically divergent. The utility in looking at Aristotle is to help sort out what is universal about man, this fundamental phenomenon, noting that in some basic ways man has not changed much, from Aristotle's study of him to our own.

Aristotle said revolutions occur from a failure of a society to realize equality. The majority segment of a society, when it revolts, does so because it sees the leading, ruling minority getting too many goods and too much honor; the minority (whether

85

distinguished by ancestry, wealth, or ability), when it revolts, does so from fear that it will lose the share of goods and honor it has come to expect as its right. All this sounds a bit like James Madison, who said in urging adoption of the United States Constitution that "the most common and durable source of faction is the various and unequal distribution of property." And it sounds like Marx, who spoke of class warfare arising from the economic exploitation of the working class by the middle class. Aristotle also described racial difference as a cause of revolution, thereby digging to some of the roots of the Sepoy Rebellion in India in 1857, of the Boxer Rebellion in China in 1900, and of the African, Arabian, and Indonesian struggles for political autonomy on a racial basis after the Second World War—and of the Black Rebellion in the United States in the 1960s.

It is when Aristotle discusses equality itself, which he sees as the foundation of justice (however inadequate his notions of distributive justice sound to modern ears) that the most striking parallels are evident. Aristotle said that the truest friends are equals (and that fathers and sons, husbands and wives, masters and slaves are not equals), adding that true friendship seeks the benefit not of the self but of the friend, whose happiness makes the self happy. Christ exorted men to do unto others as you would have them do unto you. Marx envisioned a state of spontaneous comradeship among men when the struggle for a share of goods came to an end. And Freud in his later years expanded his definition of Eros so that it included the connotations of both erotic and "Christian" love as described in the thirteenth chapter of the first letter that the Apostle Paul wrote to the people of Corinth, one of the Greek city states that Aristotle had studied.

Aristotle saw connections between equality and revolution. So did Jefferson in saying it is a self-evident truth that all men are created equal and that a government that does not treat its citizens or its subjects equally can justly be rebelled against. Twentieth-century revolutionists, whether aware or unaware of Jefferson or Marx, have also seen the connection. It is therefore reasonable to suppose that the connection is natural, innate, and that men will revolt when they believe they are being treated unequally by their government. Rebels usually discover after the event that they are justified by some such words as those in Lincoln's Gettysburg Address, which—after the American Civil War had been in progress for two years—justified that war in words written fourscore and seven years earlier.

Politics

ARISTOTLE

States of feeling

Now the principal cause, speaking generally, of the citizens being themselves disposed in a certain manner towards revolution is the one about which we happen to have spoken already. Those that desire equality enter on party strife if they think that they have too little although they are the equals of those who have more, while those that desire inequality or superiority do so if they suppose that although they are unequal they have not got more but an equal amount or less (and these desires may be felt justly, and they may also be felt unjustly); for when inferior, people enter on strife in order that they may be equal, and when equal, in order that they may be greater. We have therefore said what are the states of feeling in which men engage in party strife.

Objects

The objects about which it is waged are gain and honor, and their opposites, for men carry on party faction in states in order to avoid dishonor and loss, either on their own behalf or on behalf of their friends.

Causes and circumstances

And the causes and origins of the disturbances which occasion the actual states of feeling described and their direction to the objects mentioned, according to one account happen to be seven in number, though according to another they are more. Two of them are the same as those spoken of before although not operating in the same way: the motives of gain and honor also stir men up against each other not in order that they may get them for themselves, as has been said before, but because they see other men in some cases justly and in other cases unjustly getting a larger share of them. Other causes are insolence, fear, excessive predominance, contempt, disproportionate growth of power; and also other modes of cause are election intrigue, carelessness, pettiness, dissimilarity.

Among these motives the power possessed by insolence and gain, and their mode of operation, is almost obvious; for when the men in office show insolence and greed, people rise in revolt against one another and against the constitutions that afford the opportunity for such conduct; and greed sometimes preys on private property and sometimes on common funds. It is clear also what is the power of honor and how it can cause party faction; for men form factions both when they are themselves dishonored and when they see others honored; and the distribution of honors is unjust

when persons are either honored or dishonored against their deserts, just when it is according to desert. . . .

Fear is the motive of faction with those who have inflicted wrong and are afraid of being punished, and also with those who are in danger of suffering a wrong and wish to act in time before the wrong is inflicted, as the notables at Rhodes banded together against the people because of the law-suits that were being brought against them.

Contempt is a cause of faction and of actual attacks upon the government, for instance in oligarchies when those who have no share in the government are more numerous (for they think themselves the stronger party), and in democracies when the rich have begun to feel contempt for the disorder and anarchy that prevails, as for example at Thebes the democracy was destroyed owing to bad government after the battle of Oenophyta, and that of the Megarians was destroyed when they had been defeated owing to disorder and anarchy, and at Syracuse before the tyranny of Gelo, and at Rhodes the common people had fallen into contempt before the rising against them.

Revolutions in the constitutions also take place on account of disproportionate growth; for just as the body is composed of parts, and needs to grow proportionately in order that its symmetry may remain, and if it does not it is spoiled, when the foot is four cubits long and the rest of the body two spans, and sometimes it might even change into the shape of another animal if it increased disproportionately not only in size but also in quality, so also a state is composed of parts, one of which often grows without its being noticed, as for example the number of the poor in democracies and constitutional states. And sometimes this is also brought about by accidental occurrences, as for instance at Tarentum when a great many notables were defeated and killed by the Iapygians a short time after the Persian wars a constitutional government was changed to a democracy, and at Argos when those in the seventh tribe had been destroyed by the Spartan Cleomenes the citizens were compelled to admit some of the surrounding people, and at Athens when they suffered disasters by land the notables became fewer because at the time of the war against Sparta the army was drawn from a muster-roll. And this happens also in democracies, though to a smaller extent; for when the wealthy become more numerous or their properties increase, the governments change to oligarchies and dynasties.

And revolutions in constitutions take place even without factious strife, owing to election intrigue, as at Heraea (for they made their magistrates elected by lot instead of by vote for this reason, because the people used to elect those who canvassed); and also owing to carelessness, when people allow men that are not friends of the constitution to enter into the sovereign offices, as at Oreus oligarchy was broken up when Heracleodorus became one of the magistrates, who in place of an oligarchy formed a constitutional government, or rather a democracy. Another cause is alteration by small stages; by this I mean that often a great change of institutions takes place unnoticed when people overlook a small alteration, as in Ambracia the property-qualification was small, and finally men hold office with none at all, as a little is near to nothing, or practically the same.

Also difference of race is a cause of faction, until harmony of spirit is reached; for just as any chance multitude of people does not form a state, so a state is not formed in any chance period of time. Hence most of the states that have hitherto admitted joint settlers or additional settlers have split into factions; for example Achaeans settled at Sybaris jointly with Troezenians, and afterwards the Achaeans having become more numerous expelled the Troezenians, which was the cause of the curse that fell on the Sybarites.

Nicomachean Ethics

ARISTOTLE

LIKING seems to be an emotion, friendship a fixed disposition, for liking can be felt even for inanimate things, but reciprocal liking involves deliberate choice, and this springs from a fixed disposition. Also, when men wish the good of those they love for their own sakes, their goodwill does not depend on emotion but on a fixed disposition. And in loving their friend they love their own good, for the good man in becoming dear to another becomes that other's good. Each party therefore both loves his own good and also makes an equivalent return by wishing the other's good, and by affording him pleasure; for there is a saying, "Amity is equality," and this is most fully realized in the friendships of the good. . . .

Friendship and intercourse

Morose and elderly people rarely make friends as they are inclined to be surly, and do not take much pleasure in society; good temper and sociability appear to be the chief constituents or causes of friendship. Hence the young make friends quickly, but the old do not, since they do not make friends with people if they do not enjoy their company; and the same applies to persons of a morose temper. It is true that the old or morose may feel goodwill for each other, since they may wish each other well and help each other in case of need; but they cannot properly be called friends, as they do not seek each other's society nor enjoy it, and these are thought to be the chief marks of friendship.

The perfect kind of friendship rare

It is not possible to have many friends in the full meaning of the word friendship, any more than it is to be in love with many people at once (love indeed seems to be an excessive state of emotion, such as is naturally felt towards one person only);

and it is not easy for the same person to like a number of people at once, nor indeed perhaps can good men be found in large numbers. Also for perfect friendship you must get to know a man thoroughly, and become intimate with him, which is a very difficult thing to do. But it is possible to like a number of persons for their utility and pleasantness, for useful and pleasant people are plentiful, and the benefits they confer can be enjoyed at once.

Friendships of pleasure nearer perfect friendship than friendships of utility

Of these two inferior kinds of friendship, the one that more closely resembles true friendship is that based on pleasure, in which the same benefit is conferred by both parties, and they enjoy each other's company, or have common tastes; as is the case with the friendships of young people. For in these there is more generosity of feeling, whereas the friendship of utility is a thing for sordid souls. Also those blessed with great prosperity have no need of useful friends, but do need pleasant ones, since they desire some society; and though they may put up with what is unpleasant for a short time, no one would stand it continually: you could not endure even the Absolute Good itself for ever, if it bored you; and therefore the rich seek for friends who will be pleasant. . . . The good man, as we have said, is both useful and pleasant, but the good man does not become the friend of a superior, unless his superior in rank be also his superior in virtue; otherwise the good man as the inferior party cannot make matters proportionally equal. But potentates of such superior excellence are scarcely common.

But to resume: the forms of friendship of which we have spoken are friendships of equality, for both parties render the same benefit and wish the same good to each other, or else exchange two different benefits, for instance pleasure and profit. (These are less truly friendships, and less permanent, as we have said; and opinions differ as to whether they are really friendships at all, owing to their being both like and unlike the same thing. In view of their likeness to friendship based on virtue they do appear to be friendships, for the one contains pleasure and the other utility, and these are attributes of that form of friendship too; but in that friendship based on virtue is proof against calumny, and permanent, while the others quickly change, besides differing in many other respects, they appear not to be real friendships, owing to their unlikeness to it.)

Friendships of unequals

But there is a different kind of friendship, which involves superiority of one party over the other, for example, the friendship between father and son, and generally between an older person and a younger, and that between husband and wife, and between any ruler and the persons ruled. These friendships also vary among themselves. The friendship between parents and children is not the same as that between ruler and ruled, nor indeed is the friendship of father for son the same as that of son for father, nor that of husband for wife as that of wife for husband; for each of these persons has a different excellence and function, and also different motives for their regard, and so the affection and friendship they feel are different. Now in these unequal friendships the benefits that one party receives and is entitled to claim from the other are not the same on either side; but the friendship between parents and children will be enduring and equitable, when the children render to the parents the services due to the authors of one's being, and the parents to the children those due to one's offspring. The affection rendered in these various unequal friendships should also be proportionate: the better of the two parties, for instance, or the more useful or otherwise superior as the case may be, should receive more affection than he bestows; since when the affection rendered is proportionate to desert, this produces equality in a sense between the parties, and equality is felt to be an essential element of friendship.

Equality in friendship, however, does not seem to be like equality in matters of justice. In the sphere of justice, "equal" (fair) means primarily proportionate to desert, and "equal in quantity" is only a secondary sense; whereas in friendship "equal in quanity" is the primary meaning, and "proportionate to desert" only secondary. This is clearly seen when a wide disparity arises between two friends in point of virtue or vice, or of wealth, or anything else; they no longer remain nor indeed expect to remain friends. This is ... seen with princes: in their case also men much below them in station do not expect to be their friends, nor do persons of no particular merit expect to be the friends of men of distinguished excellence or wisdom. It is true that we cannot fix a precise limit in such cases, up to which two men can still be friends; the gap may go on widening and the friendship still remain; but when one becomes very remote from the other, as God is remote from man, it can continue no longer. ...

Inequality redressed by affection

Most men however, because they love honor, seem to be more desirous of receiving than of bestowing affection. Hence most men like flattery, for a flatterer is a friend who is your inferior, or pretends to be so, and to love you more than you love him; but to be loved is felt to be nearly the same as to be honored, which most people covet. They do not however appear to value honor for its own sake, but for something incidental to it. Most people like receiving honor from men of high station, because they hope for something from them: they think that if they want something, the great man will be able to give it them; so they enjoy being honored by him as a token of benefits to come. Those on the other hand who covet being honored by good men, and by persons who know them, do so from a desire to confirm their own opinion of themselves; so these like honor because they are assured of their worth by their confidence in the judgement of those who assert it. Affection on the other hand men like for its own sake; from which we infer that it is more valuable than honor, and that friendship is desirable in itself.

But in its essence friendship seems to consist more in giving than in receiving affection: witness the pleasure that mothers take in loving their children. Some mothers put their infants out to nurse, and though knowing and loving them, do not ask to be loved by them in return, if it be impossible to have this as well, but are content if they see them prospering; they retain their own love for them even though the children, not knowing them, cannot render them any part of what is due to a mother. As then friendship consists more especially in bestowing affection, and as we praise men for loving their friends, affection seems to be the mark of a good friend. Hence it is friends that love each other as each deserves who continue friends and whose friendship is lasting.

*Equality and rising
expectations*

By now in this collection of readings, the conclusions of Tocqueville should not appear to be new hat. Like Aristotle, he mentions what we now call the failure of empathy between rulers and ruled. In France this failure occurred during the very time that the ruling class heaped ashes on its own collective head over injustices perpetrated on the subject classes. He also discusses long-range developments which brought France, on the eve of revolution, to an economically and socially more advanced stage than it had ever known. The concluding excerpt discusses the tenacious demand for equality and liberty, and it briefly alludes to the search of Frenchmen for "the man of genius destined at once to carry on and to abolish the Revolution."

What is so remarkable about Tocqueville is precisely that he does synthesize a variety of phenomena. His synthesis has a dynamic, evolutionary quality. People's values change slowly over time. Social institutions change and get out of whack with people's increasingly equalitarian values. Political institutions get out of whack with both the changed values and the changed social institutions.

Tocqueville is notable on grounds of both his synthesis and his systematic introduction of the idea of change, of processes taking place over long periods of time. Marx ranged farther back into the history of incongruities between modes of production and social and political institutions, but Tocqueville seemed to be more aware that even degraded working men do not regard themselves simply as instruments of production, that they are sensitive, perceptive human beings.

How the spirit of revolt was promoted by well intentioned efforts to improve the people's lot

ALEXIS DE TOCQUEVILLE

Copyright by and reprinted with the permission of William Collins Sons & Co. Ltd., London, and Doubleday & Co., Inc., New York. From *The Old Regime and the French Revolution*, by Alexis de Tocqueville, translated by Stuart Gilbert. Doubleday Anchor edition, 1955, pp. 180–182, 174–177, 207–209.

For a hundred and forty years the French people had played no part on the political stage and this had led to a general belief that they could never figure there. So inert did the working class appear that it was assumed to be not only dumb but hard of hearing, with the result that when at long last the authorities began to take an interest in the masses, they talked about them in their presence, as if they were not there. Indeed, there seems to have been an impression that only the upper classes could use their ears and the sole danger was that of failing to make oneself understood by them.

Thus the very men who had most to fear from the anger of the masses had no qualms about publicly condemning the gross injustice with which they had always been treated. They drew attention to the monstrous vices of the institutions which pressed most heavily on the common people and indulged in highly colored descriptions of the living conditions of the working class and the starvation wages it received. And by thus championing the cause of the underprivileged they made them acutely conscious of their wrongs. The people of whom I now am speaking, be it noted, were not our literary men but members of the government, high officials, the privileged few.

When thirteen years before the Revolution the King attempted to abolish forced labor, his preamble to the measure ran as follows: "Outside a few provinces (the *pays d'états*) almost all the roads in the kingdom have been made by the unpaid labor of the poorest of our subjects. Thus the whole burden has fallen on those who till the soil and make relatively little use of the highways; it is the landed proprietors, nearly all of them privileged persons, who stand to gain, since the value of their estates is enhanced by the making of these roads. When the poor man is constrained to bear the brunt, unaided, of keeping the roads in order and forced to give his time and toil without remuneration, the one and only means he has of avoiding poverty and hunger is being taken from him and he is being forced to work for the benefit of the rich."

When an attempt was made at the same time to do away with the injustices and restrictions of the guild system, the King issued a declaration to the effect that "the right to work is a man's most sacred possession and any law that tampers with it violates a natural right and should be treated as null and void. The existing trade and craft corporations are unnatural and oppressive organizations stemming from self-regarding motives, greed, and a desire to domineer." It was indiscreet enough to utter such words, but positively dangerous to utter them in vain. For some months later the guild system and forced labor were reinstated.

It was Turgot, we are told, who put these words into the mouth of the King. And most of Turgot's successors followed his example. When in 1780 the King announced that notice would be given by publication in the register offices of any increases in the *taille* he made a point of referring to the hardships of those subject to this tax. "Already aggrieved by the inconsiderate manner in which the *taille* is collected, the taxpayer until now has often had to face quite unexpected increases in the sum demanded; indeed, the taxes imposed on the poorest of our subjects have risen out of all proportion to other forms of taxation." Though the King did not venture as yet to level out the incidence of taxation in general, he attempted, anyhow, to apply the same methods of collection to all taxpayers, great and small. "His Majesty trusts that the rich will not feel aggrieved if they are treated on an equal footing with the rest of his subjects. After all, they will only be shouldering a burden that for a long time past they should have shared more equally with others."

But it was especially in times of scarcity that it almost seemed as though the authorities were aiming less at providing relief for the poor than fuel for their passions. Wishing to encourage the rich to show more generosity, an Intendant denounced the lack of human feeling and any sense of justice on the part of landowners, "who owe all that they possess to the poor man's toil, yet are quite ready to let him die of starvation at the very time when he is working his hardest to keep their estates productive." The King spoke to much the same effect on a similar occasion. "His Majesty is doing his utmost to protect the worker from malpractices that deprive him even of the bare necessities of life by forcing him to work at any wage, however small, that his rich employer thinks fit to give him. The King will not tolerate rapacity of this sort and the exploitation of one class of his subjects by another."

As long as the monarchy lasted, the hostility between the various administrative authorities gave rise to declarations of this order, in which each party blamed the other for the sufferings of the laboring class. A good example is the conflict which arose in 1772 between the parlement of Toulouse and the King. According to the spokesman of the former "our poor folk are on the brink of starvation as a result of the ill-conceived measures taken by the government." To which the King retorted that the arrogance of the parlement of Toulouse and the greed of the rich were responsible for the misfortunes of the people. On one point, it will be noticed, both parties concurred: on giving the public to understand that their superiors were to blame for the evils that befell them.

How, though the reign of Louis XVI was the most prosperous period of the monarchy, this very prosperity hastened the outbreak of the revolution

ALEXIS DE TOCQUEVILLE

A STUDY of comparative statistics makes it clear that in none of the decades immediately following the Revolution did our national prosperity make such rapid forward strides as in the two preceding it. Only the thirty-seven years of constitutional monarchy, which were for us a time of peace and plenty, are in any way comparable in this respect with the reign of Louis XVI.

At first sight it seems hard to account for this steady increase in the wealth of the country despite the as yet unremedied shortcomings of the administration and the obstacles with which industry still had to contend. Indeed, many of our politicians, being unable to explain it, have followed the example of Molière's physician, who declared that no sick man could recover "against the rules of medicine"—and simply denied its existence. That France could prosper and grow rich, given the inequality of taxation, the vagaries of local laws, internal customs barriers, feudal rights, the trade corporations, the sales of offices, and all the rest, may well seem hardly credible. Yet the fact remains that the country did grow richer and living conditions improved throughout the land, and the reason was that though the machinery of government was ramshackle, ill regulated, inefficient, and though it tended to hinder rather than to further social progress, it had two redeeming features which sufficed to make it function and made for national prosperity. Firstly, though the government was no longer despotic, it still was powerful and capable of maintaining order everywhere; and secondly, the nation possessed an upper class that was the freest, most enlightened of the day and a social system under which every man could get rich if he set his mind to it and keep intact the wealth he had acquired.

The King still used the language of a master but in actual fact he always deferred to public opinion and was guided by it in his handling of day-to-day affairs. Indeed, he made a point of consulting it, feared it, and bowed to it invariably. Absolute according to the letter of the law, the monarchy was limited in practice. In 1784 Necker frankly recognized this as an accepted fact in an official declaration. "Few foreigners have any notion of the authority with which public opinion is invested in present-day France, and they have much difficulty in understanding the nature of this invisible power behind the throne. Yet it most certainly exists."

The belief that the greatness and power of a nation are products of its administrative machinery alone is, to say the least, short-sighted; however perfect that machinery, the driving force behind it is what counts. We have only to look at England, where the constitutional system is vastly more complicated, unwieldy, and erratic than that of France today. Yet is there any other European country whose national wealth is greater; where private ownership is more extensive, takes so many forms, and is so secure; where individual prosperity and a stable social system are so well allied? This is not due to the merits of any special laws but to the spirit animating the English constitution as a whole. That certain organs may be faulty matters little when the life force of the body politic has such vigor.

It is a singular fact that this steadily increasing prosperity, far from tranquilizing the population, everywhere promoted a spirt of unrest. The general public became more and more hostile to every ancient institution, more and more discontented; indeed, it was increasingly obvious that the nation was heading for a revolution.

Moreover, those parts of France in which the improvement in the standard of living was most pronounced were the chief centers of the revolutionary movement. Such records of the Ile-de-France region as have survived prove clearly that it was in the districts in the vicinity of Paris that the old order was soonest and most drastically superseded. In these parts the freedom and wealth of the peasants had long been better assured than in any other *pays d'élection*. Well before 1789 the system of forced labor (as applied to individuals) had disappeared in this region. The *taille* had become less onerous and was more equitably assessed than elsewhere. The Order in amendment of this tax must be studied if we wish to understand how much an Intendant of the time could do by way of improving—or worsening— the lot of an entire province. As set forth in this Order the impost in question assumes a very different aspect from that with which we are familiar. Tax commissioners were to be sent by the government yearly to each parish and all the inhabitants were to be summoned to appear before them. The value of all property subject to tax was to be assessed in public, the means of each tax- payer to be determined after hearing both parties, and finally, the incidence of the *taille* was to be fixed by the authorities in concert with all the taxpayers. The arbitrary powers of the Syndic and uncalled-for measures of coercion were abolished. No doubt the vices inherent in the whole system of the *taille* could not be eradicated; whatever improvements were made in the manner of collecting it, it affected only one class of taxpayers and was levied not only on their chattels but on the industries they carried on. Nevertheless, the *taille* as levied in the Ile-de-France was very different from the tax which still bore that name in nearby revenue subdivisions of the country.

Around the Loire estuary, in the Poitou fenlands, and the *landes* of Brittany the methods of the past were kept to more tenaciously than in any other part of France. Yet it was in these regions that civil war blazed up after the outbreak of the Revolu- tion and the inhabitants put up the most passionate and stubborn resistance to it.

Thus it was precisely in those parts of France where there had been most improve- ment that popular discontent ran highest. This may seem illogical—but history is full of such paradoxes. For it is not always when things are going from bad to worse that revolutions break out. On the contrary, it oftener happens that when a people which has put up with an oppressive rule over a long period without protest suddenly finds the government relaxing its pressure, it takes up arms against it. Thus the social order overthrown by a revolution is almost always better than the one immediately preceding it, and experience teaches us that, generally speaking, the most perilous mo- ment for a bad government is one when it seeks to mend its ways. Only consummate statecraft can enable a King to save his throne when after a long spell of oppressive rule he sets to improving the lot of his subjects. Patiently endured so long as it seemed beyond redress, a grievance comes to appear intolerable once the possibility of removing it crosses men's minds. For the mere fact that certain abuses have been remedied draws attention to the others and they now appear more galling; people may suffer less, but their sensibility is exacerbated. At the height of its power feudalism did not inspire so much hatred as it did on the eve of its eclipse. In the reign of Louis XVI the most trivial pinpricks of arbitrary power caused more resentment than the thorough- going despotism of Louis XIV. The brief imprisonment of Beaumarchais shocked Paris more than the *dragonnades* of 1685.

In 1780 there could no longer be any talk of France's being on the downgrade; on the contrary, it seemed that no limit could be set to her advance. And it was now that theories of the perfectibility of man and continuous progress came into fashion. Twenty years earlier there had been no hope for the future; in 1780 no anxiety was felt about it. Dazzled by the prospect of a felicity undreamed of hitherto and now within their grasp, people were blind to the very real improvement that had taken place and eager to precipitate events.

How, given the facts set forth in the preceding chapters, the revolution was a foregone conclusion

ALEXIS DE TOCQUEVILLE

Actually it was to these very conditions that our peasantry owed some of their outstanding qualities. Long enfranchised and owning some of the land he worked, the French peasant was largely independent and had developed a healthy pride and much common sense. Inured to hardships, he was indifferent to the amenities of life, intrepid in the face of danger, and faced misfortune stoically. It was from this simple, virile race of men that those great armies were raised which were to dominate for many years the European scene. But their very virtues made them dangerous masters. During the many centuries in which these men had borne the brunt of nation-wide misgovernment and lived as a class apart, they had nursed in secret their grievances, jealousies, and rancors and, having learned toughness in a hard school, had become capable of enduring or inflicting the very worst.

It was in this mood that gripping the reins of power, the French people undertook the task of seeing the Revolution through. Books had supplied them with the necessary theories, and they now put these into practice, adjusting the writers' ideas to their lust for revenge.

Readers of this book who have followed carefully my description of 18th-century France will have noticed the steady growth amongst the people of two ruling passions, not always simultaneous or having the same objectives. One of these, the more deeply rooted and long-standing, was an intense, indomitable hatred of inequality. This inequality forced itself on their attention, they saw signs of it at every turn; thus it is easy to understand why the French had for so many centuries felt a desire, inveterate and uncontrollable, utterly to destroy all such institutions as had survived from the Middle Ages and, having cleared the ground, to build up a new society in which men were as much alike and their status as equal as was possible, allowing for the innate differences between individuals. The other ruling passion, more recent and less deeply rooted, was a desire to live not only on an equal footing but also as free men.

Toward the close of the old régime these two passions were equally sincerely felt and seemed equally operative. When the Revolution started, they came in contact, joined forces, coalesced, and reinforced each other, fanning the revolutionary ardor of the nation to a blaze. This was in '89, that rapturous year of bright enthusiasm, heroic courage, lofty ideals—untempered, we must grant, by the reality of experience: a historic date of glorious memory to which the thoughts of men will turn with admiration and respect long after those who witnessed its achievement, and we ourselves, have passed away. At the time the French had such proud confidence in the cause they were defending, and in themselves, that they believed they could reconcile freedom with equality and interspersed democratic institutions everywhere with free institutions. Not only did they shatter that ancient system under which men were divided into classes, corporations, and castes, and their rights were even more unequal than their social situations, but by the same token they did away with all the more recent legislation, instituted by the monarchy, whose effect was to put every Frenchman under official surveillance, with the government as his mentor, overseer, and, on occasion, his oppressor. Thus centralization shared the fate of absolute government.

But when the virile generation which had launched the Revolution had perished or (as usually befalls a generation engaging in such ventures) its first fine energy had dwindled; and when, as was but to be expected after a spell of anarchy and "popular" dictatorship, the ideal of freedom had lost much of its appeal and the nation, at a loss where to turn, began to cast round for a master—under these conditions the stage was set for a return to one-man government. Indeed, never had conditions been more favorable for its establishment and consolidation, and the man of genius destined at once to carry on and to abolish the Revolution was quick to turn them to account.

Actually there had existed under the old régime a host of institutions which had quite a "modern" air and, not being incompatible with equality, could easily be embodied in the new social order—and all these institutions offered remarkable facilities to despotism. They were hunted for among the wreckage of the old order and duly salvaged. These institutions had formerly given rise to customs, usages, ideas, and prejudices tending to keep men apart, and thus make them easier to rule. They were revived and skillfully exploited; centralization was built up anew, and in the process all that had once kept it within bounds was carefully eliminated. Thus there arose, within a nation that had but recently laid low its monarchy, a central authority with powers wider, stricter, and more absolute than those which any French King had ever wielded. Rash though this venture may have been, it was carried through with entire success for the good reason that people took into account only what was under their eyes and forgot what they had seen before. Napoleon fell, but the more solld parts of his achievement lasted on; his government died, but his administration survived, and every time that an attempt is made to do away with absolutism the most that could be done has been to graft the head of Liberty onto a servile body.

Nothing to lose and regain but
your dogmas and righteousness

The bourgeoisie, say Marx and Engels at the end of the selection here presented, is preparing for its own interment. They say: "Its fall and the victory of the proletariat are equally inevitable." In advanced industrial nations, some of which are mixed private and public capitalist in their economic organization and some (like the Soviet Union) are something else, the statement is equally true as to both classes. It is equally true, first, that the middle class remains strong and has been enlarged by the inclusion of many skilled manual laborers and, second, that the working class has not been victorious. The working class indeed has won greater equality vis-à-vis the middle class in countries with mixed economies. Men who work with their hands have more goods, more honor, and more political power than hitherto. And in some socialist countries trade unions have much in common with what is increasingly outmoded in capitalist countries: namely, company unions.

On this basis we could dismiss Marx and Engels as false prophets. Yet they remain more widely known throughout the world than Tocqueville. The *Communist Manifesto* was first published in 1848 and *The Old Régime and the French Revolution* in 1856. So far as I know there was no connection between the writing of the former and the latter. Tocqueville was a French product and student of the old, semifeudal régime; Marx and Engels were products and students of the German bourgeoisie. This may help explain not only the lack of resonance between the French nobleman and the two German bourgeoisie but also the enormous success of the two bourgeois writers, who perhaps helped make the fall of the bourgeoisie inevitable.

Another part of the success of Marx and Engels goes back to Boeke's village colliding with capitalism. It is clear that the writings of Marx and Engels have taken deepest root in the parts of the world that are underdeveloped, that is, the ones in which the exchange economy and industrial capitalism are most primitively and crudely exploitive of rural and urban poor people. The admixture of elements of hierarchized feudalism, atomizing industrialism, and scarcely inhibited exploitation was more clearly portrayed by Marx and Engels than by Tocqueville. The latter was an aloof, acutely observant, but uninvolved member of the prerevolutionary, prebourgeois nobility; the former two were alienated members of the middle class and passionately committed to the working class.

Another part of any explanation for the success of Marx and Engels is this: As scientists they share Aristotle's focus on equality. As moralists they are descendants of Christian prophets ranging from the Apostle Paul to Martin Luther. There is a deep rumble of anger in the writing of Marx and Engels that is nearly absent from Tocqueville. They strike their fists on the lectern, contemning the atavism only of the most recent class to enjoy the swing toward congruence between modes of production and political power. The bourgeoisie sounds uniquely unjust, uniquely determined to grasp to themselves all social goods and social honor and to treat all men who work with their hands as only hands who are expendable when they become ill, inefficient, or old.

Still another part of an explanation lies in the mode of analysis. Marx and Engels make their assertions about inevitability as the certain conclusion of a scientific analysis of historical processes. In the 20th century, for much of the world, conventional religion is associated with conservative churches: a new generation is most likely to accept a new religion of fundamental reform if it is presented in the style of Science, the religion of the century.

In the 16th century the Holy Bible gave the followers of Luther and Calvin a fresh faith by which they could live, die, and kill. In the 18th century, the followers of the French Revolution could pursue the gleaming grail of Reason. In the 20th century the writings of Marx and Engels and Mao Tse-tung have served precisely the same function. They have given revolutionaries of our time a faith by which they could justify their reactions to old régimes and their subsequent actions, as they first endured and then inflicted suffering of every imaginable kind.

Bourgeois and proletarians

KARL MARX
AND
FRIEDRICH ENGELS

THE history of all hitherto existing society is the history of class struggles.

Freeman and slave, patrician and plebeian, lord and serf, guildmaster and journeyman, in a word, oppressor and oppressed, stood in constant opposition to one another, carried on an uninterrupted, now hidden, now open fight, a fight that each time ended, either in a revolutionary reconstitution of society at large, or in the common ruin of the contending classes.

In the earlier epochs of history, we find almost everywhere a complicated arrangement of society into various orders, a manifold gradation of social rank. In ancient Rome we have patricians, knights, plebeians, slaves; in the Middle Ages, feudal lords, vassals, guild-masters, journeymen, apprentices, serfs; in almost all of these classes, again, subordinate gradations.

The modern bourgeois society that has sprouted from the ruins of feudal society, has not done away with class antagonisms. It has but established new classes, new conditions of oppression, new forms of struggle in place of the old ones.

Our epoch, the epoch of the bourgeoisie, possesses, however, this distinctive feature: It has simplified the class antagonisms. Society as a whole is more and more splitting up into two great hostile camps, into two great classes directly facing each other—bourgeoisie and proletariat.

From the serfs of the Middle Ages sprang the chartered burghers of the earliest towns. From these burgesses the first elements of the bourgeoisie were developed.

The discovery of America, the rounding of the Cape, opened up fresh ground for the rising bourgeoisie. The East Indian and Chinese markets, the colonization of America, trade with the colonies, the increase in the means of exchange and in commodities generally, gave to commerce, to navigation, to industry, an impulse never before known, and thereby, to the revolutionary element in the tottering feudal society, a rapid development.

The feudal system of industry, in which industrial production was monopolized by closed guilds, now no longer sufficed for the growing wants of the new markets. The manufacturing system took its place. The guild-masters were pushed aside by the manufacturing middle class; division of labor between the different corporate guilds vanished in the face of division of labor in each single workshop.

Meantime the markets kept ever growing, the demand ever rising. Even manufacture no longer sufficed. Thereupon, steam and machinery revolutionized industrial production. The place of manufacture was taken by the giant, modern industry, the place of the industrial middle class, by industrial millionaires—the leaders of whole industrial armies, the modern bourgeois.

Modern industry has established the world market, for which the discovery of America paved the way. This market has given an immense development to commerce, to navigation, to communication by land. This development has, in its turn, reacted on the extension of industry; and in proportion as industry, commerce, navigation, railways extended, in the same proportion the bourgeoisie developed, increased its capital, and pushed into the background every class handed down from the Middle Ages.

We see, therefore, how the modern bourgeoisie is itself the product of a long course of development, of a series of revolutions in the modes of production and of exchange.

Each step in the development of the bourgeoisie was accompanied by a corresponding political advance of that class. An oppressed class under the sway of the feudal nobility, it became an armed and self-governing association in the medieval commune; here independent urban republic (as in Italy and Germany), there taxable "third estate" of the monarchy (as in France); afterwards, in the period of manufacture proper, serving either the semi-feudal or the absolute monarchy as a counterpoise against the nobility, and, in fact, cornerstone of the great monarchies in general—the bourgeoisie has at last, since the establishment of modern industry and of the world market, conquered for itself, in the modern representative state, exclusive political sway. The executive of the modern state is but a committee for managing the common affairs of the whole bourgeoisie.

The bourgeoisie has played a most revolutionary role in history.

The bourgeoisie, wherever it has got the upper hand, has put an end to all feudal, patriarchal, idyllic relations. It has pitilessly torn asunder the motley feudal ties that bound man to his "natural superiors," and has left no other bond between man and man than naked self-interest, than callous "cash payment." It has drowned the most heavenly ecstasies of religious fervor, of chivalrous enthusiasm, of philistine sentimentalism, in the icy water of egotistical calculation. It has resolved personal worth into exchange value, and in place of the numberless indefeasible chartered freedoms, has set up that single, unconscionable freedom—Free Trade. In one word, for exploitation, veiled by religious and political illusions, it has substituted naked, shameless, direct, brutal exploitation.

The bourgeoisie has stripped of its halo every occupation hitherto honored and looked up to with reverent awe. It has converted the physician, the lawyer, the priest, the poet, the man of science, into its paid wage-laborers.

The bourgeoisie has torn away from the family its sentimental veil, and has reduced the family relation to a mere money relation.

The bourgeoisie has disclosed how it came to pass that the brutal display of vigor in the Middle Ages, which reactionaries so much admire, found its fitting complement in the most slothful indolence. It has been the first to show what man's activity can bring about. It has accomplished wonders far surpassing Egyptian pyramids, Roman aqueducts, and Gothic cathedrals; it has conducted expeditions that put in the shade all former migrations of nations and crusades.

The bourgeoisie cannot exist without constantly revolutionizing the instruments of production, and thereby the relations of production, and with them the whole relations of society. Conservation of the old modes of production in unaltered form, was, on the contrary, the first condition of existence for all earlier industrial classes. Constant revolutionizing of production, uninterrupted disturbance of all social conditions, everlasting uncertainty and agitation distinguish the bourgeois epoch from all earlier ones. All fixed, fast-frozen relations, with their train of ancient and venerable prejudices and opinions, are swept away, all new-formed ones become antiquated before they can ossify. All that is solid melts into air, all that is holy is profaned, and man is at last compelled to face with sober senses his real conditions of life and his relations with his kind.

The need of a constantly expanding market for its products chases the bourgeoisie over the whole surface of the globe. It must nestle everywhere, settle everywhere, establish connections everywhere.

The bourgeoisie has through its exploitation of the world market given a cosmopolitan character to production and consumption in every country. To the great chagrin of reactionaries, it has drawn from under the feet of industry the national ground on which it stood. All old-established national industries have been destroyed or are daily being destroyed. They are dislodged by new industries, whose introduction becomes a life and death question for all civilized nations, by industries that no longer work up indigenous raw material,

but raw material drawn from the remotest zones; industries whose products are consumed, not only at home, but in every quarter of the globe. In place of the old wants, satisfied by the production of the country, we find new wants, requiring for their satisfaction the products of distant lands and climes. In place of the old local and national seclusion and self-sufficiency, we have intercourse in every direction, universal interdependence of nations. And as in material, so also in intellectual production. The intellectual creations of individual nations become common property. National one-sidedness and narrow-mindedness become more and more impossible, and from the numerous national and local literatures there arises a world literature.

The bourgeoisie, by the rapid improvement of all instruments of production, by the immensely facilitated means of communication, draws all nations, even the most barbarian, into civilization. The cheap prices of its commodities are the heavy artillery with which it batters down all Chinese walls, with which it forces the barbarians' intensely obstinate hatred of foreigners to capitulate. It compels all nations, on pain of extinction, to adopt the bourgeois mode of production; it compels them to introduce what it calls civilization into their midst, i.e., to become bourgeois themselves. In a word, it creates a world after its own image.

The bourgeoisie has subjected the country to the rule of the towns. It has created enormous cities, has greatly increased the urban population as compared with the rural, and has thus rescued a considerable part of the population from the idiocy of rural life. Just as it has made the country dependent on the towns, so it has made barbarian and semibarbarian countries dependent on the civilized ones, nations of peasants on nations of bourgeois, the East on the West.

More and more the bourgeoisie keeps doing away with the scattered state of the population, of the means of production, and of property. It has agglomerated population, centralized means of production, and has concentrated property in a few hands.

The necessary consequence of this was political centralization. Independent, or but loosely connected provinces, with separate interests, laws, governments, and systems of taxation, became lumped together into one nation, with one government, one code of laws, one national class interest, one frontier, and one customs tariff.

The bourgeoisie, during its rule of scarce 100 years, has created more massive and more colossal productive forces than have all preceding generations together. Subjection of nature's forces to man, machinery, application of chemistry to industry and agriculture, steam-navigation, railways, electric telegraphs, clearing of whole continents for cultivation, canalization of rivers, whole populations conjured out of the ground—what earlier century had even a presentiment that such productive forces slumbered in the lap of social labor?

We see then that the means of production and of exchange, which served as the foundation for the growth of the bourgeoisie, were generated in feudal society. At a certain stage in the development of these means of production and of exchange, the conditions under which feudal society produced and exchanged, the feudal organization of agriculture and manufacturing industry, in a word, the feudal relations of property became no longer compatible with the already developed productive forces; they became so many fetters. They had to be burst asunder; they were burst asunder.

Into their place stepped free competition, accompanied by a social and political constitution adapted to it, and by the economic and political sway of the bourgeois class.

A similar movement is going on before our own eyes. Modern bourgeois society with its relations of production, of exchange and of property, a society that has conjured up such gigantic means of production and of exchange, is like the sorcerer who is no longer able to control the powers of the nether world whom he has called up by his spells. For many a decade past the history of industry and commerce is but the history of the revolt of modern productive forces against modern conditions of production, against the property relations that are the conditions for the existence of the bourgeoisie and of its rule. It is enough to mention the commercial crises that by their periodical return put the existence of the entire bourgeois society on trial, each time more threateningly. In these crises a great part not only of the existing products, but also of the previously created productive forces, are periodically destroyed. In these crises there breaks out an epidemic that, in all earlier epochs, would have seemed an absurdity—the epidemic of overproduction. Society suddenly finds itself put back into a state of momentary barbarism; it appears as if a famine, a universal war of devastation had cut off the supply of every means of subsistence; industry and commerce seem to be destroyed. And why? Because there is too much civilization, too much means of subsistence, too much industry, too much commerce. The productive forces at the disposal of society no longer tend to further the development of the conditions of bourgeois property; on the contrary, they have become too powerful for these conditions, by which they are fettered, and no sooner do they overcome these fetters than they bring disorder into the whole of bourgeois society, endanger the existence of bourgeois property. The conditions of bourgeois society are too narrow to comprise the wealth created by them. And how does the bourgeoisie get over these crises? On the one hand, by enforced destruction of a mass of productive forces; on the other, by the conquest of new markets, and by the more thorough exploitation of the old ones. That is to say, by paving the way for more extensive and more destructive crises, and by diminishing the means whereby crises are prevented.

The weapons with which the bourgeoisie felled feudalism to the ground are now turned against the bourgeoisie itself.

But not only has the bourgeoisie forged the weapons that bring death to itself; it has also called into existence the men who are to wield those weapons—the modern working class—the proletarians.

In proportion as the bourgeoisie, i.e., capital, is developed, in the same proportion is the proletariat, the modern working class, developed—a class of laborers, who live only so long as they find work, and who find work only so long as their labor increases capital. These laborers, who must sell themselves piecemeal, are a commodity, like every other article of commerce, and are consequently exposed to all the vicissitudes of competition, to all the fluctuations of the market.

Owing to the extensive use of machinery and to division of labor, the work of the proletarians has lost all individual character, and, consequently, all charm for the workman. He becomes an appendage of the machine, and it is only the most simple, most monotonous, and most easily acquired knack, that is required of him. Hence, the cost of production of a workman is restricted, almost entirely to the means of subsistence that he requires for his maintenance, and for the propagation of his race. But the price of a commodity, and therefore also of labor, is equal to its cost of production. In proportion, therefore, as the repulsiveness of the work increases, the wage decreases. Nay more, in proportion as the use of machinery and division of labor increases, in the same proportion the burden of toil also increases, whether by prolongation of the working hours, by increase of the work exacted in a given time, or by increased speed of the machinery, etc.

Modern industry has converted the little workshop of the partriarchal master into the great factory of the industrial capitalist. Masses of laborers, crowded into the factory, are organized like soldiers. As privates of the industrial army they are placed under the command of a perfect hierarchy of officers and sergeants. Not only are they slaves of the bourgeois class, and of the bourgeois state; they are daily and hourly enslaved by the machine, by the overlooker, and, above all, by the individual bourgeois manufacturer himself. The more openly this despotism proclaims gain to be its end and aim, the more petty, the more hateful and the more embittering it is.

The less the skill and exertion of strength implied in manual labor, in other words, the more modern industry develops, the more is the labor of men superseded by that of women. Differences of age and sex have no longer any distinctive social validity for the working class. All are instruments of labor, more or less expensive to use, according to their age and sex.

No sooner has the laborer received his wages in cash, for the moment escaping exploitation by the manufacturer, than he is set upon by the other portions of the bourgeoisie, the landlord, the shop-keeper, the pawnbroker, etc.

The lower strata of the middle class—the small tradespeople, shopkeepers, and retired tradesmen generally, the handicraftsmen and peasants—all these sink gradually into the proletariat, partly because their diminutive capital does not suffice for the scale on which modern industry is carried on, and is swamped in the competition with the large capitalists, partly because their specialized skill is rendered worthless by new methods of production. Thus the proletariat is recruited from all classes of the population.

The proletariat goes through various stages of development. With its birth begins its struggle with the bourgeoisie. At first the contest is carried on by individual laborers, then by the work people of a factory, then by the operatives of one trade, in one locality, against the individual bourgeois who directly exploits them. They direct their attacks not against the bourgeois conditions of production, but against the instruments of production themselves; they destroy imported wares that compete with their labor, they smash machinery to pieces, they set factories ablaze, they seek to restore by force the vanished status of the workman of the Middle Ages.

At this stage the laborers still form an incoherent mass scattered over the whole country, and broken up by their mutual competition. If anywhere they unite to form more compact bodies, this is not yet the consequence of their own active union, but of the union of the bourgeoisie, which class, in order to attain its own political ends, is compelled to set the whole proletariat in motion, and is moreover still able to do so for a time. At this stage, therefore, the proletarians do not fight their enemies, but the enemies of their enemies, the remnants of absolute monarchy, the landowners, the nonindustrial bourgeois, the petty bourgeoisie. Thus the whole historical movement is concentrated in the hands of the bourgeoisie; every victory so obtained is a victory for the bourgeoisie.

But with the development of industry the proletariat not only increases in number; it becomes concentrated in greater masses, its strength grows, and it feels that strength more. The various interests and conditions of life within the ranks of the proletariat are more and more equalized, in proportion as machinery obliterates all distinctions of labor and nearly everywhere reduces wages to the same low level. The growing competition among the bourgeois, and the resulting commercial crises, make the wages of the workers ever more fluctuating. The unceasing improvement of machinery, ever more rapidly developing, makes their livelihood more and more precarious; the collisions between individual workmen and individual bourgeois take more and more the character of collisions between two classes. Thereupon the workers begin to form combinations (trade unions) against the bourgeoisie; they club together in order to keep up the rate of wages; they found permanent associations in order to make provision beforehand for these occasional revolts. Here and there the contest breaks out into riots.

Now and then the workers are victorious, but only for a time. The real fruit of their battles lies, not in the immediate result, but in the ever expanding union of the workers. This union is furthered by the improved means of communication which are created by modern industry, and which place the workers of different localities in contact with one another. It was just this contact that was needed to centralize the numerous local struggles, all of the same character, into one national struggle between classes. But every class struggle is a political struggle. And that union, to attain which the burghers of the

Middle Ages, with their miserable highways, required centuries, the modern proletarians, thanks to railways, achieve in a few years.

This organization of the proletarians into a class, and consequently into a political party, is continually being upset again by the competition between the workers themselves. But it ever rises up again, stronger, firmer, mightier. It compels legislative recognition of particular interests of the workers, by taking advantage of the divisions among the bourgeoisie itself. Thus the ten-hour bill in England was carried.

Altogether, collisions between the classes of the old society further the course of development of the proletariat in many ways. The bourgeoisie finds itself involved in a constant battle. At first with the aristocracy; later on, with those portions of the bourgeoisie itself whose interests have become antagonistic to the progress of industry; at all times with the bourgeoisie of foreign countries. In all these battles it sees itself compelled to appeal to the proletariat, to ask for its help, and thus, to drag it into the political arena. The bourgeoisie itself, therefore, supplies the proletariat with its own elements of political and general education, in other words, it furnishes the proletariat with weapons for fighting the bourgeoisie.

Further, as we have already seen, entire sections of the ruling classes are, by the advance of industry, precipitated into the proletariat, or are at least threatened in their conditions of existence. These also supply the proletariat with fresh elements of enlightenment and progress.

Finally, in times when the class struggle nears the decisive hour, the process of dissolution going on within the ruling class, in fact within the whole range of old society, assumes such a violent, glaring character, that a small section of the ruling class cuts itself adrift, and joins the revolutionary class, the class that holds the future in its hands. Just as, therefore, at an earlier period, a section of the nobility went over to the bourgeoisie, so now a portion of the bourgeoisie goes over to the proletariat, and in particular, a portion of the bourgeois ideologists, who have raised themselves to the level of comprehending theoretically the historical movement as a whole.

Of all the classes that stand face to face with the bourgeoisie today, the proletariat alone is a really revolutionary class. The other classes decay and finally disappear in the face of modern industry; the proletariat is its special and essential product.

The lower middle class, the small manufacturer, the shopkeeper, the artisan, the peasant, all these fight against the bourgeoisie, to save from extinction their existence as fractions of the middle class. They are therefore not revolutionary, but conservative. Nay more, they are reactionary, for they try to roll back the wheel of history. If by chance they are revolutionary, they are so only in view of their impending transfer into the proletariat; they thus defend not their present, but their future interests; they desert their own standpoint to adopt that of the proletariat.

The "dangerous class," the social scum (*Lumpenproletariat*), that passively rotting mass thrown off by the lowest layers of old society, may, here and there, be swept into the movement by a proletarian revolution; its conditions of life, however, prepare it far more for the part of a bribed tool of reactionary intrigue.

The social conditions of the old society no longer exist for the proletariat. The proletarian is without property; his relation to his wife and children has no longer anything in common with bourgeois family relations; modern industrial labor, modern subjection to capital, the same in England as in France, in America as in Germany, has stripped him of every trace of national character. Law, morality, religion, are to him so many bourgeois prejudices, behind which lurk in ambush just as many bourgeois interests.

All the preceding classes that got the upper hand, sought to fortify their already acquired status by subjecting society at large to their conditions of appropriation. The proletarians cannot become masters of the productive forces of society, except by abolishing their own previous mode of appropriation, and thereby also every other previous mode of appropriation. They have nothing of their own to secure and to fortify; their mission is to destroy all previous securities for, and insurances of, individual property.

All previous historical movements were movements of minorities, or in the interest of minorities. The proletarian movement is the self-conscious, independent movement of the immense majority, in the interest of the immense majority. The proletariat, the lowest stratum of our present society, cannot stir, cannot raise itself up, without the whole superincumbent strata of official society being sprung into the air.

Though not in substance, yet in form, the struggle of the proletariat with the bourgeoisie is at first a national struggle. The proletariat of each country must, of course, first of all settle matters with its own bourgeoisie.

In depicting the most general phases of the development of the proletariat, we traced the more or less veiled civil war, raging within existing society, up to the point where that war breaks out into open revolution, and where the violent overthrow of the bourgeoisie lays the foundation for the sway of the proletariat.

Hitherto, every form of society has been based, as we have already seen, on the antagonism of oppressing and oppressed classes. But in order to oppress a class, certain conditions must be assured to it under which it can, at least, continue its slavish existence. The serf, in the period of serfdom, raised himself to membership in the commune, just as the petty bourgeois, under the yoke of feudal absolutism, managed to develop into a bourgeois. The modern laborer, on the contrary, instead of rising with the progress of industry, sinks deeper and deeper below the conditions of existence of his own class. He becomes a pauper, and pauperism develops more rapidly than population and wealth. And here it becomes evident, that the bourgeoisie is unfit any longer to be the ruling class in society, and to impose its conditions of existence upon society as an overriding law. It is unfit to rule because it is incompetent to assure an existence to its slave within his slavery, because it cannot help letting him sink into such a state, that it has to feed him, instead of being fed by him. Society can no longer live under this bourgeoisie, in other words, its existence is no longer compatible with society.

The essential condition for the existence and sway of the bourgeois class, is the formation and augmentation of capital; the condition for capital is wage-labor. Wage-labor rests exclusively on competition between the laborers. The advance of industry, whose involuntary promoter is the bourgeoisie, replaces the isolation of the laborers, due to competition, by their revolutionary combination, due to association. The development of modern industry, therefore, cuts from under its feet the very foundation on which the bourgeoisie produces and appropriates products. What the bourgeoisie therefore produces, above all, are its own gravediggers. Its fall and the victory of the proletariat are equally inevitable.

Some dynamics of revolutionary behavior

In his writings Marx left enough food for moral sustenance and self-examination for a very wide variety of people. He has been variously chewed and digested and regurgitated. Like other writers producing new ideas and ideology, he felt inclined to say, about some interpretations of his works, that he could not be a good Marxist. When *Das Kapital* became quickly popular among Russian intelligentsia, in the late 19th century, he commented that Russians always were inclined toward extreme doctrine.

Marx wrote about class conflict and about what more recent writers have called dyssynchronization—that is, various social practices that were inappropriate for the political institutions of the time. He wrote about the alienation of working men from their work, their families, and from their societies as they increasingly became appendages of the machines they tended. Marx was by any measure a fully developed economist and sociologist, but as a psychologist he was at best a novice. He nevertheless intuitively sensed one of the central social and psychic consequences of the industrial process—alienation. Durkheim wrote with surgical elegance about the social psychology of the division of labor and the attendant breakup of established interpersonal ties—alienation. Perhaps less systematically and surely less directly, Marx had already explored that consequence.

It has taken a new generation of scholars, more systematically trained in psychology, to bring a deeper understanding of the mental processes that underlie social processes. The usual sociological units of analysis are large social aggregates like class and race, or social and ethnic marginality. A major psychological unit of analysis is the individual human being.

The following article by David Schwartz combines such older sociological units of analysis with the newer psychological ones. And he adds historical perspective. This latter is somewhat akin to the grand sweep of Marxian analysis of slavery, feudalism, mercantilism, and the growth of capital and industry. It is more closely tied to the style of analysis of a still-contemporary and I think ageless student of revolution, Crane Brinton. The following article shows what can be done when the traditional units of analysis do not hobble thought but are used to move it a few steps farther along the road to greater knowledge of why revolutions occur.

A theory of revolutionary behavior

DAVID C. SCHWARTZ*

David C. Schwartz, "A Theory of Revolutionary Behavior," is printed with the permission of the author. Copyright by the Free Press, New York, 1970.

Notes to this section will be found on pages 335–338.

I. INTRODUCTION: PROBLEMS AND OPPORTUNITIES IN UNDERSTANDING REVOLUTIONARY BEHAVIOR

THE phenomena of revolutions—objects of long, continuous, and increasing attention in social study—have not yet been explained in a comprehensive, theoretically integrated manner. Rather, the considerable variety of competing approaches, foci, models, and methods current in the study of structured political violence give evidence of a vigorous, but not yet theoretically coherent, research tradition.[1] The present state of this growing and groping tradition is characterized by unresolved problems and unfinished tasks but at least some preconditions for the effective development of broader, integrating theory seem to have been met. This paper is an attempt to state such a theory: the introductory section is a sketch of some of the problems and opportunities to which the paper is responsive.

Initially, revolutionary situations have been described extensively.[2] The already large and fast growing body of descriptive or "case study" literature should prove most useful for the generation and testing of theoretical formulations. Presently, however, the bases on which descriptive efforts have been proceeded generally remain implicit or imprecise and case-specific. Accordingly, comparative secondary analysis is difficult and the findings lack synthesis. A more comprehensive theoretical conception of revolutionary behavior might be expected to effect improvement and perhaps consensus in the definition, refinement, and selection of categories for description and in ordering the descriptive material. This alone would facilitate the development of more cumulative knowledge about revolutionary phenomena.

Other, more systematic efforts to explain revolutionary occurrences have resulted in the identification of a number of relevant organizational foci — (individuals, socio-psychologically defined "people-types," small revolutionary groups, crowds, mobs, mass movements, political parties, existing regimes, social systems)—and have yielded some insightful hypotheses regarding the role of these different units in the development and incidence of revolutions. This task of modeling different levels of analysis separately is far from completion. Our understanding of all of the organizational levels is marked by alternative explanations and too little in the way of codification, testing and reconciliation of partial theories. In addition, a good deal more is known about the reaction to revolutionary conditions of some social units than others, and social units in general have historically been better investigated than has the behavior of individuals in revolutionary circumstances. More recently, some promising lines of inquiry regarding the needs, aspirations, and expectations relevant to revolutions have been identfied,[3] and both the systematization of these and their relationship to various social conditions which can produce them have found preliminary and insightful statement.[4] Still it seems likely that a general theory of revolutionary behavior will have to redress these imbalances, to substantially augment our understanding of the psychology of such behavior.

* I am indebted to the following persons for their advice and encouragement during the preparation of this paper: Crane Brinton, Peter Ch'en, James C. Davies, Daniel L. Dolan, Shel Feldman, Morton Gorden, Ted Gurr, the late Rex Hopper, William R. Kintner, Robert Melson, S. Sankar Sengupta and Robert Strausz-Hupé. Parts of this paper were written at the Foreign Policy Research Institute of the University of Pennsylvania with the support of the U.S. Navy (Nonr 551–60).

Limitations on our understanding of the causes and character of revolution are also reflected in a lack of theoretical linkages between levels of analysis. To be sure, there has long been a conception of revolution as a multilevel process—which notion seems adequately to stress the interrelatedness of phenomena ordered at individual, group, institutional, and systemic levels—and today, the explication of revolution in processual terms is rather generally accepted as a goal toward which theory-building should be directed. But most of the recent analysis of revolutions has focused more intensively on one stage in the process, or on the correlation of various other (especially psychological) phenomena with the fact of, or one or another stage in, revolution.[5] Thus far, moreover, much processual analysis has been restricted to descriptive or comparative "natural histories" in which a sequential pattern of events, couched largely in macrosocial terms, is identified.[6] On the other hand, there have been a few recent efforts at synthesis[7] and even if contemporary and previous process modelling of revolutions is not yet predictively powerful or widely applied, it has nevertheless given rise to a specification of some of the significant stages which characterize the phenomena under review.

Thus the tasks of initial observation, preliminary description and tentative classification seem well begun, if not well or uniformly advanced, and some uniformities, patterns and stages have been identified. The logic of process as an ordering principle and the ordinary course of theory construction both suggest that the next step in the development of a more comprehensive, operational, dynamic theory of revolutionary behavior is to seek the conditions or "transition rules" which are regularly associated with the movement of political systems through various stages toward (and into) revolution; to discover the dynamics of the revolutionary process. There is patently a need for such effort, and our present level of understanding seems to provide at least some encouragement, some realistic opportunities for efforts in this direction. We may hope, moreover, that attempts at more comprehensive theorizing (including the statement of an informing framework) may also help to resolve some of the recognized problems. Such theorizing may effect improvements in the definition and refinement of concepts and categories, in the measurement and combination of these (an interest which is fast moving ahead)[8] in the reexamination of extant data, in the stimulation and direction of further research—in the process of making our knowledge of revolution more cumulative. In sum, the attempt to theorize confronts the prior problems of delimitation, classification, analysis and reformulation of problems—what Eckstein has cogently called the "pretheoretical processing"[9]—and may advance the cause of meeting these preconditions of understanding. The framework and theory tentatively advanced in this paper are proffered in the hope that they may contribute to the realization of some of these advantages.

To locate this paper in a field of theories, one other approach or viewpoint must be mentioned. This is the idea that revolutions can and should be explained by applying one or another embryonic or developing general social science theory — conflict theories, communications theories, social action theories and the like.[10] These are fascinating proposals, deserving of trial, for they remind us that revolution may ultimately be properly explicable and subsumable under more general rubrics. To date, however, no one of these theories has been shown to provide an adequate baseline for explaining revolutionary behavior; indeed the prerequisites for employment (and necessary combination) of these theories, the establishment of correspondences between elements of the theory and units recognized in the revolutionary situation, have not yet been met. This paper aims at a "theory of the middle range," at providing something of the supporting infrastructure for the use and combination of more general constructs, at the same time that it facilitates more specific analyses of revolutions.

II. THE STAGES OF POLITICAL REVOLUTIONS

I propose to explain the essential features of political revolutions, (i.e., the origin, development and interactions of revolutionary organizations and the outbreak and course of revolutionary violence) by means of a multistage process model. Accordingly, the theory to be stated here will comport with the basic epistemological requirements inherent in the notion of process. These requirements prescribe certain forms to be employed and suggest certain types of relationships to be sought. The forms and types of relationships differ, of course, from those implied by other ordering principles, such as equilibrium or evolution, which may also be potentially useful in the study of political violence.

More specifically, a process may be thought of as a series of changes, through time, in the state of an object or, as here, a political system and some of its relevent subsystems. Process analysis requires that: (1) initial and terminal stages or states be described; (2) significant intermediate stages be specified; (3) conditions or behaviors within each stage or time period be explained; (4) the rules by which (or conditions under which) transitions occur between the stages, along a temporal continuum, be stated. The most powerful process analyses seem to be those in which the same variable or variables (though not necessarily the same variable magnitudes) account for all of the transitions between the stages or states (e.g., the transformation process by which some materials in an initially solid state pass through a liquid to a gaseous state as a function, *ceteris paribus*, of the variable, heat). The explanation of conditions or behaviors within the stages of a process may be quite different from the transition rules (i.e., may be different from the relationships which obtain between the stages), although, of course, a comprehensive processual analysis will include both the dynamic and the relatively more static or cross-sectional aspects of the phenomena under review.

If revolution is a process, its ultimate explanation must be a series of conditional probabilistic statements of the following form: "given that a political system is in state n, there exists a specifiable probability that it will move to (be transformed into) state $n+1$ (under identified conditions), will move then to $n+2$ ... to $n+n$. A precise description and comprehensive explanation of the cause of a modal form of revolution, then, would be an equation in conditional probabilities where the combination of the probabilities were equal to the probability of the end-state (terminal state, final result).

The theory to be stated here is an attempt to facilitate this kind of explanation, it does not itself achieve it. Some of the stages which lead to and through a revolution and some of the conditions under which political systems will undergo transitions among these stages toward revolution are roughly identified herein; the precise probabilities are not stated. They are, however, specifiable in principle and the kind of comparative inquiry which I hope this paper will encourage should lead us toward a more exact assessment of these probabilities.

In our theory, the stages of political revolution are defined in terms of the principal actors or units (political subsystems) which are operating in the given time period and their behaviors and interactions. Explanation of behavior within the stages will be generally couched in the language of individual and social psychology, with some especial reference to (and extensions of) the psychological theories of ambivalence, conflict, and cognitive consistency. Transitions between the stages are here generally explained in terms of the effects which the intrastage interactions of actors or subsystems have upon the political system as a whole. In a sense, the outcomes of the interactions within any one stage are conceived of as the (changed) systemic environment which constitutes the starting point for the subsequent stage. The (changed) character of the system at the start of the new phase, acting as stimulus or constraint (and, frequently as both—to different actors), operates to affect the behaviors and interactions in the new stage. In this way, both the unit or actor and the systems level of analysis are included and related in this theory. As a result, some interesting relationships between political development and political violence seem to suggest themselves. These will be presented in a concluding section of this paper, following the discussion of the theory itself.

In analyzing the general case of "complete" revolution (defined generally as a mass-linked social movement oriented to the acquisition of political power through the use of the social disruption and/or violence —including insurgencies, civil wars, and nationalist movements, but excluding most *coups*), it seems useful to identify at least ten separate stages or subprocesses. These are:

1. Initial political alienation;
2. Origination of revolutionary organizations;
3. Revolutionary appeals;
4. Revolutionary coalition and movement-building;
5. Nonviolent revolutionary politics;
6. The outbreak of revolutionary violence;
7. Rule of the moderates;
8. Accession of the extremists;
9. Reigns of terror;
10. Thermidor.

These stages constitute a partial "political space" (a partially defined matrix of possible states of a political system). The transition rules by which a political system moves through these stages are stated in the theory below.[11] If the transition conditions for movement between, say, stages 1 and 2 are not met, the system will either remain in Stage 1 or move to an unspecified state. This theory, of course, does not identify every possible alternative political condition (so, other revolutionary paths and patterns may exist). But the behavior rules within each stage (i.e., the relationships which govern behavior and interactions within each stage) may help explain changes to alternative states.

Before proceeding to a detailed systematic examination of each of the stages it will be useful to say something about the relationship of this model of the extant research tradition in which it resides. Initially, it will be immediately observed that at least the titles of some of these stages (i.e., stages 7 to 10) are taken over from the classical historio-sociological work of Edwards and of Brinton.[12] This should not be surprising in an effort to build upon and to systematize existing work. Any such theory must recognize and perhaps restate, but not merely "rediscover" ancient truths.

But these classical stages of revolution are not merely "borrowings" included in the present analysis to insure comprehensiveness of foci. Rather they are familiar constructs which will here be at least briefly reanalyzed in an attempt to explain the phenomena more effectively. Thus, for example, it will be argued that the same cognitive consistency formulations which seem to account for behavior in the pre-violence stages of revolution also provide explanatory increments regarding the more familiar stages of revolution. Indeed, such explanatory increments will be a principal data form adduced in support of the theory.[13]

Secondly, I am concerned here with the commonalities of revolutions and revolutionary behavior; with those theories which, in application, tend to provide at least a baseline explanation for the behavior of all revolutionary actors. Manifestly, a great disparity in the initial conditions represented by two societies or polities will result in systematic differences in the kind of revolution that can or does take place therein. Differences in the combination, magnitude or relative importance of variables will, as clearly, produce differences in outcome. Here, the emphasis is on the identification of generally relevant variables and the discovery and preliminary testing of typical relationships. Admittedly, political culture conditions revolutions no less than it affects other political processes, but it now seems legitimate, important and feasible to seek general formulations for which cultural considerations would serve as correction factors. In sum, this processual theory deemphasizes those obvious differences among revolutions which are the stuff of which typologies are made, in favor of distilling the central similarities of which all typologies will be variants.

Stage 1: Initial political alienation: withdrawal

Revolutions, like all political phenomena, originate in the minds of men and, thus, it is there that at least part of the explanation of revolutionary behavior is to be sought. This, of course, has long been recognized, if not systematically treated: "The state of mind which creates revolutions" having been a subject of Aristotelian inquiry[14] and much consideration since.

As understanding of human psychology has advanced, initially speculative, and later, empirical applications of psychological insights to the study of revolutions have taken place. Thus, implicitly, if not explicitly, emphases have shifted from manifest to latent psychic functions or causes and, within the latter category, from supposed revolutionary "instincts"[15] to some rather sophisticated operational formulations regarding the political consequences of certain aspiration–frustration–aggression relationships.[16] But though the psychopolitical disturbances which end in revolution begin in the psyche, if they remain there they are of interest only to the psychiatrist. Accordingly, of course, identification of the real world (or social) phenomena which produce, activate, and channel these sets of psychological elements is also an important aspect of the research tradition and of this paper.

All theories of collective behavior presuppose a theory of motivation.[17] In this regard the study of revolutions has been consonant with most modern analyses of macrosocial and political processes. The fundamental difficulty here has been the absence of a synthetic, general psychological theory to integrate the less complete middle-range theories which have been applied in revolution studies. Frustration–aggression–displacement,[18] the outplay of guilt,[19] the operation of cognitive consistency tendencies,[20] to name but a few, have all been recently applied to the phenomena

of structured violence and all seem to suggest useful research. At present, however, there exist neither adequate experimental data to allow us to choose among these psychic processes nor well articulated theory about the simultaneous interplay of these processes should they prove equally relevant. It seems likely that different processes will be elaborated by different personality types, but the psychological materials on this are embryonic and not yet applied (if applicable) to the analysis of revolution.

Fortunately, there have been several recent efforts to integrate heretofore seemingly disparate psychological theories;[21] and we shall use these below to construct a plausible psychodynamic of alienation—moving from ambivalence, through conflict, to cognitive consistency and adjustment.

More important for our purposes is the fact that each of the middle-range theories (i.e., those concerned with frustration, guilt, conflict, or cognitive consistency) yields the same initial deduction: revolutions begin with the attempted withdrawal from politics of individual and especially intellectual's attention, affection and involvement. Each of these theories, in application, posits that psychopolitical disturbances, which result when stimuli from the political system evoke conflictful or contradictory response tendencies (e.g., both positive and negative evaluations of the policy), can and in the short run will be reduced by weakening or removing the stimulus, initially by withdrawing attention from the political system. "Conflicts must decline if the strengths of both [conflictful] tendencies can be reduced to an ineffective level or if the difference between them can be markedly increased."[22] Just as the alcoholic seeking a cure can avoid his conflicts, to a degree, by staying away from the stimuli provided by taverns—the loyal citizen for whom political conditions have come to contravene basic values (or induce guilt or arouse frustrations) can, to a degree avoid the pain of such conflicts by avoiding the political clubs, the newspaper, etc. Whether, as in Wolfenstein's interpretation of Ghandi, one seeks "to escape his guilt by fleeing from a guilt provoking environment,"[23] or displaces political frustration onto private objects, or cognitively adjusts a perceived negative relationship between two positively valued elements (polity and politicized values)—the behavioral manifestation is the same, withdrawal. We shall also indicate below how, after a failure or effective withdrawal, the relearning process which markedly increases the difference between conflictful response tendencies augurs for revolution.

Let us be more precise. A cognitive structure which exists in persons who have undergone effective political socialization experiences and who support an existing political system—at least by regarding themselves as citizens or participants therein —may be represented either as: (1) an identity between images of the political system and politicized values (such that typically no distinction is made between the two); or (2) a balanced cognitive set of highly positive relationships between images of the self, the polity and politicized values.[24] These cognitive structures may be iconically represented as:

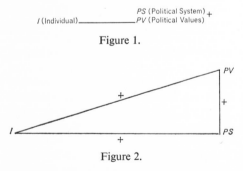

Figure 1.

Figure 2.

Figures 1 and 2 are balanced triads or sets (multiply the 3 signs, $+$ = balance, $-$ = imbalance), connoting that governments are deemed legitimate when they are perceived to be facilitative of, or consonant with, the significant politicized values of the population.

Such a sense of legitimacy and support for government are jeopardized when the political system comes to be viewed as inconsonant with, or nonsupportive of, an individual's basic politicized values (i.e.,

that the political system is either discriminating against, or is unable to protect or create the conditions requisite for holding or enjoying the values. An ambivalence, a potentially unbalanced cognitive structure results in: (1) the political system and the set of politicized values becoming (more) separate and therefore potentially conflictful; and (2) reevaluation of the polity becomes necessary. This is represented in Figure 3.

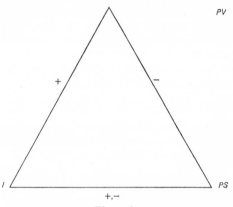

Figure 3.

The ambivalence represented in Figure 3 has motivational implications; above a "tolerance of ambiguity" threshold, some political behavior may be expected. Three gross directions which this behavior might take can be identified. First, the individual can "remain where he is," reducing the psychopolitical disturbance of ambivalence by modifying some of his less salient political values. Second, he may "move toward the system," modifying his behavior to become more politically active (e.g., reformist) and thereby seeking to influence the government in ways he regards as desirable. Finally, he may "move away from the system," reducing disturbance by entering a phase of withdrawal or passive alienation from politics.

These possibilities suggest that the structure of our problem may be akin to basic spatial conflict forms in psychology (i.e., approach–approach, approach–avoidance, avoidance–avoidance, and double approach–avoidance situations).[25] We can eliminate both the avoidance–avoidance and the simple approach–avoidance condition, because in our situation the polity and the politicized values have initial positive valuation. This leaves only the approach–approach and the double approach–avoidance forms.

In approach–approach conflict environments, two points of reinforcement (herd polity and politicized values) are desirable objects. Any movement toward either object tends to place the individual in a position of reinforced stimulation from that object, resulting in further movement toward the object. In periods of "early political ambivalence" (in the absence of effective stimuli from revolutionary organizations) movement is likely to be toward the system.

Under the circumstances of every day living, however, it is doubtful whether pure approach–approach conditions ... ever exist. In nearly every case, the choice of one goal generates an avoidance tendency due to the fact that the other goal may have to be relinquished ... such double approach–avoidance conflicts are not readily resolved. By and large, these ... conflicts reduce to a kind of avoidance–avoidance paradigm ... where conflict must continue unless withdrawal is feasible.[26]

Under certain circumstances (psychological conditions) psychopolitical disturbances are likely to be structured as double approach–avoidance conflict and withdrawal is likely to be attempted. These are: (1) the condition that the values at stake are basic or fundamental in character and/or many in number. (These may be economic, religious, cultural, social structural or power-role related values; they may be personal aspirations, new identities, or values concerning the procedures of government.) Revolutions have been made for all of these. The only relevant limitations are that they be basic and politicized;[27] and/or (2) the political system is perceived to be inherently incapable (inefficacious) to maintain or create the significant politicized values; and/or (3) the individual perceives himself to be incapable (inefficacious) to operate within the political system to bring about the changes he desires; but that (4) early and continuing socialization and daily life

patterns establish and reinforce positive identifications with the polity so that the negative evaluations fostered by 1 through 3 above produce fundamental conflict or psychopolitical disturbance.

The perceptions of personal and systemic inefficacy posited above in the operating salient political sphere, produce strong feelings of frustration and aggression. In addition, the disturbance is associated with significant tension or threat. There are three reasons for this: (1) a perceived negative relationship between one's basic values and one's organized society is, itself, threatening (e.g., as a separation anxiety); (2) the cognitive conflict or imbalance is itself tensionful, and; (3) some free floating anxiety is likely to become fixed on politics (i.e., on the dislocation between ego and politics). As the bonds between self and society weaken, latent rage tends to reinforce feelings of frustration and aggression and threat. Such rage results from the too constraining character of general socialization, when the conditions to which one has been socialized fail.

These, then, are the conditions conducive to the occurrence of at least passive alienation in the participant sectors of a polity: (1) a perceived incongruity between significant politicized values and the operations and/or structures and/or directions of government; (2) a sense of personal political futility; (3) a sense of systemic political futility; (4) a syndrome of associated, mutually reinforcing frustration, aggression, rage, threat and tension.

Under these conditions, an individual is likely to at least try to withdraw attention and affection (support, sense of legitimacy) from the government and from the political system. Thus:

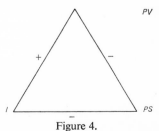

Figure 4.

Before turning to the behavioral manifestations of withdrawal or to its social implications (which constitute the transition conditions for the onset of Stage 2), something should be said of those ambivalent or conflictful persons who move toward the political system instead of withdrawing from it. Even where it is an individuals basic values with which a political system is in conflict, one may be able to reduce disturbance by moving toward the system *if he can psychologically differentiate the political system as a whole from some part of the system which can be reformed.* If he perceives that, though the actions of the system contravene his basic values, it is only some separable personnel, or process, or structure or even cultural norm that needs change (and not the fundamental character of the system), he is likely to enter, not withdraw from the system. Illustratively, he moves from:

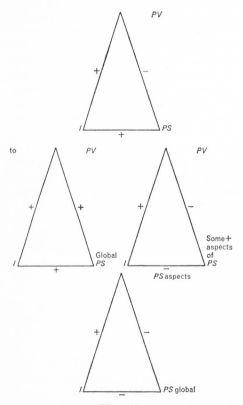

Figure 5.

An example of this is the widely prevalent and persistent notion that "the Czar would help us if only he knew our plight" which delayed any Russian revolution for some time as it reduced peasant support for governmental overthrow. Here the peasantry were differentiating the personnel of the system from its central authoritarian character as manifested in the Czar.

Any national political system is sufficiently complex that this process of differentiation–rationalization can go on for some time and this may explain why Stage 1 subprocesses sometimes take place over several generations. As the reformer continues to eliminate differentiable elements of the system as possible causes of his value conflict, or fails to change the plausible conflictful features of a polity it becomes increasingly difficult simultaneously to adjust his preceptions along cognitively consistent lines[28] and still stay within the system. Accordingly, frustrations rise (i.e., this is a thwarted approach–approach conflict wherein one cannot achieve one's basic values in an acceptable time frame—a lifetime, perhaps).[29] The probability of passive or active alienation increases with time and the escalation of revolutionary potential builds up within the system. Criticism of the regime (including its legitimacy) becomes commonplace, therefore. This occurs first among intellectuals either before they withdraw or because they can't effectively withdraw (see Stage 2 below). Here the decades of philosophic, political and artistic criticism before both the French and Russian revolutions are the type-cases.

Disgusted (and tired) one drops out or, as we will show in Stages 2 and 4, stays in until an appealing revolutionary organization develops. The major point to be made here is that the pool of withdrawn passively alienated persons is made up not only of those who opt out early but also of a subset of reformers who are thoroughly familiar with the system. When the time comes for infiltration of the polity, requiring a knowledge of and contacts in the system, these men become strategically crucial.

A nice illustration of the range of alienation possibilities can be observed in the Algerian revolution. There, the three top FLN leaders—Krim, Ben Bella and Abbas—exhibit three different time frames for the evaluation of, and alienation from, a central system. Whereas Krim's first evaluation of the polity produced revolutionary behavior at the early age of 17 (see Stage 3 below for the conditions of prepolitical "going revolutionary"), Ben Bella entered the political system (as an elected orthodox party representative for approximately two years) then opted out, and Abbas spent much of his adult life being forced to progressive stages of reevaluation and alienation. When the time comes for "revolution termination" (i.e., peace negotiations, for not all revolutions are duels to the death) men like Abbas—who know the language and styles of the older system—may again play historic roles, even as Abbas did at Evian.

However it develops, the behavioral manifestations of withdrawal include individuation, privatization, reduction in the scope of loyalties, a sense of public purposelessness, nonvoting, decrease in political interactions (as in membership and meetings of organizations) and the like. Such behavior, under conditions of threat and futility, is a recurrent theme in revolutions. "There is a good deal of evidence that as revolutions go on, a very large number of people just drop out of active politics, make no attempt to register their votes."[30]

The notion of a withdrawal phase in the subprocess of alienation helps to explain the "earliest sympton of revolution which is an increase in restlessness."[31] This restlessness, as noted by Edwards and Brinton, manifests itself in "aimless interactions" and "purposeless activity."[32] Hopper aptly calls this "The Milling Process"[33] wherein individual restlessness tends to spread and become social as is evidenced, *inter alia*, by "the wandering of attention from one individual, object, or line of action to another. . . ."[34]

The analysis presented above suggests that at least part of what these scholars are observing are *the normal social interactions* of persons who no longer share common

orientations to the political system; that different people withdraw different degrees of attention, salience, and affection from different institutions and symbols at different rates of speed (e.g., the greater the disturbance, the more rapid and complete the withdrawal). Change in attitude sets and attention foci are posited by the very notions of privatization and withdrawal. Previously effective interactions might well become or appear aimless under these circumstances, and even the fragmentary data which have sometimes been marshaled in support of the inference of restlessness[35] comports with the idea of privatization or individuation which results from political withdrawal.

The social isolation, extreme individuation and reinforced aggression which characterizes political withdrawal also seems useful in explaining other phenomena which have been associated with early stages of revolution. An increase in crime—especially violent crime—observed by Edwards and others is consonant with the properties of political withdrawal, as the direct outplay of the associated rage or aggression. The increased focus on the self which is the privatization aspect of political withdrawal may also account, in part, for the increase in personal "disorders" (vice, insanity, suicide) noted by Hopper[36] as an early indicator of revolution. Political withdrawal also explains the relationship between high crime and suicide rates and low voting turnout which Jack L. Walker and Robert A. Dahl have recently found of interest.[37] Certainly, the ambivalence, conflict, cognitive adjustment model identifies a principal source of the increased tension which characterizes incipient revolutionary situations as observed by Hopper and others.[38]

Perhaps more important is the fact that political withdrawal helps to explain the "availability" of persons for revolutionary behavior. Political withdrawal effects social isolation and atomization by breaking down common orientations to the social and political system. The consequent "loss of community" (in both real and perceived terms) constitutes an essential aspect of mass society, the "high availability of a population for mobilization by elites,[39] for people who are atomized readily become mobilized."[40]

Mass society is not only objectively atomized but is composed of subjectively alienated populations.[41] Political extremism, to cite but one example, has frequently been found to be positively associated with social isolation—by Lipset and others.[42] But if conditions of subjective politicized threat and futility can inure toward objective social atomization, it is interesting that we may also state that the social effects of this political withdrawal reinforce the very conditions of subjective or felt—"loss of community," which induced or created that objective social situation. This mutually reinforcing psychosocial process of alienation, then, can indeed lead to the sociopsychological crises which Cantril had identified as requisite for mass movement availability.[43] Also the cognitive adjustment formulations are consonant with Davies' important finding that it is sharp reversals in development, rather than increasing economic debilitation, which correlate with revolution. A continuing development (really a continuous improvement in the conditions under which any basic politicized value may be enjoyed), creates certain views of the world and positive expectations. A reversal of conditions is inconsistent with these perceptions and expectations and produces disturbance. While continuing debilitation certainly contravenes positive aspirations, it may be expected to produce less disturbance because it is more consonant with perceptions. Also, positive aspirations are less likely to be produced under such circumstances.[44]

The cognitive processes discussed above also operate among nonparticipants (i.e., the prepolitical or nonpolitically socialized or conscious elements of a national population as we will show in Sections 3 and 4, below.

In sum, the theory which is tentatively advanced here suggests that the process by which persons become alienated from a central government, become "available" for, and ultimately become predisposed toward,

revolutionary behavior can be represented as a series of identifiable and predictable changes in cognitive patterns. Each pattern or stage in the subprocess of alienation is also associated with a particular perceptual screen through which the world is filtered. An adequate identification of the range of cognitive patterns extant in a given polity, and a reconceptualization of the composition of a population in cognitive terms would provide early assessment of the revolution potential of a society. This could be of considerable utility to development planners seeking greater national unification and mobilization.

Stage 2: The origin of revolutionary organizations

In the absence of an appropriate "change-agent" (e.g., revolutionary organization or "antisystem"), it is conceivable that substantial elements of previously participant population sectors could remain in the stage of initial, passive alienation. Under these circumstances, the political system shifts to a lower level of functional integration.

It can be shown, however, that the social consequences or outcomes of political withdrawal serve as a partial stimuli for the development of revolutionary organization. The particular transition rule seems to be that a critical minimum of perceived passive alienation is a precondition for the origin of antisystems which are revolutionary from their inception. This is the less well understood of the two principal modes of revolutionary organization and, as such, will be emphasized here. The second predominant mode of antisystem development, the increasing radicalization of existing, reformist interest groups (i.e., the transition from "system-alternative" to antisystem), has been elaborated upon by Brinton,[45] Willer and Zollschan[46] and others. Accordingly, I will treat it somewhat more briefly.

"Organizations [which] were, from the very start, violently revolutionary[47] have been observed even in the socalled classical revolutions. How do such organizations originate? The problem can be stated more concretely. One may wish to explain the development of mass revolutionary movements in terms of the mass public appeals or propaganda of a small revolutionary corps or cadre; as the activation of basic, politically relevant predispositions in the population. This is a now-familiar formulation, to be reanalyzed below. Manifestly, however, the origin of the activators, of the revolutionary corps—cannot be so explained. What is to be said of these self-starters?

If there is a "typical" social science response to this problem, it is one which is couched in terms of the personality of the revolutionary leader.[48] This is certainly an intuitively reasonable type of response (especially in light of the leadership principle [*Fuhrer prinzip*] common to many revolutionary organizations),[49] and one for which Erikson has provided a theoretical base.[50] One might well wish, then, for considerably more in the way of comparative and systematized political biography.

The analysis which follows, however, is an effort to explain the origin of revolutionary antisystems in terms of more general cognitive processes (i.e., again, the operation of cognitive consistency principles under specified social conditions). Within it, certainly "personality counts" (e.g., the greater the generalized or politicized need affiliation, the greater the disturbance which results from "loss of community") but the emphasis here is on the cognitive rather than, for example, the need structural aspects of personality. As the two foci are clearly complimentary, increased findings of political biography may be expected to improve, but perhaps not wholly to supplant, these formulations.

The cognitive structure associated with passive alienation was represented above, as follows:

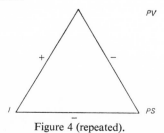

Figure 4 (repeated).

This may appear as a stable balanced triad. In actuality, for persons situated in certain social roles, the attempted withdrawal of attention, affect and involvement from politics is unlikely to be either total or very successful. The modern sectors of most political systems emit a more or less steady bombardment of symbols about themselves and, therefore, some evidences of government (and its nonsupport of basic values) will inevitably get through the perceptual screen of individuals who are receptive to, or tied to, communications media. By and large it is the urbanized intelligentsia who are most closely wedded to these media, whose attention to the channels of modern communication must be regular if not continuous, and hence it is that political withdrawal is least effective for intellectuals. This explanation for the much-discussed "alienation of the intellectuals" differs markedly from those which rely on the assumption or assertion that intellectuality necessarily imputes political awareness. Intellectuals, like other men, may be or become passively alienated and may strive mightily to remain so; as a group, they are simply less likely than others to succeed at political withdrawal.

Then too, the behavioral aspects of withdrawal may imbalance other cognitive structures. For example, withdrawal is clearly inconsistent with the participant's (especially intellectual's) value of political participation (VP). This value of participation as a factor in revolution is especially clear in student-led rebellions. Not only Castro's July 26 movement but, even more, the Directoria Revolucionario organization had this character. The entire Korean Revolution of 1961 is of this character.

Finally, where they exist, real and powerful social threats will continue to impinge on the individual despite political withdrawal. Passive alienation is no substitute for emigration.

The motivational implications of these cognitive inconsistencies and of the intellectual's often generally ineffective efforts at political withdrawal, cannot alone account for the origin of revolutionary organizations;

there are many more conflictful intellectuals, constrained to look at the system than there are revolutionary organizers.

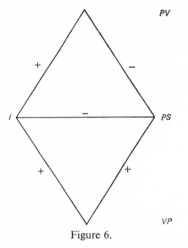

Figure 6.

If the media constrain one to view the system, creating and reinforcing conflicts, they also constitute an outlet for the behavior motivated. The predominant form of relevant intellectual endeavor is, at first, not revolution but criticism. Governmental activity is evaluated, the cultural norms underlying governmental behavior are questioned. What may begin, as vague malaise becomes intellectualized and hence manifest the potentially politicizable. Through the media (sometimes in special media—once pamphlets, now more often transistor radios) the passively alienated proliferate and "find each other."

This is crucial, for the existence and perception of a critical threshold of passive alienation is the primary precondition of revolutionary organization. In this respect, as in others to be noted below, the formation of revolutionary organizations is somewhat similar to that of ordinary interest groups.[51] The perception of common interests, of similarity, is a functional prerequisite for collective action. On the psychological level this provides reinforcement, the well known "protection of the group." This corresponds, in part, to what Edwards has called "rapport among the discontented."[52]

Other preconditions for revolutionary organization include:

1. A perception of the necessity for group action to achieve common goals;

2. A perception of the efficacy of the particular projected organization;

3. At least some compatibility or congruence in personal style among potential members;

4. Common acceptable symbols (or common foci, backgrounds, and beliefs out of which revolutionary symbols, shibboleths and myths can be constructed).

When these preconditions are met, revolutionary organization is likely to occur.[53] The specific character of the resulting organization, a matter which becomes crucial in the ensuing stages, is not wholly given (stated) in the establishment of these preconditions. Here, three factors are determinative: leadership, strategy, constraints imposed by the system.[54] Revolutionary leadership is likely to come from those who most clearly perceive the need for, and efficacy and existence of, commonality. We may also hypothesize that the most highly motivated and energized (perhaps because most conflictful or dissonant) persons will seek leadership positions. In any case, the styles, symbols, shibboleths, myths and mystique of revolutionary organizations are most often a function of (are forged by) the leadership.

Leadership is also most likely to be the source of strategy but once adopted, there is an almost independent logic or dynamic which strategy imposes on behavior. So too, with constraints imposed by the system. Typically, the strategy includes at least the potentiality (contingent planning) of violent takeover, and the regime's hostility imposes secrecy on the revolutionaries. It should not be surprising therefore, that the form of many modern revolutionary organizations is that of the military or militant conspiracy.[55] From this flows such revolutionary practices as: assumed names, a secret language, training in arms, iron discipline.[56]

The type of revolutionary organization which emerges in a given case will, of course, be that which is psychologically functional, economically feasible and strategically required. These factors may also help to explain behavior, especially in eliminating classes of behavior which were not exhibited. But they are far too general to be maximally useful.

At present, there has been very little sub-conceptualization of the "psychologically functional" category; more work has been done on identifying the roles and behaviors which meet the requirements of revolution. We know that there are multiple, complementary functions which any revolutionary group must organize itself to perform. The tasks of organization-building, or organization-maintenance and the changing of men (thus, the incessant indoctrination of recruits as well as potential revolutionaries and supporters) and of attaining power—all call for specialization and a certain division of labor.

Two modes of analysis seem useful in predicting that division of labor. First, one can examine the behavioral models available to the revolutionaries. There is some imitative behavior in any collective movement, but who are likely to be chosen as behavioral models? With the rapidly increasing diffusion of tactical knowledge about revolution (including foreign advisors), the revolutionary organization and behaviors of a given movement may be conscious parallels of some preceding successful revolution. Previous successes elsewhere increase the sense of efficacy of would-be revolutionaries. Another, less well grasped possibility is that the revolutionaries will adopt the organization, styles and behaviors of those low-level authority figures (from the central system) with whom they have been in contact. It is no accident that the Bolshevik revolutionary and the Czarist secret police are nearly indistinguishable in effect.[57]

The second mode of analysis which seems useful in explaining the types and behaviors of revolutionary organizations which develop involves examination (analytic combination) of needs and resources. Revolutionaries, like all political men, must make some reconciliation between what they want to do and what they can accomplish.

Some important, nonimitative factors relevant to the character and behavior of revolutionary organization are its "resource mix" (e.g., cohesion, discipline, numbers, money, organizational capacity, political skills, weapons, or access to these) and its "political orientation" (e.g., general strategy, risk and action preferences, recruitment policy, coalition potential). These "nuts and bolts" features of revolutionary organizations have too generally been neglected in the scholarly literature with unfortunate consequences for our understanding of revolutionary behavior. At least some of these matters will be considered in the discussion of later stages of revolution.

The second principal mode of revolutionary organization, the increasing radicalization of existing political groups, has been considered to be the more important organizing process. Yet, "There seems to be no simple and sole test to determine when and under what conditions the existence of pressure groups may be taken as a symptom of approaching political instability."[58] The difficulties are compounded by the fact that some modern writers on revolution use the term interest group to include organizations which are revolutionary from the outset.[59]

Similar to the alienative processes of individuals discussed above, it seems that interest groups and opposition party factions will work within the ongoing political system so long as they (the leadership) perceive themselves and the polity to be at least potentially efficacious and further perceive relevant threats to be tolerable. Increases in perceived threat and futility produce dissonances which are likely to be associated with pulls toward anti-system behavior. The political "clubs" of 18th century France, the student organizations in Cuba during the Batista period, and the UDMA in Algeria, are cases in point. Needless to say, the suppression of such groups (usually of reformist groups) by existing regimes often produces the requisite perceptions, and groups may go underground under these conditions. Where the existing regime tends to force (ascribe) a revolutionary or illegitimate status onto a reformist group, the revolutionary fervor of the group may markedly increase due to the ensuing cognitive inconsistency (dissonance). Postdecision dissonance (after deciding to go revolutionary) may effect the same result. The Diem regime in South Vietnam and Syngman Rhee's South Korean role were characterized by this kind of behavior.

It should be clear that modes 1 and 2 can and do coexist. All real revolutions are "mixed" processes, involving revolutionary organizations of both types. For the increasing radicalization of interest organizations to produce a revolution, there must be a relatively stable differentiation of interests in the political community. The existence of such a predictable "switching matrix" among the population means that, for the politicized, attraction to new revolutionary organizations will be small. Thus, the stability of the pattern of interests becomes an indicator of the type of revolution, if any, which a society may undergo.

One other type of group radicalization need be mentioned. This is the radicalization of those analytically defined groupings, called secondary elites. Where the reasonable expectation of upward mobility is violated, producing futility, threat to aspirant values and hence psychopolitical disturbance, radicalization takes place. Thus youthful Westernized professionals in societies dominated by still-young, more provincial, nationalists often constitute an alienated technocratic subelite. This is the oft-discussed matter of intellectual underemployment. I submit that the whole "circulation of elites" notion of revolution is but a special case of group radicalization (though, of course, no less important for that).

Stage 3: Revolutionary appeals

As with all of the stages of revolution identified here, the phase of revolutionary appeals could well be (and has been) a voluminous subject. The objective here is, as it must be in a paper of appropriate size, to state some basic general relationships; to stimulate and to facilitate, but not to achieve here comprehensiveness of treatment. Therefore, I shall emphasize the psychological and sociopolitical functions performed by such appeals, generally leaving aside their fascinating ideational characteristics. The goals of science and the practices of scholarly communication do limit the charm of political study.

There is considerable intellectual justification and scholarly precedent for handling revolutionary appeals in this fashion. A long string of studies, including those of LeBon,[60] Edwards,[61] Arendt,[62] Cantril,[63] Almond,[64] and Pye,[65] have shown the importance of latent functions, or preconscious identifications in the attraction of mass movements. This, of course, can be overdone and perhaps it has been. However internally inconsistent revolutionary social myths may sometimes be, their manifest content is somewhat influential and comparative analyses of the manifest ideational content of recent revolutionary appeals, for example, might well add much to our explication of the phenomenon. Nevertheless, most of what follows in this stage, is in the tradition of the social–psychological explanation and is an attempt to advance that tradition.

Once formed, a revolutionary organization is likely to seek such support as its strategy requires, typically as wide a base of support as is feasible. Although it is possible that some revolutionary corps have become "locked in" at, or "hung up" on, the organizational stage (including the building of infrastructure and resources prerequisite to mass appeals) and thereby neglected support-building, in the usual instance no new transition rule is needed to explain the beginnings of revolutionary appeal. If organization is needed to mobilize a perceived, passively alienated "potential group," so are the appeals of that organization. Although in some cases the mere fact that an organization existed to act as a focus or vehicle of discontent has been appealing, the same conditions that make for revolutionary organization affect the behaviors and appeals of that organization. Basically, we must distinguish between four disparate audiences for revolutionary appeal. These are: (1) those who are already passively alienated; (2) those who have never been politically conscious (the pre-politicals); (3) those who remain participants in the ongoing system; and (4) personnel of the central regime itself. The basic task of the revolutionary propagandist is to evolve an "appeal mix" which recognizes the differences between these audiences and which produces mutually reinforcing (or, at least, nonmutually interfering) effects. Of course, even within each of these gross "audience types," different subgroups exist and selective appeal is necessary. Not only do followers make revolutions for reasons which differ from those of the leaders, but among the followers, there is always a mix of motives. Thus, the revolutionary is a practicing coalition theorist, suggesting the potential explanatory utility of such theory.

The passively alienated person, as we have seen, has been subjected to conditions of (and has salient perceptions of) politicized threat, futility, loss of community, and a syndrome of associated aggression, or rage and tension.[66] The general intrastage explanation involving disturbance-reduction, suggests that such as person is likely to give at least tacit support to a revolutionary movement if it meets the following criteria:

1. It is perceived to be less threatening than the ongoing political system (and all other antisystems);
2. It is perceived to be less futile than these;
3. It explains the "loss of community" (or other crises in the society);
4. It is perceived to permit or encourage the more or less direct outplay of aggression or rage (usually by creating a scapegoat).

Some of the techniques by which these perceptions are induced are well known. They include: (1) the focusing of dissatisfaction (and free floating anxiety) on a small set of political symbols; (2) providing a sense (even if fictionalized) of prideful historical community; (3) explaining (simplifying) the threat and futility in terms of a loss of that community; (4) asserting that

the sense and fact of once glorious community can be readily and directly reestablished (both via the exorcism of community destroying factors or groups and by finding a place in the revolutionary movement); (5) projecting the hostility of alienation out onto the identified condition or group. The creation of this "out symbol" can help to develop the group or class consciousness relied on in the Marxian explication of revolution.

It can also be seen that the revolutionary is engaged in politicizing some of the most basic human needs—identity, belonging, worthiness, efficacy. Where unimpeded by a belief in God, revolutionaries tend to add salvation or immortality to the list of politicized goals. For groups that have no other social power, and hence are available for political revolution as a means to coerce society, these goals legitimize aspirations and behavior which embody these goals.

Ennobling or at least high sounding goals may make life (and revolutionary support) meaningful but, for some, activity is more important than: rationale. Basic to the notion of an "appeal mix" is that one message may be heard differently by two different sectors of the audience and yet be equally effective with each sector—for different reasons. The revolutionary propagandist who calls for the direct outplay of aggression against a scapegoat, for example, may be principally appealing to the frustrated, but may also gain adherents from young, bored persons who are "out for kicks" or perhaps just something to do. Our general intrastage behavior rule (involving the reduction of psychopolitical disturbance) however integrative of a part of human motivation, does not, of course cover the whole of men's motives. Indeed, most of contemporary psychological theory seems to be "old men's theory"—wherein man is depicted as seeking to reduce stimulation and its effects—whereas many revolutionary followers are young men, stimulation seekers more *homo-ludens* than *homo politicus*. Rulers reign safe not by bread alone, but also by circuses.

If attracting support among the passively

alienated is important, modern revolutionary organizations have relied still more heavily on activating the "prepolitical" sectors. This was as true for the Nazis in urbanized, industrial Germany, (where Nazi support was greatest among those who had never previously voted or were wholly new to the political scene) as it is now true in the underdeveloped world (where peasant support is crucial). Thus revolutionaries typically have notions about what and who is properly politicizable which are very different from those of the system's functionaries.

In a sense, the antisystem's task may be somewhat easier as regards the prepoliticals. Little, save inattention to politics needs to be unlearned by those who have never been effectively socialized to the ongoing political system. For these people to become available to "hear" revolutionary appeals, their traditional social insulation must break down. In modern societies, economic depression, rapid secularization, the enervation of familial ties are relevant. In the rural areas of the underdeveloped world, the migration of youthful potential leaders, the inability of traditional leaders to cope with modern problems or to compare favorably with more modern types, a general decline in the relevance and efficacy of traditional ways and persons—all conspire to make men available for revolutionary appeal. Then too, political and military considerations dictate that revolutionists operate in the more inaccessible rural areas. Often, central regimes ignore or cannot staff rural installations. Little wonder, under these conditions, that the critical balance of rural power often goes early and by default to the revolutionist. To the extent that the revolutionary organization succeeds at appearing as a cohesive, familial, even traditional grouping, it can attract support among traditional, rural persons. Personal needs for affiliation often lie back of revolutionary support. All these formulations seem relevant, for example, to the Chinese Communist Revolution.

It is often easier to attract support by being against something rather than for something. This is especially true among prepoliticals. So Castro became "the Robin Hood of the Sierra Maestras," exploiting the hated landlords and gaining peasant support. Also, stressing what one is against increases one's coalition potential. Thus, very disparate groups can converge on the one agreed on point: overthrow of the hated regime.

The participants in and personnel of the ongoing system are also "target audiences" for the revolutionary organization. Here the goal is neutralization of opponents by virtue of the inducement of self-doubt, and perceptions of futility, and the inevitability of revolutionary victory. This can be effective at several levels. In the Nazi and Gaullist situations, for example, men at the top who felt trapped by the inefficacy of the system, expecting the antisystem to be similarly ensnarled, have simply handed power over. In other instances, it has been the neutralization of the army and other security forces (often because of perceived inefficacy and self-doubts) which has secured revolutionary victory. (Sometimes the power structure, sensing the impotence of the moderate revolutionaries and fearing the extremists, grant power to the former, in the hope of preventing takeover by the latter.) Even in the absence of such clearcut system-collapse, revolutionary propaganda can divide and weaken a regime for a later takeover.

Stage 4: Revolutionary coalition and movement building

A small revolutionary corps formed from among the most dissonant of the passively alienated, with some wider support attracted by selective appeals within a mass social myth—these we have sought thus far to explain. They are the necessary but generally insufficient conditions for sustained revolutionary activity. For that effort what is required is a coalition of leadership elements, a firm and organized mass movement base—a party. This typically involves something of a power struggle at the top, and the development of such total identification with the movement at the mass base that recruitment and role specification can take place—

two interrelated processes which mark the stage of organizational consolidation for revolution.

The social consequences of successful revolutionary mass appeals (i.e., of the development of some critical minimum of political support in Stage 3) include: (1) the infusion of new and broader elements into the revolutionary movement which may vie for, or affect the infighting of, top leadership and the beginnings of the violence-relevant polarization of the political community; and (2) a new type, or level, of political commitment. These outcomes are intimately, and intricately, interrelated.

It is not the case that coalition-building and power struggles in the revolutionary organization wait upon a threshold of public support; far from it. The organization process discussed above as Stage 2 minimally implies the achievement of at least a temporary coalition and of some consensus on structure, strategy and tactics. In the earlier stage of organization building, however, there is rather little room for dissident persons or factions to maneuver in and still remain in the organization. In the absence of mass support, moreover, there is little inhibition on opting out and, as a result, the relatively early stages of revolution often witness a proliferation of revolutionary organizations.

The situation is appreciably changed; however, when one of these achieves some critical minimum of public support or, what is the same thing, the notion of revolution attains such support and one revolutionary organization comes to be associated with that notion (as with the Bolsheviks in the Soviet Union). Now the shibboleths and other isolation devices used to integrate the insurgents also serve to indicate that society is split into two main factions.[67] Under these more polarized circumstances (which is the transition condition), the rewards for joining and remaining with the supported organization multiply as do the punishments for opting out or staying out. The supported organization appears (is) more efficacious; to be on the outside is to be a less effective revolu-

tionist. Because the supported organization is, at this stage, still likely to have an open, inclusivist policy (seeking a maximal winning coalition), it usually is rather easy to join or rejoin their ranks. A veritable bandwagon among the discontented may result.

The augmented support has ramifications internal to the organization, too. As new elements are admitted and "dropouts" reinstated, these can be appealed to or warned and militated against. The point is that they change the room for maneuver and, often the timing and terminology of that maneuvering.

Perhaps more important in deciding the outcome of power struggles at the top is the character and speed of mass formation, the rate at which, and groups among which, a new type of total identification takes place. As a rule, the faster and more general the process of mass formation is, the more likely it is for the leader or group which held power at the end of Stage 3 to continue to rule. Conversely, when mass formation moves too slowly to suit the second level of revolutionary leadership, the policies of the top power holders may be modified or scrapped and the top leadership may itself be replaced. As this usually takes place early in the history of a movement and is often cloaked in informal and/or clandestine maneuverings, we tend to forget that many revolutionary leaders were not the founders of their movement and that many movement founders have been retained, if at all, only as figureheads. A contemporary example is the position of Holden Roberto in the Angolan Independence Movement. Where the revolutionary organization is disproportionately recruiting its totally committed cadres from among certain, identifiable groupings (e.g., labor unions, students, coreligionists), those who share the characteristics or seem to command the prior loyalties of these groupings may rise to positions of eminence in the supported revolutionary organization. This is another example of the interaction between the two modes of organization. Here, an already revolutionary group admits to prominence a leader still "in" the system who then brings along his following. The leaders of private armies in the Ukraine were thus attracted to the Bolshevik movement. We know, too, that the successful propagandists are often ranged against the organizers of the newly created revolutionary military units, at this stage. Even where the leadership principle is retained and the charismatic revolutionary figure retains and/or expands his power, this jockeying for position importantly affects the behavior of the movement in subsequent stages. Following Mosca[68] and others, we may assert that—in all stages of revolution —leadership positions are likely to go to men whose resources are relevant for that particular phase.

Below the top leadership level, there is constant selective recruitment and constant aggressive indoctrination to the cause. This is especially true in the communist revolutionary strategy. Whatever the splits that recur at the top, continuous reinforcement of the loyalty of recruits is necessary if the revolutionary movement is to be built. For the revolutionary goals to be attained both the conquest of power and the consolidation of power by the revolutionary party is required.[69] Thus it is necessary to make the party or movement an object of dedication and commitment, to have recruits allegiant to the movement and not be "mere fighters for better conditions."[70]

It remains for us to say something about the "new" totalistic commitment, used as an exploratory factor above.[71] This is a subject at once fascinating and frightening to the political analyst who is jolted by the differences between the limited purpose, shortrange, instrumental political identifications he is familiar with and the total, self-defeating, violence justifying commitment to "the cause," the movement. Arendt,[72] Fromm,[73] and Hoffer[74] have written insightfully on this matter—to the effect that total political commitment arises principally from a rejection of the worth of the self. Under this condition, the political arena is less painful an object of attention than is person. As autonomy requires one to "know thyself," to introspect, to continuously

review the perceived inadequate self, autonomy is yielded in favor of either ideology and abstraction (far removed from the self) or the banal routines of organization. The notions of cognitive dissonance are compatible with these explanations. Political withdrawal involves turning inward. Those who, then, poignantly find this even more threatening and futile than the previously rejected polity will be the most dissonant of persons. But these dissonances can be reduced by avidly fleeing the self and returning to political interest with more passion, but less realism, than before.

Another cognitive consistency explanation for the rejection of self and its consequent total immersion in politics can be stated. An individual can reduce the disturbance generated by profound inconsistencies between the sociopolitical order and his politicized values by placing a negative, relative value on the self. Thus:

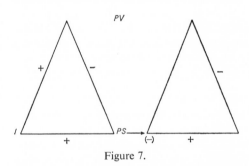

Figure 7.

Colonial situations require this of many subjects. The rejection of self, however, almost always causes severe imbalances in the cognitive set—especially with reference to aspirant values. The result may be a kind of "total dissonance" which produces "total commitment" to a political movement, to a "self-surrogate."[75] It may be reasoned that this blurring of the distinction between ego and nonego facilitates violent behavior, for it obviates a sense of person and hence personal responsibility. Those who are most dissonant are likely to be most quickly recruited to active revolutionary behavior and to be most steadfast because most satisfied by that behavior.

In sum, revolutions are made to change the self as well as society; perhaps to change the self in order to change the society. "You have to go through 15, 20, 50 years of civil wars . . .," Lenin wrote, not merely to change your conditions but to change yourself and to become qualified for political power.[76]

Stages 5 and 6: Nonviolent revolutionary politics and the outbreak of revolutionary violence

Thus far we have been focusing almost exclusively on the antisystem. This has been done for illustrative purposes only as we have known, since Aristotle, that the character of a revolution is directly related to the character of the political system in which it takes place. We know, too, that the actions which central regimes take during the early stages of a revolution are very important. Some of these matters will be considered in the concluding section of this paper.

In Stages 5 and 6 of a revolution the interactions between the political system and the antisystem are most clear and immediate. Here, as between these protagonists the situation becomes increasingly akin to a two-person, zero-sum game; the behavior of both the regime and the revolutionists being a function of the perceptions and evaluations of: (1) the character and the likely strategies and actions of its opponents; and (2) the effects of these actions on the loyalty of the general population.

·The importance of these three basic social units (i.e., regime, revolutionists, and population) derives from the social consequences of the previous stage. One outcome of mass movement consolidation accomplished in Stage 4, is a sharp increase in social polarization. Thus, much as movement-building required some previous polarization as its transitional precondition, the effective use of that movement for political purposes requires a further transitional increase in polarization which is brought about by movement-building. Under these circumstances, nascent coalitions of status quo interests are likely to be activated as the mass movement grows and becomes increasingly active. It also becomes increasingly difficult for loyal, reformist groups (system alternatives) to maintain and stress the differences between themselves and either the system or antisystem. Very often the system itself, equating dissent with disloyalty or goaded into indiscriminate repression by revolutionary terrorism, will suppress such reform groups. The unfortunate consequence of this is that the revolutionary movement becomes the only alternative to the system. In these cases, the central regime accomplishes the very thing that the revolutionary has been seeking to do, a further polarization of the polity.

To paraphrase Brinton, the existence of antagonisms among social units and classes is a ubiquitous fact of modern and modernizing societies.

But in a normal society the various antagonisms, by no means purely economic, which set class against class are subordinated by other concerns, . . . cut across by other conflicts subdued by other interests. At any rate, they are not concentrated, embittered, strengthened . . . [and we might add, cumulative].[77]

When the issue is finally joined between the competing systems, the antagonisms are concentrated, strong, embittered and cumulative and relative violence results.[78] By that time, both sides see the other as employing (or about to employ) violence effectively and hold their own use of violence as legitimate and efficacious.

Where the polarization is less strong, the uncommitted population larger, the system more open, the status quo elements weaker (or, sometimes, wiser), and/or the antisystem holds to a nonviolent ideology—the antisystem can work within the system. As we have seen in postwar France and Italy, such situations can be characterized by some level of political stability. Even if stability fails, the period of nonviolent politics serves several important revolutionary purposes. First, where the revolutionary strategy calls for infiltrating rather than (or before) mass assault on the system, this period provides time and opportunity to learn the language, styles, rules and behaviors of the system.[79]

Secondly, the revolutionary can go before the people and say "we tried." Sometimes the system is "open" to the antisystem in another sense. Plagued by confusion, self-doubt, a loss of intellectual leadership and the like, the elite may simply fail to fill elite roles, fail to fulfill elite functions. When this occurs, the system does not exactly collapse, it rather more lies empty awaiting revolutionary possession.

Where, however, the two sides see implacable hostility (i.e., futility in working out a *modus vivendi*) and significant threat, the cognitive processes discussed above operate to effect a greater likelihood of violent behavior. *The transition rule by which the revolutionary moves from non-violent politics to violence* again involves a perceived critical minimum of support for the behavior. Lenin, for example, made this decision-rule explicit when he changed Blanqui's technique by insisting that military insurrection not be attempted until agitational preparation had won a necessary minimum of the masses and had neutralized groups who otherwise might have opposed armed revolt.[80] It is commonplace to assert that, under these conditions, any "spark" can touch off the revolution. This is almost always used to escape responsibility for explaining the immediate or provocative cause of violence. Accordingly, we have nothing like an adequate understanding of these incidents. This is clearly an area which requires future study, yet it does seem both clear and important that the failure of non-violent politics causes the transition to internal war.

Stages 7 through 10: The postviolent stages of revolution

That stage of revolution which is the actual conduct of internal war requires far more consideration than can be given it here, although I shall say a few things relevant to it in the next section of this paper. Passing over this stage, there are then the four classically identified phases of revolution: (1) the rule of the moderates; (2) accession of the extremists; (3) reigns of terror; and (4) Thermidor. My objective here is to note briefly the extent to which, and the ways in which, the formulations elaborated above help to explain these phenomena.

The conduct and character of internal war and of the takeover of power do, of course, importantly influence behavior in the postviolent stages. Recruitment affects role performance and the lessons learned in recruitment by successful revolution are likely to be reapplied once power is attained. There is excellent evidence, for example, that the views of the world which revolutionaries learn (adopt) in the mountains or jungles (however distorted these may be, usually in the direction of overperception of hostility and conspiracy) constitute basic orientations to both domestic and foreign policy, later. In relatively neglecting such variables as the length and intensity of revolutionary struggle, the role of other nations in that struggle, the socioeconomic and political constraints or "confining conditions" which the successful revolutionary confronts, I am not asserting their triviality, but rather, delimiting the goals of inquiry.

It may be pointed out that one essential difference between revolutionary moderates and revolutionary extremists is in their degree of dissonance (or psychopolitical conflict); after takeover, the revolutionary leaders who have themselves attained national power are likely to be considerably less dissonant than many of their followers. The takeover of power is itself a demonstration of their efficacy, the overthrow or collapse of the system reduces or eliminates theretofore threatening objects. The valued objects for which the revolution was made can now be either created or enjoyed.

But contra to revolutionary social myths, revolutions do not create utopias. Often, indeed, they leave a good deal unchanged. For some followers, that fact of subordination means that even power relationships remain unchanged. In revolutions, as in other political situations, followers are often more radical than leaders. The more elements of the old system which are inconsistent with base values and the more of these which remain, the greater the dissonance among the revolution's second level leadership and rank and file. Under these circumstances, there is need for more change to reduce disturbance. Therefore, radicalism of extremism increases.

There is also the fact that, once power is attained and the revolutionary leadership therefore has more tangible rewards to bestow, there may be a tendency for the leaders to switch from their former inclusivist, maximal winning coalition idea to an exclusivist, minimum winning coalition basis for rewarding followers. Then too, many followers do not see themselves as yet having been personally efficacious. This produces or maintains dissatisfactions. Finally, for those who have rejected the self, there is still profound disturbance for that corporeal and psychicentity also remains, often insufficiently transformed. Hence, the effort of the extremists to capture power. Where, as in nationalist revolutions, the coalition includes both men who have made the revolution in order to modernize and those who have fought to restore tradition, some extremist effort is virtually certain and not one, but several extremisms may emerge. Thus, the common revolutionary front of Stage 4 falls apart and a Nkrumah must put down the Ashanti chieftains he had hailed as "our national rulers," or a Castro must replace the transitional Urritria.

Where the extremists are scattered and weak, this challenge may be short and sporadic or even obviated. Where the radicals are numerous and organized, the challenges come quickly and are sustained. Confronted with the problems of power, which centrally include a revolution-ravaged society, the revolutionary moderates may be seriously disadvantaged. The extremists can use the very symbols, organization and, at least some resources which the moderates developed, against the "betrayers of the revolution." Suppression of their former comrades, as Brinton indicated, may itself be dissonance-producing for the moderates. Under these conditions, the accession of the extremists takes place, rarely without some violence.

Now the outplay of aggression has been legitimized by success (perhaps twice), the efficacy of extremism has also been reinforced. The enactment of the revolutionary myth is now possible. If the utopian constructions of that myth are difficult to achieve, the tools and skills to effect the exorcism and destructive aspects of the myth abound. The attainment of power does not wholly fulfill these aspects of the myth; the reign of terror does. The followers of the extremists can reduce their dissonance, can play out their aggression, in the bloodbath. This may also effect or demonstrate the efficacy and sincerity of the new regime through the slaughtering or terrorizing of virtually all articulate potential counterrevolutionary opposition.[81]

In the long run the responsibilities and requirements of power absorb and channel the energies once allocated to the terror. Thermidor takes place when the terror is sufficiently dysfunctional for the revolutionary regime and the society it rules that it begins to produce motivating dissonance.

III. SOME INFERENCES AND QUESTIONS OF POLITICAL DEVELOPMENT AND POLITICAL VIOLENCE

From the frequency of the incidence of revolution in the developing areas, and the apparent correlation between political violence and conditions of socioeconomic development, it is clear that a theory of revolutionary behavior ought to be related to development. At this point, several alternative hypotheses and approaches suggest themselves. Is it the case, for example, that structured political violence is an integral part of, or one or more choice points in, a general developmental process: possibly a kind of systemic dysfunction regularly associated with some identifiable stages of nation-building? Alternatively, political development might well be defined, at least in part, in psychological terms such that one may identify the "violence potential" inherent in a given developmental state. Combining these two notions, it may well be that certain social-structural (and economic) conditions of development are necessary but insufficient conditions for revolution and that the reactions of human beings to these conditions supply the rest of the explanation. This would cast the problem into a series of stimulus-organism (organization)-response problems.

It certainly seems clear that political development either breaks up or is the break up of the constellation of needs, values and perceptions which inhibit revolution. Where the polity is less salient, the imbalance between polity and valued objects seems less disturbing. The more fixed or less threatened one's status, the less salient the polity. The lower one's aspirations for and from the polity, the less the dissonance. The more otherwordly a man's focus, and the less he expects to understand a rational political world, the less likely is either aspiration or alienation.

With political development all these psychological conditions become changed, untenable. The modern circumstance is more politicized, more status mobile, more aspirant, more secular, more rationalized, more intellectualized than is traditional society. Then too, modern governments tend to interpenetrate a great number of social spheres, making themselves salient to (relevant to) a greater number of personal valued objects. This may act as an "alienation-multiplier" if development fails.

Obviously, this implies neither that nations should shun development, nor that they should become paralyzed by fear that each developmental step may produce revolutionary counter effects. In the present situation there is little likelihood of either of these eventualities. The foregoing does suggest that national leaders and development planners be somewhat more sophisticated about the unwanted consequences of development. Perhaps, too, it suggests some means to attain some increased sophistication.

Initially, the population of a nation might be reconceptualized, for development policy planning, in terms of its distribution of cognitive patterns. Groups which appear to be ethnically or geographically homo-geneous may actually have a great diversity of cognitive patterns (and degrees of alienation) within it, and thus constitute not one, but several subpopulations for which different integrational symbols and development policies may be required. Conversely, groups which appear to be very different from each other, when looked at in terms of socioeconomic factors may actually be in quite similar cognitive conditions and hence constitute a single functional subpopulation.

Secondly, there is the matter of over-extending or overselling development. Particularly with reference to chronically under-developed regions within a developing society, there is often the view that "anything we can do will be useful, will provide more than they now have. That may sometimes be true, but it may also raise aspirations above realistic levels. This comes down to walking the thin line between attempting too little and too much, between promising too little to produce positive identifications and overselling (with negative effects).

In all of this, there is the matter of "development style." A confident style of development can produce substantive results, whereas substantive programs are not always able to impute confidence and legitimacy. This is particularly true in the earlier stages of revolution, as Pye has pointed out. When, for example, an individual first perceives an imbalance between his values and his polity, he may hunt around for an alternative within the ongoing political system on which to peg his hopes. The more there are loyal reformist alternatives, the more people will find their aspirations tied to the center. When the only choice that is left open is between status quo elites and the insurgents, a greater percentage of the population are likely to become at least passively alienated. This suggests that the growth and proliferation of interest organizations be at least tolerated if not encouraged. However untidy this may seem to planners, such organizations constitute the vital intermediate associations which link men to the polity and which, by insulating both elites and nonelites, inhibit the conditions of mass society.

On the other hand, if forceful responses are to be employed, a confident, timely and discriminating use of force is indicated. The vacillating fits and starts approach to violence produces the very perception of governmental inefficacy which induces initial alienation. Delays moreover, may mean that the harsher, less discriminating force which activates passive alienation will have to be used later.

Finally, our theory has something to say regarding psychological operations and general policy in counterinsurgency. As revolutions are made by men who feel inefficacious within the political system, a "preventive counterinsurgency" can be effected by keeping the system open, permeable. Political symbols, to effect national integration, should be inclusivist, not exclusivist. The new institutions created in the process of political development should be accessible (as to policy, personnel and structure) to those who politicization is effected in the same process. To open men's eyes and minds to the possibilities of change and close to them the political system through which those changes may be brought about, may be political development for some, but it is surely a formula for violence.

These are the generalities, perhaps too value-laden and not even glittering. We can be more specific. The revolutionary is necessarily under great psychological cross pressure, and, hence, is available or amenable for manipulation by psychological operations. The theory of cognitive consistency suggests that his perceptual screen (predispositions) have two important elements: (1) he perceives (and very much wants to perceive) a great difference between the central government and his movement (band) or its future government; (2) he prefers the latter. If the propaganda of the central government insists that "yes, there is a great difference between the two 'governments' but that the existing government is better," all that he may hear is "yes, there is a great difference." This reinforces his insurgency behavior.

Cognitive dissonance may also help to explain the passive alienation of mature populations caught between revolutionaries and counterinsurgents. Caused to pay taxes and to perform services for the insurgents, when they don't feel much loyalty to the revolution creates what cognitive consistency theorists call "counter-attitudinal dissonance." When the counter insurgents weaken or remove the stimulus by partially or completely protecting the native population from the revolutionaries, they often expect to recover peasant loyalties quickly. This would be a legitimate expectation if the peasant behavior was simply fear-motivated. As it is not, but is rather driven by complex motivation (i.e., is reinforced by dissonance), the response tendency extinguishes much more slowly. Governments are well advised to meet their people's needs before passive alienation occurs; for though withdrawal may appear to yield decision-latitude in the short run, it produces the conditions for revolution in the not-so-long-run.

IV. CONCLUSION

Men have been slaying each other over political things forever. In this, is our past but prologue, and revolution the inevitable condition of man? The very conception of revolution as a process implies the notion of choice-points. To speak of structural violence as a social process is not to celebrate the operation of impersonal forces but rather to emphasize the special responsibilities of those empowered to choose by societies and social groupings. The scholar analyzes revolution as a process in order to identify more precisely the conditions under which revolutionary behavior obtains, connoting by his emphasis on social (and especially developmental) policy, that men can alter their conditions in peaceful, as well as, revolutionary fashion.

No political system can perfectly represent the distinctive genius of its people nor instantly adjust to the ever-shifting distribution of power and purposes within a society. If such were the conditions of social peace there would be, could be, no surcease from civil strife. Revolutions are surely more than the outplay of personal processes, but neither do they occur in the absence of revolutionary men. The modern social scientist tends increasingly to seek the relevant conditions of revolutions in those which touch and energize the actor.

To him who makes it, a revolution becomes a reason for being, an engagement with the cosmic, an identification of the self with history; indeed, a transmutation of the self. Revolutions occur when the core of that self—the self-defining characteristics of a people—are threatened or demeaned. The, of course, personal processes become politicized and one wages internal war for to do other is to be less than a man.

If we have been at political slaughter forever, may it not be that our politics has profoundly threatened or demeaned some of us that long? Those who sow the wind of repression, heedless of their fellows aspirations and identities, may not reap the whirlwind, but others shall!

Though no political system can be perfectly integrated nor instantly self-regulating, revolutions are not the constant consequence, for neither are the grossly demeaning mismatches between politics and person ever-present. To establish and maintain an appropriately adaptive polity, to identify and adopt responsive social practices, so as to inure to social peace—these are the tasks, the problems and opportunities of political men. Unlike inefficient repression, but not unlike that force which is good governance, these tasks require knowledge; perhaps a revolution in our political knowledge-making. Here, the unevenly increasing power of the social sciences may be useful. Here, the problems and opportunities of the scholar become historic. Understanding the causes, character and consequences of political violence appears today to be at once both more necessary and more feasible than in the past. Both the problems and the opportunities are growing.

This paper has been an effort to provide a more comprehensive understanding of one form of political violence, revolution. Any such effort, it is said, may be expected to raise as many questions as it answers. This is certainly true of this chapter but it is, in itself, a limited virtue. Unless the new questions are better questions, unless they are better grounded in theory (i.e., unless we know why the questions arise) and unless we can anticipate how important the questions are (i.e., unless we are seeking "correction factors" for the general formulations from which the new questions arise), we may merely be engaged in pursuit of the trivial.

The theory propounded above does give rise to a variety of new questions; hopefully these are better formulated, theoretically derived objects of inquiry. To answer these questions, much work must be done. Each stage of the theory must be related to an existing related set of theories. The notion of initial alienation set forth here can and should be fructified by new work of sociologists and psychologists on alienation and anomie. The development of revolutionary organizations should be related to organization theory. Communications analysts need be consulted on the mass appeals stage of revolution. And so on.

Then too, culture and area specialists may provide both regional and national correction factors. Historical knowledge is required to test out propositions regarding revolutionary periodicity. Economists and international relations specialists would also quickly find important problems to turn their hands to.

The same thing is also true as regards the other forms of political violence—coup, riot, violence as interest articulation. Interdisciplinary skills and perspectives are called for. Indeed, other and better efforts at comprehensive theory building than this one are called for.

The phenomena of revolution—objects of long, continuous and increasing attention in social study—have not yet been explained in a comprehensive, theoretically integrated manner. But we may seek better to do so.

The revolutionary state of mind

The following article in some of its language appears to be in the conventional tradition of socioeconomic analysis, because it flatly says that revolution is most likely to occur when a prolonged period of socioeconomic upswing is followed by a short and sharp reversal of the long upswing. From discussions that others and I have had with the author, it appears that there has been legitimate grounds for some confusion. The graph below (Figure 1) of the J curve more accurately represents his viewpoint than the abovementioned socioeconomic statement.

The thesis is a fundamentally psychological one, referring to individuals rather than social aggregates: revolution is most likely to occur when a long period of rising expectations and gratifications is followed by a period during which gratifications (socioeconomic or otherwise) suddenly drop off while expectations (socioeconomic or otherwise) continue to rise. The rapidly widening gap between expectations and gratifications portends revolution. The most common case for this widening gap of individual dissatisfactions is economic or social dislocation that makes the affected individual generally tense, generally frustrated. That is, the greatest portion of people who join a revolution are preoccupied with tensions related to the failure to gratify the physical (economic) needs and the needs for stable interpersonal (social) relationships.

These are the ones, the following theory says, who are most likely to be the hewers of wood for scaffolds and the drawers of tumbrels—and to form the massive crowds that witness the execution of the old régime. The majority of revolutionaries thus are likely to be poor people at loose ends who have made some progress toward a new and better life and see themselves now failing to do so.

But socioeconomically deprived poor people are unlikely to make a successful rebellion, a revolution, by themselves. Their discontent needs the addition of the discontents developing among individuals in the middle class and the ruling class when they are rather suddenly deprived (socioeconomically or otherwise). Without the support of disaffected bourgeoisie, disaffected nobles, and disaffected intellectuals, the French Revolution might have been some kind of grand, episodic upheaval. But it would not likely have amounted to the successful assault on the political power structure that a revolution amounts to. The same may be said for the American

Revolution. Those who signed the Declaration of Independence and/or became rulers of the new nation were gentlemen farmers like Washington and Jefferson rather than callous-handed yeomen, who became the rank and file of the Continental Army. The Russian Revolution, particularly in its 1905 phase, depended on the disaffection not solely of factory workers and peasants but also of urban bourgeoisie and—almost incredibly it seemed at first glance—of substantial numbers of the landed nobility.

The unit of analysis below is therefore not a vast or a small social aggregate, a peasantry or an elite, but consists of individual human beings. Whatever their state of advancement—from men who work with their hands and lose factory jobs or see prices fall for the product of their fields to intellectuals who graduate from university with high honors and find themselves without jobs that fit their training—such individuals see a gap widening between their rising expectations and downturning gratifications. The interests of these visibly very different people may in the long run be directly counter to those of others with whom they for a time work together. But during the revolution they all share a high degree of frustration directed toward the government and the incumbent ruling "class." It is this frustrated state of mind, shared and focused on the government, that produces their cooperation.

In addition to the *J* curve hypothesis there are alternative and additional explanations for the development of the revolutionary state of mind. It may be that gratifications do not suddenly fall but continue to rise, but not so rapidly as expectations rise, with the result that the gap between the two widens without a downturn in gratifications. There may be cases in which violence breaks out after a steady but too-slow rise in gratifications. On the other hand, a close look at the events immediately preceding the outbreak of a period of violence always seems to reveal such acts as the violent suppression of a demonstration, the roughing-up of a worker or poor farmer or a black—or some other event in which there is a clearcut but scarcely visible downturn in the (mental) belief that rewards will continue to meet expectations. Tear gas or a billy club are not rising gratifications, nor do they produce rising expectations. They dash the expectation that tear gas will not be used and that the public park will at last be integrated. And so they hurt.

Toward a theory of revolution

JAMES C. DAVIES

James C. Davies, "Toward a Theory of Revolution," is reprinted with permission of the author. Copyright by and reprinted with permission of The American Sociological Association, from the *American Sociological Review*, 6(1), pp. 5–19, February 1962.

Notes to this section will be found on pages 338-339,

Revolutions are most likely to occur when a prolonged period of objective economic and social development is followed by a short period of sharp reversal. People then subjectively fear that ground gained with great effort will be quite lost; their mood becomes revolutionary. The evidence from Dorr's Rebellion, the Russian Revolution, and the Egyptian Revolution supports this notion; tentatively, so do data on other civil disturbances. Various statistics—as on rural uprisings, industrial strikes, unemployment, and cost of living—may serve as crude indexes of popular mood. More useful, though less easy to obtain, are direct questions in cross-sectional interviews. The goal of predicting revolution is conceived but not yet born or matured.

In exhorting proletarians of all nations to unite in revolution, because they had nothing to lose but their chains, Marx and Engels most succinctly presented that theory of revolution which is recognized as their brain child. But this most famed thesis, that progressive degradation of the industrial working class would finally reach the point of despair and inevitable revolt, is not the only one that Marx fathered. In at least one essay he gave life to a quite antithetical idea. He described, as a precondition of widespread unrest, not progressive degradation of the proletariat but rather an improvement in workers' economic condition which did not keep pace with the growing welfare of capitalists and therefore produced social tension.

A noticeable increase in wages presupposes a rapid growth of productive capital. The rapid growth of productive capital brings about an equally rapid growth of wealth, luxury, social wants, social enjoyments. Thus, although the enjoyments of the workers have risen, the social satisfaction that they give has fallen in comparison with the increased enjoyments of the capitalist, which are inaccessible to the worker, in comparison with the state of development of society in general. Our desires and pleasures spring from society; we measure them, therefore, by society and not by the objects which serve for their satisfaction. Because they are of a social nature, they are of a relative nature.[2]

Marx's qualification here of his more frequent belief that degradation produces revo-

lution is expressed as the main thesis by Tocqueville in his study of the French Revolution. After a long review of economic and social decline in the 17th century and dynamic growth in the 18th, Tocqueville concludes:

So it would appear that the French found their condition the more unsupportable in proportion to its improvement. . . . Revolutions are not always brought about by a gradual decline from bad to worse. Nations that have endured patiently and almost unconsciously the most overwhelming oppression often burst into rebellion against the yoke the moment it begins to grow lighter. The regime which is destroyed by a revolution is almost always an improvement on its immediate predecessor. . . . Evils which are patiently endured when they seem inevitable become intolerable when once the idea of escape from them is suggested.[3]

On the basis of Tocqueville and Marx, we can choose one of these ideas or the other, which makes it hard to decide just when revolutions are more likely to occur—when there has been social and economic progress or when there has been regress. It appears that both ideas have explanatory and possibly predictive value, if they are juxtaposed and put in the proper time sequence.

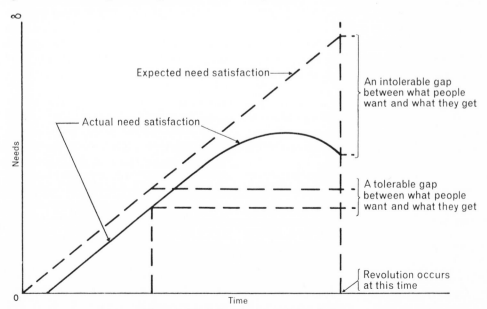

Figure 1. Need Satisfaction and Revolution.

Revolutions are most likely to occur when a prolonged period of objective economic and social development is followed by a short period of sharp reversal.[4] The all-important effect on the minds of people in a particular society is to produce, during the former period, an expectation of continued ability to satisfy needs—which continue to rise—and, during the latter, a mental state of anxiety and frustration when manifest reality breaks away from anticipated reality. The actual state of socioeconomic development is less significant than the expectation that past progress, now blocked, can and must continue in the future.

Political stability and instability are ultimately, dependent on a state of mind, a mood, in a society. Satisfied or apathetic people who are poor in goods, status, and power can remain politically quiet and their opposites can revolt, just as, correlatively and more probably, dissatisfied poor can revolt and satisfied rich oppose revolution. It is the dissatisfied state of mind rather than the tangible provision of "adequate" or "inadequate" supplies of food, equality, or liberty which produces the revolution. In actuality, there must be a joining of forces between dissatisfied, frustrated people who differ in their degree of objective, tangible welfare and status. Well fed, well educated high-status individuals who rebel in the face of apathy among the objectively deprived can accomplish at most a coup d'état. The objectively deprived, when faced with solid opposition of people of wealth, status, and power, will be smashed in their rebellion as were peasants and Anabaptists by German noblemen in 1525 and East Germans by the Communist élite in 1953.

Before appraising this general notion in light of a series of revolutions, a word is in order as to why revolutions ordinarily do not occur when a society is generally impoverished—when, as de Tocqueville put it, evils that seem inevitable are patiently endured. They are endured in the extreme case because the physical and mental energies of people are totally employed in the process of merely staying alive. The Minnesota starvation studies conducted during World War II[5] indicate clearly the constant preoccupation of very hungry individuals with fantasies and thoughts of food. *In extremis*, as the Minnesota research poignantly demonstrates, the individual withdraws into a life of his own, withdraws from society, withdraws from any significant kind of activity unrelated to staying alive. Reports of behavior in Nazi concentration camps indicate the same preoccupation.[6] In less extreme and barbarous circumstances, where minimal survival is possible but little more, the preoccupation of individuals with staying alive is only mitigated. Social action takes place for the most part on a local, face-to-face basis. In such circumstances the family is a—perhaps the major—solidary unit[7] and even the local community exists primarily to the extent families need to act together to secure their separate survival. Such was life on the American frontier in the 16th through 19th centuries. In very much attenuated form, but with a substantial degree of social isolation persisting, such evidently is rural life even today. This is clearly related to a relatively low level of political participation in elections.[8] As Zawadzki and Lazarsfeld have indicated,[9] preoccupation with physical survival, even in industrial areas, is a force strongly militating against the establishment of the community-sense and consensus on joint political action which are necessary to induce a revolutionary state of mind. Far from making people into revolutionaries, enduring poverty makes for concern with one's solitary self or solitary family at best and resignation or mute despair at worst. When it is a choice between losing their chains or their lives, people will mostly choose to keep their chains, a fact which Marx seems to have overlooked.[10]

It is when the chains have been loosened somewhat, so that they can be cast off without a high probability of losing life, that people are put in a condition of proto-rebelliousness. I use the term protorebelliousness because the mood of discontent may be dissipated before a violent outbreak occurs. The causes for such dissipation may be natural or social (including economic and political). A bad crop year that threatens a return to chronic hunger may be succeeded by a year of natural abundance. Recovery from sharp economic dislocation may take the steam from the boiler of rebellion.[11] The slow, grudging grant of reforms, which has been the political history of England since at least the Industrial Revolution, may effectively and continuously prevent the degree of frustration that produces revolt.

A revolutionary state of mind requires the continued, even habitual but dynamic expectation of greater opportunity to satisfy basic needs, which may range from merely physical (food, clothing, shelter, health, and safety from bodily harm) to social (the affectional ties of family and friends) to the need for equal dignity and justice. But the necessary additional ingredient is a persistent, unrelenting threat to the satisfaction of these needs: not a threat which actually returns people to a state of sheet survival but which puts them in the mental state where they believe they will not be able to satisy one or more basic needs. Although physical deprivation in some degree may be threatened on the eve of all revolutions, it need not be the prime factor, as it surely was not in the American Revolution of 1775. The crucial factor is the vague or specific fear that ground gained over a long period of time will be quickly lost. This fear does not generate if there is continued opportunity to satisfy continually emerging needs; it generates when the existing government suppresses or is blamed for suppressing such opportunity.

Three rebellions or revolutions are given considerable attention in the sections that follow: Dorr's Rebellion of 1842, the Russian Revolution of 1917, and the Egyptian Revolution of 1952. Brief mention is then made of several other major civil disturbances, all of which appear to fit the *J* curve pattern.[12] After considering these specific disturbances, some general theoretical and research problems are discussed.

No claim is made that all rebellions follow the pattern, but just that the ones here presented do. All of these are "progressive" revolutions in behalf of greater equality and liberty. The question is open whether the pattern occurs in such markedly retrogressive revolutions as Nazism in Germany or the 1861 Southern rebellion in the United States. It will surely be necessary to examine other progressive revolutions before one can judge how universal the *J* curve is. And it will be necessary, in the interests of scientific validation, to examine cases of serious civil disturbance that fell short of producing profound revolution—such as the Sepoy Rebellion of 1857 in India, the Pullman Strike of 1894 in America, the Boxer Rebellion of 1900 in China, and the Great Depression of the 1920s and 1930s as it was experienced in Austria, France, Great Britain, and the United States. The explanation for such stillborn rebellions —for revolutions that might have occurred— is inevitably more complicated than for those that come to term in the "normal" course of political gestation.

DORR'S REBELLION OF 1842

Dorr's Rebellion[13] in nineteenth-century America was perhaps the first of many civil disturbances to occur in America as a consequence, in part, of the Industrial Revolution. It followed by three years an outbreak in England that had similar roots and a similar program—the Chartist agitation. A machine-operated textile industry was first established in Rhode Island in 1790 and grew rapidly as a consequence of domestic and international demand, notably during the Napoleonic Wars. Jefferson's Embargo Act of 1807, the War of 1812, and a high tariff in 1816 further stimulated American industry.

Rapid industrial growth meant the movement of people from farms to cities. In Massachusetts the practice developed of hiring mainly the wives and daughters of farmers, whose income was thereby supplemented but not displaced by wages. In Rhode Island whole families moved to the cities and became committed to the factory system. When times were good, industrialized families earned two or three times what they got from the soil; when the mills were idle, there was not enough money for bread.[14] From 1807 to 1815 textiles enjoyed great prosperity; from 1834 to 1842 they suffered depression, most severely from 1835 to 1840. Prosperity raised expectations and depression frustrated them, particularly when accompanied by stubborn resistance to suffrage demands that first stirred in 1790 and recurred in a wave-like pattern in 1811 and then in 1818 and 1820 following suffrage extension in Connecticut and Massachusetts. The final crest was reached in 1841, when suffrage associations met and called for a constitutional convention.[15]

Against the will of the government, the suffragists held an election in which all adult males were eligible to vote, held a constitutional convention composed of delegates so elected and in December 1841 submitted the People's Constitution to the same electorate, which approved it and the call for an election

new government. The next day the People's legislature met and respectfully requested the sheriff to take possession of state buildings, which he failed to do. Violence broke out on the 17th of May in an attempt to take over a state arsenal with two British cannon left over from the Revolutionary War. When the cannon misfired, the People's government resigned. Sporadic violence continued for another month, resulting in the arrest of over 500 men, mostly textile workers, mechanics, and laborers. The official legislature called for a new constitutional convention, chosen by universal manhood suffrage, and a new constitution went into effect in January, 1843. Altogether only one person was killed in this little revolution, which experienced

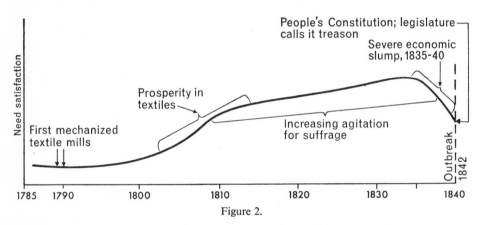

Figure 2.

of state officers the following April, to form a new government under this unconstitutional constitution.[16]

These actions joined the conflict with the established government. When asked—by the dissidents—the state supreme court rendered its private judgment in March 1842 that the new constitution was "of no binding force whatever" and any act "to carry it into effect by force will be treason against the state." The legislature passed what became known as the Algerian law, making it an offense punishable by a year in jail to vote in the April election, and by life imprisonment to hold office under the People's Constitution.

The rebels went stoutly ahead with the election, and on May 3, 1842 inaugurated the

violence, failure, and then success within the space of nine months.

It is impossible altogether to separate the experience of rising expectations among people in Rhode Island from that among Americans generally. They all shared historically the struggle against a stubborn but ultimately rewarding frontier where their self-confidence gained strength not only in the daily process of tilling the soil and harvesting the crops but also by improving their skill at self-government. Winning their war of independence, Americans continued to press for more goods and more democracy. The pursuit of economic expectations was greatly facilitated by the growth of domestic and foreign trade and the gradual establishment of industry. Equalitarian expectations in politics were satisfied and without severe struggle—in most Northern states—by suffrage reforms.

In Rhode Island, these rising expectations —more goods, more equality, more self-rule —were countered by a series of containing forces which built up such a head of steam that the boiler cracked a little in 1842. The textile depression hit hard in 1835 and its consequences were aggravated by the Panic of 1837. In addition to the frustration of seeing their peers get the right to vote in other states, poor people in Rhode Island were now beset by industrial dislocation in which the machines that brought them prosperity they had never before enjoyed now were bringing economic disaster. The machines could not be converted to produce food and in Rhode Island the machine tenders could not go back to the farm.

When they had recovered from the preoccupation with staying alive, they turned in earnest to their demands for constitutional reform. But these were met first with indifference and then by a growing intransigence on the part of the government representing the propertied class. Hostile action by the state supreme court and then the legislature with its Algerian law proved just enough to break briefly the constitutional structure which in stable societies has the measure of power and resilience necessary to absorb social tension.

THE RUSSIAN REVOLUTION OF 1917

In Russia's tangled history it is hard to decide when began the final upsurge of expectations, that, when frustrated, produced the cataclysmic events of 1917. One can truly say that the real beginning was the slow modernization process begun by Peter the Great over two hundred years before the revolution. And surely the rationalist currents from France that slowly penetrated Russian intellectual life during the reign of Catherine the Great a hundred years before the revolution were necessary, lineal antecedents of the 1917 revolution.

Without denying that there was an accumulation of forces over at least a 200-year period,[17] we may nonetheless date the final

upsurge as beginning with the 1861 emancipation of serfs and reaching a crest in the 1905 revolution.

The chronic and growing unrest of serfs before their emancipation in 1861 is an ironic commentary on the Marxian notion that human beings are what social institutions make them. Although serfdom had been shaping their personality since 1647, peasants became increasingly restive in the second quarter of the 19th century.[18] The continued discontent of peasants after emancipation is an equally ironic commentary on the belief that relieving one profound frustration produces enduring contentment. Peasants rather quickly got over their joy at being untied from the soil after two hundred years. Instead of declining, rural violence increased.[19] Having gained freedom but not much free land, peasants now had to rent or buy land to survive: virtual personal slavery was exchanged for financial servitude. Land pressure grew, reflected in a doubling of land prices between 1868 and 1897.

It is hard thus to tell whether the economic plight of peasants was much lessened after emancipation. A 1903 government study indicated that even with a normal harvest, average food intake per peasant was 30 per cent below the minimum for health. The only sure contrary item of evidence is that

Table 1. *Population of European Russia (1480–1895)*

	POPULATION IN MILLIONS	INCREASE IN MILLIONS	AVERAGE ANNUAL RATE OF INCREASE*
1480	2.1	—	—
1580	4.3	2.2	1.05%
1680	12.6	8.3	1.93%
1780	26.8	14.2	1.13%
1880	84.5	57.7	2.15%
1895	110.0	25.5	2.02%

* Computed as follows: dividing the increase by the number of years and then dividing this hypothetical annual increase by the population at the end of the preceding 100-year period.
Source for gross population data: *Entsiklopedicheskii Slovar*, St. Petersburg, 1897, vol. 40, p. 631. Russia's population was about 97% rural in 1784, 91% in 1878, and 87% in 1897. See Masaryk, *op. cit.*, p. 162n.

the peasant population grew, indicating at least increased ability of the land to support life, as the table shows.

The land-population pressure pushed people into towns and cities, where the rapid growth of industry truly afforded the chance for economic betterment. One estimate of net annual income for a peasant family of five in the rich blackearth area in the late nineteenth century was 82 rubles. In contrast, a "good" wage for a male factory worker was about 168 rubles per year. It was this difference in the degree of poverty that produced almost a doubling of the urban population between 1878 and 1897. The number of industrial workers increased almost as rapidly. The city and the factory gave new hope. Strikes in the 1880s were met with brutal suppression but also with the beginning of factory legislation, including the requirement that wages be paid regularly and the abolition of child labor. The burgeoning proletariat remained comparatively contented until the eve of the 1905 revolution.[20]

There is additional, noneconomic evidence to support the view that 1861 to 1905 was the period of rising expectations that preceded the 1917 revolution. The administration of justice before the emancipation had largely been carried out by noblemen and landowners who embodied the law for their peasants. In 1864 justice was in principle no longer delegated to such private individuals. Trials became public, the jury system was introduced, and judges got tenure. Corporal punishment was alleviated by the elimination of running the gauntlet, lashing, and branding; caning persisted until 1904. Public joy at these reforms was widespread. For the intelligentsia, there was increased opportunity to think and write and to criticize established institutions, even sacrosanct absolutism itself.

But Tsarist autocracy had not quite abandoned the scene. Having inclined but not bowed, in granting the inevitable emancipation as an act not of justice but grace, it sought to maintain its absolutist principle by conceding reform without accepting anything like democratic authority. Radical political and economic criticism surged higher. Some strong efforts to raise the somewhat lowered floodgates began as early as 1866, after an unsuccessful attempt was made on the life of Alexander II, in whose name serfs had just gained emancipation. When the attempt succeeded fifteen years later, there was increasing state action under Alexander III to limit constantly rising expectations. By suppression and concession, the last Alexander succeeded in dying naturally in 1894.

When it became apparent that Nicholas II shared his father's ideas but not his forcefulness, opposition of the intelligentsia to absolutism joined with the demands of peasants and workers, who remained loyal to the Tsar but demanded economic reforms. Starting in 1904, there developed a "League of Deliverance" that coordinated efforts of at least seventeen other revolutionary, proletarian, or nationalist groups within the empire. Consensus on the need for drastic reform, both political and economic, established a many-ringed circus of groups sharing the same tent. These groups were geographically distributed from Finland to Armenia and ideologically from liberal constitutionalists to revolutionaries made prudent by the contrast between their own small forces and the power of Tsardom.

Events of 1904–05 marked the general downward turning point of expectations, which people increasingly saw as frustrated by the continuation of Tsardom. Two major and related occurrences made 1905 the point of no return. The first took place on the Bloody Sunday on January 22, 1905, when peaceful proletarian petitioners marched on the St. Petersburg palace and were killed by the hundreds. The myth that the Tsar was the gracious protector of his subjects, however surrounded he might be by malicious advisers, was quite shattered. The reaction was immediate, bitter, and prolonged and was not at all confined to the working class. Employers, merchants, and white-collar officials joined in the burgeoning of strikes which brought the economy to a virtual standstill in October. Some employers even continued to pay wages to strikers. University students and faculties joined the revolution. After the great October strike, the peasants ominously sided with the workers and engaged in riots and assaults on landowners. Until peasants became involved, even some landowners had sided with the revolution.

The other major occurrence was the disastrous defeat of the Russian army and navy in the 1904–05 war with Japan. Fundamentally an imperialist venture aspiring to hegemony over the people of Asia, the war was not regarded as a people's but as a Tsar's war, to save and spread absolutism. The military defeat itself probably had less portent than the return of shattered soldiers from a fight that was not for them. Hundreds of thousands, wounded or not, returned from the war as a visible, vocal, and ugly reminder to the entire populace of the weakness and selfishness of Tsarist absolutism.

The years from 1905 to 1917 formed an almost relentless procession of increasing misery and despair. Promising at last a constitutional government, the Tsar, in October, 1905, issued from on high a proclamation renouncing absolutism, granting law-making power to a duma, and guaranteeing freedom of speech, assembly, and association. The first two dumas, of 1906 and 1907, were dissolved for recalcitrance. The third was made pliant by reduced representation of workers and peasants and by the prosecution and conviction of protestants in the first two. The brief period of a free press was succeeded in 1907 by a reinstatement of censorship and confiscation of prohibited publications. Trial of offenders against the Tsar was now conducted by courts martial. Whereas there had been only 26 executions of the death sentence, in the 13 years of Alexander II's firm rule (1881–94), there were 4,449 in the years 1905–10, in six years of Nicholas II's soft regimen.[21]

But this "white terror," which caused despair among the workers and intelligentsia in the cities, was not the only face of misery. For the peasants, there was a bad harvest in 1906 followed by continued crop failures in several areas in 1907. To forestall action by the dumas, Stolypin decreed a series of

agrarian reforms designed to break up the power of the rural communes by individualizing land ownership. Between these acts of God and government, peasants were so preoccupied with hunger or self-aggrandizement as to be dulled in their sensitivity to the revolutionary appeals of radical organizers.

After more than five years of degrading terror and misery, in 1910 the country appeared to have reached a condition of exhaustion. Political strikes had fallen off to a new low. As the economy recovered, the insouciance of hopelessness set in. Amongst the intelligentsia the mood was hedonism, or despair that often ended in suicide. Industrialists aligned themselves with the government. Workers worked. But an upturn of expectations, inadequately quashed by the police, was evidenced by a recrudescence of political strikes which, in the first half of 1914—on the eve of war—approached the peak of 1905. They sharply diminished during 1915 but grew again in 1916 and became a general strike in February 1917.[22]

Figure 3 indicates the lesser waves in the tidal wave whose first trough is at the end of serfdom in 1861 and whose second is at the end of Tsardom in 1917. This fifty-six year period appears to constitute a single long phase in which popular gratification at the termination of one institution (serfdom) rather quickly was replaced with rising expectations which resulted from intensified industrialization and which were incompatible with the continuation of the inequitable and capricious power structure of Tsarist society. The small trough of frustration during the repression that followed the assassination of Alexander II seems to have only briefly interrupted the rise in popular demand for more goods and more power. The trough in 1904 indicates the consequences of war with Japan. The 1905–06 trough reflects the repression of January 22, and after, and as followed by economic recovery. The final downturn, after the first year of war, was a consequence of the dislocations of the German attack on all kinds of concerted activities other than production for the prosecution of the war. Patriotism and governmental repression for a time smothered discontent. The inflation that developed in 1916 when goods, including food, became severely scarce began to make workers self-consciously discontented. The conduct of the war, including the growing brutality against reluctant, ill-provisioned troops, and the enormous loss of life, produced the same bitter frustration in the army.[23] When civilian discontent reached the breaking point in February, 1917, it did not take long for it to spread rapidly into the armed forces. Thus began the second phase

national rather than religious grounds and helped establish a fairly unified community—in striking contrast to late 19th-century Russia.

But nationalist aspirations were not the only rising expectations in Egypt of the 1920s and 1930s. World War I had spurred industrialization, which opened opportunities for peasants to improve, somewhat, their way of life by working for wages in the cities and also opened great opportunities for entrepreneurs to get rich. The moder-

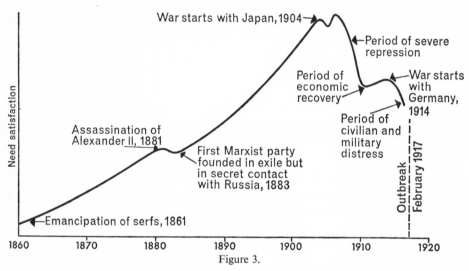

Figure 3.

of the revolution that really started in 1905 and ended in death to the Tsar and Tsardom —but not to absolutism—when the Bolsheviks gained ascendancy over the moderates in October. A centuries-long history of absolutism appears to have made this post-Tsarist phase of it tragically inevitable.

THE EGYPTIAN REVOLUTION OF 1952

The final slow upsurge of expectations in Egypt that culminated in the revolution began when that society became a nation in 1922, with the British grant of limited independence. British troops remained in Egypt to protect not only the Suez Canal but also, ostensibly, to prevent foreign aggression. The presence of foreign troops served only to heighten nationalist expectations, which were excited by the Wafd, the political organization that formed public opinion on

ately wealthy got immoderately so in commodity market speculation, finance, and manufacture, and the uprooted peasants who were now employed, or at any rate living, in cities were relieved of at least the notion that poverty and boredom must be the will of Allah. But the incongruity of a money-based modern semi-feudality that was like a chariot with a gasoline engine evidently escaped the attention of ordinary people. The generation of the 1930s could see more rapid progress, even for themselves, than their parents had even envisioned. If conditions remained poor, they could always be blamed on the British, whose economic and military power remained visible and strong.

Economic progress continued, though unevenly, during World War II. Conventional exports, mostly cotton, actually declined, not even reaching depression levels until 1945, but direct employment by Allied military forces reached a peak of over 200,000 during the most intense part of the African war. Exports after the war rose steadily until 1948, dipped, and then rose sharply to a peak in 1951 as a consequence of the Korean war. But in 1945 over 250,000 wage earners[24]—probably over a third of the working force—became jobless. The cost of living by 1945 had risen to three times the index of 1937.[25] Manual laborers were hit by unemployment; white-collar workers and professionals probably more by inflation than unemployment. Meanwhile the number of millionaires in pounds sterling had increased eight times during the war.[26]

Frustration, exacerbated during the war by German and thereafter by Soviet propaganda, were at first deflected against the British[27] but gradually shifted closer to home. Egyptian agitators began quoting the Koran in favor of a just, equalitarian society and against great differences in individual wealth. There was an ominous series of strikes, mostly in the textile mills, from 1946–48.

At least two factors stand out in the postponement of revolution. The first was the insatiable postwar world demand for cotton and textiles and the second was the surge of solidarity with king and country that followed the 1948 invasion of the new state of Israel. Israel now supplemented England as an object of deflected frustration. The disastrous defeat a year later, by a new nation with but a fifteenth of Egypt's population, was the beginning of the end. This little war had struck the peasant at his hearth, when a shortage of wheat and of oil for stoves provided a daily reminder of a weak and corrupt government. The defeat frustrated popular hopes for national glory and—with even more portent—humiliated the army and solidified it against the bureaucracy and the palace which had profiteered at the expense of national honor. In 1950 began for the first time a direct and open propaganda attack against the king himself. A series of peasant uprisings, even on the lands of the king, took place in 1951 along with some 49 strikes in the cities. The skyrocketing demand for cotton after the start of the Korean War in June, 1950 was followed by a collapse in March, 1952. The uncontrollable or uncontrolled riots in Cairo, on January 26, 1952, marked the fiery start of the revolution. The officers' coup in the early morning of July 23 only made it official.

OTHER CIVIL DISTURBANCES

The *J* curve of rising expectations followed by their effective frustration is applicable to other revolutions and rebellions than just the three already considered. Leisler's Rebellion in the royal colony of New York in 1689 was a brief dress-rehearsal for the American Revolution eighty-six years later. In an effort to make the colony serve the crown better, duties had been raised and were being vigorously collected. The tanning of hides in the colony was forbidden, as was the distillation of liquor. An embargo was placed on unmilled grain, which hurt the farmers. After a long period of economic growth and substantial political autonomy, these new and burdensome regulations produced a popular rebellion that for a year displaced British sovereignty.[28]

The American Revolution itself fits the *J* curve and deserves more than the brief mention here given. Again prolonged economic growth and political autonomy produced continually rising expectations. They became acutely frustrated when, following the French and Indian War (which had cost England so much and the colonies so little), England began a series of largely economic regulations having the same purpose as those directed against New York in the preceding century. From the 1763 Proclamation (closing to settlement land west of the Appalachians) to the Coercive Acts of April, 1774 (which among other things, in response to the December 1773 Boston Tea Party, closed tight the port of Boston), Americans were beset with unaccustomed manifestations of British power and began to resist forcibly in 1775, on the Lexington–Concord road. A significant decline in trade with England in 1772[29] may have hastened the maturation of colonial rebelliousness.

The curve also fits the French Revolution,

which again merits more mention than space here permits. Growing rural prosperity, marked by steadily rising land values in the 18th century, had progressed to the point where a third of French land was owned by peasant-proprietors. There were the beginnings of large-scale manufacture in the factory system. Constant pressure by the bourgeosie against the state for reforms was met with considerable hospitality by a government already shifting from its old landed-aristocratic and clerical base to the

deed be said to have precipitated the revolution. But less well known is the fact that 1787 was a bad harvest year and 1788 even worse; that by July, 1789 bread prices were higher than they had been in over seventy years; that an ill-timed trade treaty with England depressed the prices of French textiles; that a concurrent bumper grape crop depressed wine prices—all with the result of making desperate the plight of the large segment of the population now dependent on other producers for food. They had

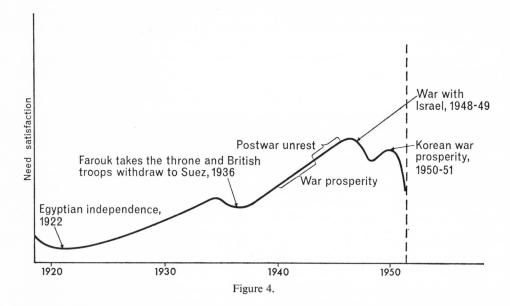

Figure 4.

growing middle class. Counter to these trends, which would *per se* avoid revolution, was the feudal reaction of the mid-18th century, in which the dying nobility sought in numerous nagging ways to retain and reactivate its perquisites against a resentful peasantry and importunate bourgeoisie.

But expectations apparently continued rising until the growing opportunities and prosperity rather abruptly halted, about 1787. The fiscal crisis of the government is well known, much of it a consequence of a 1.5 billion livre deficit following intervention against Britain in the American war of independence. The threat to tax the nobility severely—after its virtual tax immunity— and the bourgeoisie more severely may in-

little money to buy even less bread. Nobles and bourgeoisie were alienated from the government by the threat of taxation; workers and some peasants by the threat of starvation. A long period of halting but real progress for virtually all segments of the population was now abruptly ended in consequence of the government's efforts to meet its deficit and of economic crisis resulting from poor crops and poor tariff policy.[30]

The draft riots that turned the city of New York upside down for five days in July, 1863 also follow the *J* curve. This severe local disturbance began when conscription threatened the lives and fortunes of workingmen whose enjoyment of wartime prosperity was now frustrated not only by military service (which could be avoided by paying $300 or furnishing a substitute—neither means being available to poor people) but also by inflation.[31]

Even the riots in Nyasaland, in February and March, 1959, appear to follow the pattern of a period of frustration after expectations and satisfactions have risen. Nyasaland workers who had enjoyed the high wages they were paid during the construction of the Kariba dam in Rhodesia returned to their homes and to unemployment, or to jobs paying $5 per month at a time when $15 was considered a bare minimum wage.[32]

One negative case—of a revolution that did not occur—is the depression of the 1930s in the United States. It was severe enough, at least on economic grounds, to have produced a revolution. Total national private production income in 1932 reverted to what it had been in 1916. Farm income in the same year was as low as in 1900; manufacturing as low as in 1913. Construction had not been as low since 1908. Mining and quarrying was back at the 1909 level.[33] For much of the population, two decades of economic progress had been wiped out. There were more than sporadic demonstrations of unemployed, hunger marchers, and veterans. In New York City, at least 29 people died of starvation. Poor people could vividly contrast their own past condition with the present—and their own present condition with that of those who were not seriously suffering. There were clearly audible rumbles of revolt. Why, then, no revolution?

Several forces worked strongly against it. Among the most depressed, the mood was one of apathy and despair, like that observed in Austria by Zawadzki and Lazarsfeld. It was not until the 1936 election that there was an increased turnout in the national election. The great majority of the public shared a set of values which since 1776 had been official dogma—not the dissident program of an alienated intelligentsia. People by and large were in agreement, whether or not they had succeeded economically, in a belief in individual hard work, self-reliance, and the promise of success. (Among workers, this non-class orientation had greatly impeded the establishment of trade unions, for example.) Those least hit by the depression—the upper middle-class businessmen, clergymen, lawyers, and intellectuals—remained rather solidly committed not only to equalitarian values and to the established economic system but also to constitutional processes. There was no such widespread or profound alienation as that which had cracked the loyalty of the nobility, clergy, bourgeoisie, armed forces, and intelligentsia in Russia. And the national political leadership that emerged had constitutionalism almost bred in its bones. The major threat to constitutionalism came in Louisiana; this leadership was unable to capture a national party organization, in part because Huey Long's arbitrariness and demagogy were mistrusted.

The major reason that revolution did not nonetheless develop probably remains the vigor with which the national government attacked the depression in 1933, when it became no longer possible to blame the government. The ambivalent popular hostility to the business community was contained by both the action of government against the depression and the government's practice of publicly and successfully eliciting the cooperation of businessmen during the crucial months of 1933. A failure then of cooperation could have intensified rather than lessened popular hostility to business. There was no longer an economic or a political class that could be the object of widespread intense hatred because of its indifference or hostility to the downtrodden. Had Roosevelt adopted a demagogic stance in the 1932 campaign and gained the loyalty to himself personally of the Army and the F.B.I., there might have been a Nazi-type "revolution," with a potpourri of equalitarian reform, nationalism, imperialism, and domestic scapegoats. Because of a conservatism in America stemming from strong and long attachment to a value system shared by all classes, an anti-capitalist, leftist revolution in the 1930s is very difficult to imagine.

SOME CONCLUSIONS

The notion that revolutions need both a period of rising expectations and a succeeding period in which they are frustrated qualifies substantially the main Marxian notion that revolutions occur after progressive degradation and the de Tocqueville notion that they occur when conditions are improving. By putting de Tocqueville before Marx but without abandoning either theory, we are better able to plot the antecedents of at least the disturbances here described.

Half of the general, if not common, sense of this revised notion lies in the utter improbability of a revolution occurring in a society where there is the continued, unimpeded opportunity to satisfy new needs, new hopes, new expectations. Would Dorr's rebellion have become such if the established electorate and government had readily acceded to the suffrage demands of the unpropertied? Would the Russian Revolution have taken place if the Tsarist autocracy had, quite out of character, truly granted the popular demands for constitutional democracy in 1905? Would the Cairo riots of January, 1952 and the subsequent coup actually have occurred if Britain had departed from Egypt and if the Egyptian monarchy had established an equitable tax system and in other ways alleviated the poverty of urban masses and the shame of the military?

The other half of the sense of the notion has to do with the improbability of revolution taking place where there has been no hope, no period in which expectations have risen. Such a stability of expectations presupposes a static state of human aspirations that sometimes exists but is rare. Stability of expectations is not a stable social condition. Such was the case of American Indians (at least from our perspective) and perhaps Africans before white men with Bibles, guns, and other goods interrupted the stability of African society. Egypt was in such a condition, vis-a-vis modern aspirations, before Europe became interested in building a canal. Such stasis was the case in Nazi concentration camps, where conformism reached the point of inmates cooperating

with guards even when the inmates were told to lie down so that they could be shot.[34] But in the latter case there was a society with externally induced complete despair, and even in these camps there were occasional rebellions of sheer desperation. It is of course true that in a society less regimented than concentration camps, the rise of expectations can be frustrated successfully, thereby defeating rebellion just as the satisfaction of expectations does. This, however, requires the uninhibited exercise of brute force as it was used in suppressing the Hungarian rebellion of 1956. Failing the continued ability and persistent will of a ruling power to use such force, there appears to be no sure way to avoid revolution short of an effective, affirmative, and continuous response on the part of established governments to the almost continuously emerging needs of the governed.

To be predictive, my notion requires the assessment of the state of mind—or more precisely, the mood—of a people. This is always difficult, even by techniques of systematic public opinion analysis. Respondents interviewed in a country with a represssive government are not likely to be responsive. But there has been considerable progress in gathering first-hand data about the state of mind of peoples in politically unstable circumstances. One instance of this involved interviewing in West Berlin, during and after the 1948 blockade, as reported by Buchanan and Cantril. They were able to ascertain, however crudely, the sense of security that people in Berlin felt. There was a significant increase in security after the blockade.[35]

Another instance comes out of the Middle Eastern study conducted by the Columbia University Bureau of Applied Social Research and reported by Lerner.[36] By directly asking respondents whether they were happy or unhappy with the way things had turned out in their life, the interviewers turned up data indicating marked differences in the frequency of a sense of unhappiness between countries and between "traditional," "transitional," and "modern" individuals in these countries.[37] There is no technical reason why such comparisons could not be made chronologically as well as they have been geographically.

Other than interview data are available with which we can, from past experience, make reasonable inferences about the mood of a people. It was surely the sense for the relevance of such data that led Thomas Masaryk before the first World War to gather facts about peasant uprisings and industrial strikes and about the writings and actions of the intelligentsia in nineteenth-century Russia. In the present report, I have used not only such data—in the collection of which other social scientists have been less assiduous than Masaryk—but also such indexes as comparative size of vote as between Rhode Island and the United States, employment, exports, and cost of living. Some such indexes, like strikes and cost of living, may be rather closely related to the mood of a people; others, like value of exports, are much cruder indications. Lest we shy away from the gathering of crude data, we should bear in mind that Durkheim developed his remarkable insights into modern society in large part by his analysis of suicide rates. He was unable to rely on the interviewing technique. We need not always ask people whether they are grievously frustrated by their government; their actions can tell us as well and sometimes better.

In his *Anatomy of Revolution*, Crane Brinton describes "some tentative uniformities" that he discovered in the Puritan, American, French, and Russian revolutions.[38] The uniformities were: an economically advancing society, class antagonism, desertion of intellectuals, inefficient government, a ruling class that has lost self-confidence, financial failure of government, and the inept use of force against rebels. All but the last two of these are long-range phenomena that lend themselves to studies over extended time periods. The first two lend themselves to statistical analysis. If they serve the purpose, techniques of content analysis could be used to ascertain trends in alienation of intellectuals. Less rigorous methods would perhaps serve better to ascertain the effectiveness of government and the self-confidence of rulers. Because tensions and frustrations are present at all times in every society, what is most seriously needed are data that cover an extended time period in a particular society, so that one can say there is evidence that tension is greater or less than it was N years or months previously.

We need also to know how long is a long cycle of rising expectations and how long is a brief cycle of frustration. We noted a brief period of frustration in Russia after the 1881 assassination of Alexander II and a longer period after the 1904 beginning of the Russo-Japanese War. Why did not the revolution occur at either of these times rather than in 1917? Had expectations before these two times not risen high enough? Had the subsequent decline not been sufficiently sharp and deep? Measuring techniques have not yet been devised to answer these questions. But their unavailability now does not forecast their eternal inaccessibility. Physicists devised useful temperature scales long before they came as close to absolute zero as they have recently in laboratory conditions. The far more complex problems of scaling in social science inescapably are harder to solve.

We therefore are still not at the point of being able to predict revolution, but the closer we can get to data indicating by inference the prevailing mood in a society, the closer we will be to understanding the change from gratification to frustration in people's minds. That is the part of the anatomy, we are forever being told with truth and futility, in which wars and revolutions always start. We should eventually be able to escape the embarrassment that may have come to Lenin six weeks after he made the statement in Switzerland, in January, 1917, that he doubted whether "we, the old [will] live to see the decisive battles of the coming revolution."[39]

4

Some mental and social antecedents of revolution

The nonpolitics of survival

Revolutions come about in the classic physical form of irresistible forces of change meeting immovable objects of stasis. The origin of these forces is complex. A good way to commence an understanding of these forces is to observe circumstances that are so overwhelming as to preclude the generation of revolution in the minds of men.

In his hypothetical, prehistorical primitive state, man is mainly preoccupied simply with staying alive. He has little time—as he forages for food, gets sick and gets well— to be much more than an animal.

Two times in modern history some men have degraded others to the condition of living only to survive. The first was the slave trade. It is estimated that two-thirds of those Africans who were captured and sold in Africa died either before leaving Africa or before entering plantation life in the New World. The second was the concentration camp. In the Nazi camps that flourished in Central Europe in the 1930s and 1940s, the mortality rate was roughly ninety percent. The Africans and the concentration camp inmates who survived have shown what happens when man is stripped of all but the most rudimentary civilization and normal social interaction.

This selection from Stanley Elkins' remarkable study shows what political behavior is like when relentless pressure from the environment forces men to concentrate individually on life itself. Between capture and enslavement or encampment, protest took almost entirely the form of individual or collective suicide or resignation to death.

This gives us some notion of the starting point for political behavior and revolutionary behavior. So long as there is constant preoccupation with survival and determined, unrestrained willingness to coerce on the part of those who possess the means thereof, there will be no revolution and no other political behavior among the general public. There is lacking the physical or mental energy for people to work together, to seek recognition of the sense of dignity and worth and identity that they had hitherto acquired.

So it has been among people who had been moderately well off before enslavement or encampment. So, we may suppose and only suppose, it was in the primitive condition of man before there was the organized and continuous institution of public power that has to do with government. People were too busy staying alive and protecting their families to do much more. People on the slave plantations and in the camps lived like this. They were a long way from having frustrations or aggressions that could have political content. Most of the mental antecedents of political protest did not yet exist.

To literate people reading this, it may seem redundant to belabor such an obvious reality. But life for a continuing majority of people on this earth is more like the life of primitive, preliterate man or like life on the slave plantation or in the concentration camp than it is like the life of students of politics. While far more people survive than previously, survival is still the main concern. Such people are very unlikely to rebel.

One warning is in order against oversimplification. Elkins points out that there were occasional revolts among slaves in Latin America—more than in North America. The reader will see for himself Elkins' explanation for this. Such a revolt in French-colonized Haiti at the end of the 18th century was successful. And occasional outbreaks did occur in the Nazi concentration camps. These awesome, puzzling outbreaks must, however, be seen in context. They were mostly small, infrequent, brief, and they mostly failed.

If the revolts on plantations and in camps are forgotten, we are apt to oversimplify. If the proportions of people who did in such circumstances revolt is forgotten, we are then apt to forget the still rather significant fact that—with the Haitian exception—the revolts among slaves and inmates did not have the same outcome as did the classic revolutions of France in 1789, Russian in 1905 and 1917, and China in 1949. And in the Haitian-case, the main result was to change the skin color of the oppressors. That is to say, the slave and inmate revolts did not much change life for the rebels or their adherents. Nevertheless, their occurrence remains inadequately explained.

Slavery and personality

STANLEY M. ELKINS

Notes to this section will be found on pages 339–344.

I. PERSONALITY TYPES AND STEREOTYPES

AN examination of American slavery, checked at certain critical points against a very different slave system, that of Latin America, reveals that a major key to many of the contrasts between them was an

institutional key: The presence or absence of other powerful institutions in society made an immense difference in the character of slavery itself. In Latin America, the very tension and balance among three kinds of organizational concerns—church, crown, and plantation agriculture — prevented slavery from being carried by the planting class to its ultimate logic. For the slave, in terms of the space thus allowed for the development of men and women as moral beings, the result was an "open system": a system of contacts with free society through which ultimate absorption into that society could and did occur with great frequency. The rights of personality implicit in the ancient traditions of slavery and in the church's most venerable assumptions on the nature of the human soul were thus in a vital sense conserved, whereas to a staggering extent the very opposite was true in North

American slavery. The latter system had developed virtually unchecked by institutions having anything like the power of their Latin counterparts; the legal structure which supported it, shaped only by the demands of a staple-raising capitalism, had defined with such nicety the slave's character as chattel that his character as a moral individual was left in the vaguest of legal obscurity. In this sense American slavery operated as a "closed" system—one in which, for the generality of slaves in their nature as men and women, *sub specie aeternitatis*, contacts with free society could occur only on the most narrowly circumscribed of terms. The next question is whether living within such a "closed system" might not have produced noticeable effects upon the slave's very personality. . . .

Two kinds of material will be used in the effort to picture the mechanisms whereby this adjustment to absolute power—an adjustment whose end product included infantile features of behavior—may have been effected. One is drawn from the theoretical knowledge presently available in social psychology, and the other, in the form of an analogy, is derived from some of the data that have come out of the German concentration camps. It is recognized in most theory that social behavior is regulated in some general way by adjustment to symbols of authority—however diversely "authority" may be defined either in theory or in culture itself—and that such adjustment is closely related to the very formation of personality. A corollary would be, of course, that the more diverse those symbols of authority may be, the greater is the permissible variety of adjustment to them—and the wider the margin of individuality, consequently, in the development of the self. The question here has to do with the wideness or narrowness of that margin on the antebellum plantation.

The other body of material, involving an experience undergone by several million men and women in the concentration camps of our own time, contains certain items of relevance to the problem here being considered. . . .

[1] Although the majority of Southern slaveholders were not planters, the majority of slaves were owned by a planter minority. "Considerably more than half of them lived on plantation units of more than twenty slaves, and one-fourth lived on units of more than fifty. That the majority of slaves belonged to members of the planter class, and not to those who operated small farms with a single slave family, is a fact of crucial importance concerning the nature of bondage in the ante-bellum South." Stampp *Peculiar Institution*, p. 31.

The experience showed that infantile personality features could be induced in a relatively short time among large numbers of adult human beings coming from very diverse backgrounds. The particular strain which was thus placed upon prior theory consisted in the need to make room not only for the cultural and environmental sanctions that sustain personality (which in a sense Freudian theory already had) but also for a virtually unanticipated problem: actual change in the personality of masses of adults. It forced a reappraisal and new appreciation of how completely and effectively prior cultural sanctions for behavior and personality could be detached to make way for new and different sanctions, and of how adjustments could be made by individuals to a species of authority vastly different from any previously known. The revelation for theory was the process of detachment.

These cues, accordingly, will guide the argument on Negro slavery. Several million people were detached with a peculiar effectiveness from a great variety of cultural backgrounds in Africa—a detachment operating with infinitely more effectiveness upon those brought to North America than upon those who came to Latin America. It was achieved partly by the shock experience inherent in the very mode of procurement but more specifically by the type of authority-system to which they were introduced and to which they had to adjust for physical and psychic survival. The new adjustment, to absolute power in a closed system, involved infantilization, and the detachment was so complete that little trace of prior (and thus alternative) cultural sanctions for behavior and personality remained for the descendants of the first generation. For them, adjustment to clear and omnipresent authority could be more or less automatic—as much so, or as little, as it is for anyone whose adjustment to a social system begins at birth and to whom that system represents normality. We do not know how generally a full adjustment was made by the first generation of fresh slaves from Africa. But we do know —from a modern experience—that such an adjustment is possible, not only within the same generation but within two or three years. This proved possible for people in a full state of complex civilization, for men and women who were not black and not savages. . . .

II. SHOCK AND DETACHMENT

We may suppose that every African who became a slave underwent an experience whose crude psychic impact must have been staggering and whose consequences superseded anything that had ever previously happened to him. Some effort should therefore be made to picture the series of shocks which must have accompanied the principal events of that enslavement.

The majority of slaves appear to have been taken in native wars,[2] which meant that no one—neither persons of high rank nor warriors of prowess—was guaranteed against capture and enslavement.[3] Great numbers were caught in surprise attacks upon their villages, and since the tribes acting as middlemen for the trade had come to depend on regular supplies of captives in order to maintain that function, the distinction between wars and raiding expeditions tended to be very dim.[4] The first shock, in an experience destined to endure many months and to leave its survivors irrevocably changed, was thus the shock of capture. It is an effort to remember that while enslavement occurred in Africa every day, to the individual it occurred just once.[5]

The second shock—the long march to the sea—drew out the nightmare for many weeks. Under the glaring sun, through the steaming jungle, they were driven along like beasts tied together by their necks; day after day, eight or more hours at a time,

they would stagger barefoot over thorny underbrush, dried reeds, and stone. Hardship, thirst, brutalities, and near starvation penetrated the experience of each exhausted man and woman who reached the coast.[6] One traveler tells of seeing hundreds of bleaching skeletons strewn along one of the slave caravan routes.[7] But then the man who must interest us is the man who survived—he who underwent the entire experience, of which this was only the beginning.

The next shock, aside from the fresh physical torments which accompanied it, was the sale to the European slavers. After being crowded into pens near the trading stations and kept there overnight, sometimes for days, the slaves were brought out for examination. Those rejected would be abandoned to starvation; the remaining ones—those who had been bought—were branded, given numbers inscribed on leaden tags, and herded on shipboard.[8]

The episode that followed—almost too protracted and stupefying to be called a mere "shock"—was the dread Middle Passage, brutalizing to any man, black or white, ever to be involved with it. The holds, packed with squirming and suffocating humanity, became stinking infernos of filth and pestilence. Stories of disease, death, and cruelty on the terrible two-month voyage abound in the testimony which did much toward ending the British slave trade forever.[9]

The final shock in the process of enslavement came with the Negro's introduction to the West Indies. Bryan Edwards, describing the arrival of a slave ship, writes of how in times of labor scarcity crowds of people would come scrambling abroad, manhandling the slaves and throwing them into panic. The Jamaica legislature eventually "corrected the enormity" by enacting that the sales be held on shore. Edwards felt a certain mortification at seeing the Negroes exposed naked in public, similar to that felt by the trader Degrandpré at seeing them examined back at the African factories.[10] Yet here they did not seem to care. "They display . . . very few signs of lamentation for their past or of apprehension for their future condition; but ... commonly express great eagerness to be sold."[11] The "seasoning" process which followed completed the series of steps whereby the African Negro became a slave.

The mortality had been very high. One-third of the numbers first taken, out of a total of perhaps fifteen million, had died on the march and at the trading stations; another third died during the Middle Passage and the seasoning.[12] Since a majority of the African-born slaves who came to the North American plantations did not come directly but were imported through the British West Indies, one may assume that the typical slave underwent an experience something like that just outlined. This was the man—one in three—who had come through it all and lived and was about to enter our "closed system." What would he be like if he survived and adjusted to that?

Actually, a great deal had happened to him already. Much of his past had been annihilated; nearly every prior connection had been severed. Not that he had really "forgotten" all these things—his family and kinship arrangements, his language, the tribal religion, the taboos, the name he had once borne, and so on—but none of it any longer carried much meaning. The old values, the sanctions, the standards, already unreal, could no longer furnish him guides for conduct, for adjusting to the expectations of a complete new life. Where then was he to look for new standards, new cues —who would furnish them now? He could now look to none but his master, the one man to whom the system had committed his entire being: the man upon whose will depended his food, his shelter, his sexual connections, whatever moral instruction he might be offered, whatever "success" was possible within the system, his very security —in short, everything. . . .

The only mass experience that Western people have had within recorded history comparable in any way with Negro slavery was undergone in the nether world of Nazism. The concentration camp was not only a perverted slave system; it was also— what is less obvious but even more to the point—a perverted patriarchy.

The system of the concentration camps was expressly devised in the 1930s by high officials of the German government to function as an instrument of terror. The first groups detained in the camps consisted of prominent enemies of the Nazi regime; later, when these had mostly been eliminated, it was still felt necessary that the system be institutionalized and made into a standing weapon of intimidation—which required a continuing flow of incoming prisoners. The categories of eligible persons were greatly widened to include all real, fancied, or "potential" opposition to the state. They were often selected on capricious and random grounds, and together they formed a cross-section of society which was virtually complete: criminals, workers, businessmen, professional people, middle-class Jews, even members of the aristocracy. The teeming camps thus held all kinds—not only the scum of the underworld but also countless men and women of culture and refinement. During the war a specialized objective was added, that of exterminating the Jewish populations of subject countries, which required special mass-production methods of which the gas chambers and crematories of Auschwitz–Birkenau were outstanding examples. Yet the basic technique was everywhere and at all times the same: the deliberate infliction of various forms of torture upon the incoming prisoners in such a way as to break their resistance and make way for their degradation as individuals. These brutalities were not merely "permitted" or "encouraged"; they were prescribed. Duty in the camps was a mandatory phase in the training of SS guards, and it was here that particular efforts were made to overcome their scruples and to develop in them a capacity for relishing spectacles of pain and anguish.

The concentration camps and everything that took place in them were veiled in the utmost isolation and secrecy. . . . The results, therefore, contained elements of the diabolical. The undenied existence of the camps cast a shadow of nameless dread over the entire population; on the other hand the *individual* who actually became a prisoner in one of them was in most cases devastated with fright and utterly demoralized to discover that what was happening to *him* was not less, but rather far more terrible than anything he had imagined. The shock sequence of "procurement," therefore, together with the initial phases of the prisoner's introduction to camp life, is not without significance in assessing some of the psychic effects upon those who survived as long-term inmates.

The arrest was typically made at night, perferably late; this was standing Gestapo policy, designed to heighten the element of shock, terror, and unreality surrounding the arrest. After a day or so in the police jail came the next major shock, that of being transported to the camp itself. "This transportation into the camp, and the 'initiation' into it," writes Bruno Bettelheim (an ex-inmate of Dachau and Buchenwald), "is often the first torture which the prisoner has ever experienced and is, as a rule, physically and psychologically the worst torture to which he will ever be exposed."[13] It involved a planned series of brutalities inflicted by guards making repeated rounds through the train over a twelve- to thirty-six hour period during which the prisoner was prevented from resting. If transported in cattle cars instead of passenger cars, the prisoners were sealed in, under conditions not dissimilar to those of the Middle Passage.[14] Upon their arrival—if the camp was one in which mass exterminations were carried out—there might be sham ceremonies designed to reassure temporarily the exhausted prisoners, which meant that the fresh terrors in the offing would then strike them with redoubled impact. An SS officer might deliver an address, or a band might be playing popular tunes, and it would be in such a setting that the initial "selection" was made. The newcomers would file past an SS doctor who indicated, with a motion of the forefinger, whether they were to go to the left or to the right. To one side went those considered capable of heavy labor;

to the other would go wide categories of "undesirables"; those in the latter group were being condemned to the gas chambers.[15] Those who remained would undergo the formalities of "registration," full of indignities, which culminated in the marking of each prisoner with a number.[16]

There were certain physical and psychological strains of camp life, especially debilitating in the early stages, which should be classed with the introductory shock sequence. There was a state of chronic hunger whose pressures were unusually effective in detaching prior scruples of all kinds; even the sexual instincts no longer functioned in the face of the drive for food.[17] The man who at his pleasure could bestow or withhold food thus wielded, for that reason alone, abnormal power. Another strain at first was the demand for absolute obedience, the slightest deviation from which brought savage punishments.[18] The prisoner had to ask permission—by no means granted as a matter of course—even to defecate.[19] The power of the SS guard, as the prisoner was hourly reminded, was that of life and death over his body. A more exquisite form of pressure lay in the fact that the prisoner had never a moment of solitude: he no longer had a private existence; it was no longer possible, in any imaginable sense, for him to be an "individual."[20]

Another factor having deep disintegrative effects upon the prisoner was the prospect of a limitless future in the camp. In the immediate sense this meant that he could no longer make plans for the future. But there would eventually be a subtler meaning: it made the break with the outside world a *real* break; in time the "real" life would become the life of the camp, the outside world an abstraction. Had it been a limited detention, whose end could be calculated, one's outside relationships—one's roles, one's very "personality"—might temporarily have been laid aside, to be reclaimed more or less intact at the end of the term. Here, however, the prisoner was faced with the apparent impossibility of his old roles or even his old personality ever having any future at all; it became more and more difficult to imagine himself resuming them.[21] It was this that underlay the "egalitarianism" of the camps; old statuses had lost their meaning.[22] A final strain, which must have been particularly acute for the newcomer, was the omnipresent threat of death and the very unpredictable suddenness with which death might strike. Quite aside from the periodic gas-chamber selections, the guards in their sports and caprices were at liberty to kill any prisoner any time.[23]

In the face of all this, one might suppose that the very notion of an "adjustment" would be grotesque. The majority of those who entered the camps never came out again, but our concern here has to be with those who survived—an estimated 700,000 out of nearly eight million.[24] For them, the regime must be considered not as a system of death but as a way of life. These survivors did make an adjustment of some sort to the system; it is they themselves who report it. After the initial shocks, what was the nature of the "normality" that emerged?

A dramatic species of psychic displacement seems to have occurred at the very outset. This experience, described as a kind of "splitting of personality," has been noted by most of the inmates who later wrote of their imprisonment. The very extremity of the initial tortures produced in the prisoner what actually amounted to a sense of detachment; these brutalities went so beyond his own experience that they became somehow incredible—they seemed to be happening no longer to him but almost to someone else. "[The author] has no doubt," writes Bruno Bettleheim, "that he was able to endure the transportation, and all that followed, because right from the beginning he became convinced that these horrible and degrading experiences somehow did not happen to 'him' as a subject, but only to 'him' as an object."[25] This subject-object "split" appears to have served a double function: not only was it an immediate psychic defense mechanism against shock,[26] but it also acted as the first thrust toward a new adjustment. This splitting-off of a special "self"—a self which endured the tortures but which was not the "real" self—also provided the first

glimpse of a new personality which, being not "real," would not need to feel bound by the values which guided the individual in his former life. "The prisoners' feelings," according to Mr. Bettleheim, "could be summed up by the following sentence: 'What I am doing here, or what is happening to me, does not count at all; here everything is permissible as long and insofar as it contributes to helping me survive in the camp. . . .' "[27]

"If you survive the first three months you will survive the next three years." Such was the formula transmitted from the old prisoners to the new ones,[28] and its meaning lay in the fact that the first three months would generally determine a prisoner's capacity for survival and adaptation. "Be inconscpicuous": this was the golden rule.[29] The prisoner who called attention to himself, even in such trivial matters as the wearing of glasses, risked doom. Any show of bravado, any heroics, any kind of resistance condemned a man instantly. There were no rewards for martyrdom: not only did the martyr himself suffer, but mass punishments were wreaked upon his fellow inmates. To "be inconspicuous" required a special kind of alertness—almost an animal instinct[30]—against the apathy which tended to follow the initial shocks.[31] To give up the struggle for survival was to commit "passive suicide"; a careless mistake meant death. There were those, however, who did come through this phase and who managed an adjustment to the life of the camp. It was the striking contrasts between this group of two- and three-year veterans and the perpetual stream of newcomers which made it possible for men like Bettelheim and Cohen to speak of the "old prisoner" as a specific type.

The most immediate aspect of the old inmates' behavior . . . was its *childlike* quality. "The prisoners developed types of behavior which are characteristic of infancy or early youth. Some of these behaviors developed slowly, others were immediately imposed on the prisoners and developed only in intensity as time went on."[32] Such infantile behavior took innumerable forms. The inmates' sexual impotence brought about a disappearance of sexuality in their talk;[33] instead, excretory functions occupied them endlessly. They lost many of the customary inhibitions as to soiling their beds and their persons.[34] Their humor was shot with silliness and they giggled like children when one of them would expel wind. Their relationships were highly unstable. "Prisoners would, like early adolescents, fight one another tooth and nail ... only to become close friends within a few minutes."[35] Dishonesty became chronic. "Now they suddenly appeared to be pathological liars, to be unable to restrain themselves, to be unable to make objective evaluation, etc."[36] ... Bruno Bettelheim remarks on the extravagance of the stories told by the prisoners to one another. "They were boastful, telling tales about what they had accomplished in their former lives, or how they succeeded in cheating foremen or guards, and how they sabotaged the work. Like children they felt not at all set back or ashamed when it became known that they had lied about their prowess."[37]

This development of childlike behavior in the old inmates was the counterpart of something even more striking that was happening to them: *Only very few of the prisoners escaped a more or less intensive identification with the S.S.*[38] As Mr. Bettelheim puts it: "A prisoner had reached the final stage of adjustment to the camp situation when he had changed his personality so as to accept as his own the values of the Gestapo."[39] The Bettelheim study furnishes a catalogue of examples. The old prisoners came to share the attitude of the SS toward the "unfit" prisoners; newcomers who behaved badly in the labor groups or who could not withstand the strain became a liability for the others, who were often instrumental in getting rid of them. Many old prisoners actually imitated the SS; they would sew and mend their uniforms in such a way as to make them look more like those of the SS—even though they risked punishment for it. "When asked why they did it, they admitted that they loved to look like ... the guards." Some took great enjoyment in the fact that

during roll call "they really had stood well at attention." There were cases of nonsensical rules, made by the guards, which the older prisoners would continue to observe and try to force on the others long after the SS had forgotten them.[40] Even the most abstract ideals of the SS, such as their intense German nationalism and anti-Semitism, were often absorbed by the old inmates—a phenomenon observed among the politically well-educated and even among the Jews themselves.[41] The final quintessence of all this was seen in the "Kapo"—the prisoner who had been placed in a supervisory position over his fellow inmates. These creatures, many of them professional criminals, not only behaved with slavish servility to the SS, but the way in which they often outdid the SS in sheer brutality became one of the most durable features of the concentration-camp legend.

To all these men, reduced to complete and childish dependence upon their masters, the SS had actually become a father-symbol. "The SS man was all-powerful in the camp, he was the lord and master of the prisoner's life. As a cruel father he could, without fear of punishment, even kill the prisoner and as a gentle father he could scatter largesse and afford the prisoner his protection."[42] The result, admits Dr. Cohen, was that "for all of us the SS was a father image. ..."[43] The closed system, in short, had become a kind of grotesque patriarchy.

The literatures provides us with three remarkable tests of the profundity of the experience which these prisoners had undergone and the thoroughness of the changes which had been brought about in them. One is the fact that few cases of real resistance were ever recorded, even among prisoners going to their death.

With a few altogether insignificant exceptions, the prisoners, no matter in what form they were led to execution, whether singly, in groups, or in masses, never fought back! ... there were thousands who had by no means relapsed into fatal apathy. Nevertheless, in mass liquidations they went to their death with open eyes, without assaulting the enemy in a final paroxysm, without a sign of fight. Is this not in conflict with human nature, as we know it?[44]

Even upon liberation, when revenge against their tormentors at last became possible, mass uprisings very rarely occurred. "Even when the whole system was overthrown by the Allies," says David Rousset writing of Buchenwald, "nothing happened. . . . The American officer appointed to command of the camp was never called upon to cope with any inclination toward a popular movement. No such disposition existed."[45]

A second test of the system's effectiveness was the relative scarcity of suicides in the camps.[46] Though there were suicides, they tended to occur during the first days of internment, and only one mass suicide is known; it took place among a group of Jews at Mauthausen who leaped into a rock pit three days after their arrival.[47] For the majority of prisoners the simplicity of the urge to survive made suicide, a complex matter of personal initiative and decision, out of the question. Yet they could, when commanded by their masters, go to their death without resistance.

The third test lies in the very absence, among the prisoners, of hatred toward the SS. This is probably the hardest of all to understand. Yet the burning spirit of rebellion which many of their liberators expected to find would have had to be supported by fierce and smoldering emotions; such emotions were not there. "It is remarkable," one observer notes, "how little hatred of their wardens is revealed in their stories."[48]

III. THREE THEORIES OF PERSONALITY

The immense revelation for psychology in the concentration-camp literature has been the discovery of how elements of dramatic personality change could be brought about in masses of individuals. And yet it is not proper that the crude fact of "change" alone should dominate the conceptual image with which one emerges from this problem. "Change" per se, change that does not go beyond itself, is productive of nothing; it leaves only destruction, shock, and howling bedlam behind it unless some future basis of stability and order lies wait-

ing to guarantee it and give it reality. So it is with the human psyche, which is apparently capable of making terms with a state other than liberty as we know it. The very dramatic features of the process just described may upset the nicety of this point. There is the related danger, moreover, of unduly stressing the individual psychology of the problem at the expense of its social psychology.

These hazards might be minimized by maintaining a conceptual distinction between two phases of the group experience. The process of detachment from prior standards of behavior and value is one of them, and is doubtless the more striking, but there must be another one. . . . The other phase of the experience should be considered as the "stability" side of the problem, that phase which stabilized what the "shock" phase only opened the way for. This was essentially a process of adjustment to a standard of social normality, though in this case a drastic *re*adjustment and compressed within a very short time—a process which under typical conditions of individual and group existence is supposed to begin at birth and last a lifetime and be transmitted in many and diffuse ways from generation to generation. The adjustment is assumed to be slow and organic, and it normally is. Its numerous aspects extend much beyond psychology; those aspects have in the past been treated at great leisure within the rich provinces not only of psychology but of history, sociology, and literature as well. What rearrangement and compression of those provinces may be needed to accommodate a mass experience that not only involved profound individual shock but also required rapid assimilation to a drastically different form of social organization, can hardly be known. But perhaps the most conservative beginning may be made with existing psychological theory.

The theoretical system whose terminology was orthodox for most of the Europeans who have written about the camps was that of Freud. . . . Elie Cohen . . . specifically states that "the superego acquired new values in a concentration camp."[49] The old values, according to Dr. Cohen, were first silenced by the shocks which produced "acute depersonalization" (the subject-object split: "It is not the real 'me' who is undergoing this"), and by the powerful drives of hunger and survival. Old values, thus set aside, could be replaced by new ones. It was a process made possible by "infantile regression"—regression to a previous condition of childlike dependency in which parental prohibitions once more became all-powerful and in which parental judgments might once more be internalized. In this way a new "father-image," personified in the SS guard, came into being. That the prisoner's identification with the SS could be so positive is explained by still another mechanism: the principle of "identification with the aggressor." "A child," as Anna Freud writes, "interjects some characteristic of an anxiety-object and so assimilates an anxiety-experience which he has just undergone. ... By impersonating the aggressor, assuming his attributes or imitating his aggression, the child transforms himself from the person threatened into the person who makes the threat."[50] In short, the child's only "defense" in the presence of a cruel, all-powerful father is the psychic defense of identification. ...

A second theoretical scheme is better prepared for crisis and more closely geared to social environment than the Freudian adaptation indicated above, and it may consequently be more suitable for accommodating not only the concentration-camp experience but also the more general problem of plantation slave personality. This is the "interpersonal theory" developed by the late Harry Stack Sullivan. ...

Sullivan's great contribution was to offer a concept whereby the really critical determinants of personality might be isolated for purposes of observation. Out of the hopelessly immense totality of "influences" which in one way or another go to make up the personality, or "self," Sullivan designated one—the estimations and expectations of others—as the one promising to

unlock the most secrets. He then made a second elimination: the *majority* of "others" in one's existence may for theoretical purposes be neglected; what counts is who the *significant* others are. Here, "significant others"[51] may be understood very crudely to mean those individuals who hold, or seem to hold, the keys to security in one's own personal situation, whatever its nature. Now as to the psychic processes whereby these "significant others" become an actual part of the personality, it may be said that the very sense of "self" first emerges in connection with anxiety about the attitudes of the most important persons in one's life (initially, the mother, father, and their surrogates—persons of more or less absolute authority), and automatic attempts are set in motion to adjust to these attitudes. In this way their approval, their disapproval, their estimates and appraisals, and indeed a whole range of their expectations become as it were internalized, and are reflected in one's very character. Of course as one "grows up," one acquires more and more significant others whose attitudes are diffuse and may indeed compete, and this "significance," in Sullivan's sense, becomes subtler and less easy to define. The personality exfoliates; it takes on traits of distinction and, as we say, "individuality." The impact of particular significant others is less dramatic than in early life. But the pattern is a continuing one; new significant others do still appear, and theoretically it is conceivable that even in mature life the personality might be visibly affected by the arrival of such a one—supposing that this new significant other were vested with sufficient authority and power. In any event there are possibilities for fluidity and actual change inherent in this concept which earlier schemes have lacked. ...

Consider the camp prisoner—not the one who fell by the wayside but the one who was eventually to survive; consider the ways in which he was forced to adjust to the one significant other which he now had—the SS guard, who held absolute dominion over every aspect of his life. The very shock of his introduction was perfectly designed to dramatize this fact; he was brutally mal-treated ("as by a cruel father"); the shadow of resistance would bring instant death. Daily life in the camp, with its fear and tensions, taught over and over the lesson of absolute power. It prepared the personality for a drastic shift in standards. It crushed whatever anxieties might have been drawn from prior standards; such standards had become meaningless. It focused the prisoner's attention constantly on the moods, attitudes, and standards of the only man who mattered. A truly childlike situation was thus created: utter and abject dependency on one, or on a rigidly limited few, significant others. All the conditions which in normal life would give the individual leeway—which allowed him to defend himself against a new and hostile significant other, no matter how powerful—were absent in the camp. No competition of significant others was possi-ble; the prisoner's comrades for practical purposes were helpless to assist him. He had no degree of independence, no lines to the outside, in any matter. Everything, every vital concern, focused on the SS: food, warmth, security, freedom from pain, all depended on the omnipotent significant other, all had to be worked out within the closed system. Nowhere was there a shred of privacy; everything one did was subject to SS supervision. The pressure was never absent. It is thus no wonder that the prisoners should become "as children." It is no wonder that their obedience became unquestioning, that they did not revolt, that they could not "hate" their masters. Their masters' attitudes had become *inter-nalized* as a part of their very selves; those attitudes and standards now dominated all others that they had. They had, indeed, been "changed". . . .

It is hoped that the very hideousness of a special example of slavery has not dis-qualified it as a test for certain features of a far milder and more benevolent form of slavery. But it should still be possible to say, with regard to the individuals who lived as slaves within the respective systems, that just as on one level there is every difference between a wretched childhood and a care-free one, there are, for other purposes, limited features which the one may be said to have shared with the other.

Both were closed systems from which all standards based on prior connections had been effectively detached. A working adjust-ment to either system required a childlike conformity, a limited choice of "significant others." Cruelty per se cannot be considered the primary key to this; of far greater importance was the simple "closedness" of the system, in which all lines of authority descended from the master and in which alternative social bases that might have supported alternative standards were system-atically suppressed.[52] The individual, con-sequently, for his very psychic security, had to picture his master in some way as the "good father,"[53] even when, as in the concentration camp, it made no sense at all.[54] But why should it not have made sense for many a simple plantation Negro whose master did exhibit, in all the ways that could be expected, the features of the good father who was really "good"? If the concentration camp could produce in two or three years the results that it did, one wonders how much more pervasive must have been those attitudes, expectations, and values which had, certainly, their benevolent side and which were accepted and trans-mitted over generations.

For the Negro child, in particular, the plantation offered no really satisfactory father-image other than the master. The "real" father was virtually without authority over his child, since discipline, parental responsibility, and control of rewards and punishments all rested in other hands; the slave father could not even protect the mother of his children except by appealing directly to the master. Indeed, the mother's own role loomed far larger for the slave child than did that of the father. She con-trolled those few activities—household care, preparation of food, and rearing of children —that were left to the slave family. For that matter, the very etiquette of plantation life removed even the honorific attributes of fatherhood from the Negro male, who was addressed as "boy"—until, when the vigorous years of his prime were past, he was allowed to assume the title of "uncle."

From the master's viewpoint, slaves had been defined in law as property, and the master's power over his property must be absolute. But then this property was still human property. These slaves might never be quite as human as *he* was, but still there were certain standards that could be laid down for their behavior: obedience, fidelity, humility, docility, cheerfulness, and so on. Industry and diligence would of course be demanded, but a final element in the master's situation would undoubtedly qualify that expectation. Absolute power for him meant absolute dependency for the slave—the dependency not of the developing child but of the perpetual child. For the master, the role most aptly fitting such a relationship would naturally be that of the father. As a father he could be either harsh or kind, as he chose, but as a *wise* father he would have, we may suspect, a sense of the limits of his situation. He must be ready to cope with *all* the qualities of the child, exasperating as well as ingratiating. He might conceivably have to expect in this child—besides his loyalty, docility, humility, cheerfulness, and (under supervision) his diligence—such additional qualities as irresponsibility, playfulness, silliness, laziness, and (quite possibly) tendencies to lying and stealing. Should the entire prediction prove accurate, the result would be something resembling "Sambo". . . .

Why should it be, turning once more to Latin America, that there one finds no Sambo, no social tradition, that is, in which slaves were defined by virtually complete consensus as children incapable of being trusted with the full privileges of freedom and adulthood?[55] There, the system surely had its brutalities. The slaves arriving there from Africa had also undergone the capture, the sale, the Middle Passage. They too had been uprooted from a prior culture, from a life very different from the one in which they now found themselves. There, however, the system was not closed.

Here again the concentration camp, paradoxically enough, can be instructive.

There were in the camps a very small minority of the survivors who had undergone an experience different in crucial ways from that of the others, an experience which protected them from the full impact of the closed system. These people, mainly by virtue of wretched little jobs in the camp administration which offered them a minute measure of privilege, were able to carry on "underground" activities. In a practical sense the actual operations of such "undergrounds" as were possible may seem to us unheroic and limited: stealing blankets; "organizing" a few bandages, a little medicine, from the camp hospital; black market arrangements with a guard for a bit of extra food and protection for oneself and one's comrades; the circulation of news; and other such apparently trifling activities. But for the psychological balance of those involved, such activities were vital; they made possible a fundamentally different adjustment to the camp. To a prisoner so engaged, there were others who mattered, who gave real point to his existence—the SS was no longer the *only* one. Conversely, the role of the child was not the only one he played. He could take initiative; he could give as well as receive protection; he did things which had meaning in adult terms. He had, in short, alternative roles; this was a fact which made such a prisoner's transition from his old life to that of the camp less agonizing and destructive; those very prisoners, moreover, appear to have been the ones who could, upon liberation, resume normal lives most easily. It is, in fact, these people—not those of the ranks— who have described the camps to us.[56]

It was just such a difference—indeed, a much greater one—that separated the typical slave in Latin America from the typical slave in the United States. Though he too had experienced the Middle Passage, he was entering a society where alternatives were significantly more diverse than those awaiting his kinsman in North America. Concerned in some sense with his status were distinct and at certain points competing institutions. This involved multiple and often competing "significant others."

His master was, of course, clearly the chief one—but not the only one. There could, in fact, be a considerable number: the friar who boarded his ship to examine his conscience, the confessor; the priest who made the rounds and who might report irregularities in treatment to the *procurador*; the zealous Jesuit quick to resent a master's intrusion upon such sacred matters as marriage and worship (a resentment of no small consequence to the master); the local magistrate, with his eye on the king's official protector of slaves, who would find himself in trouble were the laws too widely evaded; the king's informer who received one-third of the fines. For the slave the result was a certain latitude; the lines did not all converge on one man; the slave's personality, accordingly, did not have to focus on a single role. He was, true enough, primarily a slave. Yet he might in fact perform multiple roles. He could be a husband and a father (for the American slave these roles had virtually no meaning); open to him also were such activities as artisan, peddler, petty merchant, truck gardener (the law reserved to him the necessary time and a share of the proceeds, but such arrangements were against the law for Sambo); he could be a communicant in the church, a member of a religious fraternity[57] (roles guaranteed by the most powerful institution in Latin America—comparable privileges in the American South depended on a master's pleasure). These roles were all legitimized and protected *outside* the plantation; they offered a diversity of channels for the development of personality. Not only did the individual have multiple roles open to him as a slave, but the very nature of these roles made possible a certain range of aspirations should he some day become free. He could have a fantasy-life not limited to catfish and watermelons; it was within his conception to become a priest, an independent farmer, a successful merchant, a military officer.[58] The slave could actually—to an extent quite unthinkable in the United States—conceive of himself *as a rebel*. Bloody slave revolts, actual wars, took place in Latin America; nothing on this order occurred in the United States.[59] But even without a rebellion, society here had a network of customary arrangements, rooted in antiquity, which made possible at many points a smooth transition of status from slave to free and which provided much social space for the exfoliation of individual character.

To the typical slave on the antebellum plantation in the United States, society of course offered no such alternatives. But that is hardly to say that something of an "underground"—something rather more, indeed, than an underground—could not exist in Southern slave society. And there were those in it who hardly fitted the picture of "Sambo."

The American slave system, compared with that of Latin America, was closed and circumscribed, but, like all social systems, its arrangements were less perfect in practice than they appeared to be in theory. It was possible for significant numbers of slaves, in varying degrees, to escape the full impact of the system and its coercions upon personality. The house servant, the urban mechanic, the slave who arranged his own employment and paid his master a stipulated sum each week, were all figuratively members of the "underground."[60] Even among those working on large plantations, the skilled craftsman or the responsible slave foreman had a measure of independence not shared by his simpler brethren. Even the single slave family owned by a small farmer had a status much closer to that of house servants than to that of a plantation labor gang. For all such people there was a margin of space denied to the majority; the system's authority-structure claimed their bodies but not quite their souls.

Out of such groups an individual as complex and as highly developed as William Johnson, the Natchez barber, might emerge. Johnson's diary reveals a personality that one recognizes instantly as a type—but a type whose values came from a sector of society very different from that which formed Sambo. Johnson is the young man on the make, the ambitious free-enterpriser of American legend. He began life as a slave, was manumitted at the age of eleven, and rose from a poor apprentice barber to become one of the wealthiest and most influential Negroes in antebellum Mississippi. He was respected by white and black alike, and counted among his friends some of the leading public men of the state.[61]

It is of great interest to note that although the danger of slave revolts (like Communist conspiracies in our own day) was much overrated by touchy Southerners; the revolts that actually did occur were in no instance planned by plantation laborers but rather by Negroes whose qualities of leadership were developed well outside the full coercions of the plantation authority-system. Gabriel, who led the revolt of 1800, was a blacksmith who lived a few miles outside Richmond; Denmark Vesey, leading spirit of the 1822 plot at Charleston, was a freed Negro artisan who had been born in Africa and served several years aboard a slave-trading vessel; and Nat Turner, the Virginia slave who fomented the massacre of 1831, was a literate preacher of recognized intelligence. Of the plots that have been convincingly substantiated (whether they came to anything or not), the majority originated in urban centers.[62]

For a time during Reconstruction, a Negro elite of sorts did emerge in the South. Many of its members were Northern Negroes, but the Southern exslaves who also comprised it seem in general to have emerged from the categories just indicated. Vernon Wharton, writing of Mississippi, says:

A large portion of the minor Negro leaders were preachers, lawyers, or teachers from the free states or from Canada. Their education and their independent attitude gained for them immediate favor and leadership. Of the natives who became their rivals, the majority had been urban slaves, blacksmiths, carpenters, clerks, or waiters in hotels and boarding houses; a few of them had been favored body-servants of affluent whites.[63]

The William Johnsons and Denmark Veseys have been accorded, though belatedly, their due honor. They are, indeed, all too easily identified, thanks to the system that enabled them as individuals to be so conspicuous and so exceptional and, as members of a group, so few.

Aggression follows frustration

The following selection is from a book that is the joint effort of eight psychologists. It is perhaps the most tightly reasoned theoretical statement of the relationship between frustration and aggression that has thus far been written. It builds on Freud's genetic psychology and on stimulus–response (that is, behavioral) psychology. The result is a general theoretical statement that does help explain why the child aggresses when he becomes frustrated. It also helps us understand the adult citizen who, not getting what he expects to get from action by his government, either displaces his aggression from government to other objects or directs his aggression toward government, possibly to the point of revolt.

The authors define instigators to actions, goal responses to instigators, interferences between the desired responses to instigations which constitute frustration, and the aggression that follows frustration. We end with a more systematic notion of how that form of aggression called civil violence comes about.

We are also told that aggression may leave unaffected the original instigation and therefore the impulse to aggress. The thesis is that only actual gratification of the original instigation can do it. Watching a football game's attenuated violence will not satisfy the man whose frustration derives from the inability to get the kind of job he wants. Nor will hate campaigns by a Nazi government against Jews; a Soviet government against capitalists; a Chinese government against capitalists, Russians, and Americans; or an American government against communists, Russians, or Chinese—none of these displacements of aggression serves as a satisfactory substitute for the gratification of the various original instigators of citizens' frustrations.

165

Frustration and aggression: Definitions

JOHN DOLLARD,
LEONARD W. DOOB,
NEAL E. MILLER,
O. H. MOWRER,
AND
ROBERT R. SEARS

Copyright by and reprinted with the permission of Yale University Press, New Haven and London, from John Dollard, Leonard W. Doob, Neal E. Miller, O. H. Mowrer, Robert R. Sears, *Frustration and Aggression* (1939), Yale University Press paperback edition, 1967, pp. 1–54. Portions of the original text have been omitted.

Notes to this section will be found on page 344.

THE problem of aggression has many facets. The individual experiences difficulty in controlling his own temper and often sees others carrying on an unwitting struggle with their hostilities. He fears justified revenge or writhes at the blow or taunt that appears from an unexpected source. Children are often expert at annoying their elders by sly mischief or a sudden tantrum. Helpless minorities are persecuted. The lynching mob has a grimness and cruelty not to be expected from people who are so gentle and kind in other situations. Primitive tribesmen slay one another and even civilized people are frightened by the prospect of new and increasingly destructive wars. This book represents an attempt to bring a degree of systematic order into such apparently chaotic phenomena.

THE BASIC POSTULATE

This study take as its point of departure the assumption that *aggression is always a consequence of frustration*. More specifically the proposition is that the occurrence of aggressive behavior always presupposes the existence of frustration and, contrariwise, that the existence of frustration always leads to some form of aggression. From the point of view of daily observation, it does not seem unreasonable to assume that aggressive behavior of the usually recognized varieties is always traceable to and produced by some form of frustration. But it is by no means so immediately evident that, whenever frustration occurs, aggression of some kind and in some degree will inevitably result. In many adults and even children, frustration may be followed so promptly by an apparent acceptance of the situation and readjustment thereto that one looks in vain for the relatively gross criteria ordinarily thought of as characterizing aggressive action. It must be kept in mind, however, that one of the earliest lessons human beings learn as a result of social living is to suppress and restrain their overtly aggressive reactions. This does not mean, however, that such reaction tendencies are thereby annihilated; rather it has been found that, although these reactions may be temporarily compressed, delayed, disguised, displaced, or otherwise deflected from their immediate and logical goal, they are not destroyed. With this assumption of the inevitability of aggression following frustration, it is possible to bring a new measure of integration into a variety of types of facts which have hitherto been considered more or less isolated phenomena and to consider reasonable many instances of human conduct that have commonly been regarded and lightly dismissed as simply irrational, perverse, or abnormal.

The plausibility of the systematic position just suggested—which will be more fully developed in subsequent pages—is, of course, dependent to an important degree upon the formal definitions which are given to frustration, aggression, and certain related concepts; and an attempt will be made to provide these terms with as high a degree of exactness and operational specificity as possible. Formal terminology in this field, however, is still so new and unsettled that it is necessary to rely at least in a supplementary way upon the use of denotative examples in order to convey intended meanings in many instances. In this and subsequent chapters, therefore, frequent recourse is had to illustrative materials, a procedure which in no sense is intended to constitute proof of the propositions being elucidated. Evidence of a more compelling character is not entirely lacking and will be presented from time to time; but even this latter material should be regarded also as evidence, not as proof. The whole intent and aim of this book may be said, in fact, to be simply the exploration, in both a logical and empirical sense, of the implications and applications of a particular hypothesis which, despite its apparent plausibility and usefulness, is to be regarded as still an *hypothesis*.

FUNDAMENTAL CONCEPTS

At three-thirty on a hot afternoon the bell of an ice-cream vendor is heard on the street. James, aged four, runs toward his mother and announces: "Mother, the ice-cream man! I want an ice-cream cone!" Then he looks up very appealingly, puckers his lips, grasps his mother's skirt, and starts tugging her toward the front door.

At this point an observer who had been studying the behavior of this family might make a prediction. He might say: "Now James is going to try to take his mother out to the push cart. He may attempt to take her down the right or the left branch of the walk. In either case we can say that, unless something stops him, he will be holding a cone in his hand within three minutes and will have consumed it within ten. The act of consuming the cone will put an end to the sequence which I am predicting."

It is probable, however, that such an observer would find it more convenient for his purpose to deal abstractly with some of the significant aspects of the situation than with the actual events themselves. In referring to the origin of James' behavior sequence he might say, in the terminology to be used in this book, that James is *instigated* to take his mother out to buy him an ice-cream cone. An *instigator* is some antecedent condition of which the predicted response is the consequence. It may be directly observable as in the case of the vendor's

bell; or it may be an internal condition that can only be inferred—in this instance from James' statement that he wants ice cream. The statement itself is not the instigator, of course, but it may be used to indicate that an instigator exists because on previous occasions the statement has been observed to be correlated with the predicted response. The bell and the vendor are likewise interpreted as instigators because of such a previously observed correlation. The concept of instigator is clearly much broader than that of stimulus; whereas the latter refers only to energy (as physically defined) exerted on a sense-organ, the former refers to any antecedent condition, either observed or inferred, from which the response can be predicted, whether this condition be a stimulus, a verbally reported image, idea, or motive, or a state of deprivation.

The directly observable instigators to James' behavior are the bell and the ice-cream vendor. But the presence of internal instigators not directly observed could be inferred from what James says and does. To the extent that specific predictions could be made from the *appealing look*, the *puckering of the lips*, the *tugging on the skirt*, and the *statement* "I want an ice-cream cone!" that efforts would be made to get the ice cream, there would be justification for inferring the existence of instigators. All that is necessary, in order to infer their presence, is for the organism to have revealed some measurable, or at least denotable, behavior which has been shown previously to be correlated with the occurrence of the predicted response. Any refinements in either observational technique or theoretical analysis that enable one to predict responses more accurately also improve the inferences concerning the presence of instigators.

Several instigators to a certain response may operate simultaneously, and their combined effect represents the total amount of instigation to the response.[1] Instigation, therefore, is a quantitative concept and so some consideration must be given to the problem of *strength of instigation*. This strength is measured by the degree to which the instigated response competes successfully with simultaneously instigated incompatible responses, or in different technical words, by the prepotency of the instigated responses.

James might notice that the lawn sprinkler was spraying water in such a way as to cut off his path to the ice-cream vendor. He might say that he did not want to get wet or display other behavior from which it could be infered that there was instigation to avoid the sprinkler. Owing to the position of the sprinkler, this instigation would be incompatible with the instigation to get an ice-cream cone. On one occasion James might walk in the path of the sprinkler and on another he might not; the instigation to have an ice-cream cone would have competed successfully with the same simultaneous instigation to an incompatible response in the first case and not in the second. The instigation to obtain a cone, therefore, might be said to have been stronger when James ran through the water than when he did not. Any conditions which allow one to predict that James will run through more or less water to reach the cone are conditions from which an increase or decrease in the strength of instigation may be inferred.

In many instances of everyday behavior it is impractical to determine directly by an obstruction technique the degree to which simultaneously instigated incompatible responses can be overcome. In such instances it is desirable to use certain subsidiary measures for inferring the strength of instigation to the predicted response. The speed, duration, force, and probability of occurrence of a given response are presumably functions of the degree to which the response competes successfully with simultaneously instigated incompatible responses. Under properly constant conditions, these indicators may be used in lieu of the more exact measure. If James ran immediately and very rapidly toward the ice-cream vendor, it would be proper to assume that the instigation to this response was fairly strong. If, on the contrary, he dawdled, it would be reasonable to assume that the

instigation to get ice cream was relatively weak.

In the example that has been cited, it has been said that the act of consuming the cone would put an end to the predicted sequence of behavior. This means that James is known, from observation of previous ice-cream episodes, to be very much less likely to respond to the ringing of the bell with the predicted sequence of behavior for some time after he has had an ice-cream cone than he was before eating the cone. An act which terminates a predicted sequence will be called a *goal-response*. The goal-response may be defined as that reaction which reduces the strength of instigation to a degree at which it no longer has as much of a tendency to produce the predicted behavior sequence. The hungry rat eats and no longer seeks food; because the behavior sequence is terminated, the eating is considered to be the goal-response. The ticket-buyer reaches the box-office, purchases his ticket, and no longer stands in line; the purchase of the ticket is therefore said to be the goal-response.

Later on, however, James may give the same appealing look, may tug his mother's skirt again, and announce he wants another ice-cream cone; thus he will be giving further evidence from which instigation can be inferred. The termination of a behavior sequence is frequently only temporary. If there is reason to believe that the instigation exists again, James will be expected to perform the predicted sequence a second time. In fact, he will be expected to be even more apt to repeat the previous acts which had led successfully to the ice cream, since goal-responses have a *reinforcing effect* that induces the learning of the acts preceding them.

So far it has been assumed that nothing goes wrong to stop James. His mother, however, may insist that he wait until dinner time for his ice cream. His father may arrive on the scene, reprimand the mother for being so indulgent, and threaten to spank James for going to the cart. Or the ice-cream man may not have any more cones. In any of these cases the expected sequence of action will be interrupted and James will be prevented from consuming the cone. Such an interference with the occurrence of an instigated goal-response at its proper time in the behavior sequence is called a *frustration*.

Normally a series of acts ripples through without interruption, but interference may occur through punishment incident to the goal-seeking activities or through inaccessibility of the goal itself. The interference may be slight, as when a mosquito hums near a person absorbed in thought, or great, as when an individual suffers the effects of kidney disease. It is, nevertheless, the same form of interference that induces the frustration. Such expressions as "to disappoint a person," "to let someone down," "to cause pain to someone," and "to block somebody in carrying out an act" indicate that one person is imposing a frustration on another.

Neither the nature nor the origin of the interrupted behavior sequence need be considered here. It is essential only that it can be identified as in the process of occurring and that the mode of interference be specified. The goal-response may involve gross overt activity such as the manipulation of a physical object or it may involve but little overt activity as in the case of receiving congratulations for work well done. And it is irrelevant whether thumb-sucking in an eighteen-months-old child occurs as an unlearned response, or whether the physical integrations necessary to it have been learned in other stimulus contexts. To have the object-manipulation or the receiving of congratulations or the thumb-sucking blocked, however, constitutes a frustration. The instigations remain and the adequate goal-responses are interdicted. In order to say that a frustration exists, then, one must be able to specify two things: (1) that the organism could have been expected to perform certain acts, and (2) that these acts have been prevented from occurring.

It must be noted here that either the goal-response of eating the ice cream or a degree of prevention caused by an interfering agent can terminate James' activity; it may be difficult to tell whether the behavior sequence has stopped because of the first or the second circumstance. This is especially true when the interfering agent is an emotional conflict within the organism itself. From an operational standpoint, however, an infallible criterion exists. A goal-response reinforces the behavior sequence leading up to it, while interference does not. If it were not known from previous experience that eating ice cream was the goal-response to James' behavior sequence, it might be difficult to tell, if interference be assumed, whether the last act carried out (e.g., giving an appealing look) before the sequence was terminated was a goal-response or not; but by determining whether this act produced a stronger tendency for James to carry out the sequence a second time a decision could be reached.

Still another concept can be gleaned from this overworked example. In the past James might always have consumed vanilla cones. Interference with this response by the fact that the vendor had no vanilla ice cream would be a frustration. A chocolate cone, however, might be found to be a more or less acceptable substitute for vanilla. A response which substitutes for the goal-response, in that it also tends to terminate and reinforce the same preceding action, is called a substitute response.

A *substitute response* is any action which reduces to some degree the strength of the instigation, the goal-response to which was prevented from occurring. It has, therefore, one property of the goal-response itself: it too can reduce the strength of instigation. This reduction may occur as a result of a quantitatively reduced goal-response, as when a child is given an opportunity to enjoy some praise for turning a somersault instead of much praise for a handspring. Or the reduction of instigation may result from the occurrence of a goal-response to some more or less discrete element of the total instigation, as when a person lights a cigarette or drinks a glass of water while awaiting a delayed luncheon.

As may be supposed, substitute responses

occur with great frequency in the face of frustrations of all kinds. Eating raisin pie when there is no mince, reading romantic stories when real romance is unavailable, producing amateur theatricals when having a professional career has been prevented are characteristic substitutions. Some responses of this kind are even so apparent that they approach caricatures and are recognized by all adults in our culture— the childless woman who pampers her lap dog, the jilted lover who marries his ex-fiancée's sister, the smoker who, renouncing his practice, chews gum. These examples may give denotative definition to the concept of substitute response.[2]

Substitute responses, moreover, can be either less or more effective as terminating and reinforcing agents than the original response. To the extent that they are equally or more effective, they put an end to the frustrations preceding them and to the aggression produced by these frustrations.

At times James may kick or scream or say he hates his mother. Any such sequence of behavior, the goal-response to which is the injury of the person toward whom it is directed, is called *aggression*. According to the hypothesis, this is the primary and characteristic reaction to frustration, and will occur when something happens to interfere with James' efforts to get the ice-cream cone.

Many of the common forms of aggression can be instantly recognized by almost any observer who belongs to Western society. Acts of physical violence are perhaps the most obvious. Fantasies of "getting even" with galling superiors or rivals, calculated forays against frustrating persons (whether the weapon is a business deal, a gun, a malicious rumor, or a verbal castigation is of little moment), and generalized destructive or remonstrative outbursts like lynchings, strikes, and certain reformist campaigns are clearly forms of aggression as well. It hardly needs special emphasis that tremendously complex learned skills, such as the use of the boomerang and machine gun, may occur in these aggressive behavior sequences.

Aggression is not always manifested in overt movements but may exist as the content of a fantasy or dream or even a well thought-out plan of revenge. It may be directed at the object which is perceived as causing the frustration or it may be displaced to some altogether innocent source or even toward the self, as in masochism, martyrdom, and suicide. The target of aggression quite as readily may be inanimate as animate, provided that the acts would be expected to produce injury were the object animate. In fact, the aggression may be undirected toward any object— a man swears after striking his thumb with a hammer—when the action would cause pain if it were directed toward a person. Such nouns as anger, resentment, hatred, hostility, animus, exasperation, irritation, and annoyance carry something of the meaning of the concept. Verbs such as destroy, damage, torment, retaliate, hurt, blow up, humiliate, insult, threaten, and intimidate refer to actions of an aggressive nature.[3]

Although the frustration-aggression hypothesis assumes a universal causal relation between frustration and aggression, it is important to note that the two concepts have been defined *independently* as well as *dependently*. The dependent definition of aggression is *that response which follows frustration, reduces only the secondary, frustration-produced instigation, and leaves the strength of the original instigation unaffected.* Frustration is independently defined as *that condition which exists when a goal-response suffers interference.* Aggression is independently defined as *an act whose goal-response is injury to an organism* (or *organism-surrogate*)[4]. . . .

Although frustration as such can occur only to an individual organism, any given frustrating condition may occur to several individuals simultaneously. In such a case, a "group" is viewed distributively rather than as a collective thing. If all or most of the individuals in a group are hungry, the "group" may be said, after this distributive fashion, to be hungry. A group of laborers, for example, had gathered around a boarding-house table at six o'clock for dinner, as was their practice at the end of the day. On ordinary days they ate without much conversation but with a fair approximation of dignity and good manners. On the day in question, the group sat down at the usual hour but no waiters appeared. There were soon murmurs of protest to the general effect that, if the landlady were to stay home, dinner could be served on time; and threats were made that they might stop boarding at that house. Gradually the self-restraints usually governing behavior at the table disappeared and there was a rhythmic stamping of feet. Someone shouted, "We want food"—the rest took up the cry and produced a tremendous uproar. Hard rolls were seized from the table and thrown at the kitchen door, presumably in the direction of the landlady. Soon the object of their aggression appeared and explained the reason for the delay. Dinner was eventually served and the unusual behavior gradually died down, but with many threats and mutterings. Frustration was induced by the inability to continue those responses habitually connected with sitting down at a table and aggressive acts assumed the form of the breaches of etiquette, vociferous demands, shouted threats, and bread-throwing. . . .

A young man and his wife moved to a small town and began the process of finding a position in the social hierarchy of the city. It was important for their self-esteem as well as for the business success of the husband that this position should be as high as possible. They therefore welcomed an invitation from the wife of one of the leading bankers of the town to attend an informal party at his house. Both of the young people made every reasonable attempt to be agreeable and, in fact, succeeded very well. This success seemed to be attested by a further invitation which was accepted and which also resulted in a pleasant evening.

The observer who reported on this incident was also a witness of the expressions of satisfaction which came from both husband and wife at their successful plunge into the social mill-pond. The banker and his wife were regarded cordially and their friendliness was warmly appreciated. The same observer had, however, the opportunity to witness a sharp change in the attitudes of this young couple toward their older friends. The young woman became critical of the appearance and clothes of the banker's wife; she seemed to notice for the first time also that the older woman displayed an unseemly flirtatious attitude toward men more youthful than herself. In the conversation of the banker there was discovered an emptiness and pomposity which had not been sensed before. Discussions with friends suddenly revealed, strangely enough, that the banker was a mere figurehead in his own bank and that he was kept there because of his wealth rather than because of his business skill or judgment. There was a complete change of front from a cordial and admiring attitude to a markedly critical and hostile one. The visits to the big house stopped and a marked bitterness remained. No explanation was given for this change.

It was a number of months before the participant observer discovered, during an intimate conversation, the cause of the reversal of feeling. After several visits to the home of the banker, the young couple had thought they perceived a growing intimacy between the two families. They also experienced some dissatisfaction at accepting so much from their older friends while not themselves returning any of the favors received. After a suitable time they asked the banker family to come to dinner, with the wish to make at least a token payment on their social debt. Difficulties, however, developed at this point. After several weeks it seemed to be impossible to find any date which would be suitable to the banker and wife, and the only conclusion to be drawn was that they did not wish to come. This left the young couple with very distressing feelings of having been patronized and of not actually existing on the social horizon of the older couple. Their reactions of humiliation were inevitable.

An analysis of these data indicates that the frustrated responses were those connected with pleasure and satisfaction at securing recognition in the social life of the small town in which the young couple's lot was cast. The frustration ensued from the refusal of leaders in the hierarchy to confirm this status by accepting a dinner invitation. The refusal was frustrating, in that it put an effective end to all further action of self-betterment in the social sphere. It was undoubtedly at this point that the reaction of the young people toward the banker and his wife changed from an amiable and friendly one to an extremely resentful one. In this case, of course, the frustration itself was concealed because every admission of the humiliation to another person was in itself experienced as frustrating. . . .

In Marxian doctrine, the theories of the class-struggle and of the nature of the state depend to some extent, again by implication on the frustration-aggression principle. Surplus value, the materialistic interpretation of history, the nature of ideologies, these are subjects that can be treated adequately in a somewhat pure sociological or economic frame of reference. But when Marxists have described the dynamic human interrelationships involved in the class struggle and in the preservation and destruction of the state, they have introduced unwittingly a psychological system involving the assumption that aggression is a response to frustration.

The clearest and most concise statement of the nature of the class-struggle is to be found in *The Communist Manifesto*, the general *motifs* of which pervade most of the writings of Marx and Engels. The reasoning is as follows. The proletariat can be called oppressed, i.e., frustrated, since "These laborers, who must sell themselves piecemeal, are a commodity, like every other article of commerce, and are consequently exposed to all the vicissitudes of competition, to all the fluctuations of the market"; and, "owing to the extensive use of machinery and to division of labor," their work "has lost all individual character, and, consequently, all charm" (99, p. 21). The resulting aggression "goes through various states of development":

With its [the proletariat's] birth begins its struggle with the bourgeoisie. At first the contest is carried on by individual laborers, then by the work people of a factory, then by the operatives of one trade, in one locality, against the individual bourgeois who directly exploits them. They direct their attacks not against the bourgeois conditions of production, but against the instruments of production themselves: they destroy wares that compete with their labor, they smash to pieces machinery, they set factories ablaze, they seek to restore by force the vanished status of the workman of the Middle Ages. (99, p. 23).

This blind aggression is fruitless, since the frustration or exploitation continues to increase: "The growing competition among the bourgeois, and the resulting commercial crises, make the wages of the workers ever more fluctuating." In short, "The unceasing improvement of machinery, ever more rapidly developing, makes their livelihood more and more precarious; the collisions between individual workmen and individual bourgeois take more and more the character of collisions between two classes." As a result of these increased frustrations, the aggression assumes the following form:

The workers begin to form combinations (trades' unions) against the bourgeois; they club together in order to keep up the rate of wages; they found permanent associations in order to make provision beforehand for these occasional revolts. Here and there the contest breaks out into riots. (99, p. 24).

This aggression, however, is not yet completely directed against the frustrating agents, the bourgeoisie, for the "organization of the proletarians into a class, and consequently into a political party, is continually being upset again by the competition between the workers themselves." Finally, "when the class-struggle nears the decisive hour," the proletariat has organized its aggression and is "a really revolutionary class."

An extremely important instrument of the ruling class which prevents the frustrated from expressing their aggression against their frustrators is the state. It was Lenin, the practical strategist as well as Marxian theorist, who developed, as he himself has said, the implications of Marx and Engels in respect to the functioning of that state. In his *The State and Revolution*, he states plainly:

The State is the product and the manifestation of the *irreconcilability* of class antagonisms. The State arises when, where, and to the extent that the class antagonisms *cannot* be objectively reconciled. And, conversely, the existence of the State proves that the class antagonisms *are* irreconcilable. (87, p. 154; italics his).

The capitalistic state, then, with its "special bodies of armed men," enables "imperialism" and "banks" to create "to an unusually fine art both these methods of defending and asserting the omnipotence of wealth in democratic republics of all descriptions"; or, in Engels' words (which Lenin quotes with approval), the state is a "special repressive force."

It is evident that Marxian theory assumes the existence of profound frustrations in each member of the proletariat. These derive from many circumstances, among which are: the destruction of his pride by being forced to work at a machine and by being treated as another commodity; exploitation by his employers; the crises of the economic system; and the repressive measures of the state. These frustrations lead inevitably to aggression and eventually, according to the Marxian prediction, to the triumph of the oppressed class.

Psychological principles: I

JOHN DOLLARD AND OTHERS

Notes to this section will be found on pages 344–345.

STRENGTH OF INSTIGATION TO AGGRESSION

THE first step in elaborating the basic hypothesis is to restate it in the following quantitative form: the strength of instigation to aggression varies directly with the amount of frustration. The next step is to consider the factors which are responsible for the amount of frustration and therefore also responsible for the strength of instigation to aggression. It is assumed that there are three such factors: *the strength of instigation to aggression should vary directly with* (1) *the strength of instigation to the frustrated response*, (2) *the degree of interference with the frustrated response, and* (3) *the number of frustrated response-sequences.* Each of these factors will now be discussed and illustrated.

1. Strength of instigation to the frustrated response

According to this principle, withdrawal of food from a hungry dog should produce more growling and baring of teeth than similar withdrawal from a satiated dog. Loss of a crucial page from a detective story should exasperate a twelve-year-old boy more than loss of an equally crucial page from his history lesson.

An appeal to common experience gives this proposition an appearance of obvious validity which relevant experimental data are not yet completely adequate to check. Those that are cited here are regarded primarily as further illustrations and not as final proofs. An experiment by Sears and Sears (144) was designed to utilize variations in the strength of a five-months-old baby's hunger instigation as the independent variable. During a three-week period, at two of the four daily feedings, the child's feeding was systematically interrupted by withdrawal of the bottle from the mouth after varying amounts of milk had been taken. With this method, frustration of sucking and eating occurred when the instigation to those acts was of several different strengths. The strength of the aggressive reaction was measured in terms of the immediacy of crying following the withdrawal. When withdrawal occurred after only .5 oz. had been taken, crying began, on the average, after 5.0 seconds; after 2.5 oz. had been taken, the latency was 9.9 seconds; and after 4.5 oz. had been taken, it was 11.6 seconds. These figures indicate that as the child became more nearly satiated, i.e., as the strength of instigation decreased, frustration induced a less and less immediate aggressive response.

Two questionnaire studies by Doob and Sears (37) and Miller (106) have yielded additional relevant data. In the first, college students were given descriptions of various frustrating situations they had encountered in real life. Below each situation was listed a series of aggressive actions and substitute responses which might have occurred in the situation. The subjects were instructed to indicate which responses they had actually made and to rate on a four-point scale the strength of the instigator whose goal-responses had suffered interference. The proportion of responses which were aggressive was reliably greater as the strength of the instigation was rated higher.[1]

The proverbial violence of lovers' quarrels is probably a consequence of this same principle. Since two lovers presumably have greater instigation to affectional behavior involving each other than two non-lovers have, interference with this behavior by one of the former produces a more serious frustration than would be the case with the latter. The consequences of a somewhat similar difference in strength of instigation were illustrated in the study by Miller. He employed an annoyance test which permitted subjects to indicate the degree of annoyance caused by (*a*) being snubbed by various persons whom the subject liked to different degrees, and (*b*) being "off form" in sports for which the subject had different degrees of instigation to be successful. Ratings from a large group of college students indicated that in these situations the principle that the stronger the instigation the stronger the annoyance (aggression) held true. Being snubbed by an acquaintance was rated as more annoying than being snubbed by a stranger. Being snubbed by a close friend was, in turn, worse than being snubbed by an acquaintance. Similar results were obtained from the items pertaining to sport; the stronger the liking for a sport, the greater the annoyance exhibited at being "off form" in it. All these differences had critical ratios greater than 3.00.

2. Degree of interference with the frustrated response

According to this principle, a slight distraction producing a little interference with a golfer's drive at a crucial moment should be less likely to cause him to swear than a stronger distraction producing a much greater interference. Delays are also thought of as interferences. An employee, therefore, should be more likely to be severely reprimanded for keeping his busy employer waiting idly for thirty minutes than for being but three minutes tardy.

Empirical data illustrative of this second factor may be obtained from various kinds of social statistics. While these statistics undoubtedly involve a greater number of uncontrolled variables than would the results of an appropriate laboratory experiment, the facts which they represent are of such social significance that even a tentative attempt to elucidate them is of some interest.

Two correlations can be cited to demonstrate that aggression increases with an increase in interference with the goal-response. Indices of economic conditions were assumed by Hovland and Sears (69) to reflect the ease, or difficulty, with which customary economic activities of the members of a group can be carried out. Low indices, or bad economic conditions, should represent a greater interference with customary goal-responses than do high indices or good business conditions. The annual numbers of lynchings and property crimes with violence were taken as measures of aggression. As one index of the severity of interference with economic actions, the annual per acre value of cotton was computed for fourteen Southern states for the years 1882 to 1930. The correlation between this index and the number of lynchings in these same fourteen states was —.67; i.e., the number of lynchings (aggression) increased when the amount of interference increased. Similarly, Thomas (170) has found that property crimes with use of violence are correlated —.44 with economic indices.

Miller's study of annoyances (106) has also furnished results bearing on the same problem. The subjects reported that they felt much more irritated at being completely "off form" in their favorite sport than at being only slightly "off form." The critical ratio of this difference was 5.5.

3. Number of frustrated response-sequences

In addition to the variations in strength of any frustration, the amount or strength of aggressive response will depend in part on the amount of residual instigation from previous or simultaneous frustrations, which instigation summates to activate the response under observation. Minor frustrations add together to produce an aggressive response of greater strength than would normally be expected from the frustrating situation that appears to be the immediate antecedent of the aggression. The temporal factor is of great importance in this connection, but there are no data available at present to indicate precisely how long after the removal of the primary frustration the secondary instigation to aggression will persist. Further reference to this problem of "readiness to be aggressive" will be made in Chapter IV.

Morgan (113, pp. 245–246) has suggested an everyday kind of situation to indicate the potentialities (for aggression) of summation of previous frustrations:

Suppose we get up in the morning with the decision that, no matter what happens during this day, we will be sweet-tempered. In spite of our determination things may go wrong. We may stub our toe, lose our collar button, cut outselves while shaving, be unable to find the styptic to stop the bleeding, get to breakfast late and discover that the toast is burned and the coffee cold, but through all this we keep cool and even-tempered. Then some trivial thing occurs and we unexpectedly have a violent outburst. Those around us cannot understand why we are so irritable. If they knew all the facts, the repressed anger impulses that have at last gained an outlet, they would not be so surprised.

Studies of sleep-deprivation (75; 143) indicate the ease with which minor frustrations can bring about explosions of wrath when there is a background of serious frustration. In one investigation (143) a man who had previously been a willing subject for several arduous experiments complained vigorously at having to give free associations to fifty stimulus words. Another gave zero ratings to a series of jokes and added the comment that there was a limit to what could be called funny; he rated as mildly funny similar series of dull jokes both the day before and the day after the experiment.

INHIBITION OF ACTS OF AGGRESSION

It is evident, of course, that all frustrating situations do not produce overt aggression. Few arrested motorists jeer at the policeman; guests at formal dinners do not complain when the meat is tough; German Jews do not strike Nazi storm-troopers. To assume, however, that in such cases there is no aggression would be clearly false. Careful questioning may elicit the statement that the frustrated person "feels angry" or is "annoyed" or is "simply furious inside." These verbal expressions refer to implicit or partially inhibited aggressive actions which may be called *non-overt* as opposed to the *overt* aggression of fighting, striking, swearing, and other easily observed actions. It is not supposed that these terms refer to discrete classes of aggressive behavior but simply to the extremes of a descriptive continuum.

The basic variable that determines the degree to which any specific act of aggression will be inhibited appears to be anticipation of punishment. Provisionally it may be stated that *the strength of inhibition of any act of aggression varies positively with the amount of punishment anticipated to be a consequence of that act.* A boy who has been severely spanked for hitting his little brother should be somewhat less apt to hit him again under similar circumstances.

In essence this principle derives from the law of effect; those actions cease to occur which, in the past, have been followed by punishment.[2] It may be supposed that each frustration acts as an instigator to a great variety of aggressive responses. Some of these are overt in the sense that other persons can perceive them and some are so minimal (nonovert) that only the subject himself is aware of them. If past experience has taught him that certain of these aggressions are followed by punishment, those forms will tend to be eliminated and there will remain a residue of the forms that have not been punished. The overt vs. nonovert dimension achieves its importance primarily from the fact that in our own society, as well as in many others, it is the overt aggressions which are so frequently punished.[3] It must be recognized, however, that the general principle that punishment may eliminate any specific act of aggression can apply equally well, whether that act be overt, nonovert, or in some other descriptive dimension.

Some consideration must be given to a definition of punishment as it is used in this connection. There can be little question that such responses on the part of the social environment as physical injury, insults, ostracism, and deprivation of goods or freedom constitute punishment, but the term as it refers to these experiences has a connotation of "intention" on the part of the punishing persons. No such implication is essential nor is it desirable. Punishment, in essence, is equivalent to the occurrence of pain, but refers to the objective conditions of the infliction of pain rather than to facts of immediate experience.

In this sense two occurrences not ordinarily considered under the rubric of punishment may be added to the forms mentioned above. (1) *Injury to a loved object is punishment.* Since human love seems, almost universally, to involve an identification of the lover with the loved object, any punishment which the latter suffers is essentially a punishment of the lover himself. Aggression clearly has an injurious effect when it is expressed overtly and hence any aggression expressed toward the loved object serves to injure the person who has identified himself with the loved object. (2) *Anticipation of failure is equivalent to anticipation of punishment.*[4] The failure may be anticipated either because of a lack of a suitable object or because there are insuperable difficulties involved in carrying out the act.[5]

Psychological principles: II

JOHN DOLLARD AND OTHERS

Notes to this section will be found on page 345.

CONFLICT BETWEEN INSTIGATION AND INHIBITION

UNDERLYING the statement that anticipation of punishment decreases the degree to which any aggressive act is expressed is the assumption that the strength of instigation to the aggression is held constant. If the strength of this instigation is increased, however, it may become strong enough to overcome the anticipation of punishment.

In other words, a sufficiently "infuriated" (frustrated) person may "throw caution to the winds" and attack the frustrating agent. The overcoming of the anticipation of punishment depends on the assumption that *the strengths of antagonistic or incompatible responses summate negatively in some algebraic manner.* Although this assumption may have to be qualified, Hovland and Sears (68) and Bugelski and Miller (28) have demonstrated its usefulness in the theoretical explanation of conflicts. The conflict in the present instance is between the two incompatible action-sequences of expressing a specific act of aggression and of avoiding the punishment anticipated for such expression.

Tentative evidence for assuming some

form of algebraic summation of the two antagonistic factors called instigation and inhibition may be obtained from the same questionnaire study of Doob and Sears (37). Not only did the proportion of aggressive responses increase with increase in the strength of the instigation, as rated by the subjects; but also, in line with the fact that more punishment was anticipated for overt than for non-overt aggression, the proportion of aggressive acts which were overt rather than non-overt increased in the same way. Of the aggressive responses to those situations in which the drive was rated as "very weak," only 39.0 per cent were overt aggression; the next strongest rating produced 44.7 per cent overt; the next strongest, 47.6 per cent; and the strongest, 61.6 per cent. The progressive increase in the amount of overt aggression as the instigation to aggression becomes stronger is evidence that the successively stronger instigations are able to override progressively more of the inhibitions against acts of overt aggression. . . .

In order to begin the task of describing the direction which aggression will be expected to take, it is necessary to make a further assumption: *the strongest instigation, aroused by a frustration, is to acts of aggression directed against the agent perceived to be the source of the frustration and progressively weaker instigations are aroused to progressively less direct acts of aggression.*[1] A man who had just had his vacation plans disrupted by his employer will be expected, on the basis of this assumption, to be most angry at his employer but also somewhat more irritable toward the world in general.

The principle that the strongest instigation is to aggression against the agent perceived to be the source of the frustration finds a social application in war propaganda. Lasswell (83, p. 47) has shown that one of the techniques for making people aggressive toward the enemy during the World War was to make them believe that this enemy was the actual or potential source of important frustrations. Further evidence, indirectly supporting this principle, is suggested by the fact that the subjects in the study by Doob and Sears (37) definitely reported acts of direct aggression to be much more satisfying to them than other forms of aggression.

A given frustration will instigate direct aggression. The next logical step is a consideration of the behavior to be expected when a strongly instigated act of direct aggression is prevented from occurring by a strong anticipation of punishment specific to that act. Since it is thus assumed that the act of direct aggression is strongly instigated, interference with this direct aggression constitutes in itself an additional frustration. And, according to the principles already stated, this additional frustration will be expected: (1) directly to instigate acts of aggression against the agent perceived to be responsible for the interference with the original aggression, and (2) indirectly to heighten the instigation to all other forms of aggression.

Obviously this vicious circle—frustration, aggression, interference with aggression, more frustration—tends to be repeated as long as successive acts of aggression suffer interference.[2] From this it follows that *the greater the degree of inhibition specific to a more direct act of aggression, the more probable will be the occurrence of less direct acts of aggression.*

When the argument is carried further, it is clear that, if all the acts of aggression directed at a given object are prevented, there will be a tendency for other acts of aggression, not directed at this object, to occur. A person may kick a chair instead of his enemy. In Freudian terminology, such aggression is *displaced* from one object to another.[3] If, on the other hand, the prevention is specific to the type of act which would be direct aggression, there will be a tendency for other acts of different types to occur.[4] An individual may bring a lawsuit against his enemy instead of attempting to murder him; thus a *change in the form* of aggression may occur. Although these two kinds of change are not necessarily distinct functionally, they will be discussed separately.

DISPLACEMENT OF AGGRESSION

The principle which has just been derived, that there should be a strong tendency for inhibited aggression to be displaced, is supported by a wide variety of observations from different fields of investigation. In turn, these observations are integrated and made more meaningful by the principle of displacement.

Superficially puzzling instances of behavior in which a tremendous amount of aggression suddenly explodes without apparent cause are often explicable on the basis of displaced aggression. A Southern girl whose life history was being studied had severely berated a porter who merely failed to have the exact change immediately on hand. Such behavior was exceedingly rare in this ordinarily mild-mannered girl. She herself was for some time most perplexed and dismayed by such a sudden, violent, and seemingly irrational outburst of temper. When questioned briefly, she revealed that on this particular morning she had had a severely exasperating experience with her landlord, but had completely inhibited all aggressive tendencies toward him. As soon as this fact was called to her attention, she understood her own atypical anger toward the porter as displaced aggression.

On occasion, displaced aggression may have a somewhat happier fate and even serve socially approved ends. Lasswell (84) reports the case of a political reformer, part of whose zeal, the investigator believed, could be traced back definitely to basic hatreds against his father and brother. These hatreds were displaced to objects whose destruction was highly approved by the followers of the reformer. Some such displacements may be called sublimations.

A different type of evidence tending to support the principle of displacement is afforded by three simple exploratory experiments on aggression. In one of these, Miller and Davis (110) trained albino rats to commence striking one another, at the signal of a mild shock, in a manner similar to the way in which rats strike at one another when normally fighting. This behavior was reinforced by turning off the shock as soon as the rats were observed to strike one another vigorously. A small celluloid doll was then placed in the arena along with a pair of the trained rats; these particular animals tended to strike each other. Different animals, similarly trained, were placed *one at a time* in the same apparatus with the doll; these tended to strike the doll. A rat first attempted, in short, to strike the other animal, but when this was prevented by the absence of that animal it struck the doll.

In another study Miller and Bugelski (108) used an experimental situation to frustrate human subjects. The subjects were told that they were working in an experiment on co-operation and competition, and by proper urging they were instigated to do their very best. Then they were paired, one at a time, with a partner who, they thought, was just another subject but who was actually a confederate of the experimenters. During "cooperation" this partner caused the subjects to fail by bungling his part of all the cooperative tasks. During "competition" the partner caused the subjects to fail by succeeding well himself and making distracting remarks and invidious comparisons. A variety of other little annoyances, such as mispronouncing the subject's name, were also provided. Immediately after experiencing this frustrating situation the subjects tended to rate their friends lower on a simple personality scale than did control subjects who had not been subjected to these frustrations. Since the friends had not been present and could not possibly have been to blame for the frustrations which the subjects had just undergone, the more critical attitude of the subjects toward their friends may be taken as tentative evidence of the spread or displacement of aggression.

A third experiment, also by the same writers (109), took advantage of a frustrating situation in a natural setting. By chance it was known that, as part of a general testing program, boys at a camp were going to be forced to sacrifice a portion of their leisure activity in order to take long, dull examinations composed of questions which, on the whole, were too difficult for them to answer.

At the outset the boys were relatively unaware of what was in store for them. Later it became obvious that the tests were running overtime and were preventing them from making the strongly instigated response of attending Bank Night at the local theatre; thus they were compelled to miss what they considered to be the most interesting event of the week. In order to exploit this situation, so loaded with frustrations, all of the boys were given brief attitude tests before and after the main examination. Half of them rated Mexicans before and Japanese after the main examination. The other half rated Japanese before and Mexicans afterwards. As would be expected, the attitude toward either set of foreigners was more unfavourable after the frustration of taking the examinations and missing Bank Night than before.

An apparently similar tendency is to be observed in the behavior of groups of Southern whites toward the Negro. The positive correlation between low economic indices and number of lynchings, cited in Chapter II, represents not only the variation in aggression with variation in strength to frustration but also the displacement of aggression to the Negroes. By no stretch of imagination could it be assumed that the lynched Negroes were the *source* of the frustration represented by low per acre value of cotton. That politicians as well as Negroes may be the target of displaced aggression is indicated by two studies which suggest that there is a greater tendency for rural districts to vote the incumbents out of office following years of poor rainfall than of good (10; 98). Since the politicians could not conceivably have been thought to be responsible for the rainfall, such a trend is perhaps an even more striking example of displacement than the well-known tendence for the public to vote against the party which was holding office at the onset of an economic depression. The processes involved in bringing about such displacements, to be sure, may actually be found to be quite complex. . . .

CATHARSIS: EQUIVALENCE OF FORMS

It has been assumed that the inhibition of any act of aggression is a frustration which increases the instigation to aggression. Conversely, *the occurrence of any act of aggression is assumed to reduce the instigation to aggression.* [5] In psychoanalytic terminology, such a release is called *catharsis.* . . .

These similar dynamics seem to be exhibited in a case . . . in which a wife frustrated her husband by withdrawing money for household expenses from their savings account. The money was being saved slowly and arduously through the husband's rigorous self-denial of small luxuries. His wife's careless dependence on the account to tide her over when she ran out of her supposedly adequate household budget constituted a serious frustration to the husband's careful program of investment. Instead of being angry at her, however, he berated himself. He said, "I don't blame you for not paying any attention to my wishes; they aren't worth worrying about. I'm no good to anybody anyway." Then he shut the door of his room and the wife heard him sobbing bitterly. Her abject apologies only brought more tears and self-recrimination. Nothing she could do was of any avail until finally she happened to say a few sharp words to him. This brought down an avalanche of vituperation on her head and afterwards the husband seemed to feel much better and could be comforted. Soon he cheerfully began to plan new ways in which the savings account could be restored.

In this instance aggression toward the self was evidently a characteristic direction for aggression to take. When a further frustration occurred in which the wife was clearly perceived as the frustrating agent, direct aggression was expressed. The "avalanche of vituperation" was presumably a much stronger aggression than would normally have been called forth by the "few sharp words" and was a response to the total instigation produced by the original frustration plus the later relatively mild one. This final aggression apparently served to reduce the strength of instigation to the self-aggression, since no further self-aggression occurred after the object-directed outburst. . . .

SUMMARY

1. The strongest instigation aroused by a frustration is to acts of aggression directed against the agent perceived to be the source of the frustration, and progressively weaker instigations are aroused to progressively less direct acts of aggression.

2. The inhibition of acts of direct aggression is an additional frustration which instigates aggression against the agent perceived to be responsible for this inhibition and increases the instigation to other forms of aggression. There is, consequently, a strong tendency for inhibited aggression to be displaced to different objects and expressed in modified forms. Socially approved modifications are called sublimations.

3. Since self-punishment is necessarily involved, aggression turned against the self must overcome a certain amount of inhibition and therefore tends not to occur unless other forms of expression are even more strongly inhibited. If the amount of inhibition of various acts of aggression is held relatively constant, the tendency to self-aggression is stronger both when the individual believes himself, rather than an external agent, to be responsible for the original frustration and when direct aggression is restrained by the self rather than by an external agent.

4. The expression of any act of aggression is a catharsis that reduces the instigation to all other acts of aggression. From this and the principle of displacement it follows that, with the level of original frustration held constant, there should be an inverse relationship between the expression of various forms of aggression.

5. It is the functional unity represented by the phenomena of catharsis and displacement that justifies attaching the label of aggression to the variety of responses considered in this theoretical presentation.

Aggression, nature, and nurture

The clarity of the frustration–aggression hypothesis has not solved the problem of the origins of aggression. Freud believed that aggression was an innate tendency in man. A now very popular European natural scientist, Konrad Lorenz, has amassed a great array of data arguing substantially the same belief. All such writing opposes the usually implicit assumption of many social scientists that Society is to blame for man's aggressiveness. An American psychologist, Leonard Berkowitz, by implication depreciates the ill-disguised moralism of man's original guilt or his original innocence. His findings argue that people and aggression are more complicated than that.

Berkowitz, in short, in the following essay argues that the factors involved in producing that overt behavior described as aggressive are too intertwined to produce a simple conclusion, scientific or moral. For anyone who wishes to oversimplify and confirm what he knew all along about the origin of aggression—finding it altogether in the nature of man or altogether in his nurture—a careful selection of only some of the items in the bibliography is guaranteed to produce that inner peace which certainty generates. However, when this certainty is confronted with inconsistent facts, frustration may result, to be followed by aggression against the ambivalent environment. The editor himself remains unsure who would be at fault for such aggression.

The study of Urban violence

Some implications of laboratory
studies of frustration and
aggression*

LEONARD BERKOWITZ

Notes to this section will be found on page 345.

THE frustration-aggression hypothesis is
the easiest and by far the most popular
explanation of social violence—whether
political turmoil, the hot summers of riot
and disorder, or robberies and juvenile
delinquency. We are all familiar with this
formulation, and there is no need to spell
out once again the great number of economic, social, and psychological frustrations
that have been indicted as the source of
aggression and domestic instability. Espoused
in the social world primarily by political
and economic liberals, this notion contends
that the cause of civil tranquility is best
served by eliminating barriers to the satisfaction of human needs and wants. Indeed,
in the version that has attracted the greatest
attention, the one spelled out by Dollard
and his colleagues at Yale in 1939, it is
argued that "agression is always the result
of frustration."[1]

The widespread acceptance of the frustration-aggression hypothesis, however, has
not kept this formula safe from criticism.

* Author's Note: *This is a slightly revised
version of a paper delivered at the annual meeting
of the American Political Science Association,
Chicago, September 1967. The research reported
in this paper has been sponsored by grants GS 1228
and GS 1737 from the National Science Foundation.*

Since we are here concerned with the roots
of violence, it is important to look closely
at the relationship between frustration and
aggression and consider the objections that
have been raised. These criticisms have
different, sometimes radically divergent,
implications for social policy decisions.
Before beginning this discussion, two points
should be made clear. One, I believe in the
essential validity of the frustration–aggression
hypothesis, although I would modify it
somewhat and severely restrict its scope.
Two, with the Yale psychologists I prefer
to define a "frustration" as the blocking of
ongoing, goal-directed activity, rather than
as the emotional reaction to this blocking.

One type of criticism is today most clearly
associated with the ideas and writings of
the eminent ethnologist, Konrad Lorenz.
Throughout much of his long and productive
professional career Lorenz has emphasized
that the behavior of organisms—humans
as well as lower animals, fish, and birds—
is largely endogenously motivated; the
mainsprings of action presumably arise from
within. Behavior, he says, results from the
spontaneous accumulation of some excitation or substance in neural centers. The
external stimulus that seems to produce the
action theoretically only "unlocks" inhibi-
tory processes, thereby "releasing" the
response. The behavior is essentially not a
reaction to this external stimulus, but is
supposedly actually impelled by the internal
force, drive, or something, and is only let
loose by the stimulus. If a sufficient amount
of the internal excitation or substance
accumulates before the organism can encounter a releasing stimulus, the response
will go off by itself. In his latest book, *On
Aggression*, Lorenz interprets aggressive
behavior in just this manner. "It is the
spontaneity of the [aggressive] instinct," he
maintains, "that makes it so dangerous"[2]
(p. 50). The behavior "can 'explode' without
demonstrable external stimulation" merely
because the internal accumulating *something*
had not been discharged through earlier
aggression. He strongly believes that
"present-day civilized man suffers from insufficient discharge of his aggressive drive

...." (p. 243). Lorenz's position, then, is that frustrations are, at best, an unimportant source of aggression.

We will not here go into a detailed discussion of the logical and empirical status of the Lorenzian account of behavior. I should note, however, that a number of biologists and comparative psychologists have severely criticized his analysis of animal behavior. Among other things, they object to his vague and imprecise concepts, and his excessive tendency to reason by crude analogies. Moreover, since Lorenz's ideas have attracted considerable popular attention, both in his own writings and in *The Territorial Imperative* by Robert Ardrey, we should look at the evidence he presents for his interpretation of human behavior. Thus, as one example, he says his views are supported by the failures of "an American method of education" to produce less aggressive children, even though the youngsters have been supposedly "spared all disappointments and indulged in every way" (*On Aggression*, p. 50). Since excessively indulged children probably expect to be gratified most of the time, so that the inevitable occasional frustrations they encounter are actually relatively strong thwartings for them, Lorenz's observation must leave the frustration–aggression hypothesis unscathed. His anthropological documentation is equally crude. A psychiatrist is quoted who supposedly "proved" that the Ute Indians have an unusually high neurosis rate because they are not permitted to discharge the strong aggressive drive bred in them during their warlike past (p. 244). Nothing is said about their current economic and social frustrations. Again, we are told of a psychoanalyst who "showed" that the survival of some Bornean tribes is in jeopardy because they can no longer engage in head-hunting (p. 261). In this regard, the anthropologist Edmund Leach has commented that Lorenz's anthropology is "way off," and reports that these Bornean tribes are actually having a rapid growth in population.

Another citation also illustrates one of Lorenz's major cures for aggressive behavior. He tells us (p. 55) that quarrels and fights often tear apart polar expeditions or other isolated groups of men. These people, Lorenz explains, had experienced an unfortunate damming up of aggression because their isolation had kept them from discharging their aggressive drive in attacks on "strangers or people outside their own circle of friends" (p. 55). In such circumstances, according to Lorenz, "the man of perception finds an outlet by creeping out of the barracks (tent, igloo) and smashing a not too expensive object with as resounding a crash as the occasion merits" (p. 56). According to this formulation, then, one of the best ways to prevent people from fighting is to provide them with "safe" or innocuous ways of venting their aggressive urge. Efforts to minimize their frustrations would presumably be wasted or at least relatively ineffective.

I must strongly disagree with Lorenz's proposed remedy for conflict. Informal observations as well as carefully controlled laboratory experiments indicate that attacks upon supposedly safe targets do not lessen, and can even increase, the likelihood of later aggression. We know, for example, that some persons have a strong inclination to be prejudiced against almost everyone who is different from them. For these prejudiced personalities, the expression of hostility against some groups of outsiders does not make them any friendlier toward other persons. Angry people may perhaps feel better when they can attack some scapegoat, but this does not necessarily mean their aggressive tendencies have been lessened. The pogroms incited by the Czar's secret police were no more successful in preventing the Russian Revolution than were the Russo-Japanese and Russo-Germanic wars. Attacks on minority groups and foreigners did not drain away the hostility toward the frustrating central government. Aggression can stimulate further aggression, at least until physical exhaustion, fear, or guilt inhibits further violence. Rather than providing a calming effect, the destruction, burning, and looting that take place during the initial stages of a riot seem to provoke still more violence. Further, several recent laboratory studies have demonstrated that giving children an opportunity to play aggressive games does not decrease the attacks they later will make upon some peer, and has a good chance of heightening the strength of these subsequent attacks.[3]

These misgivings, it should be clear, are not based on objections to the notion of innate determinants of aggression. Some criticisms of the frustration–aggression hypothesis have argued against the assumption of a "built-in" relationship between frustration and aggression, but there is today a much greater recognition of the role of constitutional determinants in human behavior. However, we probably should not think of these innate factors as constantly active instinctive drives. Contemporary biological research suggests these innate determinants could be likened to a "built-in wiring diagram" instead of a goading force. The "wiring" or neural connections makes it easy for certain actions to occur, but only in response to particular stimuli.[4] The innate factors are linkages between stimuli and responses—and an appropriate stimulus must be present if the behavior is to be elicited. Frustrations, in other words, may inherently increase the likelihood of aggressive reactions. Man might well have a constitutional predisposition to become aggressive after being thwarted. Clearly, however, other factors—such as fear of punishment or learning to respond in non-aggressive ways to frustrations—could prevent this potential from being realized.

It is somewhat easier to accept this interpretation of the frustration–aggression hypothesis, if we do not look at frustration as an emotionally neutral event. Indeed, an increasing body of animal and human research suggests that the consequences of a severe thwarting can be decidedly similar to those produced by punishment and pain. In the language of the experimental psychologists, the frustration is an aversive stimulus, and aversive stimuli are very reliable sources of aggressive behavior. But setting aside the specific emotional quality of the

frustration, more and more animal and human experimentation has provided us with valuable insights into the frustration–aggression relationship.

This relationship, first of all, is very widespread among the various forms of life; pigeons have been found to become aggressive following a thwarting much as human children and adults do. In a recent experiment by Azrin, Hutchinson, and Hake,[5] for example, pigeons were taught to peck at a key by providing them with food every time they carried out such an action. Then after the key-pressing response was well established, the investigators suddenly stopped giving the bird food for his behavior. If there was no other animal present in the experimental chamber at the time, the pigeon exhibited only a flurry of action. When another pigeon was nearby, however, this burst of responding did not take place and the thwarted bird instead attacked the other pigeon. The frustration led to aggression, but only when a suitable target was present. This last qualification dealing with the nature of the available target is very important.

Before getting to this matter of the stimulus qualities of the target, another aspect of frustrations should be made explicit. Some opponents of the frustration–aggression hypothesis have assumed a person is frustrated whenever he has been deprived of the ordinary goals of social life for a long period of time. This assumption is not compatible with the definition of "frustration" I put forth at the beginning of this paper or with the results of recent experimentation. Contrary to traditional motivational thinking and the motivational concepts of Freud and Lorenz, many psychologists now insist that deprivations alone are inadequate to account for most motivated behavior. According to this newer theorizing, much greater weight must be given to anticipations of the goal than merely to the duration or magnitude of deprivation per se. The stimulation arising from these anticipations—from anticipatory goal responses—is now held to be a major determinant of the vigor and persistence of goal-seeking activity. As one psychologist (Mowrer) put it, we cannot fully account for goal-striving unless we give some attention to "hope." Whether a person's goal is food, a sexual object, or a color TV set, his goal-seeking is most intense when he is thinking of the goal and anticipating the satisfactions the food, sexual object, or TV set will bring. But similarly, his frustration is most severe when the anticipated satisfactions are not achieved.[6]

The politico-social counterpart of this theoretical formulation is obvious; the phrase "revolution of rising expectations" refers to just this conception of frustration. Poverty-stricken groups who had never dreamed of having automobiles, washing machines, or new homes are not frustrated merely because they had been deprived of these things; they are frustrated only after they had begun to hope. If they had dared to think they might get these objects and had anticipated their satisfactions, the inability to fulfill their anticipations is a frustration, Privations in themselves are much less likely to breed violence than is the dashing of hopes.

James Davies has employed this type of reasoning in his theory of revolutions.[7] The American, French, and Russian Revolutions did not arise because these people were subjected to prolonged, severe hardships, Davies suggests. In each of these revolutions, and others as well, the established order was overthrown when a sudden, sharp socioeconomic *decline* abruptly thwarted the hopes and expectations that had begun to develop in the course of gradually improving conditions. Some data recently reported by Feierabend and Feierabend[8] can also be understood in these terms. They applied the frustration–aggression hypothesis to the study of political instability in a very impressive crossnational investigation. Among other things, they observed that rapid change in modernization within a society (as indicated by changes in such measures as the percentage of people having a primary education and the per capita consumption of calories) was associated with a relatively great increase in political instability (p. 265).

It could be that the rapid socioeconomic improvements produce more hopes and expectations than can be fulfilled. Hope outstrips reality, even though conditions are rapidly improving for the society as a whole, and many of the people in the society are frustrated. Some such process, of course, may be occurring in the case of our present Negro revolution.

Let me now return to the problem of the stimulus qualities of the target of aggression. Recall that in the experiment with the frustrated pigeons that thwarted birds did not display their characteristic aggressive behavior unless another pigeon was nearby. The presence of an appropriate stimulus object was evidently necessary to evoke aggression from the aroused animals. Essentially similar findings have been obtained in experiments in which painful electric shocks were administered to rats.[9] Here too the aroused animals only attacked certain targets; the shocked rats did not attack a doll placed in the experimental chamber, whether the doll was moving or stationary. Nor did they attack a recently deceased rat lying motionless in the cage. If the dead animal was moved, however, attacks were made. Comparable results have been obtained when electrical stimulation was applied to the hypothalamus of cats.[10] Objects having certain sizes or shapes were attacked, while other kinds of objects were left alone.

This tendency for aroused animals to attack only particular targets can perhaps be explained by means of Lorenz's concept of the releasing stimulus. The particular live and/or moving target "releases" the animal's aggressive response. But note that the action is not the product of some gradually accumulating excitation or instinctive aggressive drive. The pigeon, rat, or cat, we might say, was first emotionally aroused (by the frustration, pain, or hypothalamic stimulation) and the appropriate stimulus object then released or evoked the action.

Similar processes operate at the human level. A good many (but not all) aggressive acts are impulsive in nature. Strong emotional arousal creates a predisposition to aggression, and the impulsive violent be-havior occurs when an appropriate aggressive stimulus is encountered. Several experiments carried out in our Wisconsin laboratory have tried to demonstrate just this. Simply put, our basic hypothesis is that external stimuli associated with aggression will elicit rela-tively strong attacks from people who, for one reason or another, are ready to act aggressively. A prime example of such an aggressive stimulus, of course, is a weapon. One of our experiments has shown that angered college students who were given an opportunity to attack their tormentor exhibited much more intense aggression (in the form of electric shocks to their frus-trator) when a rifle and pistol were nearby than when a neutral object was present or when there were no irrelevant objects near them.[11] The sight of the weapons evidently drew stronger attacks from the subjects than otherwise would have occurred in the absence of these aggressive objects. Several other experiments, including studies of children playing with aggressive toys, have yielded findings consistent with this anal-ysis.[12] In these investigations, the aggressive objects (guns) acquired their aggressive stimulus properties through the use to which they were put. These stimulus pro-perties can also come about by having the object associated with aggression. Thus, in several of our experiments, people whose name associated them with violent films shown to our subjects later were attacked more strongly by the subjects than were other target-persons who did not have this name-mediated connection with the observed aggression.[13]

These findings are obviously relevant to contemporary America. They of course argue for gun-control legislation, but also have implications for the riots that have torn through our cities this past summer. Some of our political leaders seem to be looking for single causes, whether this is a firebrand extremist such as Stokely Car-michael or a history of severe social and economic frustrations. Each of these factors might well have contributed to this summer's rioting; the American Negroes' frustrations

undoubtedly were very important. Never-theless, a complete understanding of the violence, and especially the contagious spread from one city to another, requires consideration of a multiplicity of causes, all operating together. Some of these causes are motivational; rebellious Negroes may have sought revenge, or they may have wanted to assert their masculinity. Much more simply, a good deal of activity during these riots involved the looting of desirable goods and appliances. Not all of the violence was this purposive, however. Some of it arose through the automatic operation of aggressive stimuli in a highly emotional atmosphere.

This impulsive mob violence was clearly not part of a calculated war against the whites. Where a deliberate antiwhite cam-paign would have dictated attacks upon whites in all-white bastions, it was often Negro property that was destroyed. More-over, aggressive stimuli had an important role. A lifetime of cruel frustrations built up a readiness for aggression, but this readiness had to be activated and inhibi-tions had to be lowered in order to produce the impulsive behavior. Different types of aggressive stimuli contributed to the aggres-sive actions. Some of these stimuli originated in the news reports, photographs, and films from other cities; research in a number of laboratories throughout this country and Canada indicates that observed aggression can stimulate aggressive behavior. This media-stimulated aggression may not always be immediately apparent. Some aggressive responses may operate only internally, in the form of clenched fists and violent ideas, but they can increase the probability and strength of later open aggression. The news stories probably also lower restraints against this open violence. A person who is in doubt as to whether destruction and looting are safe and/or proper behavior might have his doubts resolved; if other people do this sort of thing, maybe it isn't so bad. Maybe it is a good way to act and not so dangerous after all. And again the likelihood of aggression is heightened.

Then a precipitating event occurs in the

Negro ghetto. The instigating stimulus could be an attack by whites against Negroes—a report of police brutality against some Negro—or it might be the sight of aggressive objects such as weapons, or even police. Police probably can function as stimuli automatically eliciting aggression from angry Negroes. They are the "head thumpers," the all-too-often hostile enforcers of laws arbitrarily imposed upon Negroes by an alien world. Mayor Cavanagh of Detroit has testified to this aggression-evoking effect. Answering criticisms of the delay in sending in police reinforcements at the first sign of rioting, he said experience in various cities around the country indicates the presence of police can inflame angry mobs and actually increase violence (*Meet the Press*, July 30, 1967). Of course the events in Milwaukee the week after Mayor Cavanagh spoke suggest that an army of police and National Guardsmen swiftly applied can restrain and then weaken mob violence fairly effectively. This rapid, all-blanketing police action obviously produces strong inhibitions, allowing time for the emotions inflamed by the precipitating event to cool down. Emptying the streets also removes aggression-eliciting stimuli; there is no one around to see other people looting and burning. But unless this extremely expensive complete inhibition can be achieved quickly, city officials might be advised to employ other law-enforcement techniques. Too weak a display of police force might be worse than none at all. One possibility is to have Negroes from outside the regular police department attempt to disperse the highly charged crowds. There are disadvantages, of course. The use of such an extra-police organization might be interpreted as a weakening of the community authority or a sign of the breakdown of the duly constituted forces of law and order. But there is also at least one very real advantage. The amateur law enforcers do not have a strong association with aggression and arbitrary frustration, and thus are less likely to draw out aggressive reactions from the emotionally charged people.

There are no easy solutions to the violence in our cities' streets. The causes are complex and poorly understood, and the possible remedies challenge our intelligence, cherished beliefs, and pocketbooks. I am convinced, however, that the roots of this violence are not to be found in any instinctive aggressive drive, and that there is no easy cure in the provision of so-called "safe" aggressive outlets. The answers can only be found in careful, systematic research free of the shopworn, oversimplified analogies of the past.

Conflict, cooperation, and revolution

Georg Simmel was a German social scientist who wrote early in the 20th century. To sociologists, he is a sociologist—one of them (Everett Hughes) describing him as "the Freud of the study of society." To the editor of this volume, a political scientist, Simmel reads more like a psychologist than a psychoanalyst. All of this goes to show how arbitrary and contrived are the fences separating academic disciplines.

Simmel's great contribution has been to emphasize the ambivalence of interpersonal relationships. He discusses friendly and hostile interaction between husbands and wives and between large social aggregates like churches. He concludes that co-operation sometimes produces conflict and that conflict sometimes produces co-operation.

Ambivalence is the central theme of social relationships as Simmel sees them. It is indeed ambivalence of the profoundest sort toward other people that runs through the minds of people on the verge of revolt. Revolution ("internal war") is an act of violence, so to speak within the family. It is conflict that follows from a history of both friendship and hostility, love and hate, between various people who have been in more or less close contact. Simmel indicates how the ambivalence and closeness can produce first conflict and then an intensification of the prior positive bonds that revolution separates. Unfortunately he does not provide us with means of measuring the intensity of cooperation and conflict—the affection, the hatred, the release, and then the remorse and friendship that occur during successive stages of revolution. The measurement problem remains, leaving uncertain the distinction between the hostility that produces contained conflict within the social system and that produces conflict so intense as to break the system.

Conflict and the web of group affiliations

GEORG SIMMEL

Notes to this section will be found on page 346.

THE PRIMARY NATURE OF HOSTILITY

SKEPTICAL moralists speak of natural enmity between men. For them, *homo homini lupus* [man is wolf to man], and "in the misfortune of our best friends there is something which does not wholly displease us." But even the diametrically opposed moral philosophy, which derives ethical selflessness from the transcendental foundations of our nature, does not thereby move very far from the same pessimism. For after all, it admits that devotion to the Thou cannot be found in the experience and observation of our will. Empirically, rationally, man is pure egoist, and any deflection of this natural fact can occur in us, not through nature, but only through the *deux ex machina* of a metaphysical being. Hence natural hostility as a form or basis of human relations appears at least side by side with their other basis, sympathy. The strange lively interest, for instance, which people usually show in the suffering of others, can only be explained on the basis of a mixture of the two motivations. This deep-lying antipathy is also suggested by the phenomenon, not at all rare, of the "spirit of contradiction" (*Widerspruchsgeist*). It is found not only in those nay-sayers-on-principle who are the despair of their surroundings among friends, in families, in committees, and in the theatre public. Nor does this spirit celebrate its most characteristic triumphs in the realm of politics, in those men of opposition whose classical type Macaulay has described in the person of Robert Ferguson: "His hostility was not to Popery or to Protestantism, to monarchical government or to republican government, to the house of Stuarts or to the house of Nassau, but to whatever was at the time established." All these cases which are usually considered to be types of "pure opposition" do not *necessarily* have to be such: ordinarily, the opponents conceive of themselves as defenders of threatened rights, as fighters for what is objectively correct, as knightly protectors of the minority.

It appears to me that much less striking phenomena reveal more clearly an abstract impulse to opposition—especially the quiet, often hardly known, fleeting temptation to contradict an assertion or demand, particularly a categorical one. This instinct of opposition emerges with the inevitability of a reflex movement, even in quite harmonious relationships, in very conciliatory persons. It mixes itself into the overall situation even though without much effect. One might be tempted to call this a protective instinct—just as certain animals, merely upon being touched, automatically use their protective aggressive apparatus. But this would precisely prove the primary, basic character of opposition. It would mean that the individual, even where he is not attacked but only finds himself confronted by purely objective manifestations of other individuals, cannot maintain himself except by means of opposition. It would mean that the first instinct with which the individual affirms himself is the negation of the other.

It seems impossible to deny an *a priori* fighting instinct, especially if one keeps in mind the incredibly picayunish, even silly, occasions of the most serious conflicts. An English historian reports that not long ago two Irish parties, whose enmity developed from a quarrel over the color of a cow, fought each other furiously throughout the whole country. Some decades ago, grave rebellions occurred in India as the consequence of a feud between two parties which knew nothing about one another except that they were, respectively, the party of the right hand and the party of the left. And this triviality of the causes of conflicts is paralleled by the childish behavior in which conflicts often end. In India, Mohammedans and Hindus live in a constant latent enmity which they document by the Mohammedans buttoning their outer garments to the right, and the Hindus to the left; by the Mohammedans, at common meals, sitting in a circle, and the Hindus in a row; by the poor Mohammedans using one side of a certain leaf for a plate, and the Hindus the other. In human hostility, cause and effect are often so heterogeneous and disproportionate that it is hard to determine whether the alleged issue really is the cause of the conflict or merely the consequence of long-existing opposition. The impossibility of ascertaining any rational basis of the hostility presents us with this uncertainty in regard to many details of the conflicts between the Roman and Greek circus parties, between the Homoousians and the Homoiousians, and of the Wars of the Roses and of the Guelfs and Ghibellines. The general impression is that human beings never love one another because of such picayunish trivia as lead them to violent hatred.

THE SUGGESTIBILITY OF HOSTILITY

There is finally another phenomenon which seems to me to point to a wholly primary need for hostility. This is the uncanny ease with which hostility can be suggested. It is usually much easier for the average person to inspire another individual with distrust and suspicion toward a third, previously indifferent person than with confidence and sympathy. It is significant that this difference is particularly striking in respect to these favorable or unfavorable moods and prejudices if they are at their beginning or have developed only to a slight degree. For, higher degrees, which lead to practical application, are not decided by such fleeting leanings (which, however, betray the fundamental instinct) but by more conscious considerations. The same fundamental fact is shown in merely another version, as it were, by the circumstance that quite indifferent persons may successfully suggest those slight prejudices which fly over the image of another like shadows, whereas only an authoritative or emotionally close individual succeeds in causing us to have the corresponding *favorable* prejudice.

Without this ease or irresponsibility with which the average person reacts to suggestions of an unfavorable kind, the *aliquid haeret* [social, emotional inertia] would perhaps not be so tragically true. The observation of certain antipathies, factions, intrigues, and open fights might indeed lead one to consider hostility among those primary human energies which are not provoked by the external reality of their objects but which create their own objects out of themselves. Thus it has been said that man does not have religion because he believes in God but that he believes in God because he has religion, which is a mood of his soul. In general, it is probably recognized that love, especially in youth, is not a mere reaction evoked by its object (as a color sensation is evoked in our optical apparatus), but that on the contrary, we have a need for loving and ourselves seize upon some object which satisfies this need—sometimes bestowing on it those characteristics which, we alleged, have evoked our love in the first place.

THE HOSTILITY DRIVE AND
ITS LIMITED POWER

There is nothing to suggest that all this does not also hold of the development of the opposite emotion (except for a qualification, of which presently). There is nothing to suggest that the soul does not also have an inborn need for *hating* and *fighting*, and that often this need alone injects into the objects it takes for itself their hate-provoking qualities. This interpretation of hatred is not so obvious as is that of love. The reason probably is that the need for love, with its tremendous physiological pointedness in youth, is so palpably spontaneous, that is, so palpably determined by the actor (lover) rather than by the beloved, that, by comparison, the hate drive is only seldom found in stages of comparable acuteness which would make us equally conscious of its subjective, spontaneous character.[1]

Assuming that there indeed exists a formal hostility drive as the counterpart of the need for sympathy, it seems to me that historically it stems from one of those processes of distillation by which intra-individual movements leave an independent impulse as the residue of the forms which are common to them. All kinds of interests so often lead to conflicts over particular objects or to opposition against particular persons that, possibly as a residue of these conflicting interests, a general state of irritation, which by itself presses for manifestations of antagonism, has become part of the hereditary inventory of our species. It is well known that (for reasons often discussed) the mutual relation of primitive groups is almost always one of hostility. Perhaps the most decisive example comes from the American Indians, among whom every tribe was on principle considered in a state of war with every other tribe with which it had not concluded an explicit peace treaty. It must not be forgotten, however, that in early stages of culture, war is almost the only form in which contact with alien groups is brought about at all. As long as inter-territorial commerce remains undeveloped, individual travel is something unknown, and intellectual communities do not transcend the boundaries of the group, war is the only sociological relation between different peoples. At such a stage, relations of the group *members* with one another have forms which are diametrically opposed to the interrelations among the *groups*. *Within* the closed circle, hostility usually means the termination of relations, withdrawal, or avoidance of contact, and these negative characteristics even accompany the passionate interaction of open fight. By contrast, these groups, as whole units, live in mutual indifference side by side as long as there is peace, while they gain active reciprocal significance for one another only in war. For this reason, the same drive to expand and to act, which *within* the group

requires unconditional peace for the integration of interests and for unfettered interaction, may appear to the outside as a tendency toward war.

No matter how much psychological autonomy one may be willing to grant the antagonistic drive, this autonomy is not enough to account for all phenomena involving hostility. For in the first place, even the most spontaneous drive is restricted in its independence in as much as it does not apply to *all* objects but only to those which somehow appeal to it. Although hunger certainly originates in the subject without first being actualized by the object, it nevertheless does not seize on stones and wood but only on what is edible. Similarly, love and hate, too, however little their drives may derive from external stimuli, nevertheless seem to need some appealing structure of their objects with whose cooperation alone they yield the total phenomena that go by their names.

On the other hand, it seems probable to me that on the whole, because of its formal character, the hostility drive merely adds itself as a reinforcement (like the pedal on the piano, as it were) to controversies which are due to concrete causes. And where a conflict springs from the purely formal lust to fight—that is, from something entirely impersonal, fundamentally indifferent toward any content, even toward the adversary—even there, hatred and rage against the enemy as a person, and if possible interest in a prize for victory, inevitably grow in the course of the conflict because such emotions feed and increase its psychological strength. It is *expedient* to hate the adversary with whom one fights (for any reason), just as it is expedient to love a person whom one is tied to and has to get along with. The truth expressed by a popular Berlin song, "What one does out of love goes twice as well" ("*Was man aus Liebe tut, Das geht noch mal so gut*"), also goes for what one does out of hatred. The mutual behavior between people can only be understood by appreciating the inner adaptation which trains in us feelings most suitable to a given situation, whether they are to exploit or assert this situation, or are to bear or end it. By means of psychological connections, these feelings produce the forces which are necessary to execute the given task and to paralyze inner counter-currents. Hence no serious conflict probably lasts any length of time without being sustained by a *complex* of psychological impulses, even though this complex grows only gradually. This is of great sociological significance: the purity of conflict for the sake of conflict thus is seen to become interspersed partly with more objective interests, partly with impulses which can be satisfied by other means than fight, and which in practice form the bridge between conflict and other forms of interaction.

ANTAGONISTIC GAMES

I really know only a single case in which the fascination of fight and victory itself—elsewhere only an *element* in the antagonisms over particular contents—is the exclusive motivation: this is the antagonistic game (*Kampfspiel*), more precisely, the game which is carried on without any prize for victory (since the prize would lie outside of it). The purely sociological attraction of becoming master over the adversary, of asserting oneself against him, is combined here, in the case of games of skill, with the purely individual enjoyment of the most appropriate and successful movement; and in the case of games of luck, with favor by fate which blesses us with a mystical, harmonious relation to powers beyond the realm of the individual and social. At any rate, in its *sociological motivation*, the antagonistic game contains absolutely nothing except fight itself. The worthless chip which is often contested as passionately as is a gold piece, suggests the formal nature of this impulse, which even in the quarrel over gold often greatly exceeds any material interest.

But there is something else most remarkable: the realization of precisely this complete dualism presupposes sociological forms in the stricter sense of the word, namely, unification. One *unites* in order to fight, and one fights under the mutually recognized control of norms and rules. To repeat, these unifications do not enter into the *motivation* of the undertaking, even though it is through them that it takes shape. They rather are the technique without which such a conflict that excludes all heterogeneous or objective justifications could not materialize. What is more, the norms of the antagonistic game often are rigorous and impersonal and are observed on both sides with the severity of a code of honor—to an extent hardly shown by groups which are formed for cooperative purposes.

LEGAL CONFLICT

The principles of conflict and of unification, which holds the contrasts together in one whole, are shown in this example with the purity of almost an abstract concept. It thus reveals how each principle attains its full sociological meaning and effect only through the other. The same form which dominates the antagonistic game also governs legal conflict, even though not with the same neatness and separateness of the two factors involved. For legal conflict has an *object*, and the struggle can be satisfactorily terminated through the voluntary concession of that object. This does not occur in fights for the lust of fighting. In most cases, what is called the lust and passion of legal quarrels, is probably something quite different, namely, a strong feeling of justice or the impossibility of bearing an actual or alleged interference with the sphere of law with which the ego feels identified. All the uncompromising stubbornness and obstinacy with which parties at a trial so often bleed themselves to death has, even on the defendant's part, hardly the character of an offensive but, in a deeper sense, that of a defensive, since the question is the self-preservation of the person. This self-preservation is so inseparable from the person's possessions and rights that any inroad on them destroys it. It is only consistent to fight with the power of one's whole existence. Hence it probably is this individualistic drive, rather than the sociological drive to fight, which determines such cases.

In respect to the *form* of conflict, however, legal quarrel is indeed absolute. That is, on both sides the claims are put through with pure objectivity and with all means that are permitted; the conflict is not deflected or attenuated by any personal or in any other sense extraneous circumstances. Legal conflict is pure conflict in as much as nothing enters its whole action which does not belong to the conflict *as such* and serves its purpose. Elsewhere, even in the wildest struggles, something subjective, or some mere turn of fate, or some interference by a third party is at least possible. In legal conflict, all this is excluded by the objectivity with which only the fight and absolutely nothing else proceeds.

This elimination of all that is not conflict can of course lead to a formalism which becomes independent of all contents. On the one hand, we here have legal pettifoggery. In legal pettifoggery, it is not objective points which are weighed against one another; instead, concepts lead an entirely abstract fight. On the other hand, the conflict is sometimes delegated to agents which have no relation to what their contest is to decide. The fact that in higher cultures, legal quarrels are carried out by professional counsels, certainly serves the clean separation of the controversy from all personal associations which have nothing to do with it. But if Otto the Great decrees that a legal question must be decided through ordeal by combat, only the mere form—the occurrence of fighting and winning itself— is salvaged from the whole conflict of interests; only the form is the element common to the fight to be decided and to the individuals who decide it.

This case expresses in exaggeration or caricature the reduction and restriction of legal conflict to the mere element of fight itself. It is the most merciless type of contestation because it lies wholly outside the subjective contrast between charity and cruelty. But precisely because of its pure objectivity, it is grounded entirely in the premise of the unity and commonness of the

parties—and this to a degree of severity and thoroughness hardly required by any other situation. Legal conflict rests on a broad basis of unities and agreements between the enemies. The reason is that both parties are equally subordinated to the law; they mutually recognize that the decision is to be made only according to the objective weight of their claims; they observe the forms which are unbreakably valid for both; and they are conscious that they are surrounded in their whole enterprise by a social power which alone gives meaning and certainty to their undertaking. The parties to a negotiation or a commercial affair form a unity in the same manner, even though to a less extent, for they recognize norms binding and obligatory to both, irrespective of the opposition of their interests. The *common* premises which exclude everything personal from legal conflict have that character of pure objectivity to which (on the other hand) correspond the inexorability and the acute and unconditional character of the conflict itself. Legal conflict thus shows the interaction between the dualism and the unity of sociological relations no less than antagonistic games do. The extreme and unconditional nature of conflict comes to the fore in the very medium and on the very basis of the strict unity of common norms and conditions.

CONFLICTS OVER CAUSES

This same phenomenon is characteristic, finally, of all conflicts in which both parties have objective interests. In this case, the conflicting interests, and hence the conflict itself, are differentiated from the personalities involved. Here two things are possible. The conflict may focus on purely objective decisions and leave all personal elements outside itself and in a state of peace. Or on the contrary, it may involve precisely the persons in their subjective aspects without, however, thereby leading to any alteration or disharmony of the coexisting objective interests common to the two parties. The second type is characterized by Leibnitz's saying that he would run even after a deadly enemy if he could learn something from him. Such an attitude can obviously soften and attenuate the hostility itself; but its possible opposite result must also be noted. Hostility which goes along with solidarity and understanding in objective matters is indeed, so to speak, clean and certain in its justification. The consciousness of such a differentiation assures us that we do not harbor personal antipathy where it does not belong. But the good conscience bought with this discrimination may under certain circumstances lead to the very intensification of hostility. For where hostility is thus restricted to its real center, which at the same time is the most subjective layer of personality, we sometimes abandon ourselves to it more extensively, passionately, and with more concentration than when the hostile impulse carries with it a ballast of secondary animosities in areas which actually are merely infected by that center.

In the case in which the same differentiation inversely limits the conflict to impersonal interests, there too are two possibilities. On the one hand, there may be the elimination of useless embitterments and intensifications which are the price we pay for personalizing objective controversies. On the other hand, however, the parties' consciousness of being mere representatives of supraindividual claims, of fighting not for themselves but only for a cause, can give the conflict a radicalism and mercilessness which find their analogy in the general behavior of certain very selfless and very idealistically inclined persons. Because they have no consideration for themselves, they have none for others either; they are convinced that they are entitled to make anybody a victim of the idea for which they sacrifice themselves. Such a conflict which is fought out with the strength of the whole person while the victory benefits the cause alone, has a noble character. For, the noble individual is wholly personal but knows nevertheless how to hold his personality in reserve. This is why objectivity strikes us as noble. But once this differentiation has been achieved and the conflict thus objectified, it is, quite consistently, not subjected

to a second restriction, which in fact would be a violation of the objective interest to which the fight has been limited. On the basis of this mutual agreement of the two parties, according to which each of them defends only his claims and his cause, renouncing all personal or egoistic considerations, the conflict is fought with unattenuated sharpness, following its own intrinsic logic, and being neither intensified nor moderated by subjective factors.

The contrast between unity and antagonism is perhaps most visible where both parties really pursue an identical aim—such as the exploration of a scientific truth. Here any yielding, any polite renunciation of the merciless exposure of the adversary, any peace prior to the wholly decisive victory would be treason against that objectivity for the sake of which the personal character has been eliminated from the fight. Ever since Marx, the social struggle has developed into this form, despite infinite differences in other respects. Since it has been recognized that the condition of labor is determined by the objective conditions and forms of production, irrespective of the desires and capacities of particular individuals, the personal bitterness of both general and local battles has greatly decreased. The entrepreneur is no longer a bloodsucker and damnable egoist, nor does the worker suffer from sinful greediness under all circumstances. Both parties have at least begun no longer to burden each other's consciences with their mutual demands and tactics as acts of personal meanness. In Germany, this objectification was started more nearly by means of theory, in as much as the personal and individualistic nature of antagonism was overcome by the more abstract and general character of the historical and class movement. In England, it was launched by the trade unions, and was furthered by the rigorously supra-individual unity of their actions and those of the corresponding federations of entrepreneurs. The violence of the fight, however, has not decreased for that. On the contrary, it has become more pointed, concentrated, and at the same time

more comprehensive, owing to the consciousness of the individual involved that
he fights not only for himself, and often not
for himself at all, but for a great super-
personal aim.

An interesting example of this correlation
is the workers' boycott of the Berlin brew-
eries in 1894. This was one of the most
violent local fights in recent decades,[2]
carried out with the utmost force by both
sides, but without any personal hatred of
the brewers by the leaders of the boycott,
or of the workers by the business leaders.
In fact, in the middle of the fight, two
leaders of the two parties published their
opinions of the struggle in the same periodical, both being objective in their presenta-
tions of the facts and hence agreeing on
them, but differing, in line with their
respective parties, on the practical consequences that were to be drawn from the
facts. It thus appears that conflict can
exclude all subjective or personal factors,
thus quantitatively reducing hostility, en-
gendering mutual respect, and producing
understanding on all personal matters, as
well as the recognition of the fact that both
parties are driven on by historical necessities. At the same time, we see that this
common basis increases, rather than decreases, the intensity, irreconcilability, and
stubborn consistency of the fight.

The objective common to the conflicting
parties on which alone their fight is based,
can show itself in a much less noble manner
than in the cases just discussed. This is true
when the common feature is not an objective
norm, an interest that lies above the egoism
of the fighting parties, but their secret
understanding in respect to an egoistic
purpose which they both share. To a certain
extent this was true of the two great English
political parties in the eighteenth century.
There was no basic opposition of political
convictions between them, since the problem
of both equally was the maintenance of the
aristocratic regime. The strange fact was that
two parties which between themselves completely dominated the area of political
struggle, nevertheless did not fight each
other radically—because they had a silent

mutual pact against something which was
not a political party at all. Historians have
connected the parliamentary corruptibility
of that period with this strange limitation
of the fight. Nobody thought too badly of
a party's selling its conviction in favor of
the opposing party because the conviction
of that opposing party had a rather broad,
even though hidden common basis, and the
fight lay elsewhere. The ease of corruption
showed that here the restriction of the
antagonism through a common feature did
not make the conflict more fundamental
and objective. On the contrary, it blurred it
and contaminated its meaning as necessarily
determined by objective circumstances.

In other, purer cases, when unity is the
point of departure and the basis of the
relationship, and conflict arises over this
unity, the synthesis between the monism
and antagonism of the relation can have
the opposite result. A conflict of this sort is
usually more passionate and radical than
when it does not meet with a prior or
simultaneous mutual belongingness to the
parties. While ancient Jewish law permitted
bigamy, it forbade marriage with two
sisters (even though after the death of one
her husband could marry the other), for this
would have been especially apt to arouse
jealousy. In other words, this law simply
assumes as a fact of experience that antagonism on the basis of a common kinship tie is
stronger than among strangers. The mutual
hatred of very small neighboring states
whose whole outlooks, local relations, and
interests are inevitably very similar and
frequently even coincide, often is much
more passionate and irreconcilable than
between great nations, which both spatially
and objectively are complete strangers to
one another. This was the fate of Greece
and of post-Roman Italy, and a more
intensive degree of it shook England after
the Norman Conquest before the two races
fused. These two lived scattered among one
another in the same territory, were mutually
bound by constantly operating vital interests,
and were held together by one national idea
—and yet intimately, they were complete
mutual strangers, were, in line with their

whole character, without reciprocal understanding, and were absolutely hostile to one another in regard to their power interests. Their reciprocal hatred, as has rightly been said, was more bitter than it can ever be between externally and internally separate groups.

Some of the strongest examples of such hatred are church relations. Because of dogmatic fixation, the minutest divergence here at once comes to have logical irreconcilability—if there is deviation at all, it is conceptually irrelevant whether it be large or small. A case in point are the confessional controversies between Lutherans and Reformed, especially in the seventeenth century. Hardly had the great separation from Catholicism occurred, when the whole, over the most trivial matters, split into parties which frequently said about one another that one could more easily make peace with the Popists than with the members of the other Protestant group. And in 1875 in Berne, when there was some difficulty over the place where Catholic services were to be held, the Pope did not allow them to be performed in the church used by the Old-Catholics, but in a Reformed church.

COMMON QUALITIES VS. COMMON
MEMBERSHIP IN A LARGER SOCIAL
STRUCTURE AS BASES OF CONFLICT

Two kinds of commonness may be the bases of particularly intense antagonisms: the common qualities and the common membership in a larger social structure. The first case goes back simply to the fact that we are discriminating beings (*Unterschiedswesen*). A hostility must excite consciousness the more deeply and violently, the greater the parties' similarity against the background of which the hostility rises. Where attitudes are friendly or loving, this is an excellent protective measure of the group, comparable to the warning function of pain in the organism. For it is precisely the keen awareness of dissonance against the prevailing general harmony which at once warns the parties to remove the grounds of conflict lest conflict half-consciously creep on and endanger the basis of the relation itself. But where this fundamental intention to get along under all circumstances is lacking, the consciousness of antagonism, sensitized as this consciousness is by similarity in other respects, will sharpen the antagonism itself. People who have many common features often do one another worse or "wronger" wrong than complete strangers do. Sometimes they do this because the large area common to them has become a matter of course, and hence what is temporarily different, rather than what is common, determines their mutual positions. Mainly, however, they do it because there is only little that is different between them; hence even the slightest antagonism has a relative significance quite other than that between strangers, who count with all kinds of mutual differences to begin with. Hence the family conflicts over which people profoundly in agreement sometimes break up. That they do so does by no means always prove that the harmonizing forces had weakened before. On the contrary, the break can result from so great a similarity of characteristics, leanings, and convictions that the divergence over a very insignificant point makes itself felt in its sharp contrast as something utterly unbearable.

We confront the stranger, with whom we share neither characteristics nor broader interests, objectively; we hold our personalities in reserve; and thus a particular difference does not involve us in our totalities. On the other hand, we meet the person who is very different from us only on certain points within a particular contact or within a coincidence of particular interests, and hence the spread of the conflict is limited to those points only. The more we have in common with another *as whole persons*, however, the more easily will our totality be involved in every single relation to him. Hence the wholly disproportionate violence to which normally well controlled people can be moved within their relations to those closest to them. The whole happiness and depth of the relation to another person with whom, so to speak, we feel identical, lies in the fact that not a single contact, not a single word, not a single common activity or pain remains isolated but always clothes the whole soul which completely gives itself in it and is received in it. Therefore, if a quarrel arises between persons in such an intimate relationship, it is often so passionately expansive and suggests the schema of the fatal "Not you" ("*Du-überhaupt*"). Persons tied to one another in this fashion are accustomed to invest every direction in which they may turn with the totality of their being and feeling. Hence they also give conflicting accents and, as it were, a periphery by virtue of which it far outgrows its occasion and the objective significance of that occasion, and drags the total personalities into it.

CONFLICT IN INTIMATE RELATIONS

At the highest level of spiritual cultivation it is possible to avoid this, for it is characteristic of this level to combine complete mutual devotion with complete mutual differentiation. Whereas undifferentiated passion involves the totality of the individual in the excitement of a part or an element of it, the cultivated person allows no such part or element to transcend its proper, clearly circumscribed domain. Cultivation thus gives relations between harmonious persons the advantage that they become aware, precisely on the occasion of conflict, of its trifling nature in comparison with the magnitude of the forces that unify them.

Furthermore, the refined discriminatory sense, especially of deeply sensitive persons, makes attractions and antipathies more passionate if these feelings contrast with those of the past. This is true in the case of unique, irrevocable decisions concerning a given relationship, and it must be sharply distinguished from the everyday vacillations within a mutual belongingness which is felt, on the whole, to be unquestionable. Sometimes between men and women a fundamental aversion, even a feeling of hatred— not in regard to certain particulars, but the

reciprocal repulsion of the total person—is the first stage of a relation whose second phase is passionate love. One might entertain the paradoxical suspicion that when individuals are destined to the closest mutual emotional relationship, the emergence of the intimate phase is guided by an instinctive pragmatism so that the eventual feeling attains its most passionate intensification and awareness of what it has achieved by means of an opposite prelude —a step back before running, as it were.

The inverse phenomenon shows the same form: the deepest hatred grows out of broken love. Here, however, not only the sense of discrimination is probably decisive but also the denial of one's own past—a denial involved in such change of feeling. To have to recognize that a deep love—and not only a sexual love—was an error, a failure of intuition (*Instinkt*), so compromises us before ourselves, so splits the security and unity of our self-conception, that we unavoidably make the object of this intolerable feeling pay for it. We cover our secret awareness of our own responsibility for it by hatred which makes it easy for us to pass all responsibility on to the other.

This particular bitterness which characterizes conflicts within relationships whose nature would seem to entail harmony is a sort of positive intensification of the platitude that relations show their closeness and strength in the absence of differences. But this platitude is by no means true without exception. That very intimate groups, such as marital couples, which dominate, or at least touch on, the whole content of life, should contain no occasions for conflict is quite out of the question. It is by no means the sign of the most genuine and deep affection never to yield to those occasions but instead to prevent them in far-ranging anticipation and to cut them short immediately by mutual yielding. On the contrary, this behavior often characterizes attitudes which though affectionate, moral, and loyal, nevertheless lack the ultimate, unconditional emotional devotion. Conscious of this lack, the individual is all the more anxious to keep the relation free from any shadow and to compensate his partner for that lack through the utmost friendliness, self-control, and consideration. But another function of this behavior is to soothe one's own consciousness in regard to its more or less evident untruthfulness which even the most sincere or even the most passionate will cannot change into truthfulness—because feelings are involved which are not accessible to the will but, like fate itself, exist or do not exist.

The felt insecurity concerning the basis of such relations often moves us, who desire to maintain the relation at all cost, to acts of exaggerated selflessness, to the almost mechanical insurance of the relationship through the avoidance, on principle, of every possibility of conflict. Where on the other hand we are certain of the irrevocability and unreservedness of our feeling, such peace at any price is not necessary. We know that no crisis can penetrate to the foundation of the relationship—we can always find the other again on this foundation. The strongest love can stand a blow most easily, and hence it does not even occur to it, as is characteristic of a weaker one, to fear that the consequences of such a blow cannot be faced, and it must therefore be avoided by all means. Thus, although conflict among intimates can have more tragic results than among less intimate persons, in the light of the circumstances discussed, precisely the most firmly grounded relation may take a chance at discord, whereas good and moral but less deeply rooted relationships apparently follow a much more harmonious and conflictless course.

This sociological sense of discrimination and the accentuation of conflict on the basis of similarity have a special nuance in cases where the separation of originally homogeneous elements occurs on purpose. Here separation does not follow from conflict but, on the contrary, conflict from separation. Typical of this is the way the renegade hates and is hated. The recall of earlier agreement has such a strong effect that the new contrast is infinitely sharper and bitterer than if no relation at all had existed

in the past. Moreover, often both parties realize the difference between the new phase and the similarity remembered (and the unambiguousness of this difference is of the greatest importance to them) only by allowing it to grow far beyond its original locus and to characterize every point which is at all comparable. This aim of securing the two respective positions transforms theoretical or religious defection into the reciprocal charge of heresy in respect to all moral, personal, internal and external matters—a charge not necessarily ensuing where the same difference occurs between strangers. In fact, the degeneration of a difference in *convictions* into hatred and fight ordinarily occurs only when there were essential, original similarities between the parties. The (sociologically very significant) "respect for the enemy" is usually absent where the hostility has arisen on the basis of previous solidarity. And where enough similarities continue to make confusions and blurred borderlines possible, points of difference need an emphasis not justified by the issue but only by that danger of confusion. This was involved, for instance, in the case of Catholicism in Berne, mentioned earlier. Roman Catholicism does not have to fear any threat to its identity from external contact with a church so different as the Reformed Church, but quite from something as closely akin as Old-Catholicism.

CONFLICT AS A THREAT TO THE GROUP

This example already touches upon the second type which is relevant here, although in practice it more or less coincides with the first. It is the case of hostility whose intensification is grounded in a feeling of belonging together, of unity, which by no means always means similarity. The reason for treating this type separately is that instead of the sense of discrimination, it shows a very different fundamental factor, namely, the peculiar phenomenon of social hatred. This hatred is directed against a member of the group, not from personal motives, but because the member represents a danger to the preservation of the group. In so far as intragroup conflict involves such a danger, the two conflicting parties hate each other not only on the concrete ground which produced the conflict but also on the sociological ground of hatred for the enemy of the group itself. Since this hatred is mutual and each accuses the other of responsibility for the threat to the whole, the antagonism sharpens—precisely because both parties to it belong to the same social unit.

Most characteristic here are the cases which do not lead to the proper breakup of the group. For once the group is dissolved, there is a certain release of the conflict; personal differences have been discharged sociologically; the thorn of ever new irritation has been removed. The tension between intragroup antagonism and group continuation must, on the contrary, lead to continued conflict. Just as it is terrible to be in conflict with a person to whom one is tied—externally or, in the most tragic cases, by an internal bond—but from whom one cannot tear oneself loose even if one wished to, so the bitterness is equally intensified when one does not *want* to leave the group because one feels this unit to be an objective value, a threat to which calls for fight and hatred. From this constellation springs the violence characteristic of conflicts within a political faction, a labor union, a family, etc.

Here, conflicts within the individual offer an analogy. In certain cases, they may be held down by the feeling that a struggle between sensuous and ascetic, egoistic and moral, practical and intellectual tendencies not only does injustice to one or both of these contrasting claims—not allowing full life to either of them—but menaces the very unity, equilibrium, and strength of the whole individual. Where on the contrary this feeling is not enough to check the conflict, it gives it a bitter and desperate accent—as if the fight were about something much more essential than the immediate issue in question. The energy with which each of the conflicting tendencies wishes to subjugate the other, feeds not only on its own egoistic interest, so to speak, but on the much more comprehensive interest in the maintenance of the ego which is torn apart and destroyed by the conflict, unless the conflict ends in unambiguous victory. Just so, conflict within a closely knit group often enough grows beyond the extent justified by its occasion and by the interest to the group immediately attendant on this occasion; for in addition, this conflict is associated with the feeling that the discord is not a matter only of the two parties but of the group as a whole. Each party fights, as it were, in the name of the whole group and must hate in its adversary not only its own enemy but at the same time the enemy of the higher sociological unit.

JEALOUSY

Finally, there is a fact by which the extreme violence of antagonistic excitement is linked to the closeness of belonging together. This fact, though apparently quite individual, actually is of great sociological significance. It is jealousy. Linguistic usage is ambiguous in regard to this concept; often it does not distinguish it from envy. Both affects are undoubtedly of the greatest importance for the shaping of human conditions. In both a value is at stake which a third party actually or symbolically prevents us from attaining or keeping. Where it is a matter of attaining, we shall here speak of envy; where of keeping, of jealousy. But the use of definitions is of course quite irrelevant as long as the psychological–sociological processes are clearly distinguished. It is characteristic of the jealous individual to have a rightful claim to possession, whereas envy refers to the desirability of what is denied it, not to the legitimacy of any claim. To the envious individual it is irrelevant whether the good is denied him because somebody else possesses it or whether even its loss or renunciation by that other individual would not let him obtain it. Jealousy, on the contrary, is determined in its inner direction and color precisely by the fact that we are prevented from possession because the possession is in somebody else's hands, and that if this were otherwise, we would become the possessors at once. The feeling of the envious individual turns more around possession, that of the jealous person more around the possessor. One can envy somebody's fame even though one has not the slightest claim to fame, but one is jealous of a famous man if one thinks that one deserves fame as much or more than he does. What is embittering and gnawing to the jealous individual is a certain fiction of feeling—no matter how unjustified or even nonsensical it may be—that the other has, so to speak, stolen the fame from him. Jealousy, whatever the exceptional psychological constellation from which it may have arisen, is a sensation of such a specific kind and power that it internally complements its typical situation.

Midway on the continuum between the phenomena of envy and jealousy thus described, there is a third one which may be designated as begrudging (*Missgunst*). "Begrudging" is the envious desire of an object, not because it is especially desirable but because the other has it. This kind of feeling may grow to either of two extremes, both of which end up by negating one's own possession. One form is that passionate begrudging which dispenses with the object or in fact destroys it, rather than leaving it in the hands of the other. The second form is complete indifference or even aversion toward the object, accompanied by the utter unbearability of the thought that the other possesses it. Such forms of begrudging are enmeshed in a thousand degrees and mixtures in the reciprocal behavior of human beings. They cover considerable portions of the large problem area in which people's relations to things are revealed as causes or effects of their relations to one another. For here it is not only the question of desiring money or power, affection or social position, through competing with another person or through surpassing or eliminating him, whereby these activities are techniques, identical in their inner meaning with conquering physical obstacles. Rather, in these modifications of begrudging, the feeling which accompanies such external and secondary relations among persons develops into autonomous sociological forms in which the desire for the object has become mere *content*. That this is so can be seen in the fact that the interest in the objective purpose has been slouched off or, rather, has been reduced to the intrinsically irrelevant material around which the personal relation crystallizes.

This is the general basis on which emerges the significance of jealousy for our problem, conflict. More particularly, this is so when the content of jealousy is a person or the relation of a given individual to that person. In fact, it seems to me linguistic usage does not recognize jealousy in regard to a purely impersonal object. What concerns us here is the relation between a jealous individual and the person for whose sake his jealousy is directed toward a third individual. The relation to that third individual itself has a very different, sociologically much less specific and complicated, formal character. For, the rage and hatred, contempt and cruelty against *him* are built precisely on the premise of a *belonging together*, of an external or internal, real or presumed claim to love, friendship, recognition, union of some sort. Whether felt on both sides or on one only, the antagonism is the more intensive and extensive, the more unconditional the unity from which it started and the more passionate the longing to overcome it. The frequent, apparent vacillation of the jealous person between love and hate means that these two layers (of which the second covers the first in its whole expanse) alternatively command his stronger awareness.

Here it is very important to remember the condition indicated earlier, namely, the *right* that the jealous individual believes he has to the psychological or physical possession, the love or the veneration of the person who is the object of his jealousy. A man may *envy* another's possession of a woman, but he is jealous only if he himself has some *claim* to possessing her. This claim may well consist exclusively in the mere passion of his desire, for it is a general human trait to derive a right from such a desire. The child excuses himself for taking something forbidden to him by saying that he "wanted it so much." At a duel, the adulterer, if he has the slightest trace of conscience, could not aim at the offended husband if he did not see in his own love for the other's wife a right to her, which he defends against the husband's merely legal right. Everywhere the mere fact of possession is considered the right to possession.

Just so, the stage preceding possession, namely, the desire for it, may grow into such a right. In fact, the double meaning of "claim"—simple desire and legally grounded desire—alludes to the fact that the will likes to increase the right of its strength by the strength of its right. To be sure, precisely because of this legal claim, jealousy often is the most pitiful spectacle; for to make *legal* claims to such feelings as love and friendship is to make an attempt with wholly inadequate means. The level on which one can operate on the basis of any right, external or internal, does not even touch the level on which these feelings lie. To wish to enforce them through a right, no matter how profound and well-acquired in other respects, is as senseless as if one wanted to order back back to its cage a bird which has escaped from it beyond the reach of sight and hearing. This hopelessness of the right to love produces the phenomenon characteristic of jealousy, that is, the eventual hanging on to the *external proofs* of feeling, which can indeed be enforced by an appeal to duty. By means of this miserable satisfaction and self-deception, jealousy preserves the "body" of the relationship—and does as if it had caught in it something of its "soul."

The *claim* advanced by the jealous person is often fully recognized by the other party. Like every right between persons, this claim means or produces a sort of unity. It is the ideal or legal content of a group, or a positive relationship of some sort, or at least their subjective anticipation. To this existing and continuing unity is added its simultaneous negation, and thus the situa-tion ripe for jealousy is created. Contrary to other situations in which unity and antagonism interact, in the situation conducive to jealousy these two forces are not distributed among different areas, being held together and against one another only by the total personality. On the contrary, there is the denial of the very unity which still exists in some inner or outer form and is felt by at least one of the two parties so to exist, actually or ideally. The feeling of jealousy interjects a very peculiar, blinding, irreconcilable bitterness between two persons. For, the separation between them revolves precisely around the point of their *connection*, and the negative element in the tension between them thus attains the highest possible sharpness and accentuation.

The complete control of the inner situation by this formal-sociological constellation explains the strange, actually unlimited, range of motives upon which jealousy may feed. It also explains why its development is often incomprehensible as far as its content is concerned. Where either the very structure of the relation or the psychology of the individual is disposed toward such a synthesis of synthesis and antithesis, any occasion will develop the consequences—and these consequences, obviously, will be the more appealing, the more often they have been developed in the past. The jealous person can never see more than *one* interpretation. Thus, jealousy finds a completely malleable instrument in the fact that all human deeds and words admit of *several* interpretations of their intentions and attitudes. Jealousy can combine the most passionate hatred with the continuation of the most passionate love, and the lingering of the most intimate unity with the destruction of both parties—for, the jealous individual destroys the relation just as much as that relation invites him to destroy his partner. Thus, jealousy is perhaps that sociological phenomenon in which the building of antagonism upon unity attains its subjectively most radical form.

5

How some social scientists have combined theory and research

Inequality in land

We have already seen that Aristotle regards inequality as a, perhaps the, basic cause of revolution. And the theme of equality is central to the American Declaration of Independence and to the rallying cries of many revolutions since. But just what kinds and degrees of inequality produce a revolutionary state of mind was not adequately specified by either Aristotle or Jefferson.

What is clear is that in the 20th century one of the commonest forms of politically explosive inequality is in land use and distribution. This means that a person who feels land ownership and use are unjustly distributed feels unequally treated: his relationship to land is central to his outlook toward the government. Rents and living conditions are a major cause of unrest in urban slums. In nations with a substantial rural population—which includes most nations in the world, even late in the 20th century—land tenure remains a dominant political issue. It was so in the 16th-century German peasant revolt, the 18th-century French Revolution, and the 20th-century Russian and French Revolutions.

The following article is one of the first head-on attempts to find out just what relationships there are between rural land tenure and political stability. Bruce Russett comes to the tentative conclusion that there can be a wide range in the amount of land owned by individuals without producing instability. What is critical is this: when those who have the smallest amount of land are unable to make a steady and decent living off of it, instability becomes high.

The forms of land tenure, the amounts of land actually owned, the productivity of that amount of land, and other aspects of man's relation to the soil are all related to political stability. It is evident that the relationships are complicated. Land-tenure problems were multifaceted in imperial Russia after the 1861 emancipation of serfs gave them some dignity. Long after this, Ukrainian peasants retained sullen and bitter hostility to land collectivization in the 1920s and 1930s. Stalin and virtually everyone else has not adequately understood why. This is to say that land—more exactly, the man who works it—remains pretty much unexplored territory as far as politics is concerned. The following is one of the few efforts systematically and quantitatively to relate land tenure to revolution.

Inequality and instability

The relation of land tenure to politics*

BRUCE M. RUSSETT

Bruce M. Russett, "Inequality and Instability: The Relation of Land Tenure to Politics," is reprinted with the permission of the author. Copyright by and reprinted with the permission of Princeton University Press, Princeton, from *World Politics*, 16(3), pp. 442–454, April 1964.

Notes to this section will be found on pages 346–347.

I

At least since the ancient Greeks many thinkers have regarded great diversity of wealth as incompatible with stable government. According to Euripides:

> In a nation there be orders three:—
> The useless rich, that ever crave for more;
> The have-nots, straitened even for sustenance,
> A dangerous folk, of envy overfull,
> Which shoot out baleful stings at such as have,
> Beguiled by tongues of evil men, their "champions":
> But of the three the midmost saveth states;
> They keep the order which the state ordains.[1]

Alexis de Tocqueville, writing many centuries later, declared: "Remove the secondary causes that have produced the great convulsions of the world and you will almost always find the principle of inequality at the bottom. Either the poor have attempted to plunder the rich, or the rich to enslave the poor. If, then, a state of society can ever be founded in which every man shall have something to keep and little to take from others, much will have been done for the peace of the world."[2]

Many modern writers echo the same thought. Merle Kling, for example, blames

* This article is part of the research of the Yale Political Data Program, supported by a grant from the National Science Foundation. I am grateful to John Shingler and Seth Singleton for research assistance. An earlier version was presented at the Annual Meeting of the American Political Science Association, September 1963.

political instability in Latin America on the extreme concentration of economic bases of power in what he terms "colonial economies." Land ownership, he says, is so heavily concentrated that no individual not already possessing great tracts of agricultural land can reasonably hope to achieve wealth through farming. Foreign exploitation of mineral resources effectively blocks the ambitious native from that source of wealth. Industry remains rudimentary. Of the possible sources of enrichment, only government is open to competition. Political office provides such a unique source of gain that "large segments of the population are prepared to take the ultimate risk of life, in a revolt, in a *coup d'état*, to perpetuate a characteristic feature of Latin American politics—chronic political instability."[3]

Both Plato and Karl Marx so despaired of the pernicious effects of wealth that they saw no way to abolish the evil except to abolish private property itself. Tocqueville, on the other hand, thought that he found in America a society which had been able to reach another solution: "Between these two extremes [very few rich men and few poor ones] of democratic communities stands an innumerable multitude of men almost alike, who, without being exactly either rich or poor, possess sufficient property to desire the maintenance of order, yet not enough to excite envy. Such men are the natural enemies of violent commotions; their lack of agitation keeps all beneath them and above them still and secures the balance of the fabric of society."[4]

Yet if we check the matter empirically with present-day polities the answer is not so clear-cut. Wealth is everywhere distributed unequally; even in the most egalitarian societies the income of the rich is many times that of the poor. And one can readily point to a number of instances—such as Spain—where, despite an impressionistic judgment that goods are distributed highly unequally, the polity is seemingly stable under the rule of a dictator.

Part of the difficulty stems from a conceptual problem, a lack of clarity about just what is the dependent variable. Is economic inequality incompatible with *stable* government, or merely with *democratic* or "*good*" government? If we mean stable government, do we mean regimes in which the rulers maintain themselves in power for long periods despite the chronic outbreak of violence (Colombia and South Vietnam), or simply the avoidance of significant violence even though governments may topple annually (France throughout most of the Third and Fourth Republics)? Or must "stable" government be both peaceful and reasonably long-term? Finally, what do we mean by the government? A particular individual (Spain), a particular party (Uruguay), the essential maintenance of a particular coalition (France under the system of "replastering"), or the continued dominance of a particular social stratum (Jordan)?

Another part of the difficulty stems from the absence of comparative study. Numerous authors have examined the distribution of agricultural land in particular countries or areas, and its contribution to a particular political situation. Several books have drawn together studies giving attention to many different nations.[5] But none of these have been based on the same concepts or have presented data for the same variables in a manner necessary for true comparative analysis. Case studies are essential for providing depth and insight, but generalization requires eventual attention to many cases.

Comparative analysis is dependent on the provision of comparable data. For instance, one may know that in contemporary England the upper 5 percent of income earners receive over fifteen percent of all current income, even after taxes.[6] Is this high or low compared with other nations? All too often the necessary data simply are not available or, if they are, they are not in comparable form. For another country one may, for instance, know the proportion of income going to the top 10 percent and top one percent of earners, but not to the top five percent, as in England.

In this article we shall attempt to clarify the problem conceptually, present for the first time a large body of distribution data, and test some hypotheses about the relation between economic inequality and politics. First, the data. We shall be concerned with information on the degree to which agricultural land is concentrated in the hands of a few large landholders. Information on land tenure is more readily available, and is of more dependable comparability, than are data on the distribution of other economic assets like current income or total wealth.[7] Material on land distribution is available for many countries about which we know nothing precise or reliable in regard to income distribution. In addition, land distribution is intrinsically of major interest. Kling's theory of Latin American political instability was built in large part on land inequality; the United States government has long warned its allies in poorer nations about the need for land reform. In Japan, and to a lesser extent in South Korea, the American military government took upon itself a major redistribution of land with the intention of providing the necessary bases for political democracy.

II

I have discussed elsewhere the uses of various summary statistical measures designed to indicate the degree of inequality in a distribution.[8] Here we shall employ three separate indices, each of which measures somewhat different aspects of land distribution. The first two are directed to the relative size of farms, the last to tenancy.

1. The *percentage of landholders who collectively occupy one-half of all the agricultural land* (starting with the farmers with the *smallest* plots of land and working toward the *largest*).

2. *The Gini index of concentration.* We begin with a Lorenz curve (Figure 1) drawn by connecting the points given in a cumulative distribution (e.g., the proportion of land held by each decile of farmers). All farms are ranked in order from the smallest to the largest, so that one can say what proportion of the total *number* of farms accounts for a given proportion of the total *area* of agricultural land. In Figure 1 the cumulated percentage of farms is given along the

horizontal axis, and the cumulated percentage of the area along the vertical axis. The 45° line represents the condition of perfect equality, wherein each percentile of farmers would make an equal contribution to the cumulated total of agricultural land. Thus, under complete equality each ten percent of the population would have exactly ten percent of the land; any two-thirds of the

distribution and the line of equality we have the Gini index, a simple summary measure of the total inequality of a distribution.[9] The Gini index calculates over the whole population the difference between an "ideal" cumulative distribution of land (where all farms are the same size) and the actual distribution. The higher the Gini index, the greater the inequality.

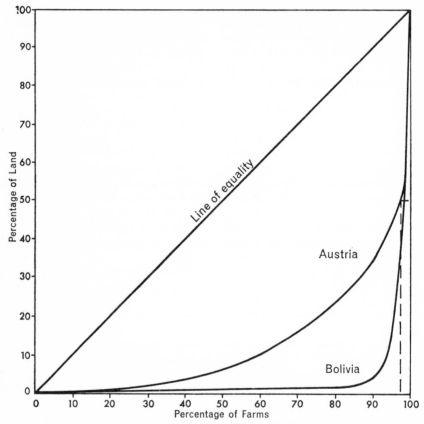

Figure 1. Lorenz Curves of Land Distribution:
Austria and Bolivia.

population would have exactly two-thirds of the land. How far in fact the curve for a particular distribution departs from the "line of equality" gives us a visual measure of the inequality involved.

The Lorenz curve provides an extremely useful way of showing the complete pattern of a distribution, but it is impractical to try to compare whole Lorenz curves for any substantial number of countries. But if we measure the *area* between the cumulated

Though the percentage of farmers with one-half the land is simple and useful, the more comprehensive Gini index, by examining the whole distribution, is in many ways superior. The curves for the two countries in Figure 1, for example, both show virtually the same percentage of farmers with half the land. But below the fifty percent mark, the distribution for Bolivia is much more unequal than is that for Austria. In Bolivia the top 10 percent of all farmers owned nearly ninety-five percent of the land; in Austria the top 10 percent of farmers owned only about sixty-five percent of the land. The implications for a theory of political stability are obvious. (The Bolivian figures actually apply to 1950. Since that date Bolivia has experienced a social revolution.)

3. Probably less important than the relative size of farms, but still relevant, is the question of *ownership*. If a farmer tills a substantial piece of land but nevertheless must pay much of the produce to a landlord, the effect may be much the same as if he actually owned a much smaller plot. Therefore we also present data, where available, on *farm households that rent all their land as a percentage of the total number of farms.*

It is even more difficult to find a satisfactory operational definition of stability than to measure inequality. In our effort to account for different aspects of "stability," we shall use several quite different indices.

1. *Instability of Personnel.* One measure of stability is simply the term of office of the chief executive. As the numerator of our index, we have used the number of years during the period 1945–1961 in which a country was independent; and, as the denominator, the number of individuals who held the post of chief executive during the same period. By subtracting this figure from seventeen (the number of years in the period) we obtain what we shall term the index of "personnel instability." It may vary from zero to seventeen; in fact, the highest figure in our sample is 16.32 for France.[10]

2. *Internal Group Violence.* Rudolph Rummel, in his Dimensionality of Nations Project, collected data on the number of people killed as a result of internal group violence—i.e., civil wars, revolutions, and riots—during the years 1955–1957. We have extended the time period to 1950–1962, and have modified the data to allow for the size of the total population in question, making the index deaths per million people.[11]

3. *Internal War.* As an alternative to the violent-death material, we shall use Harry Eckstein's data on internal war for the period 1946–1961.[12] These data include the total

number of violent incidents, from plots to protracted guerrilla warfare.

4. Quite a different problem is the *Stability of Democracy.* With a few adaptations we shall use the distinctions employed by Seymour Martin Lipset. "Stable democracies" will be defined as states that have been characterized by the uninterrupted continuation of political democracy since World War I, *and* the absence over the past thirty years of a totalitarian movement, either Fascist or Communist, which at any point received as much as twenty percent of the vote. "Unstable democracies," again following Lipset, are countries which, although unable to meet the first criteria, nevertheless have a "history of more or less free elections for most of the post-World War I period."[13] "Dictatorships" are those countries in which, perhaps despite some democratic interludes, free elections have been generally absent. These judgments are impressionistic and do not permit precise rankings from most to least democratic; nevertheless they generally agree with those of other scholars and with widely accepted standards.[14]

Note again that our political dependent variables measure distinctly different aspects —stability of executive personnel, the incidence of violence, and "democracy." No one is by itself an adequate measure of all the conditions to which land distribution has been thought relevant.

Table 1 (see pp. 210–211) indicates the rankings of forty-seven countries (all those for which distribution data are available) on the first six of these indices. It also gives 1955 *GNP per capita*, in U.S. dollars, and the *percentage of the labor force employed in agriculture* in the most recent year for which we have data. The possible relevance of these additional variables will be discussed below.

III

Land is everywhere distributed unequally. In even the most egalitarian states, about four-fifths of the farmers are concentrated on only half the land. Still, the degree of inequality varies widely from state to state.

Table 1. Land distribution and politica stability, forty-seven countries†

Country	LAND DATA			POLITICAL DATA			ECONOMIC DATA	
	Gini Index	Percentage of Farms with ½ Land	Percentage of Farms Rented	Personnel Instability	Eckstein Internal War	Deaths from Civil Group Violence per 1,000,000	GNP per Capita ($-1955)	Percentage Labor Force in Agriculture
Yugoslavia	43.7	79.8	0*	0	9	0	297	67
Poland	45.0	77.7	0*	8.5	19	5.0	468	57
Denmark	45.8	79.3	3.5	14.6	0	0.1	913	23
Japan	47.0	81.5	2.9	15.7	22*	0	240	40
Canada	49.7	82.9	7.2	11.3	0	0	1667	12
Switzerland	49.8	81.5	18.9	8.5			1229	10
India	52.2	86.9	53.0	3.0	83	14.0	72	71
Philippines	56.4	88.2	37.3	14.0	15	292.0	201	59
Sweden	57.7	87.2	18.9	8.5	0	0	1165	13
France	58.3	86.1	26.0	16.3	46	0.3	1046	26
Belgium	58.7	85.8	62.3	15.5	8	0.9	1015	10
Ireland	59.8	85.9	2.5**	14.2	9	0	509	40
Finland	59.9	86.3	2.4	15.6	4	0	941	46
Netherlands	60.5	86.2	53.3	13.6	2	0	708	11
Luxembourg	63.8	87.7	18.8	12.8	0	0	1194	23
Taiwan	65.2	94.1	40.0	0	3	0	102	50
Norway	66.9	87.5	7.5	12.8	1	0	969	26
South Vietnam	67.1	94.6	20.0*	10.0	50*	1000	133	65
West Germany	67.4	93.0	5.7	3.0	4	0	762	14
Libya	70.0	93.0	8.5	14.8	8	0*	90	75
United States	70.5	95.4	20.4	12.8	22*	0	2343	10
United Kingdom	71.0	93.4	44.5	13.6	12	0	998	5
Panama	73.7	95.0	12.3	15.6	29	25.0	350	54
Austria	74.0	97.4	10.7	15.8	4	0	532	32
Egypt	74.0	98.1	11.6	12.8	45	1.6	133	64
Greece	74.7	99.4	17.7	15.8	9	2.0	239	48
Honduras	75.7	97.4	16.7	15.8	45	111.0	137	66
Nicaragua	75.7	96.4	n.a.	13.6	16	16.0	254	68
New Zealand	77.3	95.5	22.3	12.8	0	0	1249	16
Spain	78.0	99.5	43.7	12.8	22	0.2	254	50
Cuba	79.2	97.8	53.8	0	100	2900.0*	361	42
Dominican Rep.	79.5	98.5	20.8	13.6	6	31.0	205	56

(Table 1. cont'd.)

Country	LAND DATA			POLITICAL DATA			ECONOMIC DATA	
	Gini Index	Percentage of Farms with ½ Land	Percentage of Farms Rented	Personnel Instability	Eckstein Internal War	Deaths from Civil Group Violence per 1,000,000	GNP per Capita ($-1955)	Percentage Labor Force in Agriculture
Italy	80.3	98.0	23.8	15.5	51	0.2	442	29
Uruguay	81.7	96.6	34.7	14.6	1	0.3	569	37
El Salvador	82.8	98.8	15.1	15.1	9	2.0	244	63
Brazil	83.7	98.5	9.1	15.5	49	10	262	61
Colombia	84.9	98.1	12.1	14.6	47	316.0	330	55
Guatemala	86.0	99.7	17.0	14.9	45	57.0	179	(68)
Argentina	86.3	98.2	32.8	13.6	57	217.0	374	25
Ecuador	86.4	99.3	14.6	15.1	41	18.0	204	53
Peru	87.5	96.9	n.a.	14.6	23	2.60	140	60
Iraq	88.1	99.3	75.0*	16.2	24	344.0	195	81
Costa Rica	89.1	99.1	5.4	14.6	19	24.0	307	55
Venezuela	90.9	99.3	20.6	14.9	36	111.0	762	42
Australia	92.9	99.6	n.a.	11.3	0	0.0	1215	14
Chile	93.8	99.7	13.4	14.2	21	2.0	180	30
Bolivia	93.8	97.7	20.0	15.3	53	663.0	66	72

† Sources: GNP: Norton Ginsburg, *Atlas of Economic Development* (Chicago, 1962), p. 22. Land, Personnel Instability, Violent Deaths, and Percentage of Labor Force in Agriculture: Russett, *World Handbook* (forthcoming). Internal War: Eckstein, Appendix I.

* Yale Data Program estimate—very approximate.

** Percentage Area (not farms) rented.

Table 2 presents the correlation coefficients (*r*) indicating the degree of association between each of the three measures of land distribution and each of the first three indices of instability.[15]

Table 2. *Correlation coefficients (r) for measures of land equality with measures of political instability for forty-seven countries*

	PERSONNEL INSTABILITY	VIOLENT POLITICAL DEATHS (per 1,000,000)	ECKSTEIN INTERNAL WAR DATA
Percentage of Farms with ½ Land	.24	.45	.35
Gini Index	.33	.46	.29
Percentage of Farms Rented (44 countries only)	.01	.27	.11

For the three indices of inequality there is in each case a positive relationship to instability, though in two instances the correlation is extremely slight. The highest correlation is between violent deaths and the Gini index. Judged by the standards of most social science this is a fairly high correlation, with a significance level of .001 (i.e., unless there really were a positive relationship between land distribution and instability, this high a correlation would not occur, purely by chance, as often as one time in a thousand). Nevertheless, these correlations indicate that much remains unexplained. Even the highest (.46) gives an r^2 of only .21. (The squared product moment coefficient—r^2—can be interpreted as the percentage of the total variation in one index that can be explained by another.) Inequality of land distribution does bear a relation to political instability, but that relationship is not a strong one, and many other factors must be considered in any attempted explanation.[16] The degree to which farm land is rented is not a factor of great explanatory power, given the low level of the correlations of rental with all the stability indices.

A more complex hypothesis, closely related to Kling's, might read as follows: extreme inequality of land distribution leads to political instability only in those poor, predominantly agricultural societies where limitation to a small plot of land almost unavoidably condemns one to poverty. In a rich country, the modest income a farmer can produce from even a small holding may satisfy him. Or, if that is not the case, at least in wealthy countries there are, besides agriculture, many alternative sources of wealth.[17] Finally, one might assert that the *combination* of inequality *and* a high rate of tenancy would cause instability. While neither by itself would necessarily lead to violence or frequent change of government, the combination almost inevitably would.

To test these hypotheses we examined simultaneously the effect of GNP per capita, percentage of labor force in agriculture, tenancy, and land distribution on our various indices of political stability.[18] These refinements improved our explanation rather strikingly in some cases. The strongest relationship was between the Gini index and violent deaths; r^2 was raised to .50. By far the most important variables in the equations for "predicting" instability were first the Gini index and then the percentage of the population in agriculture, as suggested by our first hypothesis. The percentage of farms rented again added little explanatory power. Qualifications of this sort help to explain the stability of a country like Australia, despite a highly unequal distribution of agricultural land. Venezuela's land distribution is also very unequal (but no more so than Australia's), yet Venezuela is somewhat poorer and has three times as many people (proportionately) employed in agriculture.[19] All the indices of instability are quite high for Venezuela. Nevertheless, even the strongest relationship found among these variables leaves over half the variance "unexplained"

—as the sophisticated student of politics might expect. The old saws about equality can be accepted only with caution.

There remains one other possibility yet to be explored—that equality may be related to the stability of a *democratic regime*. That is, there may or may not be sporadic outbreaks of violence; there may or may not be frequent changes of personnel at the highest level; but it is highly unlikely that a stable democracies, whereas only three of 24 more unequal countries can be classified as stable democracies. And of these three, each is a fairly rich state where agriculture is no longer the principal source of wealth. Tocqueville's basic observation would therefore appear correct: no state can long maintain a democratic form of government if the major sources of economic gain are divided very unequally among its citizens. American

Table 3. *Stable democracies, unstable democracies, and dictatorships by degree of inequality in land distribution*

GINI INDEX	STABLE DEMOCRACIES	UNSTABLE DEMOCRACIES	DICTATORSHIPS
Greater than Median Equality	Denmark Canada Switzerland India Philippines Sweden Belgium Ireland Netherlands Luxembourg Norway United States United Kingdom	Japan France Finland West Germany	Yugoslavia Poland Taiwan South Vietnam Libya Panama
Median Equality or Less	New Zealand Uruguay Australia	Austria Greece Italy Brazil Colombia Argentina Costa Rica Chile	Egypt Honduras Nicaragua Spain Cuba Dominican Rep. El Salvador Guatemala Ecuador Peru Iraq Venezuela Bolivia

nation with a grossly unequal pattern of distribution of a major source of wealth, like agricultural land, will have a consistently democratic government. Table 3 presents a sixfold table showing each of the countries in our sample classified, after Lipset, as a "stable democracy," an "unstable democracy," or a "dictatorship."[20] and also listed as above or below the median for the Gini index of land inequality.

The results are again quite striking. Of the twenty-three states with the more equal pattern of land distribution, thirteen are policy in urging the governments of underdeveloped nations to undertake massive land reform programs seems essentially wellfounded. A "sturdy yeomanry" may be a virtual *sine qua non* for democratic government in an underdeveloped land. Nevertheless there are many instances where relative equality of land tenure is not associated with stable democracy; it is no *guarantee* of democratic development. Land reform may provide the soil to nourish free institutions, but the seed must first be planted.

Socioeconomic change and political instability

This article has to do with the political consequences of socioeconomic development. Earlier articles have stated that such development preceded the Protestant Reformation and the French Revolution. Olson reinforces and generalizes the statements of Engels and Tocqueville. He argues that economic change when it is rapid—upward or downward—produces instability.

The reader by now is prepared to appraise and evaluate this article better than if he had read it *de novo*, but not all the material relevant to a close analysis is available, in this book or anywhere. Psychological research has associated race prejudice with downward (and upward) mobility; this article says that rapid change produces social mobility, which helps produce political instability. Durkheim argued that the disruption of established communal life led both to the growth of industrial civilization and to anomy (rootlessness and normlessness); this article says that rapid change aggravates the crisis that Durkheim analyzed.

Some questions remain. It seems evident that people prefer socioeconomic mobility to stasis. If this were not so, the appeals of modernization would never have been heard in subsistence economies. What people hear depends on what they want. If they had no wants beyond staying alive and well, they would not hear such appeals. It should be apparent that above all they do not want the maximum stability that stasis amounts to. On the other hand, they do not want only mobility and change. Postrevolutionary governments are often repressive, in the name of law and order. These régimes are popularly tolerated and even supported. This suggests that people also do not want maximum instability.

So we have remaining the quantitative question: just what rate of change (between zero change and ultrarapid change) produces instability. If, as Olson persuasively argues, change that is too rapid produces instability, so also does change that is too slow. As he argues, accelerated economic development was followed by the Protestant Reformation. But what caused the development to accelerate? People must not have been altogether content with their material status or they would not have undertaken to destroy the feudal system, which produced subsistence (in principle) for all within it. If comparable people in the 20th century in Africa and Asia were content with the stability of their static societies, they would surely not have so positively

214

responded to unstabilizing external influences that were introduced by traders and missionaries, Christian or Marxist.

The ultimate goal of Olson's line of investigation might be threefold: ascertaining (a) the slowest rate of change that people in a particular culture will tolerate without becoming violent against their rulers; (b) the rapidest rate of change they will tolerate without becoming violent, and (c) the optimum rate of growth that will minimize violent instability. To find this optimum rate takes us into problems in sociology and psychology about which there simply is not enough information to calculate the optimum. We know that England made a transition from feudal to industrial society, with only one major revolution. The process took hundreds of years. We know that France, Russia, and China have had gigantic revolutions in the course of accomplishing the same. It appears that the transition from a subsistence to a wealth-producing society did not take so long in these three cases. To ascertain whether this is true requires that we know what is to be called the starting point for change in all cases.

One of the most provocative aspects of Olson's essay is precisely that it raises so many more questions than it answers. Where—between the English and other cultures—the optimum growth rate lies is a continuing unknown in social science. In terms of the frustration–aggression hypothesis, this article is an instigator to frustration, leading hopefully to an aggressive but nonviolent attack on the scientific problem.

Rapid growth as a destabilizing force*

MANCUR OLSON, JR.

Mancur Olson, Jr., "Rapid Growth as a De-stabilizing Force," is reprinted with the permission of the author. Copyright by and reprinted with the permission of The Economic History Association, New York, from the *Journal of Economic History*, 23(4), pp. 529–552, December 1963.

Notes to this section will be found on pages 347–349.

* I am thankful to the Center of International Studies at Princeton University and to the Institute for Defense Analysis of Washington, D.C., for the support they have given my research, and particularly to Dr. Stephan Enke of the latter organization, from whose writings I have drawn several of the examples used to support the argument of this paper. Professors Kenneth Curran and William Hochman of Colorado College, Lt. Gerald Garvey of the Air Force Academy, Mr. Richard Zeckhauser of Harvard University, and my wife, Alison G. Olson, have also offered very helpful criticisms. But I am alone responsible for the errors.

I

Many writers—some of them reputable scholars, others important public officials—have implicitly assumed or explicitly argued that economic growth leads toward political stability and perhaps even to peaceful democracy. They have argued that "economic development is one of the keys to stability and peace in the world";[1] that it is "conditions of want and instability on which communism breeds";[2] and that economic progress "serves as a bulwark against international communism."[3] A recent and justly famous book on revolution by Hannah Arendt ascribes the most violent forms of revolutionary extremism mainly to poverty.[4]

This view has had an influence on American foreign aid policy and more often than not foreign economic aid is regarded as "an investment in peace and orderly political evolution toward a democratic world."[5] In one of his presidential messages to Congress, for example, Eisenhower justified a request for foreign aid funds by saying that unless the underdeveloped nations "can hope for reasonable economic advance, the danger will be acute that their governments will be subverted by communism."[6] A committee of scholars, so distinguished that they nearly make up a *Who's Who* of American students of economic development, has prepared for the guidance of the Senate Foreign Relations Committee a report which later was published as a book on *The Emerging Nations,*[7] and which argues that the United States should offer most of its economic aid to the countries in the "takeoff" stage of economic development. The countries that are not yet ready for this stage of rapid development should get only modest amounts of aid, mainly in the form of technical assistance. This favoritism in the allocation of aid is justified on the grounds that a given amount of aid will bring about more growth if it is concentrated in the nations that are, in any case, in a stage of rapid development. This prescription for policy is justified, not on straightforward humanitarian grounds, but rather in the long term political interest of the United States, particularly in view of the cold war with the Soviet Union. While at least some of these students of economic development have denied that they accept a "crude materialist" explanation of the causes of political stability,[8] the obvious premise of their policy is that the rapid economic growth of selected underdeveloped countries is the "key to an effective foreign policy" for the United States in its cold war with the Soviet Union. Many communists have also shared the faith that poverty was the prelude to revolution: the poor, they argue, "have nothing to lose but their chains."

Several scholars, however, have suggested that the assumed connection between economic growth and political stability was much too simple, or that there was no such connection. But their denials of any positive relationship between economic growth and political stability have too often been mere *obiter dicta*. They have at least failed to convince many people. It is not, therefore, enough simply to deny that economic growth necessarily brings political stability.

What is needed instead is a bold and sustained argument in the opposite direction. What is needed now is, not a cautious qualification of the argument that economic growth leads toward political stability, but rather a clear and decisive argument stating that rapid economic growth is a major force leading toward revolution and instability. Many of the reasons why rapid economic growth should lead to political instability have apparently never been discussed, at least in print; it is thus time that these reasons were stated and put together in an attempt to show that rapid economic growth is a profoundly destabilizing force.

II

Any adequate analysis of the relationship between economic growth and revolutionary political changes must consider the problem in terms of the individuals who bring revolutions about. Students of the sociology of revolution often argue that those people who participate in "mass movements" of the radical left or radical right—movements designed to bring about revolutionary rather than evolutionary change—tend to be distinguished by the relative absence of bonds that tie them to the established order. They tend to lack close attachments to any of the social subgroups that comprise a society— to extended families, for example, or to voluntary associations, professional groups, or social classes.

Thus some of these scholars have argued, not without evidence, that labor unions, which are often regarded as particularly likely sources of strength for communist revolutionaries, are in fact a force tending to reduce the chances for communist revolutions, mainly because they provide one more group connection that can hold the worker to the prevailing system. The social class, which Marx thought was the engine of revolutionary change, some sociologists regard instead as a stabilizing institution. Those who are *déclassé*, whose class ties are weakest, are most apt to support revolutionary changes, while those who are firmly caught up in a class are least likely to do so.

Even those who are firmly caught up even in the lowest and least fortunate class are not normally in the revolutionary vanguard, for they are secure in their modest place in the social hierarchy. Those who are very poor, after meeting the exigencies of life, have in any case very little energy left for agitation for a better political system, even if they had much hope that real improvement was possible. "There is thus a conservatism of the destitute," says Eric Hoffer, "as profound as the conservatism of the privileged."[9] It is not those who are accustomed to poverty, but those whose place in the social order is changing, who resort to revolution.

III

The next thing is to ask how rapid economic growth might affect the number of individuals who are *déclassé*, or who have lost their identification with other social groups, and who are thus in circumstances conducive to revolutionary protest.

It is now generally understood that economic growth proceeds not so much through simple capital accumulation—through continuing the old methods of production with more capital—as it does through innovation and technical change. Economic growth—especially rapid economic growth—therefore involves vast changes in the methods of production. It involves vast changes in the importance of different industries, in the types of labor demanded, in the geographical configuration of production. It means vast changes in the ways and places in which people live and work. Above all, economic growth means vast changes in the distribution of income.

The fact that some gain a lot and others lose a lot, in a rapidly growing economy, means that the bonds of class and caste are weakened. Some rise above the circumstances of their birth and others fall behind. Both groups are normally *déclassé*. Their economic status keeps them from belonging wholly to the class or caste into which they were born, and their social situation keeps them from belonging to the caste or class

into which their income bracket should put them. Rapid economic growth therefore loosens the class and caste ties that help bind men to the social order.

But castes and social classes are not the only social groupings which rapid economic growth breaks down. Even the family group, and especially the clan or extended family, can be destroyed by the occupational and geographic mobility associated with economic growth. The replacement of subsistence agriculture and cottage industry, normally organized around the family, with factory production by workers hired individually, can weaken family ties. Similarly, modern business institutions are bound to weaken or even to destroy the tribe, the manor, the guild, and the rural village. The uprooted souls torn or enticed out of these groups by economic growth are naturally susceptible to the temptations of revolutionary agitation.

IV

When the focus is on the fact that rapid economic growth means rapid economic change, and that economic change entails social dislocation, it becomes clear that *both the gainers and the losers from economic growth can be destabilizing forces.* Both will be imperfectly adjusted to the existing order. This paper will argue, first, that economic growth increases the number of *nouveaux riches*, who may use their economic power to change the social and political order in their interest; and second, that economic growth may paradoxically also create a surprisingly large number of "*nouveaux pauvres*," who will be much more resentful of their poverty than those who have known nothing else.

The fact that there will be some who gain disproportionately from economic growth means that there will be a new distribution of economic power. But there will be an (almost Marxian) "contradiction" between this new distribution of economic power and the old distribution of social prestige and political power. Certain individuals are left in places in the economic order that are incompatible with their positions in the old social and political hierarchy. This means, not only that these people are in socially ambiguous situations that may leave them "alienated" from society; it means also that they have the resources with which they can ultimately change the social and political order in their own interest. The economic system, the social system, and the political system are obviously interdependent parts of a single society, and if one part changes quickly, there must also be instability in other parts of the society. The fact that the distribution of wealth will have both social and political effects is beyond dispute. In time, those groups who have gained the fruits of economic growth (or their children) will probably have built a new social and political order that is suited to the new distribution of economic power. But, especially if the economic growth is very rapid, the path to any new equilibrium may be highly unstable.

Something very like this seems to have happened in Europe as a result of the commercial and industrial revolutions. The growth of commerce and industry in early modern Europe created a larger and wealthier middle class; and as this middle class gained in numbers and in wealth, especially in relation to the landed aristocracy, it demanded, and it got, extra political power to match that wealth. These demands were obviously behind the middle class participation in the French Revolution, and were also fundamental to many of the other instances of political instability in the history of modern Europe. Liberalism and laissez-faire economic doctrine were also related to the newly achieved gains that the industrial revolution brought to Europe, and these ideas in turn tended further to destabilize the political environment.

The middle class in early modern and modern Europe was not the only group of gainers from economic growth that destabilized its environment. There are other types of gainers from economic growth who have also attempted to change the prevailing order. Urban areas, for example, normally grow disproportionately during periods of economic growth, and those who move from farm to city in pursuit of the more remunerative opportunities there are often also discontented gainers. The man who has been tempted away from his village, his manor, his tribe, or his extended family, by the higher wages of burgeoning urban industry may well be a disaffected gainer from economic growth. He has been, albeit voluntarily, uprooted and is not apt soon to acquire comparable social connections in the city. He is, therefore, prone to join destabilizing mass movements. Those who leave rural areas for the higher wages or other gains that economic growth brings to the cities often display a nostalgia for the economically poorer, but socially more secure, life they left. The Chartists, for example, at one time proposed schemes that would give factory workers small agricultural estates.[10] But after British workers had had some time to adjust to the urban, industrial order, this sort of scheme lost its popularity to programs designed to improve the conditions of urban industrial life. The degree of extremism of the different labor movements in the Scandinavian countries has also been related to the varying proportions of migrants from rural areas in the industrial work force, which in turn resulted from different rates of economic growth. The first and most gradual industrialization took place in Denmark, and there the rate at which migrants from rural areas were recruited into the urban work force was slow. In Sweden, and still more in Norway, industrialization and the absorption of rural migrants was later and faster, and the labor movements in turn revealed, especially in Norway, more disaffection and political extremism.[11] The fact that the concentration of population in cities can sometimes make agitation cheaper and the spread of new ideas faster is also important, as is the fact that riots and revolts are often technically easier to organize in cities. Whenever an ideology, like Marxism, designed explicitly for the urban proletariat, is in the air, the growth of cities induced by economic expansion will be particularly conducive to revolt.

The movement from farm to city is moreover only one of the types of geographic mobility brought about by economic growth. Some industries and localities will expand rapidly with economic growth, and others, urban as well as rural, will decline. Individuals may move from city to city or from rural area to rural area in search of the gains from economic growth. These sorts of mobility can also lead to a frustrating severance of social ties. The radical elements in Jacksonian democracy, in Populism, in the unusually strong Socialist parties of some of the frontier states of the Great Plains, in the violent western mining unions, and in the Non-Partisan League, cannot be adequately explained by any hypothesis of economic decline or stagnation. The western areas near the frontier were growing rapidly when these destabilizing movements began, and they were often filled with people who had gained from this expansion. Perhaps in frontier areas, or in areas that have only recently been on the frontier, the social groupings that bind people to the social order have not had time to develop, and as a result there is a susceptibility to protests against established governments and inherited conventions. This factor may explain Turner's alleged "quasi-revolutionary" or rebellious frontier democracy, which has sometimes been ascribed to "self-reliant pioneer" and "labor safety valve" theories.

v

Just as the gainers can be a destabilizing force, so, of course, can the losers. Their position in the social order is changing too, and they are also imperfectly adjusted to the existing society.

Moreover, contrary to what is usually assumed, economic growth can significantly increase the number of losers. It can be associated with a decided increase in the number whose standard of living is falling. This may seem absurd at first glance, since economic growth by definition leads to an increase in average income—to a situation such that the gains of the gainers are more than sufficient to compensate for the losses of the losers. But when average income

increases, the number who are getting poorer may nonetheless increase. The gains of a small percentage of large gainers may be so large that they may exceed the combined losses of a larger percentage of losers; median income might fall while average income rises. In other words, while average income is increasing, the income of the average man may be falling.

It is not only a logical possibility, but also at times a practical probability, that the number getting poorer will increase with rapid economic growth.[12] This is because in periods of rapid economic growth there are often several forces that work toward a concentration of most of the gains in a relatively small number of hands and to a widespread diffusion of the losses. One of the forces that can work in this direction is the tendency for wages to be more sticky than prices. Thus, as demand increases with economic growth, businessmen may raise prices *pari-passu* with the increase in demand, but wages may rise much more slowly. The particular importance of this phenomenon during periods of inflation, which also seem to be correlated somewhat with economic growth, is of course familiar to every economic historian, because this same argument has been used to contend that inflation leads to a redistribution of income from wage earners to entrepreneurs.[13]

Another force that leads toward inequality in the distribution of the fruits of rapid economic growth is the change of technology involved in economic growth. When one firm, or some group of firms, begins to use a new technique, a technique sufficiently superior to the old techniques to lead to rapid increases in productivity and efficiency, those firms with the old technology are apt to fail or at least to suffer falling profits. Unless the new technology is adopted by all firms in an industry at the same time, one would expect that the introduction or the arrival of this technology would increase the differences in profits or lead to the failure of some of the firms. When the factors of production—especially the labor—that the declining firms employ are considered, the problem becomes more important in human, and political, terms. The unskilled laborers or skilled craftsmen replaced by machines are apt to be a destabilizing force.

The increased productivity of the modern machinery and new techniques introduced in periods of rapid economic growth will no doubt in the long run increase the income of all classes. But those who suffer in the short run know that in the long run they will be dead and are all too apt to be susceptible to disruptive agitation. The British weavers who were left unemployed in the advance of the industrial revolution certainly lost a great deal in a period when the nation's total wealth and per capita income doubtless increased. The Luddite-type movements against new machinery that increased productivity illustrate the reactions against the unevenness of the short-run benefits of growth.

The fact that some groups in the population may in the short run lose from rapid economic growth is made all the worse by the fact that societies in the early stages of industrialization rarely have suitable institutions for mitigating the adversities that the losers in the process suffer. While traditional social institutions, like the tribe, the extended family, and the manor will often have appropriate ways of helping those among them who suffer adversities, and while mature industrial societies have developed welfare institutions, the society in an early stage of rapid industrialization will probably not have adequate institutions to care for those who suffer from the economic advance. Unemployment is not normally a serious problem for the preindustrial society. It could hardly have meaning in, say, a tribal society. The word "unemployment" is indeed a rather recent coinage. The unemployment, frictional or otherwise, that may result when a traditional society begins to industrialize and grow will therefore lead to serious losses for some parts of the society. And, since the problem is new, the society is not apt to deal with it successfully. The United States and Great Britain certainly had not yet developed systems for dealing with the unemployment that was becoming increasingly serious in their societies in the nineteenth century.

In short, rapid economic growth will bring about a situation where some lose part of their incomes, and others, because of the new problem of unemployment, lose *all* of their incomes. Thus a sense of grievance and insecurity may be a destabilizing force resulting from the fact that with economic growth, as with so many other things, there are both winners and losers.

In those cases where the number of gainers from economic growth exceeds the number of losers, there is apt to be a number of those who, while they have gained in absolute terms, have lost in relative terms; that is, they have come to have a lower position relative to the rest of the income earners in that society. Some of those whose gains from economic growth are rather modest may find that they have fallen in the economic scale because of the larger advances of some of the other gainers. There have been some studies that provide interesting indirect evidence about the reactions of people who are experiencing an absolute increase in income and a relative decline in their economic position. These studies, arising out of the controversies over the Keynesian consumption function, have suggested that families with a given level of income tend to spend a smaller percentage of that income when the others in that society have low incomes than they do when the others in that society have high incomes. A family's consumption, in sort, is affected, not only by that family's level of income, but also by the level of incomes of the other people in that society. The evidence on this point Professor James S. Duesenberry has explained in terms of the "demonstration effect." The demonstration or evidence of higher consumption patterns in one's neighbors will increase one's desire for additional consumption, in the sense that it leads to saving a smaller proportion of income. From this in turn one can perhaps infer that, when a group's position in the economic hierarchy falls, there may be some dissatisfaction—dissatisfaction that would not necessarily be counteracted by an absolute increase in that group's level of income.

Therefore, quite apart from the fact that

even the relative gainers may, as earlier parts of this paper argued, be destabilizing, and quite apart from the possibility that economic growth may increase the number of losers, there is still the further fact that, when the number of gainers from economic growth exceeds the number of losers, some of the gainers may have lost ground relative to the society in general and may display some degree of disaffection.[14]

VI

But the most important error involved in the all-too-common assumption, "when the economy grows, the standard of living improves," is that it neglects the very important possibility that the level of consumption will decline when the rate of economic growth increases greatly. This can best be explained by using an elementary Domar-type model. Let the marginal propensity to save be equal to the average propensity to save, and let it be symbolized by the letter S. Let the marginal capital-output ratio be symbolized by the letter R, and income by the letter Y. Then the increase in income with economic growth will be given by the equation $dY = dS/dR$. Assume a rather typical capital-output ratio of, say, 3 to 1. The shortcomings of the capital-output ratio as a tool of prediction, or planning, or rigorous analysis, are obvious enough, but they are not relevant to the merely illustrative use of the concept here. Whether capital accumulation is as fundamental a force in economic growth as some have assumed is doubtful, but there can be no question that capital accumulation is associated with growth. Let us therefore accept the usual assumption that a stagnant underdeveloped nation will normally be saving only about five percent of its income, and growing at less than two percent per year—that is, at a rate barely sufficient to compensate for normal population growth. Now, suppose such a nation is, through its own efforts, going to increase its growth to five percent per year. Then it must, as long as the capital-output ratio remains constant, increase its rate of savings until it saves fifteen percent of its total income: it

must *reduce* its standard of living by ten percent, in order to triple its rate of savings. So when growth is financed primarily out of domestic sources, as it normally is, a rapid increase in the rate of growth will tend to be associated with a decline in the standard of living.[15] To be sure, the increased rate of growth will after a time put a nation in a position such that it can reduce its rate of savings again and enjoy a higher standard of living than before (provided that population growth doesn't then catch up with this increase in income). It can even, if it waits long enough, get a higher standard of living than it had before without reducing the rate of its savings, for in time it will have grown so much that the smaller fraction of this larger income will still mean more consumption than it had before. Yet the fact remains that a nation that greatly increases the rate at which it grows through its own efforts must normally sustain a reduction in its standard of living for a significant period.

The all-too-common argument that hunger and deprivation breed discontent and disaffection and that economic growth therefore reduces the chances for revolt is, apart from its other shortcomings, ruined by the simple fact that there is in the short run no necessary, or even likely, connection between economic growth and amelioration of hunger and the other deprivations of poverty. There may, instead, very well be a general decrease in living standards with rapid economic growth.

It may be only a remarkable coincidence that Marx, writing during a period of rapid economic growth and tremendous capital accumulation in Europe, emphasized the "rising organic composition of capital" (the increased importance of capital invested in things other than labor) as the fundamental reason why the *advance* of capitalism would lead to the immiseration of the workers. But it is an interesting coincidence: perhaps Marx's insight was better than his logic.

The upshot of the foregoing arguments, then, is that the gainers from economic growth may themselves be a destabilizing influence because their position in the social order is changing. Those who lose from economic growth will also find that their position in the social order is changing, and they are apt to be much more resentful of poverty, and aware of the possibilities of a better life, than those who have known nothing but privation. The assumption that economic growth ameliorates social discontents is, in addition to its other shortcomings, weakened by the fact that there is no necessary connection between rapid economic growth and short-run increases in the incomes of the mass of the people. And even when the incomes of the mass of the people are increasing, it does not follow that their standards of living are increasing, for the increased rate of saving concomitant with economic growth may reduce the level of consumption.

VII

Since economic growth is associated, not only with capital accumulation, but also with the advance of education, skill, and technology, it will be connected in underdeveloped countries with an increasing knowledge of the possibilities of a better life, of new ideologies, and of new systems of government. It will be associated with a "revolution of rising expectations" that is apt to involve, above all, rising expectations about what the government should do. Economic growth, since it leads to higher incomes for some people who were previously at a lower standard, will itself stimulate and exacerbate these rising expectations. Thus it is possible that there may be something in the economic sphere corresponding to the tendency for the demands for reform to increase as soon as reform is begun. Alexis de Tocqueville made this point particularly clearly.

It is not always by going from bad to worse that a society falls into revolution. It happens most often that a people, which has supported without complaint, as if they were not felt, the most oppressive laws, violently throws them off as soon as their weight is lightened. The social order destroyed by a revolution is almost always better than that which immediately preceded it, and experience shows that the most dangerous moment for a bad government is generally that in which it sets about reform. Only great genius can save a prince who undertakes to relieve his subjects after a long oppression. The evil, which was suffered patiently as inevitable, seems unendurable as soon as the idea of escaping from it is conceived. All the abuses then removed seem to throw into greater relief those which remain, so that their feeling is more painful. The evil, it is true, has become less, but sensibility to it has become more acute. Feudalism at the height of its power had not inspired Frenchmen with so much hatred as it did on the eve of its disappearing. The slightest acts of arbitrary power under Louis XVI seemed less easy to endure than all the despotism of Louis XIV.[16]

The awareness of racial injustice and the willingness to do something about it seem to be higher among American Negroes now than they have been for a long time. The discontent seems to have increased *after* the historic Supreme Court decision outlawing segregated schools and *after* a series of other steps in the direction of racial justice. (This discontent also appears to have been correlated with an economic improvement in the position of American Negroes.) Many other cases could be cited where reform nourishes revolt; but the relevant point here is that economic growth, like political reform, can awaken a people to the possibilities of further improvement and thereby generate additional discontent.

There is, however, at least one situation where economic growth need *not* be correlated with increased knowledge of new ideologies, new systems of government, and the like, or perhaps even with the possibilities of a better material life. That is in a modern totalitarian country, where the media of communication are controlled in such a way that they glorify the existing situation and keep out any ideas that would threaten the existing system. Modern totalitarian regimes of the Stalinist and Hitlerian kinds will also have other techniques for guaranteeing their own stability, most notably the practice of liquidating anyone who shows any lack of enthusiasm for the prevailing regime. There was rapid growth in the Soviet Union under Stalin's five-year plans; yet the nation was relatively stable, and for obvious reasons.[17] Some other despotic regimes have been less thoroughgoing in their repression that Stalin or Hitler yet have nonetheless managed to control dissent fairly effectively. Japan before World War II would provide an example of this sort of situation.

Repression is not, of course, the only thing besides economic growth that can affect the degree of political instability. Clearly, charismatic leadership, religious controversy, ideological change, and probably other things as well, also have an independent influence on the degree of instability in any country. It would be absurd to attempt to explain political instability through economic growth alone. Indeed, a severe depression, or a sudden *decrease* in the level of income, could of course also be destabilizing—and for many of the same reasons that rapid economic growth itself can be destabilizing. A rapid economic decline, like rapid economic growth, will bring about important movements in the *relative* economic positions of people and will therefore set up contradictions between the structure of economic power and the distribution of social and political power. (Severe inflation of the German and Chinese types will have the same effect.) There is, accordingly, nothing inconsistent in saying that both rapid economic growth and rapid economic decline would tend toward political instability.[18] It is economic stability—the absence of rapid economic growth or rapid economic decline —that should be regarded as conducive to social and political tranquility. But it would be absurd to suppose that economic stagnation would guarantee political stability. Since there are many factors in addition to rapid economic change that cause political instability, there can be political instability in a wide range of economic conditions.

This makes it extremely difficult to test the hypothesis that rapid economic growth is conducive to political instability. The hypothesis would not be proven even if every period of rapid economic growth were shown to be politically destabilizing, for the instability in these periods of rapid economic growth could be due to other factors that were operating at the same time. Similarly, the hypothesis that rapid economic growth

is destabilizing would not be disproven if there were a negative relationship between rapid economic growth and political instability, for the extent of totalitarian repression or the presence of other stabilizing forces might keep the destabilizing tendencies of rapid economic growth from being manifest. If rapid economic change and political instability are positively or negatively correlated, all this will do is establish some tentative *presumption* that rapid economic growth is, or is not, destabilizing. A final judgment, if one could ever be made, would have to rest on detailed historical studies of a vast variety of cases. These historical studies would have to be so careful and so detailed that they looked, not only at the connection over time between economic and political change, but also at the complex of detailed economic, social, and political changes. They would have to identify both the gainers and the losers from rapid economic growth and all of the other factors affecting political stability, and then attempt to come to a judgment about the role of the economic changes. A massive set of historical studies of the kind needed, covering all historical periods and countries in which there has been rapid economic growth or political instability, is obviously out of the question in a brief paper, even if it were within my competence, which it is not. But it is nonetheless important that historians should start studying at least parts of the problem, however difficult, as soon as possible.

VIII

There are several important historical situations in which the relationship between economic growth and political instability seems particularly worth studying.[19] Consider, for example, the Reformation, the English civil wars, the French Revolution, the middle class upheavals of nineteenth-century Europe, the rise of continental Marxism, and the Russian Revolution.

It is clear, first, that the Reformation followed a period of economic growth. Partisans of medieval and early modern institutions may debate the exact timing of the speedup in the European economy, but there can be little doubt that the pace of economic change quickened well before the Protestant Reformation became a major mass movement. This Reformation, moreover, continued through the Age of Exploration and the Commercial Revolution. Nor can there be any doubt that the Reformation was a profoundly destabilizing movement—one which destroyed much of what was left of the medieval order and which threatened the existence of the dominant institution of that order. While Henry VIII's renunciation of the Pope and the conversions of some of the German Princes were of course important, the Reformation was nonetheless in large part a genuine popular uprising. It featured spontaneous peasant revolts and thousands upon thousands of voluntary conversions, many in spite of governmental opposition or repression. The Thirty Years War certainly involved the mass of the people as well as the rulers, and it affected every facet of German life. There was obviously a fertile soil in Early Modern Europe for dissident and destabilizing popular movements, and the fertility of this soil could hardly be attributed to economic stagnation.

The continuing religious controversy that finally culminated in the English civil wars also had deep roots in the popular consciousness. But before and during these popular religious controversies there had been a great deal of rapid growth.[20] Thus economic stagnation could hardly explain the deep divisions in English life that ultimately led to the civil wars.

British life after the civil wars, was, for a considerable time, less disruptive than it had been. It was only with the onset of the Industrial Revolution that the pace of popular dissent again began to quicken. The last half of the eighteenth century and the first half of the nineteenth century in Great Britain saw the near revolution of the 1780's, the Luddite movement, the Chartist agitation, the Great Reform bill, and a considerable assortment of riots and minor uprisings. Yet this was of course a period of rapid growth. By the second half of the 19th

century, the basis of a modern industrial order had been built, and the rate of economic growth soon began to slow down.[21] Economic growth was no longer working to destroy traditional life, and this in turn led to a calmer political climate.

It has been argued, at least since Tocqueville's book on the Ancient Regime, that the French Revolution also followed upon a period of economic growth. Tocqueville also argues that the revolutionary fervor was strongest in those parts of France that were advancing most rapidly and weakest in those places that were advancing least.[22] The leading participants in the French Revolution (as in other revolutions) were, moreover, not generally drawn from the poorest classes—as Crane Brinton has told us. The rising middle class, swelled by those who had gained from the economic growth, was perhaps the dominant force, though the aristocratic and lower classes at times also played important roles.

Farther east in Europe, the economic advances were much later in coming. It was the last half of the nineteenth century before Prussian economic growth reached a rapid rate. And during this period of the Prussian or German take off, the political life of Germany was seething with discontent. Germany had the largest Marxist party anywhere, in spite of the fact that both the stick of repression and the carrot of social insurance were used in attempts to destroy German Marxism.

In Russia, the take off was still later.[23] It was only in the last quarter of the 19th century and the first years of the 20th that Russian industrialization gathered speed. The Russian labor force was growing rapidly in the years before World War I, and the incidence of strikes and riots was correlated with the speed at which the economy advanced.[24] The revolutionary ferment which characterized Russia in this period and which reached its climax in the revolutions of 1917 may, therefore, have been related to the take off of the Russian economy.

In the currently underdeveloped countries, too, there is some evidence linking rapid economic growth and political instability.

Of all the underdeveloped countries, few had progressed as far or as quickly as Cuba in the years before Castro. In other countries of Latin America as well there seems to be a positive association between increasing incomes and political discontent. It was in Argentina, which had nearly completed an industrial revolution, that Peron staged his Fascist–Socialist revolution. Venezuela, which has grown to the point where it is one of the wealthiest of underdeveloped countries, is considered one of the most likely candidates for a Communist takeover. Brazil is said to be in the midst of a take off, but its political life is scarcely stable. By contrast, Paraguay, Peru, and Ecuador are among the slowest to develop, and they seem furthest removed also from any genuine social revolution. In the Middle East, the states that have advanced furthest, like Egypt, are less stable than the most stagnant, like Saudi Arabia. Many of the most progressive parts of India are said to have displayed the most discontent, while some of the most stagnant areas have been relatively quiet.[25] The nation as a whole made significant economic progress between 1952 and 1957, yet the Communist vote increased from 4 million to 12 million in this period. In underdeveloped Eastern Europe before World War II, Czechoslovakia had the most progressive economy and the largest Communist party.[26] In poor but rapidly growing Italy there is one of the largest Communist parties outside the Iron Curtain.[27]

IX

Thus, both European history and contemporary experience provide concrete situations against which the hypothesis that rapid economic growth leads to political stability can usefully be compared. Moreover, even the most casual glance at these situations establishes some presumption that this hypothesis would be supported by further study. If this paper is correct in suggesting that there are reasons why political instability should be associated with economic growth and that (at least until there is further research) the presumption should be that this hypothesis is generally consistent with the empirical or historical evidence, then some current prescriptions for American policy need rethinking.

There are those students of economic development, mentioned earlier, who argue that the United States should give most of its foreign aid to nations in the takeoff stage of economic development, at the expense of those nations that have yet to establish the "preconditions" for the take off. This policy is justified, at least partly, in terms of the American political interests during the cold war. But if it is true, as this paper argues, that rapid economic growth of the kind that might be expected in the takeoff stage is politically destabilizing, such a policy would work to the advantage, not of the United States, but of the Soviet Union. Such a policy would place those governments that the United States thinks are worth aiding in additional jeopardy by stimulating destabilizing forces. In view of the current world political situation, there is a very large chance that the destabilizing forces will be Communist and linked with the Soviet Union or Communist China. Thus, a policy designed to make those nations already in the fastest stage of growth grow yet faster through economic aid does not seem to be consistent with the announced purposes of American foreign policy.

It would be more nearly consistent with American policy to give the nations in the earliest stages the larger amount of aid. While it may be true that nations in this stage cannot now grow *rapidly* even with large infusions of aids, they can be enabled to move through the preconditions stage much faster than they would otherwise do. The aid given to them, while it might not result in a rapid growth rate *now*, could still move much nearer to the present the date when these nations become developed industrial states. If the efficacy of aid is measured, not in terms of current growth rates, but rather in terms of how much it moves ahead the date when these nations become modernized, it might well be more efficient to give aid to the nations that have not yet reached the take off stage.

Moreover, aiding such nations could encourage a somewhat steadier type of progress that would be more conducive to constructive political evolution. The most serious political problems seem to occur in those countries that industrialize with a violent advance because their industrialization has been greatly postponed. Compare Britain and the Soviet Union. Britain was the first nation to experience an industrial revolution, and as a result its economy was modernized and changed *relatively* slowly and steadily. Important and revolutionary as the improvements in Britain industry were during the Industrial Revolution, they nonetheless involved a less dramatic break with the economic practices of the past than Russia experienced. Britain's Industrial Revolution followed in the path broken long before by its commercial revolution. When modern techniques were brought to Russia and led to its take off in the late nineteenth and early twentieth centuries, there was a far more violent change. In Russia, there was very nearly an abrupt change from a fourteenth-century feudalism to a twentieth-century industrialism. Modern technology was superimposed upon a backward society, and the process of adjustment was therefore particularly painful.[28] The contrast between the types of economic development in Britain and in Russia may have had something to do with the democratic evolution of Great Britain and the Bolshevik Revolution in the Soviet Union.

The underdeveloped countries today may face even more abrupt and painful transitions into modern economic life than Russia faced. The take off in these countries may therefore be even more traumatic than Russia's. It can only make the transition more painful for these countries, however, if the United States curtails aid to the most backward of these nations, thus postponing their (presumably inevitable) industrialization. If, when these nations reach the takeoff stage, the United States then gives them vast amounts of aid and makes the transition to a modern economy even more abrupt and disruptive than it would otherwise be, this will surely stimulate political and social instability.

If, on the other hand, the United States gives a great deal of emphasis to *preparing* the poorest countries to survive the storm and stress of delayed industrialization and attempts to build a basis for steady and sustained growth, it may help spare these countries some of the political turmoil that industrialization so often involves. By strengthening the educational institutions, the civil services, the military organizations, the labor unions, and the business institutions of emerging nations, the United States can in some degree promote their economic growth, while at the same time increasing their capacity to endure the growing pains that industrialization will involve. By starting now to promote the modernization of backward countries, the United States would at least reduce the extent to which the industrialization of the underdeveloped nations is retarded and thus make the industrialization process a little less revolutionary than it would otherwise be.

The primary purpose of the foregoing argument is to show the inadequacy of the conventional contention that economic aid should be given mainly to nations in the takeoff stage. Hopefully, this purpose has been served by showing that the opposite policy is, if anything, more plausible and more nearly consistent with American objectives. It would be going too far, however, to suggest that it is enough simply to concentrate aid in the nations that are not yet in the take off stage. Those who (like myself) advocate economic aid must appreciate the incredible complexity of the problem and be more wary of general policy prescriptions than some previous writers have been. The genuinely philanthropic and purely political justifications for certain aid grants need to be studied more sympathetically. It is not enough simply to concentrate economic aid in the take off stage or even to justify economic aid solely in terms of the economic growth it is supposed to bring about.

x

If there is indeed a connection between

rapid economic growth and political instability, then those Western scholars who criticize the underdeveloped countries for attempting to provide some of the services of the modern welfare state may be a bit off the mark. It is no doubt true that the underdeveloped countries cannot afford modern welfare measures as well as the advanced nations can. But it is perhaps also true that they need these modern welfare institutions more than the advanced countries do. These welfare measures, though they might retard growth, could nonetheless be a profitable investment in social peace. They could ease the plight and alleviate the discontents of those who lose from economic growth.

Those who assume that, because certain welfare measures in underdeveloped countries might decrease the rate of growth, they are therefore undesirable, make the mistake that Karl Polanyi discussed in *The Great Transformation*. Polanyi was, in my opinion, quite correct in emphasizing that the relative merits of alternative economic policies had not been decided when it was shown that one led to a faster rate of growth than the others. The differing impacts of capitalistic and socialistic economic systems on the political and social life of a society also had to be considered. Polanyi felt that, while laissez-faire capitalism led to a high rate of growth, it imposed too great a burden of adjustment on society. His argument is indeed interesting; but to me he is quite wrong in identifying the social disorganization resulting from economic change with capitalism alone. Whatever the organization and control of the means of production, rapid economic growth must require painful adjustments. In few places has economic growth involved such painful adjustments as in the Soviet Union in Stalin's first five-year plan. And in the underdeveloped countries today, nationalized industries are often playing a major role in the struggle for economic growth. It would be hard to see how the nationalization of industry itself would reduce the disruption that economic growth causes. The person who leaves the tribe, the manor, the peasant village, or the extended family for the modern factory in the growing city will find that he is in an alien environment, no matter who runs the factory. If the factory is to be run in the interest of maximum production, under socialist or private management, it cannot fail to impose a new and burdensome discipline and a new style of life upon the recently recruited work force.

Thus the point is that rapid economic growth, whatever the nature of the economic system, must involve fast and deep changes in the ways that things are done, in the places that things are done, and in the distribution of power and prestige. Most people spend such a large proportion of their time working for a living and draw such a large part of their social status and political influence from their economic position that changes in the economic order must have great effects on other facets of life. This is especially true in underdeveloped societies, where the institutions that exist were developed in relatively static conditions and are not suited to making rapid adjustments.[29] Therefore, until further research is done, the presumption must be that rapid economic growth, far from being the source of domestic tranquility it is sometimes supposed to be, is rather a disruptive and destabilizing force that leads to political instability. This does not mean that rapid economic growth is undesirable or that political instability is undesirable. It means, rather, that no one should promote the first without bracing to meet the second.

The cross-national analysis of
political instability

In this study two major ingredients of social research are combined: psychological theory and the quantitative analysis of aggregate data. The psychological theory is the frustration–aggression hypothesis of Dollard and his colleagues that we have already looked at. The aggregate data are statistics indicating various internal conditions of all the nations in the world. Included are data on such things as number of telephones and doctors per capita and on such unstable events as riots, strikes, assassinations, etc.

The work of the Feierabends and their associates is already a fundamental contribution to the method and substance of research in revolution. They have systematized various barometric and thermometric indicators so as to make possible a comparison of the *degree* of civil turmoil in all times and places where data are available. Perhaps their most enduring contribution is the scaling of various kinds of instability—from labor strikes at one end to assassinations to coups d'état and actual civil war at the other. In the candor with which they report their measures and how they are made, they provide tools testable and usable by any interested person. This is one of the things science is about.

The result is a rich and elegant establishment of comparisons between what the authors call want formation and want satisfaction. Like many bold advances in research, this continuing work of the Feierabends has raised almost as many questions as it has answered. The precedent for their use of such indicators as physicians, newspapers, and radios is in Lipset's pioneering article, "Some Social Requisites of Democracy." As they use the indicators, the Feierabends provide no justification for calling urbanization and education want-formers or for calling doctors, newspapers, and radios want-satisfiers. A person who is ill wants a doctor; when he has recovered, he not only no longer wants a doctor but wants other things that presuppose good health but have nothing else to do with the desire for health. A person may want to read the newspaper and listen to the radio, but the things he reads or hears in these media inescapably lead to the generation of new wants. If reading or listening to news or music were ultimate satisfiers, newspapers and radios would not be so heavily used to advertise consumer products. The classifying of want-formers and want-satisfiers remains an unsolved problem.

228

Two other research questions are relevant. The first has to do with time. The Feierabends have taken blocks of time for their data but, for the most part, at the time they wrote this article, had not yet separated out for analysis the *differences* in instability within a nation over time. They have made only tantalizing beginnings at analysis of changes within nations in the levels of stability.

The second question has to do with population size. The Feierabends do not control for a nation's population. Thus the United States, with a population nearing 200 million in the period 1955–1961, is in the same stability category as Switzerland with less than 5.5 million people and Portugal with less than 10 million. One unstable occurrence in Portugal should be roughly equal to twenty instances of the same kind of instability in the United States. There is no evidence that the authors take into account this widely varying variable of national population. On the other hand, not all the stable nations are small and not all the large nations are unstable by their analysis.

The effort to relate theory and research which the Feierabends and their associates continue to make remains one of the most successful and promising thus far. They have established a structure out of the seeming chaos of data that bodes well for further research and in time for some increasingly dependable predictions. And their work continues to develop.*

Aggressive behaviors within polities, 1948–1962

A cross-national study[1]

IVO K. FEIERABEND

AND

ROSALIND L. FEIERABEND

Ivo K. Feierabend and Rosalind L. Feierabend, "Aggressive Behaviors within Polities, 1948–1962, A Cross-national Study," is reprinted with the permission of the authors. Copyright by and reprinted with the permission of the University of Michigan, Ann Arbor, from *The Journal of Conflict Resolution*, 10(3), pp. 249–271, September 1966.

Notes to this section will be found on pages 349–350.

* See, for example, their paper in the Historical and Comparative Task Force Report to the National Commission on the Causes and Prevention of Violence, in *Violence in America*, edited by H. D. Graham and T. R. Gurr (published by the U.S. Government Printing Office and as a New American Library Signet paperback in June 1969).

A RECENT trend in behavioral research is the systematic and empirical analysis of conflict behaviors both within and among nations. External conflict behaviors among nations are typified by wars, embargoes, interruption of diplomatic relations, and other behaviors indicative of aggression between national political systems. Internal conflict behaviors within nations, on the other hand, consist of such events as demonstrations, riots, *coups d'état*, guerrilla warfare, and others denoting the relative instability of political systems.

There are a few studies which have attempted systematic empirical analyses of internal conflict, more or less broadly based in crossnational studies (Kling, 1959; LeVine, 1959; Davies, 1962; Eckstein, 1962, 1964; Feierabend, Feierabend, and Nesvold, 1963; Haas, 1964; Russett, 1964; Nesvold, 1964; Hoole, 1964; Conroe, 1965; Walton, 1965). Furthermore, crossnational inquiry, as a method, is being used by many researchers (Cattell, 1949, 1950, 1952; Rokkan, 1955; Lerner, 1957, 1958; Lipset, 1959, 1960; Inkeles, 1960; Deutsch, 1960, 1961; Deutsch and Eckstein, 1961; Fitzgibbon and Johnson, 1961; McClelland, 1961;

Cantril and Free, 1962; Cantril, 1963, 1965; Banks and Textor, 1963; Almond and Verba, 1963; Russett *et al.*, 1964; Gregg and Banks, 1965; Merritt and Rokkan, 1966; Singer and Small, 1966; Rokkan, forthcoming). All of these efforts have in common an interest in abstracting relevant dimensions on which to compare large numbers of nations. Some (McClelland, 1961; Cantril and Free, 1962; Cantril, 1963, 1965; Almond and Verba, 1964) are concerned with measuring psychological dimensions. Others (especially Banks and Textor, 1963; Russett *et al.*, 1964) are directed toward a largescale empirical assessment of the interrelationships among all available ecological variables—political, economic, and societal. A very few (Rummel, 1963, 1965, 1966; Tanter, 1964, 1966; Hoole, 1964; Feierabend, Feierabend, and Litell, 1966) attempt to discover the structure of the complex universe of internal or external conflict behavior through factor analysis.

The studies here described are directly concerned with the measurement of political instability and, furthermore, with a search for the correlates of internal conflict behaviors. As a first step, a theoretical framework is adopted to aid in the analysis of the problem.

THEORETICAL FRAMEWORK

Although political instability is a concept that can be explicated in more than one way, the definition used in this analysis limits its meaning to aggressive, politically relevant behaviors. Specifically, it is defined as the degree or the amount of aggression directed by individuals or groups within the political system against other groups or against the complex of officeholders and individuals and groups associated with them. Or, conversely, it is the amount of aggression directed by these officeholders against other individuals, groups, or officeholders within the polity.

Once this meaning is ascribed, the theoretical insights and elaborations of frustration—aggression theory become available (Dollard *et al.*, 1939; Maier, 1949; McNeil, 1959; Buss, 1961; Berkowitz, 1962). Perhaps the most basic and generalized postulate of the theory maintains that "aggression is always the result of frustration" Dollard *et al.*, 1939, p. 3), while frustration may lead to other modes of behavior, such as constructive solutions to problems. Furthermore, aggression is not likely to occur if aggressive behavior is inhibited through devices associated with the notion of punishment. Or it may be displaced onto objects other than those perceived as the frustrating agents.[2]

The utility of these few concepts is obvious. Political instability is identified as aggressive behavior. It should then result from situations of unrelieved, socially experienced frustration. Such situations may be typified as those in which levels of social expectations, aspirations, and needs are raised for many people for significant periods of time, and yet remain unmatched by equivalent levels of satisfactions. The notation:

$$\frac{\text{social want satisfaction}}{\text{social want formation}} = \text{systemic frustration}$$

indicates this relationship. Two types of situations which are apt to produce high levels of systemic frustration are investigated in this research, although certainly many other possibilities are open to study.

In applying the frustration–aggression framework to the political sphere, the concept of punishment may be identified with the notion of coerciveness of political regimes. And the constructive solution of problems is related to the political as well as the administrative, entrepreneurial, and other capabilities available in the environment of politics. The notion of displacement may furthermore be associated with the occurrence of scapegoating against minority groups or aggression in the international sphere or in individual behaviors.

The following general hypotheses are yielded by applying frustration–aggression theory to the problem of political stability:

1. Under a situation of relative lack of systemic frustration, political stability is to be expected.

2. If systemic frustration is present, political stability still may be predicted, given the following considerations:

a. It is a nonparticipant society. Politically relevant strata capable of organized action are largely lacking.

b. It is a participant society in which constructive solutions to frustrating situations are available or anticipated. (The effectiveness of government and also the legitimacy of regimes will be relevant factors.)

c. If a sufficiently coercive government is capable of preventing overt acts of hostility against itself, then a relatively stable polity may be anticipated.

d. If, as a result of the coerciveness of government, the aggressive impulse is vented or displaced in aggression against minority groups and/or

e. against other nations, then stability can be predicted.

f. If individual acts of aggression are sufficiently abundant to provide an outlet, stability may occur in the face of systemic frustration.

3. However, in the relative absence of these qualifying conditions, aggressive behavior in the form of political instability is predicted to be the consequence of systemic frustration.

A more refined set of hypotheses concerning socially aggressive behaviors and frustration can be achieved by interpreting the frustration–aggression hypothesis within the framework of theories of social and political action and political systems (Merton, 1949; Parsons and Shils, 1951; Lasswell, 1951; Almond, 1960; Parsons *et al.*, 1961; Deutsch, 1963; Easton, 1965a, 1965b; Gurr, 1965).

METHODOLOGY

The methodology of the studies is indicated by the scope of the problem. Concern is not with the dynamics underlying stability in any one particular country but with the determinants of stability within all national political systems. As many cases as possible, or at least an appropriate sample of cases, must be analyzed. Thus the present studies are crossnational endeavors in which data are collected and analyzed for as many as eighty-four polities. (The eight-four nations

are listed in Table 1.) The crossnational method is here conceived in similar terms as the crosscultural studies of anthropology (Whiting and Child, 1953; Murdock, 1957; Feierabend, 1962).

A crucial aspect of the research is the collection of relevant crossnational data. Although data are available on ecological variables of political systems through the Yale Political Data Program, the Dimensionality of Nations Project, and the Cross-Polity Survey, data collections on the political stability dimension are scarcer.

In order to carry out the research, data on internal conflict behaviors were collected for eight-four nations for a fifteen-year period, 1948–1962. The data derive from two sources: *Deadline Data on World Affairs* and the *Encyclopaedia Britannica Yearbooks*. They are organized into a particular format in which each instability event is characterized according to country in which it occurs, date, persons involved, presence or absence of violence, and other pertinent characteristics (Feierabend and Feierabend, 1965a). The data are on IBM cards, creating a storage bank of some 5,000 events.[3]

STUDY 1
The Analysis of the Dependent Variable: Political Stability

with Betty A. Nesvold, Frances W. Hoole, and Norman G. Litell

In order to evaluate the political stability–instability continuum, data collected on internal conflict behavior were scaled. The ordering of specific instability events into a scale was approached from the viewpoint of both construct validity and consensual validation (Nesvold, 1964).

A seven-point instrument was devised, ranging from 0 (denoting extreme stability) through 6 (denoting extreme instability). Each point of the scale was observationally defined in terms of specific events representing differing degrees of stability or instability. An illustration may be given of one item typical of each position on the scale. Thus, for example, a general election is an item associated with a 0 position on the rating instructions. Resignation of a cabinet official falls into the 1 position on the scale; peaceful demonstrations into the 2 position; assassination of a significant political figure into the 3 position; mass arrests into the 4 position; *coups d'état* into the 5 position; and civil war into the 6 position.

Consensual validation for this intensity scale was obtained by asking judges to sort the same events along the same continuum. The level of agreement among judges on the distribution of the items was fairly high (Pearson $r = .87$). Other checks performed on the reliability of the method were a comparison of the assignment of items to positions on the scale by two independent raters. Their level of agreement for the task, involving data from eighty-four countries for a seven-year time period, was very high (Pearson $r = .935$).

Using this scaling instrument, stability profiles for the sample of eighty-four nations were ascertained for the seven-year period, 1955–1961. Countries were assigned to groups on the basis of the most unstable event which they experienced during this seven-year period. Thus countries which experienced a civil war were placed in group 6; countries which were prey to a *coup d'état* were placed in group 5; countries with mass arrests were assigned to group 4, and so on. The purpose of this assignment was to weight intensity (or quality) of instability events equally with the frequency (or quantity) of events.

Following the allotment to groups, a sum total of each country's stability ratings was calculated. Countries were then rank-ordered within groups on the basis of this frequency sum total. The results of the ratings are given in Table 1.[6]

In this table, it may be seen first of all that the distribution is skewed. Instability is more prevalent than stability within the sample of nations, and the largest proportion of countries are those experiencing an instability event with a scale weighting of 4. Furthermore, there is an interesting combination of countries at each scale position. The most stable scale positions, by and large, include modern nations but also a

sprinkling of markedly underdeveloped polities and some nations from the Communist bloc. Again, the small group of extremely unstable countries at scale position 6 comprise nations from Latin America, Asia, and the Communist bloc. The United States, contrary perhaps to ethnocentric expectations, is not at scale position 1 although it is on the stable side of the scale.

Another approach to the ordering of internal conflict behavior was based upon frequency alone (Hoole, 1964).[5] The frequency of occurrence of thirty types of internal conflict behaviors was determined for the eighty-four countries for the time period, 1948–1962. Analysis in terms of frequency was used in three different ways:

1. A global instability profile for all types of events, for all countries, was drawn to show changes in world level of instability during the time period under study. As may be seen in Figure 1, instability has been on the increase in recent years, reaching one peak in the late 1950s and an even higher level in the early 1960s.

2. Frequencies of particular types of instability behaviors were compared for the entire sample of countries. The range of frequencies was from 18 (execution of significant persons) to 403 (acquisition of office). When the events were rank-ordered in terms of frequency of occurrence and the rank-ordering divided into quartiles, the first quartile, with the highest frequency of occurrence (1,555 occurrences) included events denoting routine governmental change (such as acquisition of office, vacation of office, elections, and significant changes of laws). The second quartile (704 occurrences) appeared to be one of unrest, including such events as large-scale demonstrations, general strikes, arrests, and martial law. The third quartile (333 occurrences) indicated serious societal disturbance, in the form of *coups d'état*, terrorism and sabotage, guerrilla warfare, and exile. And the fourth quartile (150 occurrences) consisted primarily of events connoting violence: executions, severe riots, civil war. Thus an inverse relationship was revealed between the frequency of

Table 1. Frequency distribution of countries in terms of their degree of relative political stability, 1955–1961. (Stability score shown for each country)

0	1	2	3	4	5	6
New Zealand 000	Norway 104	W. Germany 217	Tunisia 328	France 499	India 599	Indonesia 699
	Netherlands 104	Czechoslovakia 212	Great Britain 325	U. of S. Africa 495	Argentina 599	Cuba 699
	Cambodia 104	Finland 211	Portugal 323	Haiti 478	Korea 596	Colombia 681
	Sweden 103	Romania 206	Uruguay 318	Poland 465	Venezuela 584	Laos 652
	Saudi Arabia 103	Ireland 202	Israel 317	Spain 463	Turkey 583	Hungary 652
	Iceland 103	Costa Rica 202	Canada 317	Dominican Rep. 463	Lebanon 581	
	Philippines 101		U.S. 316	Iran 459	Iraq 579	
	Luxembourg 101		Taiwan 314	Ceylon 454	Bolivia 556	
			Libya 309	Japan 453	Syria 554	
			Austria 309	Thailand 451	Peru 552	
			E. Germany 307	Mexico 451	Guatemala 546	
			Ethiopia 307	Ghana 451	Brazil 541	
			Denmark 306	Jordan 448	Honduras 535	
			Australia 306	Sudan 445	Cyprus 526	
			Switzerland 303	Morocco 443		
				Egypt 438		
				Pakistan 437		
				Italy 433		
				Belgium 432		
				Paraguay 431		
				U.S.S.R. 430		
				Nicaragua 430		
				Chile 427		
				Burma 427		
				Yugoslavia 422		
				Panama 422		
				Ecuador 422		
				China 422		
				El Salvador 421		
				Liberia 415		
				Malaya 413		
				Albania 412		
				Greece 409		
				Bulgaria 407		
				Afghanistan 404		

STABILITY ——————————————————————————————————————— INSTABILITY occurrence of an event and the intensity of violence which it denotes.

3. Finally, countries were compared for the relative frequency of occurrence of all thirty instability behaviors during this time period. The range was from 136 events (France) to one event (Switzerland). The median of this distribution was represented by Laos and Burma, with 28 and 26 events, respectively.

cating the Rummel variables for the years 1958–1960, found a two-factor solution: turmoil and internal war. Recently, Rummel (1966) factor-analyzed thirteen variables obtained from Eckstein's collection of internal conflict behaviors (Eckstein, 1962) for the time period 1946–1950. This factor analysis again yielded three dimensions, which Rummel identifies with the three dimensions of the 1963 factor solution,

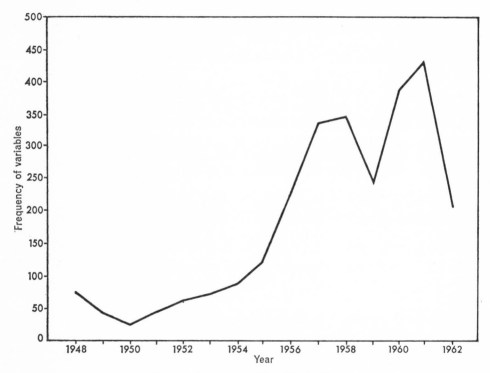

Figure 1. Frequency of Variables by Year,
1948–1962.

An additional refinement in the understanding of political instability is achieved by factor analysis, which reduces the large number of observed variables to a smaller number of underlying dimensions. Four previous factor analyses of internal conflict behaviors have been performed. Rummel (1963), factor-analyzing nine types of internal conflict behaviors for a three-year time period (1955–1957), emerged with three underlying dimensions: turmoil, revolution, and subversion. Tanter (1964, 1966), repli-

namely, revolution, subversion, and turmoil. Hoole (1964) factor-analyzed thirty variables collected over a fifteen-year time span, 1948–1962, from a single source (see note 5), and emerged with five major and five minor factors. The five major factors were labeled: demonstrations, change of office-holder, riots, guerrilla warfare, and strikes.

Most recently, Feierabend, Feierabend, and Litell (1966), using Hoole's thirty variables for the fifteen-year period 1948–1962 and the complete data bank derived

Table 2. *Rotated factor matrix of domestic conflict measures*

FACTORS*

VARIABLES	Mass participation —Turmoil	Palace revolution —Revolt	Power struggle —Purge	Riot	Election	Demonstration	Imprisonment	Civil war	Guerrilla warfare
1. Elections	29	-02	09	-18	70*	-10	-17	-05	-23
2. Vacation of office	38	08	74*	-14	20	-11	-15	-25	09
3. Significant change of laws	38	41	41	-01	31	15	-16	-23	-11
4. Acquisition of office	29	06	75*	-19	15	-04	-25	-19	22
5. Crisis within a nongovernmental organization	40	13	12	-21	04	-09	62*	07	-23
6. Organization of opposition party	08	10	-02	02	56*	36	19	-39	-10
7. Repressive action against specific groups	46	61*	27	01	-03	16	12	04	12
8. Micro strikes	67*	00	-15	-26	-16	05	12	03	23
9. General strikes	73*	13	04	-42	09	-06	03	08	-18
10. Macro strikes	43	-22	-11	-35	15	-17	-33	-12	-19
11. Micro demonstrations	61*	19	-02	02	20	59*	10	03	02
12. Macro demonstrations	73*	-01	00	26	06	19	18	-21	03
13. Micro riots	46	11	-06	68*	27	-03	-03	-15	11
14. Macro riots	69*	28	-04	33	20	02	04	-08	-05
15. Severe macro riots	64*	-03	-04	53*	11	-19	-02	-20	14
16. Arrests of significant persons	09	64*	54*	07	-14	-06	23	-10	-01
17. Imprisonment of significant persons	-14	12	49	17	-05	16	38	-33	-22
18. Arrests of few insignificant persons	42	09	05	-08	07	75*	07	07	21
19. Mass arrests of insignificant persons	52*	33	14	54*	-12	-02	-01	05	01
20. Imprisonment of insignificant persons	26	-08	09	-12	08	34	64*	-03	-14
21. Assassination	17	40	23	06	24	23	-07	-10	56*
22. Martial law	11	71*	03	03	15	09	-27	-06	-08
23. Execution of significant persons	-08	01	54*	31	-26	14	-04	31	05
24. Execution of insignificant persons	01	-10	63*	32	-07	12	-02	47	-02
25. Terrorism and sabotage	62*	28	12	-21	13	-01	10	07	38
26. Guerrilla warfare	04	42	07	-19	19	-35	25	21	55*
27. Civil war	-14	25	31	14	45	08	-08	60*	02
28. Coup d'etat	03	69*	07	01	-02	12	-40	07	-32
29. Revolts	06	75*	-01	11	07	-01	-10	32	16
30. Exile	-09	40	00	03	-36	32	-19	-13	04
Percentage of common variance	23.37	16.30	13.20	9.67	8.33	8.00	7.99	6.76	6.40 = 100.0
Percentage of total variance	23.33	11.11	7.52	6.77	5.89	5.32	4.18	3.82	3.62 = 71.46

* Asterisks indicate loadings > .50. Decimals omitted from loadings.

from two sources, performed a factor analysis with a principal components solution and an orthogonal Varimax rotation. (See Table 2 for the rotated factor matrix.) Nine factors emerged. The first three of these, ranked according to importance in terms of the amount of variance accounted for after rotation, were labeled, first, a turmoil dimension (characterized by violence and mass participation); second, a palace-revolution–revolt dimension (distinguished by a marked lack of mass support); and, third, a power-struggle–purge dimension (connoting violent upheavals and changes of office within regimes). It will be noted that there is definite correspondence between the first two factors revealed in this analysis and the factors discovered by both Rummel and Tanter.

Looking at the variables with the highest loadings on each factor, we see that the first factor comprises strikes of all types; demonstrations and riots, large and small, violent and severe; and also mass arrests and terrorism. One could say that it denotes serious, widespread disturbance, anomie, popular mass participation, and some governmental retaliation.

The second factor presents a sharp contrast to this mass turmoil dimension. It encompasses revolts, *coups d'état*, martial law, arrests of politically prominent leaders, and governmental action against specific groups. These events do not connote mass participation but rather extreme instability created by highly organized and conspiratorial elites and cliques. And the third factor presents yet another divergent pattern, including acquisition and loss of office, arrests and executions of politically significant figures, and some punitive action. Mass turmoil is not evident, as on the first factor; neither is the situation one of revolt and *coup d'état*. This is an instability dimension of violent internal power struggles, purges, depositions, and changes within ruling parties and cliques, which nevertheless remain in power.

The nine factors in combination account for 71.5% of the total variance. After rotation the three first factors combined account for over half of the common variance (53%).

The remaining six factors, accounting in combination for less than half of the common variance, seem to reveal the following patterns: a specific riot dimension; an election dimension; two factors connoting mild, limited unrest; and, finally, two separate dimensions of civil war and guerrilla warfare, respectively, the extreme forms of political instability.

STUDY 2

The Relation of Social Frustration and Modernity to Political Stability

with Betty A. Nesvold

Once the data for the dependent variable, political stability, were collected, factor-analyzed, and scaled, the major step of seeking correlates of instability became feasible. In this attempt, two generalized and related hypotheses were investigated. (1) *The higher (lower) the social want formation in any given society and the lower (higher) the social want satisfaction, the greater (the less) the systemic frustration and the greater (the less) the impulse to political instability.* (2) *The highest and the lowest points of the modernity continuum in any given society will tend to produce maximum stability in the political order, while a medium position on the continuum will produce maximum instability* (Nesvold, 1964).

These hypotheses embody the basic propositions of the frustration–aggression theory, as well as insights gained from the literature on processes of modernization (Lerner, 1958; Deutsch, 1961; Cutright, 1963). In the first hypothesis, the discrepancy between social wants and social satisfactions is postulated to be the index of systemic frustration. The relationship is represented as follows:

$$\frac{\text{want satisfaction low}}{\text{want formation high}} = \text{high frustration}$$

$$\frac{\text{want satisfaction low}}{\text{want formation low}} = \text{low frustration}$$

$$\frac{\text{want satisfaction high}}{\text{want formation high}} = \text{low frustration}$$

A variety of social conditions may satisfy or leave unsatisfied the social wants of different strata of the population within social systems. In our present century the process of modernization is certain to create new wants and aspirations, as well as to lead in the long run to their satisfaction.

The notion of modernity denotes a very complex set of social phenomena. It includes the aspiration and capacity in a society to produce and consume a wide range and quantity of goods and services. It includes high development in science, technology, and education, and high attainment in scores of specialized skills. It includes, moreover, new structures of social organization and participation, new sets of aspirations, attitudes, and ideologies. Modern affluent nations, with their complex of economic, political, and social systems, serve best as models of modernity to nations emerging from traditional society. In these transitional nations, the growing, politically relevant strata of the population are all participants in modern life. Lerner (1957), for one, states categorically that once traditional societies are exposed to the modern way of life, without exception they desire benefits associated with modernity.

The acquisition of modern goals, although an integral aspect of modernity, is hardly synonymous with their attainment. The notion of "the revolution of rising expectations" (Lerner, 1958), also termed "the revolution of rising frustrations," points to the essentially frustrating nature of the modernization process. The arousal of an underdeveloped society to awareness of complex modern patterns of behavior and organization brings with it a desire to emulate and achieve the same high level of satisfaction. But there is an inevitable lag between aspiration and achievement which varies in length with the specific condition of the country. Furthermore, it may be postulated that the peak discrepancy between systemic goals and their satisfaction, and hence the maximum frustration, should come somewhere in the middle of the transitional phase between traditional society and the achievement of modernity. It is at this middle stage that awareness of modernity and exposure to modern patterns should be complete, that is, at a theoretical ceiling, whereas achievement levels would still be lagging far behind. Prior to this theoretical middle stage, exposure and achievement would both be lower. After the middle stage, exposure can no longer increase, since it already amounts to complete awareness, but achievement will continue to progress, thus carrying the nation eventually into the stage of modernity. Thus, in contrast to transitional societies, it may be postulated that traditional and modern societies will be less frustrated and therefore will tend to be more stable than transitional societies.

The most direct way to ascertain systemic frustration is through field work in the many countries, administering questionnaires (see Inkeles, 1960; Doob, 1960; Cantril, 1963, 1965; Almond and Verba, 1964). For the purpose of this study, an inexpensive and very indirect method was adopted.

The highly theoretical notions of want satisfaction and want formation were translated into observable definitions. For this purpose, available collections of cross-national statistical data were consulted and a few statistical items were chosen as appropriate indicators. The following selection of indicators was made. GNP and caloric intake per capita, physicians and telephones per unit of population were singled out as indices of satisfaction. Newspapers and radios per unit of population were also included. Many other indicators denoting material or other satisfactions could have served the purpose. The selection was guided by parsimony as well as availability of data.

The indicators, of course, have different significance in referring to the satisfaction of different wants. Furthermore, their significance may vary at different levels of relative abundance or scarcity. A great deal of theorizing is necessary to select and use the indicators wisely. For example, it is possible that a country with many physicians and telephones may still be starving. Or, beyond a certain point, caloric intake cannot measure the satisfaction of some other less basic needs than hunger, while GNP per capita may do so.

For want formation, literacy and

Table 3. *Relationship between level of systemic frustration and degree of political stability**

DEGREE OF POLITICAL STABILITY	INDEX OF SYSTEMIC FRUSTRATION			
	Ratio of Want Formation to Want Satisfaction			
	High systemic frustration		*Low systemic frustration*	*Total*
Unstable	Bolivia	Iran	Argentina	
	Brazil	Iraq	Belgium	
	Bulgaria	Italy	France	
	Ceylon	Japan	Lebanon	
	Chile	Korea	Morocco	
	Colombia	Mexico	Union of South Africa	
	Cuba	Nicaragua		
	Cyprus	Pakistan		
	Dominican Rep.	Panama		
	Ecuador	Paraguay		
	Egypt	Peru		
	El Salvador	Spain		
	Greece	Syria		
	Guatemala	Thailand		
	Haiti	Turkey		
	India	Venezuela		
	Indonesia	Yugoslavia		
	34		6	40
Stable	2		20	22
	Philippines		Australia	New Zealand
	Tunisia		Austria	Norway
			Canada	Portugal
			Costa Rica	Sweden
			Czechoslvakia	Switzerland
			Denmark	United States
			Finland	Uruguay
			West Germany	
			Great Britain	
			Iceland	
			Ireland	
			Israel	
			Netherlands	
Total	36		26	62

Chi square** $= 30.5$, $p = . < 001$; Yule's $Q = .9653$.

* The number of cases in this and the following tables varies with the data available in the UN statistical sources. This table includes only those countries with data on all eight indices.
** All chi squares in this and the following tables are corrected for continuity in view of the small frequencies in the nonconfirming cells.

urbanization were chosen as indicators. This selection was influenced by the notion of exposure to modernity (Lerner, 1958; Deutsch, 1961). Exposure to modernity was judged a good mechanism for the formation of new wants, and literacy and city life were taken as the two agents most likely to bring about such exposure.

These eight indices (GNP, caloric intake, telephones, physicians, newspapers, radios, literacy, and urbanization) were used to construct both a frustration index and a modernity index. The modernity index was formed by combining scores on all of the eight indicators. Raw scores were first transformed into standard scores and then a mean standard score was calculated for each of the eighty-four countries on the basis of the available data. The frustration index was a ratio. A country's combined coded score on the six satisfaction indices (GNP, caloric intake, telephones, physicians, newspapers, and radios) was divided by either the country's coded literacy or coded urbanization score, whichever was higher.[6]

The data on the independent variables were collected for the years 1948–1955 whereas the stability ratings were made for

Table 4. *Relationships between the eight indicators of systemic frustration and degree of political stability*

A. LITERACY:

	Percentage literate		
	Low (*below 90%*)	High (*above 90%*)	Total
Unstable	48	5	53
Stable	10	19	29
Total	58	24	82

Chi square = 25.83; p = <.001
Yule's Q = .90

B. RADIOS:

	Per 1,000 population		
	Low (*below 65*)	High (*above 65*)	Total
Unstable	45	6	51
Stable	9	20	29
Total	54	26	80

Chi square = 25.02; p = <.001
Yule's Q = .887

C. NEWSPAPERS:

	Per 1,000 population		
	Low (*below 120*)	High (*above 120*)	Total
Unstable	48	5	53
Stable	6	10	16
Total	54	15	69

Chi square = 17.34; p = <.001
Yule's Q = .88

D. TELEPHONES:

	Percentage of population owning telephones		
	Low (*below 2%*)	High (*above 2%*)	Total
Unstable	35	6	41
Stable	7	18	25
Total	42	24	66

Chi square = 19.68; p = <.001
Yule's Q = .875

E. CALORIES:

	Per capita per day		
	Low (*below 2,525*)	High (*above 2,525*)	Total
Unstable	39	10	49
Stable	8	20	28
Total	47	30	77

Chi square = 17.42; p = <.001
Yule's Q = .81

F. PHYSICIANS:

	People per physician		
	Low (*above 1,900*)	High (*below 1,900*)	Total
Unstable	40	13	53
Stable	6	19	25
Total	46	32	78

Chi square = 11.41; p = <.001
Yule's Q = .81

G. GNP:

	Per capita (in US dollars)		
	Low (*below 300*)	High (*above 300*)	Total
Unstable	36	8	44
Stable	9	18	27
Total	45	26	71

Chi square = 14.92; p = <.001
Yule's Q = .80

H. URBANIZATION:

	Percentage of population living in urban centers		
	Low (*below 45%*)	High (*above 45%*)	Total
Unstable	38	6	44
Stable	11	15	26
Total	49	21	70

Chi square = 13.08; p = <.001
Yule's Q = .79

the years 1955–1961. It was assumed that some lag would occur before social frustrations would make themselves felt in political aggressions, that is, political instabilities.

RESULTS

The main finding of the study is that the higher the level of systemic frustration, as measured by the indices selected, the greater the political instability. The results are shown in Table 3. The stable countries are those which experience the least amount of measured systemic frustration. Conversely, the countries beset by political instability also suffer a high level of systemic frustration, although certain interesting exceptions occur.

Each indicator of want formation and satisfaction is also significantly related to political stability. The relationships between each indicator and stability are presented in Table 4. Another finding of interest in this table is that all eight indicators do not predict degree of stability with equal efficiency. Level of literacy is the best single predictor, as seen by the .90 degree of relationship (Yule's Q) between literacy and stability. Comparatively, GNP is one of the weaker predictors, along with percent of urbanization, population per physician, and caloric intake per capita per day.

These data on the predictors of political stability also determine empirical threshold values for each indicator. Above these values, countries are predominantly stable; below them, countries are predominantly unstable. The cutting point for each of the indicators was selected so as to reveal the maximum difference between stable and unstable countries.

From these empirical thresholds, a composite picture of the stable country emerges. It is a society which is 90 percent or more literate; with 65 or more radios and 120 or more newspapers per 1,000 population; with two percent or more of the population having telephones; with 2,525 or more calories per day per person; with not more than 1,900 persons per physician; with a GNP of 300 dollars or more per person per year; and with 45 percent or more of the population living in urban centers. If all of these threshold values are attained by a society, there is an extremely high probability that the country will achieve relative political stability. Conversely, if gratifications are less than these threshold values, the more they fail to meet these levels, the greater the likelihood of political instability.

In order to investigate the relationship between modernity and stability, countries were rank-ordered on the modernity index and the distribution was broken into three groups representing modern countries, transitional countries, and traditional countries. The cutting points for these three groups were to some extent arbitrary: the twenty-four countries which were highest on the modernity index were selected as the modern group. The traditional group was chosen to be equal in size to the modern group, while ranking at the opposite end of the modernity continuum. The remaining countries, falling between the modern and traditional groups, were designated transitional. The difficulty in determining the true state of the countries lies not so much in finding the cutting point for the modern group as in selecting the traditional one. Truly traditional countries do not report data and hence have no way of being included in the study. The countries designated traditional are simply less modern than those classed as transitional, but they have nonetheless been exposed to modernity.[7]

A mean stability score was calculated for each group of countries. The differences between the mean stability scores for the three groups were then estimated. According to the hypothesis, the difference in mean stability score should be greatest between the transitional group and either of the other two groups. The difference in mean stability score between modern and traditional countries should not be significant. The results are given in Table 5.

As may be seen in the table, the predicted difference between the stability level of modern and of transitional countries emerges as highly significant. The difference between modern and traditional countries is less but nonetheless also significant. And the dif-

Table 5. *Relationship between modernity and stability*

MODERNITY LEVEL	N	MEAN STABILITY SCORE	t	p*	t	p*
Modern countries	24	268 ⎫				
			6.18	< .001 ⎫		
Transitional countries	37	472 ⎬			3.71	< .01
			1.53	> .05 ⎭		
Traditional countries	23	420 ⎭				

* Probability levels are two-tailed.

ference between traditional and transitional countries does not reach significance. The difficulty in obtaining data on truly traditional countries undoubtedly contributes to the lack of significant difference between countries labeled in this sample as transitional and traditional.

In view of the lack of support in these eighty-four nations for the hypothesized curvilinear relationship between modernity and stability, the assumption may be made that all of the countries have been exposed to modernity. Hence want formation should be at a relatively high level throughout the sample. One might hypothesize that want formation reaches an early maximum with exposure to modernity, after which further awareness of the modern world can no longer increase desire for modernity. Under these conditions, the modernity index is also in fact a frustration index, indicating the extent to which these measured economic satisfactions are present within a society which may be presumed to have already been exposed to modernity.

To compare the relative efficacy of these two frustration indices, product-moment correlations were calculated between each index and stability. The results show that while both indices are significantly correlated with stability, the correlation between the so-called modernity index and stability is the higher of the two. The product-moment correlation between modernity and stability is .625; the correlation between the so-called frustration index and stability is the so-called frustration index and stability is .499. An *eta* calculated between the modernity index and the stability index, to show curvilinearity of relationship, is $\eta =$

.667, which is not significantly different from the Pearson *r* of .625. Thus again the hypothesis of cuvilinearity between modernity and stability is not supported.

STUDY 3
The Prediction of Changes in Political Stability Over Time

with Wallace R. Conroe

In the previous study, stability, modernity, and the frustration index were all calculated as static measures. Each variable was represented by a single score, indicating an overall estimate of the level of the variable during the time period under study. The question raised in this study concerns the effect of relative rates of change over time in the ecological variables. It seeks to uncover dynamic relationships which would supplement the static ones.

The assumptions made in this study of dynamic trends are based on a view of change as essentially disruptive in character. The process of transition toward modernity, discussed in the previous study, is one during which, almost inevitably, goals and demands will exceed achievements. It is also a process during which former patterns of behavior, outdated technologies, established roles, statuses and norms, must all give way to new, unfamiliar patterns. The transitional personality is frustrated by his breakoff from the past and the uncertainty of the present.

To this picture of a society in ferment is now added the notion of the relevance of time. Insofar as the transitional process is a gradual one, there is a possibility that new patterns may be adopted and adjusted to before old ones are completely abandoned. There is also the further possibility that achievements may begin to approximate the level at which aspirations are set, before aspirations move even further ahead. Where the transitional process is rapid, however, the effect will be to decrease the possibility of adaptation, thus increasing the probability of disruption, chaos, and feelings of personal discontent. Furthermore, the more rapid the process of change, the greater the likelihood of opening new perspectives of modernity, that is, of creating higher and higher levels of aspiration, thus inevitably increasing the gap between aspiration and achievement, at least in the early stages.

Thus the hypothesis promulgated in this study is that: *the faster (the slower) the rate of change in the modernization process within any given society, the higher (the lower) the level of political instability within that society* (Conroe, 1965).

As a first step in investigating that hypothesis, yearly changes in instability pattern for each of the eighty-four countries were calculated for the time period under study, 1948–1962. From the evidence accumulated on the global frequency of occurrence of instability events (Figure 1), it was clear that the world instability level increased sharply during the fifteen years, reaching its highest peak in the last six years. In order to compare countries as to their relative position on the instability continuum over time, the period was split in half and country instability scores were calculated for each seven-year period separately. The country scores for the second period tended to be higher than for the first one. A rank-order correlation between stability levels in the two seven-year periods for the eighty-four countries showed a moderate degree of relationship (Spearman $r = .43$). Not only was the instability level generally on the increase, but there was a tendency for countries to maintain their relatively stable or unstable positions over time.

As a further, more refined method of analyzing the stability–instability continuum over time, stability scores for the eighty-four nations were calculated on a year-by-year

basis and plotted as a function of time. To characterize the time function, at least two measures were necessary: the slope of a best-fit line, indicating the average instability trend, over the fifteen-year period; and amplitude of change from year to year, as estimated by variance.

A calculation of the relationship between these two measures showed them to be independent and unrelated dimensions (Spearman $r = .06$). Of the two, only amplitude was related to static stability level as measured by the intensity scale (Spearman $r = .64$). This indicates that the meaning of instability as empirically ascertained in these studies is identified with the fluctuation of instability rather than with the average trend over time. Furthermore, it is the measure of amplitude and not the average trend over time which is directly related to rate of change in the independent variables. The average instability trend over time (increases or decreases) is related to the ecological variables only when combined with the data on yearly fluctuations in stability levels.

Turning to the predictors of instability, interest was in the effect of changes in levels of ecological variables upon changes in stability. The general hypothesis of this study was that rapid change will be experienced as an unsettling, frustrating societal condition and hence will be associated with a high level of internal conflict. To test the hypothesis, nine predictor indices were selected for study: caloric intake, literacy, primary and postprimary education, national income, cost of living, infant mortality, urbanization, and radios per thousand population. Data for these indices were collected for a 28-year period from 1935 through 1962. Plotting of the data revealed a consistent trend for substantially all countries in the sample to improve their position on all indices over time. Hence a yearly percent rate of change was calculated for each indicator.[8] These indicators are not identical to those of the previous study, although there is overlap. The new choice was determined by the availability of data for as many years as possible and for a

Table 6. *Relationship between mean rate of change on ecological variables and rate of change in stability*

MEAN RATE OF CHANGE ON ECOLOGICAL VARIABLES (PERCENT)	CHANGE IN STABILITY		
	Amplitude of Fluctuations in Yearly Stability Scores		
	Low change (amplitude)	*High change (amplitude)*	*Total*
Low change	Argentina Mexico	Belgium	
	Australia Netherlands	Cuba	
	Austria New Zealand	Greece	
	Bulgaria Norway	Hungary	
	Canada Pakistan	Paraguay	
	Chile Philippines		
	Denmark Spain		
	Ecuador Sweden		
	Finland Switzerland		
	France Taiwan		
	Guatemala Un. of S. Africa		
	Iceland United Kingdom		
	Ireland United States		
	Israel Uruguay		
	Italy West Germany		
	Luxembourg		
	31 5		36
High change	Ceylon	Bolivia Japan	
	Ghana	Brazil Korea	
	India	Burma Malaya	
	Syria	Cambodia Morocco	
	Turkey	Colombia Panama	
		Costa Rica Peru	
		Dominican Rep. Poland	
		Egypt Portugal	
		El Salvador Thailand	
		Haiti Tunisia	
		Honduras U.S.S.R.	
		Indonesia Venezuela	
		Iraq Yugoslavia	
	5	26	31
Total	36	31	67*

Chi square = 30.0; $p = <.001$.

* The N on this and some of the following tables is reduced to include only those countries with data on six or more indices, from which to calculate the mean rate of change score.

maximum number of countries in the sample.

To summarize the results of the interrelationship between rates of change in the independent indices and rate of change in stability, it may be said that the higher the rate of change on the indices, the greater the increase in instability. A contingency table showing the relationship between mean rate of change on six or more of the nine indices and instability, as measured only by variation in pattern (amplitude), is given in Table 6.

As may be seen from the table, the countries experiencing a highly erratic instability pattern are those also undergoing a rapid rate of change in the ecological variables selected for study. On the other hand, countries experiencing political stability in the sense of a steady pattern are the static countries in which ecological change proceeds at a slower pace.

Furthermore, the rate at which modernization occurred from 1935 to 1962 is correlated with static stability level in the 1955–1961 time period (as measured in Study 1). A Pearson r of .647 was found between rate of change (calculated as a combined measure on six or more of the nine indices) and static stability score. Relationships were also calculated between rates of change on each of the nine independent indices taken separately and instability

Table 7. *Rank-order correlations (rho) between rate of change on ecological variables and two measures of stability, 1948–1962*

	N	STATIC STABILITY	DYNAMIC STABILITY (AMPLITUDE)
Primary education	70	.61	.57
Calories per capita per day	39	.49	.35
Postprimary education	30	.36	.41
Cost of living	72	.36	.21
Radios	82	.34	.31
Infant mortality rate	60	.33	.36
Urbanization	69	.17	.14
Literacy	82	.03	.01
National income	70	− .34	− .45

level, measured both as a static score and as a dynamic fluctuation (variance measure) for the 1948–1962 period (see Table 7).

The pattern is somewhat the same for both sets of calculations, indicating primary education to be the best single predictor of instability and literacy the worst.[9] The most interesting finding is the inverse relationship revealed between rate of change in national income and instability. In the case of this indicator, the higher the rate of change, the greater the likelihood of stability. This finding may be understood when one contrasts the pattern of rate of change on national income to that for the nine indices taken together (see Tables 8 and 9).

From Table 8 it is clear that all countries except the modern show a high rate of change on ecological variables. (This again confirms the point made earlier that no truly traditional countries are included in the sample. By definition, a traditional country should be characterized by lack of change.) The modern countries are those undergoing the least amount of change. They are also those experiencing the least amount of instability.

In Table 9, however, we find the situation reversed for growth in national income. On this indicator, it is the modern countries which show the highest rate of change over time. National income may be viewed as a variable with no intrinsic ceiling and one on which marked improvement will not occur until a country is well advanced toward modernity and has achieved a relatively high standard on other ecological variables,

such as literacy, education, caloric intake, and infant mortality. Thus again it is the modern countries which are the most stable and which show the greatest growth rate in national income.

A final comparison between rate of change in modernization and instability level was made by grouping countries on instability in terms of both amplitude of yearly fluctuations and general trend in instability over time (variance and slope). Three groups of countries were distinguished: stable countries (in which yearly fluctuations are low and the trend over time is either stationary or improving); unstable countries in which yearly fluctuations are high and the trend over time is either stationary or worsening); and indeterminate countries which represent conflicting combinations of trend and fluctuation. Four levels of rate of change were also distinguished. With these refinements, the relationship between rate of modernization and instability level over time appears more clearly (see Table 10).

The countries with the lowest rate of change are predominantly stable, as measured both by a low level of yearly fluctuations in instability and by a lack of any worsening trend toward instability over time. Conversely, the countries with the highest rate of change on the ecological variables are beset by instability, as measured both by yearly fluctuations in instability levels and the absence of evidence of any improvement in trend toward stability over time. Furthermore, countries experiencing intermediate rates of change toward modernization are

Table 8. *Relationship between modernity level and mean rate of change on ecological variables*

MEAN RATE OF CHANGE (PERCENT)	Traditional countries	Transitional countries	Modern countries	Total
Low change	Pakistan, Philippines, Taiwan	Bulgaria, Chile, Cuba, Guatemala, Hungary, Italy, Mexico, Paraguay, Spain, Union of South Africa	Argentina, Australia, Austria, Belgium, Canada, Denmark, Finland, France, Iceland, Ireland, Israel, Luxembourg, Netherlands, New Zealand, Norway, Sweden, Switzerland, United Kingdom, United States, Uruguay, W. Germany	
	3	10	21	34
High change	Bolivia, Burma, Cambodia, Ghana, Haiti, India, Indonesia, Iraq, Malaya, Morocco	Brazil, Ceylon, Colombia, Costa Rica, Dom. Rep., Ecuador, Egypt, El Salvador, Greece, Honduras, Japan, Korea, Panama, Peru, Poland, Portugal, Syria, Thailand, Tunisia, Turkey, Venezuela, Yugoslavia	U.S.S.R.	
	10	22	1	33
Total	13	32	22	67

Chi square = 31.0; $p = <.001$.

Table 9. *Relationship between modernity level and rate of change in national income*

RATE OF CHANGE IN NATIONAL INCOME (PERCENT)	Traditional countries	Transitional countries	Modern countries	Total
Low change	Burma, Cambodia, China, Ghana, Haiti, India, Iraq, Jordan, Indonesia, Malaya, Morocco, Pakistan, Philippines, Sudan	Bulgaria, Colombia, Costa Rica, Dom. Rep., Ecuador, Egypt, El Salvador, Guatemala, Honduras, Lebanon, Panama, Poland, Portugal, Syria, Tunisia, Venezuela	E. Germany, Ireland, Switzerland, U.S.S.R., United Kingdom	
	14	16	5	35
High change	Taiwan	Brazil, Chile, Ceylon, Cuba, Greece, Hungary, Italy, Japan, Korea, Mexico, Paraguay, Peru, Spain, Thailand, Turkey, Un. of S. Africa, Yugoslavia	Argentina, Australia, Austria, Belgium, Canada, Denmark, Finland, France, Iceland, Israel, Luxembourg, Netherlands, New Zealand, Norway, Sweden, United States, W. Germany	
	1	17	17	35
Total	15	33	22	70

Chi square = 17.8; $p = <.001$.

Table 10. *Relationship between mean rate of change on ecological variables and change in stability as measured by variance and slope*

MEAN RATE OF CHANGE ON ECOLOGICAL VARIABLES	STABLE — Low variance and either		INDETERMINATE — Low variance/positive slope or high variance/negative slope		UNSTABLE — High variance and either		Total
	negative or slope	zero slope			positive or slope	zero slope	
Low change	Norway New Zealand W. Germany Australia Denmark Iceland Israel	United States Canada Sweden Switzerland Netherlands Luxembourg	Great Britain Austria			Belgium	
	13		2		1		16
Moderately low change	Ireland Guatemala Bulgaria Taiwan	Finland Italy Chile Philippines	France Un. S. Africa Mexico Pakistan Greece	Argentina Uruguay Spain Ecuador	Cuba Paraguay Hungary		
	8		9		3		20
Moderately high change			Thailand Colombia Egypt Ceylon Poland	Costa Rica Ghana Turkey India	Peru Portugal Panama Brazil Haiti Iraq	Japan Yugoslavia Tunisia Burma U.S.S.R.	
	0		9		11		20
High change	Syria		Korea Malaya		El Salvador Bolivia Venezuela Dom. Rep.	Cambodia Morocco Honduras Indonesia	
	1		2		8		11
Totals	22		22		23		67

also intermediate in instability, showing some conflicting combination of fluctuation and trend over time.

In conclusion, one might speak of a syndrome which is exemplified by the modern group of nations. With interesting exceptions, they are relatively satisfied economically and relatively stable politically, no longer changing rapidly on many economic dimensions, although making sizable gains in national income. In contrast are the transitional nations, some moving more rapidly toward modernity than others but, by and large, all characterized by relative economic deprivation, a high rate of change on many economic dimensions but a low rate of growth on national income, and a strong tendency to political instability, finding overt expression in many diverse events such as strikes, demonstrations, riots, *coups d'état*, and even civil war.

The results of these studies are an encouraging indication that cross-national, correlational, and scaling methods can profitably be applied to complex areas such as the analysis of internal conflict behaviors. The scaling, as well as the identification of the dimensions of internal conflict behavior, show that these events can be classified and disentangled.

Furthermore, the results of the studies provide empirical corroboration for many current notions regarding the determinants of political instability. The fact that change may lead to unrest has been suggested. By applying postulates drawn from the frustration–aggression model to this area of internal conflict behavior, and by subjecting the area to empirical analysis, new insights are also obtained. On the basis of these findings, it may be suggested that one compelling reason for the greater stability of modern countries lies in their greater ability to satisfy the wants of their citizens. The less advanced countries are characterized by greater instability because of the aggressive responses to systemic frustration evoked in the populace. It could be argued simply that the increase in instability resulting from a change in ecological conditions is due to the disruptive effect of change. But it is also possible that the satisfaction of wants has a feedback effect, adding to the strength of the drive for more satisfactions. As wants start to be satisfied, the few satisfactions which are achieved increase the drive for more satisfactions, thus in effect adding to the sense of systemic frustration. It is only when a high enough level of satisfaction has been reached that a country will tend toward stability rather than instability.

Although exploratory in nature, the findings are sufficiently striking and persuasive to argue for continuing with additional designs. A large-scale series of studies utilizing a wider scope of ecological, psychological, and political variables, an inventory of other, complementary aggressive behaviors, and a longer time period should lead to more refined results.

REFERENCES

Gabriel A. Almond and James S. Coleman (eds.), *The Politics of the Developing Areas* (Princeton: Princeton University Press, 1960).
────── and Sidney Verba, *The Civic Culture* (Princeton, N.J.: Princeton University Press, 1963).
Arthur S. Banks and Robert B. Textor, *A Cross-Polity Survey* (Cambridge, Mass.: Massachusetts Institute of Technology Press, 1963).
Leonard Berkowitz, *Aggression: A Social Psychological Analysis* (New York: McGraw-Hill, 1962).
──────, "The Concept of Aggressive Drive: Some Additional Considerations." In L. Berkowitz (ed.), *Advances in Experimental Social Psychology*, Vol. 2 (New York: Academic Press, 1965).
Arnold H. Buss, *The Psychology of Aggression* (New York: Wiley, 1961).
Hadley Cantril, "A Study of Aspirations," *Scientific American*, February 1963, pp. 41–45.
──────, *The Pattern of Human Concerns* (New Brunswick, N.J.: Rutgers University Press, 1965.)
────── and Lloyd A. Free, "Hopes and Fears for Self and Country," *American Behavioral Scientist*, 6, 2 (October 1962), pp. 3–30.
Raymond Cattell, H. Breul, and H. Parker Hartman, "An Attempt at More Refined Definition of the Cultural Dimensions of Syntality in Modern Nations," *American Sociological Review*, 16 (1951), pp. 408–421.
──────, "The Principal Culture Patterns Discoverable in the Syntal Dimensions of Existing Nations," *Journal of Social Psychology* (1950), pp. 215–253.
──────, "The Dimensions of Culture Patterns of Factorization and National Characters," *Journal of Abnormal and Social Psychology* (1949), pp. 443–469.
Wallace W. Conroe, *A Cross-National Analysis of the Impact of Modernization Upon Political Stability*. Master's thesis, San Diego State College, 1965.
Philips Cutwright, "National Political Development: Measurement and Analysis," *American Sociological Review*, 28 (April 1963), pp. 253–264.
James C. Davies, "Toward a Theory of Revolution," *American Sociological Review*, 27 (January 1962), pp. 5–19.
Karl W. Deutsch, *The Nerves of Government* (New York: Free Press, 1963).
──────, "Social Mobilization and Political Development," *American Political Science Review*, 55 (September 1961), pp. 493–514.
──────, "Toward an Inventory of Basic Trends and Patterns in Comparative and International Politics," *American Political Science Review*, 54 (March 1960), pp. 34–57.
John Dollard *et al.*, *Frustration and Aggression* (New Haven: Yale University Press, 1939).
Leonard W. Doob, *Becoming More Civilized: A Psychological Exploration* (New Haven: Yale University Press, 1960).
David Easton, *A Framework for Political Analysis* (Englewood Cliffs, N.J.: Prentice-Hall, 1965a).
──────, *A Systems Analysis of Political Life* (New York: Wiley, 1965b).
Harry Eckstein (ed), *Internal War* (New York: Free Press, 1964).
──────, *Internal War: The Problem of Anticipation*. A Report submitted to the Research Group in Psychology and the Social Sciences, Smithsonian Institution, Washington, D.C., January 15, 1962.

Ivo K. Feierabend, "Exploring Political Stability: A Note on the Comparative Method," *Western Political Quarterly* (*Supplement*), 15, 3 (September 1962), pp. 18–19.

—— and Rosalind L. Feierabend, *Cross-National Data Bank of Political Instability Events* (*Code Index*). Public Affairs Research Institute, San Diego College, January 1965a.

——, ——, "Aggressive Behaviors Within Polities: A Cross-National Study." Paper delivered at the Annual Meeting of the American Psychological Association, Chicago, Illinois, September 1965b.

——, ——, and Norman G. Littell, "Dimensions of Political Unrest: A Factor Analysis of Cross-National Data." Paper delivered at the annual meeting of the Western Political Science Association, Reno, Nevada, March 1966.

——, ——, and Betty A. Nesvold, "Correlates of Political Stability." Paper delivered at the Annual Meeting of the American Political Science Association, New York City, September 1963.

R. H. Fitzgibbon and Kenneth Johnson, "Measurement of Latin American Political Change," *American Political Science Review*, 55 (September 1961).

Philip M. Gregg and Arthur S. Banks, "Dimensions of Political Systems: Factor Analysis of a *Cross Polity Survey*," *American Political Science Review*, 59 (September 1965), pp. 602–614.

Ted Gurr, *The Genesis of Violence: A Multivariate Theory of the Preconditions of Civil Strife.* Ph.D. dissertation, New York University, 1965.

Michael Haas, *Some Societal Correlates of International Political Behavior* (Stanford, Calif.: Studies in International Conflict and Integration, Stanford University, 1964).

Francis W. Hoole, *Political Stability and Instability Within Nations: A Cross-National Study.* Master's thesis, San Diego State College, August 1964.

Alex Inkeles, "Industrial Man: The Relation of Status to Experience, Perception and Value," *American Journal of Sociology* (July 1960), pp. 1–31.

Merle Kling, "Taxes on the 'External' Sector: An Index of Political Behavior in Latin America," *Midwest Journal of Political Science* (May 1959), pp. 127–150.

Harold D. Lasswell, *The Political Writings of Harold D. Lasswell* (Glencoe, Ill.: Free Press, 1951).

Daniel Lerner, "Communication Systems and Social Systems: A Statistical Exploration in History and Policy," *Behavioral Science*, 2, 4 (October 1957), pp. 266–275.

——, *The Passing of Traditional Society* (Glencoe, Ill.: Free Press, 1958).

Robert A. LeVine, "Anti-European Violence in Africa: A Comparative Analysis," *Journal of Conflict Resolution*, 3, 4 (December 1959), pp. 420–429.

Seymour H. Lipset, *Political Man* (Garden City, N.Y.: Doubleday, 1960).

——, "Some Social Requisites of Democracy," *American Political Science Review*, 53 (March 1959), pp. 69–105.

Norman R. F. Maier, *Frustration: The Study of Behavior Without a Goal* (New York: McGraw-Hill, 1949).

David McClelland, *The Achieving Society* (Princeton: Van Nostrand, 1961).

Elton B. McNeil, "Psychology and Aggression," *Journal of Conflict Resolution*, 3, 3 (September 1959), pp. 195–293.

Richard L. Merritt and Stein Rokkan, *Comparing Nations: The Uses of Quantitative Data in Cross National Research* (New Haven: Yale University Press, 1966).

R. K. Merton, *Social Theory and Social Structure* (New York: Free Press, 1949).

George P. Murdock, "Anthropology as a Comparative Science," *Behavioral Science*, 2, 4 (October 1957), pp. 249–254.

Betty A. Nesvold, *Modernity, Social Frustration, and the Stability of Political Systems: A Cross-National Study.* Master's thesis, San Diego State College, June 1964).

Talcott Parsons and Edward A. Shils, *Toward a General Theory of Action* (Cambridge, Mass.: Harvard University Press, 1951).

——, ——, K. Naegele, and J. Pitts, *Theories of Society* (New York: Free Press, 1961).

Stein Rokkan, "Comparative Cross-National Research: II. Bibliography," *International Social Science Bulletin*, 1955, pp. 622–641.

—— (ed.), *Comparative Research Across Cultures and Nations* (forthcoming).

Rudolph J. Rummel, "Dimensions of Conflict Behavior Within Nations, 1946–59," *Journal of Conflict Resolution*, 10, 1 (March 1966), pp. 65–74.

——, "A Field Theory of Social Action and Political Conflict Within Nations," *General Systems Yearbook*, 10 (1965).

——, "Dimensions of Conflict Behavior Within and Between Nations," *General Systems Yearbook*, 8 (1963), pp. 1–50.

Bruce M. Russett, "Inequality and Instability: The Relation of Land Tenure and Politics," *World Politics*, 16, 3 (April 1964), pp. 442–454.

—— et al., *World Handbook of Social and Economic Indicators* (New Haven: Yale University Press, 1964).

J. David Singer and Melvin Small, "The Composition and Status Ordering of the International System: 1815–1940," *World Politics*, 18, 2 (January 1966), pp. 236–282.

Raymond Tanter, *Dimensions of Conflict Be-*

havior Within and Between Nations, 1958–1960. Monograph prepared in connection with research supported by National Science Foundation Contract NSF-GS224, 1964.

——, "Dimensions of Conflict Behavior Within and Between Nations, 1958–60," *Journal of Conflict Resolution*, 10, 1 (March 1966), pp. 41–65.

Jennifer G. Walton, *Correlates of Coerciveness and Permissiveness of National Political Systems: A Cross-National Study.* Master's thesis, San Diego State College, 1965).

John W. Whiting and Irvin L. Child, *Child Training and Personality: A Cross-Cultural Study* (New Haven: Yale University Press, 1953).

Cross-national interviewing on
political instability

To ascertain the mood of a people, it is most useful actually to talk with individual citizens and not rely only on the aggregate data available in the statistical reports of national census bureaus. Such gross data are potentially very rich and have not been exhaustively mined, even by such pioneers as Russett, Olson, and the Feierabends. But we need also direct evidence of the state of mind of individual citizens. This can most surely be ascertained by asking them questions in interviews taken by opinion surveyors: pollsters.

Perhaps the boldest and most innovative pioneers in the field of international opinion surveying have been in the group that has grown under the guidance of Hadley Cantril. In research technology they have developed what promises to be a major instrument, what they call the "self-anchoring scaling" device: a ladder with ten rungs which interviewers show to people and ask them where on the ladder they would place themselves. In research substance, the Cantril group has rather systematically used the psychological principles of frustration and aggression, relying on the ten-rung ladder to get indications of popular frustration.

Lloyd Free with inappropriate modesty but appropriate trepidation here reports on studies done by the Cantril group in Brazil, Nigeria, Cuba, the Dominican Republic, and the United States. He indicates that the data are suggestive but not conclusive: they predicted political instability rightly in Brazil, wrongly in Nigeria, rightly in Cuba and the Dominican Republic, and equivocally in forecasting the Black Rebellion in the United States in the 1960s.

In the process, Free implicitly and explicitly suggests the rather exciting possibilities for asking people how they feel about their past, present, and future expectations. This gets rather centrally at the mood of a public and should lead to the ability to predict better the likelihood of that mood becoming rebellious.

The weakness of the Cantril–Free–Kilpatrick line of analysis, as I see it, lies in the lack of theoretical underpinning. If people in *varying* stages of material well-being—poor people *and* rich people—can join in revolution, then the ten-rung ladder is a brilliantly simple research instrument. But such research may presume that, because people are satisfied with regard to one set of needs, they therefore are generally satisfied. Such research, like that using the gross indicators of newspapers

250

and radios, fails to appreciate the dynamic, changing nature of frustrations as individuals move from a concern for physical to social to dignity needs. We have to remember that it was somehow frustrated Southern plantationers, enjoying "ample" satisfaction of their physical, social, and dignity needs, who wrote the Declaration of Independence or commanded the Continental rebel armies or flamboyantly shouted from a safe distance from battle: "Give me liberty or give me death."

Gauging thresholds of frustration

LLOYD A. FREE

Lloyd A. Free, "Gauging Thresholds of Frustration," was first presented as a paper at the September 1967 meeting of The American Political Science Association. Reprinted with permission of the author and of the copyright holder, The American Political Science Association.

To avoid any suspicion of false pretenses, I must confess at the outset that I am not a political scientist, but a rough-and-ready pollster and political analyst, illiterate in the modern vocabulary and literature of the social sciences. I shall therefore leave the propounding of sweeping theories, principles, and generalizations to others, and confine myself to some of the data and implications flowing from our field research.

At the level of theory, all I shall say is that I began our research Odyssey on the unquestioned premise that something loosely denominated frustration was at the root of violence and revolution. And, however frustration may be defined, it is indubitably a psychological condition. It may be inferred or estimated through the manipulation and analysis of objective data; but our own approach has rested on the thesis that, if you want to find out what people are thinking and feeling, the most direct way is to go out and talk to them through systematic interviewing procedures. More specifically, I am here to describe a device which we believe has a potential for determining in a rough, simple way, capable of application to large groups, whether or not people are significantly frustrated; and, if so, how intensely frustrated they are and what they are frustrated about, that is, what is actually "bugging" them, not in theory but in practice.

THE SELF-ANCHORING STRIVING SCALE

We call this device the Self-Anchoring Striving Scale. It was developed by my associate Hadley Cantril, with the assistance of Franklin P. Kilpatrick. It provides a method of obtaining comparative, quantifiable data, without superimposing fixed categories. The technique involves asking a person to describe in his own words and in his own terms, from his own behavioral center, on the basis of his own assumptions, perceptions, goals and values (not those imposed by the researcher designing the study), what he feels would be the best possible life for himself. Thus, for example, the first question reads as follows:

All of us want certain things out of life. When you think about what really matters in your own life, what are your wishes and hopes for the future? In other words, if you imagine your future in the *best* possible light, what would your life look like, if you are to be happy?

At the other extreme, the respondent is asked to define the worries and fears involved in his own conception of the *worst* possible life. In answering these questions he thus delineates the spectrum of values he is concerned about and by means of which he evaluates his own life.

The interviewee is then confronted with a nonverbal ladder device, which consists of a picture of a ladder with steps numbered from zero at the bottom to ten at the top, and is told that this is symbolic of the "ladder of life". The top represents the best possible life as he has defined it, the bottom the worst. He is asked to point out where he stands on the ladder today; where he stood in the past—usually five years ago; and where he thinks he will stand in the future—usually five years from now. Obviously, the ladder ratings a person assigns himself are entirely subjective, being based on the spectrum of values which he as a unique individual brings to bear in evaluating his own life. This, of course, is why we refer to our scale as *self-anchoring*.

Similar questions are put to him about the best and the worst possible situations for his country, so his aspirations and fears at the national level can be identified. His answers reveal the spectrum of values he brings to bear in judging the state of the nation. Again, he is asked to indicate on the ladder where he believes the country stands in the present, where it stood in the past, and where he thinks it will stand in the future.

The replies are carefully coded by specially trained people according to a scheme comprising 145 different categories, worked out empirically, which has proved reliable in a goodly number of studies. This standardized coding scheme permits comparisons on a quantified basis of results from different countries or from different groups within countries.

The juxtaposition of the ladder ratings for the past with those for the present indicates whether those interviewed have a sense of progress or not, both at the personal and the national levels. Similarly, by comparing the ladder ratings for the future with those for the present, it is possible to determine whether respondents are generally optimistic or pessimistic about their own and the country's future. The patterning of these ratings provides a rough indicator of how much confidence they have in the existing politico-socio-economic system under which they live and in the regime which governs them. More specifically from the point of view of our topic today, a combination of sense of progress from past to present and of optimisim from present to future points

to an absence of significant frustration. The reverse pattern can be taken as a signal that frustration is present and with roughly what intensity. Then, by studying the aspirations and fears, personal and national, of those exhibiting frustration symptoms, it is possible to get some idea of what they are frustrated about.

By now, our Institute has administered this device in some fourteen countries, sampling national publics whose total numbers equal almost one-third of the world's population. The methodology is described and the results reported and analyzed in Hadley Cantril's book *The Pattern of Human Concerns* (Rutgers University Press, 1965).

In designing our studies we did not have the subject of violence and revolution specifically in view, although we were interested, among other things, in frustration and political stability. Nevertheless, by good luck, it happens that we have done surveys in one country *following* a revolution (Cuba, after Castro's victory); in two others *before* political upheavals (Brazil, preceding the military takeover; and Nigeria, before the present civil war); in a fourth *between* two violent political explosions (the Dominican Republic, after the overthrow of Trujillo and before the domestic turbulence which led to American intervention); and in the United States, both *before* and *during* the series of riots which have been plaguing our cities.

BRAZIL

In reporting on our batting average to date, let us first take the Brazilian study we did in 1961, just because it is the least relevant and spectacular. The average ladder ratings that emerged from a national cross-section of Brazilians are given below. Incidentally, in all the figures I shall give on ladder ratings, a difference of 0.2 is significant at the 5 percent level.

	PERSONAL LADDER	NATIONAL LADDER
Past	4.1	4.9
Present	4.6	5.1
Future	7.3	7.6

Based on these and other data, I reached the following conclusion, among others, in my report:

In a basic way, the general picture in terms of popular protest or revolt is encouraging from the point of view of the political stability of the Brazilian nation. The people, both urban and rural, appear not to be overly frustrated at this stage, despite their very real problems in connection with standard of living. They have some sense of progress over the past five years, both personal and national. They are highly optimistic both about their own personal future and the nation's future. They appear to have confidence in the existing system and way of life.

Yet three years later, there was a *coup d'etat* in which the military ousted the leftist-leaning Goulart. Goulart, who had been elected Vice-President with the backing of the Communists, had succeeded to the Presidency following the dramatic resignation of Quadros, who was President at the time of our study.

Does this indicate that my reading of the situation was inadequate or faulty at the time of my report? I do not think that it does. In discussing the problem of political stability, I had expressly distinguished between what I called "the 'palace revolution' type of upset ... which results merely in a shift of control among power elements at the top and a real, popularly based revolution", saying that there were no very strong reasons for believing that the former type might not occur again. And I had pointed out specifically that the military in Brazil "can exert ultimate control over the course of the nation whenever it decides with a fair degree of unanimity to flex its muscles in concerted fashion."

Then, if no popular revolt was involved, why do I mention the Brazilian case at all? Principally, just because there was *no* violence, *no* riots, not even any demonstrations when the military overthrew Goulart, who was the symbol of the left and of radical reform. The Brazilian people as a whole were so unfrustrated that they backed the army, which appeared as the defender of the status quo.

NIGERIA

If you will agree with me that, on the whole, I emerged from the Brazilian venture unscathed, I am sure you will also agree that, in the case of my Nigerian study, I badly missed the boat. The mean ladder ratings that a national sample of Nigerians assigned themselves and their country at the end of 1962 were as follows:

	PERSONAL LADDER	NATIONAL LADDER
Past	2.8	4.0
Present	4.8	6.2
Future	7.4	8.2

Taking all the data into account, I came up with this conclusion in my report:

At the time of our study, the psychology of the Nigerian people, the most numerous in Africa, appeared to be relatively sound, unfrustrated and optimistic. The prevailing sense of progress and mood of optimism were indicative of general confidence in the existing set up ...

For the time being at least, the psychological picture of this promising country was generally reassuring, both at the level of the Nigerian public and of the political elite.

As we all know, a little over three years later, the country erupted in bloody tribal strife and at the moment is in a state of civil war. Now, it is true that, in connection with the optimistic statement just quoted, I added this qualifier:

But potentially serious complications and trouble spots could unquestionably be seen on the horizon.

On the political front, the threat to national unity and domestic tranquility was very real. Taking into account the rivalry among Regional (i.e., tribal) leaders, nothing seemed easier than to stir up dissension and turmoil on a tribal and/or religious basis. Yet the threat to national unity appeared lessened by the fact that there was so much awareness of the danger and desire to avert it, both at the level of the public and of the new national-minded elite.

The desire for unity that I was referring to highlights the poignancy of the current Nigerian tragedy. Our study negated the frequently heard claim that Nigerians did not even know what "Nigeria" is. More than eight out of ten of the public displayed a sense of nationhood, at least at the level of word symbols. When asked about their national aspirations, more than one-half of the public and three-quarters of the members of the National Legislature (whom we also surveyed) mentioned their desire for national unity and political stability. And three-quarters of the people and almost nine out of ten of the Legislators listed disunity and instability among their national fears.

My miscalculation on Nigeria points up an extremely difficult problem in research in violence and revolution. Once all the data are in, and even assuming that every significant variable is measured and taken into account, there remains the final step of assigning relative weights to these variables in predicting probabilities. In this case, I allowed my own hope and optimism for this promising country to lead me to assume that the newly acquired aspiration for national unity would somehow win out over what I well know to be historically deep-seated, highly emotional tribal animosities. I was wrong.

However, I still believe I was right in concluding that, at the time of our study at least, the Nigerian people as a whole were not frustrated in any significant degree; nor, in the absence of subsequent data, am I really sure that they became so later. The fact of the matter is that the initial steps which launched this bloody revolution were taken, not by the people, as such, but by a small group of disgruntled Ibo army officers, who assassinated various officials of Northern origins, including the Prime Minister and a good many high-ranking army officers, whom they saw as standing in the way of their own ambitions. Although, eventually, elements of the public joined in the violence, this was not a revolt which welled up from popular frustration—at least that is my considered opinion.

These facts, in my mind, raise three additional problems in research in violence and revolution. The first is the difficulty of identifying in advance the elements in a country which are apt to become violence- or revolution-prone. It is significant that in the Nigerian case, not one of the many people, highly knowledgeable about the country, whom I interviewed for background information, including not only Americans and Britishers but many Nigerians themselves, and nothing I had ever read on the subject, ever pointed to the Nigerian Army as a significant element of power in the nation (unlike Brazil) or as a potential threat to national unity.

Secondly, even if I had been alerted to this possibility, I probably could not have done anything about it. After attempting to do research on military personnel in several countries (including Brazil), we have found that contacts with the military are generally considered so sensitive that interviewing them systematically is difficult if not impossible. Yet, in country after country these days, the military is proving to be not only *a* but *the* decisive element.

The third problem the Nigerian case points up is even more fundamental. Perhaps the Ibo officers who started the violence were frustrated in some meaningful sense of the term, I do not know. But I have come to question whether, after all, this notion of frustration is, primarily and alone, at the root of violence and revolution. Perhaps in a good many situations, such as the Nigerian one, we must focus also on such old-fashioned, interdependent notions as ambitions, rivalries, hatreds, and sheer antipathies, in this case of a tribal nature, which are related to or associated with frustration but not precisely the same as frustration.

CUBA AND THE DOMINICAN REPUBLIC

Having admitted that our Brazilian survey was largely irrelevant to the subject of violence and revolution, and that the conclusions I drew from our Nigerian study were inadequate and misleading, if not just plain erroneous, I now feel entitled to boast about one case where we really did hit the nail on the head: namely, the job I did in the Dominican Republic ten months after the assassination of Trujillo. One might have assumed that the fall of this brutal dictator would have issued in a period of euphoria similar to that we found in Cuba a year after Castro vanquished Batista. In that case, and I will quote the figures for purposes of comparison with the Dominican ones, the Cubans exhibited a perfectly enormous sense particularly of national progress and were highly optimistic about the future.

	PERSONAL LADDER	NATIONAL LADDER
Past (Batista)	4.1	2.2
Present (Castro)	6.4	7.0
Future	8.4	8.8

(Incidentally, on the basis of these and other findings, we came to the conclusion that, at least in the spring of 1960, Castro was overwhelming popular with the Cuban people. There was a small opposition, but it was confined almost entirely to the City of Havana. We were, therefore, not at all surprised when there was no popular uprising in support of the Bay of Pigs invasion a year later.)

In the Dominican case, the figures could hardly have been more different than in the Cuban one.

	PERSONAL LADDER	NATIONAL LADDER
Past (Trujillo)	1.6	1.7
Present (Spring, 1960)	1.6	2.7
Future	5.8	7.0

At the national level, the ratings indicated a slight sense of national progress, but nothing like what might have been expected from a people who had just emerged, assumedly exultantly, from thirty years of oppressive dictatorship. On top of the modestness of the increment from past to present, the average rating assigned the Dominican Republic as of the time of our survey was the lowest rating for the present we have ever encountered in any country we have studied to date.

The real shocker, however, emerged on the personal ladder ratings. A comparison of the past and present averages showed no sense of personal progress whatsoever. Irrespective of this factor of lack of personal progress, the Dominicans obviously felt they were very badly off in the present in absolute terms. The rating they assigned their lives in the present was very much lower than we

have ever registered elsewhere. Most amazingly of all, *no less than one-third of our sample assigned themselves, in terms of their own personal lives, the lowest possible score of zero.*

Connected with this, the aspiration for an improved standard of living was mentioned by the Dominicans, both at the personal and the national levels, with a frequency never before encountered, often at the elemental level of sheer hunger.

On the basis of these and other findings, we made this flat statement in our report issued in June of 1962:

An extremely serious situation of popular discontent and frustration, fraught with a dangerous potential for upheaval, exists in the Dominican Republic. Never have we seen the danger signals so unmistakably clear.

Despite this urgent warning, the United States Government went ahead devising well merited but long-range solutions to Dominican problems, to the neglect of short-term emergency programs, which might have helped alleviate population discontent and frustration. Three years later, the Dominican situation exploded in such violent fashion that American intervention was felt to be imperative.

THE LAND OF THE FREE

Finally, let us turn from these distant shores and talk about the recent violence in American cities. Our data in this case derive from two administerings of the Self-Anchoring Striving Scale, one by Hadley Cantril in 1959, a second by me in the fall of 1964. The mean ladder ratings registered by the Negro Americans in our sample in 1959 were as follows:

	PERSONAL LADDER	NATIONAL LADDER
Past	5.9	6.6
Present	5.3	6.3
Future	7.3	7.2

The Negroes were optimistic about their own and the country's future. (It might be pointed out in passing in this connection that unrealistic optimism in certain circumstances can be taken as a warning of trouble ahead, since the greatest danger period often is when the hopeless begin to hope.) But the Negroes not only had no sense of personal or national progress at all, but actually felt that their own personal situation and that of the country had retrogressed. Objectively, of course, this was not the case. Both they and the nation were better off than five years before. But what had obviously happened was that this improvement had in itself raised expectations and heightened aspirations which caused them to judge the present situation more critically than they evaluated the past. Despite their optimism about the future, the patterning of past and present ratings clearly suggested considerable frustration. Yet there were no substantial riots in our cities in 1959, nor, indeed, any of

major importance until the summer of 1964. In this case, then, at least in any immediate sense, frustration did not produce instantaneous violence.

Now let us turn to our study conducted in the fall of 1964, after the initial major riots in the summer of that year, and preceding those that have followed during the past three summers. First, we shall have a look at what Negro Americans were really concerned about at that time—in other words, at what seemed to be "bugging" them. With the figures for the whites given for purposes of comparison, here are selected examples of the percentages of Negroes mentioning various subjects, either by way of an aspiration, or a fear, or both, at the level of their own personal lives:

	NEGROES	WHITES
Health of self and/or family	50%	67%
Standard of living	40	40
Better housing	34	9
Children—opportunities for them (particularly education)	29	39
Employment	28	18
Social justice	21	4

It will be noted that more Negroes were concerned about health than any other item, although proportionately fewer than among whites. They were highly preoccupied with the question of their standard of living, but no more so than the whites. Fewer of them, actually, were concerned about opportunities for their children. Where the Negro figures vastly exceeded the white percentages were in three fields: housing, employment, and

social justice, which under our coding scheme is defined as "greater equality in the treatment, benefits and opportunities afforded all elements of the population irrespective of race, color, etc.; the elimination of discrimination."

At the national level, a comparison of the percentages of Negroes and of whites mentioning various selected items, either as a national aspiration, a national fear, or both, is equally revealing:

	NEGROES	WHITES
Problems of race or of integration	48%	32%
Employment—jobs for everyone	30	17
Standard of living	22	30
Social justice—equality in the treatment, benefits, and opportunities afforded all elements of the population	19	5
Elimination of discrimination based on color	17	4
Education—more and/or better schools	15	11
Housing—elimination of slums	14	2
Elimination of discrimination based on class or economic status	5	2

Negro Americans showed little more concern than whites about education, just as they talked less at the personal level about opportunities for their children. This suggests that the situation in our schools is not really one of their compelling preoccupations. They

were also significantly less concerned than the whites with the question of standard of living. In addition to the obvious ones of employment and to a less extent housing, the items that really seemed to be "bugging" them were a related complex having to do with racial problems, social justice and elimination of discrimination based on color.

Daniel Patrick Moynihan, the eminent expert on urban problems, was recently quoted (in the *New York Times*, July 25, 1967) as saying that class, rather than race, was at the root of the recent riots; that the violence was essentially caused by "a large, desperately unhappy and disorganized lower-class community" in American cities that happened to be prevalently nonwhite. Although he may be very largely correct, the Negroes apparently do not see it that way. They appear to feel that, rather than being rooted in economics as such, their problems stem in the broadest sense from a denial of social justice because of their color. In these terms, they had—and still have—plenty to be frustrated about. But were Negro Americans, as a group, actually frustrated in the fall of 1964 (a few months after the passage of the sweeping civil rights act of that year) as they unquestionably had been frustrated in 1959? Here are the later ladder ratings:

	PERSONAL LADDER	NATIONAL LADDER
Past	5.11	4.89
Present	5.84	6.62
Future	7.72	8.97

Unlike 1959, at the personal level the Negroes had a substantial sense of progress in their own lives from past to present, and, along with young people in general, were the most optimistic of all elements of the population about their personal futures. As to the national ladder ratings, the Negroes had a much greater sense of national progress during the preceding five years than any other group. And they were by far the most optimistic about the country's future.

In short, I can only conclude that, as of the fall of 1964 at least, *Negro Americans as a whole were not frustrated.* Whether they again became so later, as is likely, we do not know for sure because we have not been able to administer our Self-Anchoring Striving Scale again. (This points, of course, to the compelling need in such matters for repeated measurements to permit the charting of trends—a very costly business, however.)

If the Negroes as a group were not frustrated in the fall of 1964, then how do we explain, consistently with the theory that frustration is at the root of violence, the rioting that occurred during the preceding summer and the violent explosion that followed half a year later in Watts, anticipating the recent holocausts in Newark and Detroit?

One possible explanation, which seems to be an accepted fact, is that in no case has more than a minority of Negroes in the ghettos of this country actually been involved in the riots. And perhaps *they* were frustrated even though their Negro compatriots as a whole were not. Unfortunately, our study can throw no light on this. Our surveys carried out in the fall of 1964 were parts of a study, not on violence or prospective violence in the United States, but on *The Political Beliefs of Americans* as a whole (which, incidentally, will soon be published in book form by the Rutgers University Press). The samples consisted of cross-sections of the total national adult population of the United States of all races and colors, so that the number of Negroes interviewed was too small to permit much in the way of breakdowns among Negro respondents. We were thus unable to take a look at Negro Americans living in the ghettos as a separate group, let alone at segments of this group, such as younger urban Negroes in particular cities. Again, this points to the problem in research in violence and revolution of identifying and separating out for special study elements in a given population which may be more inclined to violence.

However, beyond this, our finding that Negro Americans as a whole were not frustrated in the fall of 1964 also points to another possibility, mentioned before in connection with the Nigerian civil war. Perhaps frustration, as such, is not so much the central key to violence and revolution as I had originally thought. Perhaps to explain the violence and anarchy in our ghettos we must also look to various other interrelated factors: to desperation (which is associated with frustration but adds elements of intensity and of action-proneness which go beyond mere frustration); to hatred and fear (which may or may not be associated with frustration); to a need to prove masculinity (what the Latins call "*machismo*"); to a desire to raise hell just for the sheer exhilaration of raising hell; and even to an unadulterated spirit and habit of lawlessness.

Do not misunderstand me. I share the feelings of guilt and shame of most white liberals because of the decades of unthinking but systematic discrimination against, and exploitation of our Negro fellow-countrymen which we Americans allowed for so long to go unchecked. I still believe that misery and frustration are the bedrock of our present crises. But I am suggesting that in all probability something else needs to be added to explain the riots and anarchy of the last few years.

In this connection, President Johnson posed some very pertinent questions in summoning his National Advisory Commission on Civil Disorders: Why do riots occur in some cities (and I might add, revolutions in some countries) and not in others? Why does one man (or I might add, one group) break the law, while another, living in the same circumstances, does not? I don't think we have the answers to these questions today; at least, I am sure I don't. In my heart of hearts, I feel reasonably sure by now that the answers do not lie in sheer frustration or degree of frustration alone. There are other interrelated aspects—and I am speaking of psychological aspects—which must be taken into account. Whether we pollsters or you political scientists can successfully identify, isolate and study these variables to a point where we can accurately predict the likelihood of violence or rebellion on the basis of gross, quantified indicators, I frankly do not know. But, continue to try we must.

*Violence as end, means, and
catharsis*

This article, like several of its predecessors, builds on an intellectual tradition. But what is unique is the theoretical synthesis of some past writers who are rather hard to synthesize and the application of the synthesis to the events of the ten-year dictatorship of Pérez Jiménez and of the fundamentally constitutional rule of Romulo Betancourt that followed the Jiménez era in Venezuela. The author goes far to explain the failure of violence perpetrated by extreme leftist and rightist groups to overthrow Betancourt.

This paper is a story of skilled statecraft on the part of Betancourt. This paper is also a skillful integration of theoretical writing about violence with a study of its practice. Gude at one point says that Sorel and Fanon advocate violence as a means or an end. And he points out the failure of antirégime violence during the Betancourt era, a failure attributable in part to popular hostility to continued violence. This raises for examination in light of the Venezuelan experience the question whether violence is indeed a means or an end. It raises the third possibility: that violence is a kind of catharsis, which people take to no more as a steady diet than purge victims in prison take to castor oil.

Political violence in
Venezuela: 1958–1964

EDWARD W. GUDE

Edward W. Gude, "Political Violence in Venezuela: 1958–1964," was first presented as a paper at the September 1967 meeting of The American Political Science Association. Reprinted with permission of the author and of the copyright holder, The American Political Science Association.

Notes to this section will be found on page 350.

POLITICAL violence happens relatively rarely and for one reason or another has received relatively scant treatment in the literature of social science. This was particularly true until about 1960. After that date the civil rights movement and foreign adventures such as the Bay of Pigs, the Dominican intervention, and the escalation of the Vietnam war have focused attention on this oldest of problems: How can man manage conflict within societies without resort to large-scale violence and how does violence operate as part of ongoing political processes? . . .

In order to develop reasonable theory, it may be worthwhile to remember that violence was treated extensively in classical literature. Aristotle devoted Book V of his *Politics* to revolution as the cause of systemic change. The emphasis was certainly on political violence that brought about major change rather than simply a conflict management technique. He did, however, identify both general and particular causes that lead men to employ violence. His most general analysis is the "it is the passion for equality which is thus at the root of sedition."[1]

Aristotle then translated this into the psychological dimension when he states that:

The principle and general cause of an attitude of mind which disposes men toward change is the cause of which we have just spoken. There are some who stir up sedition because their minds are filled by a passion for equality, which arises from their thinking that they have the worst of the bargain in spite of being the equals of those who have got the advantage. There are others who do it because their minds are filled with a passion for inequality (i.e., superiority), which arises from their conceiving that they get no advantage over others (but an equal amount, or even smaller amount) although they are really more than equal to others.[2]

From this start several typologies of causes are developed which fairly completely enumerate the types of grievances peoples and governments feel. It is also clear from his analysis that counterviolence alone is not adequate to curb revolution. Petty lawlessness must be prevented but the basis of prevention lies in "the quality of goodness and justice, in the particular form that suits the nature of each constitution."[3]

Such an analysis is useful in providing insight into the causes that lead to the outbreak of political violence but tells us little of the dynamics. Aristotle, however, did not carefully differentiate governmental violence from that used to control "petty lawlessness," thus blurring the situation in which segments of the polity viewed the violence as unjust. What are the effects of police brutality? Why do people support insurgents? Under what conditions can an insurgency mobilize increasing membership?

Machiavelli, among the classical theorists, comes the closest to providing an operational theory of political violence as a conflict management technique for princes or governments and to recognizing both its strengths and weaknesses. Violence was conceptualized as an ongoing part of the political process, something governments could not avoid. While Machiavelli provides some theoretical and practical guides to government, it was not until later that similar treatises were abundantly available to insurgents or revolutionaries. Engels, Marx, Lenin, Blanqui, Bakunin, Necaev, Sorel, and others put out a stream of material from the middle of the 19th century on. This later literature dealt almost exclusively with revolutionary violence, ways of capitalizing on the weakness of governments enumerated by Aristotle. Again little attention was given to the role of violence in socalled normal political processes.

Max Weber provides an analysis which provided a link between revolution, violence, and other conflict management techniques. In his essay, "Politics as a Vocation," Weber stressed the intimate relationship between politics and violence. He did this first of all by defining the state in terms of a monopoly on the legitimate use of violence and second in terms of the role of a politician as follows:

It is the specific means of legitimate violence as such in the hands of human associations that determines the peculiarity of all ethical problems of politics. Whosoever contracts with violent means for whatever ends—and every politician does—is exposed to its specific consequences.[4]

This analysis clearly places violence in the center of political action. This does not assert that violence is the only or even the dominant means but merely one of the means.

Violence does, however, have some unique characteristics. It is violence as a means in the political process, particularly its unique characteristics, that is our central concern.

Before turning to the development of a specific framework for the study of violence, it seems desirable to mention some work which discusses violence as an end as well as a means. Specifically the work of Sorel[5] and Fanon[6] come to mind. These treatises see in political violence not only the tactical use for securing demands or seizing power but also the psychological benefit of providing a means of identification and mobilization. For Sorel, the tactic and end was the general strike, and for Fanon it is violence. Data for these interpretations are difficult to obtain and for the present will not be treated in the theoretical and case study analysis. That there is something to these formulations is supported by considerable anecdotal evidence. Most widely experienced recently are the frequent TV interviews with rioters in American cities who say, "I smile every time I see Whitey get it." There is a sense in which the rioting becomes a shared experience by those who have been kept outside the American experience. Fanon cites evidence of a clinical nature from his practice in which the use of violence becomes part of the personality structure and an integrative mechanism in the context of the exercise of oppressive authority.

One of the important determinants of the role that violence plays in the analysis of political processes is the character of the definition. The frequent conceptualization of force and violence tends to cloud the distinction between legality, legitimacy, and specific acts. Often force is taken to mean legal, legitimate governmental use of violence for the protection of the state; violence is taken to mean illegal and illegitimate acts carried out by non-governmental individuals. Because then, a particular type of act, i.e., violence, is connected to notions of illegality and illegitimacy, it is difficult to be sensitive to cases where force is not considered legitimate by important sectors of a society. We prefer to treat the concept of violence as the characterization for a particular type of act, independent of actor. Thus we define violence as a physical act carried out by an individual or individuals against another individual or individuals and/or property with the intent to cause injury or death to persons and/or damage or destruction to property. For violence to be political, there must also be the intent of affecting the political process. The political process is considered to be the system of distribution

of values carried out by specific individuals within specific institutions. The crux of this definition lies in the intent of initiating actors to cause damage or injury and to cause changes in the political process. That is to say, all violence that affects politics is not necessarily political violence.

Such a definition excludes accident and criminal actions for personal gain but includes acts of both representatives of a government or insurgents. The immediately important question then becomes to consider the legitimacy of acts as perceived by significant groups within a polity. The following table illustrates the various possibilities:

Table 1

VIOLENCE PERCEIVED AS:	VIOLENCE INITIATED BY:	
	Government	Insurgent
Legitimate	I	II
Illegitimate	III	IV

In a stable society one would expect governmental violence to be perceived as legitimate (I) and insurgent violence as illegitimate (IV). Similarly a society would be quite unstable if the violence of the government were perceived as illegitimate and that of the insurgent perceived as legitimate.

It is important to recognize that rarely is there total agreement on the assessment of any act of a government or of insurgents. It is necessary then to identify what significant groups in a polity perceive acts as legitimate or illegitimate. Shifts from the axis of I & IV to the Axis of II & III would then indicate an increase in instability. Note that the notion of stability is independent of the level of violence except as the level of violence is reflected in the perception of legitimacy. A decrease in stability would indicate a relationship between violence and change. Case study material seems to confirm the notion that stability of a political system is not directly correlated with the level of violence in that system. For example, Manfred Halpern has discussed the stability of Islamic political systems in the context of high levels of violence as follows:

The Muslims' extraordinary achievement of a way of life that endured 1300 years because of a system of balanced tensions in which political violence and what may be called antagonistic collaboration became integrative and homeostatic rather than destructive forces in society.[7]

Changes in the level of violence and/or changes in the perception of the violence are important determinants of social change. Perceptions of violence of type I & IV would be homeostatic and types II & III disruptive. Similarly, if significant groups were to change their perception of the legitimacy of act, changes in the system can be anticipated.

Political violence by itself does not necessarily determine the type of change in a political system. This is true in terms of openness or closedness, development orientation or non-development orientation, or any particular value orientation or ideology. In addition political violence does not always operate in an antisystem context. Political violence is not solely a revolutionary phenomenon indicating goals of complete reordering of society. Violence often involves limited goals. To repeat, it is primarily a means for the political management of conflict.

So far we have spoken about actual acts of violence. While this is central, threatened violence also must be considered. In fact, they are closely related, as Neiburg has nicely stated:

Violence has two inextricable aspects: its actual use ... and its potential (threatened) use. The outbreak or demonstration of violence must occur from time to time in order to give plausibility to its threatened outbreak, and thereby to gain efficacy for the threat as an instrument of social and political change. The two aspects, demonstration and threat, therefore cannot be separated.[8]

The occasional use of violence is necessary, then, to demonstrate credibility, capability, and will on the part of initiating actors. Threat of violence is certainly a more frequent occurrence in politics than actual use and in terms of police, national guards, and military a daily reminder of governmental capability. In addition to the actual verbalized threat, the tacit threat of violence is a real one. Tacit threat is more often a capability of a government because of the claim on a monopoly of legitimate violence and the availability of means in being able to carry out threats. An insurgency has much greater difficulty demonstrating capability and must usually carry out actual violence in order to gain credibility. Threat operates with actual violence as an integral part of this particular means for conflict management.

In spite of the governmental claim of a more or less monopoly on the use of legitimate violence, insurgents have equal access to this means. In every polity the physical means are available in such number that absolute control is impossible. A few rifles, pistols, Molotov cocktails, home-made bombs are easily attainable. Even communications equipment, logistical support (automobiles), and field gear (camping equipment) are readily attainable with the proceeds of a small robbery. As will be discussed later, violence becomes an attractive means when others are blocked. It is difficult for a government to control. Access to elected or appointed bodies, press, public gatherings, legitimate institutions are all relatively easy to control as compared to violence as a means in the political arena.

Once violence becomes the effective means, the process becomes one of a competition for mobilization among the uncommitted portion. In most, if not all, situations utilizing political violence, the number of actual participants is small relative to the population as a whole. An insurgency is faced with the task of recruiting cadre and sympathizers. It is the sympathizers that provide the cover and protection from governmental authorities that is essential to the growth of a movement. A government is faced with a similar task of mobilizing the uncommitted and particularly the target population of an insurgency. This target population can be an ethnic, religious, economic or other type of group whose real or perceived grievances are being ignored or infringed upon by the government.

Many of the tactics of both government

and insurgent units are aimed more at this uncommitted group than at the direct opponents. This means that governments are sensitive (if not always successfully) to the perceptions of their acts by target populations. Thus, they try to use tactics that will fall in cell I of the previous table even though this may not be technically the most "efficient" means for eliminating an insurgency. Similarly, an insurgency attempts to commit acts that will be perceived in cell II. Governments often take calculated risks in using tactics in cell III if the payoff is perceived to be high enough. Similarly, insurgents use tactics falling in cell IV if they can stimulate governmental acts in cell III. This is a frequent tactic and response. The assassination of a policeman often stimulates a police sweep that further alienates the target population, although they may not have been in sympathy with the terrorist act in the first place. Thus, in many ways a government has the opportunity to set the style of a violent political encounter.

The initial decisions of a government confronted with the threat of internal war are usually the most fateful and long-lasting of any it will be called upon to make throughout an insurrection.[9]

Professor Pye attributes British success in controlling colonial violence to a non-moralistic, unemotional response to various outbreaks during their colonial experience.[10] Such an approach does not require "total victory" or "unconditional surrender" for an insurgent movement. By maintaining various options, a government is least likely to further alienated target populations and most likely to get the degree of cooperation from the polity necessary to deal with the situation.

If, on the other hand, a government responds totally, the die is cast for the insurgents for they must "fight to the death" and every member, regardless of his possible desire for compromise, must continue the action because his access back into society is blocked. This strategy might be successful if the government is quite secure and has considerable support in a target population. In situations where insurgency is a serious

threat, this is rarely the case. The affront of having demonstrated that a government cannot in fact command a monopoly on legitimate violence severely shakes the self-confidence of a regime as well as the public assessment of it. One of the objectives of insurgents is to create a condition under which a government has difficulty maintaining effectiveness and responsiveness or at a minimum the myth of it. Government strategy and response to a threat of insurgency is therefore critical in determining the course of mobilization.

Rarely do governments distinguish between system and anti-system oriented insurgencies. If one considers insurgency as at a minimum involving the explicit threat of violence, then there are many cases in which the demands of an insurgent are not total. In fact, most revolutionary movements have gone through phases of the employment of violence for purposes less than the complete overthrow of a given political system. In such cases, overresponse of a government is particularly counterproductive. The distinction between system and anti-system oriented behavior is thus an important determinant of governmental strategy although not often recognized as such.

Turning from governmental strategy to that of the insurgent, we see that they are confronted with the basic organizational tasks facing any organization. Such an organization becomes a system within a system, having many of the same problems of management as the government. It must recruit members; socialize them; formulate doctrine and tactics; communicate to others; interact with significant others, in this case the government, in such a way as to increase their own strength. Violence, for an insurgency, plays a role in each of these processes. The activism of an insurgent movement attracts the very type of "true believer" that is needed to expand an organization. Without resorting to the argument of Fanon, it is clear that insurgent organizations are perceived by potential members as an outlet for their frustrations, both personal and with society at large. Participation in acts of violence, at first in less critical roles, becomes an important part of the socialization process of becoming a respected member of the organization. In addition, having thus participated, leaving the movement becomes difficult since reentry into the polity is difficult. Maintaining outside contact becomes too risky, thereby reducing cross-pressures on members. Participation in acts of violence becomes an expression of total commitment, and full acceptance into central roles in such acts becomes confirmation of having passed all the tests of membership.

In such a context it is not surprising that violence becomes one of the central concerns of doctrine and tactics. Violence is the dominant means of insurgency. Every major movement has produced reams of literature on the role of violence in doctrine and tactics. Most leadership and organization crises focus on disagreement about the role of violence in doctrine and tactics. Once a movement has adopted its own style with regard to the use of violence as well as substantive policies, violence is used as a means of communicating them. Whereas insurgents cannot get on the front page of newspapers with nonviolent means, violence almost insures major coverage. Even in situations of tight censorship, some coverage must be given because of the effectiveness and distortions of informal means of communication. In target populations not sympathetic to the government, the distortion would favor the insurgents and among groups supporting a government considerable anxiety would result from no coverage in the press of known violence. Small coverage in tightly censored press is as effective as larger coverage in an uncensored press because the fact of lack of freedom of the media would be well known.

The military tactics of insurgents are most frequently designed to avoid major contact with government forces. Symbolic targets are attacked, such as foreign-owned business, police, individuals in the elite who are particularly hated, and sometimes merely representatives of a government, such as the case of the school teachers and hamlet chiefs in Vietnam. The purpose of much of this violence, in addition to gaining publicity, is to trigger governmental repression that can provide a basis for recruitment into an insurgent movement. This is the trap that is set repeatedly by insurgents for governments, and it is surprising the regularity with which the military and the police fall for it. This possibly results from the fact that insurgents can keep the tactical nature of violence paramount whereas governments tend to view such outbreaks either in narrow legal or moral terms.

The foregoing might suggest that violence, as an integral part of the political process, is a frequent and recurring event. On the contrary, violence is employed rarely as a means in politics, although its threatened use is ever present. Acts of political violence attract a lot of attention, whereas we never think about, much less attempt to count, the enormous number of significant nonviolent political acts which occur all the time. Even the press makes little effort to report them all, so violence often appears to be a more prevalent phenomenon than it is. The psychic and physical costs of violence are such as to preclude its frequent use. In some cases it seems a more difficult task to explain why violence did not occur than to explain in other cases why it did. However, in this paper we are not dealing with the question of why or why not violence was employed in a particular situation. We have been concerned with developing some theoretical notions of how violence operates in political processes when it does occur.

This discussion can be summarized in a series of propositions that will be useful in analyzing the insurgency in Venezuela. The oversimplification can help to keep central notions in mind but should not be taken as more than initial statements on what might become a theoretical base for a better understanding of political violence. The following will provide the basis of the subsequent analysis.

1. If nonviolent means of access to conflict management processes are blocked, violence tends to become a feasible means for dissidents.

2. If nonviolent means of access to conflict

management processes are not blocked, an antisystem insurgency stands little likelihood of success.

3. If nonviolent means of access to conflict management processes are blocked, then violence becomes an effective means of political communication.

4. If governmental violence is perceived by significant groups to be illegitimate or if insurgent violence is perceived to be legitimate by significant groups, then considerable change in the system can be expected.

5. If a government overresponds to the threat of insurgency, it runs the risk of fostering proinsurgent mobilization.

6. If a government loses support among its military and police, then its probability of successfully countering an insurgency is minimal.

7. If an insurgency is to become self-sustaining, then it needs to use violence as a means of recruitment and socialization.

These propositions provide a window through which to examine the use of political violence in Venezuela from the fall of the Pérez Jiménez regime to the election of Leoni as President. The socalled Betancourt years were ones of severe testing by both leftwing and rightwing violence. That Betancourt succeeded in completing his term is both a credit to his government and a measure of the ineptitude of the insurgents.

The political history of Venezuela is one in which violence has played a singularly important role. The achievement of independence was the culmination of the period marked by considerable violence against the agents of the Spanish only to be followed by a similarly violent century of attempts at constitutional rule. The system became, however, quite regularized. Violence and *caudillo* armies were the predictable means of political succession. This was the *de facto*, if not *de juri*, and accepted style of Venezuelan politics.

Bolívar, the aristocratic revolutionary, led the successful defeat of the Spanish after several abortive attempts only to lose control

to José Antonio Páez, originally an illiterate *illanero* general. Páez did, however, conduct himself with greater sensitivity than perhaps any ruler until the fall of Gómez in 1935. The period from the death of Páez until the rise of Juan Vincente Gómez in the early part of this century was marked by a succession of one corrupt regime after another, with some slightly less corrupt than others. Most ran the country as a personal fief, for their own benefit and that of their friends and retainers.

Gómez was the first modern ruler in Venezuela in that he developed the art of dictatorship to a high level. He also developed the seeds of destruction of his system by professionalizing the military. This was done through the establishment of an academy, introduction of achieved promotion, modern equipment and tactics, and an ethos that was not wholly personal but national. In addition, his exploitation of oil transformed the country from a largely agricultural country to one that had the beginnings of industrialization. One manifestation of these developments was the beginnings of a middle class and educational aspiration. While there were several attempted revolts against the Gómez regime, probably the most significant outbreak occurred when some university students took advantage of student week celebrations to speak out against the dictatorship. The subsequent arrests generated large support among the students and gave birth to the "generation of '28." Romulo Betancourt and Jóvito Villalba were among the speakers arrested. Out of these events developed the modern political party structure and personnel of the country.

Gómez was to die in his bed in 1935. But the Minister of War, General Eleazar López Coutreras, who was selected by the cabinet to fill out the "term" of Gomez, had different ideas of how to govern. He introduced what, in the context of Venezuela at that time, were significant reforms. He seemed to view his tenure in office as a transition between dictatorship and democracy.

I began my government by giving liberty to thousands of political prisoners detained in jail and labor camps; I authorized the return to their homeland of all the exiles, and gave them the opportunity of working with me; I inaugurated a great number of public works; I permitted the organization of trade unions and political parties; I allowed freedom of the press and speech, and supported electioneering—and in these elections, in many cases, the opposition won. I put all my efforts into setting up a system entirely different from the one just ended, a new system with all the advantages and privileges of a democratic government.[11]

The fact that López Contreras felt it necessary to indicate that "in many cases the opposition won" raises some doubts about the effectiveness of the reforms. Nevertheless, the symbols and a beginning toward the meaning of democracy had been established. The attempt of Pérez Jiménez to revert to the Gómez style was doomed to failure. General Isaías Medina Augarita, elected by Congress to succeed Lopez Contreras, continued the reforms to the point of legalizing the Acción Democrátia (AD) party in 1941 headed by Romulo Betancourt.

The reforms were slow in affecting the basic structure of Venezuelan society that had labored so long under dictatorial rule. The constitution that provided for Congressional election of the present and the election laws virtually assured the victory of conservative factions. A faction within the military, the Unión Patriótria Militar (UPM), primarily concerned with the slow pace of modernization within the military, joined forces with the AD party and staged a successful coup against Medina in 1945. The resulting junta consisted of two military officers plus Romulo Betancourt and Raul Leone from the AD party and one civilian.

Betancourt, as head of the junta, sought to introduce rapidly the party platform of the AD party on oil policy and other social reforms. A new constitution was promulgated and elections held on December 14, 1947. The AD party candidate, Romulo Gallegos, the well known novelist, was elected. Unfortunately, the rapid social change proposed by the new government and carried out by the junta had caused the military to be wary. The UPM supported the overthrow of Medina for reasons largely internal to the military. Many of the same officers that had supported the coup in 1945 now were in favor of overthrowing Gallegos. The coup on November 24, 1948, resulted in a junta composed of Lt. Col. Carlos Delgade Chalbaud, Lt. Col. Marcos Pérez Jiménez, and Lt. Col. Llovera Páez. Chalbaud was a leader of the UPM and Jiménez was the leader of the Tachira faction which had supplied so many of the politically oriented military leaders in the past, such as Gómez, López Contreras, and Medina. The country was in for another ten years of repressive dictatorship. Whereas the first two years of the junta were marked in general by a continuation of the AD program, with the murder of Chalbaud and the ascendency of Jiménez, the more negative aspects of the dictatorship emerged.

Because of the Suez crisis in 1956, Venezuela accumulated tremendous oil profits as well as windfall profits from selling more oil concessions contrary to the policy of the AD. This money was largely squandered on graft, the military, and major public works. The AD party and one faction of the Communist Party were outlawed, but the URD (Unión Republicana Democrática), COPIE Christian Democratic), and the socalled Black Communist Party continued at the sufferance of the regime; however, no effective political activity was permitted during this period. A crude repudiation of rigged elections that didn't come out as expected, a growing economic crisis, and an increasing reaction to political repression all led to large-scale support for those who thought they had won an election. Even the military withdrew its support of Jiménez, and he was given a diplomatic passport, sent to an awaiting plane and exile. Even though the junta had representatives of the Army, Air Force, and Navy and was headed by Admiral Wolfgang Larrazábal, this did not prevent serious attempts at overthrow because of the move toward rapid elections. Attempted coups on July 22 and 23, 1958, and September 7 and 8 failed in large measure because civilian political leaders were able to mobilize mass support for the provisional government and the majority of the military remained loyal.

The Larrazábal government returned to some of the policies of the period of 1945–1948, but adopted many short-term, provisional policies with regard to many of the basic problems facing the country. This left the solution or management to the forthcoming government. The elections of December, 1958, resulted in a victory for the AD party and Romulo Betancourt. The victory extended to control of both houses of the legislature as well as most of the state legislatures. The URD/Communist coalition with Larrazábal as candidate ran a strong second, controlling some state legislatures as well as the city councils of Caracas and Maracay among the principal cities. Achieving power was only the first of the problems for the AD party. The economic crisis, disrupted public services and administration, lack of trust on the part of the military, and opposition in urban areas were some of the problems that Betancourt had to deal with. As if this were not enough, many were willing to use violence to compound problems and hopefully seize power.

Initially, the threat was primarily from the right, a coalition of military, supporters of Pérez Jiménez, and aided by Trujillo of the Dominican Republic. This move was finally discredited with an abortive attempt on the life of Betancourt in June of 1960. At no time did this group generate mass support or even much sympathy within the military. The acts were isolated and few in number as compared with the attempts of the left. The threat was certainly serious, however, and at times it was not at all clear that the Betancourt government would survive. One of the political mistakes of the first period of AD rule was to ignore the military—that was not to happen again. President Betancourt spent a great deal of time talking to various military at all levels about their special problems. These conversations resulted in improving the living conditions of noncommissioned officers and enlisted men, providing loans for officers to build homes, and major technical upgrading of military training and equipment.

Nevertheless, when it became obvious that the junta was serious in its intent of holding elections and turning the government over to civilians, a sizable portion of the officer corps along with some conservative civilian factious felt severely threatened. They rightly perceived the popularity of Betancourt and feared his return to power. Therefore, on July 22, 1958, General Jesús María Castro Leon led an attempted coup against the junta. This was quickly put down and, as in the case of the overthrow of Pérez Jiménez, popular support was shown in terms of mass demonstrations and strikes— a relatively rare form of political mobilization in Latin America. Castro Leon, in Latin-American tradition, was exiled at full pay along with some of his close associates. This was a repeat of his exile from 1945–1948 during the first period of AD rule.

On September 7, 1958, another attempt was made against the junta, this time led by Lt. Col. Juan de Dias Moncada Vidal who had been exiled along with Castro Leon in July. Again the mass support for the junta was critical in holding the loyalty of the majority of the military. After Betancourt achieved power, there were several more serious attempts by right-wing factions, and on October 12, 1959, and January 21, 1960, minor plots were uncovered and suppressed.

Castro Leon, almost pathologically opposed to the AD rule under Betancourt, tried again in April of 1960 to organize a revolt. This time, again with the help of Trujillo, he entered Venezuela through Colombia and attempted to rally troops to his side in San Cristóbal. This is the capital of Tachira state, which had produced so many of Venezuela's military officers and dictators. Some of the garrison joined him, but loyal troops and National Guardsmen quickly put down the attempt. This time Castro Leon was not offered exile, and he received a long prison term.

Two months later the last serious attempt was launched from the right against Betancourt. This was a bomb attack on the President which failed by the narrowest of margins. In this case it is generally believed that Trujillo played a major role in collaboration with some Venezuelans. In all of the cases the program and ideology of the conspirators were never well articulated, there was no popular support, and the majority of the military remained loyal to first the provisional government and then to Betancourt. The Pérez Jiménez regression had apparently convinced most, both within the military and outside, that constitutional goverment would provide maximum benefit for all. The changes instituted by López Contreras, followed by Medina Augarita, had started the movement out of the political nadir of the Gómez era.

The form of political violence utilized by the rightist military was of a particular type: it depended for its success in not mobilizing the uncommitted. For the classic coup to be successful, much of the military must be involved, the rest neutralized; some civilian backing is necessary; the population must be presented with a *fait accompli*; and the action must be carried out in the shortest possible time. This is quite different from the type of violence that is characteristic of mass-based political movement. Violence becomes more a means for seizing power than a means of conflict management. The coup, in one sense, represents the whole process of political violence in one swift blow. Once the attempt is made, the government must respond immediately, mobilizing its forces and popular support. The confrontation places time on the side of a government if it can maintain support within the military as well as the polity. It is clear that the attempted rightwing coups during the 1958–1963 time period in Venezuela lacked sufficient support within the military to succeed. In addition, the ability of the government to mobilize popular support minimized the appeal of the military revolt leaders within their own ranks. These attempts represent a standard (in the sense of being common) type of threat in most Latin-American countries and particularly in Venezuela. Betancourt had learned from bitter experience the possibility of military intervention and did his best to cultivate support within the military. In this he largely succeeded. It must be added, however, that the skill and organization of the dis-

contented military was not the highest.

These right-wing attempts at seizing power are in in sharp contrast to the sustained left-wing violence during this time period. Young activists in the AD party actively conspired with Communist Party members during the regime of Pérez Jiménez. The hesitancy of Betancourt, or rather his political prudence, offended these younger elements who split from the AD in April 1960, and in July formed the Movemiento de Izquierda Revolucionaria (MIR). This group was strongly aligned with the Communist Party and on certain issues, such as the use of violence, was considerably more radical. The MIR took the position that violence would be their decisive means of achieving the reordering of society deemed necessary. In this judgment, they were probably correct in the sense that Betancourt was not going to carry out the massive expropriation of foreign and domestically owned business and other measures demanded. It was also equally clear that there was almost no chance of the MIR winning power at the polls. Against the advice of more seasoned and older Communist Party leaders, the MIR launched a major campaign of urban violence almost immediately, reaching its first peak of intensity in November 1960. This represented the break within the left in the universities, labor unions, and political parties. The MIR attempted unsuccessfully to gain control. The rioting and strikes in this case revealed the weakness of their forces rather than their strength. The rioting resulted in eight deaths and more than one hundred wounded. There is some indication, however, that this move was not anticipated by the MIR leadership and grew out of reaction to some arrests.[12] In response to this failure, a plan was developed which envisioned successful overthrow of the system in some two years. According to this plan, 1961 was to be mainly a testing period with 1962 the start of extensive operations.

The wild assumptions of the MIR strategic planning brought forth considerable opposition from Communist Party circles who had a better understanding of the realities and the requirements for insurgency and the

strength of the radical left forces. Nevertheless, incidents in urban areas began to
accumulate during 1961. Originally at a
rate of approximately one a week, the
violence increased to several incidents a
week by the end of the year. It appears
possible that initially many of the attacks
were kept out of the press by informal and
formal control of the media, although this

percent increase. This reflects the greater
training and tactical skill acquired during
this period.

The early violence, although not particularly effective militarily, assured maximum
attention in both formal and informal communication. Even with the relatively few
acts committed in 1960, forty-six, the MIR
was a factor to be reckoned with in Vene-

Table 2. *Percentage distribution of reported left-wing political violence*
by means employed*

	1960	1961	1962	1963
Riot	17%	3%	13%	5%
Assassination	4	9	12	6
Robbery	0	6	9	12
Terrorism	63	60	50	42
Sabotage	11	15	10	33
Other	5	7	6	2
	100%	100%	100%	100%
n	(46)	(33)	(120)	(181)

* Source, *El Universal*, Caracas.

cannot be documented. This period of
learning for the insurgents was coincidental
with the worsening of relations between
Cuba and the Betancourt government.
While it appears that Castro refrained from
supplying the insurgents with arms, considerable ideological and training support
was apparently forthcoming. Money is
reported to have been slipped into the
country by Communist deputies who were
immune to customs search, and students
were reportedly trained in guerrilla warfare
in Cuba.

The early attempts were not systematic
and were comprised of a high percentage of
terrorist acts which were quite indiscriminate.
It might be said that this activity was a
training mission since random terrorism
takes less planning and skill than robbery
or sabotage. In addition the chances of
getting caught are considerably less for the
random terrorist. From Table 2, it can be
seen that random terror declined by 21
percentage points (thirty percent) as a
portion of total acts from 1960 to 1963.
During this same period robbery and
sabotage rose from a combined total of
eleven percent to forty-five percent, a 400

zuelan politics. The specter of Castro and
Communism was present, but the gross
problems in the Venezuelan polity made the
threat real. The new system inaugurated by
President Betancourt had not had time to
demonstrate that it was capable of dealing
with these problems or that it would be
responsive to the aggrieved sectors of the
society. This was compounded by the necessary austerity imposed in the wake of the
ruinous economic policies and corruption of
the Pérez Jiménez regime and the lack of
significant improvement during the tenure
of the provisional government. During 1960
and 1961 the basis was developed for a major
attempt at seizure of power by the left. In
1962 the number of reported incidents
increased fourfold, and coordinated moves
by the left wing in the military compounded
the threat.

The military risings at Carúpano in May
and Puerto Cabello in June represented the
most serious immediate threat to the
Betancourt government. Early in 1962 the
government pressed its campaign against the
MIR with considerable success, but this did
not change the intrusion of leftwing factions
within the military. Their attempted revolt

on the fourth of May was triggered by the arrest of the brother of the leader. The marines and some national guards were overcome within a day or so by loyal forces. The premature rising at Carúpano broke the insurgent strategy of coordinated attacks there and at Puerto Cabello. When the second uprising of marines occurred on June 2, it was again suppressed but at the cost of several hundred dead and many more wounded. The Army and Air Force remained loyal, and all service chiefs, including the head of the Navy, condemned the action. Little popular support was generated and, as in previous situations of military rebellion, workers struck to demonstrate support for the government and some 20,000 marched to show their commitment.[13] The government used these risings as an opportunity to suspend constitutional guarantees and ban the Communist Party and the MIR. Betancourt was careful, however, to limit the action to the CP and MIR and not to other opposition groups. While government action against the leaders of the attempted coup was severe, no generalized repression was used. The leader of the attempt, Lt. Comdr. Jesus Teodoro Villegas, was given 15 years, and others from 4 to 14. With the back of the immediate threat broken, the government restored the constitutional guarantees on the thirty-first of July. They were not ignorant of future problems; as a government release said, "The national government has proof that the groups which have promoted and carried out subversive action against the constitution and democratic organization of the republic continue preparing acts of rebellion with the manifest intention of overthrowing the legitimately constituted powers."

The strategy of the MIR and CP had been predicated on a much larger expansion of the urban insurgency as well as the rural guerrilla warfare. The latter was almost a complete failure, with the peasant more often than not reporting activity immediately to government authorities. The strong support given Betancourt and the AD party in rural areas was certainly a factor in this. Even after the failure of the military uprising, plans were laid for further activity. On July 21, Minister of the Interior Carlos Andres Pérez announced the discovery of a training camp in Portuguese state. Seeds of self-doubt started to become apparent among the rebels, particularly in the Communist Party. It was obvious that the insurgency was not providing a basis for mobilizing large numbers of cadre or passive supporters. The only convivial places were the university and mountain redoubts.

This failure did not mean, however, a decline in insurgency activity. In fact, the opposite occurred. The attacks became threatening enough that Betancourt again suspended constitutional guarantees on the seventh of October. Many were immediately arrested as the result of extensive raids by the police. The government was careful to gather considerable support from many sectors of society. In addition to the military leaders and other elite groups, the Venezuelan Workers Confederation council met on the tenth of October to declare their total support of the government. The first of five resolutions was "to call on all workers, employees, and peasants to declare themselves, as of this moment, on a war footing on the side of the government, prepared to combat any act of violence." As the public resentment at the insurgents increased, Betancourt also accelerated his pressure through both public exhortation and police action.

The Communist Party remained publicly optimistic as indicated by an analysis of the situation that appeared in *Tribuna Popular*, the party newspaper, on the twenty-fifth of November. Privately, however, the doubts were coming to the surface. Probably about this time a secret study was written by a faction within the Party strongly criticizing the plan for rapid victory. This document was published by *El Universal* in March of 1963.[14] A strong attack on the tactics and lack of preparation of the MIR, the study called for adoption of a strategy of protracted conflict—a familiar theme in communist revolutionary doctrine. One of the interesting facts revealed was the lack of coordination and control of the military uprisings. The program of violence had, by the end of 1962, been exposed for its weakness both by the success of the government action and the internal criticism within the Communist Party. The situation had improved to the point where some constitutional guarantees could be restored on the fifteenth of December.

military was of great importance. The level of overt action by the guerrillas is indicated by the following monthly totals.

At first, the government moved cautiously so as not to alienate sectors potentially susceptible to MIR/CP influence. A particularly brazen raid was made by the insurgents on an excursion train on 29 September,

Table 3. *MIR/CP violence, 1963*[15]

	Jan.	Feb.	Mar.	Apr.	May	June	July	Aug.	Sept.	Oct.	Nov.	Dec.
MIR/CP violence	14	12	10	8	5	5	6	11	17	23	51	19

During this rapid push of 1962, the insurgents had clearly failed to increase their base of recruitment or discredit the government. Operating under great restraint, Betancourt had minimized the use of troops in urban areas, minimized the overt use of large-scale police tactics, and created the impression at least that the government was completely in control and using legitimate means in dealing with the situation. Walking the narrow path, he maintained the support of the police, military and other elite factions, as well as that of labor and moderate left-wing groups. The governmental response measured in terms of reported acts closely followed that of the insurgents. The correlation on a month-by-month basis for the years 1957–1964 was $r = .78$, significant at .001 percent. The correlation for leading and lagging governmental response dropped to .39 in both cases. This is still significant at the .001 percent level but is considerably reduced. This indicates that the government response kept pace with the insurgency, rather than leading or following it.

The last year of Betancourt's term, 1963, was marked by another push on the part of the insurgents. In this case, however, the objective had shifted from seizure of power to overthrow of the Betancourt regime. Never in Venezuelan history had a popularly elected president turned power over to another popularly elected official. If Betancourt succeeded in this, it was surmised that the opportunities for the extreme left would be hurt severely. It is in this context that the care taken by Betancourt in dealing with the

1963, killing four National Guardsmen. This attack seemed to crystalize popular antagonism. Capitalizing on this sentiment, Betancourt clamped down hard, arresting MIR/CP Deputies, instituted emergency measures, and used regular troops in urban areas. This strong response insured continued support by the military and was welcomed by the population at large.

The rest of the Fall preceding the election on December 1 was marked by considerable terrorism. The effects were slight as compared to the expectations of the insurgents. These actions tended to increase the support for Betancourt and forced postponement of many petty disputes among the moderate political factions. The discovery of a cache of Cuban weapons on the first of November was a brilliant stroke of luck for the government. The public stayed solidly behind Betancourt, refusing a call for a general strike and refusing to be intimidated by the violence. Election day brought a terrorist threat to kill anyone on the streets but also brought a remarkable turnout of over ninety percent, only a fraction lower than in 1958. This is the best documentation of the failure of violence of the left.

In reviewing this attempt at violent political change, it would be wise to get inside the minds and eyes of the insurgents. That could tell us a lot about the motivation for violent solutions and insurgent perceptions of political processes. Such data is rarely available and often unreliable when interviews are granted either willingly as part of an attempt at publicity (it is doubtful that scientific interests are sufficient) or unwillingly in jail cells where results are equally unreliable. Those who defect present another range of problems. The data we do have also present problems. Many factors enter into the process of news-gathering and publishing which tend to distort. Over a period of several years a largely competitive press and a largely competitive political system impose some measure of reliability. On setting out to explore some largely theoretical ideas on how violence operates in political processes, we have selected a single case study. This has begged some important questions of operationalization of key concepts which would be necessary for adequate comparative analysis. That remains a next step. Notions such as those explored here need to be sharpened and made amenable to quantification before much of an advance in our theoretical knowledge can be made. An exercise of our present sort is primarily concerned with whether a given conceptual framework provides insight in terms of description, explanation, and prediction. If the results then prove heuristic, additional case studies and comparative analysis may be undertaken.

Focusing on the competitiveness or openness of the political system, perceived legitimacy of violent acts, and insurgent and military skills, several initial relationships have appeared important as expressed in the suggested propositions. For review then, it is possible to look at the attempt to use political violence to manage conflict in these terms. It is clear in the Venezuelan context that access to the process of allocation of valuables was not blocked under the Betancourt regime. At a minimum it can be said that the alternatives of a rightist or leftist dictatorship were perceived as promising a greater block by the vast majority. The insurgents were not able to convince more than a handful of people that violence was necessary to gain access to effective politics. In this context the insurgency had little likelihood of success, although this is more obvious in retrospect than at the time. Even though the insurgents may have had little likelihood of success, they were able to

use violence as a means of access to the communications system out of proportion to their actual strength. Their position and strength precluded their commanding much attention in nonviolent politics.

The dynamics of this particular case of political violence can be examined largely in the context of the extent to which the government was able to carry out its operations in such a way that they were perceived as legitimate by the significant sectors in the society. By undertaking major moves in response to major insurgent acts, the government was able to maintain a sense of legitimacy. Contributing to this was the largely successful attempt to stay within the legal code. The insurgents, on the other hand, continually committed acts that were considered illegitimate. They were unable to shift the focus to the illegitimacy of governmental acts and legitimacy of their own. This is the crux of the success of Betancourt and the failure of the insurgents. Contributing to this outcome was the recent political history that seemed to weaken the potential for mobilization on the part of the insurgents. Betancourt established the myth that his government and the constitutional system offered greater opportunity than the alternatives. The substantive accomplishments were taken as an indication of the future trend.

The restraint of the government, the constant support given by the service chiefs, trade unions, opposition parties, church and other important sectors of society, contributed to the maintenance of public support. As stated above, one common mistake of governments under the threat of insurgency is to overrespond, thus alienating many who would otherwise not be predisposed to support insurgents. Even if this support is limited to protecting and not reporting insurgent activity, a government finds itself in serious trouble. Betancourt showed considerable adroitness on this score and did not provide indirect aid to the insurgents.

An additional feature of the success of the Betancourt government was the ability to maintain the support of the military. By continuing many of the benefits enjoyed by the services under the Jiménez dictatorship and in some cases extending them, the government did not give economic cause for discontent. In terms of political influence, the military was advised and consulted on major policy and given quite a free hand in dealing with strictly military matters. By cracking down hard occasionally on the insurgent when public and political opinion was ready, the government convinced the military of their willingness to deal with force when necessary. In the 1963 insurgent campaign one tactical alternative of the insurgents was to stimulate a military revolt which the CP and MIR felt would provide a basis for legitimacy themselves. Betancourt also used this to convince the military of the necessity of loyalty.

Above all, the failure of the insurgency can be laid to their inability to expand recruitment. It appears that the total cadre at its height was about a thousand men. In assessing this figure it should be remembered that it is considerably more men than Castro had in the Spring of 1958, six months before he achieved power. The difference is that Castro rapidly recruited and that he had supporting underground movements in major urban areas. While the distribution of violent acts suggests that 1961 was used for training, there is little indication that this group was enlarged upon during the next two years. A movement of this sort must grow if it is to avoid defeat; it cannot just stand still. Violence was not sufficiently attractive as the decisive means for political action.

This review suggests that perception of legitimacy of violent acts may indeed be an important determinant in explaining the relation between violence and political processes. Much more work is necessary before any claim could be made to testing theory or even developing it. Nevertheless, there are important theoretical implications of this analysis. Some of the more popular images of violence as the breakdown of politics have led to theoretical formulation that may quite seriously distort not only analysis but action. Faced as we are by increasing levels of violence in domestic and international politics, it is certainly desirable to spend some time learning how to avoid mistakes.

One question that still is not adequately answered relates to whether the failure of the insurgency was due to the adroitness of Betancourt, the stupidity of the insurgents, or the conviction of significant groups that constitutional government provided the best alternative in the context of the other choices of a right or leftwing dictatorship and possible civil war. Such questions in politics can probably not be definitively answered. In this case all three factors were important. Had Betancourt made gross errors in political judgment, the outcome might well have been different. Had the insurgents been better trained, organized, and led, it is still unlikely they could have defeated the government as long as the majority of significant groups remained loyal. There is one last nagging thought. It is possible that Betancourt survived because of and not in spite of the violence since it was a lever to hold the coalition, moderate opposition, and military together. That would be strange irony for the insurgents indeed.

Instability in Latin America

Professor Bwy's article provides additional evidence of the ability of theory and prior research techniques and findings to help explain revolution. He has here combined ideas and techniques from Brinton, Russett, the Feierabends, Lipset, Rummell, Tanter and Midlarsky, and notably Cantril, Free, and Kilpatrick. With these people in his mind and work, Bwy here meticulously analyzes the factors he deems crucial for Turmoil (which does not necessarily end in revolution) and Internal War (which is revolution). He emphasizes that both unconcerted and concerted civil violence result from many of the same causes.

The style of the article is quite different from Free's and Gude's. But the substance of all three of these articles has much in common: an effort to explain revolution in South America, the exciting laboratory for social research which has resisted Yankee imperialism and challenged Yankee social research. In time it will become increasingly apparent that Latin America is a laboratory for understanding not just Latin America but also basic phenomena of revolution everywhere. The ultimate synthesis of those who have worked on political stability in Latin America remains to be done, and Bwy's article is perhaps the biggest step toward that elusive synthesis. As such it is a big step toward overall synthesis on the causes of revolution.

Dimensions of social conflict in Latin America*

DOUGLAS BWY

Douglas P. Bwy, "Dimensions of Social Conflict in Latin America," is reprinted from *Riots and Rebellion: Civil Violence in the Urban Community* (1968), pp. 201–236, edited by Louis H. Masotti and Don R. Bowen, by permission of the author and the publisher, Sage Publications, Inc., Beverly Hills, California.

Notes to this section will be found on pages 350–354.

* Author's Note: *In addition to the National Science Foundation, which partially supported this research under Grant NSF–GS789, the author is also indebted to the Vogelback Computing Center, Northwestern University, and the Andrew Jennings Computing Center, Case Western Reserve University.*

THIS research proposes to take a close empirical look at political aggression, to extract from the extensive bodies of literature a theoretical model which might account for much of the variance about political instability, and to systematically apply the model within a common socio-cultural environment.

Politically relevant aggression, here, is defined as *behavior designed to injure* (either physically or psychologically) *those toward whom it is directed.*[1] Politically relevant violence, on the other hand, is defined as *any action* (attack or assault) *with intent to do physical harm* (injury or destruction) *to persons or property.* Violence, then, is on one end of the aggressive continuum (events such as riots, clashes, assassinations, and so on, appear to fall here); while more subtle forms of aggression, the nonviolent forms, fall at the opposite end of the continuum (and generally seem to find expression in such activities as threats, protests, boycotts, and so on).[2]

Because of a personal research interest in the politics of the Latin American republics, and because of the eclectic nature of the political aggression there, this region was selected as the natural laboratory in which to test the model of political instability.

THE DIMENSIONS OF SOCIAL CONFLICT
IN LATIN AMERICA

Social conflict is so much a part of the Latin American political process that "to treat violence . . . as [an] aberration, places one in the awkward position of insisting that practically all significant political events in the past half century are deviations."[3] While such "deviations" are: (a) chronic, it is equally true that the majority of them are (b) frequently accompanied by limited violence, and that they (c) generally produce no basic shifts in economic, social, or political policies.[4] The so-called "revolutions" of Latin America range from the Chilean "revolution" of 1924 (when, in the throes of a continuous cycle of cabinet instability. Arturo Alessandri resigned), to the rather violent removal of Porfirio Díaz, or Jorge Ubico, or Enrique Peñaranda, and the kind of socioeconomic uprooting which took place in Mexico during 1911 and after, in Guatemala during 1945 and after, and in Bolivia in 1943 and 1952. "Revolutions" have taken place after the central decision-maker has spent as little as twenty-eight hours in office (which was Arturo Rawson's

tenure after being "installed" by the Perón revolution), or as many as forty-four years, in the case of Mexico's Díaz, or twenty-eight years, in the case of Venezuela's Juan Vicente Gómez. They have been as brutal and bloody as the guerrilla insurrection taking place in Cuba, and as peaceful as the kind of game of "musical chairs" played out year after year in Paraguay. They are more often the result of precision and planning among elites (as for example, the recent *coup* in Argentina, which saw Arturo Illia's government fall prey to the militarism of General Juan Carlos Onganía) than events of mass participation (as exemplified in Colombia's *bogotazo*, which cost the lives of over 5,000 residents of Bogotá, or Guatemala's *huelga de los brazos caidos* [the strike of the fallen arms], or the 1958 full-scale uprising in Caracas which brought down Pérez Jiménez).

When looked at from the point of view of "revolution," then, the domain of political instability in Latin America appears as eclectic as it is unmanageable. Underpinning each of these "revolutions," however, is a character of interpersonal or intergroup conflict,[5] and whether each reflects an aggregate of conflict (e.g., civil uprising, guerrilla warfare) or a specific act (e.g., resignation, assassination), the conflict behavior itself is measurable. Thinking of the domain of political instability in terms of specific and aggregate instances of aggression, then, the conflict landscape can be reduced to: demonstrations and boycotts, protests and threats, riots, nonpolitical and political clashes, instances of *machetismo* [peasant rebellion], *cuartelazo* [barracks revolt], *imposición* [imposing oneself in office], and *candidato único* [single candidate], strikes and general strikes, acts of terrorism and sabotage, guerrilla warfare, plots, revolutionary invasions, military *coups*, civil wars, private warfare, banditry, and others.

In the belief that each of these instances of conflict could be empirically defined so as to yield mutually exclusive events for analysis, a set of over forty conflict events (generally involving either (a) aggressive activity from a populace to a government, or (b) that directed from a government to a

CODE SHEET: DOMESTIC CONFLICT

1 2 3 [ ][ ][ ] Actor (sub-sets)

(Description)

Distance from unit-of-analysis actor

4 [ ]=0 Actor located in sub-set
4 [ ]=1 Actor located in outer fringes of sub-set
4 [ ]=2 Actor located in same province or state as sub-set

Specific locality where action took place ________

Object

5 [ ]=0 National Govt.
5 [ ]=1 State/ Provincial Govt.
5 [ ]=2 Local Govt.
[ ]=3 Other Authority

Specify*3 ________

6 7 [ ][ ] Day
8 9 [ ][ ] Month
10 11 [ ][ ] Year
12 [ ] Data Source
13 [ ] Data Collector

14 [ ]=0 Complete Data
14 [ ]=1 Incomplete Data
15 [ ]=0 Non-Composite (discrete event)
15 [ ]=1 Composite (continuous event)

Non-Violent Behavior

16 17 [ ][ ]=01 Nonviolent behavior (Actor)

18 [ ]
1 Legal
2 Extralegal

19 20 [ ][ ]
01=Antigovernment demonstration
02=Antigovernment demonstrating
03=Printed protests
04=Threat
05=Political boycott
06=Antiforeign demonstration
07=Antiforeign threat
99=Other (specify) ________

16 17 [ ][ ]=02 Nonviolent behavior (Object)

21 [ ]
1=Legal
2=Extralegal

22 23 [ ][ ]
01=Imposición
02=Candidato único
03=Continuismo
99=Other (specify) ________

Unplanned Violence

16 17 [ ][ ]=03 Unplanned Violence

24 25 [ ][ ]
01=Riot or Manifestaciones
02=Rioting
03=Political Clashes
04=Non-Political Clashes
05=Anti-Foreign Riot
06=Machetismo or Peasant Rebellion
99=Other (specify) ________

Figure 1A.

populace) was developed,[6] and incorporated into a Domestic Conflict Code Sheet (see Figures 1A and 1B). In applying the Code Sheet to journalistic data, it was decided that the conflict behavior sought should: (a) focus on aggressive activity taking place within nations on which detailed survey research data were also available,[7] (b) be applied to both comprehensive and comparable data sources;[8] and (c) have the quality of being able to be aggregated across specific city or provincial units of analysis.

Thirty-four of the events collected on the Code Sheet dealt with conflict directed by "individuals or groups within the political system against other groups or against the complex of officeholders and individuals and groups associated with them." It was these which were selected as measures of political instability. In an effort to reduce them to a smaller set of conceptual variables, the data were: (a) aggregated by provincial (state) units[9] for the total nine-year period over which they had been collected, and (b) factor analyzed.[10] The results of this analysis appear in Table 1, below.

Planned Violence

16 17 ☐☐=04
Planned Violence

26 27 ☐☐
01=Strike
02=General Strike
03=Terroristic Act/Sabotage
04=Terrorism/Continuing Sabotage
05=Guerrilla Action
06=Guerrilla Warfare
07=Golpe de Estado/Coup d'Etat
08=Cuartelazo
09=Plots
10=Assassination
11=Civilian Political Revolt
12=Private Warfare
13=Banditry
14=Revolutionary Invasion
99=Other (specify)_____

Governmental Response

16 17 ☐☐=05
Governmental Response

28 29 ☐☐
01=Limited State of Emergency
02=Martial Law
03=Arrest/Imprisonment of Politically Insignificant Persons
04=Execution of Politically Insignificant Persons
05=Governmental Action against Specific Groups
99=Other (specify)_____

16 17 ☐☐=06
Quality of Governmental Response

30 31 ☐☐
01=Resignations of Political Elite
02=Dismissals of Political Elite
03=Dissolution of Legislature
04=Cabinet Instability
05=Mutiny
06=Arrest/Imprisonment of Politically Significant Persons
07=Exile
08=Execution of Politically Significant Persons
09=Political Boycott
99=Other (specify)_____

Individual Statistics

Duration

32 ☐=0 32 ☐=1
<Day   ≥Day

33 34 35 36 ☐☐☐☐ Days   Or duration based on intuitive rating:

37 ☐=0 37 ☐=1 37 ☐=2
1-7 Days 8-30 Days 31-365 Days

Numbers Involved

38 39 40 41 42 43 ☐☐☐☐☐☐ For Actor

44 45 46 47 48 49 ☐☐☐☐☐☐ For Object

50 ☐=0 Numbers involved for both Actor and Object

Numbers Injured

51 52 53 54 55 ☐☐☐☐☐

56 ☐=0 Injured for Actor

56 ☐=1 Injured for Actor and Object

Numbers Killed

57 58 59 60 61 ☐☐☐☐☐

Or if no data on killed or injured:

62 63 64 65 66 ☐☐☐☐☐ Casualties

67 ☐=0 Killed for Actor

67 ☐=1 Killed for Actor and Object

Numbers Arrested

68 69 70 71 ☐☐☐☐

Amount of Property Damage (in $100's)

72 73 74 75 76 ☐☐☐☐☐

Figure 1B.

Each entry or "factor loading" of the matrix represents the correlation between the conflict measures and a given factor. By squaring these factor loadings and summing them (h^2) we have an approximation of the amount of variance in social conflict (taken as the dependent variable) explained by the underlying factors. In addition to indicating the weight of each factor in explaining the observed measures, the matrix of factor loadings also provides the basis for grouping the measures into common factors. The various operational measures have clustered into two basic (and a third, primarily negative) configurations, with high intercorrelations within the clusters and relatively low correlations between them. By examining the nature of the operational measures, we are in a position to identify the basic dimension, or "latent variable," which "causes" the array of variables along the factor.

By adopting the value of +.50 as that necessary for assigning "significant" variables to any one dimension, the operational measures in Table 1 were shuffled into two interpretable factors (contained with the boxes).

Factor 1, Turmoil. Factors are computed in the order of their ability to explain the variation in the domestic conflict measures used. The first dimension to be extracted accounts for 58% of the common variance. Among the highest loading conflict measures on this dimension are: Anti-Government

know it within the Latin American context?

This finding is not unique. R. J. Rummel, and after him Raymond Tanter, reported[11] the existence of a basic dimension indexed by such things as Demonstrations, Riots, Strikes, Governmental Crises,[12] and Assassinations. With the possible exception of

Table 1. *Rotated factor matrix for twenty-four domestic conflict measures, sixty-five provincial units, nine-year time period*

	ROTATED FACTOR LOADINGS			
DOMESTIC CONFLICT MEASURES	F_1	F_2	F_3	h^2
1. Antigovernment Demonstration	.86	.35	−.16	.896
2. Riot or Manifestacion	.90	.21	−.18	.881
3. Antiforeign Demonstration	.96	−.01	−.02	.936
4. Political Clash	.93	−.03	−.15	.890
5. Antiforeign Riot	.94	−.02	−.05	.899
6. Strike	.82	.39	−.16	.849
7. Golpe de Estado/Coup d'Etat	.87	.12	−.01	.764
8. Cuartelazo	.69	−.05	.06	.493
9. Plots	.62	−.04	−.29	.476
10. Assassination	.72	.45	.09	.734
11. Deaths from Domestic Group Violence	.91	.27	.10	.908
12. Numbers Involved in Civil Violence	.84	−.03	−.37	.843
13. Numbers Injured in Civil Violence	.78	.11	−.12	.631
14. Numbers Arrested	.92	.10	−.19	.890
15. Terroristic Act/Sabotage	.52	.64	−.09	.705
16. Antigovernment Demonstrating	.22	.51	.39	.470
17. Terrorizing/Sabotaging	−.01	.92	.05	.855
18. Guerrilla Action	.48	.79	.08	.868
19. Guerrilla Warfare	−.07	.93	.03	.879
20. Revolutionary Invasion	−.04	.91	.04	.822
21. Threat	.49	.04	−.65	.678
22. Rioting	.22	−.03	−.79	.684
23. Nonpolitical Clash	.01	−.03	−.92	.842
24. General Strike	.07	−.14	−.85	.741
Percentage Total Variance	45.41	18.84	13.38	77.63
Percentage Common Variance	58.49	24.27	17.24	100.00

Riots [*Manifestaciones*], Political Clashes, Anti-Foreign Riots and Demonstrations, Arrests, and Deaths from Domestic Violence —most suggesting a kind of spontaneous, sporadic, and essentially nonorganized conflict behavior dimension. The next highest loading measures—Strikes, Coups, *Cuartelazos*, Injuries, Assassinations, and Numbers Involved (all of which are not always spontaneous in nature)—also come out on this dimension.

Two inquiries are suggested by these data: first the methodological question (a) What about the stability of these findings? and secondly, the substantive question (b) Are they interpretable with such behavior as we

Governmental Crises (which may find partial expression in the measure "Plots" (9) from the present analysis), all of the variables in the Rummel and Tanter matrices also come out with strong factor loadings in the first dimension of Table 1. To use the name they applied to such a cluster, Factor 1 reflects the degree of Turmoil among the provincial units.

As to the substantive question of the fit of such findings to the Latin American scene, there seems to be little or no evidence challenging the fact that such a cluster of conflict events does not covary. The occurrence of one set of variables on the first continuum, however, may appear questionable: Coups

(7), *Cuartelazos* (8), and Plots (9). That these events occur together (even though defined in a mutually exclusive manner), is not a point of contention; since we would indeed expect this to be the case. That they come out on the first dimension is, however, of legitimate concern. How can such loadings be explained in the light of the substantive literature which places such activities within the framework of highly organized and clandestine events? A previous analysis[13] has suggested the strongest correlate (negative) of highly organized violence (such as guerrilla warfare) to be the populace's perception of the legitimacy of the political system. Organized violence increased linearly as system legitimacy decreased. There was, however, little or no association with what was termed Anomic (or spontaneous) Violence and Legitimacy. That is, something other than challenges to the legitimacy of the system seemed to be at work in "causing" Anomic Violence. Since the vast majority of Latin American coups are relatively bloodless and of short duration (generally because of the lack of interest and participation of the masses), they rarely appear to be serious challenges to the legitimacy of the systems involved. Instead, they appear more in the form of a frequent game of rotation between the set of upper class "ins" and "outs." The coup d'etat, or palace revolution, then, as it is practiced in Latin America, appears to be as institutionalized a form of challenging governments as the ballot, or as viable a mechanism of protest (although more often practiced by an elite clientele) as the *manifestacion*, or demonstration, or strike. As such, its emergence on the first factor, in association with these events, is more than acceptable.

Factor 2, Internal War. The second basic factor computed for Table 1 accounts for 24% of the common variance. In the order of the strength of their association with the factor, the highest loading variables are: continuing Guerrilla Warfare, Terrorizing/Sabotaging, Revolutionary Invasion, Guerrilla Action, and discrete Terroristic Act/Sabotage. Only two other conflict measures produce factor loadings at or near the +.50

level established earlier: Antigovernment Demonstrating, and Assassinations. Together, the extreme loading conflict measures on Factor 2, then, generally refer to aggressive actions defined by high degrees of planning and organization. Or, to use Tanter's concept for such a cluster, Factor 2 reflects the degree of Internal War among the political units.

The two questions posed earlier, with respect to the first factor, can now be put to the results here, namely: (a) What about the stability of this second factor? and (b) Are these factor loadings interpretable within the context of Latin American behavior?

When Rummel factor analyzed data for 77 nations on nine domestic conflict variables gathered for the three-year period 1955–1957, three basic dimensions emerged. The first was a dimension we have already described as having a nice fit to what we have also called a Turmoil dimension. The second and third dimensions were labeled by Rummel as Revolutionary and Subversive. In describing them, he notes that they "appear to represent organized conflict behavior, i.e., behavior that is planned with definite objectives and methods in mind."[14] When Tanter replicated Rummel's study, using 1958–1960 data, the Revolutionary and Subversive dimensions were pulled together into a single basic factor which he labeled Internal War. Indexed by such variables as Revolutions,[15] Domestic Killed, Guerrilla War, and Purges, Tanter noted that "these activities are generally associated with organized conflict behavior of a highly violent nature."[16]

With respect to the second question asked about Factor 2, what we have labeled as Internal War has variously been referred to in the literature as "unconventional warfare," "protracted conflict," "irregular warfare," "paramilitary operations," or "guerrilla warfare."[17] Internal War is certainly not a new phenomenon to the Latin American scene. The most dramatic of the recent occurrences is, of course, Fidel Castro's 26th of July movement against the Batista regime from 1956 to 1959. Examples of guerrilla activities, while infrequent, go back to the

1800's and before, one of the earliest being Antonio Conselheiro's open rebellion against the Brazilian government in the northeastern sectors of the country at the end of the nineteenth century. In analyzing the Cuban Revolution, however, Merle Kling notes that it was a case of the insurgents employing ". . . violence in a manner which deviated from the traditional Latin American practice."[18] The dimensions of this "deviation" appear to be embodied in the high loading variables on the Internal War factor in Table 1. The traditional pattern, to Kling, conforms more ". . . to the restraints inherent in a coup d'etat or *golpe de estado* or palace revolution. Such revolts, while abruptly terminating the tenure of government personnel, do not disturb the prevailing pattern of social and economic relations."[19] The dimensions of this pattern are embodied in the high loadings on the Turmoil factor. With respect to the briefest review of the literature on the subject, then, the factor loadings in Table 1 appear interpretable within the context of Latin American conflict behavior.

THE PRECONDITIONS OF TURMOIL
AND INTERNAL WAR: SYSTEMIC
DISSATISFACTION, LEGITIMACY, AND
RETRIBUTION

Psychosocial Dissatisfaction and Political Instability. While the conflict literature has strongly suggested a (causal) linkage between discontent and political instability, it has often been at odds with respect to the *direction* of such a relationship. From Marx, for example, we can extract the proposition: "As a group experiences a *worsening* of its conditions of life, it will become increasingly dissatisfied until it eventually rebels."[20] A number of recent empirical studies have appeared which corroborate this proposition. Through a correlational analysis, Bruce Russett demonstrated that as the inequitable distribution of land (among 47 nation-units) increased, the number of violent political deaths also increased.[21] Through a regression analysis, he established the fact that an even stronger association existed when other indices of discontent (i.e., low GNP per capita, and high percentage of the labor force in the agricultural sector) were taken into consideration. In "A Theory of Revolution," Raymond Tanter and Manus Midlarsky also tested the relationship between land inequality and the occurrence of successful or unsuccessful revolution, and concluded that successful revolutions occurred in those polities with a higher degree of land inequality.[22] And finally, much of the work done by Lipset,[23] Cutright,[24] and Lerner[25] suggests, at least implicitly, that "satisfied" (i.e., wealthy) polities are stable polities. In propositional terms: Political instability increases as economic development decreases.

As reasonable as this argument seems, in both theory and empirical findings, it runs oblique, if not counter, to the propositional relationship between satisfaction and political instability often credited to Edwards, Tocqueville, Brinton, Hoffer, and Davies; namely: "As a group experiences an *improvement* in its conditions of life, it will also experience a rise in its level of desires. The latter will rise more rapidly than the former, leading to dissatisfaction and rebellion."[26] Tocqueville concluded, for example ",. . . so it would appear that the French found their condition the more unsupportable in proportion to its improvement." Eric Wolf has perhaps couched this relationship in its most dramatic form when he said: "Revolt occurs not when men's faces are ground into the dust; rather, it explodes during a period of rising hope, at the point of sudden realization that only the traditional controls of the social order stand between men and the achievement of still greater hopes."[27] James Davies finds that both Marx and Tocqueville's notions have explanatory and possibly predictive value, if they are but juxtaposed and put into the proper time sequence: "Revolutions are most likely to occur when a prolonged period of objective economic and social development is followed by a short period of sharp reversal."[28] "Revolutions," according to these views, are not born in societies that are economically retrograde (downswing), but, on the contrary, in those which are economically progressive (upswing). And, as for the Marxian proposition before it, the evidence in support of the "upswing thesis" is considerable. Brinton finds it applies to the French, Russian, English, and American revolutions,[29] while Davies notes its unique fit to Dorr's Rebellion, the Egyptian Revolution of 1952, and the Bolshevik Revolution of 1917,[30] and Blasier sees it as a reasonably accurate description of conditions leading to the Mexican, Bolivian, and Cuban revolutions.[31]

While discontent, then, appears to be an important correlate of political instability, the direction of the association is very much in doubt. Even admitting a consistent finding as to direction, however, the highest correlations obtained in much of the quantified literature suggest that only a little over half of the variance about instability can be "explained" by measures of dissatisfaction. It appears, therefore, that the causes of political instability are numerous, and that the relationship is indeed complex. Let us look at another predictor variable—legitimacy—which may account for some of this unexplained variance.

Legitimacy and Political Instability. While it has been suggested that the effectiveness of a political system in satisfying demands is primarily an instrumental dimension, legitimacy is more an affective, or evaluative, dimension. Perhaps the most often quoted definition of legitimacy (or what has also been termed "political allegiance") has been given by Lipset, who noted that it involved the capacity of a political system to engender and maintain the belief that existing political institutions were the most appropriate ones for the society.[32] The strength of this variable in predicting instability is emphasized by Lipset, who claims that the political stability of any given nation depends more on this factor than on its effectiveness in satisfying wants.

Despite their separate treatment here, certainly the model's first two variables—discontent and political legitimacy—cannot be considered independent. Actually, psychosocial satisfaction and notions of legitimacy are closely related subsystems of phenomena, which can only be separated for analytic purposes. For example, when explaining how political systems manage to maintain a steady flow of support (legitimacy), Easton concluded that it is (a) through a process of "politicization" (by which attachments to the political system are built into the maturing member), and (b) through *outputs* that meet the demands of the members of society, as well.[33]

It should be emphasized, however, that legitimacy (or allegiance) is not the exclusive province of Western democracies, or what have been referred to as "participant" political cultures. Many closed or hierarchically organized systems, or "subject" political cultures as Almond and Verba[34] would call them, enjoy positive affect, or high feelings of legitimacy. For example, many American Indian political communities or African tribal communities are traditionally oriented, and more often than not hierarchically organized and authoritarian; nevertheless, their inhabitants feel that the systemic arrangements are morally right and proper. The simple fact of the matter is that the members of any type of political system may or may not take pride in it or like it; in short, may or may not ascribe legitimacy to it.

It appears clear, however, that the members of a political system will ascribe legitimacy to the system if the political structure is congruent with the political culture. According to Almond and Verba, when the political structure (regardless of whether traditional, centralized-authoritarian, or democratic) is cognized, and when the frequency of affective (or positive feeling) and evaluative orientations are high, a congruence between culture and structure occurs and is accompanied by high amounts of allegiance or legitimacy. The congruence between culture and structure is weak when the political structure is cognized, but the frequency of positive feeling and evaluation approaches indifference or zero. Here, in place of allegiance, one finds apathy or anomie. Incongruence between political culture and structure begins when the indifference point is passed and negative affect and evaluation grow in frequency. The end product of this mechanism is alienation. Almond and Verba suggest further that such a continuum can also be thought of as one of stability/instability. As political systems move toward allegiant or legitimate orientations, they also tend to become more stable; while movement away from legitimacy, toward apathy and alienation, is often associated with instability. And furthermore, if forced to choose, as correlates of political instability, either low system output (what could roughly be equated with dissatisfaction) or low system legitimacy, Almond and Verba suggest, as did Lipset earlier, that "long-run political stability may be more dependent on a more diffuse sense of attachment or loyalty to the political system—a loyalty not based specifically on system performance."[35]

Retribution: The Correlates of Force. Some notions freely translated from psychology, and particularly those of Arnold Buss, indicate the relationship between force (punishment) and aggression to be curvilinear. From this premise, therefore, it is hypothesized that very little political instability is found at the two extremes of a permissive-coercive continuum, but great quantities of instabilty should be observed at the center. Buss notes, for example, that low levels of punishment do not serve as inhibitors; it is only high levels which are likely to result in anxiety or flight. Punishment in the mid-levels of intensity acts as a frustrator and elicits further aggression, maintaining an aggression–punishment–aggression sequence.[36] Robert LeVine, in his study of African violence against colonial regimes, came to similar conclusions. He found that if colonial policy is consistently repressive toward African self-rule (as was supported by the cases of the Union of South Africa, Portugal's Mozambique, and Angola), or if it is consistently permissive toward self-rule (as seemed to be the case in Nigeria, Ghana, Sudan, and Uganda), then violence against Europeans was relatively low. Only if colonial policy toward self-rule was ambivalent, therefore arousing conflicting expectations of political autonomy (as was the case in Nyasaland and Kenya), did

LeVine find violence to be greater.[37] And finally, some recent research which distinguishes between basic types of domestic conflict is beginning to suggest that such a curvilinear model may only apply to non-organized (or disorganized) and spontaneous violence (such as riots or demonstrations); and that the linear model is a more accurate reflection of more organized types of violent behavior (such as guerrilla warfare and armed rebellions).[38]

OPERATIONALIZING THE MODEL AND TESTING IT WITH OVER-TIME DATA

Satisfaction: An assessment through self anchoring scaling

The Self-Anchoring Striving Scale is a survey research technique developed by Hadley Cantril and F. P. Kilpatrick[39] which attempts to locate an individual on a scale in terms of a spectrum of values he is preoccupied or concerned with, and by means of which he evaluates his own life. The respondent describes, as the top anchoring point, his wishes and hopes as he personally conceives them, the realization of which would constitute for him the best possible life. At the other extreme, he describes the worries and fears, the preoccupations and frustrations, embodied in his conception of the worst possible life he could imagine. Then, utilizing a non-verbal ladder device, he is asked where he thinks he stands on the ladder today, with the top (or tenth rung) being the best life as he had defined it, and the bottom being the worst life as he has defined it. He is also asked where he thinks he stood in the past (five years ago), and where he thinks he will stand in the future (five years from now). Similar questions are then asked about the best and worst possible situations he can imagine for his country, so his aspirations and fears on the national level can be learned. And again, the ladder is used to find out where he thinks his country stands today, where it stood in the past, and where it will stand in the future.[40] By avoiding the pitfalls of imposing a predetermined set of structures on the respondent, and talking in terms of each individual's perceptions of reality (in terms of his own "reality world," as Cantril and Kilpatrick would say), the scale provides a remarkably comparable cross-cultural tool for measuring similar phenomena (namely, frustrations or dissatisfactions) across often divergent populations.

Among the fourteen national surveys in which the scale was administered under the direction of the Institute for International Social Research, four were in Latin American polities: Brazil, Cuba, the Dominican Republic, and Panama. These interviews (numbering over 8,000 units) were obtained,[41] "cleaned,"[42] and aggregated by city[43] and provincial[44] units of analysis.

The Striving Scale produces at least six numerical ladder ratings, which in turn can be used to generate additional measures. One can move from static to dynamic measures, for example, by calculating the difference (or change) in ladder ratings given by respondents from one period to the next. While many different operationalizations were employed, the descriptions of the five below should suffice as a general guide for the procedures followed.

P-SAT$_2$. Personal satisfaction at t_2 (where t_1 = five years ago; t_2 = present, the time of the interview; t_3 = five years into the future). The datum, then represents the mean ladder rating (or personal standing), ranging from 0–10, on the Self-Anchoring Striving Scale, aggregated for provincial units for the present time (the time of the interview, which for Brazil and Cuba was 1960, while for the Dominican Republic and Panama it was 1962).

P-SAT$_1$. Same as above, with the exception that the ladder rating given by the respondent refers to his perceptions of where he stood on the (self-anchored) ladder approximately "five years ago."

PSAT$_{21}$. Δ P-SAT$_1$—P-SAT$_2$; the amount of *change* from the respondent's personal ladder rating "five years ago" to the personal ladder rating "at the present time" the time of the interview).

NSAT$_{23}$. The first unrotated factor score of the mean ladder ratings for the nation for three time periods (N-SAT$_1$ = five years ago, N-SAT$_2$ = present, N-SAT$_3$ = five

years in the future); where the highest loading variables on the factor were: N-SAT$_2$ (+.83), N-SAT$_3$ (+.92), N-SAT$_1$ (−.56). The factor scores are, therefore, measuring a combination of the *present*, plus *future*, satisfaction at the national level.

PN-SAT. The first unrotated factor score of an analysis composed of the following four input variables: Δ P-SAT$_1$—P-SAT$_2$ (personal satisfaction), Δ P-SAT$_2$—P-SAT$_3$ (personal aspiration), Δ N-SAT$_1$—N-SAT$_2$ (national satisfaction), ΔN-SAT$_2$—N-SAT$_3$ (national aspiration). The factor scores are measuring personal (+.89) and national (+.84) *satisfaction*, since personal (−.78) and national *aspiration* (−.59) came out with negative factor loadings on this dimension.

Legitimacy: Measuring positive affect toward political structures

The basic measure of legitimacy consists of, first (a) separating from the total number of individuals in any one sampling site (province) those responding in terms of political considerations[45] when asked to describe their worries and fears (or wishes and hopes) for the future of the nation; and of this group, (b) a calculation (mean) of their perceptions of the *nation's* ladder standing at the present time. The higher the perception of the nation's standing, presumably the less concerned the respondent (with respect to the political hope or fear he may have mentioned), and the higher the feeling of positive affect.

LGLAD1 represents the mean ladder rating of individuals responding only in terms of "national worries and fears," and LGLAD2 the ladder rating of individuals responding only in terms of "national hopes and wishes." LGLAD3 and LGLAD4 correspond identically to the first two measures, with the exception that the political response "Political Stability (Instability). Internal Peace (Chaos), and Order (Civil War)" has been eliminated. The variable LGTMCY consists of the first unrotated factor scores resulting from a factor analysis of the four individual measures of legitimacy; and since the loadings were: +.96, +.93, +.84, and +.95, respectively, all four measures participate equally in this composite variable.

Operationalizing mechanisms of social control: Force

An inspection of the fourteen different types of "governmental response to domestic

mental Response.

Factor 1, Internal Response: Elite Instability. The operational measures loading highest on the first factor, itself accounting for a large portion (31.3%) of the total variance, are: Cabinet Instability, Resignations of Political Elite, Arrest/Imprisonment of Politically Significant Persons, Dismissals of Political Elite, Exiles, Dissolution of the

Table 2. *Rotated factor matrix for thirteen variables measuring governmental response, sixty-five provincial units, nine-year time period*

	ROTATED FACTOR LOADINGS			
GOVERNMENTAL RESPONSES MEASURES	F_1	F_2	F_3	h^2
1. Resignations of Political Elite	.90	.01	.28	.890
2. Dismissals of Political Elite	.67	.18	.62	.864
3. Dissolution of the Legislature	.56	.13	.37	.499
4. Cabinet Instability	.92	.02	.28	.932
5. Mutiny	.49	−.47	−.29	.556
6. Arrest/Imprison Politically-Significant Persons	.71	.23	.59	.914
7. Exiles	.65	.63	.33	.932
8. Limited State of Emergency	.13	.54	.48	.534
9. Martial Law	.07	.91	−.09	.847
10. Arrest/Imprison Politically-Insignificant Persons	.31	.23	.82	.857
11. Execution of Politically-Insignificant Prsns	.12	−.07	.89	.807
12. Governmental Acts Against Specific Groups	.37	.15	.76	.739
13. Execution of Politically-Significant Persons	.41	.08	.71	.675
Percentage Total Variance	31.29	15.21	30.75	77.25
Percentage Common Variance	40.50	19.70	39.80	100.00

conflict" gathered across the sixty-five provincial units in Brazil, Cuba, the Dominican Republic, and Panama (see Figure 1B), suggested that the application of social control may be a more complex phenomenon than was envisioned in the earlier theoretical discussion of the model. In order to test whether these measures would empirically break down into a smaller set of independent clusters, the force data were intercorrelated and factor analyzed,[46] and the results appear in Table 2, above.

When the original operational indices are "assigned" to factors on the basis of high loadings (i.e., the correlation between an index and a given factor), and made more visible by their location within boxes, a definite picture of three independent dimensions emerges. Once again, taking the factor loadings as a clue to the identity of the basic factor, or latent variable, the three dimensions have been named: (a) Elite Instability, (b) Nonviolent, and (c) Violent Govern-

Legislature, and Mutiny. It appears, therefore, that Factor 1 may be interpreted as representing a kind of elite insecurity, fractionation, and reshuffling that often accompanies political instability. It reflects both the small-scale individual behavior in both resignations and dismissals, as well as the more macro-behavior of dissolutions of the legislature and cabinet instabilities. It seems worth noting that Mutiny is positively associated with Elite Instability ($r = +.49$), but negatively associated with both Factors 2 and 3, which appear to index instances of solidarity among elites.

Factor 2, External Response: Non-Violent. The second rotated factor is related to three of the operational indices—Martial Law, Limited States of Emergency, and Exiles— and unrelated to the rest. Although Mutiny also comes out on this dimension, it is negatively ($r = −.47$) related to the latent factor itself. As one observes the declaration of more and more Limited States of Emergency and instances of Martial Law across units, one also observes the less frequent occurrences of Mutiny. It is important to recall that the factor matrix in Table 2 has been rotated to fit the three clusters with perpendicular, or orthogonal, factors; and, therefore, that Non-Violent External Response on the part of the government (Factor 2) occurs independently of Elite Instability (Factor 1).

Factor 3, External Response: Violent. The third factor also accounts for a large proportion of the total variance (30.7%), and therefore continues to support strong inferences. This factor is related to four of the operational measures, and unrelated to the rest: Executions of Politically Insignificant Persons, Arrest/Imprisonment of Politically Insignificant Persons, Governmental Action Against Specific Groups, and Execution of Politically Significant Persons. What differentiates this dimension from the rest is the violent nature of the response itself. Once again, it should be noted that the operational measures were defined so as to make them mutually exclusive, and thus the associations discovered are functions of the observed occurrences of the phenomena themselves.

In order to take advantage of overtime data, and to provide a closer approximation to a "causal" test of the instability model, the nine years of conflict data were aggregated: (a) by the number of specific events (see Figures 1A and 1B), (b) by over 21 provincial units, (c) by two four-year time periods (yielding a "before" and "after" measure about the available survey research data). Thus, conflict data for Brazil and Cuba (from which survey data were available for 1960) were aggregated from 1956–1959 for the first time period, and from 1960–1964 for the second. For the Dominican Republic and Panama (which were sampled in 1962), data corresponding to the first time period were aggregated across the years 1958–1961, and, for the second time period, across the years 1962–1966.

A series of composite variables representing the three basic force dimensions were created out of the first unrotated factor scores

from separate factor analyses, which were themselves composed of variables selected on the basis of the results presented in Table 2. *Elite Instability* for both the first (ELITE$_1$) as well as the second time period ELITE$_2$), therefore, consists of the first unrotated factor scores across the variables: Resignations, Dismissals, Dissolutions, Cabinet Instability, and Mutiny. *Nonviolent Governmental Response* (NVLNT) is a composite of: States of Emergency, Martial Law, and Exiles.[47] And the third dimension, *Violent Governmental Response* (VIOLNT), consists of factor scores from the analysis of: Arrest/Imprisonment of Politically Insignificant Persons, Execution of Politically Insignificant and Significant Persons, and Governmental Actions Against Specific Groups.

Finally, the dependent variables themselves, the Turmoil and Internal War dimensions discussed earlier, were "created" out of the first unrotated factor scores from separate analyses for the two time periods among the 21 provincial units. The most compatible factor solutions across the two time periods for the *Turmoil* dimension were yielded from an analysis of the following variables: Antigovernment Demonstration, Antigovernment Demonstrating,[48] Antiforeign Demonstration, Antigovernment Riot or *Manifestacion*, Antigovernment Rioting, Political Clash, Strike, and the Number of Deaths from Domestic Violence. The composite-variables TURMOIL$_1$ and TURMOIL$_2$, then, consist of the sum of: (a) the occurrences of these separate events (within each of the 21 provincial units) in standard score form, (b) weighted by the respective factor loading for that event.

The same procedures were followed in the "creation" of the measures of *Internal War* for the provincial units, with the following variables participating in the index: discrete Guerrilla Action, continuing Guerrilla Warfare, Revolutionary Invasion, Terroristic Act/Sabotage, continuing Terrorizing/Sabotaging, and the Number of Violent Political Deaths.

With each of the model's variables operationalized over time, we are in a position to input these dimensions directly into multiple regression (or predictive) equations. Such mathematical equations provide linear "explanations" of a dependent variable, such as Turmoil, as the sum of separate contributions from several "independent' variables, such as Elite Instability, Violent Governmental Response, Discontent, and so on. In the two-variable cases, the regression coefficient represents the degree of list, or "slope," the dependent variable (Y) has on the independent variable (X). In raw score form, this slope is known as a *b*-weight; while in standard score form it is known as *beta*. A b-constant larger than unity indicates a steeper slope. The steeper the slope, the larger the change in Y for a given change in X. And, likewise, if the b-constant is less than one but greater than zero, it will take a larger change in X to produce a given change in Y. For example, in terms of the first regression coefficient in Equation 1A, every unit change in X_1 (or Elite Instability) is accompanied by a $-.435$ unit loss in Y (or Turmoil).

When faced with a number of independent variables, as we are with the provincial data, it makes sense to look at the effects of these independent variables on each other, as they cause changes in the dependent variable. In other words, we are interested in observing the effect of Elite Instability on Turmoil, while controlling for Legitimacy, Satisfaction, Violent Governmental Response, and so on.[49] In addition, since we have admitted that theroretically it is impossible to explain all the variance about one variable (Internal War, for example), in terms of only one other (Discontent, for example), the technique of *multiple* regression analysis seems especially appropriate. Now instead of explaining the variance in the dependent variable by just one independent variable, the multiple *correlation* coefficient allows one to indicate how much of the total variation in the dependent variable can be explained by all the independent variables acting together. By squaring the multiple correlation (R^2), as is done in the two-variable case (r^2), therefore, we can determine the explanatory strength of the linear combination of the independent variables. The multiple R's for the following regression equations are unusually high by the normal standards of social research, and indicate that in most cases over 90% of the variance (or practically all the variation) in both Turmoil and Internal War occurring in the twenty-one provinces can be "explained" in terms of the various independent variables within the equations.

The b-coefficients in the following equations are given with the independent variables, while their corresponding *beta* weights appear in parentheses below. Since all but the last two variables of "satisfaction" and "legitimacy" represent factor scores (all with zero means, and standard deviations ranging from .5 to .7),[50] the b and *beta* weights for these variables are comparable. Since the two dependent variables (Turmoil and Internal War) were in standard score form, *beta* coefficients for the remaining variables ($P\text{-}SAT_1$, $P\text{-}SAT_2$, $PSAT_{21}$, LGLAD1, LGLAD2, and LGLAD3) were obtained by multiplying the b-coefficients times the standard deviation of their respective independent variables.[51] B-weights identify changes in the dependent variable "produced" by changes in the independent variables in terms of the measurement units involved, and therefore are not comparable. If we wish to compare the independent variables as to their *relative* abilities to bring about changes in the dependent variable, we must correct for the scale differences involved. In standardizing the variables, we obtain adjusted slopes, or what we have called *beta* weights, which are comparable from one variable to another. The *beta* weights, then, indicate how much of a change in the dependent variable is produced by a standardized change in one of the independent variables, when the others are controlled.

Elite Instability (ELITE) during both time periods is strongly related to the occurrence of Internal War$_2$ as well as to Turmoil$_2$, but the *signs* of the coefficients are reversed for the two conflict dimensions. Elite Instability at t_2 is positively related ($+.27$) to Turmoil during the same time period; that is, Resignations, Dismissals, and Dissolution of Governmental Bodies come during periods of Domestic Turmoil (i.e., Demonstrations, Riots, Strikes, and Political Clashes). Just the opposite occurs with respect to Organized Violence, however, and here elites cohere (Elite Instability is low, $-.14$) when Internal War events (such as Guerrilla Warfare, Revolutionary Invasion, and Terrorism) take place.

The signs of the coefficients for Elite Instability at t_1 are again reversed for the two dimensions of social conflict. Organized Violence at t_2 seems to be a partial product of Elite Instability at t_1, for Internal War increases $(+.18)$ in relationship to the fragmentation of elites. And, likewise, it

to Internal War. Harry Eckstein has also concluded that "... internal wars[53] are unlikely wherever the cohesion of an elite is intact, for the simple reason that insurgent formations require leadership and other skills and are unlikely to obtain them on a large scale without some significant break in the ranks of an elite."[54] Again, the regression coefficients seem to support this assertion. The greater the Elite Instability at $(t_1$ the greater the recruitment potential for the insurgent forces, according to Eckstein's notion), the greater the occurrence of Internal War at t_2. The same does not hold true for the occurrence of Turmoil. In mathematizing an Internal War Potential

$$\text{1A } (R = .97)$$

$$\text{TURMOIL}_2 = \underset{(-0.43)}{-.435 \text{ ELITE}_1} + \underset{(+0.27)}{.275 \text{ ELITE}_2} + \underset{(+0.06)}{.062 \text{ NVLNT}_1} - \underset{(-0.41)}{.413 \text{ VIOLNT}_1}$$

$$+ \underset{(+1.16)}{1.16 \text{ VIOLNT}_2} + \underset{(+0.02)}{.025 \text{ NSAT}_{23}} - \underset{(-0.01)}{.001 \text{ LGLAD}_1}$$

$$\text{1B } (R = .95)$$

$$\text{INTERNAL WAR}_2 = \underset{(+0.18)}{+.176 \text{ ELITE}_1} - \underset{(-0.14)}{.140 \text{ ELITE}_2} + \underset{(+0.48)}{.477 \text{ NVLNT}_1} - \underset{(-0.87)}{.869 \text{ VIOLNT}_1}$$

$$+ \underset{(+1.30)}{1.30 \text{ VIOLNT}_2} + \underset{(+0.18)}{.181 \text{ NSAT}_{23}} - \underset{(-0.01)}{.001 \text{ LGLAD}_1}$$

decreases if elites coalesce. The greater elites are characterized as coalescing at t_1 (low Elite Instability), however, the greater provincial units seem to experience domestic turmoil at t_2 $(-.43)$. These conclusions appear to be extremely stable, with the direction (and often the strength) of the regression coefficients of Elite Instability for the two time periods on the two dimensions remaining essentially the same for a number of regression equations (see Equations 2 and 3, below).

One of the consistent features Crane Brinton finds occurring *prior* to basic revolutions (a type of conflict we have suggested to be more adequately reflected in the Internal War dimension), is what he calls "the disorganization of the government," or "a loss of self-confidence among many members of the ruling class."[52] As we have seen from the first equation, Elite Instability does seem to occur prior (at t_1)

model, Manuel Avila hypothesized that as Elite Cohesiveness increased linearly, Internal War potential decreased.[55] The relationship, in other words, was negative. Again, these data seem to support such an inference; elites cohere (Elite Instability is low, $-.14$) as Internal War events take place.

Nonviolent Governmental Response (NVLNT) at t_1 (indexed by the first unrotated factor scores of variables: Limited States of Emergency, Martial Law, and Exiles) is much more important in explaining Internal War than Turmoil events. In Equations 2 and 3 (below), in addition to Equation 1, as Nonviolent Governmental Responses at t_1 increase, both organized (Internal War) and spontaneous (Turmoil) events occur. However, Acts of Terrorism, Guerrilla Insurrections, and Revolutionary Invasions (Internal War events) break out at higher levels in provinces experiencing

States of Emergency, Martial Laws, and a high Exile rate in *earlier* time periods. Again, these findings are extremely stable across all regression equations.

Violent Government Response (VIOLNT) (indexed by the unrotated factor scores of the extremely high loading variables of: Arrests of Politically Insignificant Persons, Executions of Politically Insignificant Persons, and of Significant Persons, and Governmental Actions against Specific Groups) taking place at t_1 inhibits both Organized ($-.87$, Equation 1B) and Spontaneous ($-.41$, Equation 1A) Violence at t_2. This finding is not stable, however, since the direction of the regression coefficient did

curvilinear (and there is some preliminary evidence to indicate that Violence is curvilinearly related to Turmoil, but linearly related to Internal War), then the slightest change in any one province's position in a scatter plot, vis-a-vis the others, might easily change the direction of the relationship (than if the association were linear).[56]

In an earlier study,[57] the strongest correlate (curvilinear) of what was referred to as Anomic Violence (indexed by such events as Riots, Strikes, and Demonstrations) was found to be a measure of Retribution (i.e., Expenditure on Defense as a Percentage of GNP). When force was both very permissive as well as very restrictive among nation-

2A ($R = .96$)

$$TURMOIL_2 = +.628\ ELITE_2 \underset{(+0.63)}{} +.132\ NVLNT_2 \underset{(+0.13)}{} -.056\ VIOLNT_2 \underset{(-0.06)}{} -.000\ P\text{–}SAT_1 \underset{(-0.00)}{} -.013\ LGTMCY \underset{(-0.01)}{}$$

2B ($R = .92$)

$$INTERNAL\ WAR_2 = +.384\ ELITE_1 \underset{(+0.38)}{} +.543\ NVLNT_1 \underset{(+0.54)}{} +.003\ VIOLNT_1 \underset{(+0.00)}{} +.052\ PSAT_{21} \underset{(+0.07)}{} -.009\ LGLAD3 \underset{(-0.04)}{}$$

3A ($R = .89$)

$$TURMOIL_2 = -.417\ LITE_1 \underset{(-0.42)}{} +.285\ NVLNT_1 \underset{(+0.28)}{} +.722\ VIOLNT_1 \underset{(+0.72)}{} -.036\ PSAT_{21} \underset{(-0.05)}{} -.028\ NSAT_{21} \underset{(-0.06)}{} +.026\ LGLAD1 \underset{(+0.14)}{} -.012\ LGLAD_2 \underset{(-0.07)}{}$$

3B ($R = .92$)

$$INTERNAL\ WAR_2 = +.435\ ELITE_1 \underset{(+0.43)}{} +.614\ NVLNT_1 \underset{(+0.61)}{} -.126\ VIOLNT_1 \underset{(-0.13)}{} +.059\ P\text{–}SAT_2 \underset{(+0.29)}{} -.055\ LGLAD1 \underset{(-0.28)}{}$$

change with a change in the other variables composing separate regression analyses. Any conclusions on the relationship between Violence and the two dimensions of Political Instability, then, will have to remain extremely tentative. One possible reason for the instability of the findings with respect to Violence is the fact that a *linear* model (regression analysis) is being applied to what has earlier been theoretically specified as a curvilinear function. If the data are indeed

units, Anomic Violence was found to be negligible. Force in the mid-levels of intensity, however, elicited high levels of Anomic Violence. No such relationship was found when associating the same force measures to the occurrence of what was called Organized Violence (i.e., Armed Rebellions, Guerrilla Warfare). Not respecting a series of caveats pointed out at the time (the primary one being the problem of "ecological" inferences), one could conclude that: "Guerrilla Warfare, Terrorism, and Sabotage . . . occur and continue irrespective of the extent and quality of governmental force. That is, they may break out just as readily among militarily strong as militarily weak regimes; and they may continue in the face of what would appear to be overwhelmingly adverse inhibiting power." There is some suggestion that these conclusions might tentatively be applied to the present data. In Equation 2B, for example, Violent Governmental Response, yields little or no association with Internal War; while in Equations 2A and 3A we find a tighter relationship between Violent Governmental Response and Turmoil. As a matter of fact, the higher *beta* weight of Violent Governmental Response$_2$ on Internal War (1B) (than Violent Governmental Response$_2$ on Turmoil, Equation 1A), suggests that when violence is higher at t_2 there is a greater chance of Internal War than Turmoil occurring.

While the results with respect to Violent Governmental Response are not at all conclusive, this cannot be said to be the case for the remaining variables: (a) Satisfaction (P-SAT, N-SAT), and (b) Legitimacy (LGTMCY, LGLAD). Equations 2 and 3 offer the clearest examples of a consistent pattern: Legitimacy is negatively related to both Internal War and Turmoil, but the stronger effect appears to occur among Organized Violent Activity. The higher the illegitimacy (or negative affect) ascribed to the government (low Legitimacy), the higher the prospect of Internal War ($-.28$, Equation 3B) than Turmoil ($-.07$, Equation 3A). Satisfaction, on the other hand, is positively related to Internal War ($+.29$, Equation 3B; $+.07$, Equation 2B), but negatively related to Turmoil ($-.05$, Equation 3A; $-.00$, Equation 2A).

The finding that Legitimacy is more tightly related to Organized than Spontaneous Violent Behavior also finds support in an earlier study. On the basis of findings reported in *The Civic Culture* (namely, that the ability to participate in a system leads directly to the building of positive affect toward it),[58] Legitimacy was operationalized

across nation-units, as the degree of change a polity experienced in ratings of "system openness," prior to experiencing either Anomic or Organized Violence. In this and other operationalizations of the concept, Legitimacy proved to be the strong negative correlate of Organized Violence. In all cases, as Political Legitimacy decreased, Organized Violence increased. When the effect of Political Legitimacy on Anomic Violence was tested, however, the negative association proved to be considerably weaker. Once again, dismissing the pitfalls of ecological correlations, it was concluded that ". . . the participants in Organized Violent Activity[i.e., Guerrilla Warfare, Terrorism, Armed Rebellion] seem to be challenging the Legitimacy of the political systems involved . . ."[59]

The Personal Satisfaction of respondents (and their perception of the national standing) among 21 provinces was measured in a variety of ways. P-SAT$_2$, it will be recalled, represents the mean ladder rating (personal standing) on the Self-Anchoring Striving Scale aggregated across province-units for the time of the interview (which for Brazil and Cuba was 1960; for the Dominican Republic and Panama, 1962). P-SAT$_1$ represents the same measure, with the exception that the data consist of the respondent's evaluation of his ladder rating "five years ago." PSAT$_{21}$ is the difference between P-SAT$_2$ and P-SAT$_1$, or the amount of *change* in personal standing among respondents from "five years ago" to the present.

Regardless of the operationalization, however, Satisfaction is negatively related to Turmoil, but positively related to Internal War. That is, in provinces where respondents rate themselves *low* on the Self-Anchoring Striving Scale, or where they rate themselves as "worse off today than in the past," Demonstrations, Riots, Strikes, and Political Clashes are *high*. On the other hand, instances of Guerrilla Warfare, Revolutionary Invasion, Terroristic Acts, and Sabotage appear at times (a) when people rate themselves "better off today than in the past," and (b) in areas where people tend to rate themselves high on a scale of best and worst possible existences.

While the *beta* weights indicate these relationships are not the strongest predictors of Organized (i.e., Internal War) and Spontaneous (i.e., Turmoil) Violence, the consistent *directions* of the associations are highly suggestive of the two directions Satisfaction appears to take when associated with the occurrence of Revolution in the conflict literature. One of the dependent variables here, Internal War, is admittedly not the same as the variable Revolution discussed by Edwards, de Tocqueville, Brinton, and Davies. An affinity is, nevertheless, proposed, if by "revolution" these authors meant "behaviors attempting (or succeeding) to bring about basic social restructuring." If such is the case, and we have suggested that it is, then Guerrilla Warfare and Revolutionary Invasion (i.e., Internal War) do come closer to an approximation of attempts at basic social change than Demonstrations, Riots, and Strikes (i.e., Turmoil). The positive regression coefficients then, appear to support the notion that "revolutions are born in societies on the upswing."

The work done by Russett, Lipset, Cutright, and Lerner, on the other hand, has supported the "downswing thesis," e.g., that "satisfied" (or wealthy) polities are stable (low on Political Instability). An affinity of the findings to this proposition is likewise suggested, if by Political Instability these authors were considering behavior on the order of Riots, Demonstrations, Strikes, and Political Clashes. The negative regression coefficients indicate that as Satisfaction (regardless of operationalization) goes up, Political Instability, indexed by Turmoil events, goes down.

SUMMARY AND CONCLUSIONS

Domestic conflict in Latin America (a) empirically distributes itself into two basic clusters of activities: (b) Turmoil and Internal War, (c) which are generally independent of each other, and (d) which can generally be differentiated on the basis of structure, direction, and spontaneity. When 24 operational indices of domestic conflict behavior occurring within 65 Latin American provinces over a nine-year period were intercorrelated and factor analyzed (see Table 1), these two "families of conflict" emerged as the first two factors. This finding provided the basis for the construction of composite representations of these two dimensions: (a) the spontaneous, disorganized, or *Turmoil* dimension (which was indexed by: Demonstrations, Riots, Clashes, Strikes, and Deaths from Domestic Group Violence), and (b) the *Internal War* dimension, involving conflict behavior of a more planned and organized nature (and indexed by instances of Guerrilla Warfare, Revolutionary Invasion, Terrorism/ Sabotage, and Domestic Killed).

When a general model isolated (a) Discontent, (b) Force, and (c) Legitimacy, as the possible *causes* of Turmoil and Internal War, and the effects of these independent variables were tested, using (a) overtime data, (b) among the 21 Latin American provinces (for which detailed survey research data were also available), the following conclusions emerged from a series of multiple regression analyses:

Force was viewed as a special type of conflict—that directed by a government to a populace. Governmental response to domestic conflict is itself highly structured in terms of three independent clusters of activities (see Table 2): (a) Elite Instability, (b) Nonviolent and (c) Violent Governmental Response.

1. Elite fragmentation and disorganization consistently takes place *prior* to the occurrence of Internal War; but elite cohesion is clearly the mode of behavior as Internal War events are occurring. Elite Instability (t_1), therefore, appears to be a contributing condition to Internal War (t_2).

2. Elite Instability at t_2, on the other hand, is positively related to the occurrence of Turmoil during the same time period (t_2); that is, Resignations, Dismissals, and Dissolutions come during periods of Domestic Turmoil (i.e., Demonstrations, Riots, Strikes, and Clashes).

3. Nonviolent Governmental Response (indexed by: States of Emergency, Martial Law, and Exiles) at t_1 is positively related to

both the amount of Turmoil and Internal War which occurs in the following time period; but appears to be far more important in explaining the occurrence of Internal War.

4. Although the measure Violent Governmental Response (a composite of the variables: Arrests, Executions, and Actions Against Specific Groups) appeared in a number of regression equations, both the weight and the signs of the coefficients were too unstable to support firm conclusions.

5. When *Legitimacy* is operationalized through survey responses measuring the degree of positive and negative affect among provincial inhabitants, Legitimacy (or positive affect) proves to be the negative correlate of both Internal War and Turmoil. The stronger affect appears to occur with Organized Violent Activity, however; for the higher the Illegitimacy, the greater the prospect for the occurrence of Internal War, than Turmoil, events.

6. Whether *satisfaction* is operationalized (through survey research data also aggregated by provinces) as either: (a) the mean ladder standing at which respondents place themselves on a scale of best and worst possible existences, or (b) a change in these ladder ratings from an estimate of where they stood in the past compared to where they now stand, the results are the same. Satisfaction is (a) positively related (upswing to the occurrence of Internal War events, but negatively related (downswing) to the occurrence of Turmoil events. That is, in provinces where respondents rate themselves *low* on the Self-Anchoring Striving Scale, or when they rate themselves as *"worse off* today than in the past," Demonstrations, Riots, Strikes, and Clashes are high. When measures of discontent are used as predictors of Internal War, however, instances of Guerrilla Warfare, Revolutionary Invasion, Terroristic Acts, and Sabotage appear at times (a) when people rate themselves *"better off* today than in the past," and (b) in areas where people tend to rate themselves *high* on a scale of best and worst possible existences.

Model building and the test of
theory

The following article is very precisely titled by its author. It is a causal model for civil strife. It is most comprehensible if the reader has read each of the preceding selections in this book.

In effect Gurr says this: before you can tentatively say why a government falls, you must consider systematically both the states of mind of the people in the polities you are studying and also the institutional structures therein (including, in the broadest sense, habits of compliance to authority—which are states of mind). And you must quantify the whole complex of data before you make tentative conclusions.

The article is notable not simply for its comprehensiveness and system but also for its readiness, at times insistence, to report that the most reliable indicators of civil violence are the states of mind of individuals. Nevertheless, Gurr indicates that only inferences can be made from the data he has examined as to the state of mind and that for research purposes "psychological variables" may be treated as "unoperationalized assumptions." In so doing he states and shies away somewhat from a dilemma: we really need to know what the mood of a public is, he says, but we are unable actually to get inside people's heads and therefore can only guess and assume.

If indeed we do rest content with such a resolution of the research dilemma, do not operationalize psychological assumptions, and continue to assume that our aggregates are real people who must behave as economic or other available indicators of their mental states say they do, then as students of revolution we may suffer the embarrassment of surprise. We would rest content with data that betoken mostly the degree of deprivation of physical needs, which is what economic data for the most part relate to. We would lack data about other environmental events that can influence people's mental state, for example such data as would reflect their sense of loss of dignity and respect or of their opportunities to pursue their personal goals.

To be thus data- and concept-bound would put us as social scientists and citizens in the position of Marxists in 1914 who failed to understand that German workers were more attached to Germany than to non-German workers. We would be like revolutionists who themselves fail to predict when and where the revolution will take place. Lenin a few months before the Russian Revolution failed to foresee it and the urban-oriented members of the Communist part in China in the 1920s lacked Mao Tse-tung's understanding of the mental state of peasants in an overwhelmingly rural country.

That is to say, it is easy for people to fall into the trap, in reading the following essay, that if you haven't measures for it, it's not a variable. Gurr himself does not fall into this trap, though he seems tempted to do so. As we have seen earlier, Lloyd Free demonstrates that we can measure states of mind, directly, by interviewing people. The interviewing process is often rather difficult but it can be more valuable than aggregate data alone. However, even interviewing people provides no ultimate evidence of their civic mood. People themselves, even social scientists, often do not know how they feel or why.

The inability to conclusively measure the public state of mind need not be cause for alarm. Nuclear physicists have been studying the presumed traces left on photographic plates of the presumed passage through space of a presumed subatomic particle over a presumed historic time period of no more than a fraction of a microsecond. There seems to be no great movement among physicists to deny the existence of the phenomena that nuclear pioneers study by inference, even though, as far as I know, no nuclear physicist has actually held in his hand just one subatomic particle.

Indeed the state of mind of physicists is inseparable from their understanding of nuclear particles. If they insisted on crediting only that which has hitherto been palpable or at least measurable, physics as a discipline would not have flourished but died long ago. In his newer *Why Men Rebel* (Princeton: Princeton University Press, 1970) Gurr clearly shows and boldly explores some of the new ways to understand the revolutionary state of mind. It is to be hoped that the study of revolution will not die because its present students scoff at the softness of data derived from new and crude modes of analysis. If the present generation of social scientists does so, their mental expectations of new findings and fresh knowledge will be frustrated by an objective lack of real intellectual advance. This may not cause such social scientists to revolt against their own preconceptions. But it will rather likely cause their students, whose expectations exceed their masters' performance, to rebel.

A causal model of civil strife:
A comparative analysis using new indices[1]

TED GURR

Ted Gurr, "A Causal Model of Civil Strife: A Comparative Analysis Using New Indices," is reprinted, with the permission of the author, from *The American Political Science Review*, 62 (December 1968), pp. 1104–1124. Copyright by and reprinted with the permission of The American Political Science Association.

Notes to this section will be found on pages 354–355.

THIS article describes some results of a successful attempt to assess and refine a causal model of the general conditions of several forms of civil strife, using cross-sectional analyses of data collected for 114 polities. The theoretical argument, which is discussed in detail elsewhere, stipulates a set of variables said to determine the likelihood and magnitude of civil strife.[2] Considerable effort was given here to devising indices that represent the theoretical variables more closely than the readily-available aggregate indices often used in quantitative cross-national research. One consequence is an unusually high degree of statistical explanation: measures of five independent variables jointly account for two-thirds of the variance among nations in magnitude of civil strife ($R = .80$, $R^2 = .64$).

It should be noted at the outset that this study does not attempt to isolate the set of conditions that leads specifically to "revolution," nor to assess the social or political impact of any given act of strife except as that impact is reflected in measures of "magnitude" of strife. The relevance of this kind of research to the classic concern of political scholarship with revolution is its attempt at identification and systematic analysis of conditions that dispose men to strife generally, revolution included.

I. THEORETICAL CONSIDERATIONS

The basic theoretical proposition is that a psychological variable, relative deprivation, is the basic precondition for civil strife of any kind, and that the more widespread and intense deprivation is among members of a population, the greater is the magnitude of strife in one or another form. Relative deprivation is defined as actors' perceptions of discrepancy between their value expectations (the goods and conditions of the life to which they believe they are justifiably entitled) and their value capabilities (the amounts of those goods and conditions that they think they are able to get and keep). The underlying causal mechanism is derived from psychological theory and evidence to the effect that one innate response to perceived deprivation is discontent or anger, and that anger is a motivating state for which aggression is an inherently satisfying response. The term relative deprivation is used below to denote the perceived discrepancy, discontent to denote the motivating state which is the postulated response to it. The relationship between discontent and participation in strife is however mediated by a number of intervening social conditions. The initial theoretical model stipulated three such societal variables that are explored here, namely coercive potential, institutionalization, and social facilitation.[3] Results of a previous attempt to operationalize some

of these variables and relate them to strife suggested that a fourth variable whose effects should be controlled is the legitimacy of the political regime in which strife occurs.[4]

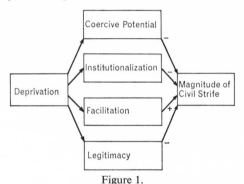

Figure 1.

The initial model, sketched in simplified form in Figure 1, specified no hierarchical or causal interactions among the mediating variables. Each was assumed to have an independent effect on the fundamental relationship between deprivation and strife. The theoretical arguments with reference to each variable are briefly stated here.

Great importance is attributed in psychological theory and equally, in theoretical and empirical studies of revolutionary behavior, to the inhibiting effects of punishment or coercion, actual or threatened, on the outcome of deprivation. The relationship is not necessarily a linear one whereby increasing levels of coercion are associated with declining levels of violence. Psychological evidence suggests that if an aggressive response to deprivation is thwarted by fear of punishment, this interference is itself a deprivation and increases the instigation to aggression. Comparative studies of civil strife suggest a curvilinear relationship whereby medium levels of coercion, indexed for example by military participation ratios or ratings of regime repressiveness, are associated with the highest magnitudes of strife. Only very high levels of coercion appear to limit effectively the extent of strife.[5] No systematic comparative study has examined whether the curvilinear relationship also holds for levels of coercion actually applied. Comparative studies have, however, emphasized the importance of the loyalty of coercive forces to the regime as a factor of equal or greater importance than the size of those forces in deterring strife, and this relationship is almost certainly linear, i.e., the greater the loyalty of coercive forces, the more effective they are, *ceteris paribus*, in deterring strife.[6] Two measures of coercion are used in this study: *coercive force size*, which is hypothesized to vary curvilinearly with levels of strife, and coercive force size weighted for the degree of loyalty of coercive forces to the regime, referred to throughout as *coercive potential*, which is expected to have a linear relationship with strife.

The second intervening variable is *institutionalization*, i.e., the extent to which societal structures beyond the primary level are broad in scope, command substantial resources and/or personnel, and are stable and persisting. Representative of the diverse arguments about the role of associational structures in minimizing strife are Huntington on the necessity of political institutionalization for political stability, Kornhauser on the need for structures intervening between mass and elite to minimize mass movements, and a variety of authors on the long-range tendencies of labor organizations to minimize violent economically based conflict.[7] Two underlying psychological processes are likely to affect the intensity of and responses to discontent. One is that the existence of such structures increases men's value opportunities, i.e., their repertory of alternative ways to attain value satisfaction. A complementary function is that of displacement: labor unions, political parties, and a range of other associations may provide the discontented with routinized and typically non-violent means for expressing their discontents.[8] The proposed relationship is linear: the greater the institutionalization, the lower the magnitude of strife is likely to be.

Given the existence of widespread discontent in a population, a great number of social and environmental conditions may be present that facilitate the outbreak and persistence of strife. They may be categorized according to their inferred psychological effects, for example, according to whether they facilitate interaction among the discontented, or provide the discontented with a sense that violent responses to deprivation are justified, or give them the means to make such responses with maximum effect, or shelter them from retribution.[9] Two aspects of facilitation are treated separately in this study: *past levels of civil strife* and *social and structural facilitation* per se. The theoretical basis for the first of these variables is that populations in which strife is chronic tend to develop, by an interaction process, a set of beliefs justifying violent responses to deprivation; the French tradition of urban "revolution" is a striking example. Social and structural facilitation (referred to below as "facilitation") comprises aspects of organizational and environmental facilitation of strife, and the provision of external assistance. The operational hypotheses are that the greater the levels of past strife, and of social and structural facilitation, the greater is the magnitude of strife.

Two considerations suggested the incorporation of the fourth intervening variable examined in this study, *legitimacy of the regime*. A study of strife for the years 1961–1963 identified a number of nations that had less strife than might be expected on the basis of characteristics they shared with more strife-ridden polities.[10] One apparent common denominator among them was a high degree of popular support for the regime. This appeared consistent with Merelman's recently-proposed learning-theory rationale for legitimacy, to the effect that people comply with directives of the regime in order to gain both the symbolic rewards of governmental action and the actual rewards with which government first associated itself, an argument that applies equally well to acceptance of deprivation and is compatible with experimental findings, in work on the frustration-aggression relationship, that people are less aggressive when they perceive frustration to be reasonable or justifiable.[11] The proposed relationship of legitimacy as an intervening variable is linear: the greater is regime legitimacy at a given level of deprivation, the less the magnitude of consequent strife.

II. OPERATIONAL MEASURES

The universe of analysis chosen for evaluating the model comprised 114 distinct national and colonial political entities, each of which had a population of one million or more in 1962.[12] Data on civil strife were collected for 1961 through 1965. Cross-sectional multiple and partial correlation techniques were used. The use of product-moment correlation coefficients was justified on grounds of their necessity for multiple regression, although not all the indicators formally meet the order-of-measurement requirements of the techniques used.

Because of the very considerable difficulties of operationalizing a number of the variables, and the fact that most of the indicators constructed are new, this article gives relatively close attention to the data collection and scaling procedures.

With the exception of magnitude of strife and its components, the underlying variables examined in this study are unmeasured and must be inferred from indicators. In most instances they are in fact unmeasureable by aggregate data, since they relate in the instance of deprivation-induced discontent to a state of mind, and in the case of the intervening variables to conditions that have their effect only insofar as the discontented perceive them, and moreover perceive them as relevant to their response to deprivation. Following Blalock's recommendation that "when dealing with unmeasured variables it will usually be advisable to make use of more than one indicator for each underlying variable," each of the summary measures used in this study is derived by combining two to seven indicators of the underlying variable. This procedure has not only the advantage Blalock attributes to it, namely of minimizing the effects of confounding variables, but also facilitates incorporation of various empirically-discrete conditions that have theoretically-identical effects.[13]

Magnitude of Civil Strife

The dependent variable of the theoretical model is magnitude of civil strife. Civil strife is defined as all collective, nongovernmental attacks on persons or property that occur within the boundaries of an autonomous or colonial political unit. By "nongovernmental" is meant acts by subjects and citizens who are not employees or agents of the regime, as well as acts of such employees or agents contrary to role norms, such as mutinies and coups d'état. Operationally the definition is qualified by the inclusion of symbolic demonstration attacks on politicla persons or policies, e.g., political demonstrations, and by the exclusion of turmoil and internal war events in which less than 100 persons take part.

A three-fold typology of civil strife is also employed, based on an empirical typology of civil strife events identified by Rummel, Tanter, and others in a series of factor analyses. The general categories, and representative subcategories, are

1. *Turmoil:* relatively spontaneous, unstructured mass strife, including demonstrations, political strikes, riots, political clashes, and localized rebellions.

2. *Conspiracy:* intensively organized, relatively small-scale civil strife, including political assassinations, small-scale terrorism, small-scale guerrilla wars, coups, mutinies, and plots and purges, the last two on grounds that they are evidence of planned strife.

3. *Internal war:* large-scale, organized, focused civil strife, almost always accompanied by extensive violence, including large-scale terrorism and guerrilla wars, civil wars, private wars, and large-scale revolts.[14]

Various measures of the relative extent of civil strife have been used in recent literature, among them counts by country of number of strife events of various types, factor scores derived from such typoloiges, number of deaths from violent strife, man-days of participation in strife, and scaling procedures that take account of both number of events and their severity.[15] One can infer from frustration-aggression theory that no single measure of magnitude of aggression, individual or collective, is likely to be sufficient. It is likely that high levels of discontent may be expressed either in intense, short-lived violence or in more protracted but less severe strife. Moreover, the proportion of a collectivity that participates in civil strife ought to vary with the modal intensity of discontent: mild discontent will motivate few to participate, whereas rage is likely to galvanize large segments of a collectivity into action.

Three aspects of civil strife thus ought to be taken into account in specifying its magnitude:

1. *Pervasiveness:* the extent of participation by the affected population, operationally defined for this study as the sum of the estimated number of participants in all acts of strife as a proportion of the total population of each polity, expressed in terms of participants per 100,000 population.

2. *Duration:* the persistence of strife, indexed here by the sum of the spans of time of all strife events in each polity, whatever the relative scale of the events, expressed in days.

3. *Intensity:* the human cost of strife, indexed here by the total estimated casualties, dead and injured, in all strife events in each polity as a proportion of the total population expressed as casualties per 10,000,000 population.

To approximate these requirements an extensive data-collection and -estimation effort was undertaken. Coding sheets and a coding manual were devised for recording a variety of information about any strife event, and a large number of sources scanned and coded to get as full as possible a representation of the strife events that occurred in the 114 polities in the 1961–1965 period. Three sources were systematically searched for data: the *New York Times* (via its *Index*), *Newsyear* (the annual volumes of *Facts on File*), and *Africa Digest*. This information was supplemented from a variety of other sources, among them *The Annual Register of World Events, Africa Diary: Weekly Record of Events in Africa, Hispanic-American Report*, and country and case studies. Some 1100 strife events were thus identified, coded, and the data punched onto IBM cards.[16] Many small-scale strife events, and some larger ones, probably went unreported in these sources and hence are not included in this civil strife data bank. More-

over, much reported and estimated data is in varying degrees inaccurate. However, neither random nor systematic error seem sufficient to affect in any substantial way the analyses or conclusions reported here; the data are adequate for the purposes to which they are put.[17]

Data estimation procedures were used to circumvent the substantial missing-data problem. Methods for determining number of initiators serve as examples. The coding sheet itself contained two "number of initiator" scales. The first was a modified geometric progression of two used to record proximate estimates of initiators, its first interval being 1 to 40, its highest 55,001 to 110,000; for purposes of summing such estimates to obtain total number of initiators, the midpoint of each interval was used. The second scale was used for recording rough estimates, sometimes coder estimates, of number of initiators, ranging from "less than 100" (set equal to 40 for purposes of computing totals) to "10,001 to 100,000" (set equal to 40,000). Data for events for which no estimate could be made were supplied by calculating and inserting means for the appropriate subcategory of event, e.g., if a riot was coded "no basis for judging" for number of initiators, it was assigned the average number of initiators of all riots for which estimates were available.

"Duration" posed little difficulty, being coded on a geometric progression whose first two intervals were "one-half day or less" and "one-half to one day," and whose upper intervals were four to nine months, nine to fifteen months, etc. No event was assigned a duration of more than five years, though some began before and/or persisted after the 1961–1965 period.

Casualties were coded similarly to number of initiators, the principal missing-data component being estimates of injuries. The ratio of injuries to deaths was calculated for all events of each subcategory for which both data were available—the general ratio for all well-reported strife being 12:1—and was used to estimate injuries for all such events for which "deaths" but not injuries estimates were given.[18]

Strife events occurred in 104 of the 114 polities during the 1961–1965 period. Pervasiveness, Duration, and Intensity scores were calculated separately, following the guidelines specified above, for turmoil, conspiracy, and internal war for each country, and for all strife taken together for each polity. All the distributions were highly skewed, hence were subjected to a log $(X+1)$ transformation. To obtain combined magnitude scores for turmoil, conspiracy, internal war, and all strife, the three component logged scores were added, divided by eight to obtain their eighth root, and the antilog used as the polity magnitude-of-strife score. The distributions remained skewed, but substantially so only in the case of internal war, which by our definitions occurred in only 25 of the 114 polities.[19]

Measures of Deprivation

A very large number of conditions are likely to impose some degree of relative deprivation on some proportion of a nation's citizens. Similarly, all men are likely to be discontented about some of their conditions of life at some point in time. On the basis of prior theoretical and empirical work, however, it was possible to construct, and subsequently to combine, a set of crossnationally comparable indices of conditions that by

inference cause pervasive and intense types of deprivation, relying in part on aggregate data and in part on indices constructed by coding narrative and historical material. In the initial stages of data collection a large number of measures were constructed, some of them representing short-term and some persisting conditions, some of each relating to economic, political, and sociocultural deprivation. Whenever possible, separate measures were included of the intensity of inferred deprivation and of its pervasiveness, i.e., of the proportion of population presumably affected, plus a third measure combining the two elements. A correlation matrix for 48 such measures and a variety of strife measures was generated, and 13 representative deprivation measures selected for combination.[20] The general rationale for the two general types of measures, short-term and persisting deprivation, and the measures finally selected, are summarized below.

Persisting Deprivation: In the very long run men's expectations about the goods and conditions of life to which they are entitled tend to adjust to what they are capable of attaining. In the shorter span, however, some groups may persistently demand and expect values, such as greater economic opportunity, political autonomy, or freedom of religious expression, that their societies will not or cannot provide.

---

1. *Economic discrimination* is defined as systematic exclusion of social groups from higher economic value positions on ascriptive bases. For each polity the proportion of population so discriminated against, if any, was specified to the nearest .05, and the intensity of deprivation coded on a four-point scale (see below). The proportion and the intensity score were multiplied to obtain a polity score.

2. *Political discrimination* is similarly defined in terms of systematic limitation in form, norm, or practice of social groups' opportunities to participate in political activities or to attain elite positions on the basis of ascribed characteristics. Proportionality and intensity scores were determined and combined in the same manner as economic discrimination scores. The "intensity" scales were defined as follows:

INTENSITY SCORE	ECONOMIC DISCRIMINATION	POLITICAL DISCRIMINATION
1	Most higher economic value positions, *or* some specific classes of economic activity, are closed to the group.	Some significant political elite positions are closed to the group, *or* some participatory activities (party membership, voting, etc.).

INTENSITY SCORE	ECONOMIC DISCRIMINATION	POLITICAL DISCRIMINATION
2	Most higher and some medium economic value positions are closed, *or* many specific classes of economic activity.	Most or all political elite positions are closed *or* most participatory activities, *or* some of both.
3	Most higher and most medium economic value positions are closed.	Most or all political elite positions and some participatory activities are closed.
4	Almost all higher, medium, and some lower economic value positions are closed.	Most or all political elite positions and most or all participatory activities are closed.

3. *Potential separatism* was indexed by multiplying the proportional size of historically separatist regional or ethnic groups by a four-point intensity measure.[21] The intensity of separatist deprivation was scored as follows:

INTENSITY SCORE	TYPE OF INFERRED SEPARATISM
1	The separatist region or group was incorporated in the polity by its own request or mutual agreement.
2	The separatist region or group was assigned to the polity by international agreement or by fiat of a former colonial or governing power, except when (3) or (4) below holds.
3	The separatist region or group was forcibly assimilated into the polity prior to the 20th century, *or* was forcibly conquered by a former colonial power prior to the 20th century.
4	The separatist region or group was forcibly assimilated into the polity during the 20th century, *or* was forcibly reassimilated in the 20th century after a period of autonomy due to rebellion or other circumstance.

4. *Dependence on private foreign capital*, indexed by negative net factor payments abroad as a percentage of Gross Domestic Product in the late 1950's, is assumed to be a chronic source of dissatisfaction in an era characterized by economic nationalism. The greater the proportion of national product that accrues to foreign suppliers of goods or capital, the greater the inferred intensity of deprivation; the extent of such deprivation was assumed equal to the proportion of population engaged in the monetary economy. The polity score is the extent score $\times$ the intensity score.[22]

5. *Religious cleavages* are a chronic source of deprivation-inducing conflict. The scale for intensity of religious cleavage takes account both of number of organized religious groups with two percent or more of total population (the major Christian and Muslim subdivisions are counted as separate groups) and of the duration of their coexistence, the greater that duration the less the inferred intensity. The extent measure is the proportion of the population belonging to any organized religious group. The polity score is the product of the two scores.

6. *Lack of educational opportunity* was indexed, in proportionality terms only, by subtracting primary plus secondary school enrollment ratios ca. 1960 from 100. Education is so widely regarded as an essential first step for individual socio-economic advancement that one can infer deprivation among the uneducated, and among the parents of children who cannot attend school if not yet among the children themselves.

Six indicators of persisting deprivation were combined to obtain a single long-run deprivation measure.

These six measures all had distributions approaching normality, and correlations with several strife measures ranging from .09 to .27. To combine them they were weighted to bring their means into approximate correspondence, and each polity's scores added and then averaged to circumvent the missing data problem.

Short-Term Deprivation: Any sharp increase in peoples' expectations that is unaccompanied by the perception of an increase in value capabilities, or any abrupt limitation on what they have or can hope to obtain, constitute relative deprivation. We inferred that short-term, relative declines in system economic and political performance were likely to be perceived as increased deprivation for substantial numbers of people. Indices were devised of five kinds of short-term economic deprivation and two of political deprivation.

1. *Short-term trends in trade value, 1957–1960 compared with 1950–1957:* The percentage change of trade value, exports + imports, for 1957–1960 was compared with the rate for 1950–1957, and any relative decrease in the later period was treated as an indicator of short-term economic deprivation. Decreases were scaled so that polities with lower rates of increase in the earlier period received greater deprivation scores than those with high rates.

2. *Short-term trends in trade value, 1960–1963 compared with 1950–1960:* Procedures identical with (1), above, were used. Both measures were incorporated in the final analysis because both were markedly correlated with strife measures but had a relatively low intercorrelation of .18.[23]

3. *Inflation 1960–1963 compared with 1958–1961:* Data on cost-of-living indices were scaled and combined in such a way that the highest deprivation scores were assigned to polities with substantial and worsening inflation in the 1958–1963 period, the lowest scores (0) to polities with stable or declining costs-of-living throughout the period.

4. *1960-1963 GNP growth rates compared with 1950's growth rate:* Economic growth rate data were scaled so that polities having low rates in the 1950's and even lower rates in the early 1960's received the highest deprivation scores; those with moderate rates in the 1950's but substantial relative decline in the early 1960's received somewhat lower deprivation scores; and those with steadily high, or moderate but steadily increasing, rates received zero deprivation scores.

5. *Adverse economic conditions 1960–1963:* To supplement aggregate data indicators of economic deprivation, several summary news sources were searched for evaluative statements about adverse internal economic conditions such as crop failures, unemployment, export market slumps, drought, etc. Each such description was coded on the following intensity and extent scales:

"SEVERITY" (INTENSITY) SCORES

Moderate	= 1
Substantial, *or* moderate and persisting for more than one year	= 2
Severe, *or* substantial and persisting for more than one year	= 3
Severe *and* persisting for more than one year	= 4

"PROPORTION AFFECTED" (EXTENT) SCORES

One region or city, *or* a small economic sector	= 0.2
Several regions or cities, *or* several economic sectors	= 0.5
Much of country, *or* several major or one dominant economic sector	= 0.7
Whole country, *or* all economic sectors	= 1.0

The score for each such condition is the product of the extent and intensity scores; the score for each polity for each year is the sum of the "condition" scores; and the score used for the summary index is the sum of annual scores for 1960 through 1963. The sources used were *Hispanic-American Report* for Latin America and the *Annual Register* for other polities.[24]

6. *New restrictions on political participation and representation by the regime* were coded from the same sources for the same years. Seventeen types of action were defined on *a priori* grounds as value-depriving political restrictions, including harrassment and banning of parties of various sizes, banning of political activity, and improper dismissal of elected assemblies and executives. These were ranked on a nine-point intensity scale.[25] The extent measure was the politically-participatory proportion of the population, crudely estimated to the nearest .10 on the basis of voting participation levels and, in lieu of voting data, on the basis of urbanization and literacy levels. The score for each action identified is the product of the intensity and extent scores; the annual polity score the sum of "action" scores; and the summary index the sum of annual scores for 1960–1963.

7. *New value-depriving policies of governments 1960–1963* were defined as any new programs or actions that appeared to take away some significant proportion of attained values from a numerically or socially significant group, for example land reform, tax increases, restrictions on trade, limitations of civil liberties, restrictive actions against ethnic, religious, or economic groups, and so forth. Two aspects of such policies were taken into account in scaling for intensity: the degree of deprivation imposed, and their equality of application. The "degree of deprivation" scale values are: small = 1, moderate = 2, substantial = 3, most or all = 4. The "equality of application" scale values are: uniform = 1, discriminatory = 2. The intensity score is the product of values on these two scales. The most intensely depriving policies are assumed to be those intentionally discriminatory and designed to deprive the affected group of most or all the relevant value, e.g. seizure of all property of absentee landlords without compensation (score = 8). Deprivation is inferred to be least intense if the policy is uniformly applicable to all the affected class of citizens and deprives them of only a small part of the value, e.g. a five percent increase in corporation tax rates (score = 1). The extent measure is a crude estimate of the proportion of the adult population likely to be directly affected, the permissible values being .01, .02, .05, .10, .20, .40, .60, .80 and 1.00. The score for each policy identified is the product of the intensity and extent scores; the annual polity score the sum of "policy" scores; and the summary index the sum of annual scores for 1960–1963. The sources are the same as for (6) and (7).[26]

Three summary short-term deprivation scores were calculated for each polity from these seven indices. The five economic variables were multiplied by constants so that their means were approximately equal and averaged to circumvent the missing-data problem. This is the "short-term economic deprivation" index referred to below. The summary measures of politically-related deprivation were similarly combined to obtain a summary "short-term political depriva-

tion" measure. The two measures were then added to comprise a single "short-term deprivation" measure for the purposes of some subsequent analyses.

Measures of the Mediating Variables

Coercive Potential and Size of Coercive Forces: A composite index was constructed to take into account four aspects of the regime's apparent potential for controlling strife. Two of the component indices represent the manpower resources available to the regime, namely military and internal security forces participation ratios, i.e., military personnel per 10,000 adults ca. 1960 ($n = 112$), and internal security forces per 10,000 adults ($n = 102$). The two distributions were normalized and their means brought into correspondence by rescaling them using 10-interval geometric progressions. The other two component indices deal respectively with the degree of *past loyalty of coercive forces to the regime*, and the extent of *illicit coercive-force participation in strife in the 1960–1965 period*.

The rationale for the five-point coercive-force loyalty scale, below, is that the more recently coercive forces had attacked the regime, the less efficacious they would be perceived to be by those who might initiate strife—and the more likely they might be to do so again themselves. Countries were scored on the basis of information from a variety of historical sources.

LOYALTY SCORE	REGIME STATUS AND MILITARY ATTEMPTS TO SEIZE CONTROL OF THE REGIME
5	As of 1960 the polity or its metropolitan power had been autonomous for 25 years or more and had experienced no military intervention since 1910.
4	As of 1960 the polity or its metropolitan power had been autonomous for 5 to 24 years and had experienced no military intervention during that period; *or* had been autonomous for a longer period but experienced military intervention between 1910 and 1934.
3	The polity last experienced military intervention between 1935 and 1950, inclusive.

| 2 | The polity last experienced military intervention between 1951 and 1957, inclusive. |
| 1 | The polity last experienced military intervention between 1958 and 1960, inclusive. |

For 28 polities that became independent after 1957 no "loyalty" score was assigned unless the military or police did in fact intervene between independence and the end of 1960. For purposes of calculating the summary score, below, a military loyalty score for these polities was derived from the "legitimacy" score.

Insofar as the military or police themselves illicitly initiated strife in the 1961–1965 period, they lost all deterrent effect. To quantify the extent of such involvement, all military or police participation in strife was determined from the data bank of 1100 events and for each polity a "coercive forces strife participation" score calculated, by weighting each involvement in a mutiny or a turmoil event as one and each involvement in any other event (typically coups and civil wars) as two, and summing for each country.

All four of the "coercive potential" measures were correlated in the predicted direction with several preliminary measures of strife levels. The participation ratios had low but consistently negative correlations with strife; the "loyalty" and "strife participation" indices had correlations of the order of −40 and +40 with strife respectively.[27] The composite "coercive potential" score was calculated by the following formula:

$$\text{Coercive potential} = 10 \cdot \sqrt{\frac{L[2(\text{HiR}) + 1(\text{loR})]}{1+P}}$$

where

L = "loyalty" score;
HiR = the higher of the scaled military and security forces participation ratios;[28]
loR = the lower of the participation ratios; and
P = "coercive forces strife participation" score.

The effect of the formula is to give the highest coercive potential scores to countries with large coercive forces characterized by both historical and concurrent loyalty to the

regime. The more recently and extensively such forces have been involved in strife, however, the lower their coercive potential score.

A second coercion measure was included in the final analysis to permit a further test of the curvilinearity hypothesis. The measure used is the expression in brackets in the coercive potential formula above, i.e., a weighted measure of the relative sizes of military and internal security forces (*coercive force size*).

Institutionalization: Indices of institutional strength and stability which I found in previous analyses to be negatively associated with strife are the *ratio of labor union membership to nonagricultural employment, central government budgeted expenditure as a percentage of Gross Domestic Product, ca. 1962,* and the *stability of the political party system.*[29] A ten-interval geometric progression was used to normalize the first of these indices, the second was multiplied by 100 and rounded to the nearest 10. To index characteristics of party systems two scales were used, one relating to the number of parties, the other to party system stability per se:

NO. OF PARTIES SCORE	CHARACTERISTICS
0	no parties, or all parties illegal or ineffective
1	one or several parties, membership sharply restricted on ascriptive bases (typically along ethnic lines) to less than twenty per cent of the population
2	one party with no formal or substantial informal restrictions on memberships
3	one party dominant
4	two-party (reasonable expectation of party rotation)
5	multiparty

PARTY SYSTEM STABILITY STABILITY SCORE	PARTY SYSTEM CHARACTERISTICS
0	no parties, or membership restricted on ascriptive bases to less than twenty per cent of population
1	unstable

PARTY SYSTEM STABILITY SCORE	PARTY SYSTEM CHARACTERISTICS
2	all parties relatively new (founded after 1945), long-range stability not yet ascertainable
3	moderately stable
4	stable

Scores on these two scales were combined on an eight-point scale using party stability as the primary indicator of institutionalization but giving highest scores at each stability level to systems with larger numbers of party structures.

The summary institutionalization measure was constructed using this formula:

$$\text{Institutionalization} = 3(\text{hiI}) + 2(\text{midI}) + 1\text{oI},$$

where $\text{hiI} =$ the highest of the three institutionalization scores, etc. This procedure gives greatest weight to the most institutionalized sector of society on the assumption that high institutionalization in one sector compensates for lower levels in others. The highest scores are attained by the Eastern European Communist states while the scores of the Western European democracies are slightly lower. The lowest-scoring polities are Ethiopia, Haiti, Nepal, and Yemen.

Facilitation: Two aspects of facilitation were indexed separately: *past levels of civil strife* and *"social and structural facilitation"* per se. The "past levels of strife" measure was derived from the Eckstein data on frequency of internal wars of various types in the period 1946–1959; although its reliability is only moderate it covers a longer period and a larger number of polities than other available data.[30] Data were collected for those of the 114 polities not included in the Eckstein tabulation, using the same procedure, a *New York Times Index* count, and recollected for a few others. Weights were assigned to events in various categories, e.g. riots = 1, coups = 5, and a summary score for each polity calculated. The distribution was normalized with a $\log(X+1)$ transformation.

The terrain and transportation network of a country constitute a basic structural limitation on the capabilities of insurgents for maintaining a durable insurrection. A complex "inaccessibility" index was constructed taking account of the extent of transportation networks related to area, population density, and the extent of waste, forest, and mountainous terrain; the highest inaccessibility scores were received by polities like Bolivia, Sudan, and Yemen, which have limited transportation networks and large portions of rugged terrain.[31]

A crucial "social" variable that facilitates strife is the extent to which the discontented can and do organize for collective action. The relative strength of Communist Party organizations was used as a partial index, taking into account both the number of party members per ten thousand population and the status of the party. Unfortunately no comparable data could be obtained for extremist parties of the right. Party-membership ratios were rescaled to an eleven-point scale based on a geometric progression of two. The party status scale, below, is based on the premise that illegal parties are more facilitative of strife because their membership is likely, because of the exigencies of repression, to be more dedicated, better organized, and committed to the more violent forms of conflict. Factionalized parties are assumed to be more facilitative because they offer more numerous organizational foci for action.

SCORE	COMMUNIST PARTY STATUS AND CHARACTERISTICS
0	In power *or* nonexistent.
1	Out of power; no serious factionalization or multiple organization; party permitted to participate in electoral activities.
2	Out of power; multiple factions or organizations; party permitted to participate in electoral activities.
3	Out of power; party excluded from electoral activities but other party activities tolerated.
4	Out of power; no serious factionalization or multiple organization; party illegal and/or actively suppressed.
5	Out of power; multiple factions or organizations; party illegal and/or actively suppressed.

The score for each polity is the scaled membership ratio times the party status score.

The third measure of facilitation is the

extent of external support for initiators of strife in the 1961–1965 period. Each strife event in the 1100-event data bank was coded for the degree of support for initiators (if any) and for the number of nations supporting the initiators in any of these ways. The scale points for "degree of support" are provision of arms and supplies ($= 1$), refuge ($= 2$), facilities and training ($= 3$), military advisors and mercenaries ($= 4$), and large ($1,000+$) military units ($= 5$). The event support score is the "degree" score times the "number of nations" score, these scores then being summed for all events for each polity to obtain a polity score. This measure alone has a relatively high correlation with strife level measures, ranging from .3 to .4; its two extreme outliers, South Vietnam and the Congo, are also among the three extreme outliers on the total magnitude of strife distribution.

The three social and structural facilitation measures were weighted to bring their means into approximate correspondence, several missing-data items estimated, and the weighted measures added to obtain the composite index.

Legitimacy: The legitimacy of a regime can be defined behaviorally in terms of popular compliance, and psychologically by reference to the extent to which its directives are regarded by its citizens as properly made and worthy of obedience. In lieu of evidence on compliance or allegiance necessary to operationalize the concept directly, I combined one indicator of an inferred cause of legitimacy, the circumstances under which the regime attained its present form, with an indicator of an inferred effect, the durability of the regime. The "character" of the regime was scored on a seven-point scale:

CHARACTER SCORE	ORIGINS OF NATIONAL POLITICAL INSTITUTIONS
7	Institutions are wholly or primarily accretive and autochthinous; reformations, if any, had indigenous roots (although limited foreign elements may have been assimilated into indigenous institutions).
6	Institutions are a mixture of substantial autochthinous and

CHARACTER SCORE	ORIGINS OF NATIONAL POLITICAL INSTITUTIONS
	foreign elements, e.g. polities with externally-derived parliamentary and/or bureaucratic systems grafted to a traditional monarchy.
5	Institutions are primarily foreign in origin, were deliberately chosen by indigenous leaders, and have been adapted over time to indigenous political conditions. (By adaptation is meant either the modification of regime institutions themselves or development of intermediate institutions to incorporate politically the bulk of the population.)
4	Institutions are primarily foreign in origin, have been adapted over time to indigenous political conditions, but were inculcated under the tutelage of a foreign power rather than chosen by indigenous leaders of their own volition.
3	Institutions are primarily foreign in origin, were deliberately chosen by indigenous leaders, but have *not* been adapted over time to indigenous political conditions.
2	Institutions are primarily foreign in origin, were inculcated under the tutelage of a foreign power, and have not been adapted to indigenous political conditions.
1	Institutions are imposed by, and maintained under threat of sanctions by, foreign powers (including polities under colonial rule as of 1965).

A similar scale, based on the number of generations the regime had persisted as of 1960 without substantial, abrupt reformation, was constructed for durability:

DURABILITY SCORE	LAST MAJOR REFORMATION OF INSTITUTIONS BEFORE 1960
7	More than eight generations before 1960 (before 1800).
6	Four to eight generations (1801–1880).
5	Two to four generations (1881–1920).
4	One to two generations (1921–1940).
3	One-half to one generation (1941–1950).
2	One-quarter to one-half generation (1951–1955).
1	Institutions originated between 1956 and 1960, or were in 1960 in the process of transition.

Examples of coding decisions about "major reformations" are that France experienced such a change in 1957; that most French tropical African polities date their basic institutional structures from the 1946 reforms, not the year of formal independence; that the Canadian regime dates from 1867, when dominion status was attained; and that many Latin American regimes, despite performance of musical chairs at the executive level, attained their basic institutional structures at various (historically specified and coded) points in the mid- or late nineteenth century.

The summary legitimacy index was constructed by summing and rescaling the "character" and "durability" scores.[32]

III. RESULTS OF CORRELATION AND REGRESSION ANALYSIS

The results of four multiple regression analyses are discussed in this paper, one of them in detail. The dependent variables in the four analyses are, respectively, total magnitude of civil strife, magnitude of conspiracy, magnitude of internal war, and magnitude of turmoil. The correlations between the ten summary independent variables and these four strife measures are given in Table 1. The independent variables all correlate with the dependent variables in the predicted direction, with the exception of coercive force size. The r's for the remaining nine independent variables are significant at the .01 level except for four correlates of internal war, three of which are significant at the .05 level.

The hypothetical curvilinear relationship between coercive force size and total magnitude of strife (TMCS) is examined graphically in Figures 2 and 3, each of which is a smoothed curve of deciles of the independent variable plotted against TMCS. Figure 2, based on all 114 polities, suggests an apparent tendency, among countries with relatively small forces, for strife to increase with the size of those forces, and also a slight increase in TMCS at very high levels of coercive forces.[33] It is quite likely that countries with protracted political violence

expand their coercive forces to meet it. It also seems likely that armies in countries facing foreign threats cause less dissatisfaction—by their presence or actions—than armies in states not significantly involved in international conflict. Both factors might contaminate the proposed curvilinear relationship, so countries with either or both characteristics were removed and the relationship plotted for the remaining 69 countries; the results, in Figure 3, show curvilinearity even more distinctly. Figure 4 indicates that the measure of coercive force potential, in which size is weighted for military loyalty to the regime, is essentially linear, as predicted. The latter measure is used in the multiple regression analyses, below.

Eight of the ten independent variables (excluding coercive force size and short-term deprivation, the sum of the two specific short-term deprivation measures) are included in the multiple regression analyses summarized in Table 2. The variables yield considerable and significant multiple correlation coefficients (R), including a high R of .806 for total magnitude of strife ($R^2 = .650$); a moderately high R for conspiracy of .630 ($R^2 = .397$); a similar R for internal war of .648 ($R^2 = .420$); and a somewhat lower R for turmoil of .533 ($R^2 = .284$).[34] There are several possible explanations for the finding that total magnitude of strife is accounted for nearly twice as well as the several forms of strife. One technical factor is that all the class-of-strife measures have greater distributional irregularities than does TMCS, hence TMCS should be somewhat better explained. It is also possible that the categorization employed has less empirical merit than other work has suggested, i.e., that conspiracy, internal war, and turmoil are not sharply distinct forms of civil strife. To qualify this possibility, the correlation matrix in Table 1 suggests that the forms of strife are only weakly related in magnitude—the highest r among the three is .32—but it may still be that they are more strongly related in likelihood, and hence that the universe of strife is more homogenous than the typology suggests. The least-predicted

Table 1. *Correlates of civil strife**

VARIABLE†	1	2	3	4	5	6	7	8	9	10	11	12	13	14
1. Economic deprivation (+)		48	83	−02	−17	−16	−36	−09	26	32	34	31	25	44
2. Political deprivation (+)			88	08	−18	03	−37	−20	33	27	44	18	30	38
3. Short-term deprivation (+)‡				04	−20	−07	−42	−17	34	34	46	28	32	48
4. Persisting deprivation (+)					−04	−21	−14	−37	−04	17	29	26	27	36
5. Legitimacy (−)						25	48	02	−05	−15	−29	−23	−29	−37
6. Coercive force size (±)							53	27	31	04	−23	−11	−01	−14
7. Coercive potential (−)								41	−14	−37	−44	−39	−35	−51
8. Institutionalization (−)									−19	−40	−35	−23	−26	−33
9. Past strife levels (+)										41	24	16	30	30
10. Facilitation (+)											42	57	30	67
11. Magnitude of conspiracy												30	32	59
12. Magnitude of internal war													17	79
13. Magnitude of turmoil														61
14. Total magnitude of strife														

* Product moment correlation coefficients, multiplied by 100. Underlined *r*'s are significant, for *n* = 114, at the .01 level. Correlations between 18 and 23, inclusive, are significant at the .05 level.

† The proposed relationships between the independent variables, nos. 1 to 10, and the strife measures are shown in parentheses, the ± for coercive force size signifying a proposed curvilinear relationship. Examination of the *r*'s between the independent and dependent variables, in the box, shows that all are in the predicted direction with the anticipated exception of coercive force size, and that all but one are significant at the .05 level.

‡ Short-term deprivation is the sum of scores on the short-term economic and short-term political deprivation measures. The separate short-term deprivation measures were used in the regression analyses reported below; the summary measure was used in the causal inference analysis.

class of strife—turmoil—might be better accounted for if turmoil events in the context of internal wars, e.g., riots and localized rebellions in such polities as the Congo and South Vietnam, were categorized as aspects of the internal wars wars in these countries rather than turmoil per se. The most likely substantive interpretation of the relatively low predictability of turmoil, however, is that much turmoil is a response to a variety of locally-incident deprivations and social conditions of a sort not represented in the indices used in this study.

The multiple regression equation for total magnitude of strife was used to calculate predicted magnitude of strife scores. Only ten polities have predicted scores that differ from their actual scores by more than one standard deviation (7.70 units of TMCS). These polities, and three others that have discrepancies approaching one standard deviation, are listed in Table 3.

In five of the thirteen polities—the Congo, Indonesia, Zambia, Rwanda, and Yemen—there is probably systematic error from data-estimation procedures. All of these countries had intense but inadequately-reported civil violence for which only rough and quite possibly exaggerated estimates of deaths were available. When estimates of "wounded" were added to deaths estimates, using a ratio of about twelve to one based on better-reported but smaller-scale events (see above), the result was almost certainly a gross inflation of actual casualties, and hence inflation of TMCS scores. The high actual TMCS score for Israel is the result of a questionable coding judgment about the extent and duration of extremist Orthodox religious conflict. More substantive questions

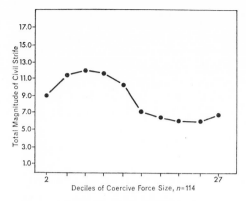

Figure 2. Magnitude of Civil Strife and Coercive Force Size, 114 Polities.

analysis has included measures of most if not all the general determinants of magnitudes of civil strife.

IV. A REVISED CAUSAL MODEL

One striking result of the regression analyses is that the partial correlations of several of the variables tend to disappear when the other variables are introduced (see Table 2). The short-term deprivation measures consistently decline in consequence, in most instances falling below the .05 level of significance. Institutionalization is in all analyses controlled for by the other variables. One or the other of the two facilitation variables declines to zero in each analysis, "past levels of strife" vanishing in three of the four. Coercive potential and legitimacy also decline in their relation to strife rather sharply.

are raised by some of the countries. Paraguay, Argentina, Ecuador, and Volta all could be argued to have had an unrealized potential for strife: in fact both Argentina and Ecuador experienced coups in the mid-1960's that according to their initiators were preventive or protective in nature, and early in 1966 the government of Volta succumbed to rioting followed by a coup. In the Dominican Republic, the Congo, and Rwanda the unexpectedly high levels of violence followed the collapse of rigid, authoritarian regimes; one can infer a time-lag effect from the deprivation incurred under the old regimes. These are special explanations rather than general ones however. The lack of apparent substantive similarities among the thirteen poorly-predicted polities suggests that the

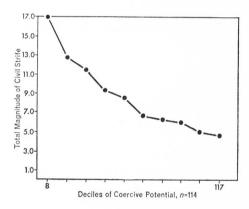

Figure 4. Magnitude of Civil Strife and Coercive Potential.

Note: The vertical axes in Figures 2, 3 and 4 give the average magnitude of civil strife scores for deciles of countries with coercive forces of increasing size (Figures 2 and 3) and for deciles of countries with increasingly large coercive forces relative to their loyalty. The range of TMCS scores for the 114 polities is 0.0 to 48.7, their mean 9.0, and their standard deviation 7.7. Units on the horizontal axes represent numbers of cases, not proportional increases in force size/loyalty; the figures represent the scores of the extreme cases. Eleven rather than ten groupings of cases were used in computations for Figures 2 and 4; the curves of all three figures were smoothed by averaging successive pairs of decile scores.

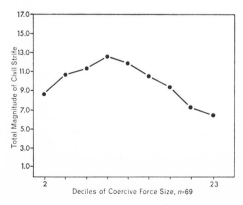

Figure 3. Magnitude of Civil Strife and Coercive Force Size, 69 Low-conflict Polities.

Table 2. *Multiple linear regression results: simple correlations, partial correlations, and standard weights**

DEPENDENT VARIABLES	Econ. Dep.	Pol. Dep.	Per. Dep.	Coerce	Instit.	Past CS	SS Facil.	Legit.	R, R²
	INDEPENDENT VARIABLES								
Total Magnitude of Strife:									
Simple r's	44	38	36	−51	−33	30	67	−37	R = .806
Partial r's	24	(09)	39	−17	(07)	(04)	55	−26	
Constant	−3.11								R² = .650
Weights	.177	.066	.271	−.140	.056	.024	.481	−.184	
Magnitude of Conspiracy:									
Simple r's	34	44	29	−44	−35	24	42	−29	R = .630
Partial r's	(10)	24	22	(−11)	(−09)	(03)	19	(−15)	
Constant	1.10								R² = .397
Weights	.094	.238	.194	−.120	−.088	.026	.181	−.135	
Magnitude of Internal War:									
Simple r's	31	18	26	−39	−23	16	57	−23	R = .648
Partial r's	(14)	(−08)	22	−17	(11)	(−07)	48	(−07)	
Constant	−3.66								R² = .420
Weights	.128	−.073	.186	−.179	.102	−.066	.513	−.063	
Magnitude of Turmoil:									
Simple r's	25	30	27	−35	−26	30	30	−29	R = .533
Partial r's	(07)	(08)	23	(−09)	(−05)	21	(04)	−19	
Constant	1.37								R² = .284
Weights	.072	.085	.223	−.102	−.056	.205	.043	−.192	

* Simple correlations from Table 1 are repeated here to facilitate comparisons. Partial correlations in parentheses have standard (beta) weights that are significant at less than the .05 level, using the one-tailed T test with n = 114. Since this analysis is concerned with what is, effectively, the entire universe of polities, all the correlations are in one sense "significant," but those in parentheses are of substantially less consequence than the others. The weights are reported to facilitate comparisons of the relative importance of the independent variables; because of the use of a variety of scaling and combination procedures for both independent and dependent variables, the weights do not permit direct interpretations, for example, of the effects of a one-unit decrease in intensity of economic discrimination on extent of turmoil.

The only variable that is consistently unaffected by the introduction of the control variables specified by the model is persisting deprivation. A preliminary analysis of the behavior of first- and second-order partials suggests what causal interactions and sequences may be involved in these results. The causal path analysis is concerned principally with the sources of the total magnitude of strife, examining the causal sequences of the specific forms of strife only when they appear to deviate from that of all strife.

A basic supposition for the evaluation of causal models is that, if X_1 is an indirect cause of X_3 whose effects are mediated by an intervening variable X_2, then if X_2's effects are controlled the resulting partial correlation between X_1 and X_3 should be approximately zero. Similarly, if several intervening variables are specified, controlling for all of them or for the last in a causal chain should, if the causal model is not to be falsified, result in a partial correlation not significantly different from zero.[35]

The initial model of the causes of civil strife (Figure 1) postulated that all the mediating variables intervened separately and simultaneously between deprivation and strife. The results indicate that this supposition is only partly correct: none of the mediating variables appear to affect the relationship between *persisting deprivation* and strife, i.e., there is a certain inevitability about the association between such deprivation and strife. Persisting deprivation is moreover equally potent as a source of conspiracy, internal war, and turmoil. With the partial and weak exception of institutionalization, no patterns of societal arrangements nor coercive potential that are included in the model have any consistent effect on its impact.

The effects of short-term deprivation on strife are substantially different—and, it should be added, uncorrelated with persisting deprivation. The intervening variables do tend to control for short-term deprivation's effects. To determine which one or ones exercise primary control, first-order partials were calculated for the several postulated

intervening variables, with these results.

1. The simple r between short-term deprivation and strife = .48[36]
2. The partial r between short term deprivation and strife is: when the control variable is:

.46	Institutionalization
.45	Legitimacy
.42	Past strife
.36	Facilitation
.34	Coercive potential

Only the last two constitute a significant reduction, and moreover when they are combined, the second-order partial, $r_d s \cdot {}_{fc,} = .27$, i.e., *coercive potential* and *facilitation* are the only consequential intervening variables affecting the outcome of short-term deprivation. Short-term deprivation taken alone accounts for $(.48)^2 = .23$ of the magnitude of strife; controlling for coercive potential and facilitation reduces the proportion of strife directly accounted for to $(.27)^2 = .07$, a relatively small but still significant amount.

The same controlling effects of coercive potential and facilitation on short-term deprivation occur among the three generic forms of strife. It is worth noting that when the mediating variables are controlled, short-term economic deprivation still accounts directly for a portion of strife, internal war in particular, while political deprivation contributes significantly to conspiracy. These relationships may reflect contamination of the independent and dependent variables because of their partial temporal overlap. Some short-term economic deprivation in the early 1960s may be attributable to protracted internal wars, and successful conspirators may impose politically-depriving policies once they are in power. The relationship between short-term deprivation of both types and the magnitude of turmoil, however, is effectively mediated or controlled by characteristics of the society and its response to strife.

The relationships among the mediating variables remain to be examined. Institutionalization has no significant relation to any measure of strife when the other variables are controlled, and in the case of magnitude of total strife and of internal war a weak *positive* relationship emerges, i.e., there is a slight though not statistically significant tendency for high institutionalization to be associated with higher levels of strife. A

total magnitude of strife, less so for turmoil and conspiracy, and inconsequential for internal war.

Coercive potential appears in several respects to be a crucial variable in the revised causal model: it is evidently attributable in

Table 3. *Polities with least-predicted total magnitude of civil strife**

POLITY	PREDICTED TMCS	ACTUAL TMCS*	RESIDUAL
Congo-Kinshasa	31.6	48.7	+17.1
Rwanda	12.7	28.2	+15.5
Yemen	9.4	23.6	+14.2
Indonesia	23.8	33.7	+9.9
Dominican Republic	12.1	21.9	+9.8
Italy	3.1	12.3	+9.2
Belgium	2.4	10.5	+8.1
Zambia	8.1	15.5	+7.4
Israel	6.9	14.0	+7.1
Argentina	20.5	13.2	−7.3
Ecuador	18.6	10.1	−8.5
Volta	9.3	0.0	−9.3
Paraguay	17.2	5.0	−12.2

* See text. A negative residual indicates that a polity had less strife than would be predicted on the basis of the characteristics it shares with other polities; a positive residual indicates more than predicted strife.
† Corrected scores. See note 34.

computation of partials between institutionalization and the other three mediating variables indicates that institutionalization has a preceding or causal relationship both to coercive potential and to the facilitation variables, as shown in the revised model in Figure 3. Polities with high levels of institutionalization tend to have high coercive potential and to have few of the conditions that facilitate strife.

Legitimacy apparently has a causal relationship with strife independent either of deprivation or the other intervening variables. About half of the initial correlation between legitimacy and strife is accounted for by the apparent causal relation between legitimacy and coercive potential, i.e., legitimate regimes tend to have large and, most importantly, loyal military and police establishments. Separately from this, however, high legitimacy is significantly associated with low levels of strife, a finding consistent with the postulate that political legitimacy itself is a desired value, one whose absence constitutes a deprivation that incites men to take violent action against their regimes. The relationship is relatively strongest for

part to both levels of institutionalization and of legitimacy, and has a major mediating effect on short-term deprivation. Nonetheless, when all variables are controlled (see Table 2), the partial r between coercive potential and strife is sharply reduced, in two instances below the .05 level of significance. This is in part due to the effects of legitimacy, which is causally linked to both strife and coercive potential.[37] The other major intervening variable is facilitation ($r_{cs} = -.52$; $r_{cs \cdot f} = -.40$, where c = coercive potential, s = strife, and f = social and structural facilitation), i.e., whether or not facilitative conditions exist for civil strife is partly dependent upon the coercive potential of the regime, and thus indirectly dependent upon legitimacy as well. (The relationship is evidently between coercive potential on the one hand and the "Communist party status" and the "external support for initiators" components of facilitation on the other; coercive potential cannot have any consequential effects on "physical inaccessibility.")

This completes the revision of the causal model with the exception of the second component of facilitation, *past strife levels.* This variable has a consistently lower relationship with strife than other variables, with the exception of the turmoil analysis. Moreover its partial correlation is reduced to zero in these analyses, with the same exception, the sole significant controlling variable being *social and structural facilitation.* Among the causes of turmoil, however, social and structural facilitation is controlled for by several variables—principally past strife,

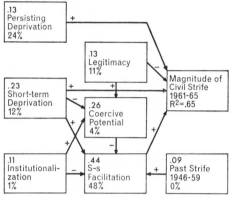

Figure 5. Revised causal model of the determinants of magnitude of civil strife. The proportion at the top of each cell is the simple r^2 between the variable and civil strike, i.e. the proportion of strife accounted for by each variable separately. The percentages are the proportion of explained variance accounted for by each variable when the effects of all others are controlled, determined by squaring each partial r, summing the squares, and expressing each as a percentage of the sum. The explained variance, R^2, is .65.

coercive potential, and institutionalization—whereas past strife remains significant when other effects are partialled out. Both findings support the theoretical argument that suggested the "past strife" measure: a history of chronic strife apparently reflects, and contributes to, attitudes that directly facilitate future turmoil, and indirectly acts to facilitate general levels of strife.

The revised model, with proportional weights inserted, is sketched in Figure 5. The most proximate and potent variable is social and structural facilitation, which accounts for nearly half the explained variance. The deprivation variables account

directly for over one-third the magnitude of strife, legitimacy and institutionalization for one-eighth. But these proportions refer only to direct effects, and in the case of both coercive potential and facilitation part of that direct effect, i.e., the illicit participation of the military in strife and the provision of foreign support for initiators, can be determined only from the characteristics of strife itself.[38] The more remote causes of strife, namely deprivation, institutionalization, legitimacy, and prior strife, are the more fundamental and persisting ones. Some additional regression analyses provide some comparisons. Four of the independent variables relate to inferred states of mind: the two short-term deprivation measures, persisting deprivation, and legitimacy. The R based on these variables is .65, compared with .81 when the remaining four variables are added. The R based on the three deprivation variables alone is .60. These analyses show that all "states-of-mind" conditions contribute significantly to magnitude of strife, but that long-term deprivation has a partial controlling effect on political deprivation. The inference is that short-term political deprivation, as indexed in this study, is most likely to lead to strife if it summates with conditions of persisting deprivation.

We can also ask, and answer, the question, To what extent do the remaining four mediating conditions alone account for magnitude of strife? The variables coercive potential, facilitation, institutionalization, and past strife give a multiple R of .73, with almost all the explained variance accounted for by the first two variables. This result should provide aid and comfort to those concerned with "levels of analysis" problems: research of this sort can focus on aggregative, societal characteristics—which the mediating variables represent—and the (inferred) psychological level can be ignored with relatively little loss of statistical explanatory power. Why these variables are strongly operative and others, like levels of development and type of political system, are relatively weak still needs answering; the answer may be to treat psychological variables as unoperationalized assumptions, or to replace them with variables whose rationale is strictly in terms of effects of social structure or processes on stability.

A further problem is identification of the set of variables that provides the most parsimonious account of magnitude of civil strife. As one approach to the answer, Figure 5 implies that three variables can be eliminated: coercive potential, institutionalization, and past strife, all of which have no consequential direct effects on TMCS. The remaining five variables—the "state of mind" variables and facilitation—give an R of .80 and R^2 of .64, results almost identical to those obtained when all eight variables are included.[39] Four of the five variables included contribute substantially to the regression equation; as expected, the effects of short-term deprivation, political deprivation in particular, are partially controlled. One important observation is that *social and structural facilitation*, though it is substantially the strongest explanatory variable,[40] has here, as in Figure 5, only a moderate direct controlling effect on short-term deprivation. One interpretation is that some of the effects of facilitation on TMCS are independent of deprivation. Two of its three component measures, Communist Party status and external support for initiators, have in common a "tactical" element, i.e., one can infer that underlying them are calculations about gains to be achieved through the employment of strife. This tactical element is not wholly independent of deprivation, inasmuch as three of the four correlations between facilitation and deprivation measures are significant, ranging from .17 to .34 (see Table 1). The basic proposition of this study, that relative deprivation is a necessary precondition for strife, is not challenged by these observations. They do, however, suggest that tactical motives for civil strife are of sufficient importance that they deserve separate operational attention comparable to the conceptual attention given them by conflict theorists.[41]

A number of additional causal inference analyses can be made which might lead to modifications of these conclusions, and of the causal model in Figure 5. Other articles will report the results of causal analyses of various subsets of the universe of polities, and of the causal sequences that can be identified for the several forms of strife.[42]

V. SUMMARY AND CONCLUSION

Quantitative comparative research cannot flourish in a theoretical vacuum, even if it makes use of an armamentarium of techniques of causal inference. This article may not be proof of that assertion, but it should suggest the usefulness of beginning with a theoretical model based on previous substantive work. The theoretical model of the causes of civil strife employed here dictated the construction of a number of aggregate indicators of not-easily-operationalized variables for 114 polities. Eight summary indicators proved to account jointly for two-thirds the variance among nations in relative magnitudes of civil strife during 1961–1965 ($R^2 = .65$). Of greater theoretical consequence, the initial analysis of partial correlation coefficients makes possible a number of more precise statements about the causal interactions among the theoretical variables.

The fundamental proposition that strife varies directly in magnitude with the intensity of relative deprivation is strongly supported; the three deprivation variables alone provide an R of .60 ($R^2 = .36$), and when a fourth state-of-mind variable, legitimacy, is added the R^2 increases to .43. One criticism of this research, and of other cross-national studies of strife that make inferences about collective manifestations of psychological variables, is that the results are not a "direct" test of the relevance of such variables, since the indices of psychological variables are derived from aggregate data rather than being obtained, for example, from cross-national surveys. It is unquestionably necessary to test all hypotheses, including psychological ones, in a variety of ways, for example to determine whether the inferentially-deprived groups are those most likely to engage in strife, and to ask highly frustrated individuals whether they would, or have, taken part in collective violence. No scientific proposition is ever *directly* confirmed or disconfirmed, but some tests are less indirect than others. However, there is only one scientifically acceptable alternative to regarding the results reported here as strong indirect evidence for the psychological propositions relating deprivation and legitimacy to civil violence. That is to provide some reasonably parsimonious, alternative explanations (substantive or technical) of the fact that indices of inferred collective states of mind account for two-thirds of the explained variance (43 percent compared with 65 percent for all variables) in total magnitude of strife.

The effects of the intervening or mediating variables on the disposition to civil violence proved considerably more complex than those of the deprivation variables. Regime legitimacy apparently has no consequential mediating effect on deprivation but acts much as deprivation itself does: low levels of legitimacy, or by inference feelings of illegitimacy, apparently motivate men to collective violence. Levels of institutionalization, as reflected in high levels of unionization, party system stability, and large public sectors, have no direct mediating effect on deprivation; they are however important determinants of coercive potential and of social facilitation, variables which in turn crucially affect the outcome of short-term deprivation. Social and structural facilitation is the most potent of the intervening variables and appears to have some independent effect on magnitudes of strife. One inference is that the index of this variable reflects tactical decisions to engage in strife as a means of goal attainment. The measure

of past levels of strife, 1946–1959, provides a partial test of what might be called the null hypotheses of human conflict, that the best predictor of future conflict is the level of past conflict.[43] The measure has relatively weak relationships with magnitude of strife measures for 1961–1965 and is an important mediating variable only among the causes of turmoil.

One striking finding is that nations' levels of persisting deprivation are consistently and directly related to their levels of strife. Deprivation attributable to such conditions as discrimination, political separatism, economic dependence, and religious cleavages tends to contribute at a relatively moderate but constant rate to civil strife whatever may be done to encourage, deter, or divert it, short only of removing its underlying conditions. One other result has important implications for theory, and also for policy, if it is supported by further research. The relation between coercive force size (the relative size of military and internal security forces) and the magnitude of civil violence is distinctly curvilinear: as the level of resources devoted to coercive forces increases, the magnitude of violence also tends to increase up to a certain point, and only at relatively high levels of coercive force does strife tend to decline. Moreover at the outer limit the relationship again tends to change direction; countries with the very largest coercive forces tend to have more strife than those with somewhat smaller forces. When one eliminates from analysis the countries that have experienced protracted internal or external conflict, the basic curvilinear relationship remains. The adage that force solves nothing seems supported; in fact force may make things worse.

6

A durable
generalization

A nontentative opinion about
"some tentative uniformities"

Crane Brinton is the person to whose memory this collection of works on revolution is dedicated. It would be doubtless polite and pseudopious enough to let things rest at that—to dedicate this collection to a pioneer and not to include anything he wrote. Readers might think his writing is by now surely outdated. The study of revolution has gained great momentum and exciting new techniques and also some new knowledge. And the new generation of social scientists appears to believe in its own unumbilicized gestation. Mere politeness would ill serve the study of revolution, but Brinton's mode and substance are not outdated.

The following selection is from that part, entitled "Some Tentative Uniformities," of the final chapter of Brinton's last (1965) edition of the book he first wrote in 1938. He first wrote before the inter- and intranational warfare that became worldwide in the 1940s and remained so a generation later. His work is still contemporary and likely to remain so for the unforeseeable future. This is asserted partly for the substance of what he says, and partly because he describes his conclusions as tentative. It is to be hoped that both apprentices and journeymen in the study of revolution in the 1970s will be as persistent and openminded in their search for knowledge by the year 2000 as Brinton has been in the nearly thirty years since he first turned his mind to the subject.

The reader of this book may have felt from time to time that either he or the authors were losing sight of the basics of revolutionary phenomena. Much of this feeling is falsely founded, because as a discipline develops, it, like an organism, becomes multicellular and complicated. Brinton is a healthy antidote for such uneasy feelings. He continued to stick to fundamentals and thereby to keep the study of revolution from wandering off into blind alleys or dry creek beds.

Eventually the study of the revolutionary state of mind, where it all begins anyhow, will lead directly to the fascinating study of the brain, including not just or primarily the cortex that is so highly developed in man but also the crucial midbrain, where signals from nerve receptors in the body are transmitted to the cortex and where signals from the cortex are transmitted to the body, causing it to act in sometimes violent ways. Such developments in knowledge are very likely to come to fruition during the next thirty years. In the interim, we continue to gain nourishment from

317

something first written more than thirty years ago and written of all things not by a social scientist in the conventional sense but by an unabashed historian.

A summary of revolutions

CRANE BRINTON

Reprinted with the permission of the author and Prentice-Hall, Inc. from Crane Brinton, *The Anatomy of Revolution*, © 1938, 1952, 1965 by Prentice-Hall, Inc., Englewood Cliffs, New Jersey, Vintage Books paperback edition, 1965, pp. 250–264.

I. SOME TENTATIVE UNIFORMITIES

WHEN all necessary concessions are made to those who insist that events in history are unique, it remains true that the four revolutions we have studied do display some striking uniformities. Our conceptual scheme of the fever can be worked out so as to bring these uniformities clearly to mind. We shall find it worth while, in attempting to summarize the work of these revolutions, to recapitulate briefly the main points of comparison on which our uniformities are based.

We must be very tentative about the prodromal symptoms of revolution. Even retrospectively, diagnosis of the four societies we studied was very difficult, and there is little ground for belief that anyone today has enough knowledge and skill to apply formal methods of diagnosis to a contemporary society and say, in this case revolution will or will not occur shortly. But some uniformities do emerge from a study of the old regimes in England, America, France, and Russia.

First, these were all societies on the whole on the upgrade economically before the revolution came, and the revolutionary movements seem to originate in the discontents of not unprosperous people who feel restraint, cramp, annoyance, rather than downright crushing oppression. Certainly these revolutions are not started by down-and-outers, by starving, miserable people. These revolutionists are not worms turning, not children of despair. These revolutions are born of hope, and their philosophies are formally optimistic.

Second, we find in our prerevolutionary society definite and indeed very bitter class antagonisms, though these antagonisms seem rather more complicated than the cruder Marxists will allow. It is not a case of feudal nobility against bourgeoisie in 1640, 1776, and 1789, or of bourgeoisie against proletariat in 1917. The strongest feelings seem generated in the bosoms of men—and women—who have made money, or at least who have enough to live on, and who contemplate bitterly the imperfections of a socially privileged aristocracy. Strong feelings, too, as James C. Davies suggests, are roused in those who find an intolerable gap between what they have come to want —their "needs"—and what they actually get. Revolutions seem more likely when social classes are fairly close together than when they are far apart. "Untouchables" very rarely revolt against a God-given aristocracy, and Haiti gives one of the few examples of successful slave revolutions. But rich merchants whose daughters can marry aristocrats are likely to feel that God is at least as interested in merchants as in aristocrats. It is difficult to say why the bitterness of feeling between classes *almost* equal socially seems so much stronger in some societies than others—why, for instance, a Marie Antoinette should be so much more hated in 18th-century France than a rich, idle, much publicized heiress in contemporary America; but at any rate the existence of such bitterness can be observed in our prerevolutionary societies, which is, clinically speaking, enough for the moment.

Third, there is what we have called the transfer of allegiance of the intellectuals. This is in some respects the most reliable of the symptoms we are likely to meet.

Here again we need not try to explain all the hows and whys, need not try to tie up this transfer of allegiance with a grand and complete sociology of revolutions. We need state simply that it can be observed in all four of our societies.

Fourth, the governmental machinery is clearly inefficient, partly through neglect, through a failure to make changes in old institutions, partly because new conditions —in the societies we have studied, pretty specifically conditions attendant on economic expansion and the growth of new monied classes, new ways of transportation, new business methods—these new conditions laid an intolerable strain on governmental machinery adapted to simpler, more primitive, conditions.

Fifth, the old ruling class—or rather, many individuals of the old ruling class— come to distrust themselves, or lose faith in the traditions and habits of their class, grow intellectual, humanitarian, or go over to the attacking groups. Perhaps a larger number of them than usual lead lives we shall have to call immoral, dissolute, though one cannot by any means be as sure about this as a symptom as about the loss of habits and traditions of command effective among a ruling class. At any rate, the ruling class becomes politically inept.

The dramatic events that start things moving, that bring on the fever of revolution, are in three of our four revolutions intimately connected with the financial administration of the state. In the fourth, Russia, the breakdown of administration under the burdens of an unsuccessful war is only in part financial. But in all our societies the inefficiency and inadequacy of the governmental structure of the society come out clearly in the very first stages of the revolution. There is a time—the first few weeks or months—when it looks as if a determined use of force on the part of the government might prevent the mounting excitement from culminating in an overthrow of the government. These governments attempted such a use of force in all four instances, and in all four their attempt was a failure. This failure indeed proved a

turning point during the first stages, and set up the revolutionists in power.

Yet one is impressed in all four instances more with the ineptitude of the governments' use of force than with the skill of their opponents' use of force. We are here speaking of the situation wholly from a military and police point of view. It may be that the majority of the people are discontented, loathe the existing government, wish it overthrown. Nobody knows. They don't commonly take plebiscites just *before* revolutions. In the actual clash—even Bastille Day, Concord, or the February Days in Petrograd—only a minority of the people is actively engaged. But the government hold over its own troops is poor, its troops fight half-heartedly or desert, its commanders are stupid, its enemies acquire a nucleus of the deserting troops or of a previous militia, and the old gives place to to new. Yet, such is the conservative and routine-loving nature of the bulk of human beings, so strong are habits of obedience in most of them, that it is almost safe to say that no government is likely to be overthrown from within its territory until it loses the ability to make adequate use of its military and police powers. That loss of ability may show itself in the actual desertion of soldiers and police to the revolutionists, or in the stupidity with which the government manages its soldiers and police, or in both ways.

The events we have grouped under the names of first stages do not of course unroll themselves in exactly the same order in time, or with exactly the same content, in all four of our revolutions. But we have listed the major elements—and they fall into a pattern of uniformities—financial breakdown, organization of the discontented to remedy this breakdown (or threatened breakdown), revolutionary demands on the part of these organized discontented, demands which if granted would mean the virtual abdication of those governing, attempted use of force by the government, its failure, and the attainment of power by the revolutionists. These revolutionists have hitherto been acting as an organized and nearly unanimous group, but with the attainment of power it is clear that they are not united. The group which dominates these first stages we call the moderates, though to emotional supporters of the old regime they look most immoderate. They are not always in a numerical majority in this stage—indeed it is pretty clear that if you limit the moderates to the Kadets they were not in a majority in Russia in February, 1917. But they seem the natural heirs of the old government, and they have their chance. In three of our revolutions they are sooner or later driven from office to death or exile. Certainly there is to be seen in England, France, and Russia a process in which a series of crises—some involving violence, street fighting, and the like—deposes one set of men and puts in power another and more radical set. In these revolutions power passes by violent or at least extralegal methods from Right to Left, until at the crisis period the extreme radicals, the complete revolutionists, are in power. There are, as a matter of fact, usually a few even wilder and more lunatic fringes of the triumphant extremists—but these are not numerous or strong and are usually suppressed or otherwise made harmless by the dominant radicals. It is therefore approximately true to say that power passes on from Right to Left until it reaches a limit usually short of the most extreme or lunatic Left.

The rule of the extremists we have called the crisis period. This period was not reached in the American Revolution, though in the treatment of Loyalists, in the pressure to support the army, in some of the phases of social life, you can discern in America many of the phenomena of the Terror as it is seen in our three other societies. We cannot here attempt to go into the complicated question as to why the American Revolution stopped short of a true crisis period, why the moderates were never ousted in this country, or at least ousted only in 1800. We must repeat that we are simply trying to establish certain uniformities of description, and are not attempting a complete sociology of revolutions.

The extremists are helped to power no doubt by the existence of a powerful pressure toward centralized strong government, something which in general the moderates are not capable of providing, while the extremists, with their discipline, their contempt for half measures, their willingness to make firm decisions, their freedom from libertarian qualms, are quite able and willing to centralize. Especially in France and Russia, where powerful foreign enemies threatened the very existence of the nation, the machinery of government during the crisis period was in part constructed to serve as a government of national defense. Yet though modern wars, as we know in this country, demand a centralization of authority, war alone does not seem to account for all that happened in the crisis period in those countries.

What does happen may be a bit over-simply summarized as follows: emergency centralization of power in an administration, usually a council or commission, and more or less dominated by a "strong man" —Cromwell, Robespierre, Lenin; government without any effective protection for the normal civil rights of the individual— or if this sounds unrealistic, especially for Russia, let us say the normal private life of the individual; setting up of extraordinary courts and a special revolutionary police to carry out the decrees of the government and to suppress all dissenting individuals or groups; all this machinery ultimately built up from a relatively small group—Independents, Jacobins, Bolsheviks—which has a monopoly on all governmental action. Finally, governmental action becomes a much greater part of all human action than in these societies in their normal condition: this apparatus of government is set to work indifferently on the mountains and molehills of human life—it is used to pry into and poke about corners normally reserved for priest or physician, or friends, and it is used to regulate, control, and plan the production and distribution of economic wealth on a national scale.

This pervasiveness of the Reign of Terror in the crisis period is partly explicable in terms of the pressure of war necessities and of economic struggles as well as of other variables: but it must probably also be explained as in part the manifestation of an effort to achieve intensely moral and religious ends here on earth. The little band of violent revolutionists who form the nucleus of all action during the Terror behave as men have been observed to behave before when under the influence of active religious faith. Independents, Jacobins, Bolsheviks, all sought to make all human activity here on earth conform to an ideal pattern, which like all such patterns, seems deeply rooted in their sentiments. A striking uniformity, in all these patterns is their asceticism or if you prefer, their condemnation of what we may call the minor as well as the major vices. Essentially, however, these patterns are a good deal alike, and all resemble closely what we may call conventional Christian ethics. Independents, Jacobins, and Bolsheviks, at least during the crisis period, really make an effort to enforce behavior in literal conformity with these codes or patterns. Such an effort means stern repression of much that many men have been used to regarding as normal; it means a kind of universal tension in which the ordinary individual can never feel protected by the humble routines to which he has been formed: it means that the intricate prerevolutionary network of customary interactions among individuals—a network which is still to the few men devoted to its intelligent study almost a complete mystery—this network is temporarily all torn apart. John Jones, the man in the street, the ordinary man, is left floundering.

We are almost at the point of being carried away into the belief that our conceptual scheme is something more than a mere convenience, that it does somehow describe "reality." At the crisis, the collective patient does seem helpless, thrashing his way through a delirium. But we must try to avoid the emotional, metaphorical appeal, and concentrate on making clear what seems to be the really important point here. Most of us are familiar with the favorite old Tory metaphor: the violent revolutionist tears down the noble edifice

society lives in, or burns it down, and then fails to build up another, and poor human beings are left naked to the skies. That is not a good metaphor, save perhaps for purpurposes of Tory propaganda. Even at the height of a revolutionary crisis period, more of the old building is left standing than is destroyed. But the whole metaphor of the building is bad. We may take instead an analogy from the human nervous system, or think of an immensely complicated gridwork of electrical communications. Society then appears as a kind of network of interactions among individuals, interactions for the most part fixed by habit, hardened and perhaps adorned as ritual, dignified into meaning and beauty by the elaborately interwoven strands of interaction we know as law, theology, metaphysics, and similar noble beliefs. Now sometimes many of these interwoven strands of noble beliefs, some even of those of habit and traditions, can be cut out, and other inserted. During the crisis period of our revolutions some such process seems to have taken place; but the whole network itself seems to have been altered suddenly and radically, and even the noble beliefs tend to fit into the network in the same places. If you kill off *all* the people who live within the network, you don't so much change the network of course as destroy it. This type of destruction is as yet rare in human history. Certainly in none of our revolutions was there even a very close approach to it.

What did happen, under the pressure of class struggle, war, religious idealism, and a lot more, was that the hidden and obscure courses which many of the interactions in the network follow were suddenly exposed, and passage along them made difficult in the unusual publicity and, so to speak, self-consciousness. The courses of other interactions were blocked, and the interactions went on with the greatest of difficulties by all sorts of detours. The courses of still other interactions were confused, short-circuited, paired off in strange ways. Finally, the pretensions of the fanatical leaders of the revolution involved the attempted creation of a vast number of new interactions.

Now though for the most part these new interactions affected chiefly those strands we have called the noble beliefs—law, theology, metaphysics, mythology, folklore, high-power abstractions in general—still some of them did penetrate at an experimental level into the obscurer and less dignified part of the network of interactions among human beings and put a further strain on it. Surely it is no wonder that under these conditions men and women in the crisis period should behave as they would not normally behave, that in the crisis period nothing should seem as it used to seem, that, indeed, a famous passage from Thucydides, written two thousand years before our revolutions, should seem like a clinical report:

When troubles had once begun in the cities, those who followed carried the revolutionary spirit further and further, and determined to outdo the report of all who had preceded them by the ingenuity of the enterprises and the atrocity of their revenges. The meaning of words had no longer the same relation to things, but was changed by them as they thought proper. Reckless daring was held to be loyal courage; prudent delay was the excuse of a coward; moderation was the disguise of unmanly weakness; to know everything was to do nothing. Frantic energy was the true quality of a man. A conspirator who wanted to be safe was a recreant in disguise. The lover of violence was always trusted, and his opponent suspected. He who succeeded in a plot was deemed knowing, but a still greater master in craft was he who detected one. On the other hand, he who plotted from the first to have nothing to do with plots was a breaker up of parties and a poltroon who was afraid of the enemy. In a word, he who could outstrip another in a bad action was applauded, and so was he who encouraged to evil one who had no idea of it. ... The tie of party was stronger than the tie of blood, because a partisan was more ready to dare without asking why.

With this we may put a quotation from a much humbler source, an obscure Siberian cooperative leader protesting against Red and White Terror alike. Mr. Chamberlin quotes:

And we ask and appeal to society, to the contending political groups and parties: When will our much-suffering Russia outlive the nightmare that is throttling it, when will deaths by violence cease? Doesn't horror seize you at the sight of the uninterrupted flow of human blood? Doesn't horror seize you at the consciousness that the deepest, most elementary bases of the existence of human society are perishing: the feeling of humanity, the consciousness of the value of life, of human personality, the feeling and consciousness of the necessity of legal order in the state? ... Hear our cry and despair: we return to prehistoric times of the existence of the human race; we are on the verge of the death of civilization and culture; we destroy the great cause of human progress, for which many generations of our worthier ancestors labored.

Certainly, however, none of our revolutions quite ended in the death of civilization and culture. The network was stronger than the forces trying to destroy or alter it, and in all of our societies the crisis period was followed by a convalescence, by a return to most of the simpler and more fundamental courses taken by interactions in the old network. More especially, the religious lust for perfection, the crusade for the Republic of Virtue, died out, save among a tiny minority whose actions could no longer take place directly in politics. An active, proselyting, intolerant, ascetic, chiliastic faith became fairly rapidly an inactive, conformist, worldly ritualistic faith.

The equilibrium has been restored and the revolution is over. But this does not mean that nothing has been changed. Some new and useful tracks or courses in the network of interactions that makes society have been established, some old and inconvenient ones —you may call them unjust if you like— have been eliminated. There is something heartless in saying that it took the French Revolution to produce the metric system and to destroy *lods et ventes* and similar feudal inconveniences, or the Russian Revolution to bring Russia to use the modern calendar and to eliminate a few useless letters in the Russian alphabet. These tangible and useful results look rather petty as measured by the brotherhood of man and the achievement of justice on this earth. The blood of the martyrs seems hardly necessary to establish decimal coinage.

Yet those who feel that revolution is heroic need not despair. The revolutionary tradition is an heroic one, and the noble beliefs which seem necessary to all societies are in our Western democracies in part a product of the revolutions we have been studying. They were initiated, even in Russia, by Peter Gay's "party of humanity." Our revolutions made tremendous and valuable additions to those strands in the network of human interactions which can be isolated as law, theology, metaphysics and, in the abstract sense, ethics. Had these revolutions never occurred, you and I might still beat our wives or cheat at cards or avoid walking under ladders, but we might not be able to rejoice in our possession of certain inalienable rights to life, liberty, and the pursuit of happiness, or in the comforting assurance that one more push will bring the classless society.

When one compares the whole course of these revolutions, certain tentative uniformities suggest themselves. If the Russian Revolution at the end of our series is compared with the English at its beginning, there seems to be a development of conscious revolutionary technique. This is of course especially clear since Marx made the history of revolutionary movements of the past a necessary preparation for revolutionists of the present. Lenin and his collaborators had a training in the technique of insurrection which Independents and Jacobins lacked. Robespierre seems almost a political innocent when his revolutionary training is compared with that of any good Bolshevik leader. Sam Adams, it must be admitted, seems a good deal less innocent. All in all, it is probable that this difference in the explicitness of self-conscious preparation for revolution, this growth of a copious literature of revolution, this increasing familiarity of revolutionary ideas, is not one of the very important uniformities we have to record. It is a conspicuous uniformity, but not an important one. Revolutions are still not a form of logical action. The Bolsheviks do not seem to have guided their actions by the "scientific" study of revolutions to an appreciably greater degree than the Independents or the Jacobins. They simply adapted an old technique to

the days of the telegraph and railroad trains.

This last suggests another conspicuous but not very important tendency in our four revolutions. They took place in societies increasingly influenced by the "Industrial Revolution," increasingly subject to those changes in scale which our modern conquests of time and space have brought to societies. Thus the Russian Revolution directly affected more people and more square miles of territory than any previous revolution; its sequence of events compresses into a few months what in England in the seventeenth century had taken years to achieve; in its use of the printing press, telegraph, radio, airplanes and the rest it seems, as compared with our other revolutions, definitely a streamlined affair. But again we may well doubt whether such changes of scale are in themselves really important factors. Men's desires are the same, whether they ride toward their achievement in airplanes or on horseback. Revolutions may be bigger nowadays, but surely not better. Our prophets of doom to the contrary notwithstanding, the loudspeaker does not change the words.

Finally, at the risk of being tedious, we must come back to some of the problems of methods in the social sciences which were suggested in our first chapter. We must admit that the theorems, the uniformities, which we have been able to put forward in terms of our conceptual scheme, are vague and undramatic. They are by no means as interesting or as alarming as the ideas of revolution held by the late George Orwell, who really believed that totalitarian revolutionary leaders have learned how to change human beings into something wholly different from their immediate predecessors. On the contrary, even Communist Russians begin to look more and more like—Russians. Our uniformities cannot be stated in quantitative terms, cannot be used for purposes of prediction or control. But at the very outset we warned the reader not to expect too much. Even such vague theorems as that of the transfer of allegiance of the intellectuals, that of the role of force in the first stages of revolution, that of the part played by "religious" enthusiasm in the period of crisis, that of the pursuit of pleasure during Thermidor, are, one hopes, not without value for the study of men in society. In themselves they amount to little, but they suggest certain possibilities in further work.

In the first place, by their very inadequacies they point to the necessity for a more rigorous treatment of the problems involved, challenging those who find them incomplete and unsatisfactory to do a better job. In the second place, they will serve the purpose of all first approximations in scientific work—they will suggest further study of the *facts*, especially in those fields where the attempt to make first approximations has uncovered an insufficient supply of the necessary facts. Notably here the facts for a study of class antagonisms are woefully inadequate. So, too, are the facts for a study of the circulation of the elite in prerevolutionary societies. But there are a hundred such holes, some of which can surely be filled. Our first approximations will then lead the way to another's second approximations. No scientist should ask more, even though the public does.

II. A PARADOX OF REVOLUTION

Wider uniformities will, to judge by the past of science, someday emerge from more complete studies of the sociology of revolutions. Here we dare not hazard much that we have not already brought out in the course of our analysis of four specific revolutions. After all, these are but four revolutions of what seems to be the same type, revolutions in what may be not too uncritically called the democratic tradition. So precious a word is "revolution" to many in that tradition, and especially to Marxists, that they indignantly refuse to apply it to such movements as the relatively bloodless but certainly violent and illegal assumption of power by Mussolini or Hitler. These movements, we are told, were not revolutions because they did not take power from one class and give it to another. Obviously

with a word in some ways as imprecise as "revolution" you can play all sorts of tricks like this. But for the scientific study of social change it seems wise to apply the word revolution to the overthrow of an established and legal parliamentary government by Fascists. If this is so, then our four revolutions are but one kind of revolution, and we must not attempt to make them bear the strain of generalizations meant to apply to all revolutions.

We need not, however, end on a note of blank skepticism. It would seem that there are, from the study of these revolutions, three major conclusions to be drawn: first, that, in spite of their undeniable and dramatic differences, they do present certain simple uniformities of the kind we have tried to bring together under our conceptual scheme of the fever; second, that they point sharply to the necessity of studying men's deeds and men's words without assuming that there is always a simple and logical connection between the two, since throughout their courses, and especially at their crises, they frequently exhibit men saying one thing and doing another; third, that they indicate that in general many things men do, many human habits, sentiments, dispositions, cannot be changed at all rapidly, that the attempt made by the extremists to change them by law, terror, and exhortation fails, that the convalescence brings them back not greatly altered.

Yet one hesitant major generalization binding all four of these revolutions together may here be made from many anticipations earlier in this book. These four revolutions exhibit an increasing scale of promises to the "common man"—promises as vague as that of complete "happiness" and as concrete as that of full satisfaction of all material wants, with all sorts of pleasant revenges on the way. Communism is but the present limit of this increasing set of promises. It is not for us here to rail or protest, but simply to record. So far, these promises in their extreme form have been fulfilled nowhere. That they are made at all offends the traditional Christian, the humanist, perhaps even the man of common sense. But they are made, more vigorously perhaps today in China, in Southeast Asia, in the Near East, wherever Communism is still a young, fresh, and active faith. It is not enough for us Americans to repeat that the promises are impossible of fulfillment, and ought not to be made. It would be folly for us to tell the world that we Americans can fill these promises, especially since we have not filled them at home. Revolution is not a fever that will yield to such innocent and deceptive remedies. For a time, at least, we must accept it as being as incurable as cancer.

As to what the experience of a great revolution does to the society that experiences it, we cannot conclude here too widely without trespassing on wider fields of history and sociology. Yet it does seem that the patient emerges stronger in some respects from the conquered fever, immunized in this way and that from attacks that might be more serious. It is an observable fact that in all our societies there was a flourishing, a peak of varied cultural achievements, after the revolutions. Certainly we may not moralize too much about the stupidities and cruelties of revolutions, may not lift up our hands in horror. It is quite possible that wider study would show that feeble and decadent societies do not undergo revolutions, that revolutions are, perversely, a sign of strength and youth in societies.

One quiet person emerges from his study, not indeed untouched by a good deal of horror and disgust, but moved also with admiration for a deep and unfathomable strength in men which, because of the softer connotations of the word, he is reluctant to call spiritual. Montaigne saw and felt it long ago:

> I see not one action, or three, or a hundred, but a commonly accepted state of morality so unnatural, especially as regards inhumanity and treachery, which are to me the worst of all sins, that I have not the heart to think of them without horror; and they excite my wonder almost as much as my detestation. *The practice of these egregious villainies has as much the mark of strength and vigor of soul as of error and disorder.*

Berkman the anarchist, who loathed the Russian Revolution, tells a story which may represent merely his own bias, but which may nonetheless serve as a brief symbolical conclusion to this study. Berkman says he asked a good Bolshevik acquaintance during the period of attempted complete communization under Lenin why the famous Moscow cabmen, the *izvoschiks*, who continued in diminished numbers to flit about Moscow and to get enormous sums in paper roubles for their services, were not nationalized like practically everything else. The Bolshevik replied, "We found that if you don't feed human beings they continue to live somehow. But if you don't feed the horses, the stupid beasts die. That's why we don't nationalize the cabmen." That is not an altogether cheerful story, and in some ways one may regret the human capacity to live without eating. But clearly if we were as stupid—or as sensible—as horses we should have no revolutions.

An elemental bibliography

How individuals and societies meet the challenge of change

The sixteenth-century Protestant Reformation

A. G. DICKENS, 1967. *Martin Luther and the Reformation.* New York: Harper and Row Perennial Library paperback. A short, psychologically sensitive analysis of the first great modern revolution and revolutionary.

DESIDERIUS ERASMUS, (1509) 1958. *The Praise of Folly* (translated 1668 by John Wilson). Ann Arbor: The University of Michigan Press paperback. A fresh, frank, and optimistic plea for acknowledging the libido as a natural and healthy fact. This polemic helps explain what it was in the medieval world that people were so determined to abandon. Prescient of the 18th-century optimism that came before the French Revolution, and arguably of 20th-century "Freudianism."

ERIK H. ERIKSON, (1958) 1962. *Young Man Luther.* New York: Norton. Very insightful on Luther's mental crises and growth, helping explain how this theological reactionary became the first great modern political revolutionary.

PRESERVED SMITH, 1913. "Luther's Early Development in the Light of Psycho-analysis," *American Journal of Psychology,* 24: 360–377. An early effort by an historian to apply psychoanalysis to Luther's family background and other experiences that shaped him.

The French Revolution of 1789

RALPH W. GREENLAW, ed., 1958. *The Economic Origins of the French Revolution.* Boston: D. C. Heath. A very useful collection of essays.

GEORGES LEFEBVRE, (1939) 1960. *The Coming of the French Revolution.* New York: Vintage. After Tocqueville's *Old Régime and the French Revolution,* excerpted in these readings, Lefebvre's succinct socioeconomic analysis is the next best starting place.

The American Civil War

W. J. CASH, (1941) 1954. *The Mind of the South.* New York: Anchor Books and Vintage Books. A classic study of the life, values, and actions of America's neofeudal old regime, which bears comparison with powerful old regimes in other eras and cultures.

ROBERT R. RUSSEL, 1924. *Economic Aspects of Southern Sectionalism: 1840–1861.* Urbana: University of Illinois Press. An excellent economic analysis of the pre-Civil War South, demonstrating the very rapid growth of that economy before the war.

The Russian Revolution of 1917

NIKITA KHRUSHCHEV, 1956. *The Crimes of the Stalin Era* (Speech to the Twentieth Party Congress in Moscow, February 1956). New York: The New Leader. One of the most awesome indictments and confessions of violence ever made by any office-holding chief of state anywhere at any time in history. The speech marked the end of the great Russian Revolution, whose violent phase began 51 years before, on Bloody Sunday in January 1905 at the Tsar's Winter Palace.

FRANCO VENTURI, (1952) 1966. *Roots of Revolution: A History of the Populist and Socialist Movements in Nineteenth-Century Russia.* New York: Grosset and Dunlap paperback. A study of the "going to the people" movement among Russian upperclass intellectuals that (negatively and positively) had so much to do with the style of revolution in Russia.

EDMUND WILSON, (1940) 1953. *To the Finland Station.* New York: Anchor Books. An interweaving of personalities and social forces in European and Russian history. Psychologically sensitive analyses of Marx, Engels, Lenin, and Trotsky show how their early experiences helped shape their later intense but different styles of revolutionary thought and action. Lacks the solid sociology of Masaryk's *Spirit of Russia,* briefly excerpted in this reader; otherwise superb.

BERTRAM D. WOLFE, (1948) 1960. *Three Who Made a Revolution.* Boston: Beacon Press. Masterful treatment of the conditions that acted on Lenin, Trotsky, and Stalin as they faced first the old regime and then the revolution they helped to shape.

The Spanish Civil War of 1936–1939

GERALD BRENAN, (1943) 1962. *The Spanish Labyrinth.* Cambridge: Cambridge University Press. A classic, balanced, and detailed historical explanation for the Spanish violence, probing deep into the past and into Spanish culture.

HUGH THOMAS, 1961. *The Spanish Civil War.* New York: Harper. Excellent in emphasizing the tensions and frustrations in all segments of Spanish society as these contributed to the savagery of the conflict.

The Nazi Revolution of 1933

THEODORE ABEL, (1938) 1966. *The Nazi Movement: Why Hitler Came to Power.* New York: Atherton. With short biographies that Abel gathered from people who joined the Nazi movement before 1933, telling why they did so, he does a rhetoric-free job of explaining the mental origins.

ALAN BULLOCK, (1952) 1961. *Hitler: A Study in Tyranny.* New York: Bantam Books. A careful study of Hitler's childhood and young manhood, to which Abel's book is a good companion piece.

ADOLF HITLER, 1943. *Mein Kampf.* Boston: Houghton–Mifflin. If modern readers can so identify with Hitler in reading this dull book as to understand how he became what he did, they may thereby lessen the likelihood of their becoming the same.

DAVID SCHOENBAUM, (1966) 1967. *Hitler's Social Revolution: Class and Status in Nazi Germany, 1933–1939.* Garden City: Anchor Books. Helps explain the strong hold that Nazism had even on those who had not joined up before 1933.

GUSTAV STOLPER, 1940. *The German Economy, 1870–1940.* New York: Reynal and Hitchcock. A source of economic indicators, from the imperial to the Nazi periods.

The Nazi concentration camps

ELIE A. COHEN, 1953. *Human Behavior in the Concentration Camp.* New York: Grosset and Dunlap Universal Library. A cool analysis of the mostly depoliticizing effects of living on the cutting edge of survival, by a participant-observer at Mauthausen. Helps explain the overt calm and covert tension of a polity in which the oppressed are unheard of and—even when seen in day-to-day contact—unlistened to. There are polities other than concentration camps which this book helps explain.

VIKTOR E. FRANKL, (1959) 1963. *Man's Search for Meaning.* New York: Washington Square Press. A study of the relationship between shock, degradation, physical deprivation, and hope in Auschwitz, again by a participant-observer. Like Cohen's book, this shows the style of political inactivity of those concerned with survival.

JEAN-FRANCOIS STEINER, (1966) 1967. *Treblinka.* New York: Simon and Schuster. This book contains information on the primitive, tenacious efforts to establish a working opposition group that in time produced an overt revolt. Of central relevance in understanding roots of revolution.

The Chinese Revolution of 1949

JEROME CH'ÊN, 1965. *Mao and the Chinese Revolution.* London: Oxford University Press. A calm but warm appraisal of how both Chiang Kai-shek and Mao Tse-tung were shaped by and shaped the modernization process in antique China.

CHIEN-NUNG LI, (1948) 1956. *The Political History of China: 1840–1928* (translated by Ssu-yu Teng and Jeremy Ingalls). Princeton: Van Nostrand. An introduction to China's traumatic, inexorable introduction to the modern world. Sometimes dull, it is nevertheless scrutable, about a culture deemed inscrutable because it has never been really scrutinized.

EDGAR SNOW, (1938) 1961. *Red Star over China.* New York: Grove Press paperback (newly revised edition by Grove Press, 1968). The most explanatory book I know of for anyone beginning a study of the Chinese Revolution.

C. K. YANG, (1959) 1965. *Chinese Communist Society: The Family and the Village.* Cambridge: M.I.T. Press paperback. A successful effort to describe two ancient Chinese institutions—the extended family and the encapsulated village—and how these institutions and the Communist revolution changed each other.

Miscellany

K. O. L. BURRIDGE, 1954. "Cargo Cult Activity in Tangu (New Guinea)," *Oceania*, 24: 241–254. A good companion piece to read with the selection in this reader from Mannoni. Describes nativist movements developing after contact with Europeans, with a motivation of injured self-esteem.

SIGMUND FREUD, 1925. *An Autobiographical Study.* London: Hogarth. This brief autobiography invites comparison with the studies already mentioned of the lives of Luther, Lenin, Trotsky, *et al.* and thereby raises the question why Freud was so apolitical a revolutionary.

JAMES H. MEISEL, 1966. *Counter-revolution.* New York: Atherton. A brilliant and sensitive set of reminiscences and essays about people who have been involved in the 16th-century English Puritan, French, and Nazi Revolutions and the Spanish Civil War.

Some general theory

LEONARD BERKOWITZ, 1962. *Aggression: A Social Psychological Analysis.* New York: McGraw-Hill. A very clear-headed and scholarly summary of theory and research on the psychologically most central phenomenon in revolution.

JAMES C. DAVIES, 1963. *Human Nature in Politics*. New York: John Wiley. A general but centrally relevant statement of this editor's views of how people act politically and why they sometimes revolt.

HARRY ECKSTEIN, 1965. "On the Etiology of Internal Wars," in George H. Nadel, ed., *Studies in the Philosophy of History*, New York: Harper Torchbooks, pp. 117–147. A sharply, sagely critical summary of theorizing on revolution.

LYFORD P. EDWARDS, 1927. *The Natural History of Revolution*. Chicago: University of Chicago Press. An early and still relevant effort to establish a general theory.

ANNA FREUD, (1936) 1946. *The Ego and the Mechanisms of Defense*. New York: International Universities Press. A pioneering work on the genesis of displacing one's aggression. Therefore a pioneering book for understanding why one becomes a revolutionary, a conformist, or a mere observer of political processes.

SIGMUND FREUD, (1923) 1927. *The Ego and the Id*. London: Hogarth. As succinct and clear a presentation of Freud's basic views as I know of. Freudians more orthodox than Freud may have other suggestions for the best approach to Freud's basic thought. The relationships between needs and their control by the reasoning powers is relevant here.

JAMES A. GESCHWENDER, 1968. "Explorations in the Theory of Social Movements and Revolutions," *Social Forces*, 47: 127–135. A synthesizing of various social psychological concepts into a theory.

LOUIS GOTTSCHALK, 1944. "Causes of Revolution," *American Journal of Sociology*, 50: 1–8. A still-relevant early theoretical synthesis.

TED GURR, 1968. "Psychological Factors in Civil Violence," *World Politics*, 20: 245–278. Emphasizes the centrality of frustration and aggression to civil violence and outlines some of the measurable indicators.

TED ROBERT GURR, 1970. *Why Men Rebel*. Princeton: Princeton University Press. A thoroughgoing analysis and synthesis of the sociopsychological theory and data bearing on the causes of civil strife.

REX D. HOPPER, 1950. "The Revolutionary Process," *Social Forces*, 28: 270–279. A successful early effort to analyze successive stages of revolution in sociological and psychological terms. Comparable to the essay by David C. Schwartz published in this reader.

CHALMERS JOHNSON, 1966. *Revolutionary Change*. Boston: Little, Brown. A somewhat hasty but provocative synthesis, burdened a bit by polysyllabilitis. It induces thought.

KONRAD LORENZ, (1963) 1967. *On Aggression*. New York: Bantam Books. Aggression here becomes virtually synonymous with all assertive interaction between people and other animals. An object lesson in the relationship between one intellectual mood at a particular time in history (the troubled mid-20th century) and a slipshod thesis that fits the mood, which now concludes man is innately aggressive.

ROLLO MAY, 1950. *The Meaning of Anxiety*. New York: Ronald Press. In the succession from Sigmund Freud and his daughter Anna, and with a theoretical assist from Soren Kierkegaard, this book is a major psychological landmark in the development of knowledge of mental tension.

WILBERT E. MOORE, 1964. "Predicting Discontinuities in Social Change," *American Sociological Review*, 29: 331–338. A relevant sociological theory.

GEORGE S. PETTEE, 1938. *The Process of Revolution*. New York: Harper. Noteworthy for its elaboration of the problem of "cramp" as an antecedent of revolution. In the same family of writings as Sorokin and Edwards that are cited in this section.

DONALD G. RIDKER, 1962. "Discontent and Economic Growth," *Economic Development and Cultural Change*, 11: 1–15. An interesting combination of psychological and economic theorizing.

PITIRIM A. SOROKIN, 1925. *The Sociology of Revolution*. Philadelphia: J. B. Lippincott. Like Edwards' *Natural History* above, this book was far ahead of its time in comprehensive theorizing. Despite a contentious tone and inelegant writing, a brilliant book.

DAVID WILLER and GEORGE K. ZOLLSCHAN, 1964. "Prolegomenon to a Theory of Revolutions," in G. K. Zollschan and W. Hirsch, eds., *Explorations in Social Change*. New York: Houghton–Mifflin, pp. 125–151. Emphasizes the structural aspects of revolutionary causation, in contrast to functional or more exactly psychological aspects.

ANTHONY F. C. WALLACE, 1956. "Revitalization Movements," *American Anthropologist*, 58: 264–281. Synthesizes biological, neural, individual, and social systems as these work together in producing demands by individuals for basic changes in society.

Some mental and social antecedents of revolution

EDWARD C. BANFIELD, 1958. *The Moral Basis of a Backward Society*. Glencoe: The Free Press. The author describes the war of each family against every family in a poor society and hints at the war of each individual against every individual which inhibits the development of a national political community. Compare Wylie's study of a French village, below.

EUCLIDES DA CUNHA, (1902) 1957. *Rebellion in the Backlands*. Chicago: University of Chicago Press paperback. An absorbing study of an almost completely uncontrived, spontaneous poor people's rebellion in Brazil in the last decade of the 19th century.

FRANTZ FANON, (1961) 1968. *The Wretched of the Earth*. Grove Press paperback. Helps explain, from analysis of the Algerian-French conflict that ended in 1958, the self-confidence and other feelings that people achieve from violence. It thus helps explain how revolutions grow.

J. R. FEAGIN and P. B. SHEATSLEY, 1968, "Ghetto Resident Appraisals of a Riot," *Public Opinion Quarterly*, 32: 352–362. With interview data from participants, argues that they view riot as a protest against social and economic inequality.

R. M. FOGELSON, 1967. "White on Black: A Critique of the McCone Commission Report on the Los Angeles Riots," *Political Science Quarterly*, 82: 337–367. Presents data radically denying the notion that rioters are only the riff-raff of ghetto society.

HUGH DAVIS GRAHAM and TED ROBERT GURR, eds., 1969. *The History of Violence in America*. New York: New American Library Signet Book. A variegated collection of historical and systematic essays on the roots of violence. Prepared for the National Commission on the Causes and Prevention of Violence.

C. L. R. JAMES, (1938) 1963. *The Black Jacobins*. New York: Vintage Books. An historical study of the successful revolt of slaves in Haiti against French colonial rule, 1791–1803. Bears comparison with J.-F. Steiner's *Treblinka* as an awesome upsurge of the heavily oppressed.

GUSTAVE LE BON, (1896) 1960. *The Crowd*. New York: Viking. A sensitive if hostile analysis of group behavior after revolution gets underway.

ELTON B. MCNEIL, 1959. "Psychology and Aggression," *Journal of Conflict Resolution*, 3: 195–293. Relates family life and the learning process to the kind of response individuals make to frustration.

BARRINGTON MOORE, JR., 1966. *Social Origins of Dictatorship and Democracy: Lord and Peasant in the Making of the Modern World*. Boston: Beacon Press. A complicated, almost encyclopedic, and very antitheoretical analysis of the interaction of land use, social habits, and people making the long transition from rural feudalism to urban industrial society.

THOMAS F. PETTIGREW, 1967. "Social Evaluation Theory: Consequences and Applications," in David Levine, ed., *Nebraska Symposium on Motivation*. Lincoln: University of Nebraska Press, pp. 241–315. A synthesis of research and theory relative to how individuals see themselves in the eyes of others. If self-esteem is indeed not separable from others' esteem of self, then this is a major contribution. It applies to the Black Rebellion of the 1960s and to the mental outlook of potential revolutionaries, anywhere and any time.

GEORGE RUDÉ, 1964. *The Crowd in History: A Study of Popular Disturbances in France and England, 1730–1848*. New York: John Wiley. An excellent, civilized blend of history, theory, and quantitative data about how crowds have helped shape revolutions.

EDGAR A. SCHULER, 1944. "The Houston Race Riot, 1917," *Journal of Negro History*, 29: 300–338. History of a race riot, describing the conditions that preceded it.

RAYMOND TANTER and MANUS MIDLARSKY, 1967. "A Theory of Revolution," *Journal of Conflict Resolution* 11: 264–280. An ingenious integration of theory and quantitative data, on sociopsychological foundations.

T. M. TOMLINSON, 1968. "The Development of a Riot Ideology among Urban Negroes," *American Behavioral Scientist*, 11: 27–31 (March–April 1968). Concise summary of characteristics and opinions of participants in the 1965 riots in Los Angeles.

DANIEL WALKER, ed., 1968. *Rights in Conflict*. New York: New American Library Signet Book. The report to the National Commission on the Causes and Prevention of Violence on the rioting by demonstrators and by police during the 1968 Democratic Party convention in Chicago. Like Fogelson's article above, a healthy antidote for those who believe rioting is what the "rabble" do.

LAURENCE WYLIE, (1957) 1964. *Village in the Vaucluse*. New York: Harper & Row paperback. A study of a French village. Helps explain the isolation of individuals and therefore the fragmentation of local communities that keep weak the political structure of a nation.

How some social scientists have combined theory and research

HADLEY CANTRIL, (1941) 1963. *The Psychology of Social Movements*. New York: John Wiley. An early and still classic study of social movements varying from lunch mobs to Nazism.

HADLEY CANTRIL, 1958. *The Politics of Despair.* New York: Basic Books. A study of the appeal of the Communist Party in France and Italy after the Second World War, making it the principal continuing party of opposition rather than the party of revolution in these countries.

HADLEY CANTRIL, 1965. *The Pattern of Human Concerns.* New Brunswick: Rutgers University Press. With elaborate data from at least thirteen nations, this work is a major source of facts and inferences about stirrings within people that may lead them to revolt.

CHALMERS A. JOHNSON, 1962. *Peasant Nationalism and Communist Power: The Emergence of Revolutionary China, 1937–1945.* Stanford: Stanford University Press. An excellent, very durable study of China in its late prerevolutionary period, making bloodily clear the great and savage contribution that the Chinese National and Japanese occupying armies made toward the Maoist victory.

ALEXANDER H. LEIGHTON, 1945. *The Governing of Men.* Princeton: Princeton University Press. A clinical history of rebellion in American detention camps for Japanese during the Second World War, as observed by a psychiatrically trained anthropologist.

ROBERT JAY LIFTON, 1961. *Thought Reform and the Psychology of Totalism: A Study of "Brainwashing" in China.* New York: Norton. An awesome, awful, Faustian soul-probing of what happens in mental laundries. May give some clues as to the conversion processes in earlier times, during the 16th-century Reformation and Counter-reformation and the 20th-century purges in the Soviet Union, Hungary, and elsewhere.

SEYMOUR MARTIN LIPSET, 1959. "Some Social Requisites of Democracy," *American Political Science Review*, 53: 69–105. This article pioneered in the search for indicators of social development, thereby much hastening the conceptualization and measurement of change.

DAVID C. McCLELLAND, 1961. *The Achieving Society.* Princeton: Van Nostrand. Updates and should upstage Max Weber's synecdoche, *The Protestant Ethic and the Spirit of Capitalism*, because it goes deeper into the forces that push toward modernization than any religious framework of institutions.

ROBERT W. McCOLL, 1967. "A Political Geography of Revolution: China, Vietnam, and Thailand," *Journal of Conflict Resolution*, 11: 153–167. Relates technical use of land position and communication links to revolution.

D. L. MEIER and W. BELL, 1959. "Anomia and Differential Access to the Achievement of Life Goals," *American Sociological Review*, 24: 189–202. Finds a positive relationship between anomia and denial of access to life goals.

CHARLES TILLY, (1964) 1967. *The Vendée.* New York: John Wiley paperback. Until Tilly, the incongruous revolution against the French Revolution in Northern France was too conveniently ignored. He heeds it and thereby tests general principles about revolution.

R. S. WEINERT, 1966. "Violence in Pre-modern Societies: Rural Colombia," *American Political Science Review*, 60: 340–347. An excellent consideration of factors other than frustration (including economic deprivation) that produced violence in Colombia. Emphasizes the breakdown of authority patterns between the former rural-dominated and now urban-dominated society.

Notes

The threat of abandonment

by O. MANNONI

1. *Solo*, in Malagasy, means substitute.

2. This verticalization of ties, with the projection of the father-image on a "patron," has often had a harmful influence and frustrated measures which might otherwise have served a useful purpose, but the reason for their failure has not been understood. Here is an example. There has been a considerable development of trade unionism of recent years in Madagascar, and this should have led to progress in psychological growth through the development of a sense of responsibility and social and occupational unity. Unfortunately the Malagasies have always chosen to lead their unions, not the men best able to protect their interests, but the "notables" most likely to exercise paternalist authority, and prone to make use of trade union activity for their own gain—which fails to shock the majority of union members. The need for dependence has almost always hindered (and even halted) the development of a real trade union spirit, and has thus deprived the Malagasies of almost all the psychological and moral benefits they might have derived from this activity. And, as usual, this experience doubles the tasks for the future; what might have been achieved without great difficulty by starting from nought and taking account of the psychological situation, can now be achieved only after a painful effort of correction has first been made.

3. A. Hesnard, in *Freud dans la Société d'après-guerre* (p. 78) says: "There is an astonishing disproportion between the childhood events which appear from the affective history of the individual to have been pathogenic, and these same events as they were in reality, that is to say on the scale and in the proportion in which they were seen by the adults who participated in or witnessed them. . . . The poisoning of entire lives by a terrible social inferiority complex . . . is thus often due to some stupid and vulgar admonition by a parent who, when questioned about the traumatic event, no longer even remembered it, so childishly unimportant did it seem."

This, no doubt, is what Künkel means by "betrayal."

4. There is a description of the behavior of the "inferior" European in Adler's *The Neurotic Constitution*. The inferior person develops a cult of means by which to attain the end he desires. He endeavors to be different from others in order to feel superior. He feels he is a martyr to his own demands. The Malagasy respects forms, desires no superiority, and does not make himself a martyr.

5. What he lacks is a certain development of the superego. His conscience remains attached to the persons in whom authority resides, to their edicts, and the social customs. He has not what the philosophers would call an "autonomous" moral authority: dependence excludes autonomy. E. Cailliet, in his *Essai sur la psychologie du Hova*, noted these psychological traits (pp. 26–31), but without analyzing them.

6. See G. Berthier, *Note sur les coutumes du peuple malgache*, p. 26 (concern for politeness in replies).

7. For further details, see Berthier, *ibid.*, p. 89. The fortune revealed by divination is somehow identified with the will of the ancestors.

8. This failure is a good example of those false verifications by experience which are so frequently met with in the study of interracial relations.

To all appearances, in fact, these Europeanized Malagasies differ from Europeans proper only by the racial characteristics determined by their genetic stock, the most obvious of these being the color of the skin. Thus it appears that the conditions are present for a verification by the "method of difference" as conceived by inductive logic. The difference in skin-color is enough, in fact, for the European colonial society to refuse to receive these evolved natives into its midst (though it finds room for them in the administration). The Malagasy reacts to these difficulties with symptoms of inferiority, a need for compensation, feelings of abandonment, and so on. But his reaction is taken by the European for a racial characteristic, and racialism, which was at first spontaneous, becomes deliberate, and claims to be based on impartial observation. Typical Malagasies, for their part, noticing what happens to Europeanized Malagasies, draw their conclusions too. Thus, paradoxically, the more "civilized" the colonial inhabitants become, the greater is the awareness on both sides of irremovable racial differences. These differences acquire exactly the importance attributed to them. Seen in this light, our old claim that we wanted to assimilate the Malagasies seems somewhat hypocritical, since in fact we denied them social assimilation. We may conclude that but for this hypocrisy assimilation would have been perfectly possible. But there is no doubt today that as a result of new unconscious convictions, this possibility has quite disappeared.

9. Malagasies today are very anxious to learn from us.

10. There are only traces—recognizable ones, however—of totemism in Madagascar. It would be arbitrary to consider them as survivals of an earlier system; we do not know. Here are some examples: among the Merina, certain families pass on *fady* (taboos) connected with various animal species. There are personal *fady* like those of the King Andrianampoinimerina connected with the dog. The dog then acquired a new name —*alika* instead of *amboa*. The ox appears to have been *fady* at one time; it is said that a king, half-legendary, removed this *fady* some centuries ago. The Tandroy, who are rather backward inhabitants of the south of Madagascar, commit suicide when they lose an ox they were fond of. Other tribes take for their ancestors lemurs or crocodiles. The commonest word for lemurs is *babakoto*, which means something like ancestor-child.

This assimilation of the image of the child with that of the ancestor can also be found in the unconscious of the European, where, indeed, it was first discovered by psychoanalysis. See Ernest Jones, *Papers on Psycho-Analysis* (3rd ed., 1923), Chapters XXXVIII and XXXIX.

11. Since this book was written, Mr. H. F. Hanneman has published an interesting article in the *Monde non chrétien* (and also in the *International Review of Missions*), called "Le culte du cargo en Nouvelle-Guinée." It shows how the image of the white man, in the eyes of

the Papuans, coincides with that of the *Tibud*— the ancestor-gods.

In his introduction to this article Maurice Leenhardt says: ". . . The Oceanians often place the paradise which is inhabited by their dead on an island they name and which they say is beyond the horizon. That of the people of Buka was called Sune. When, once a month, a ship from Sydney brought goods for trading, the natives went on board, bought freely, and delighted in all the possibilities of wealth laid out before them. One day a captain forbade them to come on board. This caused discontent among them, protests, and finally a revolt, which the administration feared it might have to quell by force of arms. Everything became clear when it was discovered that the natives, who had confused the names Sune, their paradise, and Sydney, believed that the monthly steamer and its cargo were a miraculous gift from the ancestors and that the ancestors themselves had come in the form of white men. They went on board because they felt at home there. But they could no longer see the white man as god-ancestor when he suddenly became unkind."

There is no doubt, as we shall see from Part III, Chapter V, that in a certain way white men are the ancestors. There are two observations I should like to make in connexion with the above text.

(1) Confusion of the names Sune and Sydney is not the real explanation of what happened, for it would apply only to the people of Buka, whereas the same attitude towards the whites and their cargoes is found in places where no such confusion of names is possible. That explanation is purely coincidental, therefore. The true explanation would show that the people of Buka were *prepared* to make this confusion by their general behavior as Melanesians.

(2) My second and more serious comment is that the mythical explanation is probably accidental also. The myth, like the confusion of Sune with Sydney, is a story offered by the Papuans to justify an attitude they adopt spontaneously and unconsciously, following upon the transference to the white man of deep feelings they had earlier transferred to their dead. This is easy to prove because the transference and this attitude are much more widespread than the myth. It is recognizably the attitude described by the observers quoted by Lévy-Bruhl; it is the attitude of typical Malagasies, though they would indignantly deny it or burst out laughing if anyone suggested to them that the white men were ancestors!

Mythologists think that myths are beliefs, but real beliefs are situated at a greater depth; they are the fundamental and vital attitudes of which myths are merely the reflection in the imagination: they indicate the beliefs in the way a dream might indicate psychological structure.

A mythologist reading this might think it a pity that we had not been able to find an ancient myth to explain Malagasies' present behavior. But it would be a waste of time to look for one, and even if one were to be found, it would explain nothing, but would, on the contrary, itself require explanation in terms of the deeper psychological attitudes indicated by this behavior, which psychoanalysis is able to elucidate. Otherwise we should be obliged to admit, what is absurd, that the incarnation of the ancestors by white men is an unconscious myth of the Malagasies! To the psychologist these transference reactions are elementary phenomena; the myths with which they may be embellished are purely accidental. Analysis reveals the fundamental beliefs.

It would be interesting to know how the people of Buka reacted when they were told that Sydney was not Sune, and what happened to the transference thereafter.

There is a third point which I shall refrain from commenting on because it will be cleared up later in this book; it is the difficulty of explaining why the natives should have revolted against the ancestors, in the form of white men, when they ceased being kindly—as if the dead could not prove fearsome without provoking immediate rebellion!

12. It must also be remembered that the elements which come into contact with each other first are in one way or another the most "eccentric." They would have had less chance of meeting had they been more firmly held within their respective social structures. This fact no doubt explains the exaggerated character of the acts of dependent behavior noted by the observers whom Lévy-Bruhl quotes and which I referred to earlier. The exaggeration seems to be due to a state of dissatisfaction which aggravates the hunger for dependence.

13. One of many examples of these beliefs may be found in *Notes, Reconnaissances et Explorations*, Antananarivo, 1897, 2nd vol., p. 196.

14. *Vazaha* has recently acquired a pejorative sense. After the revolt, the *boto* at the hotel where I used to dine in Antananarivo took to calling me *Rangahy*, which is the word used to address a Malagasy as "sir." Surprised by this new form of address, I looked for an explanation; it was a way of telling me that they were not confusing me with the colonialists.

15. That is the impression invariably produced on a personality psychologically dependent by a personality psychologically inferior.

16. For instance, one of the Antananarivo hotels, two steps from police headquarters and with a self-propelled gun almost on its doorstep, obtained for its defense two machine-guns which were entrusted to the residents. (They were sorely needed on the east coast where the colonials were beleaguered.) Armed Senegalese soldiers mounted guard outside the rooms of the officers' wives. Hotel residents, armed, patrolled the town. These patrols served no purpose, for there was no sign of real danger, nor did any ever arise in the town. The danger, at that moment, was over a hundred miles away. But the significant point is that two months later, when the rebellion had spread as a result of repressive measures which roused uncertain terror everywhere, danger in fact drew near to Antananarivo. Then, the European inhabitants of the town recovered their calm completely and behaved with normal good sense. What better proof could there be of the purely emotional character—to say no more—of the earlier reactions?

National independence

by O. MANNONI

1. On the *tody*, see Cailliet, *Essai sur la psychologie du Hova* (from Andriamifidy: *Ny Hevitra Malagasy, in Ny Mpanolo Tsaina*, Antananarivo, 1905, p. 206). Compare the meanings of the roots of the words *ody* and *tody* and their derivatives, in P. Malzac's Malagasy dictionary.

2. See Part III, Chapter IV.

3. It is these borrowings which give colonial movements having no real connection with each other a superficial resemblance.

4. The trial of the leaders has taken place since these pages were written, but in conditions such that no acceptable proof of their guilt has been brought forward. Nothing has become clear, except that the investigation was mishandled from the start. This can be said because the chairman of the tribunal has admitted it in as much as he has ignored the preliminary examination. The judgment given has been accepted in official circles, especially in its political implications, as a remedial measure rather than as a sentence.

Riots and rioters

by GEORGE WADA
AND JAMES C. DAVIES

1. "Anti-Communist Mob Action: a Case Study," *Public Opinion Quarterly*, XII (1948), pp. 57–67.

2. For the evacuation as a whole, see J. ten Broek, E. N. Barnhart, and F. W. Matson, *Prejudice, War, and the Constitution* (Berkeley and Los Angeles: University of California Press, 1954), Chapter 3, "The History of the Evacuation."

3. See D. S. Thomas and R. Nishimoto, *The Spoilage* (Berkeley and Los Angeles: University of California Press, 1946), pp. 49–52, for a discussion of the incident based on a report by

one of its proposed victims. The above summary is drawn largely from *The Spoilage*.

4. Leonard Bloom and Ruth Riemer, *Removal and Return* (Berkeley and Los Angeles: University of California Press, 1949), Table 28, p. 137.

5. The absolute figures: 68 reporting family businesses, 29 reporting none, and 1 not ascertained.

6. The methodological problems of interviewing in the camps are reported in Thomas and Nishimoto, *op. cit.*, pp. v–xv, and in A. Leighton, *The Governing of Men* (Princeton: Princeton University Press, 1945), pp. 373–397.

7. Only people who were sixteen years old or older in 1942 were interviewed in our sample. U.S. population figures for Japanese according to country of birth do not correspond with the proportions in our sample because of this exclusion of people under sixteen years of age in 1942.

8. The divergence would have been greater but for the fact that one of the rioting Issei was twenty-one at the time of the riot. (He had been born on a ship en route from Hawaii to Japan.) The youngest nonrioting Issei was thirty-four.

Genesis of a Communist: Childhood

by EDGAR SNOW

1. A *hsien* roughly corresponds to a U.S. county. It was the smallest territorial unit under the central government, and was ruled by a magistrate.

2. About 2.5 acres, or one hectare.

3. One *tan* is a *picul*, or $133\frac{1}{3}$ pounds.

4. Two and two-thirds miles.

5. Mao used the Chinese term *yuan*, which was often translated as "Chinese dollars"; 3,000 yuan in cash in 1900 was an impressive sum in rural China.

6. Mao used all these political terms humorously in his explanations, laughing as he recalled such incidents.

7. Literally, to "knock head." To strike one's head to the floor or earth was expected of son to father and subject to emperor, in token of filial obedience.

8. By Chung Kuang-ying, who advocated many democratic reforms, including parliamentary government and modern methods of education and communications. His book had a wide influence when published in 1898, the year of the ill-fated Hundred Days Reform.

9. The same society to which Ho Lung belonged.

10. Literally "Let's eat at the Big House," that is, at the landlord's granary.

11. Hsiao San (Emi Siao). See Bibliography.

12. Liang Ch'i-ch'ao, a talented essayist at the end of the Manchu Dynasty, was the leader of a reform movement which resulted in his exile.

K'ang Yu-wei and he were the "intellectual godfathers" of the first revolution, in 1911.

13. The poem evidently referred to the spring festival and tremendous rejoicing in Japan following the Treaty of Portsmouth and the end of the Russo-Japanese War.

14. Yao and Shun were semilegendary first emperors (3,000–2,205 B.C.?), credited with forming Chinese society in the Wei and Yellow River valleys, and taming the floods (with dikes, canals); Ch'in Shih Huang Ti (259–221 B.C.) unified the empire and completed the Great Wall; Han Wu Ti solidified the foundations of the Han Dynasty, which followed Ch'in and lasted (including the later Han) 426 years.

Days in Changsha

by EDGAR SNOW

1. The T'ung Meng Hui, a revolutionary secret society, was founded by Dr. Sun Yat-sen and was the forerunner of the Kuomintang. Most of its members were exiles in Japan, where they carried on a vigorous "brush-war" (war by writing brushes, or pens) against Liang Ch'i-ch'ao and Kang Yu-wei, leaders of the "reformed monarchist" party.

2. An absurd coalition, since K'ang and Liang were monarchists at that time, and Sun Yat-sen was antimonarchist.

3. An act perhaps more anti-Confucian than anti-Manchu. Some orthodox Confucianists held that man should not interfere with nature, including growth of hair and fingernails.

4. In 1911, the start of the revolution that overthrew the Manchu Dynasty.

5. *Han-jen* means the ethnical descendants of "men of Han," referring to the long-lived Han Dynasty (206 B.C.–220 A.D.). Europeans derived the name "China" and "Chinese" from the Ch'in Dynasty which immediately preceded the Han. China was known to *Han-jen* as Chungkuo, the "Central Realm," also translated as "Middle Kingdom." In official terminology all its inhabitants, including non-Han peoples, were called *Chung-kuo-jen*, or "Central-Realm People." Thus the Manchu were *Chung-kuo-jen* (China-men) but not *Han-jen*.

6. A *tutu* was a military governor.

7. T'ang Sheng-chih later became commander of the Nationalist armies of the Wuhan Government of Wang Ching-wei (see BN) in 1927. He betrayed both Wang and the Reds and began the "peasant massacre" of Hunan.

8. Yuan Shih-k'ai, army chief of staff to the Manchu rulers, forced their abdication in 1911. Sun Yat-sen, regarded as "father of the Republic," returned to China and was elected president by his followers in a ceremony at Nanking. Yuan held military control throughout most of the country, however. To avoid a conflict, Sun

resigned when Yuan Shih-k'ai agreed to a constitutional convention and formation of a parliament. Yuan continued to rule as a military dictator, and in 1915 proclaimed himself emperor, whereupon his warlord supporters deserted him. The proclamation was rescinded after a few months, Yuan died, and the Republic (if not constitutional government) survived, to enter a period of provincial warlordism and national division.

9. The gifted fourth emperor of the Manchu, or Ch'ing, Dynasty, who took the throne in 1736.

10. The reference is to a line in a poem by Li T'ai-po.

11. Li Li-san later became responsible for the CCP "Li Li-san line," which Mao Tse-tung bitterly opposed. Further on Mao tells of Li's struggle with the Red Army, and of its results. See also BN.

12. The Hsin-min Hsueh-hui, New People's Study Society.

13. See BN.

14. Hsiao San (Emi Siao), brother of Hsiao Yu (Saio Yu). See Bibliography.

15. Other members included Liu Shao-ch'i, Jen Pi-shih, Li Fu-ch'un, Wang Jo-fei, T'eng Tai-yuan, Li Wei-han, Hsiao Ching-kuang, and at least one woman, Ts'ai Chang, the sister of Ts'ai Ho-sen. All of these achieved high rank in the CCP. Mao's favorite professor and future father-in-law, Yang Ch'ang-chi, and Hsu T'eh-li, Mao's teacher at the First Normal School, were patrons.

16. In Tientsin it was the Chueh-wu Shih, or "Awakening Society," which led in organization of radical youth. Chou En-lai was one of the founders. Others included Teng Ying-ch'ao (Mme. Chou En-lai); Ma Chun, who was executed in Peking in 1927; and Sun Hsiao-ch'ing, who later became secretary of the Canton Committee of the Kuomintang.

Prelude to revolution

by EDGAR SNOW

1. The ex-bandit who became military dictator of Manchuria. Marshal Chang held power in Peking before the arrival of the Nationalists there. He was killed by the Japanese in 1928. His son, Chang Hsueh-liang, known as the "Young Marshal," succeeded him.

2. See BN.

3. Pei Hai and the other "seas" were artificial lakes in the former Forbidden City.

4. Considered the beginning of the "Second Revolution," and of modern Chinese nationalism.

5. Ch'en Tu-hsui was born in Anhui, in 1879, became a noted scholar and essayist, and for years headed the department of literature at Peking National University—"cradle of the literary renaissance." His *New Youth* magazine began the movement for adoption of the *pai-hua*, or vernacular Chinese, as the national language to replace the "dead" *wen-yen*, or Classical language. With Li Ta-chao, he was a chief promoter of Marxist study in China and a pioneer organizer of the Chinese Communist Party. See BN.

6. In October 1920, Mao organized a Socialist Youth Corps branch in Changsha, in which he worked with Lin Tsu-han to set up craft unions in Hunan.

7. Mao made no further reference to his life with Yang K'ai-hui, except to mention her execution. She was a student at Peking National University and later became a youth leader during the Great Revolution, and one of the most active women Communists. Their marriage had been celebrated as an "ideal romance" among radical youths in Hunan.

A theory of revolutionary behavior

by DAVID C. SCHWRATZ

1. See, for example, Lawrence Stone, "Theories of Revolution," *World Politics*, XVIII (January 1966), pp. 159–176.

2. In the absence of an authoritative, contemporary bibliography on revolution—a much needed reference tool—it is difficult to convey the scope of existing materials. A recently supplemented, select English-language bibliography on the related, but more limited, topic of counter-insurgency contains over 1100 entries and lists more than 30 other bibliographies on the same topic. See D. M. Condit *et al.*, *A Counter-Insurgency Bibliography* (Washington: SORO, The American University, 1963); See also Douglas Bwy, *Social Conflict: A Keyword-in-Context Bibliography on the Literature of Developing Areas* (Evanston: Northwestern University, 1966).

3. James C. Davies, "Toward a Theory of Revolution," *American Sociological Review*, Vol. 27, No. 1 (February 1962), pp. 5–19.

4. Davies, *op. cit.*, Harry Eckstein and Ted Gurr, working papers on *The Genesis of Civil Violence*. Center of International Studies, Princeton University; also, Ted Gurr, *The Genesis of Violence, A Multivariate Theory of the Pre Conditions for Civil Strife*, Ph.D. Dissertation, Department of Government and International Relations, New York University, 1965.

5. See, for example, Carl. J. Friedrich, ed., *Revolution: Nomos VIII* (New York: Atherton Press, 1966).

6. Lyford P. Edwards, *The Natural History of Revolution* (Chicago: University of Chicago Press, 1926); Crane Brinton, *The Anatomy of Revolution* (New York: Norton, 1938); George S. Pettee, *The Process of Revolution* (New York: Harper, 1938).

7. Rex D. Hopper, "The Revolutionary Process," *Social Forces* 28: 270–279 (March 1950); Chalmers Johnson, *Revolution and the Social System* (Stanford: Hoover Institution, 1964); Chalmers Johnson, *Revolutionary Change* (Boston: Little, Brown, 1966); James H. Meisel, *Counter-Revolution* (New York: Atherton Press, 1966), especially pp. 209 ff.

8. See, for example, Charles Tilly and James Rule, *Measuring Political Upheaval* (Princeton: Center of International Studies Monograph, 1965); also, Ted Gurr, *New Error-Compensated Measures for Contemporary Nations: Some Correlates of Civil Violence* (Princeton: Center of International Studies Monograph, 1966).

9. Harry Eckstein, ed., *Internal War* (Glencoe: The Free Press, 1964), pp. 7 ff.

10. See Talcott Parsons, "Some Reflections on the Place of Force in Social Processes," in Eckstein, *op. cit.*, pp. 33–70.

11. Reversibility rules, if they exist, have not been identified nor has the possibility of skipping a stage (i.e., the socalled "telescoping of revolution") been analyzed. The model does recognize that political change can be discontinuous and abrupt.

12. See Note 6.

13. Systematic data, designed specifically to test the validity of this theory in its own terms, is now being generated at the Foreign Policy Research Institute. Even the most cursory presentation of the available material would expand this paper beyond appropriate size. Accordingly, interpretive examples will provide the second principal evidence form.

14. *Politics*, Book V.

15. Gustav Le Bon, *The Psychology of Revolution* (New York: Macmillan, 1899), p. 65.

16. See Note 4.

17. Edwards, *op. cit.*, p. 2.

18. See Note 4.

19. E. Victor Wolfenstein, *Violence or Nonviolence: A Psychoanalytic Exploration of the Choice of Political Means in Social Change* (Princeton: Center of International Studies Monograph, 1965).

20. Earlier versions of this paper emphasized cognitive consistency.

21. Roger Brown, "Models of Attitude Change" in Brown *et al.*, *New Directions in Psychology* (New York: Holt, Rinehart and Winston, 1962), pp. 74 ff.; Judson S. Brown, "Principles of Intrapersonal Conflict," *Journal of Conflict Resolution* (Vol. 1, No 2), pp. 135 ff.; C. N. Cofer and M. H. Appley, *Motivation: Theory and Research* (New York: John Wiley, especially pp. 808 ff.

Judson S. Brown, *op. cit.*, p. 138.

Wolfenstein, *op. cit.*, p. 9.

e Gabriel A. Almond and Sidney Verba, *c Culture* (Princeton: Princeton University Press, 1963), *passim*. The alienative

process undergone by persons who are not politically conscious—the unincorporated groups or "prepoliticals"—is very similar to that described here and is set forth in Section 3, below.

25. This brief discussion of conflict theories neither presupposes nor requires reader familiarity with the material. Accordingly, it is highly simplified and abbreviated. The reader wishing to further familiarize himself with these matters is referred to: N. E. Miller, "Experimental Studies in Conflict," in J. McV. Hunt, *Personality and Behavior Disorders* (New York: 1944), and Judson S. Brown, *op. cit.*

26. Judson S. Brown, *op. cit.*, pp. 143 ff.

27. A perceived threat to basic values, in the absence of other effective, protective mechanisms, will tend toward politicization of the values. One dynamic by which this can take place is stated in this section and another is identified in Stage 3 below.

28. A highly simplified cognitive consistency paradigm might run as follows: Stable or enduring attitudes and images tend to be organized in consistent or compatible patterns. Disruption of such patterns (perceived incongruities or conflicts) produce psychic discomfort or "dissonance" which people are motivated to reduce by changing behaviors, attitudes, attention patterns and salience patterns. The greater the dissonance, the stronger is the motive to reduce it.

29. Brown, *op. cit.*, pp. 147 ff.

30. Brinton, *op. cit.*, p. 160.

31. Edwards, *op. cit.*, p. 23.

32. *Ibid.* See, for example, Brinton, *op. cit.*, p. 72.

33. Hopper, *op. cit.*, p. 271.

34. *Ibid.*

35. Edwards, *op. cit.*, pp. 23–37.

36. Hopper, *op. cit.*, p. 271.

37. Jack L. Walker, "A Critique of the Elitist Theory of Democracy," *American Political Science Review*, Vol. LX, No. 2, June 1966, p. 290; Robert A. Dahl, "Further Reflections on 'A Critique of the Elitist Theory of Democracy,'" *ibid.*, p. 303.

38. But crime and immorality need not, in themselves, be politically relevant. Intellectuals may increase the salience of such behavior as evidence that the regime cannot maintain basic values—and this is political. Moreover, a regime may clamp down too early and too hard and so block nonpolitical channels of outlet. This, too, is politically relevant.

39. William Kornhauser, *Politics of Mass Society* (Glencoe, Illinois: Free Press of Glencoe, 1959), p. 33.

40. *Ibid.*

41. *Ibid.*

42. Seymour Martin Lipset, *Political Man* (Garden City: Doubleday, 1960), *passim*.

43. Hadley Cantril, *The Psychology of Social Movements* (New York: John Wiley, 1941), *passim.* The thoughtful, passively alienated person is also likely to be guilt-ridden for, by opting out, he becomes part of the reason for the loss of community. Similarly, the minority group member can come to feel guilty for being different. When the system will not let him in, will not restore or create community despite his ardent desire to be "like them" he may seek political power to coerce the society into creating community or equality.

44. The continuing debate over the relationship of development to revolution can probably be resolved by a resort to typologies. It seems likely that revolutions take place around basic economic transition points because it is then that social dislocation (e.g., uneven development) will be maximal. On the near side of such a transition, leading sector or progressive revolutions may take place as polities are seen to impede the desired change. On the far side, lagging sectors or restorative revolutions may occur as polities are seen to administer or encourage undesired change.

45. Brinton, *op. cit.*, pp. 41 ff.

46. David Willer and George K. Zollschan, "Prolegomenon to a Theory of Revolutions," in George K. Zollschan and Walter Hirsch, *Explorations in Social Change* (Boston: Houghton Mifflin, 1964), pp. 136 ff.

47. See Note 45.

48. Recent studies on the revolutionary personality include: E. Victor Wolfenstein, *The Revolutionary Personality* (Princeton: Princeton University Press, 1967); and Stefan Possony, *Lenin: The Compulsive Revolutionary* (Chicago: Regnery, 1964).

49. Brinton, *op. cit.*, p. 165. But the *Fuhrerprinzip* is not merely functional for the power needs of the revolutionary leader, it is also required by the military style of organization which modern revolutionary organizations adopt. See William R. Kintner, *The Front is Everywhere* (Norman: University of Oklahoma Press, 1950), *passim.*

50. Erik Erikson, *Young Man Luther* (New York: W. W. Norton, 1958).

51. There are also, of course, enormous differences between a revolutionary nucleus and, say a civic improvement committee. The differences however, are obvious and hence I stress here the commonalities and the potential utility of group formation theories.

52. Edwards, *op. cit.*, p. 31.

53. As indicated in Stage 1, this criticism era may go on for considerable periods of time before revolutionary organization develops. What is critical is not merely the increasing radicalization of the reformist intellectuals and other passively alienated persons (as discussed above in Stage 1), but also that the criticism constitutes a new "antisystem" socialization for many prepoliticals. In some social sectors, a new generation is now growing up with an entirely new set of socialization experiences which centrally include (or even only include) criticisms of the polity. From these sectors arise youthful revolutionaries like Giap, Krim, and Chin Peng (Malaya) whose antisystem behaviors began at ages 14, 17 and 18 respectively.

54. See Kintner, *op. cit., passim.*

55. *Ibid.*, p. 12.

56. *Ibid.*, p. 14.

57. This is brilliantly presented in Rebecca West's novel, *The Birds Fall Down* (New York: The Viking Press, 1966).

58. Brinton, *op. cit.*, p. 41.

59. See Note 46.

60. See Note 15.

61. See Note 6.

62. Hannah Arendt, *The Origins of Totalitarianism* (Cleveland: World Publishing Company, 1958).

63. See Note 43.

64. Gabriel A. Almond, *The Appeals of Communism* (Princeton: Princeton University Press, 1954).

65. Lucian W. Pye, *Guerrilla Communism in Malaya* (Princeton: Princeton University Press, 1956).

66. For those whose perceptions produce not salient, conscious threat, futility, etc., but rather only a general sense of unease—the revolutionary organization's task is to increase the salience, to teach the requisite perceptions and conflicts which its program then is proferred as resolving.

67. Edwards, *op. cit.*, p. 119.

68. Gaetano Mosca, *The Ruling Class* (New York: McGraw Hill, 1939), *passim.*

69. Kintner, *op. cit.*, p. 11.

70. F. Brown, *ibid.*, p. 8.

71. It is clear, of course, that many vital revolutionary tasks are performed by men who are not wholly dedicated to the movement—or even alienated from the system. Both involuntary recruitment (another instance of the use of threatened violence)—as with physicians—and recruitment for money (as with demonstrators) are always used. The problem-area of revolutionary recruitment is an especially fascinating one and one that needs much work.

72. See Note 62.

73. Erich Fromm, *Escape from Freedom* (New York: Holt, Rinehart and Winston, 1960).

74. Eric Hoffer, *The True Believer* (New York: Harper, 1951).

75. See Dominique O. Mannoni, *Prospero and Caliban* (New York: Frederick A. Praeger, 1964); and Frantz Fanon, *The Wretched of the Earth* (New York: The Grove Press, 1963).

76. Cited in Kintner, *op. cit.*, p. 25.

77. Brinton, *op. cit.*, p. 60.

78. Some violence, of course, may have been

on-going from the beginning; anomic violence is not uncommon in Stage 1 organization and "goon" action in Stage 2, marches and riots in Stage 3, goading the system and dramatizing violent reprisals throughout. While a revolutionary organization merely "takes over" a lesser revolt, for example, the widespread violence takes off from there.

79. Kintner, *op. cit.*, p. 31.

80. *Ibid.*, p. 19.

81. From the controlled extent though emotional character, of several Reigns of Terror (a fraction of 1% population killed in Cromwell's and Castro's Terror) one is tempted to give at least as much credence to the strategic as to the psychological explanation. Even in the much-publicized Indonesian anti-Communist terror, less than ½ of 1% of the population have been killed.

Toward a theory of revolution

by JAMES C. DAVIES

1. Several people have made perceptive suggestions and generous comments on an earlier version of this paper. I wish particularly to thank Seymour Martin Lipset, Lucian W. Pye, John H. Schaar, Paul Seabury, and Dwight Waldo.

2. The *Communist Manifesto* of 1848 evidently antedates the opposing idea by about a year. See Edmund Wilson, *To the Finland Station* (Anchor Books edition), New York: Doubleday (n.d.), p. 157; Lewis S. Feuer, *Karl Marx and Friedrich Engels: Basic Writings on Politics and Philosophy*, New York: Doubleday, 1959, p. 1. The above quotation is from Karl Marx and Frederick Engels, "Wage Labour and Capital," *Selected Works in Two Volumes*, Moscow: Foreign Languages Publishing House, 1955, vol. 1, p. 94.

3. A. de Tocqueville, *The Old Regime and the French Revolution* (trans. by John Bonner), New York: Harper, 1856, p. 214. The Stuart Gilbert translation, Garden City: Doubleday, 1955, pp. 176–177, gives a somewhat less pungent version of the same comment. *L'Ancien régime* was first published in 1856.

4. Revolutions are here defined as violent civil disturbances that cause the displacement of one ruling group by another that has a broader popular basis for support.

5. The full report is Ancel Keys *et al.*, *The Biology of Human Starvation*, Minneapolis: University of Minnesota Press, 1950. See J. Brozek, "Semi-starvation and Nutritional Rehabilitation," *Journal of Clinical Nutrition*, 1 (January 1953), pp. 107–118 for a brief analysis.

6. E. A. Cohen, *Human Behavior in the Concentration Camp*, New York: W. W. Norton, 1953, pp. 123–125, 131–140.

7. For community life in such poverty, in Mezzogiorno Italy, see E. C. Banfield, *The Moral Basis of a Backward Society*, Glencoe, Ill.: The Free Press, 1958. The author emphasizes that the nuclear family is a solidary, consensual, moral unit (see p. 85) but even within it, consensus appears to break down, in outbreaks of pure, individual amorality—notably between parents and children (see p. 117).

8. See Angus Campbell *et al.*, *The American Voter*, New York: John Wiley, 1960, Chapter 15, "Agrarian Political Behavior."

9. B. Zawadzki and P. F. Lazarsfeld, "The Psychological Consequences of Unemployment," *Journal of Social Psychology*, 6 (May 1935), pp. 224–251.

10. A remarkable and awesome exception to this phenomenon occurred occasionally in some Nazi concentration camps, e.g., in a Buchenwald revolt against capricious rule by criminal prisoners. During this revolt, one hundred criminal prisoners were killed by political prisoners. See Cohen, *op. cit.*, p. 200.

11. See W. W. Rostow, "Business Cycles, Harvests, and Politics: 1790–1850," *Journal of Economic History*, 1 (November 1941), pp. 206–221 for the relation between economic fluctuation and the activities of the Chartists in the 1830s and 1840s.

12. This curve is of course not to be confused with its prior and altogether different use by Floyd Allport in his study of social conformity. See F. H. Allport, "The J-Curve Hypothesis of Conforming Behavior," *Journal of Social Psychology*, 5 (May 1934), pp. 141–183, reprinted in T. H. Newcomb & E. L. Hartley, *Readings in Social Psychology*, New York: Henry Holt, 1947, pp. 55–67.

13. I am indebted to Beryl L. Crowe for his extensive research on Dorr's Rebellion while he was a participant in my political behavior seminar at the University of California, Berkeley, Spring 1960.

14. Joseph Brennan, *Social Conditions in Industrial Rhode Island: 1820–1860*, Washington, D.C.: Catholic University of America, 1940, p. 33.

15. The persistent demand for suffrage may be understood in light of election data for 1828 and 1840. In the former year, only 3600 votes were cast in Rhode Island, whose total population was about 94,000. (Of these votes, 23 per cent were cast for Jackson and 77 per cent for Adams, in contrast to a total national division of 56 per cent for Jackson and 44 per cent for Adams.) All votes cast in the 1828 election amount to 4 per cent of the total Rhode Island population and 11 per cent of the total U.S. population excluding slaves. In 1840, with a total population of 109,000 only 8300 votes—8 per cent—were cast in Rhode Island, in contrast to 17 per cent of the national population excluding slaves.

16. A. M. Mowry, *The Dorr War*, Providence, R.I.: Preston & Rounds Co., 1901, p. 114.

17. There is an excellent summary in B.

Brutzkus, "The Historical Peculiarities of the Social and Economic Development of Russia," in R. Bendix and S. M. Lipset, *Class, Status, and Power*, Glencoe, Ill.: The Free Press, 1953, pp. 517–540.

18. Jacqueries rose from an average of 8 per year in 1826–30 to 34 per year in 1845–49. T. G. Masaryk, *The Spirit of Russia*, London: Allen and Unwin, 1919, Vol. 1, p. 130. This long, careful, and rather neglected analysis was first published in German in 1913 under the title *Zur Russischen Geschichts- und Religionsphilosophie*.

19. Jacqueries averaged 350 per year for the first three years after emancipation. *Ibid.*, pp. 140–141.

20. The proportion of workers who struck from 1895 through 1902 varied between 1.7 per cent and 4.0 per cent per year. In 1903 the proportion rose to 5.1 per cent but dropped a year later to 1.5 per cent. In 1905 the proportion rose to 163.8 per cent, indicating that the total working force struck, on the average, closer to twice than to once during that portentous year. In 1906 the proportion dropped to 65.8 per cent; in 1907 to 41.9 per cent; and by 1909 was down to a "normal" 3.5 per cent. *Ibid.*, p. 175n.

21. *Ibid.*, p. 189n.

22. In his *History of the Russian Revolution*, Leon Trotsky presents data on political strikes from 1903 to 1917. In his *Spirit of Russia*, Masaryk presents comparable data from 1905 through 1912. The figures are not identical but the reported yearly trends are consistent. Masaryk's figures are somewhat lower, except for 1912. Cf. Trotsky, *op. cit.*, Doubleday Anchor Books ed., 1959, p. 32 and Masaryk, *op. cit. supra*, p. 197n.

23. See Trotsky, *op. cit.*, pp. 18–21 for a vivid picture of rising discontent in the army.

24. C. Issawi, *Egypt at Mid-Century: An Economic Survey*, London: Oxford University Press, 1954, p. 262. J. & S. Lacouture in their *Egypt in Transition*, New York: Criterion Books, 1958, p. 100, give a figure of over 300,000. Sir R. Bullard, editor, *The Middle East: A Political and Economic Survey*, London: Oxford University Press, 1958, p. 221 estimates total employment in industry, transport, and commerce in 1957 to have been about 750,000.

25. International Monetary Fund, *International Financial Statistics*, Washington, D.C. See monthly issues of this report, 1950–53.

26. J. and S. Lacouture, *op. cit.*, p. 99.

27. England threatened to depose Farouk in February 1942, by force if necessary, if Egypt did not support the Allies. Capitulation by the government and the Wafd caused widespread popular disaffection. When Egypt finally declared war on the Axis in 1945, the prime minister was assassinated. See J. & S. Lacouture, *op. cit.*, pp. 97–98 and Issawi, *op. cit.*, p. 268.

28. See J. R. Reich, *Leisler's Rebellion*, Chicago: University of Chicago Press, 1953.

29. See U.S. Bureau of the Census, *Historical Statistics of the United States, Colonial Times to 1957*, Washington, D.C., 1960, p. 757.

30. See G. Lefebvre, *The Coming of the French Revolution*, Princeton: Princeton University Press, 1947, pp. 101–109, 145–148, 196. G. Le Bon, *The Psychology of Revolution*, New York: G. Putnam's Sons, 1913, p. 143.

31. The account by Irving Werstein, *July 1863*, New York: Julian Messner, Inc., 1957, is journalistic but to my knowledge the fullest yet available.

32. E. S. Munger, "The Tragedy of Nyasaland," American Universities Field Staff Reports Service, vol. 7, no. 4 (August 1, 1959), p. 9.

33. See U.S. Bureau of the Census, *Historical Statistics of the United States: 1789–1945*, Washington, D.C.: 1949, p. 14.

34. Eugen Kogon, *The Theory and Practice of Hell*, New York: Farrar, Straus & Co., 1950, pp. 284–286.

35. W. Buchanan, "Mass Communication in Reverse," *International Social Science Bulletin*, 5 (1953), pp. 577–583, at p. 578. The full study is W. Buchanan and H. Cantril, *How Nations See Each Other*, Urbana: University of Illinois Press, 1953, esp. pp. 85–90.

36. Daniel Lerner, *The Passing of Traditional Society*, Glencoe, Ill.: Free Press, 1958.

37. *Ibid.*, pp. 101–103. See also F. P. Kilpatrick & H. Cantril, "Self-Anchoring Scaling, A Measure of Individuals' Unique Reality Worlds," *Journal of Individual Psychology*, 16 (November 1960), pp. 158–173.

38. See the revised edition of 1952 as reprinted by Vintage Books, Inc., 1957, pp. 264–275.

39. Quoted in E. H. Carr, *A History of Soviet Russia*, vol. 1, *The Bolshevik Revolution: 1917–23*, London: Macmillan, 1950, p. 69.

Slavery and personality

by STANLEY M. ELKINS

2. There were other pretexts, such as crime or debt, but war was probably the most frequent mode of procurement. Snelgrave, *New Account*, p. 158; "John Barbot's Description," in Donnan, *Documents*, Vol. I, pp. 284, 289, 294, 298; "Observations on the Slave Trade, 1789" [C. B. Wadström] in *ibid.*, Vol. II, p. 599; Matthews, *Voyage to Sierra-Leone*, pp. 145–146, 163. See also below, Note 34.

3. As to "character types," one might be tempted to suppose that as a rule it would be only the weaker and more submissive who allowed themselves to be taken into slavery. Yet it appears that a heavy proportion of the slaves were in fact drawn from among the most warlike. "In a country divided into a thousand petty

states, mostly independent and jealous of each other; where every freeman is accustomed to arms, and fond of military achievements; where the youth who has practised the bow and spear from his infancy, longs for nothing so much as an opportunity to display his valour; it is natural to imagine that wars frequently originate from very frivolous provocation." Park, *Travels*, p. 328. "The most potent negroe," wrote William Bosman, "can't pretend to be insured from slavery; for if he ever ventures himself in the wars it may easily become his lot." *New and Accurate Description*, p. 183. It has often been pointed out that slavery already existed among the tribes themselves and that a considerable proportion of Africans were used to it and had in fact been born into it. It may be doubted, however, if substantial numbers of *these* slaves came to America, for apparently the native chiefs tended to sell only their war captives to the Europeans and to keep their hereditary and customary slaves—together with their most docile captives—for themselves. Park, *Travels*, p. 332. It has even been asserted that in many places the tribal laws themselves forbade the selling of domestic slaves, except for crimes, though apparently it was simple enough to trump up an accusation if one wanted to get rid of a slave. Matthews, *Voyage to Sierra-Leone*, p. 153; Edwards, *History*, Vol., II p. 312.

4. "The Wars which the inhabitants of the interior parts of the country, beyond Senegal, Gambia, and Sierra Leona, carry on with each other, are chiefly of a predatory nature, and owe their origin to the yearly number of slaves, which the Mandingoes, or the inland traders suppose will be wanted by the vessels that will arrive on the coast." "Observations" [Wadström], in Donnan, *Documents*, Vol. II, p. 599.

5. A number of excerpts describing these raids are cited in Thomas Fowell Buxton, *Letter on the Slave Trade to the Lord Viscount Melbourne* (London, 1838), pp. 34–38.

6. Descriptions of the march may be found in Park, *Travels*, pp. 371 ff.; Buxton, *Letter*, pp. 41–44; Rinchon, *La traite et l'esclavage*, pp. 174–175; L. Degrandpré, *Voyage à la côte occidentale d'Afrique, fait dans les années 1786 et 1787* (Paris, 1801), Vol. II, pp. 48–50.

7. Buxton, *Letter*, p. 43.

8. "When these slaves come to fida, they are put in prison all together, and when we treat concerning buying them, they are all brought out together in a large plain; where, by our Chirurgeons, whose province it is, they are thoroughly examined, even to the smallest member, and that naked too both men and women, without the least distinction and modesty. Those which are approved as good are set on one side; and the lame or faulty are set by as *invalides*, which are here called *mackrons*. These are such as are above five and thirty years old,

or are maimed in the arms, legs, hands or feet, have lost a tooth, are grey-haired, or have films over their eyes; as well as all those which are affected by any venereal distemper, or with several other diseases." Bosman, *New and Accurate Description*, p. 364. See also Degrandpré, *Voyage*, Vol. II, pp. 53–56; Buxton, *Letter*, pp. 47–49; Rinchon, *La traite et l'esclavage*, pp. 188–189; "John Barbot's Description," in Donnan, *Documents*, Vol. I, pp. 289, 295; Park, *Travels*, p. 360.

9. Descriptions of the Middle Passage may be found in *An Abstract of the Evidence Delivered before a Select Committee of the House of Commons in the Years 1790, and 1791 on the Part of the Petitioners for the Abolition of the Slave Trade* (London, 1791); Alexander Falconbridge, *An Account of the Slave Trade on the Coast of Africa* (London: J. Phillips, 1788); Rinchon, *La traite et l'esclavage*, pp. 196–209; Edwards, *History*, Vol. II; Brantz Mayer, *Captain Canot* (New York: D. Appleton, 1854); Averil Mackenzie-Grieve, *The Last Years of the English Slave Trade, Liverpool 1750–1807* (London: Putnam, 1941).

10. Degrandpré, *Voyage*, Vol. II, pp. 55–56.

11. Edwards, *History*, Vol. II, p 340. See also *Abstract of Evidence*, pp. 46–47, and Falconbridge, *Account*, pp. 33–36.

12. Tannenbaum, *Slave and Citizen*, p. 28. As for the total exports of slaves from Africa throughout the entire period of the trade, estimates run as high as twenty million. "Even a conservative estimate," notes Mr. Tannenbaum, "would hardly cut this figure in half." *Ibid.*, p. 32.

13. Bruno Bettelheim, "Individual and Mass Behavior in Extreme Situations," *Journal of Abnormal and Social Psychology*, XXXVIII (October 1943), p. 424.

14. A description of such a trip may be found in Olga Lengyel, *Five Chimneys: The Story of Auschwitz* (Chicago, 1947), pp. 7–10. See also Eugen Kogon, *The Theory and Practice of Hell* (New York: Farrar, Straus, 1946), p. 67.

15. Elie Cohen, *Human Behavior in the Concentration Camp* (New York: Norton, 1953), pp. 118–122; Kogon, *Theory and Practice*, pp. 66–76; Lengyel, *Five Chimneys*, pp. 12–22.

16. One aspect of this registration ceremony involved a sham "inspection" of the body, whose effect on the women prisoners in particular was apparently very profound. See Lengyel, *Five Chimneys*, p. 19; Ella Lingens-Reiner, *Prisoners of Fear* (London: Victor Gollancz, 1948), p. 26. This may be compared with Degrandpré's description of a similar "inspection" on the African slave coast in the 1780's; see his *Voyage*, Vol. II, pp. 55–56. "Apart from the fact that for every newcomer his transformation into a 'prisoner' meant a degradation," writes an ex-prisoner of Auschwitz and Mauthausen, "there was also the

loss of his name. That this was no trifling circumstance should be apparent from the great importance which, according to Freud, a man attaches to his name. This is, in Freud's view, sufficiently proven by 'the fact that savages regard a name as an essential part of a man's personality. . . .' Anyhow, whether one agrees with Freud or not, the loss of one's name is not without significance, for the name is a personal attribute. Because he no longer had a name, but had become a number, the prisoner belonged to the huge army of the nameless who peopled the concentration camp." Cohen, *Human Behavior*, pp. 145–146.

17. *Ibid.*, pp. 134–135, 140–143.

18. These punishments are discussed most vividly in Kogon, *Theory and Practice*, pp. 102–108, 207–211.

19. Bettelheim, "Individual and Mass Behavior," p. 445.

20. The effects of never being alone are noted in Cohen, *Human Behavior*, pp. 130–131, and David Rousset, *The Other Kingdom* (New York: Reynal & Hitchcock, 1947), p. 133.

21. "When the author [Bettelheim] expressed to some of the old prisoners his astonishment that they seemed not interested in discussing their future life outside the camp, they frequently admitted that they could no longer visualize themselves living outside the camp, making free decisions, taking care of themselves and their families." Bettelheim, "Individual and Mass Behavior," p 439.

22. M. Rousset tells of how, on one of the death marches, a prisoner came to him bringing a French compatriot and begging his protection for the wretched man. "He told me that he was a lawyer from Toulouse, and it was only with the greatest difficulty that I kept from laughing aloud. For this social designation, *lawyer*, no longer fitted the poor wretch in the slightest. The incongruity of the thought was irresistibly comic. And it was the same with all of us." Rousset, *Other Kingdom*, p. 77.

23. Kogon, *Theory and Practice*, p. 274; Cohen, *Human Behavior*, p. 155; Hilde O. Bluhm, "How Did They Survive?" *American Journal of Psychotherapy*, II (January 1948), p. 5.

24. Kogon, *Theory and Practice*, p. 277.

25. Bettelheim, "Individual and Mass Behavior," p. 431. See also Cohen, *Human Behavior*, pp. 116–117, 172.

26. "Many kept their bearings only by a kind of split personality. They surrendered their bodies resistlessly to the terror, while their inner being withdrew and held aloof." Kogon, *Theory and Practice*, p. 71. "I arrived at that state of numbness where I was no longer sensitive to either club or whip. I lived through the rest of that scene almost as a spectator." Lengyel, *Five Chimneys*, p. 20.

27. Bettelheim, "Individual and Mass Behavior," p. 432. "We camp prisoners," writes Mrs. Lingens-Reiner, "had only one yardstick: whatever helped our survival was good, and whatever threatened our survival was bad, and to be avoided." *Prisoners of Fear*, p. 142.

28. Bettelheim, "Individual and Mass Behavior," p. 438.

29. Cohen, *Human Behavior*, p. 169.

30. This should in no sense be considered as a calculating, "rational" alertness, but rather as something quite primitive. "Of myself," writes Dr. Cohen, "I know that I was not continuously occupied by the reflection: I am going to win through. The actions which contributed to my survival were performed instinctively rather than consciously. . . . Like animals warned by their instinct that danger is imminent, we would act instinctively at critical moments. These instinctive acts must, I think, be considered as manifestations of the life instinct. If the life instinct is not strong enough, the instinct will desert the individual, and instead of rising to the emergency, the individual will succumb, whereas a stronger life instinct would have seen him through." *Human Behavior*, p. 163.

31. Those who had in fact succumbed to this apathy—who had given up the struggle, and for whom death would be a mere matter of time—were known as "Moslems." See above, Note 17.

32. Bettelheim, "Individual and Mass Behavior," p. 141.

33. Says Dr. Cohen, "I am not asserting that sex was never discussed; it was, though not often. Frankl also states 'that in contrast to mass existence in other military communities . . . here (in the concentration camp) there is *no smut talk*.' " *Human Behavior*, p. 141.

34. "With reference to this phenomenon Miss Bluhm has pointed out that it is not at all unusual that people in extraordinary circumstances, for example soldiers in wartime, 'are able to give up their habitual standards of cleanliness without deeper disturbance; yet only up to certain limits.' The rules of anal cleanliness, she adds, are not disregarded. 'Their neglect means return to instinctual behavior of childhood.' " *Ibid.*, p. 175.

35. Bettelheim, "Individual and Mass Behavior," p. 445.

36. *Ibid.*, p. 421.

37. Bettelheim, "Individual and Mass Behavior," pp. 445–446. This same phenomenon is noted by Curt Bondy: "They tell great stories about what they have been before and what they have performed." "Problems of Internment Camps," *Journal of Abnormal and Social Psychology*, XXXVIII (October 1943), pp. 453–475.

38. Cohen, *Human Behavior*, p. 177. Italics in original.

39. Bettelheim, "Individual and Mass Behavior," p. 447.

40. *Ibid.*, pp. 448–450. "Once, for instance, a guard on inspecting the prisoners' apparel found

that the shoes of some of them were dirty on the inside. He ordered all prisoners to wash their shoes inside and out with water and soap. The heavy shoes treated this way became hard as stone. The order was never repeated, and many prisoners did not execute it when given. Nevertheless there were some old prisoners who not only continued to wash the inside of their shoes every day but cursed all others who did not do so as negligent and dirty. These prisoners firmly believed that the rules set down by the Gestapo were desirable standards of human behavior, at least in the camp situation." *Ibid.*, p. 450.

41. *Ibid.* See also Cohen, *Human Behavior*, pp. 189–193, for a discussion of anti-Semitism among the Jews.

42. Cohen, *Human Behavior*, pp. 176–177.

43. *Ibid.*, p. 179. On this and other points I must also acknowledge my indebtedness to Mr. Ies Spetter, a former Dutch journalist now living in this country, who was imprisoned for a time at Auschwitz during World War II. Mr. Spetter permitted me to see an unpublished paper, "Some Thoughts on Victims and Criminals in the German Concentration Camps," which he wrote in 1954 at the New School for Social Research; and this, together with a number of conversations I had with him, added much to my understanding of concentration-camp psychology.

44. Kogon, *Theory and Practice*, p. 284.

45. *The Other Kingdom*, p. 137.

46. "In the preference camp Bergen Belsen, only four cases of attempted suicide were witnessed by Tas, three of which were saved with great effort, while in the Stammlager Auschwitz only one successful attempt came to my knowledge. This does not mean that there were not more, but their number was certainly small. Kaas, on the other hand, witnessed several attempted suicides in Buchenwald. He has remembered three that were successful (two by hanging, one by rushing into the electric fence). He also knows of prisoners who were known to be depressive cases, and who were shot down when during the night they had deliberately gone out of bounds. As compared with the large number of prisoners, the number of suicides, however, was very small." Cohen, *Human Behavior*, p. 158.

47. Kogon, *Theory and Practice*, pp. 166–167. This occurred during fearful tortures at the quarry, where the Jews knew they were about to be killed anyway.

48. A. Hottinger, *Hungerkrankheit, Hungerödem, Hungertuberkulose*, p. 32, quoted in Cohen, *Human Behavior*, p. 197. "After the liberation many writers were struck by the callousness of the onetime prisoners, and particularly by their apathy when relating their experiences, even the most horrible." *Ibid.*, p. 144.

49. *Human Behavior*, p. 136.

50. Anna Freud, *The Ego and the Mechanisms of Defence* (London: Hogarth Press, 1948), p. 121. "In some illustrative case reports, Clara Thompson stresses the vicious circle put in motion by this defense-mechanism. The stronger the need for identification, the more a person loses himself in his omnipotent enemy—the more helpless he becomes. The more helpless he feels, the stronger the identification, and—we may add —the more likely it is that he tries even to surpass the aggressiveness of his aggressor. This may explain the almost unbelievable phenomenon that prisoner-superiors sometimes acted more brutally than did members of the SS. . . . Identification with the aggressor represented the final stage of passive adaptation. It was a means of defense of a rather paradoxical nature: survival through surrender; protection against the fear of the enemy—by becoming part of him; overcoming helplessness—by regressing to childish dependence." Bluhm, "How Did They Survive?" pp. 24–25.

51. Sullivan refined this concept from the earlier notion of the "generalized other" formulated by George Herbert Mead. "The organized community or social group [Mead wrote] which gives to the individual his unity of self may be called 'the generalized other.' The attitude of the generalized other is the attitude of the whole community. Thus, for example, in the case of such a social group as a ball team, the team is the generalized other in so far as it enters—as an organized process or social activity—into the experience of any one of the individual members of it." George H. Mead, *Mind, Self and Society: From the Standpoint of a Social Behaviorist* (Chicago: University of Chicago Press, 1934), p. 154.

52. The experience of American prisoners taken by the Chinese during the Korean War seems to indicate that profound changes in behavior and values, if not in basic personality itself, can be effected without the use of physical torture or extreme deprivation. The Chinese were able to get large numbers of Americans to act as informers and to cooperate in numerous ways in the effort to indoctrinate all the prisoners with Communist propaganda. The technique contained two key elements. One was that all formal and informal authority structures within the group were systematically destroyed; this was done by isolating officers, non-commissioned officers, and any enlisted men who gave indications of leadership capacities. The other element involved the continual emphasizing of the captors' power and influence by judicious manipulation of petty rewards and punishments and by subtle hints of the greater rewards and more severe punishments (repatriation or non-repatriation) that rested with the pleasure of those in authority. See Edgar H. Schein, "Some Observa-

tions on Chinese Methods of Handling Prisoners of War," *Public Opinion Quarterly*, XX (Spring 1956), pp. 321–327.

53. In a system as tightly closed as the plantation or the concentration camp, the slave's or prisoner's position of absolute dependency virtually compels him to see the authority-figure as somehow really "good." Indeed, all the evil in his life may flow from this man—but then so also must everything of any value. Here is the seat of the only "good" he knows, and to maintain his psychic balance he must persuade himself that the good is in some way dominant. A threat to this illusion is thus in a real sense a threat to his very existence. It is a common experience among social workers dealing with neglected and maltreated children to have a child desperately insist on his love for a cruel and brutal parent and beg that he be allowed to remain with that parent. The most dramatic feature of this situation is the cruelty which it involves, but the mechanism which inspires the devotion is not the cruelty of the parent but rather the abnormal dependency of the child. A classic example of this mechanism in operation may be seen in the case of Varvara Petrovna, mother of Ivan Turgenev. Mme. Turgenev "ruled over her serfs with a rod of iron." She demanded utter obedience and total submission. The slightest infraction of her rules brought the most severe punishment: "A maid who did not offer her a cup of tea in the proper manner was sent off to some remote village and perhaps separated from her family forever; gardeners who failed to prevent the plucking of a tulip in one of the flower beds before the house were ordered to be flogged; a servant whom she suspected of a mutinous disposition was sent off to Siberia." Her family and her most devoted servants were treated in much the same manner. "Indeed," wrote Varvara Zhitova, the adopted daughter of Mme. Turgenev, "those who loved her and were most devoted to her suffered most of all." Yet in spite of her brutality she was adored by the very people she tyrannized. David Magarshack describes how once when thrashing her eldest son she nearly fainted with sadistic excitement, whereupon "little Nicholas, forgetting his punishment, bawled at the top of his voice: 'Water! Water for mummy!' " Mme. Zhitova, who knew Mme. Turgenev's cruelty intimately and was herself the constant victim of her tyranny, wrote: "In spite of this, I loved her passionately, and when I was, though rarely, separated from her, I felt lonely and unhappy." Even Mme. Turgenev's maid Agatha, whose children were sent to another village, when still infants so that Agatha might devote all her time to her mistress, could say years later, "Yes, she caused me much grief. I suffered much from her, but all the same I loved her! She was a real lady!" V. Zhitova, *The Turgenev Family*, trans. A. S. Mills (London: Havill Press, 1954), p. 25; David Magarshack, *Turgenev: A Life* (New York: Grove, 1954), pp. 14, 16, 22.

54. Bruno Bettelheim tells us of the fantastic efforts of the old prisoners to believe in the benevolence of the officers of the SS. "They insisted that these officers [hid] behind their rough surface a feeling of justice and propriety; he, or they, were supposed to be genuinely interested in the prisoners and even trying, in a small way, to help them. Since nothing of these supposed feelings and efforts ever became apparent, it was explained that he hid them so effectively because otherwise he would not be able to help the prisoners. The eagerness of these prisoners to find reasons for their claims was pitiful. A whole legend was woven around the fact that two officers inspecting a barrack one had cleaned his shoes from mud before entering. He probably did it automatically, but it was interpreted as a rebuff of the other officer and a clear demonstration of how he felt about the concentration camp." Bettelheim, "Individual and Mass Behavior," p. 451.

55. See above, Note 4.

56. Virtually all the ex-prisoners whose writing I have made use of were men and women who had certain privileges (as clerks, physicians, and the like) in the camps. Many of the same persons were also active in the "underground" and could offer some measure of leadership and support for others. That is to say, both the objectivity necessary for making useful observations and the latitude enabling one to exercise some leadership were made possible by a certain degree of protection not available to the rank and file.

I should add, however, that a notable exception was the case of Bruno Bettelheim, who throughout the period of his detention had no privileged position of any kind which could afford him what I am calling an "alternative role" to play. And yet I do not think that it would be stretching the point too far to insist that he did in fact have such a role, one which was literally self-created: that of the scientific observer. In him, the scientist's objectivity, his feeling for clinical detail and sense of personal detachment, amounted virtually to a passion. It would not be fair, however, to expect such a degree of personal autonomy as this in other cases, except for a very few. I am told, for instance, that the behavior of many members of this "underground" toward their fellow prisoners was itself by no means above moral reproach. The depths to which the system could corrupt a man, it must be remembered, were profound.

57. See Tannenbaum, *Slave and Citizen*, pp. 64–65.

58. *Ibid.*, pp. 4 ff., 56–57, 90–93; see also Johnston, *Negro in the New World*, p. 90.

59. Compared with the countless uprisings of the Brazilian Negroes, the slave revolts in our own country appear rather desperate and futile.

Only three emerge as worthy of any note, and their seriousness—even when described by a sympathetic historian like Herbert Aptheker—depends largely on the supposed plans of the rebels rather than on the things they actually did. The best organized of such "revolts," those of Vesey and Gabriel, were easily suppressed, while the most dramatic of them—the Nat Turner Rebellion—was characterized by little more than aimless butchery. The Brazilian revolts, on the other hand, were marked by imagination and a sense of direction, and they often involved large-scale military operations. One is impressed both by their scope and their variety. They range from the legendary Palmares Republic of the seventeenth century (a Negro state organized by escaped slaves and successfully defended for over fifty years), to the bloody revolts of the Moslem Negroes of Bahia which, between 1807 and 1835, five times paralyzed a substantial portion of Brazil. Many such wars were launched from the *quilombos* (fortified villages built deep in the jungles by escaped slaves to defend themselves from recapture); there were also the popular rebellions in which the Negroes of an entire area would take part. One is immediately struck by the heroic stature of the Negro leaders: no allowances of any sort need be made for them; they are impressive from any point of view. Arthur Ramos has described a number of them, including Zambi, a fabulous figure of the Palmares Republic; Luiza Mahin, mother of the Negro poet Luiz Gama and "one of the most outstanding leaders of the 1835 insurrection"; and Manoel Francisco dos Anjos Fereira, whose followers in the *Balaiada* (a movement which drew its name from "Baliao," his own nickname) held the *entire province* of Maranhão for three years. Their brilliance, gallantry, and warlike accomplishments give to their histories an almost legendary quality. On the other hand, one could not begin to think of Nat Turner in such a connection. See Ramos, *The Negro in Brazil*, pp. 24–53; Herbert Aptheker, *American Negro Slave Revolts* (New York: Columbia University, 1943), *passim*.

60. See below, Part IV, Note 115.

61. See William R. Hogan and Edwin A. Davis (eds.), *William Johnson's Natchez: The Ante-Bellum Diary of a Free Negro* (Baton Rouge: Louisiana State University Press, 1951), esp. pp. 1–64.

62. Aptheker, *American Negro Slave Revolts*, pp. 220, 268–269, 295–296, and *passim*.

63. Vernon L. Wharton, *The Negro in Mississippi, 1865–1890* (Chapel Hill: University of North Carolina Press, 1942), p. 164.

Frustration and aggression: Definitions

by JOHN DOLLARD, LEONARD W. DOOB, NEAL E. MILLER, O. H. MOWRER, AND ROBERT R. SEARS

1. In fact a number of antecedent conditions must sometimes *all* be present before any instigation occurs.

2. *Aggressive action* may be distinguished from *substitute response* operationally. Since a substitute response reduces the instigation to the original (frustrated) goal-response, removal of the interference which caused the frustration will be followed by a reduced goal-response. Aggressive action, on the other hand, reduces only the secondary instigation to aggression set up by the frustration and does not have any effect on the strength of the original instigation. Removal of the interference following an aggressive action, therefore, will be followed by the occurrence of the original (frustrated) goal-response at its normal strength and rate.

3. Aggressive behavior, like all other forms of behavior, is frequently forced into culturally defined patterns. Some of these are prohibited, some are permitted, and some are actually rewarded by social approval. A number of these patterns will be considered in more detail in Chapters IV and VIII.

4. One person may injure another by sheer accident. Such acts are not aggression, because they are not goal-responses. In statistical investigations accidents may be ignored since they are merely chance or attenuating factors. In the individual case it is necessary, in order to be certain of the aggressive nature of a given act, to demonstrate that it was a goal-response to instigation to injure.

Psychological principles: I

by JOHN DOLLARD AND OTHERS

1. For a more extensive description of this study, see below, p. 35.

2. This "ceasing to occur" relates only to the specific form of the action and not to the occurrence of aggression itself as a response to frustration.

3. *Cf.* Chapter IV.

4. This seems to be analogous to the experimental extinction of a conditioned response and may actually follow somewhat different laws from those followed in the elimination of a response through punishment.

5. The mechanism by which anticipation of punishment operates to eliminate an action is

not of paramount importance in the present context. To use the term "anticipation" in connection with strictly behavioral concepts such as goal-response, frustration, and aggression does no violence to the unity of the level of discourse provided the term "anticipation" is also defined behaviorally. Hull (70) has presented the concept of *anticipatory goal-response* to account for foresightful and purposive behavior, and Sears (142)

Psychological principles: II

by JOHN DOLLARD AND OTHERS

1. In the absence of an acceptable stimulus-response theory of perception, this assumption must be phrased in a somewhat unsatisfactory manner. It would seem that learning which response is the most effective in removing the frustration must be an important factor in building up the type of perception upon which the definition of direct aggression is based. It would also seem that the generalization posited in this assumption is analogous to the generalization of a conditioned response: the more direct acts of aggression will be those which are more similar, or more closely bound by associational ties, to the act of most direct aggression.

2. Whether the instigation to aggression will continue to mount until some act occurs or will tend to die down until the instigation to aggression finally disappears should depend upon exact quantitative relationships beyond the scope of the present discussion.

3. To be exact, one should distinguish between (*a*) that spread of aggression which is assumed to occur whether or not the direct aggression is inhibited, and (*b*) the displacement of aggression which, as has been deduced, should occur only when the more direct form of aggression is inhibited. Since few of the observations available to date have been so controlled that such a distinction can be made with any certainty, the term displacement will be used loosely here to cover both phenomena.

4. In the absence of specific data upon which to base principles that describe independently which of two types of action both directed at the same object will be the more direct form of aggression, the most direct form of aggression is dependently defined as the type of act which would occur in the complete absence of anticipation of punishment.

5. Presumably this reduction is more or less temporary and the instigation to aggression will build up again if the original frustration persists. Also the repetition of a mode of release may presumably produce learning of it. Throughout this hypothesis both the rôle of temporal factors and the influence of learning present problems acutely in need of detailed solution.

The study of urban violence: Some implications of laboratory studies of frustration and aggression

by LEONARD BERKOWITZ

1. John Dollard *et al.*, *Frustration and Aggression* (New Haven: Yale University Press, 1939), p. 3.

2. Konrad Lorenz, *On Aggression* (New York: Harcourt, Brace & World, 1966).

3. For example, S. K. Mallick and B. R. McCandless, "A Study of Catharsis of Aggression," *Journal of Personality and Social Psychology*, IV (1966), pp. 591–596.

4. See L. Berkowitz, "The Concept of Aggressive Drive," in L. Berkowitz (ed.), *Advances in Experimental Social Psychology*, Vol. II (New York: Academic Press, 1965).

5. N. H. Azrin, R. R. Hutchinson, and D. F. Hake, "Extinction-Induced Aggression," *Journal of the Experimental Analysis of Behavior*, IX (1966), pp. 191–204.

6. See Berkowitz, *op. cit.*, for a further discussion, and also L. Berkowitz (ed.), *Roots of Aggression: A Re-examination of the Frustration-Aggression Hypothesis* (New York: Atherton Press, 1968).

7. J. C. Davies, "Toward a Theory of Revolution," *American Sociological Review*, XXVII (1962), pp. 5–19.

8. I. K. Feierabend and R. L. Feierabend, "Aggressive Behaviors Within Polities, 1948–1962: A Cross-National Study," *Journal of Conflict Resolution*, X (1966), pp. 249–271.

9. R. E. Ulrich and N. H. Azrin, "Reflexive Fighting in Response to Aversive Stimulation," *Journal of the Experimental Analysis of Behavior*, V (1962), pp. 511–520.

10. P. K. Levison and J. P. Flynn, "The Objects Attacked by Cats During Stimulation of the Hypothalamus," *Animal Behavior*, XIII (1965), pp. 217–220.

11. L. Berkowitz and A. Le Page, "Weapons as Aggression-Eliciting Stimuli," *Journal of Personality and Social Psychology*, VII (1967), pp. 202–207.

12. E.g., Mallick and McCandless, *op. cit.*

13. See Berkowitz, Note 4, *op. cit.* for a summary of some of this research.

Conflict and the web of group affiliations

by GEORG SIMMEL

1. Fundamentally, all relations to others are distinguished according to the following questions (even though with innumerable answers ranging from the clearcut affirmative to the clear cut negative): (1) Is the psychological basis of the relation a drive (of the subject) which would develop even without external stimulus and on its own seeks an adequate object, either *finding* it in adequate form or making it so through imagination and necessity? Or (2) does the psychological basis of the relation consist in the response evoked by the nature or action of another person—whereby this response, too, of course, presupposes the *possibility* of being evoked; but this possibility would have remained latent without the stimulus and would not by itself have developed into a need. Intellectual and aesthetic, sympathetic and antipathetic relations are subject to this contrast from which alone they draw the forms of their development, intensity, and changes.

2. Written, presumably, shortly after 1900. Cf. *The Sociology of Georg Simmel*, translated, edited, and with an introduction by Kurt H. Wolff (Glencoe, Illinois: The Free Press, 1950), pp. lviii, (8), and lxii, IV.-Tr.

Inequality and instability: The relation of land tenure to politics

by BRUCE M. RUSSETT

1. "The Suppliants," *The Tragedies of Euripides*, trans. by Arthur S. Way (London, 1894), p. 373.

2. Alexis de Tocqueville, *Democracy in America* (New York: Vintage ed., 1954), II, p. 266.

3. Merle Kling, "Toward a Theory of Power and Political Instability in Latin America," *Western Political Quarterly*, IX (March 1956), pp. 21–35. Note that land distribution is only one element of the "colonial economy" defined by Kling.

4. Tocqueville, p. 266.

5. See, for example, Kenneth Parsons *et al.*, eds., *Land Tenure* (Madison, 1958), and Walter Froelich, *Land Tenure, Industrialization, and Social Stability* (Milwaukee, 1961).

6. Robert M. Solow, "Income Inequality Since the War," in *Postwar Economic Trends in the United States*, ed. by Ralph Freeman (New York, 1960).

7. One must always introduce comparative data, particularly on land tenure, with certain caveats. The quality of data collection is not uniform from one country to the next, and in any case it cannot indicate the quality of the land in question. Nevertheless, while these caveats may be important with regard to a few distributions, they do not fundamentally alter the character of the data shown.

Although a few of the data presented were compiled some time ago, patterns of land tenure normally change but little over the years. Only for Bolivia, Taiwan and, to a lesser degree, Italy is there evidence of a significant change between the year given and 1960.

8. Hayward R. Alker, Jr., and Bruce M. Russett, "Indices for Comparing Inequality," in *Comparing Nations: The Use of Quantitative Data in Cross-National Research*, ed. by R. L. Merritt and Stein Rokkan (1964, forthcoming).

9. The Gini number for a Lorenz curve is actually twice the area mentioned divided by the area (10,000 for 100 by 100 axes) of the whole square. Formula:

$$G = \frac{2\int_0^{100} (x\text{-}f(x))\,dx}{10,000}$$

where x is the cumulated population percentage and $f(x)$ is the height of the Lorenz curve. Cf. Mary Jean Bowman, "A Graphical Analysis of Personal Income Distribution in the United States," *American Economic Review*, XXXV (September 1945), pp. 607–628. In Table 1 below, the Gini index is multiplied by 100.

10. With this definition, most of the indices fall between 11 and 17. Our use of logarithmic transformations in the correlations below compensates for this bunching.

In some ways it might have been more desirable to measure the average tenure of a party or coalition, but that solution raises other problems. When a government in the French Fourth Republic fell and was replaced by a new cabinet composed basically of the same parties, was this a new coalition or just the old one under a new Premier? The first answer immediately involves one in difficulties of comparability with other countries' experiences; the second answer would cause France to appear much more stable than any observer would agree was correct. Measuring the tenure of the chief executive tells nothing about the *form* of government, nor about what Kling (p. 25) describes as concealed instability. A government may appear stable only as long as its repressive techniques succeed; when they fail, it may be violently and suddenly overthrown. Thus Trujillo's Dominican Republic was "stable" for several decades. Nevertheless it is difficult to see how "hidden instability" can be allowed for other than through some definition of a democratic-dictatorial continuum, which we attempt in index D below.

11. Cf. Rudolph J. Rummel, "Dimensions of Conflict Behavior Within and Between Nations," in *General Systems*, Yearbook of the Society for the Advancement of General Systems Theory (Ann Arbor, 1963). The nature and limitations of the data used in this article will be discussed in Bruce M. Russett *et al.*, *World Handbook of*

Political and Social Indicators (New Haven, 1964, forthcoming).

12. Harry Eckstein, *Internal War: The Problem of Anticipation*, a report submitted to the Research Group in Psychology and the Social Sciences, Smithsonian Institution (Washington, 1962), Appendix I.

13. Seymour Martin Lipset, "Some Social Requisites of Democracy," *American Political Science Review*, LIII (March 1959), pp. 73–74.

14. For a similar classification of regimes in the underdeveloped countries, see Gabriel A. Almond and James S. Coleman, eds., *The Politics of the Developing Areas* (Princeton, 1960), pp. 579–581.

Lipset's categorization is of course crude and subject to a number of criticisms. For example, cf. Phillips Cutright, "National Political Development: Measurement and Analysis," *American Sociological Review*, XXVIII (April 1963), pp. 253–264. The alternative index that Cutright suggests, however, really deals with the complexity of political institutions—quite a different matter.

15. For the three political variables, I used logarithmic transformations instead of the raw data.

16. Nor is great concentration of farmland always a prelude to violent revolution in predominantly agricultural societies. Even according to figures cited by the Communists, inequality in Czarist Russia and interwar China was less than in most of the countries listed in Table 1. Cf. V. I. Lenin, *The Agrarian Program of Social Democracy*, in *Selected Works*, III (New York, n.d.), pp. 164–165; and Yuan-li Wu, *An Economic Survey of Communist China* (New York, 1956), p. 119. Wu lists several estimates, the most extreme of which was the report of the Hankow Land Commission, which he alleges was Communist-dominated. The Gini indices for Russia and China were, respectively, approximately 73.0 and 64.6.

According to George Pavlovsky, in *Agricultural Russia on the Eve of the Revolution* (London, 1930), Chapter 4, the difficulty in Russia stemmed less from the *relative* size of farm plots than from the fact that the *absolute* size of most holdings was too small to produce more than bare subsistence. Given the technological backwardness of the Russian peasant, this may well be true.

17. "Rich" countries and "societies where there are many alternative sources of wealth" are to some degree synonymous. Denmark and Australia, two rich nations often thought of as "agricultural," actually have only twenty-three and fourteen percent, respectively, of their labor forces in agriculture.

18. The technique used was multiple regression. For a description and application of this method, see Donald Stokes, Angus Campbell,

and Warren Miller, "Components of Electoral Decision," *American Political Science Review*, LII (June 1958), pp. 367–387. This procedure also allows us to test for the independent "explanatory" power of each variable with the other variables *controlled*.

19. This points up rather sharply the flaw in any attempt to use land distribution as an indicator of the degree of inequality in all wealth for *advanced* economies. Australia is widely acknowledged to be a highly egalitarian society.

20. Note that these definitions of stability say nothing about the rate of turnover among government personnel, but only about the stability of democratic forms of government. We have included India and the Philippines in the category "stable democracy" because, though independent only since the end of World War II, they met the above test. Nevertheless this decision is open to some question, as political conditions in these countries clearly are *not* the same as in Western Europe. If they instead were classified as "unstable democracies" it would, however, only very moderately change the pattern of the following table.

Rapid growth as a destabilizing force

by MANCUR OLSEN, JR.

1. Grant S. McClellan, ed., *U.S. Foreign Aid* (The Reference Shelf, Vol. XXIX, No. 5 [New York: The H. W. Wilson Company, 1957]), p. 90, taken from a speech by Eugene R. Black, made when he was President of the World Bank.

2. *Ibid.*, p. 205, taken from a report by Richard Nixon to President Eisenhower.

3. *Ibid.*, p. 140, taken from "Final Report of Eleventh American Assembly."

4. Hannah Arendt, *On Revolution* (New York: The Viking Press, 1963), pp. 15, 54–57, 61–63, 66–69, 74–76, 80–85, 87, 105–108, 135, 181, 224, 249.

5. McClellan, *Foreign Aid*, p. 122, taken from an article by Max F. Millikan.

6. *Ibid.*, pp. 53–54, taken from a message to Congress of May 22, 1957. It is significant that all five of the quotations cited so far to illustrate the view that economic growth leads to political stability could be found in one anthology. The number of writers who have accepted this argument must be very large indeed.

7. Max Millikan and Donald Blackmer, eds., *The Emerging Nations* (Boston: Little, Brown, & Co., 1962), pp. 142–145; and Andrew Shonfield, *The Attack on World Poverty* (New York: Random House, 1960), pp. 3–14.

8. Max Millikan and W. W. Rostow, *A Proposal: Key to an Effective Foreign Policy* (New York: Harper, 1957), pp. 19–23. See the criticism of this book in Edward C. Banfield's *American Foreign Aid Doctrines* (Washington,

D.C.: American Enterprise Institute, 1963), especially p. 6.

9. Eric Hoffer, *The True Believer: Thoughts on the Nature of Mass Movements* (New York: The New American Library, 1951), p. 17 and *passim*. See also William Kornhauser, *The Politics of Mass Society* (Glencoe, Ill.: The Free Press, 1959), especially pp. 14–15; Seymour Martin Lipset, *Political Man, The Social Bases of Politics* (Garden City, N.Y.: Doubleday and Co., 1960).

10. M. Beer, *A History of British Socialism* (London: George Allen and Unwin, 1940), pp. 153–154.

11. See Walter Galenson, *The Danish System of Labor Relations* (Cambridge: Harvard University Press, 1952); and "Scandinavia" in *Comparative Labor Movements*, Galenson, ed. (New York: Prentice-Hall, 1952), especially pp. 105–120. See also Lipset, *Political Man*, pp. 68–72.

12. Simon Kuznets, while pointing out that in recent times the *long-run* trend in the advanced economies is toward greater equality of incomes, has suggested that in the early phases of economic growth (which are the main concern of this paper) there is a tendency toward increasing inequality. Kuznets' focus is on the inequality of the *overall* income distribution, while this paper is concerned with the distribution of the gains and losses only; thus it would be logically possible that even when the distribution of gains and losses from economic growth was extremely unequal, the overall distribution of income could become less unequal, since the poorer people could get the gains and the richer the losses. Nonetheless, Kuznets' conclusions about changes in income distribution in the early phases of economic growth would appear to support the argument offered here. See "Economic Growth and Income Inequality," *American Economic Review*, XLV (March 1955), pp. 1–28.

13. R. A. Kessel and A. A. Alchian have in an interesting article denied the usual contention that wages rise more slowly than prices and profits during inflations, but I do not find their conclusion persuasive. See "The Meaning and Validity of the Inflation Induced Lag of Wages Behind Prices," *American Economic Review*, 50 (March 1960), pp. 43–67.

14. Is this factor offset by those who have lost in absolute terms but gained in relative terms? It is not, because in any society in which there has been economic growth, from which more have gained than have lost, all those who have lost in absolute terms will also have lost in relative terms, so there will be in this case no class of absolute losers and relative gainers to offset the class mentioned above. The only case in which there could be a class of absolute losers and relative gainers would be that in which the number of losers exceeded the number of gainers. But the Duesenberry investigations also tell us

that those whose incomes are falling absolutely have a higher propensity to consume than those people who have the same level of income but whose incomes have not been falling. Those who are absolute losers and relative gainers may therefore also feel that they are suffering from the economic advance.

15. The importance of this factor will be limited by the likelihood that most of the saving will come from the rich.

16. Alexis de Tocqueville, *L'Ancien Regime*, trans. M. W. Patterson (Oxford: Basil Blackwell, 1947), p. 186.

17. E. A. J. Johnson, after hearing this paper presented at the Economic History Association meeting, objected that totalitarian nations fit the author's hypothesis better than other nations do, in part because the subject people naturally blame the ubiquitous state for all difficult economic adjustments. He seemed to relate the opposition leading to Stalin's purges, after a period of rapid Soviet growth, and the apparent liberalization in some current communist regimes (especially Tito's), to the rapid economic development. I feel that his criticism, if I have understood it correctly, is very much worth investigating.

18. For models in which a variety of economic conditions can lead to instability, see Ronald G. Ridker, "Discontent and Economic Growth," *Economic Development and Cultural Change*, XI (October 1962), pp. 1–15, and James C. Davies, "Toward a Theory of Revolution," *American Sociological Review*, XXVII (February 1962), pp. 5–19. Davies contends that it is when a period of growth is interrupted by a depression that revolution is most likely. Davies' conclusion is not necessarily inconsistent with this paper's, which deals with growth as a cause of instability rather than with the precise timing of revolutions.

19. In pointing to cases of instability, however, it will be necessary to distinguish genuine instability of an entire society from some of the superficial changes that are occasionally mistaken for true instability. In the Third Republic in France there were frequent changes of cabinets and many complaints about "instability." But the policies of the French government were quite stable, and the different cabinets were composed of roughly the same men, and roughly the same coalitions of parties, so basically nothing in the life of France changed. The French could rightly say that there had been only a reshuffling of the political deck—that the more things changed the more they remained the same. Similarly the "palace guard" or "*coup d'etat*" type of change of government so common in Latin America should not be confused with a genuine social revolution. The changes of government brought about by the "palace guard" or by the army obviously depend mainly on what goes on inside the "palace guard" or inside the army rather than upon what goes on inside the economy.

And these changes of government often bring no changes in policy, in any event. Thus it is important to distinguish the political intrigue of the Third and Fourth Republics from true political upheavals like the French Revolution, and the routine Latin American *coup d'etat* from the Peronist or Castroist revolution.

20. See for example J. U. Nef, "The Progress of Technology and the Growth of Large Scale Industry in Great Britain, 1540–1640," and "Prices and Industrial Capitalism in France and England, 1540–1640," in *Essays in Economic History*, E. M. Carus-Wilson, ed. (London: Edward Arnold Ltd., 1954), I, pp. 88–134.

21. See J. L. Hammond, "The Industrial Revolution and Discontent," *Economic History Review*, II (January 1930), pp. 215–228, and G. D. H. Cole, *A Short History of the British Working Class Movement, 1787–1957* (London: George Allen & Unwin, 1948), pp. 121–151.

22. Tocqueville, *L'Ancien Regime*, pp. 185–186. Just as there are many scholars who subscribe to Tocqueville's argument, there are also many who dispute it.

23. W. W. Rostow, *The Stages of Economic Growth* (Cambridge [Engl.]: The University Press, 1960), pp. 38, 66–67, 93–105, and Alexander Gerschenkron, *Economic Backwardness in Historical Perspective* (Cambridge: Harvard University Press, 1962), pp. 5–30.

24. Lipset, *Political Man* (cited in Note 9), pp. 70–71.

25. Bert F. Hoselitz and Myron Weiner, "Economic Development and Political Stability in India," *Dissent*, VIII (Spring 1961), pp. 172–179. For a general, theoretical treatment of the relationship between economic and political change, with particular application to India, see Charles Wolf, *Foreign Aid: Theory and Practice in Southern Asia* (Princeton: Princeton University Press, 1960). I am indebted to Mr. Wolf for helpful suggestions on this topic.

26. I am indebted for many of these examples to Stephan Enke, *Economics for Development* (Englewood Cliffs, N.J.: Prentice-Hall, Inc., 1963), and to F. Benham, *Economic Aid to Underdeveloped Countries* (Oxford: Oxford University Press, 1961).

27. On Italy, see Robert Neville, "Catholic—Yet Communist—Why?" *New York Times Magazine* (June 2, 1963), p. 61.

28. "... great delays in industralization tend to allow time for social tensions to develop and to assume sinister proportions. ... The Soviet government can properly be described as a product of the country's economic backwardness. ... If anything is a 'grounded historical assumption,' this would seem to be one: the delayed industrial revolution was responsible for a political revolution in the course of which power fell into the hands of a dictatorial govern-

ment. ..." Gerschenkron, *Economic Backwardness*, p. 28.

29. The relatively brittle character of most institutions in traditional, underdeveloped societies is illustrated by Max Webber's analysis of the origins of castes and classes. He argued that a caste system would thrive only in a relatively static society, for it makes virtually no provision for the changes in individual rankings that changing societies require. A modern class system, by contrast, allows for some changes in the positions of individuals. See Max Weber, *From Max Weber: Essays in Sociology*, H. H. Gerth and C. Wright Mills, ed. and trans. (New York: Oxford University Press, 1946, especially pp. 193–193.) Presumably most institutions of traditional societies have not had to develop a great deal of flexibility, while those that have evolved in dynamic industrial societies have acquired some capacity to adjust to rapid change. Accordingly, the thesis of this article would explain the social and political effects of rapid growth much better in underdeveloped societies than in economically advanced societies. The thesis here would fit countries like the United States, Canada, Australia, and New Zealand least of all, for these countries of relatively recent settlement have inherited fewer feudal institutions than other nations, and their institutions have had to evolve in rather rapidly changing conditions from the beginning.

Aggressive behaviors within polities, 1948–1962: A cross-national study

by IVO K. FEIERABEND

AND ROSALIND L. FEIERABEND

1. This research was partially supported by a grant from the San Diego State College Foundation. A paper based on this article was delivered at the Annual Meeting of the American Psychological Association in Chicago, Illinois, September 1965 (Feierabend and Feierabend, 1965b).

2. More recent analyses of aggression have placed increasing emphasis on the role of stimulus in eliciting an aggressive response. (For a discussion of recent approaches, see Berkowitz, 1965.)

3. The data bank of political instability events, including the *Code Index* to the bank, instructions in raters, etc., is available through the Interuniversity Consortium for Political Research, Box 1248, Ann Arbor, Michigan.

4. These stability profiles correlate with the ordering of the same countries based on Eckstein's index, "Deaths from domestic group violence per 1,000,000 population, 1950–1962." The rank-order correlation between these two indices is Spearman $r = .69$. On the other hand, only a low correlation exists with Russett's index, "Executive stability: number of years

independent/number of chief executives, 1945–1961." The rank-order correlation between these two indices is Spearman *r* = .38.

5. The data used in Hoole's 1964 study were gathered from a single source, *Deadline Data on World Affairs.* The data bank as presently constituted comprises two sources, *Deadline Data on World Affairs* and *The Encyclopaedia Britannica Yearbooks.*

6. The difficulty of dividing these highly correlated indicators should be noted. Each contains some error component due to the unreliable reporting of crossnational data. For an estimate of error in crossnational data, see Russett (1964) and Rummel (1963).

7. This modernity ranking, based on eight indices, is highly comparable to that of Russett *et al.* (1964) based on GNP alone. A Spearman *r* calculated between the two rank-orderings is .92.

8. The yearly percent rate of change on the ecological variables was calculated by subtracting the lowest value of the variable in the twenty-eight-year period from the highest value attained, dividing by the lowest value to convert to a percentage change, and then dividing by the number of years spanned to obtain the yearly percentage change.

9. This finding is in contrast to the high level of relationship obtained between literacy and static stability level reported in Study 1. The explanation may lie in the observed inconsistency in the literacy data reported over the longer time period in various sources.

Political violence in Venezuela: 1958–1964

by EDWARD W. GUDE

1. Ernest Baker, *The Politics of Aristotle* (London: Oxford University Press, 1952), p. 205.

2. *Ibid.*, p. 207.

3. *Ibid.*, p. 231.

4. H. H. Gerth and C. Wright Mills, eds., *From Max Weber: Essays in Sociology* (New York: Oxford University Press, 1958), p. 125.

5. Georges Sorel, *Reflections on Violence* (New York: Collier Books, 1961).

6. Frantz Fanon, *The Wretched of the Earth* (New York: Grove Press, 1966); *Black Skin, White Mask* (New York: Grove Press, 1967); *Studies in a Dying Colonialism* (New York: Monthly Review Press, 1965).

7. Manfred Halpern, "The Revolution of Modernization in National and International Society," in Carl J. Friedrich, ed., *Revolution: Nomos VIII* (New York: Atherton Press, 1966), p. 202.

8. H. L. Nieburg, "The Threat of Violence and Social Change," *American Political Science Review,* LVI: 4 (December 1962), p. 865.

9. Lucian Pye, "The Roots of Insurgency and the Commencement of Rebellion," in Harry

Eckstein, ed., *Internal War: Problems and Approaches* (Glencoe: The Free Press, 1964), p. 167.

10. *Ibid.*, p. 160.

11. Guillermo Morón, *A History of Venezuela* (London: George Allan and Unwin, 1964), p. 207.

12. *Castro-Communist Insurgency in Venezuela* (Atlantic Research Corporation, Alexandria, Virginia, mimeo, 31 December 1964), p. 21.

13. *El Universal,* 7 May 1962.

14. Translated in Atlantic Research Corporation, *op. cit.*, pp. 39–53.

15. Source, *El Universal.*

Dimensions of social conflict in Latin America

by DOUGLAS BWY

1. Ivo Feierabend provides the linkage to "political instability," when he notes that it is "... the degree or the amount of *aggression* directed by individuals or groups within the political system against other groups or against the complex of officeholders and individuals and groups associated with them. Or, conversely, as the amount of aggression directed by these officeholders against other individuals, groups, or officeholders within the polity." See Ivo K. and Rosalind L. Feierabend, "Aggressive Behaviors within Polities, 1948–62: A Cross-National Study," *Journal of Conflict Resolution,* X (September 1966), p. 250.

2. The phrase "civil violence," which has also been used in this connection, might have better illustrated one of the distinctions being made; namely, that between (a) aggressive activity directed from a populace (individuals or groups) to a political system (either at the community, regime, or government level), and (b) criminal aggressive activity (generally, though not always, of an individual nature), such as murder and robbery. The latter is not the concern of this study.

3. James Payne, "Peru: The Politics of Structured Violence," *Journal of Politics,* XXVII (May 1965), p. 363.

4. Merle Kling, "Towards a Theory of Power and Political Instability in Latin America," *Western Political Quarterly,* IX (March 1956), p. 21.

5. Mack and Snyder note that "conflictful behaviors are those designed to destroy, injure, thwart, or otherwise control another party or other parties. ..." See Raymond W. Mack and Richard C. Snyder, "The Analysis of Social Conflict: Toward an Overview and Synthesis," *Journal of Conflict Resolution,* I (June 1957), p. 218.

6. D. P. Bwy, "Systematizing the Collection of Data on Aggressive Activity: A Domestic Conflict Code Sheet" (Dept. of Political Science,

Case Western Reserve University, July 1967), 26 pp. An example of the detail that was attempted in differentiating over forty instability events can be seen in one of the definitions, that of "Riots or Manifestaciones": "A *violent* Antigovernment Demonstration (1). The presence of accompanying violence differentiates 'riots' from 'demonstrations.' A mob clashing with the police or military, or attacking private property, is considered a riot as long as such violence appears to be spontaneous; otherwise it may qualify for consideration as a Civilian Political Revolt (27). Riots are considered discrete events, limited to a given group of people. Violence between rival political and nonpolitical groups is classified as either a Political (12) or Non political Clash (13)."

7. Sampling sites within four Latin American nations qualified under this criterion: Brazil, Cuba, the Dominican Republic, and Panama. Detailed and comparable national probability samples were drawn for these nations by the Institute for International Social Research, in 1960 and 1962. A research commitment was made to these nations primarily because the survey data provided much more sensitive measures of (a) a population's "satisfaction" (or "dissatisfaction"), and (b) feelings of legitimacy —two core variables of the political instability model.

8. The primary source which most adequately satisfied this criterion was the *Hispanic American Report*, which is itself a synthesis of major news media. *Hispanic American Report: A Monthly Report on Developments in Spain, Portugal, and Latin America* (Ronald Hilton, ed.); Institute of Hispanic American and Luso-Brazilian Studies, Stanford University, Vol. I (1948)–Vol. XVII (1964).

9. *Brazil:* Acre, Alagoas, Amapá, Amazonas, Bahía, Ceará, Espírito Santo, Fernando de Noronha, Goiás, Guanabara, Maranhão, Mato Grosso, Minas Gerais, Pará, Paraíba, Paraná, Pernambuco, Piauí, Rio Branco, Rio de Janeiro, Rio Grande do Norte, Rio Grande do Sul, Rondônia, Santa Catarina, São Paulo, Sergipe, Serra do Aimores, Distrito Federal.

Cuba: Pinar del Río, Havana, Matanzas, Las Villas, Camagüey, Oriente.

Dominican Republic: Distrito Nacional, Azua, Bahoruco, Barahone, Dajabón, Duarte, El Seibo, Espaillat, Independencia, La Romana, La Vega, Maria Trinidad, Monte Cristi, Pedernales, Peravia, Puerto Plata, Salcedo, Samaná, Sánchez, Santiago, Santiago Rodriguez, Valverde.

Panama: Chiriquí, Colón, Darién, Panamá, Veraguas.

In order to reduce the role of aberrations on what were meant to be general findings (thereby preventing any of the correlation input into the factor analysis from being dependent on too few cases), the criterion was established that each variable must have at least 5% participation among the units, to be included in the analysis. On the basis of this criterion, 24 variables qualified for inclusion in the analysis. The measures failing to satisfy the 5% criterion were: Printed or Broadcast Protests, Political Boycott, Antiforeign Threat, *Imposición, Candidato Único, Continuismo, Machetismo* or Peasant Rebellion, Civilian Political Revolt, Private Warfare, and Banditry.

10. The computer program which monitored these calculations was $MESA_1$, a 95×95 Factor Analytic Program with Varimax Rotation. The lower limit for eigenvalues (i.e., a proportion of variance which may vary from near zero to n, where n is the number of variables entering a factor matrix) to be included in rotation was 1.00. Rotation is carried out in order to obtain a solution which is not entirely dependent upon each particular variable in the analysis. Orthogonal rotation is the fitting of factors to clusters of variables, with the restriction that the correlation between factors is zero. The *varimax* criterion is used to rotate orthogonally to "simple structure," that is, the maximization of high and low leadings. Thus, this form of rotation continues to maintain independence among the factors.

11. R. J. Rummel, "Dimensions of Conflict Behavior Within and Between Nations," *General Systems Yearbook*, VIII (1963), pp. 1–50.

Raymond Tanter, "Dimensions of Conflict Behavior within and between Nations, 1958–60," *Journal of Conflict Resolution*, X (March 1966), pp. 41–64.

R. J. Rummel, "Dimensions of Conflict Behavior within Nations, 1946–59," *Journal of Conflict Resolution*, X (March 1966), pp. 65–73.

12. Although the other measures in the Rummel and Tanter analyses are generally comparable (by definition) to the domestic conflict measures used here, the variable "Major Governmental Crises" appears to be somewhat different. Rummel and Tanter defined this event as: "Any rapidly developing situation that threatens to bring the downfall of the present regime—excluding situations of revolt aimed at such an overthrow."

13. D. P. Bwy, "Political Instability in Latin America: The Cross-Cultural Test of a Causal Model," *Latin American Research Review*, III (Spring 1968), forthcoming.

14. Rummel "Dimensions of Conflict Behavior Within and Between Nations," *op. cit.*, p. 35.

15. "Revolutions" were defined by both Rummel and Tanter as: "Any illegal or forced change in the top governmental elite, any attempt at such change, or any successful or unsuccessful armed rebellion whose aim is independence from the central government."

It should be noted that their data on "civil

wars" and "social revolutions" were too infrequent to be used alone, and so apparently both Rummel and Tanter merged these data with those on "palace revolutions" into the general category, above, "Number of Revolutions." In view of this fact, a comparison across studies on this measure becomes somewhat difficult.

16. Tanter, *op. cit.*, p. 43.

17. To Andrew Janos, "Unconventional warfare may be said to exist if and when the adversaries confronting each other have grossly disproportionate capabilities, whether in manpower, resources, or organizational base. In unconventional warfare, one of the participants possesses either an army of inferior size, equipment, and organization, or no army at all. Whereas one side can rely on a regular army, the other will have to fight the war with scratch military units, 'part-time soldiers,' nonmilitary organizations, unorganized masses, or with tightly organized but numerically inferior groups of political activists."

See Andrew C. Janos, "Unconventional Warfare: Framework and Analysis," *World Politics*, XV (July 1963), pp. 637–638.

18. Merle Kling, "Cuba: A Case Study of a Successful Attempt to Seize Political Power by the Application of Unconventional Warfare," in J. K. Zawodny (ed.), "Unconventional Warfare," special issue of *The Annals of the American Academy of Political and Social Science*, CCCXLI (May 1962), p. 44.

19. *Ibid.*, p. 43.

20. From: James Geschwender, "Social Structure and the Negro Revolt: An Examination of Some Hypotheses," *Social Forces*, XLIII (December 1964), p. 249. (Italics added.)

21. Bruce M. Russett, "Inequality and Instability: The Relation of Land Tenure to Politics," *World Politics*, XVI (April 1964), pp. 442–454.

22. Raymond Tanter and Manus Midlarsky, "A Theory of Revolution," *Journal of Conflict Resolution*, XI (September 1967), pp. 264–280.

23. Seymour Martin Lipset, "Some Social Requisites of Democracy: Economic Development and Political Legitimacy," *American Political Science Review*, LIII (March 1959), pp. 69–105.

24. Phillips Cutright, "National Political Development: Measurement and Analysis," *American Sociological Review*, XXVIII (April 1963), pp. 253–264.

25. Daniel Lerner, "Modernizing Styles of Life: A Theory," in Lerner, *The Passing of Traditional Society: Modernizing the Middle East* (New York: Free Press, 1958), pp. 43–75.

26. Lyford P. Edwards, *The Natural History of Revolution* (University of Chicago Press, 1927). (Italics added.)

27. Eric R. Wolf, *Sons of the Shaking Earth* (University of Chcago Press, 1959), pp. 108–109.

28. James C. Davies, "Toward a Theory of Revolution," *American Sociological Review*, XXVII (February 1962), p. 6.

29. Crane Brinton, *The Anatomy of Revolution* (New York: Vintage Books, 1952).

30. Davies, *op. cit.*

31. Cole Blasier, "Studies of Social Revolution: Origins in Mexico, Bolivia, and Cuba," *Latin American Research Review*, II (Summer 1967), pp. 28–64.

32. Lipset, *op. cit.*, p. 86.

33. David Easton, "An Approach to the Analysis of Political Systems," *World Politics*, IX (April 1957), pp. 383–400.

34. "Subject" political cultures are those in which individual cognitions are primarily oriented toward *output* structures and the "system as a general political object." See Gabriel Almond and Sidney Verba, *The Civic Culture: Political Attitudes and Democracy in Five Nations* (Princeton University Press, 1963).

35. *Ibid.*, p. 246.

36. Arnold H. Buss, *The Psychology of Aggression* (New York: John Wiley, 1961), p. 58.

37. Robert A. LeVine, "Anti-European Violence in Africa: A Comparative Analysis," *Journal of Conflict Resolution*, III (December 1959), pp. 420–429.

38. Bwy, *op. cit.*

39. F. P. Kilpatrick and Hadley Cantril, "Self-Anchoring Scaling: A Measure of Individuals' Unique Reality Worlds," *Journal of Individual Psychology*, XVI (November 1960), pp. 158–173.

40. Hadley Cantril, *The Pattern of Human Concerns* (New Brunswick: Rutgers University Press, 1965), pp. 22–26.

41. The raw data, interview schedules, and code books were obtained from the Roper Public Opinion Research Center, Williams College, Williamstown, Mass. The on-site interviewing for the Institute for International Social Science Research was conducted by: Instituto de Estudios Sociais e Economicos, Ltda. (Brazil); International Research Associates, S.A. de C.V., of Mexico City (the Dominican Republic and Panama); and anonymous (Cuba).

42. See: D. P. Bwy, "RECODIGO: An All-Purpose Computer Program for 'Cleaning' Multiple-Punched Data," *Behavioral Science*, forthcoming.

43. City units: *Brazil:* Fortaleza, Niteroi, Porto Calvo, Recife, Rio de Janeiro, and São Paulo; *Cuba:* Cardenas, Havana, Remedios; *the Dominican Republic:* Santiago de los Caballeros and Santo Domingo; *Panama:* Colón, David, and Ciudad de Panamá.

44. Province units: *Brazil:* Alagoas, Amazonas, Bahía, Ceará, Guanabara, Maranhão, Minas Gerais, Paraíba, Paraná, Pernambuco, Rio de Janeiro, Rio Grande do Sul, and São Paulo; *Cuba:* Havana, Matanzas, and Las Villas;

the Dominican Republic: Distrito Nacional and Santiago; *Panama:* Chiriquí, Colón, and Panamá.

45. Coding scheme of "political" considerations, mentioned by at least 5 % of all respondents:

NATIONAL HOPES
AND ASPIRATIONS

National Unity—absence of unrest, tensions, and antagonisms based on regional, class, caste, religious, etc., differences.

Honest Government—fair and just; no corruption or nepotism.

Efficient Government—competent leadership and administration; effective party system; no excessive bureaucracy.

Socialistic Government—aspiration to become a socialistic or welfare state.

Balanced Government—adequate system of checks and balances; no excessive power in the hands of government; less central government; more power to states and provinces.

Freedom—with specific reference to freedom of speech, of religion, of occupation, of movement, etc.

Political Stability, Internal Peace, and Order.

Law and Order—maintenance of the public peace; decrease or no increase in crime, juvenile delinquency, etc.; fair courts, good or improved juridical practices, penal system, etc.

Representative Government—maintain present democracy, or become a democracy.

NATIONAL WORRIES AND FEARS

Disunity among People of the Nation—unrest, tensions, antagonisms, based on regional, class, caste, religious, etc., differences.

Dishonest Government—unfair and unjust; corruption and nepotism.

Inefficient Government—weak, indecisive leadership and administration; no effective party system; excessive bureaucracy.

Fear Country Will Become Socialistic.

Central Government Too Big and Too Powerful—no adequate system of checks and balances; not enough power for states and provinces. Also coded: Fear of Communist danger or the consequences of Communist control from within.

Lack or Loss of Freedom—in general, or with specific reference to freedom of speech, of religion, of occupation, of movement, etc.

Political Instability, Chaos, and Civil War.

Lack of Law and Order—failure to maintain public peace; prevalence of or increase in crime, juvenile delinquency, etc., unfair courts, poor or unfair juridical practices, penal system, etc.

No Representative Government—loss of democracy; totalitarianism.

46. The measure "Governmental Boycott" was the only variable which failed to qualify under the previously established criterion of at least 5 % participation among the units, and was dropped from the analysis presented in Table II.

47. The two sets of factorial solutions (across the two time periods) were generally compatible. One of the more comparable solutions, presented below, shows the remarkably similar factor loadings for the only extracted, unrotated factor. The unrotated first factor was selected to index these composite variables, since it explains the maximum amount of variance about the original operational indices.

t_1: *Brazil/Cuba: 1956–1959*
Dominican Republic/Panama: 1958–1961

Variable	Factor Loading
Limited States of Emergency	.874
Martial Law	.887
Exiles	.890

t_2: *Brazil/Cuba: 1960–1964*
Dominican Republic/Panama: 1962–1966

Variable	Factor Loading
Limited States of Emergency	.861
Martial Law	.851
Exiles	.716

48. The same as "Demonstration," with the exception that "Demonstra*ting*" refers to an indeterminate number of continuous demonstrations taking place (either within or across coding units) simultaneously.

49. Furthermore, in *multiple* regression, as in the two-variable case, b's and *beta's* which appear in the regression equations represent slopes, or the amount of change in Y that can be associated with a given change in one of the X's, *with the remaining independent variables held constant*. This technique, then, allows us to determine the distinct explanatory power of each of the independent variables in bringing about a change in the dependent variable, with the others held fixed.

50. With an N of 21, one might expect the standard deviation range about the mean of a normal distribution to be half (3.0) that for the large-sample case. Therefore, by extension, the standard deviation itself will probably be half its normal size of (1.0), which accounts for the .5 to .7 standard deviations among the variables in the present analysis. In addition, because of (a) the N of 21, and (b) a problem of unequal variances, two of the "*beta*" coefficients are greater than unity (Equation 1A: $VIOLNT_2$, and Equation 1B: $VIOLNT_2$).

51. Thus, a movement of 2.0 raw score b-units should equal a 1.2 standard deviation movement, if the standard deviation for the independent variable is 6.

52. Crane Brinton, "The Anatomy of Revolution," in Harry Eckstein and David Apter (eds.), *Comparative Politics: A Reader* (New York: Free Press, 1963), pp. 560–569.

53. "Internal War," for Eckstein, was defined as: "... attempts to change by violence, or threat of violence, a government's policies, rulers, or organization." See Harry Eckstein (ed.), *Internal War: Problems and Approaches* (New York: Free Press, 1964), p. 1.

54. Harry Eckstein, "Internal War: The Problem of Anticipation," in: Ithiel de Sola Pool *et al.*, *Social Science Research and National Security*, a report prepared by the Research Group in Psychology and the Social Sciences (Smithsonian Institution, Washington, D.C., 1963), pp. 102–147.

55. Manuel Avila, "Preliminary Model of Internal War Potential," in *Project Camelot: Report on Research Design* (Special Operations Research Office, American University, Washington, D.C., April 1965), p. D-4.

56. This could account for the considerable change about $VIOLNT_1$ in Equation 3A; while no such changes occurred in the Internal War equations.

57. Bwy, "Political Instability in Latin America," *op. cit.*

58. "... the opportunity to participate in political decisions is associated with greater satisfaction with that system and with greater general loyalty to the system. ... Everything being equal, the sense of ability to participate in politics appears to increase the legitimacy of a system and to lead to political stability." See Almond and Verba, *op. cit.*, p. 253.

59. Bwy, *op. cit.*

A causal model of civil strife: A comparative analysis using new indices

by TED GURR

1. This is a revised version of a paper read at the 1967 Annual Meeting of the American Political Science Association, Chicago, September 5–9. The research was supported in part by the Center for Research in Social Systems (formerly SORO), The American University, and by the Advanced Research Projects Agency of the Department of Defense. This support implies neither sponsor approval of this article and its conclusions nor the author's approval of policies of the U.S. government toward civil strife. The assistance of Charles Ruttenberg throughout the process of research design, data collection, and analysis is gratefully acknowledged. Substantial portions of the data were collected by Joel Prager and Lois Wasserspring. The author owes special thanks to Harry Eckstein for his advice and encouragement. Bruce M. Russett and Raymond Tanter provided useful criticisms of the paper in draft form. Research was carried out at the Center of International Studies, Princeton University.

2. Ted Gurr, "Psychological Factors in Civil Violence," *World Politics*, 20 (January 1968), pp. 245–278.

3. Coercive potential is labeled "retribution" in *ibid*. The theoretical model also stipulates a set of variables that determines the intensity of deprivation. In the research reported in the present article, deprivation was operationalized directly rather than by reference to its component variables. The causal mechanism of the theory is the frustration-aggression relationship, which the author has attempted to modify and apply to collective strife in the light of recent empirical and theoretical work, e.g., Leonard Berkowitz, *Aggression: A Social Psychological Analysis* (New York: McGraw-Hill, 1962), and Aubrey J. Yates, *Frustration and Conflict* (New York: Wiley, 1962).

4. Ted Gurr with Charles Ruttenberg, *The Conditions of Civil Violence: First Tests of a Causal Model* (Princeton: Center of International Studies, Princeton University, Research Monograph No. 28, April 1967).

5. See Douglas Bwy, "Governmental Instability in Latin America: The Preliminary Test of a Causal Model of the Impulse to 'Extra-Legal' Change," paper read at the American Psychological Association Annual Convention, New York, September 2–6, 1966; Jennifer Walton, "Correlates of Coerciveness and Permissiveness of National Political Systems: A Cross-National Study" (M.A. thesis, San Diego State College, 1965); Gurr and Ruttenberg, *The Conditions of Civil Violence . . .*, pp. 81–84.

6. See, for example, Chalmers Johnson, *Revolution and the Social System* (Stanford: The Hoover Institution on War, Revolution and Peace, 1964), pp. 14–22.

7. Samuel P. Huntington, "Political Development and Political Decay," *World Politics*, 17 (April 1965), pp. 386–430; William Kornhauser, *The Politics of Mass Society* (New York: The Free Press, 1959); and Arthur M. Ross and George W. Hartmann, *Changing Patterns of Industrial Conflict* (New York: Wiley, 1960), among others.

8. Gurr, "Psychological Factors . . ."

9. *Ibid.*

10. Gurr and Ruttenberg, *The Conditions of Civil Violence . . .*, pp. 100–106.

11. Richard M. Merelman, "Learning and Legitimacy," this *American Political Science Review*, pp. 548–561, 60 (September 1966); see also the work of Pastore and of Kregarman and Worchel, reviewed in Berkowitz, *op. cit., passim.*

12. Five polities meeting these criteria were excluded: Laos on grounds that at no time in the 1960s did it have even the forms of a unified regime, and Albania, Mongolia, North Korea, and North Vietnam for lack of sufficient reliable data. The universe nonetheless includes polities with more than 98 percent of the world's population.

13. Hubert M. Blalock, Jr., *Causal Inferences*

in Nonexperimental Research (Chapel Hill: University of North Carolina Press, 1964), pp. 166–167, italicized in original.

14. In each of a number of analyses by Rummel and others a set of "domestic conflict" measures was factor analyzed. Turmoil, indexed by riots and demonstrations, is found to be a distinct dimension in all the analyses; two other factors, labeled by Rummel "revolution" and "subversion," are in some cases separate and in others combined. Principal components of the "revolution" dimension are coups, palace revolutions, plots, and purges; the category is labeled here conspiracy. Guerrilla war and terrorism are major components of the "subversion" dimension, here labeled internal war. See Rudolph J. Rummel, "A Field Theory of Social Action With Application to Conflict Within Nations," *Yearbook of the Society for General Systems Research*, X (1965), pp. 189–195; and Raymond Tanter, "Dimensions of Conflict Behavior Within Nations, 1955–1960: Turmoil and Internal War," *Peace Research Society Papers*, III (1965), pp. 159–183. The subcategories used here are adapted, with their operational definitions, from Rummel, "Dimensions of Conflict Behavior Within and Between Nations," *Yearbook of the Society for General Systems Research*, VIII (1963), pp. 25–26.

15. See, for example, Rummel, *op. cit.*; Tanter, *op. cit.*; Bruce M. Russett, "Inequality and Instability: The Relation of Land Tenure to Politics," *World Politics*, 16 (April 1964), pp. 442–454; Charles Tilly and James Rule, *Measuring Political Upheaval* (Princeton: Center of International Studies, Princeton University, 1965); and Ivo K. and Rosalind L. Feierabend, "Aggressive Behaviors Within Polities, 1948–1962: A Cross-National Study," *Journal of Conflict Resolution*, 10 (September 1966), pp. 249–271.

16. Information coded, in addition to that required for the three measures specified, included the socio-economic class(es) of the initiators, the social context in which they acted, the category of events, the targets and apparent motives of action, the number and role of coercive forces, and the extent and types of external support for initiators and regime, if any. Although no formal reliability tests were undertaken, the four coders did extensive practice coding on the same set of materials prior to coding and reviewed points of disagreement, and the author reviewed all coding sheets for internal consistency and, where necessary, recoding or search for additional information. It should be noted that the 1100 "events" include many cumulated reports, e.g. civil rights demonstrations in the U.S. were treated as a single set of events, all European-OAS terrorism in Algeria as a single event, etc.

17. It has been suggested that strife in countries with press restrictions is underreported. As a check on this type of systematic error a nine-point measure of press freedom was incorporated in initial analyses; the measure is from Raymond B. Nixon, "Freedom in the World's Press: A Fresh Appraisal With New Data," *Journalism Quarterly* (Winter 1965), pp. 3–14. The correlations of this measure, in which high scores reflect low press freedom, with some measures of strife are: Duration, $+19$; Intensity, $+17$; Pervasiveness, -16; Total magnitude of strife, $+11$. The first two are significant at the .05 level, the third at .10. In effect, *more* strife tends to be reported from polities with low press freedom, not less, as might be expected. The results almost certainly reflect the association of high levels of economic development and press freedom in the Western nations, which tend to have less strife than the developing nations.

18. The missing-data procedures gave implausibly-high estimates for initiators and casualties for a number of events. In subsequent and comparable analysis it seems advisable to rely on estimates of deaths alone, rather than casualties, and to insert means derived from comparable events *in comparable countries* rather than such events in all countries.

19. Tables are available on request from the author listing the 114 countries, their strife scores, the summary measures of deprivation and mediating conditions discussed below, and the data sources.

20. The 48 deprivation measures, with only one statistically significant exception, were positively associated with strife, most of them at a relatively low level. The thirteen were selected with regard to their representativeness, relatively high correlations with the dependent variables, and low intercorrelations.

21. Coding judgments for both discrimination indices and for separatism were made on the basis of country studies. The proportionality measures are versions of indices reported in Ted Gurr, *New Error-Compensated Measures for Comparing Nations* (Princeton: Center of International Studies, Princeton University, 1966), pp. 67–90.

22. A crude measure of the proportion of each polity's population engaged in the monetary economy, to the nearest .10, was constructed for the purpose of weighting this and some other measures. The measure was based primarily on labor census data.

23. The two measures will be used in subsequent analyses to examine time-lag relationships between short-term economic deprivation and strife. The trade data, obtained primarily from United Nations sources, was converted to U.S. currency when necessary to maintain comparability over time.

24. The *Hispanic-American Report* is much more comprehensive a source, hence the mean

deprivation scores for Latin America were much higher than those for other polities. As a crude adjustment, the Latin American polity scores were divided by a constant so that their mean approximated that of other polities. The same procedure was followed for indices 6 and 7, below. Analyses of regional clusters of polities, not reported here, provide a check on the adequacy of the procedure.

25. Types of restrictive actions, and their scale values, are as follows:

1 Amalgamation of splinter party with larger party
1 Restriction or harrassment of splinter party
2 Banning of splinter party
2 Amalgamation of minority party with larger party
2 Restriction or harrassment of minority party
3 Banning of minority party
3 Amalgamation of a major party with another major party
3 Restriction or harrassment of major party
4 Banning of major party
4 Improper dismissal of regional representative body
4 Improper dismissal of elected regional executive
5 Ban on party activities, parties allowed to continue their organizational existence
5 Improper dismissal of national legislature, with provision for calling new one within a year
5 Improper dismissal of elected chief executive, with provision for replacement within a year
6 Dissolution of all parties, ban on all political activity
6 Improper dismissal of national legislature, no short-term provision for reestablishment
6 Improper dismissal of elected chief executive, no short term provision for reelection

26. The annual scores for (5), (6), and (7) are being used in a series of time-lagged and cross-panel correlation analyses, not reported here, in further tests of causal relationships.

27. These are product-moment correlation coefficients, the strife measures including measures of duration, pervasiveness, intensity, and total magnitude of strife for 1961–1965. The last two strife measures are defined differently from those employed in the present analysis, but are derived from the same 1100-event data bank.

28. If one or the other ratio was missing, it was assumed equal to the known ratio. Internal security force ratios for 94 polities are reported in Gurr, *New Error-Compensated Measures for Comparing Nations*, pp. 111–126.

29. The first two indices are reported in *ibid.*, pp. 33–66, 91–110. Correlations among all three and strife measures are reported in Gurr and Ruttenberg, *The Conditions of Civil Violence*,

passim. The party characteristics are recoded from Arthur S. Banks and Robert B. Textor, *A Cross-Polity Survey* (Cambridge: MIT Press, 1963), raw characteristics 41 and 43.

30. Harry Eckstein, "Internal War: The Problem of Anticipation," in Ithiel de Sola Pool *et al.*, *Social Science Research and National Security* (Washington, D.C.: Smithsonian Institution, March 5, 1963).

31. Inaccessibility appears to be an almost-but-not-quite necessary condition for protracted internal wars. With one exception all such internal wars in the post-1945 period occurred in polities with high or very high scores on this index; the exception, a notable one, is Cuba.

32. The following rescaling was used, the sum of the "durability" and "character" scores being given on the upper line, the final legitimacy score on the lower:

Sum: 3,4 5 6 7 8 9 10 11 12 13,14
Legitimacy: 0 1 2 3 4 5 6 7 8   9

33. The S-shape of this relationship is considerably more pronounced when coercive-force size is related to total magnitude of turmoil; see Ted Gurr, "Why Urban Disorder? Perspectives from the Comparative Study of Civil Strife," *American Behavioral Scientist*, 10 (March–April 1968).

34. Significant computational errors in internal war and TMCS scores of several countries were identified and corrected after completion of the analyses reported here. Robert van den Helm of Princeton University has analyzed the corrected data, using the combined short-term deprivation measure in lieu of the two separate measures, with these multiple regression results: for TMCS, $R^2 = .638$; conspiracy, $R^2 = .391$; internal war, $R^2 = .472$; and turmoil, $R^2 = .284$. The significant increase in the degree of explanation for internal war is the result of increased correlations between magnitude of internal war and short-term deprivation (from .28 in Table 1 to .34); facilitation (from .57 to .61); and legitimacy (from −.23 to −.26). The r between magnitudes of turmoil and internal war increases from .17 to .23, the r between TMCS and internal war from .79 to .86. No other results of the analyses reported here are significantly affected by the reanalysis. The actual TMCS scores shown in Table 3 are corrected ones.

35. These and other fundamental arguments about causal inference are well summarized in Blalock, *Causal Inferences . . .*, Chapters 2 and 3. A partial correlation coefficient can be most easily regarded as the correlation between X and Z after the portions of X and Z that are accounted for by Y are removed, or held constant. The results discussed below are based on the use of only one of a variety of related causal inference techniques and are open to further, more refined analysis and interpretation. For other applicable

approaches see, for example, Hayward R. Alker, Jr., *Mathematics and Politics* (New York: Macmillan, 1965), Chapters 5 and 6.

36. To simplify evaluation of the effects of the control variables, the summary short-term deprivation variable was employed rather than its economic and political components separately.

37. Analysis of the correlation coefficients does not indicate definitively that legitimacy contributes to coercive potential rather than vice versa; nor would it be impossible to argue, on the basis of the partial r's alone, that short-term deprivation is a weak intervening variable between coercive potential and facilitation, on the one hand, and strife on the other. It is the plausibility of the theoretical arguments, in each case, that gives deciding force to the interpretation proposed. For a comparable argument see Hugh Donald Forbes and Edward R. Tufte, "A Note of Caution in Causal Modeling," *American Political Science Review*, 62 (December 1968), pp. 1258–1264.

38. Tanter has examined time-lag effects between a number of measures of foreign economic and military assistance for the regime and magnitude of civil violence in 1961–1963 for Latin American nations and finds generally weak relationships. The only consequential positive relationship, an indirect one, is between levels of U.S. military assistance and subsequent strife.

Raymond Tanter, "Towards a Theory of Conflict Behavior in Latin America." (Paper read to the International Political Science Association, Brussels, September 1967.)

39. In a reanalysis using corrected data (see footnote 34), four variables—the combined short-term deprivation measure, persisting deprivation, legitimacy, and facilitation—given an R^2 of .629.

40. The partial r's for these five variables are: economic deprivation, .27; political deprivation, .13; persisting deprivation, .39; legitimacy, .36; facilitation, .61.

41. For example Kenneth E. Boulding, *Conflict and Defense: A General Theory* (New York: Harper and Row, 1962); Lewis Coser, *The Functions of Social Conflict* (New York: The Free Press, 1956); and Thomas C. Schelling, *The Strategy of Conflict* (Cambridge, Mass.: Harvard University Press, 1960).

42. See Gurr, "Why Urban Disorder?" for a causal inference analysis of the sources of turmoil. The turmoil model differs principally in that "past strife levels" has the primary mediating role that facilitation has in the TMCS model.

43. The test is less than precise because the measures are not comparable; the past strife measure is based on an arbitrary weighting of counts of number of events, whereas the magnitude of strife measures reflect levels of participation, duration, and intensity.